THE RELIGION OF THE ETRUSCANS

THE RELIGION OF THE ETRUSCANS

Nancy Thomson de Grummond
and
Erika Simon,
Editors

University of Texas Press
Austin

Selections from volumes in the Loeb Classical Library®
are reprinted in Appendix B (p. 191). The Loeb Classical
Library® is a registered trademark of the President and
Fellows of Harvard College.

Copyright © 2006 by the University of Texas Press
All rights reserved
Printed in the United States of America
First edition, 2006

Requests for permission to reproduce material from this work
should be sent to:
  Permissions
  University of Texas Press
  P.O. Box 7819
  Austin, TX 78713-7819
  www.utexas.edu/utpress/about/bpermission.html

∞ The paper used in this book meets the minimum
requirements of ANSI/NISO Z39.48-1992 (R1997)
(Permanence of Paper).

Library of Congress Cataloging-in-Publication Data
The religion of the Etruscans / Nancy Thomson
de Grummond and Erika Simon, editors.— 1st ed.
     p.   cm.
Includes bibliographical references and index.
ISBN 978-0-292-72146-3 ISBN 0-292-72146-3
1. Etruscans—Religion—Congresses.   I. De Grummond,
Nancy Thomson.   II. Simon, Erika.
BL740.R45   2006
299'.9294—dc22   2005022652

CONTENTS

Editors' Note   vii

List of Abbreviations   viii

Contributors to This Volume   ix

Preface   xi
W. Jeffrey Tatum

I. Introduction: The History of the Study of Etruscan Religion   1
Nancy Thomson de Grummond

II. Etruscan Inscriptions and Etruscan Religion   9
Larissa Bonfante

III. Prophets and Priests   27
Nancy Thomson de Grummond

IV. Gods in Harmony: The Etruscan Pantheon   45
Erika Simon

V. The Grave and Beyond in Etruscan Religion   66
Ingrid Krauskopf

VI. Votive Offerings in Etruscan Religion   90
Jean MacIntosh Turfa

VII. Ritual Space and Boundaries in Etruscan Religion   116
Ingrid E. M. Edlund-Berry

VIII. Sacred Architecture and the Religion of the Etruscans   132
Giovanni Colonna

Glossary   169

Appendix A: The Etruscan Brontoscopic Calendar   173
Jean MacIntosh Turfa

Appendix B: Selected Latin and Greek Literary Sources on Etruscan Religion   191
Nancy Thomson de Grummond

Index   219

EDITORS' NOTE

In *The Religion of the Etruscans* the abbreviations of journals and series as well as of basic reference works in classical studies are those used by the *American Journal of Archaeology* and listed in AJA 104 (2000), 10-24. An updated version is on the website: http://www.ajaonline.org/shared/s_info_contrib_7.html.

A glossary of technical terms and words that may be otherwise unfamiliar to the reader is provided at the back of this book. Words that are included in the glossary are regularly marked with an asterisk in the text the first time the term is used in a particular chapter (e.g., *templum**). There is also a glossary of the most important Etruscan gods by Erika Simon in Chapter IV.

The spellings used for the names of the gods in Chapter IV are used as much as possible throughout the book. Etruscan orthography, however, was by no means consistent, and references may be made to inscriptions in which a name has an alternate spelling. A different kind of problem arises for nomenclature because we do not know the names in Etruscan of many of the archaeological sites mentioned in this book. Many scholars use a blend of modern Italian, ancient Roman (i.e., Latin), and occasionally, Etruscan, names for Etruscan cities and other sites, and this book is no exception.

Maps showing the major Etruscan cities and mountains may be found on page 124. As much as possible we have attempted to use ancient names; these are mainly Roman. Thus we refer to Caere, Populonia, Veii, Vetulonia, and Vulci, in accordance with established custom, and also the less common forms of Tarquinii and Volaterrae. The names Cerveteri, Tarquinia, and Volterra are used to refer to the modern cities with those names. Some scholars refer to Orvieto as the ancient Volsinii and to Bologna as Felsina. When no ancient name is known or agreed upon, we use the modern Italian name. For the names of tombs, we have opted for translating the many Italian names into English as a policy that will help make the vocabulary of Etruscan scholarship more readily accessible to students and to others who may be beginning the study of the Etruscans.

The appendices provide a Greek text and an English translation of the Etruscan Brontoscopic Calendar, as well as key original texts in Latin and Greek, with English translations.

The standard chronology of the periods of Etruscan culture is as follows:

Iron Age/Villanovan — 1000/900-750/700 BCE
Orientalizing — 750/700-600 BCE
Archaic — 600-475/450 BCE
"Classical" — 475/450-300 BCE
Hellenistic — 300 BCE-first century BCE

For dates of Latin and Greek authors and of selected texts, see the appropriate entries in the index.

LIST OF ABBREVIATIONS

The following works are so frequently used throughout the book that it seemed appropriate to give abbreviations to them:

ANRW = *Aufstieg und Niedergang der römischen Welt*, ed. H. Temporini. Berlin, 1972–.

CIE = *Corpus Inscriptionum Etruscarum*.

CSE = *Corpus Speculorum Etruscorum*.

Dizionario = *Dizionario della Civiltà Etrusca*, ed. M. Cristofani. Florence, 1985.

EHCA = *An Encyclopedia of the History of Classical Archaeology*, ed. N. T. de Grummond. 2 vols. Westport, 1996.

ES = *Etruskische Spiegel*, ed. E. Gerhard, G. Körte, and A. Klügmann. 5 vols. Berlin, 1840–1897.

ET = H. Rix, *Etruskische Texte*. 2 vols. Tübingen, 1991.

Etruscan Painting = S. Steingräber, *Etruscan Painting: Catalogue Raisonné of Etruscan Wall Paintings*, ed. D. Ridgway and F. R. Ridgway. New York, 1986.

LIMC = *Lexicon Iconographicum Mythologiae Classicae*

LPRH = *Les Étrusques, les plus religieux des hommes: État de la recherche sur la religion étrusque. Actes du colloque international Grand Palais 17–19.11.1992*, ed. D. Briquel and F. Gaultier. Paris, 1997.

Rasenna = *Rasenna: Storia e civiltà degli etruschi*, ed. M. Pallottino et al. Milan, 1986.

ThLE = *Thesaurus Linguae Etruscae*, ed. M. Pandolfini Angeletti. Rome, 1978–.

TLE = *Testimonia Linguae Etruscae*, ed. M. Pallottino. 2nd ed. Florence, 1968.

CONTRIBUTORS TO THIS VOLUME

LARISSA BONFANTE is Professor of Classics at New York University. She is the author of *Etruscan Dress* (new ed., 2003) and *The Etruscan Language* (2nd ed., 2002, with Giuliano Bonfante) and is author and editor of *Etruscan Life and Afterlife: A Handbook of Etruscan Studies* (1986). Since 1974 she has served as the chair of the U.S. Committee for the Corpus of Etruscan Mirrors (*Corpus Speculorum Etruscorum*). She is the author of numerous articles on Etruscan civilization, dress, language, and art.

GIOVANNI COLONNA is Professor of Etruscology and Italic Archaeology at the University of Rome "La Sapienza." He has directed the excavations at the Etruscan sanctuary of Pyrgi since its inception in the 1950s and has published numerous reports on his results. He is the author of *Bronzi umbro-sabellici* (1970) and, with Elena di Paolo, *Castel d'Asso* (1970) and *Norchia* (1978). Many of his more than three hundred articles on various topics are now collected in *Italia ante Romanum Imperium*, I-IV, Pisa/Rome, 2005. He has curated a number of museum exhibitions, the most notable of which was his *Santuari d'Etruria* (1985).

NANCY THOMSON DE GRUMMOND is the M. Lynette Thompson Professor of Classics at Florida State University (FSU). She specializes in Etruscan, Roman, and Hellenistic art and archaeology, with a particular concentration on Etruscan myth and religion. She serves as director of excavations at Cetamura del Chianti under the auspices of the FSU Archaeology Programs in Italy. Her publications include *A Guide to Etruscan Mirrors* (Tallahassee, FL, 1982) and *Etruscan Mythology, Sacred History and Legend: An Introduction* (forthcoming, Publications of the University of Pennsylvania Museum).

INGRID E. M. EDLUND-BERRY is Professor of Classics and Classical Archaeology at the University of Texas at Austin. She is the author of *The Iron Age and Etruscan Vases in the Olcott Collection at Columbia University, New York* (1980), *The Gods and the Place* (1987), and *The Seated and Standing Statue Akroteria from Poggio Civitate (Murlo)* (1992). She has completed a publication of the Central Sanctuary of Morgantina in Sicily and in collaboration with Lucy Shoe Meritt has recently published a reissue of *Etruscan and Republican Roman Mouldings* (2003).

INGRID KRAUSKOPF is Professor at the University of Heidelberg and associate of the Heidelberg Academy of Science, where she has guided the work of the *Lexicon Iconographicum Mythologiae Classicae* (LIMC). She has published numerous articles and books on Etruscan mythology and religion, including the basic book on Etruscan demonology, *Todesdämonen und Totengötter in der vorhellenistischen Kunst* (1987), and numerous articles on Etruscan mythology in the LIMC.

ERIKA SIMON, who served as Langford Family Eminent Scholar in Classics at Florida State University in 1999, is Professor Emerita of Würzburg University, where she held the chair for Classical Archaeology and served as director of the antiquities section of the Martin-von-Wagner Museum. She is the author or editor of many books on Greek, Roman, and Etruscan art, myth, and religion, including *Ara Pacis Augustae* (1968), *Augustus: Kunst und Leben in Rom um die Zeitenwende* (1986), *Schriften zur etruskischen und italischen Kunst und Religion* (1996).

W. JEFFREY TATUM is the Olivia Dorman Professor of Classics at Florida State University. A specialist in the literature and history of the Late Roman Republic, he is the author of numerous articles and of the volume *The Patrician Tribune: Publius Clodius Pulcher* (Chapel Hill, NC, 1999). He is currently writing a commentary on the *Commentariolum Petitionis* for Oxford University Press.

JEAN MACINTOSH TURFA is a Research Associate at the University of Pennsylvania Museum. Recent publications have been in the fields of Etruscan architecture, Etruscan votive offerings, art and myth in the Greek colonies, and parasols in Etruscan art. She served as consultant for the installation of the new galleries of Etruscan and Faliscan antiquities in the University Museum, now published as *Catalogue of the Etruscan Gallery of the University of Pennsylvania Museum of Archaeology and Anthropology* (2005).

PREFACE

W. Jeffrey Tatum

During the spring term of 1999, the Department of Classics at The Florida State University organized and hosted a conference, the title of which was "The Religion of the Etruscans," in honor of Erika Simon, who was in that year the Langford Eminent Scholar in Classics. The Eminent Scholar's chair and the expenses of the conference were made possible by funding from the George and Marian Langford Family Endowment in Classics. The smooth running of the conference was owed to the congeniality of the participants and to the industry of several individuals: Susan Stetson, the department's office manager; Kimberley Christensen, Harry Neilson, and Sarah Stinson, graduate students in the department; and Nancy de Grummond and Leon Golden, who were the faculty coordinators of the conference.

It is difficult to imagine a more important, or more formidable, subject than Etruscan religion. Readers of this collection will not need telling that the Etruscans were without question the pivotal people of central Italy during the Archaic period or that their effect on later Italian culture, owing to their influence on Roman civilization, was considerable, if not yet quite completely sorted out to everyone's satisfaction. The religion of any society is crucial to its proper apprehension. All the more so for a nation that, as Livy put it, was "more than any other dedicated to religion, the more as they excelled in practicing it" (Livy 5.1.6; cf. Appendix B: Selected Latin and Greek Literary Sources on Etruscan Religion, Source no. 1.1). The significance of this remark is underscored by the fact that, from the perspective of the Greeks, the Romans themselves were quite exceptional in their scrupulous religiosity, a quality that Polybius deemed one of the strengths of the Roman constitution. Etruscan religion can hardly be said to be an unexplored topic, though it is far too little discussed in Anglophone scholarship, a state of affairs this collection will go a long way toward correcting. The extent to which past examinations of Etruscan religion have resulted in infallible conclusions, on the other hand, must remain an arguable matter.

The impediments to the recuperation of any alien religion are several and severe, and this must especially be so for an extinct tradition. Which means that the study of any ancient religion demands an inordinately high degree of methodological self-consciousness, a resistance to neat and easy conclusions that must be reinforced even more when the information for that tradition tends to derive from material evidence and from secondary sources scattered over a considerable period of history, which is the state of affairs that obtains for the study of Etruscan religion. Indeed, it is fair to say that the problematic nature of all literary sources for Etruscan culture constitutes the principal difficulty confronting Etruscan studies, a difficulty that is sometimes finessed by a perhaps too ready recourse to speculation or at least a recourse to speculation that is too ready to carry conviction among minds of an Anglo-Saxon bent.

The study of Roman religion can be illuminating in this regard. The Late Republic supplies an abundance of written sources—historical, philosophical, oratorical, and literary—for the religious practices and the religious mentalities of the Roman elite. Ample material exists from a variety of genres, all originating in a well-defined and reasonably well understood milieu. Yet only in the past twenty years have students of Roman religion succeeded in recognizing the Christianizing assumptions that have colored their interpretation of these sources, an important step forward. One may still insist, however, that scholars have to too large an extent tended to swap their Christian framework for an anthropological one, by which I mean the anthropology of the 1970s and not of the 1990s (or of the current decade), which is far from the same thing.[1]

Still, the current state of affairs is a healthy agnosticism or at the very least a sane confusion. To take only one instance, it would be a rash scholar these days who, after reading Beard or Schofield, claimed to know exactly what were Cicero's views on divination.[2] Moreover, it is becoming increasingly clear that we must be more careful in our attention to the plurality of voices that speak to us from the past, not least because, even on fundamental issues such as augural law, Romans of the elite classes held strongly conflicting opinions, none of which can legitimately or meaningfully be discarded as "wrong."[3] In sum, the recuperation of Roman religiosity in the Late Republic, a period of extraordinarily rich documentation, remains elusive and challenging, to say the very least. How much harder, then, is the recuperation of Etruscan religion.

And how suggestive, though inconclusive, are our sources! Let me avoid becoming bogged down in distinguishing Etruscan from Hellenic patterns of worship and of religious representation and turn directly to Etruscan divination. Though we enjoy an abundance of references to the *Etrusca disciplina** and its practitioners, whom the Romans called *haruspices*,* we are confronted by difficulties at every turn. In the middle of the second century, the elder Cato wondered how a *haruspex* could pass a colleague on the street without giving him a wink (Cicero, *De div.* 2.52). At about the same time, Ti. Gracchus, the consul of 177, spurned the instructions of the *haruspices* by sneering, "Who are you Etruscan barbarians to know the Roman constitution?" (Cicero, *ND* 2.11). Yet these events transpired, if Cicero is honest in recounting them, at the very time when Polybius was informing the Greek world of the Romans' punctiliousness in all matters religious, an attitude he described as their "fear of the gods." The apparent contrast matters.

By the end of the century, however, the consultation of Etruscan *haruspices* had been assimilated to the mechanisms of civic religion: the Senate could consult the *haruspices* through the mediation of the *Decimviri* (later the *Quindecimviri*) *sacris faciundis*, the college that also consulted the foreign Sibylline books. In this regard, Etruscan religion was treated by the Romans little differently from Greek religion, which, as Denis Feeney has made clear, the Romans appropriated sometimes without comment and without historical memory but sometimes through "elaborate and self-conscious mechanisms for preserving a sense of distance and difference from the Greek element in their religious life."[4] Indeed, it was by carefully maintaining Greek, and Etruscan, religion as simultaneously integral and marginal that the Romans made it *Roman*, all of which highlights an approach to religion that must render all Roman practices, and all Roman references to Etruscan religion, an interpretive challenge of the highest order.

Inscriptions are hardly more straightforward. Though we possess an inventory of Tarquinian *haruspices*, it is by no means clear that we have to do with anything more than a local organization, despite the more powerful claims that have been made for this information. We do not even know if there was a formal *ordo* during Cicero's day.[5] The orator's serious attempt to interpret the most famous of all haruspical responses in the speech *De haruspicum responso* tells us next to nothing about its authors. Nor does Cicero denigrate the importance of the *responsum* itself, the proper interpretation of which was deemed by the whole of the Roman elite to be a matter of vital concern. Indeed, Cicero's enemy, Clodius Pulcher, was endeavoring to exploit this *responsum* so as to overturn nothing less than a previous decision of the pontifical college and a decree of the Senate pertaining to (Roman) religion, strong evidence of the value placed by the Roman elite in the *Etrusca disciplina*.[6] No surprise, then, that Late Republican antiquarians, some with Etruscan credentials, endeavored to provide accounts of Etruscan religion. Let us hope they were more successful than Varro in avoiding the Hellenizing and philosophical influences that permeated the intellectual life of the time.

The status of the *haruspices*, high in the first century BCE, continued to rise. The emperor Claudius established a formal *collegium*, which he removed to the supervision of the pontiffs. As is well known, it was also the opinion of his attending *haruspices*, whether members of a state *collegium* or not we cannot say, that inspired Diocletian's distaste and distrust for Christianity. Even the *haruspices*, however, could not withstand the grey-eyed Galilean: Constantine crushed Maxentius despite their advice, and, the support of Julian notwithstanding, the *disciplina* was outlawed at the end of the fourth century by Theodosius. Even the Christians were impressed: Arnobius, in an expression that does his Latin little credit, described Etruria as *genetrix et mater superstitionum* (*Adv. nat.* 7.26; Appendix B, Source no. 1.2). Much, then, can be said about the *haruspices*, and much else about Etruscan religious practices circulating in Roman writings. But the provenance of this material ought at least to give one pause, and the dangers of selecting information from various periods of Roman history ought to be too evident to require comment.

All of which is to say that the contributors to this volume were faced with a task as daunting as it is important. I think it is fair to say, however, that their efforts show a good measure of success. Whatever the weaknesses of modern times, we are, thankfully, no longer at the mercy of the shapes and the patterns of entrails. "Diligence is the mother of good fortune," as Cervantes put it, and, in the absence of a visitation by Vegoia (cf. Source no. 11.1), diligence and good fortune must remain essential elements in the endeavor to recover the nature of the Etruscans' beliefs and practices.

NOTES

1. A brief selection of recent and fundamental work (with further literature): Beard 1994; Beard, North, and Price 1998; Liebeschuetz, 1979; Linderski 1997; North 2000; Price 1984.
2. Beard 1986; Schofield, 1986, 47-65.
3. Tatum 1999b.
4. Feeney 1998, 26.
5. Rawson 1991, 302-303.
6. Discussion of this episode: Tatum 1999a, 215-219.

BIBLIOGRAPHY

Beard, M. 1986. "Cicero and Divination: The Formation of a Latin Discourse." *JRS* 76, 33-46.

Beard, M. 1994. "Religion," in *The Cambridge Ancient History,* eds. J. A. Crook, A. Lintott, and E. Rawson, vol. 9, 2nd ed. Cambridge. 729-768.

Beard, M., J. North, and S. Price 1998. *Religions of Rome.* 2 vols. Cambridge.

Feeney, D. 1998. *Literature and Religion at Rome: Cultures, Contexts and Beliefs.* Cambridge.

Liebeschuetz, J. H. W. G. 1979. *Continuity and Change in Roman Religion.* Oxford.

Linderski, J. 1997. *Roman Questions.* Stuttgart.

North, J. A. 2000. *Roman Religion.* Oxford.

Price, S. 1984. *Rituals and Power: The Roman Imperial Cult in Asia Minor.* Cambridge.

Rawson, E. 1991. *Roman Culture and Society.* Oxford.

Schofield, M. 1986. "Cicero for and against Divination," *JRS* 76, 47-65.

Tatum, W. J. 1999a. *The Patrician Tribune: Publius Clodius Pulcher.* Chapel Hill.

———. 1999b. "Roman Religion: Fragments and Further Questions." In *Veritatis Amicitiaeque Causa: Essays in Honor of Anna Lydia Motto and John R. Clark,* eds. S. N. Byrne and E. P. Cueva. Wauconda. 273-291.

CHAPTER I

INTRODUCTION: THE HISTORY OF THE STUDY OF ETRUSCAN RELIGION

Nancy Thomson de Grummond

"Religion is in fact the best known facet of the Etruscan civilization."[1] In making this statement, Massimo Pallottino noted that very many of the archaeological remains of the Etruscans and the literary sources about the Etruscans in Latin and Greek have a connection, in one way or another, with religion. The well-known statement of Livy describing the Etruscans as being the nation most devoted to religion, excelling others in their knowledge of religious practices (5.1.6; see Appendix B, Source no. 1.1), provides evidence that the ancients also recognized the pervasiveness of religion in Etruscan civilization.

It is a little odd, given the acknowledged importance of this subject, that there are relatively few general, sustained accounts of Etruscan religion, and there is as yet none today in the English language. It is also surprising that there does not seem to exist a critical review of the history of the study of Etruscan religion, which might help to evaluate the original sources and frame the problems and methodology for current study of the topic. In this introduction we shall consider the latter subject—the history of scholarship on Etruscan religion—and at the end attempt to show how this particular book relates to the former topic: the need for a comprehensive treatment in English. Here and throughout the book, there will be an emphasis on the evidence from written sources, and accordingly, frequent reference will be made to a special feature of this volume, the appendix on Selected Latin and Greek Literary Sources on Etruscan Religion (Appendix B).

In antiquity the study of and theorizing about Etruscan religion was already well developed, with scholarship that we may distribute into three main categories: canonical texts, philosophical treatises, and historical/antiquarian writings.

THE CANONICAL TEXTS

There were studies of the many different Etruscan texts having to do with the *Etrusca disciplina*,* that body of original Etruscan religious literature describing the cosmos and the Underworld, as well as prescribing various rituals and ways to interpret and act upon messages from the gods. The names of the texts that have survived include the *Libri rituales, Libri fatales, Libri de fulguratura* ("on lightning") and *Libri Acheruntici* (concerning Acheron, i.e., the Underworld), as well as books named after the two principal Etruscan prophets, who were called Tages and Vegoia in Latin: *Libri Tagetici* and *Libri Vegoici*. Both Etruscans and Romans were involved in this study, which included translating and interpreting the old texts and teaching them to appropriate individuals. The practitioners of this type of study perhaps relate to their material in a manner similar to that of the Jewish and Early Christian scholars who studied, taught, and commented on their religious literature.

Unfortunately, we know so little of these writings and teachings that we are unable to discern what, if any, may have been their theological concerns or what debates may have enlivened their encounters.[2] Further, it is a perennial frustration in studies of Etruscan religion that little about Etruscan prophetic or priestly texts can be confidently traced back earlier than the first century BCE, when in fact Etruscan civilization had become fully submerged in the dominant Roman culture.

Among the names that have survived are individuals who lived in the first century BCE, such as Aulus Caecina from Volaterrae, friend of Cicero, who wrote *De Etrusca disciplina*, a publication that has been described as a "major event" in the intellectual life of the Late Republic;[3] the admired and erudite Nigidius Figulus, who composed books on dreams, private augury, and divining from entrails, and a brontoscopic calendar (the latter surviving in a Greek translation; see Appendix A for the text and a full account of Figulus); and Tarquitius Priscus,[4] friend of Varro, known to have written an *Ostentarium Tuscum*, a translation of an Etruscan work on prodigies and signs, as well as a book on prognosticating from trees. Tarquitius also produced a translation of the cosmic prophecies of the nymph Vegoia, a fragment of which has survived (Appendix B, Source no. II.1).[5] Another figure in this category is Cornelius Labeo, whose date is unknown but who seems to have written translations and commentaries, in fifteen books, on the prophecies of Vegoia and Tages.[6]

Also in this category are the many shadowy figures who are mentioned as being consulted for advice by the Romans, the soothsaying priests or *haruspices*,* as for example, Umbricius Melior, described as "most skilled," the Early Imperial soothsayer of Galba.[7] Sulla had his *haruspex* Postumius, and the famous Spurinna tried to warn Caesar about the Ides of March.[8] There must have been many more Romanized Etruscans involved in these pursuits (there are a few more such figures whose names alone have come down to us), for we know that as a general principle, the Romans thought the Etruscan teachings to be so important that they had a practice of sending their sons to Etruria to study this ancient lore.[9]

PHILOSOPHICAL TEXTS

The foregoing individuals we have mentioned may be recognized as real practitioners of Etruscan or Etruscan-style religion, and as such they had their own bias. Our second division is related, but it manifests a different approach: intellectuals with a concern for philosophy. There is no more significant surviving text for the study of Etruscan religious practice than the treatise on divination by Cicero, written around the time of the death of Caesar, ca. 44 BCE. In *De divinatione* Cicero presents a vivid debate on the reliability of divination in its various manifestations, with the principal interlocutors represented as his brother Quintus and himself.[10] The evidence presented on both sides is all the more interesting because Cicero had intimate knowledge of the subject from his own experiences as an augur of state religion.

This first-century Roman debate is of course sophisticated and probably shows some thought patterns well beyond any present in Etruscan religious teaching. Quintus Cicero supports credence in divination from the standpoint of Stoic philosophy, and Marcus Cicero, while rejecting actual faith in divination, in the end admits the importance of traditional rites and ceremonies solely for political aims. He has great contempt for most divinatory practices and heaps scorn upon, for example, the important Etruscan revelation myth of the prophetic child Tages.[11] What is most important in the treatise for our purposes is the abundant evidence about the principal Etruscan methods of divining, by reading of entrails and by interpretation of lightning (cf. Appendix B, Section VIII). When we can sort these out from Roman interpolation, we have some of the most meaningful reports from antiquity on Etruscan practices.

The treatise of Seneca, *Quaestiones naturales*, written shortly before his death in 65 CE, also promotes philosophy but is fascinating for its sympathetic presentation of the point of view of Etruscan priests. We have a clear statement of the contrast of thought between the two sides, in the famous declaration that "this is the difference between us [philosophers] and the Etruscans, who have consummate skill in interpreting lightning: we think that because clouds collide, lightning is emitted; but they think the clouds collide in order that lightning may be emitted" (Appendix B, Source no. VIII.1). In fact, we know little about the Etruscan studies of the natural sciences, but the passage in Seneca tends to confirm suspicions that their observation of natural phenomena was carried out with religious premises and conclusions.

HISTORICAL/ANTIQUARIAN TEXTS

A third and rather different brand of scholarship is that of the historians, philologists, and antiquarians. Livy (d. 12 or 17 CE) transmitted a great deal of information in his narratives of Roman/Etruscan politics and war, such as in his frequent references to the Etruscan federal sanctuary of the shrine of Voltumna (3.23.5, 25.7, 61.2; 5.17.6; 6.2.2). Verrius Flaccus, the tutor of the grandsons of Augustus, wrote a treatise on Etruscan matters (*Libri rerum Etruscarum*) that has not survived, but we do have some of his observations as preserved in the epitome by Festus of his *De significatu verborum*, which contained rare and obsolete words and accompanying archaic antiquarian lore. Vitruvius, a practicing architect of the time of Augustus, has left a precise account of the theoretical and practical aspects of building and locating an Etruscan temple (*De architectura* 1.7.1-2, 4.7; Appendix B, Source nos. v.2, v.3).

The pure antiquarians are especially useful. They were intrigued with the past and recorded information objectively about Etruscan religion out of curiosity. A great variety of Etruscan topics was treated by the most learned of all Romans, Varro (116-27 BCE), ranging from the practice of sacrificing a pig for a ritual pact (*De re rustica* 2.4.9), to the Etruscan rite for laying out a city (*Etruscus ritus**; *De lingua Latina* 5.143; see Appendix B, Source no. IV.2). He wrote a treatise on human and divine matters of antiquity (i.e., what was ancient at that time, 47 BCE), the loss of which is most unfortunate. It contained fascinating material on the lore of lightning, such as that other gods beside Jupiter, for example, Minerva and Juno, were allowed to throw lightning bolts (Appendix B, Source no. VIII.7). It was Varro who provided the famous and precious reference to Vertumnus as the "chief god of Etruria" (*De lingua Latina* 5.46; Appendix B, Source no. VI.3).

He was of course frequently quoted by other antiquarians, such as Pliny the Elder (d. 79 CE), who drew from him information about the decoration of Etruscan shrines, in his book on painting and modeling sculpture (*HN* 35.154), and about the tomb of Porsena, in his section on building stones and architecture (*HN* 36.91; Appendix B, Source no. V.5). Pliny included a good bit of Etruscan material in his encyclopedic *Historia Naturalis* as part of his goal of being compendious, and in this way he preserved many interesting fragments of information from various sources, such as lore about signs from the birds in his sections on zoology; he refers to an illustrated Etruscan treatise (*HN* 10.28, 30, 33, 35-49).

Among the antiquarians we may also classify selected Latin poets who drew on early Roman and Etruscan antiquities for one reason or another, during that period of the first century BCE when we detect so much other activity regarding Etruscan religion. Vergil, exposed to Etruscan culture in his native Mantua, has left us his stirring description of the warrior priest from Pisa, Asilas, skilled in the interpretation of all the signs from the gods, embracing entrails, the stars, birds, and lightning (*Aeneid* 10.246-254).

No text from the Romans is more important for studying Etruscan divinity than the poem of Propertius of Perusia about the statue of Vertumnus set up in Rome (4.2; Appendix B, Source no. VI.1). It expresses vividly the Etruscan tendency to be vague or ambivalent about the gender and other characteristics of a particular deity.

Ovid, too, has related the myth of Vertumnus, and interestingly has the god change sex to appear as an old woman in the story of the courtship of Pomona (*Meta.* 14.623-771; see Appendix B, Source no. VI.2). His calendar in the *Fasti*, replete with lore of early religion in Rome, is relevant but must be used with caution, both because the poet is sometimes inaccurate in his citations (and he does not tell his sources) and because the material on the Etruscans is certainly colored by the Roman context. Of course, all the poetic literature—of Vergil, Propertius, Ovid, and others—must be read critically as just that, rich in allusions, sometimes created for the occasion by the poet and not necessarily reflecting Etruscan belief or practice.

After this, we can note a crowd of later Roman polymaths who took an interest in Etruscan culture, probably most often using some of the writers we have already cited. Festus (second century CE), as noted, prepared an epitome of Verrius Flaccus, and this was in turn epitomized by Paulus Diaconus in the eighth century. The grammarian Censorinus (third century CE) wrote on a wide range of topics such as the origin of human life and time (Appendix B, Source no. III.6). The indefatigable and generally trustworthy Servius (fourth century CE)[12] has left an abundance of observations on the Etruscans in his commentary on Vergil's works. He took a great interest in augural lore, and though he did not always refer directly to the Etruscans, his comments are useful in augmenting our knowledge of this important branch of Etruscan religious praxis.[13] Macrobius (probably fifth century CE), whose *Saturnalia* is a potpourri of antiquarian, scientific, and especially philological lore, provides in his dilettante's way little nuggets of Etruscan information, for example, on the use of the sacred bronze plow in founding a city (*Sat.* 5.19.13 [Appendix B, Source no. IV.5]) or on the good omen seen in the wool of sheep when it was naturally tinted purple or golden (*Sat.* 3.7.2 [Appendix B, Source no. IV.6]). Finally, we may include in this group Arnobius, a rhetorician and Christian convert living in Africa in the late fourth and early fifth century CE, who assembled his text intelligently from other sources, as shown by his passage quoting Varro on the group gods such as the Penates recognized by the Etruscans (*Adv. nat.*, 3.40 [Appendix B, Source no. IX.3]).

An absolutely singular case is that of Martianus Capella. He, too, flourished in the atmosphere of North Africa in the fifth century, leaving as his chief work a compendious pedantic allegory on the marriage of Mercury and Philology (*De nuptiis Mercurii et Philologiae*).[14] Regarded as eccentric, tedious, and superficial in its discourse on the seven liberal arts, the text of Martianus is nonetheless of the greatest importance for Etruscan studies. It contains the single most significant text in Latin for understanding the Etruscan pantheon and cosmos (1.45–61; Appendix B, Source no. III.4). Martianus sets the stage for the wedding of Mercury and Philology by sending out invitations to gods all around the sky, and he depicts them as inhabiting sixteen main divisions.

Scholars are united in regarding this number as a clue that Martianus was following the Etruscan system of dividing the sky (cf. Cicero, *De div.* 2.18.42, Appendix B, Source no. III.3), and have found that the scheme agrees in some striking details with that other famous document of the Etruscan cosmos, the bronze model of a sheep's liver found near Piacenza (see Fig. 11.2).[15] The use of deities who may be readily equated with well-known Etruscan gods, along with divinities who are completely obscure in Roman religion, suggests that we may indeed have here a reflection of an original Etruscan doctrine.

The antiquarian trend continues in the Middle Ages in isolated instances, such as the writings of the Byzantine scholar Johannes Lydus, who taught Latin philosophy and championed that language in sixth-century Constantinople. It is he who recorded the thunder calendar of Nigidius Figulus (Appendix A; note the discussion of the career and writings of Lydus there). In addition, he left a quite lengthy discussion of Tages (*De ostentis,* 2.6.B; Appendix B, Source no. II.5). The texts that had come to be associated with the name of Tages continued to be of interest long after Etruscan and Roman religion were no longer operative. Isidore of Seville also mentions Tages (*Etymol.* 8.9.34–35, seventh century). The encyclopedic text, the *Suda,* has left a strange account of creation, undoubtedly affected by biblical precedents, attributed to the Etruscans (tenth century; Appendix B, Source no. III.5).

The Etruscans were largely forgotten during the medieval centuries. When interest in them was reborn during the Renaissance in the former Etruscan territories,[16] it was some time before their religion became a focus of study. That famous old fraud Annio da Viterbo (d. 1502) was interested in the mythology of Etruria, but he had as distorted a view of the gods[17] as he had of the Etruscan language, which he translated quite wrongly. In the seventeenth century, the Scotsman Thomas Dempster,[18] serving as a law professor in Pisa, pioneered serious research on the Etruscans with his treatise *De Etruria regali libri septem* ("Seven Books on Etruria of the Kings"). A section near the beginning was devoted to Etruscan religion, drawing on various texts he had available. The work was not published until over a century later and thus had little impact until the following century.

In spite of the veritable mania for the Etruscans (*Etruscheria*) of the eighteenth century,[19] few yet took an interest in the topic of religion. The Accademia Etrusca,[20] founded at Cortona in 1726, met regularly and heard papers and reports, but its members and other contemporary scholars seem to have been more interested in Etruscan architecture and material antiquities, along with the Etruscan language.[21] Their studies often embraced Roman archaeology, and of some interest for our theme is a treatise on the origins and development of shrines in the ancient world, based on Roman numismatics especially, presented by the academician Filippo Venuti and published in 1738 among the *Saggi di dissertazioni* of the Accademia Etrusca.[22] A remarkable study of "Etruscan philosophy" by Giovanni Maria Lampredi, a young priest and tutor in Florence, also belongs to this period. *Saggio sopra la filosofia degli antichi Etruschi* (1756) drawing on Seneca especially, argues that the Etruscans had an "emanative system" for the cosmos tied to Pythagoreanism and Stoicism. Lampredi went to some pains to explain the contradiction he perceived between Seneca and the account in the *Suda*.[23]

In the nineteenth century, as part of the scientific trend manifest in various branches of Etruscan studies,[24] we find the first extended consideration of Etruscan religion based on a rigorously critical assemblage of texts. The great classic handbook on the Etruscans, *Die Etrusker,* published by Karl Otfried Müller (1828) and significantly augmented by Wilhelm Deecke (1877), devoted Book 3 to a lengthy survey of Etruscan gods and spirits, the *Etrusca disciplina*, and the various branches of divination.

Following this product of German scholarship came the basic formulation of the various categories of the *disciplina* by the Swede Carl O. Thulin (1871–1921). His two essays on lightning (1905) and haruspicy (1906) and a third on the ritual books and the *haruspices* in Rome (1909) were gathered together as *Die Etruskische Disciplin* (Darmstadt, 1968). The works of Müller and Deecke and of Thulin are almost exclusively philological and historical and thus do not take into account the vast amount of archaeological material with bearing on the subject of Etruscan religion. Nor does either contain very much evidence derived from the study of the Etruscan language, which was still a pioneer discipline in the nineteenth and early twentieth century.

Nevertheless, Thulin did utilize the bronze liver found near Piacenza in 1877 (see Fig. 11.2),[25] though his listings of the inscriptions were very rudimentary. Moreover, Deecke, who was quite interested in the Etruscan language, drew upon the evidence of Etruscan mirrors, using the volumes of Gerhard's corpus of *Etruskiche Spiegel*,[26] a rich repository of representations of gods identifiable by their names labeled in Etruscan or else recognizable by their resemblance to Greek or Roman gods (e.g., see Figs. 11.8, 11, 16–19). Of great significance in this period for the study of original Etruscan texts was the recognition and publication (1892) of the astonishing linen book, an Etruscan ritual calendar, found reused as bandages for a mummy deposited in the National Museum of Zagreb (see Fig. 11.1).[27]

THE STUDY OF ETRUSCAN RELIGION IN THE TWENTIETH CENTURY

In the twentieth century, development in the study of Etruscan religion was not linear, but some trends and certainly major developments may be detected. In 1984, Pallottino summed up the scholarship by listing the chief researchers on the topic: almost all of the literature was in German, Italian, or French.[28] A further and excellent guide to this literature was provided by the "nota bibliografica" of Mario Torelli, written for his chapter on Etruscan religion in the massive *summa* of Etruscan studies, *Rasenna* (1986).[29] Historians of religion may be noted, such as Carl Clemen, who wrote the first true monograph on this topic, *Die Religion der Etrusker* (Bonn 1936). A series of articles in *Studi e Materiali di Storia della Religione* (4, 1928 and 5, 1929) featured articles by a number of different experts on ancient religion (Clemen, H. J. Rose, C. C. Van Essen, H. M. R. Leopold, Franz Messerschmidt), including such topics as the relationship between Etruscan and Greek and Roman religion. Stefan Weinstock published a series of seminal articles, including his masterful study of the text of Martianus Capella and a basic study of the books on lightning,[30] based on his careful scrutiny of the texts and intimate knowledge of the comparative religious material from the Near East.

Missing from the bibliographies of Pallottino and Torelli but worth mentioning here is the study by the comparativist Georges Dumézil, originally published in French (1966) and then translated into English as "The Religion of the Etruscans," a lengthy appendix to his *Archaic Roman Religion*.[31] At the time, the book introduced a novel attitude toward the Etruscans, rather contemptuously removing them from forming background to Roman religion and placing them at the end of his study. Dumézil was eager to prove that Roman religion conformed to an Indo-European scheme and found the Etruscans inconvenient for his theory.[32] A useful contribution to the study of sources was the *Fonti di storia etrusca* compiled by Guilio Buonamici, translations of various basic Greek and Latin texts, with a fairly full section on religion.[33]

The greatest advances were being made by scholars who were strong philologists, especially those who were on the front lines in the study of the Etruscan language. Pallottino himself, Jacques Heurgon, and in particular Ambros J. Pfiffig brought to bear the ever-increasing scientific advances in the study of the language. In addition, they placed, for the first time, appropriate emphasis on the insertion of material culture into the dialogue.

The best general account in English to date, albeit brief, is that of Pallottino (1975, ch. 7). Likewise, his articles in the encyclopedic *Roman and European Mythologies*[34] are all basic authoritative accounts. Pfiffig's *Religio etrusca* (1975) remains the only lengthy, systematic exposition of Etruscan religion that takes into account Greek and Roman literary sources, the Etruscan language, and the archaeological evidence.[35] His bibliography was exhaustive (369 items).

The basic integrated methodology of Pallottino and Pfiffig has become standard today, and those who seek to be effective in the study of religion need global knowledge of the field of Etruscan studies. The latest generation of Italian scholars exemplifies well this ideal: Mario Torelli, Mauro Cristofani, Adriano Maggiani, Francesco Roncalli, and Giovanni Colonna. But the international character of Etruscan religious studies today was clearly evident in the conference organized in Paris in 1992 by Françoise Gaultier and Dominique Briquel, *Les Plus religieux des hommes: État de la recherche sur la religion étrusque* ("The Most Religious of Men: The State of Research on Etruscan Religion"), which included sessions on iconography, the pantheon, comparative religion, cults and rituals, and the relationship between Etruscan civilization and religion. The resulting publication (Paris, 1997) has a brief preface that sums up the "state of research." In combination with use of the most current archaeological discoveries, we see light shed on an increased chronological arc (the earliest periods of the Villanovan and Orientalizing phases are now clearer), and scholars are investigating the ties of the Etruscans with external cultures: Italic, Greek, and Oriental. For the rest, the reader may deduce the state of the field from the manifold articles; twenty-two scholars of international status published their latest insights there, all translated into French. Not one native speaker of English was on the program.

As of the year 2005 there still does not exist a substantial general account of the Etruscan religion in the English language. To fill this lacuna, the present volume of *The Reli-*

gion of the Etruscans was planned as a handbook, intended to be used as an introduction to the subject, but with sufficient scholarly apparatus to be of interest and use to more advanced students and scholars as well. The chapters of the book are based largely on papers given in 1999 at the Sixth Annual Langford Conference of the Department of Classics at Florida State University. Erika Simon, in her capacity as the Langford Family Eminent Scholar of Classics for the year 1999, selected the participants for the conference from leading scholars in the field of Etruscan studies. With coordinator Nancy de Grummond, Prof. Simon requested that the presenters give a general introduction to their individual subjects and include as well some of their own latest frontline research in the field. The participants fulfilled their assignments admirably and, after lively discussions and ideas for further additions to the book, proceeded to do a formal written version of their papers, taking into account the contributions of others.

The table of contents for *The Religion of the Etruscans* reveals the range of topics. The aim is to be systematic and comprehensive. The chapter by Larissa Bonfante lays out the most important surviving Etruscan inscriptions and explains how they are relevant for Etruscan religion, including points from her latest research relating inscriptions to religious iconography. The next chapter, by Nancy de Grummond, presents information on the sacred books of the Etruscan prophets and the activities of priests in divining the will of the gods; her work on Etruscan mirrors has brought up some new ideas about the Etruscan rituals of prophecy. Erika Simon discusses her concept of the "harmonious" pantheon of gods, pointing out how much cooperation and friendship there was among Etruscan deities and how versatile individual gods were, especially in regard to their ability to come and go from the Underworld to the upper sphere.

Her chapter concludes with an alphabetical listing of the most significant Etruscan gods and brief characterizations of them.

Next, Ingrid Krauskopf gives a full survey of concepts of the Underworld and the intriguing demons inhabiting that part of the cosmos. Jean MacIntosh Turfa reviews the fascinating range of votive objects found in Etruscan sanctuaries and sacred areas, providing a most useful site-by-site summary of votive deposits of Etruria. Ingrid Edlund-Berry then discusses the delineation of space and boundaries in the cosmos, including some of her own original conclusions about the nature of Etruscan federal sanctuaries. The text concludes with a chapter on altars, shrines and temples, in which Giovanni Colonna provides a thorough overview and includes considerable detail about his own latest discoveries at Pyrgi and the nature of worship as revealed by offerings to the gods. His information about turf altars at Pyrgi, used in popular religion as opposed to the state patronage of grand temples, is integrated into the study of Etruscan religion for the first time here and provides a window on the ordinary, pious Etruscan people who sought to live in harmony with the gods. Every chapter has its own bibliography, so that the reader may follow up the scholarship on each particular topic.

NOTES

1. Pallottino 1975, 138.

2. Cicero provides a notable exception to this generalization, but he is to be classified with the philosophers. See below, p. 2.

3. Cicero, *Ad fam.* 6.5-9; Pliny, *HN* 2; Seneca, *QN* 2.3.9); Schofield 1986, 49 (quoting E. Rawson).

4. For a collection of Latin passages relevant to Tarquitius Priscus, see Thulin 1909, 22-29. There were other, later Tarquitii, from whom it is not always easy to distinguish the Late Republican figure.

5. For a full discussion of Vegoia, see below, pp. 30-31.

6. On Labeo, see Müller and Deecke 1877. For a full discussion of Tages, see below, pp. 27-30.

7. Pliny, *HN* 10.6.19, describes him as *haruspicum in nostro aevo peritissimus* ("the most skilled haruspex of our time").

8. Cicero, *De div.* 1.52.119; Suetonius, *Caesar* 81.

9. Johannes Lydus, *De ostentis*, 2.6.B, mentions as authors and translators Capito "the priest," Fonteius, and Apuleius Vicellius, but we know only the names. On the education of Romans in Etruria, cf. Heurgon 1964, 231, who argued that the literary tradition was scrambled in antiquity and that it was only young Etruscans who were sent to study the *Etrusca disciplina*. Valerius Maximus 1.1 (Appendix B, Source no. IV.9) states that Roman noble youths were thus educated, but passages in Cicero support Heurgon's idea: *De leg.* 2.21, *De div.* 1.92; Appendix B, Source no. IV.8. Cf. Livy 9.36.3, on the sending of Roman boys to Etruria to be educated.

10. Beard 1986; Schofield 1986.

11. Providing along the way some very worthwhile detail on the myth; told in full below, p. 27.

12. Perhaps augmented by a later commentator, the so-called Danielis; certainly drawing extensively on earlier authors, such as Aelius Donatus.

13. Festus also preserved many short observations in this area. See the collection of texts in Regell 1882.

14. *Martianus Capella* 1977; Ramelli 2001.

15. See van der Meer 1987 and the discussion by Bonfante below, pp. 10-11. For a detailed discussion of Martianus Capella, see de Grummond, forthcoming, ch. III, "Creation, Time and the Universe."

16. For the following section, see the account in de Grummond 1986.

17. For Annio, founders of the Etruscans included biblical figures along with Isis and Osiris, Ajax, Electra and Tyrrhenus, see de Grummond 1986, 28. See also N. T. de Grummond, "Annio da Viterbo," EHCA 1996, 1, 48-49.

18. C. Sowder, "Sir Thomas Dempster," in EHCA 1996, 1, 357-358.

19. N. de Grummond "Etruscheria," in EHCA 1996, 1, 410.

20. N. de Grummond, "Accademia Etrusca," in EHCA 1996, 1, 3-5.

21. For listings of books published in the early centuries of Etruscan studies, see esp. Barrocchi and Gallo 1985-1986, 195-196, and *Les Étrusques et l'Europe* 1992, 489-490.

22. Venuti's *Dissertazione sopra i tempietti degli antichi* was followed by a treatise on the temple of Janus in Rome (1740). See Barocchi and Gallo 1985, 154-156.

23. It is impossible to say if any Etruscans outside Rome had real knowledge of Greek philosophical systems. What is interesting about Lampredi's attempt is that he has used the basic texts critically and, in the end, describes an Etruscan cosmos not so different from that envisioned by Pallottino (1975, 140): the vague evidence "seems to point toward an original belief in some divine entity dominating the world through a number of varied, occasional manifestations which later became personified into gods."

24. F. Delpino, "L'âge du positivisme," *Les Étrusques et l'Europe*, 1992, 340-347; de Grummond 1986, 41-43. See also N. T. de Grummond, "Etruscan Tombs," in EHCA 1996, 1, 406-410; Pallottino 1975, 26-27.

25. On the liver, see his monograph, Thulin 1906.

26. ES; volumes 1 through 4 were issued by 1867. The fifth and final volume, edited by Klügmann and Körte, appeared in 1897.

27. Krall 1892; Roncalli 1985, 19.

28. Pallottino 1984, 323, lists C. Thulin, G. Herbig, R. Pettazzoni, C. Clemen, G. Furlani, C. C. Van Essen, H. M. R. Leopold, B. Nogara, G. Q. Giglioli, A. Grenier, R. Herbig, S. Weinstock, J. Heurgon, R. Bloch, and A. J. Pfiffig.

29. *Rasenna*, 159-237; bibliographical note, 234-237.

30. Weinstock 1932; Weinstock 1946.

31. Dumézil 1970, 625-696.

32. For a modern critique of Dumézil's theory, see Beard, North, and Price 1998, vol. 1, 14-16.

33. Buonamici 1939, 297-351.

34. Bonnefoy and Doniger 1992, 25-45; articles on Etruscan demonology, Etruscan and Italic divination, *Etrusca disciplina*, and other topics.

35. The recent book by J.-R. Jannot (1998) is much better illustrated than Pfiffig and constitutes a very useful album of pictures. Philologically, the book is insufficiently critical. At the time of this writing, an English translation of this work, *Religion in Ancient Etruria*, has been announced by the University of Wisconsin Press.

BIBLIOGRAPHY

Barocchi, P., and D. Gallo, eds. 1985. *L'Accademia etrusca*. Milan.

Beard, M. 1986. "Cicero and Divination: The Formation of a Latin Discourse." *JRS* 76, 33-46.

Beard, M., J. North, and S. Price. 1998. *Religions of Rome*, 2 vols. Cambridge.

Bibliotheca Etrusca, 1985-1986. *Bibliotheca Etrusca, Fonti letterarie e figurative tra XVIII e XIX secolo nella Bibliotheca dell'Istituto Nazionale di Archeologia e Storia dell'arte*. Rome.

Bonnefoy and Doniger. 1992 = *Roman and European Mythologies*, ed. Y. Bonnefoy, tr. W. Doniger et al. Chicago.

Buonamici, G. 1939. *Fonti di storia etrusca*. Florence.

De Grummond, N. T. 1986. "Chapter I, Rediscovery." In *Etruscan Life and Afterlife, A Handbook of Etruscan Studies*, ed. L. Bonfante. Detroit. 18-46.

———. Forthcoming. *Etruscan Mythology, Sacred History and Legend: An Introduction*. Philadelphia.

Dumézil, G. 1970. *Archaic Roman Religion*. Tr. P. Krapp. 2 vols. Baltimore.

EHCA 1996 = *An Encyclopedia of the History of Classical Archaeology*, ed. N. T. de Grummond, 2 vols. Westport.

ES = *Etruskische Spiegel*. Ed. E. Gerhard (vols. 1-4); A. Klügmann and G. Körte (vol. 5). Berlin. 1840-1897.

Les Étrusques et l'Europe. 1992. Catalogue of exhibition. Paris.

Heurgon, J. 1964. *Daily Life of the Etruscans*. Tr. J. Kirkup. London.

Jannot, J.-R. 1998. *Devins, dieux et démons: Regards sur la religion de l'Étrurie antique*. Paris.

Krall, J. 1982. *Die etruskischen Mumienbinden des Agramer Nationalmuseums*. In *Denkschriften der Kaiserlichen Akademie der Wissenschaften der Kaiserlichen Akademie der Wissenschaften. Philosophisch-historische Klasse*, 41, Vienna.

Martianus Capella. 1977. *Martianus Capella and the Seven Liberal Arts*. Tr. W. H. Stahl and R. Johnson. New York.

Müller and Deecke. 1877 = *Die Etrusker*, by K.-O. Müller, ed. W. Deecke. 2 vols. Repr. Graz 1965.

Pallottino, M. 1975. *The Etruscans*. Tr. J. Cremona, ed. D. Ridgway. Bloomington, IN.

———. 1984. *Etruscologia*. 7th ed. Milan.

Pfiffig, A. J. 1975. *Religio etrusca*. Graz.

Ramelli, I. 2001. *Marziano Capella: Le Nozze di Filologia e Mercurio*. Milan.

Rasenna = *Rasenna: Storia e civiltà degli etruschi*, Milan. 1986.

Regell, P. 1882. *Fragmenta auguralia (Fragments of the Books of the Augurs)*. Hirschberg. Repr. in *Roman Augury and Etruscan Divi-*

nation, in the series Ancient Religion and Mythology, ed. W. R. Connor and R. E. A. Palmer. New York, 1975.

Roncalli, F. 1985. *Scrivere etrusco: Scrittura e letteratura nei massimi documenti della lingua etrusca*. Milan.

Schofield, M. 1986. "Cicero for and against Divination." *JRS* 76, 47-65.

Thulin, C. O. 1906. *Die Götter des Martianus Capella und der Bronzleber von Piacenza*. Gieszen.

———. 1968. *Die Etruskische Disciplin*. Repr. of I. *Die Blitzlehre* (1905); II. *Die Haruspicin* (1906); III. *Die Ritualbücher und zur Geschichte und Organisation der Haruspices* (1909). Darmstadt.

Van der Meer, L. B. 1987. *The Bronze Liver of Piacenza: Analysis of a Polytheistic Structure*. Amsterdam.

Weinstock, S. 1932. "Templum." *MDAI(R)* 47, 95-121.

———. 1946. "Martianus Capella and the Cosmic System of the Etruscans." *JRS* 36, 101-129.

CHAPTER II

ETRUSCAN INSCRIPTIONS AND ETRUSCAN RELIGION

Larissa Bonfante

We have no Etruscan literature, no epic poems, no religious or philosophical texts. We learn about Etruscan life and civilization—including language and religion, the two basic aspects of a people's identity—from the remains of their cities and cemeteries. These include highly important evidence from their inscriptions, written in their own peculiar language, that reveal much about their religious rituals and beliefs.

These inscriptions are so central to the study of Etruscan religion that they will naturally be referred to frequently throughout the book. In this chapter we present an overview of this source material, including a list of the most important inscriptions and a survey of some of the intriguing religious themes that have emerged in recent studies. We shall make frequent reference to the new standard collection of Etruscan inscriptions, Helmut Rix's *Etruskische Texte* (ET),[1] and include Rix's numbers for all inscriptions possible. By consulting the index of inscriptions in Appendix C, below, the reader can locate references to other discussions of particular inscriptions throughout the book.

Rix gives a revised count for the total number of Etruscan inscriptions that have come down to us. Taking into account duplicate publications of the same inscription, counting each coin legend once—and not counting the glosses, which give us Etruscan words explained in Latin or Greek texts but which are not inscriptions—the author comes to a total of fewer than 10,000 inscriptions (some 8,600, to be precise, though a good many more have been discovered in the years since ET appeared).[2] These range in date from the seventh to the first century BCE. There are some 75 inscriptions from the seventh century, a very respectable quantity, even when compared to the 500 or so Greek inscriptions of the Archaic period (from a far wider geographical area).[3]

Any boundaries we set between religious and nonreligious areas of Etruscan civilization are artificial at any time, but this is especially true in the early period. Giovanni Colonna has pointed out the sacral and aristocratic character of writing in the Orientalizing and Archaic periods.[4] Indeed, some of the earliest and most intriguing archaic inscriptions are found in rich tombs of southern Etruria. Many present the sequence of the Greek alphabet, evidently a sign of status, adopted from the Euboean Greeks of Pithekoussai.[5] This alphabet was in time adapted to the Etruscan language, with a few changes indicating geographical or chronological differences, and was then passed on to various peoples of Italy and Europe (such as the Latins, Umbrians, and Gauls).[6]

All the inscriptions can be read, and so they need not be "deciphered." Not all can be understood, however, partly because of the nature of the language, which is not Indo-European and is different from any known language, ancient and modern; and partly because of the nature of the evidence, which is fragmentary. Yet they reveal much about Etruscan religion. Four types of Etruscan inscriptions—ritual, legal, funerary, and votive—deal with religious rituals and the gods. Other inscriptions deal with myth, notably those on Etruscan mirrors, which illustrate stories of Greek and Etruscan mythological figures and which are, as Ambros Pfiffig called them, "picture bilinguals."[7]

Most of the nine thousand or so Etruscan inscriptions are brief, consisting of only a few words: they are epitaphs or dedications, recording the names of the deceased, the donor,

11.1. Zagreb mummy wrappings. 150–100 BCE. Zagreb, National Museum. (After Bonfante and Bonfante 2002, fig. 57.)

the god to whom the object is dedicated, or the mythological character depicted. The longer texts are technical, religious, and ritual, confirming the reputation of the Etruscans as being skillful in dealing with the gods, and related to the various books of the *Etrusca disciplina.** Many of these longer inscriptions have been the objects of recent studies.[8] Let us briefly survey them here and then follow with some of the more revealing short inscriptions.

THE LONGER INSCRIPTIONS

Zagreb Mummy Wrappings

The longest and most exotic Etruscan text that survives is not, properly speaking, an inscription. It is a religious text of the Hellenistic period, originally a sacred linen book, parts of which were preserved by being used as wrappings on an Egyptian mummy (*ET*, LL; Fig. 11.1).[9] The original book, which was cut up into bandages, is of a type referred to in Roman historical sources as a *liber linteus,* a linen book, often illustrated on Etruscan funerary statues as the attribute of a priest. In 1985 Francesco Roncalli had the wrappings restored—they were spotted and damaged by blood and the unguents used for mummification—and photographed in a specialized laboratory in Switzerland. Roncalli, having worked at the Vatican, was familiar with religious texts and was able to add new readings as well as to reconstruct the original form of the book by following the folds of the cloth and the red guidelines for the text. Rubrics in red ink (cinnabar) indicated how it was used as a liturgical text, like some modern Catholic missals. The neatly inked text, with some twelve hundred words laid out in twelve vertical columns, contains a liturgical calendar of sacrifices, offerings and prayers to be made on specific dates. A typical passage runs (col. VIII, line 9, Roncalli 1985, 40): *celi* (the month of September) *huθiś zaθrumiś* (the 26th [day]) *flerχva* (all the offerings) *neθunsl* (to the god Nethuns) *śucri* (should be declared) *θezric* (and should be made).

Piacenza Liver

Another very strange object also contains the names (abbreviated, but recognizable) of divinities who received cult. This is the life-sized bronze model of a sheep's liver from northern Italy, near Piacenza, made around 100 BCE (*ET*, Pa 4.2; Fig. 11.2).[10] It may have been used by a priest in the Roman army. (Other ritual inscriptions are from an earlier period.)

The model was clearly used as a device to teach (or remind) Etruscan priests of the divinatory practice of reading the entrails of animals. As Nancy de Grummond discusses below (Chap. III) priests or seers are shown using it in Etruscan art, including representations on several mirrors. According to the place where the liver of a sacrificed animal showed some special mark, the priest could guess the future or even bend it to his will. The Etruscans were particularly skilled in this *haruspicina,** or science of reading omens, and the Romans respected, hired, and imitated them. The sections of the liver correspond to the sections of the sky that were under the protection of each of the gods. There

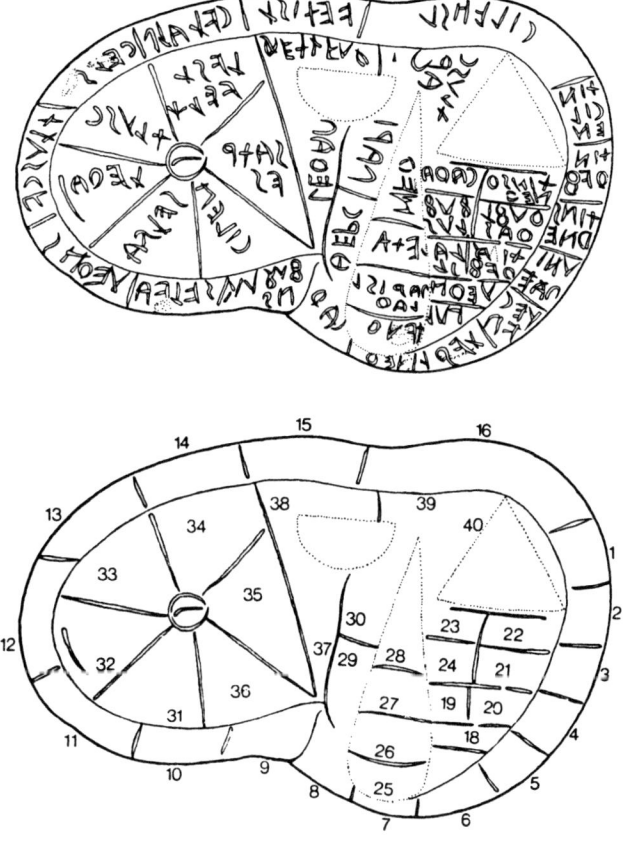

11.2. Bronze model of a sheep's liver from Piacenza. Hellenistic period. Piacenza, Museo Civico. (After Rasenna, 211.)

was a mystic correlation between the parts of a sacred area, like the sky, and the surface of the liver of a ritually sacrificed animal. Such a correlation allowed those who had mastered the technique to "read," as it were, the god's writing in the sky.[11]

Each of the forty-two sections of the liver contains the names of one or more gods; there are fifty-one names, but several are mentioned two or three times. The sixteen sections in the margin of the upper (visceral) side correspond to the sixteen regions of the heavens, according to Martianus Capella (fifth century CE). Further, a number of names of divinities on the liver appear in the description of the skies by Martianus. (See Appendix B, Source no. III.4.)[12]

The lower (venal) side of the liver has two names: Usil, the name of the Sun god, and Tivr, the Moon.[13] A number of the names of these gods are familiar from various sources: Tin (Tinia), Uni, Hercle, Cath (Cautha/Kavtha), Usil, and Tivr. Others may represent epithets of gods. The placement of the different clusters of divinities indicates their function: so, for example, the right lobe contains the gods of heaven and lights (Tin, Uni, Cath, Fufluns); the god of water Nethuns (Neptune, whose name appears so frequently on the mummy wrappings); and Cilens, perhaps a god of Fate. Bouke van der Meer[14] finds that this constellation of divinities came together in the fourth century BCE and that about half of the approximately twenty-eight different names of gods inscribed on the liver are of Etruscan origin. The other half came into Etruria from the surrounding Italic world, Umbria, and the area of Rome (Uni, Neth, and other deities).

Terracotta Tile from Capua

The "Capua Tile," a large terracotta tile used as a tablet, found at Santa Maria di Capua and now in the Berlin Museum, records a religious calendar, like the Zagreb mummy wrappings or the Roman Fasti (ET, TC; Fig. 11.3). The nail holes have been taken to show that it was publicly exhibited in a sanctuary, but they can better be explained as holes for spikes to keep a series of similar documents stored or filed horizontally, the raised edges intended to protect the text incised on the inner surface.

With sixty-two lines and almost three hundred legible words, this is the longest strictly epigraphical Etruscan inscription. Cristofani's study of 1995 dates it to the early fifth century (ca. 470 BCE). There were ten months, as in the earliest Roman calendar, in which the year began in March. Listed are offerings and sacrifices made to various divinities, including gods of the Underworld such as Letham (who appears on the Piacenza liver), Laran, Tin, and Thanr (who appears in birth scenes on Etruscan mirrors; see also Chap. 4), as well as to Uni, the mother goddess to whom the famous local cult was dedicated.[15]

Lead Strip from Santa Marinella

A text written on both sides of a strip of lead, found in fragments at Punta della Vipera near Santa Marinella on the sea, dates from around 500 BCE (ET, Cr 4.10; Fig. 11.4). Inscribed in a miniature style, it is incomplete but contains traces of at least eighty words. Little of the text can be understood, but we can read the word *cver*, "gift."[16]

Lead Plaque from Magliano

A small lead plate found at Magliano, probably dating from the fifth century BCE, has a strange spiral inscription on each side, running from the exterior margin inwards toward the center (Fig. 11.5). There are about seventy words (ET, AV 4.1). The word for "gods," *aiser*, which occurs here, in the Zagreb mummy wrappings, and elsewhere, seems to refer to a group

11.3. Terracotta tile from Capua. Ca. 500 BCE. Berlin, Staatliche Museen. (After Cristofani 1995, fig. 2.)

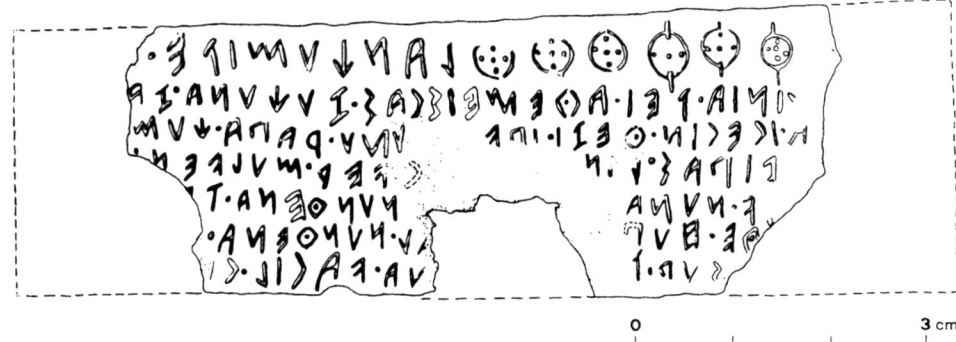
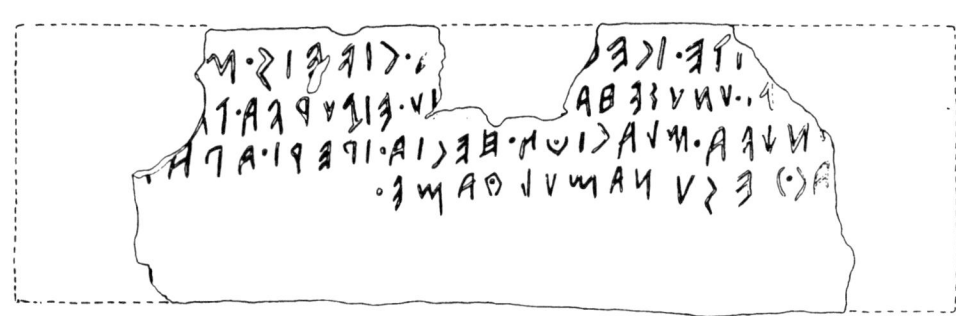

11.4. *Lead plate from Santa Marinella (near Pyrgi). Fifth century BCE. Rome, Museo Nazionale di Villa Giulia. (After Santuari d'Etruria, fig. 8.1c1.)*

11.5. *Lead tablet from Magliano, ca. 500 BCE. Florence, Archaeological Museum. (After Morandi 1982, 36.)*

or "college" of gods, something like the *dii consentes, Penates,* or other collective divinities.[17]

Gold Tablets from Pyrgi

The three gold tablets, two written in Etruscan and one in Phoenician, found in 1964 at the sanctuary at Pyrgi, the harbor of Caere, record a dedication with important historical implications (*ET*, Cr 4.3–4.8; Fig. 11.6).[18] They date from around 500 BCE and constitute the nearest thing to the long-sought Etruscan bilingual. They record in both Etruscan and Phoenician a religious event: the dedication of a gift, perhaps a statue, by the king of Caere, in gratitude for the protection of the goddess. The identification of the goddess Astarte with Uni, rather than with Turan-Aphrodite, is particularly striking. Another tablet mentions Thesan. The longer Etruscan inscription has sixteen lines, thirty-six or thirty-seven words.

Sarcophagus of Laris Pulenas

Another long inscription is funerary: the *elogium* or epitaph of L(a)ris Pulenas (or Pulena) of Tarquinii, engraved on a scroll that the figure of the dead man holds in his hands (*ET*, Ta 1.17; Fig. 11.7).[19] The date is the Hellenistic period, third century BCE, and the text contains nine lines and fifty-nine words. The text can be in part interpreted by means of a comparison with the Latin *elogia* (honorary epitaphs) of the Scipios at Rome. Laris Pulenas was the great-grandson of Laris Pule, the Greek (*Creice*; the latter was possibly related to the famous Greek seer, Polles). Pulenas wrote a book on divination, like the scroll or *volumen* he is proudly exhibiting to the viewer. Like his great-grandfather, he devoted himself to religious duties, perhaps including the cult of ancestors. Recorded are the titles he held in his lifetime, most of them religious, including the priesthoods of Catha and Pacha, the latter equivalent to Fufluns or Dionysos (Pacha is Etruscan for Bacchus). Catha and Fufluns are connected elsewhere too in a joint worship. The name of Culśu can also be recognized.

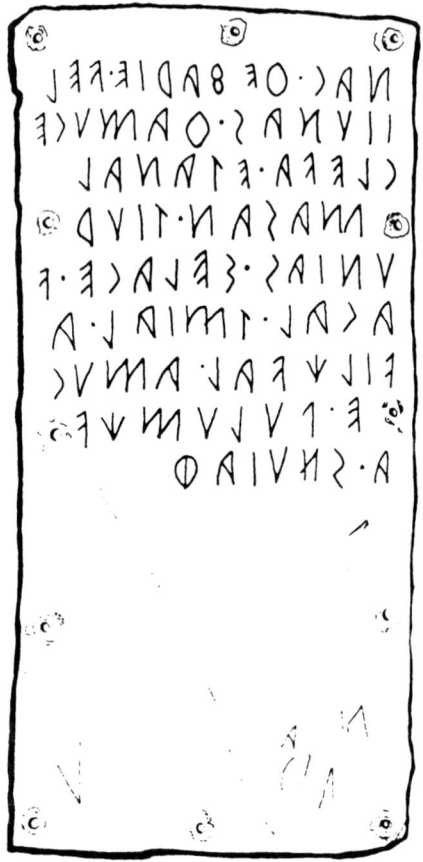 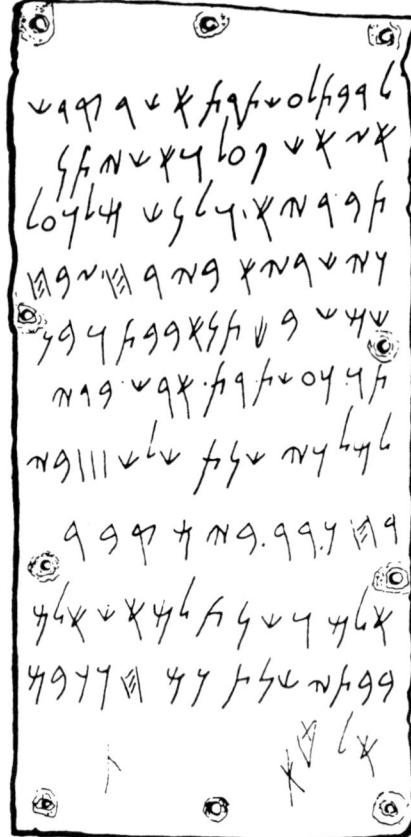 

11.6. Gold tablets from Pyrgi, the harbor of Caere. End of sixth century BCE. Copies in Rome, Museo Nazionale di Villa Giulia. (After Morandi 1991, figs. 12–14.)

SOME SHORTER INSCRIPTIONS

Boundary Stones from Tunisia

Tin was a god who protected boundaries. His name appears as the guarantor on three boundary stones with identical inscriptions found in Tunisia, originally placed there by Etruscan colonists, perhaps in the time of the Gracchi: *m vnata zvtas tvl dardanivm tinś* Φ "M. Unata Zutas. Boundaries of the Dardanians. Of Tin. 1000 [paces]" (ET, Af 8.1–8.8).[20]

Bronze Mirror from Volaterrae

Clearly religious in character is an engraved bronze mirror from Volaterrae (ET, Vt S2; Fig. 11.8) whose inscription, a legal-religious document, has important implications. An imposingly regal, enthroned female figure, Uni, is pictured nursing a full-grown Hercle, while four gods stand by as witnesses. Among these are Apollo, recognizable by his laurel branch, and an older god holding a trident or lightning bolt, either Nethuns or Tinia. He points to a tablet on which the

11.7. Sarcophagus of Laris Pulenas. 250–200 BCE. Tarquinia, Museo Nazionale. (After Morandi 1991, fig. 20.)

11.8. Bronze mirror from Volaterrae with Hercle nursing at Uni's breast. 325–300 BCE. Florence, Museo Archeologico. (After ES, 5.60.)

significance of the scene is explained: *eca: sren: tva: iχnac hercle:unial clan: θra:sce,* "This picture shows how Hercle became Uni's son (or: drank milk)." This mother goddess, Uni, is carrying out an adoption ritual witnessed by four other gods. While Greek myth tells the story of the nursing of Herakles by Hera, his jealous stepmother, in the context of the conflict between the goddess and the hero, the story is not illustrated in the Greek art that has come down to us.[21] In Etruria, in contrast, there are a number of representations of this mythological nursing scene: as on this mirror, Uni is reconciled with Hercle by means of a ritual familiar from the Near East and Egypt but downplayed in Greece. It is in fact the Etruscan version that best illustrates for us the meaning of his name in Greek, "Glory of Hera."

Bronze Chimaera from Arezzo

The famed bronze Chimaera of Arezzo (Arretium), dating to the fourth century BCE, depicts the Greek monster with the body of a lion and, on its back, the head of a goat. The tail shaped like a serpent is a restoration. On the leg is incised an inscription dedicating it to the god, *tinścvil*, "gift to Tin" (ET, Ar 3.2; Fig. VI.1). This was indeed a splendid gift, for the animal, which is life size, was evidently a part of a large group representing Bellerophon and Pegasus attacking the monster.[22]

Bronze Statuette of Culśanś

A bronze statuette of a double-faced divinity from Cortona is dedicated to Culśanś (*ET*, Co 3.4; Fig. 11.9): *v. cvinti. arntiaś. culśanśl alpan. turce*, "V[elia] Cuinti, Arnt's (daughter) to Culśanś (this object) gladly gave."[23]

Bronze Statuette Dedicated to Selvans Tularias

A bronze statuette of an athlete, from an unknown provenance (Fig. 11.10), has the following inscription: *ecn:turce: avle:havrnas:tuθina:apana: selvansl tularias*, "This gave Avle Havrnas [*tuthina apana*, meaning unknown] to Selvans of the Boundaries."[24]

Bronze Mirror from Praeneste

Not only are inscriptions in Etruscan useful. From Praeneste comes a mirror with Latin inscriptions, now in the Metropolitan Museum of Art, dated ca. 300 BCE (Fig. 11.11),[25] that presents an Italic view of the relationship between Uni and Hercle. It shows *Iovei* (i.e., Jupiter, in the dative case), reconciling *Iuno* and *Hercele*. A female herm and a phallus put the picture in a sexual context that may be religious, though it is hard for us to interpret.

Rectangular Boundary Stone from Perugia

The protection of boundaries, *tular*,* was an important divine responsibility. It was mentioned in the text of the prophecy of Vegoia (Appendix B, Source no. 11.1) and serves as the epithet of the god Selvans in a votive inscription. It also occurs in the sharply chiseled inscription (forty-six lines and 130 words) on two of the four faces of a boundary stone (*cippus**) from Perugia, dating from the second or first century BCE (*ET*, Pe 8.4; Fig. 11.12).[26] The inscription does not name any gods and would not be overtly religious according to our modern definition of the word. But Roncalli suggests that the two holes on the top were made for *cippi*, perhaps aniconic images of Silvanus-Terminus, and that there were two of them in relation to the two families, the Velthina and the Afuna, whose boundaries they protected.[27]

Bronze Tablet from Cortona

The context may be similar for a remarkable recent find, the *Tabula Cortonensis*, which takes its place, at sixty words, as one of the longest Etruscan inscriptions to have come down

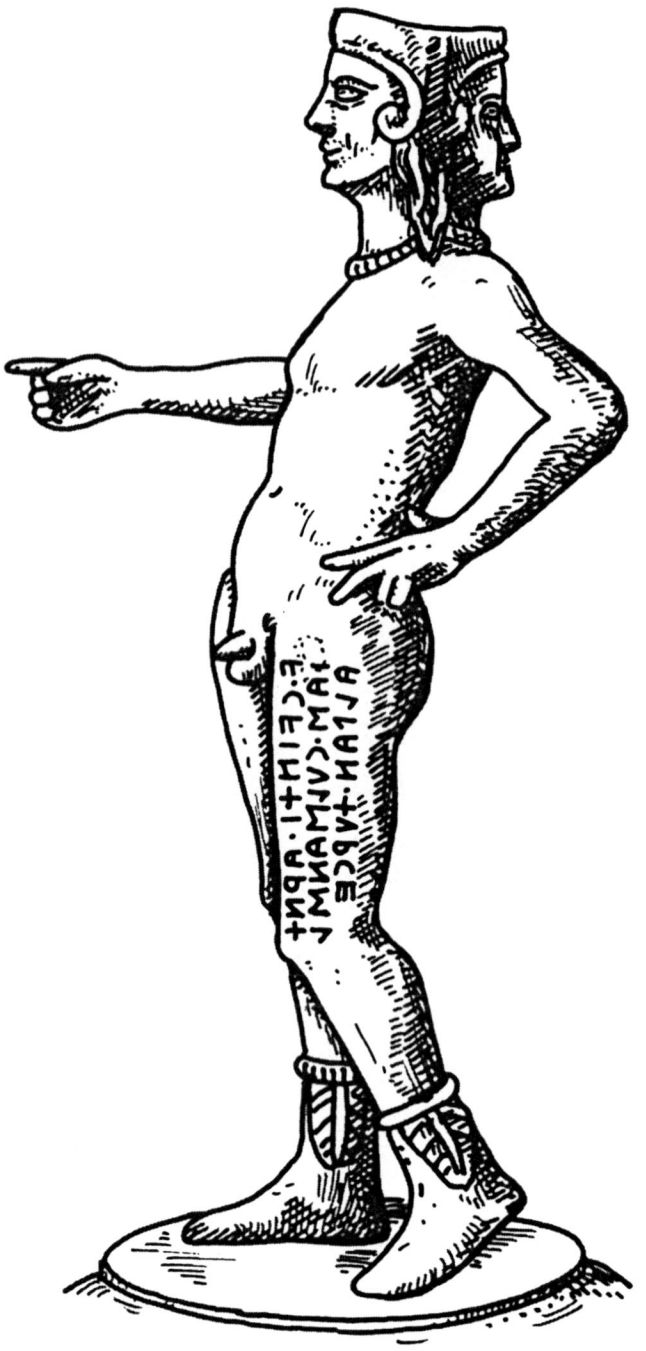

11.9. Bronze statuette of Culśanś. Third century BCE. Cortona, Museum. (After A. Pfiffig, Religio etrusca, Graz, 1975, fig. 108.)

to us (Fig. 11.13).[28] The bronze tablet, of Hellenistic date, came to light in 1992 in Cortona but was publicly announced only in June 1999, causing a flurry of excitement in newspapers and on Italian television. It records a legal contract or religious ritual, including a long list of the names of the

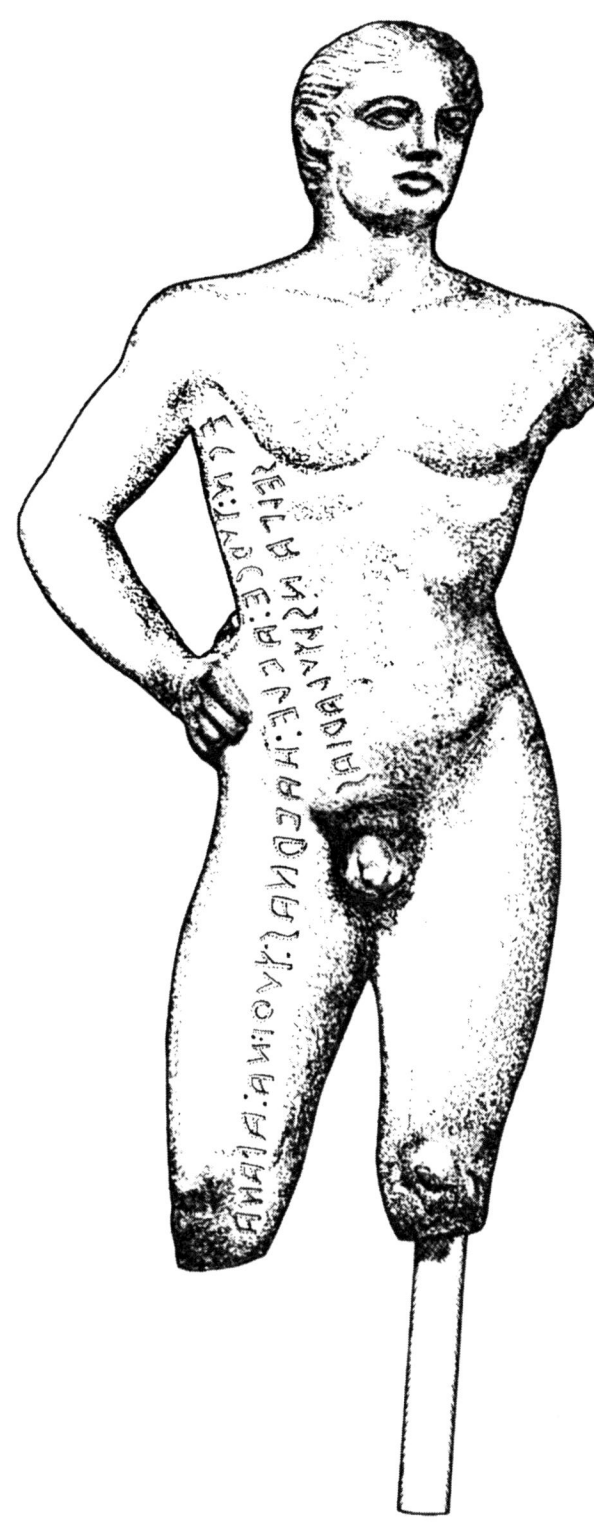

11.10. Bronze statuette dedicated to Selvans Tularias. End of fourth century BCE. Malibu, CA. The J. Paul Getty Museum. (After Bonfante 1991, 836, fig. 1.)

11.11. Praenestine mirror with Juno, Jupiter, and Hercules. Ca. 300 BCE. New York, The Metropolitan Museum of Art. (After CSE USA 3.7.)

parties involved and another list of the witnesses' names. No gods seem to be mentioned, but the fact that it was folded over into eight pieces, apparently in a ritual destruction, suggests that the content was religious.

Dedications to Hercle

Several inscriptions came to light in the late 1970s and early 1980s to a cult in honor of Hercle. A votive inscription on a bronze base in the Manchester Museum (Fig. 11.14), incompletely preserved, tells us that a certain Prisnius gave it to Hercle on behalf of his son, . . . *esi p.ri.snius turce hercles clen ceχa munis en ca eluruve itruta: ala alpnina luθs inpa ulχn.* . . . *Luθs* may also be the name of a god, and *ala alpnina* may be compared to *alpan turce*, "gladly gave" (Latin: *libens dedit*).[29] A sanctuary at Caere seems to account for a number of inscriptions to Hercle. A large bronze club, a bronze statuette of Hercle in Toledo (Fig. 11.15), a bronze weight, and a red-

II.12. Rectangular boundary stone from Perugia. Third or second century BCE. Perugia, Museo Archeologico. (Photo: Schwanke, DAI Rome 82.1151.)

figured Attic cup by Euphronios (returned to Rome in 1999 by the J. P. Getty Museum) all have inscriptions that testify to an important cult place for Hercle.[30]

Dedications to Other Deities

Inscribed dedications at the sanctuary of Graviscae, the port of Tarquinii, point to the worship of Turan, Uni, Vei, Atunis (Adonis), and Aplu.[31] A group of bronze statues and statuettes with votive inscriptions also provide the names of gods to whom cult is paid. The inscriptions are incised on the

II.13. Bronze tablet from Cortona, Tabula Cortonensis. Third or second century BCE. Florence, Museo Archeologico. (After Agostiniani and Nicosia 2000, pls. 8–9.)

11.14. Bronze base dedicated to Hercle. Hellenistic period. Manchester Museum. (After Bonfante and Bonfante 2002, fig. 52.)

bodies of these figures, illustrating the continuity of an archaic custom that was usual in early Greek inscriptions but that in Greece was abandoned in favor of writing the names on a separate base, in order, no doubt, to avoid defacing the image.[32] This is one of the many cases in which the Etruscans maintain archaic customs, not a surprising tendency given the aristocratic character of their society.

RECURRING THEMES

Etruscan mirrors and wall paintings constitute a rich repertoire of Etruscan mythological scenes. Often the labels on the figures give us an insight into points of view of images, themes, and motifs that are either strictly Etruscan or differ in significant ways from Greek religious and mythological iconography. The following appear to be characteristically Etruscan: (1) the prevalence of couples and "dyads," (2) the importance of mothers, (3) representations of scenes of the birth of gods, with related midwives and other medical subject matter, and (4) the frequent appearance of souls or ghosts. Let us now consider each of these themes at greater length.

The Prevalence of Couples and "Dyads"

As regards gods in groups, we have already noted the implications of the word *aiser*. The tendency to put gods in pairs or dyads is also deduced through inscriptions. Besides Fufluns and Catha, couples include Turan and Atunis, often representing Turan as an older woman with Atunis as a boy or very young man; Aita (Hades) and Phersipnei (Persephone or Proserpina); Atmite (Admetus) and Alsctei (Alkestis). Some couples turn out to be mother-and-son groups like Semla and Fufluns. Other "dyads," as Pallottino calls them, are twins like the Dioskouroi, *tinas cliniiar*, Castor and Pollux.[33]

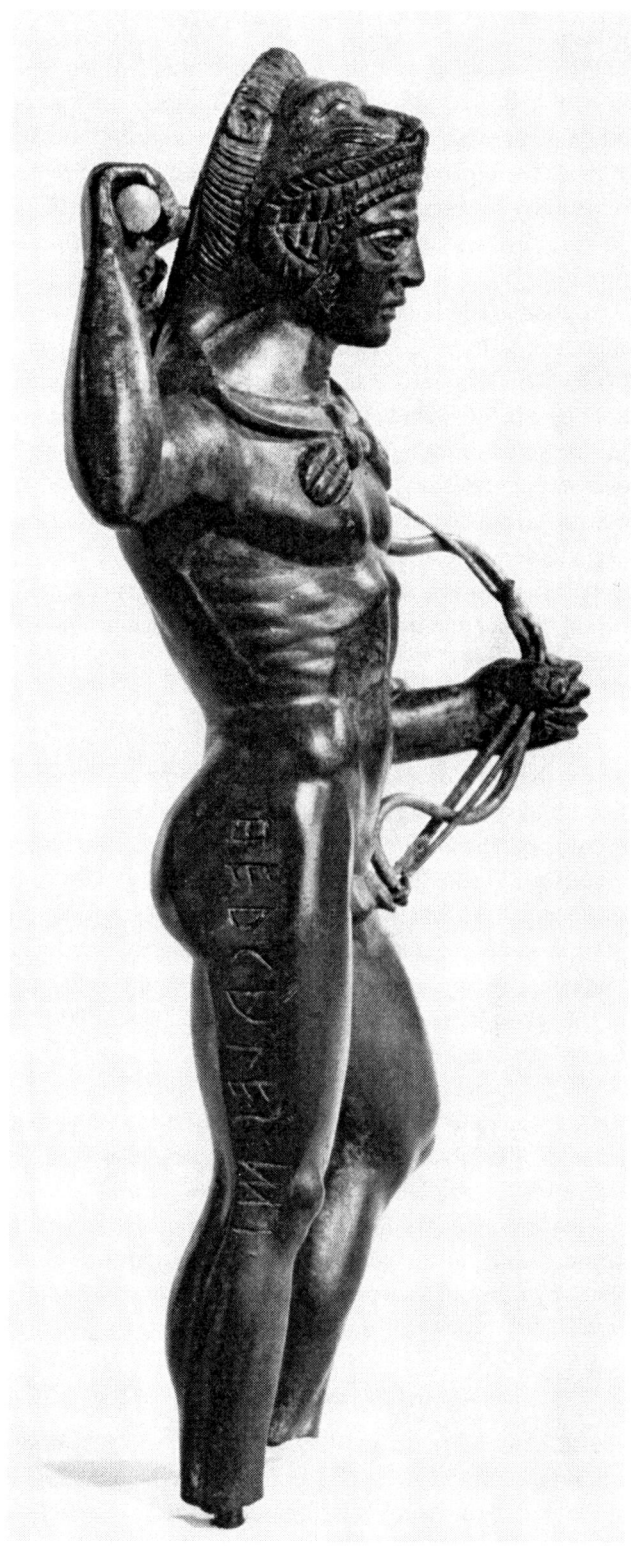

11.15. Bronze statuette of Hercle. Ca 300 BCE. Toledo Museum of Art. (Acc. 78.22, gift of Edward Drummond Libbey. Courtesy of Toledo Museum of Art.)

The Importance of Mothers

The importance of mothers is shown by the frequent epithets of goddesses who are called *ati*, "mother," such as *cel ati*, "mother earth" (Celsclan= son of Cel), *turan ati*, "mother Turan." These parallel the early and frequent artistic representations of mothers and children, many of them nursing — an image that was shunned in Greek art until the fourth century BCE.[34]

A good example of a mother is the third-century votive stone statue from Volaterrae known as the *kourotrophos* Maffei*. This life-sized marble statue of a standing woman holding a baby might be thought to be a cult statue, except for the votive inscription that runs along the figure's right arm and shoulder (*ET*, Vt 3.3). Though the statue is based on a Greek fourth-century model, the baby is a peculiarly Etruscan addition. The inscription gives us the word for "image," *cana*.[35] It reads *mi: cana: larθiaś: zanl: velχinei: śe[lv]ansĺ[: tu]rce*, "I (am) the image of Larthia Zan. Velchina [to Selvans?] gave (me)."

The Birth of Gods

As for the birth of gods, not only is the subject favored in Etruscan art but there are surprising twists and additions to the stories. The birth of Fufluns (Dionysos, Bacchus) has a precedent: a scene shows the conception of the god by Tinia and Semla.[36] Thalna, who appears on a number of mirrors of birth scenes together with Thanr, or Ethausva, as a divine midwife, also appears as a male, illustrating the ambiguity of the sex of certain divine figures and a different attitude towards their anthropomorphism.[37]

Such a practical view of myths is typically Etruscan. Artists show the birth of Menerva (Athena), a scene that takes on special emphasis in Etruscan art because of her importance, with divine "nurses" — Thalna, Thanr — realistically assisting Tinia. Other medical scenes include Prumathe (Prometheus), at the moment of his liberation, who is assisted by Esplace (Asclepius), in what looks to us like a similarly realistic approach (Fig. 11.16).[38]

The Frequent Appearance of Souls or Ghosts

Ingrid Krauskopf discusses (below, Chap. 5) evidence of the importance of the afterworld in Etruscan religion. Around the area of the ancient Volsinii (modern Orvieto) we find the custom of dedicating an object to the dead, especially a precious object, by scratching on it the word *suθina*, "for the grave." In the case of a mirror, scratching the word across the reflecting surface makes it useless for the living. One mirror at the Metropolitan Museum of Art has *suθina* on the disc,

11.16. Bronze mirror with Prometheus Unbound. Early third century BCE. New York, The Metropolitan Museum of Art. (After CSE USA 3.11.)

while another has the word *cracna* in the same position; perhaps it is the name of the deceased. The custom of "killing" the object to make it unfit for use by the living is known from other cultures, and indeed elsewhere in Etruria as well. It belongs in the context of the world of the dead and of ghosts.[39]

In fact, we have several depictions of ghosts, which can be identified because they are clearly labeled with one of the words we know best in Etruscan: *hinθial*, which means "soul" or "image." There is *hinθial teriasals* (*ET*, Ta 7.67), "the ghost of Teiresias," and a vase painting shows the ghosts of two Amazons, *pentasila* and *aturmuca* (*ET*, Vc 7.36), Penthesilea and Andromache.[40] A mirror in the Metropolitan Museum with Odysseus and Kirke (Fig. 11.17) shows a thin, wan

11.17. Bronze mirror with Uthste, Cerca, and Velparun. 350–300 BCE. New York, The Metropolitan Museum of Art. (After CSE USA 3.15.)

11.18. Bronze mirror with Lasa, Hamphiar, and Aivas. 350–300 BCE. London, British Museum. (After CSE Great Britain 1, I, 28.)

figure of Velparun, that is, Elpenor, whose ghost comes up to Odysseus (Uthste) in the Underworld scene in the *Odyssey*: the ghost is present along with Cerca (Kirke) as two scenes from the epic are merged in the same picture.[41]

Legends on Etruscan coins provide source material for the religious, as well as the political and commercial life of the Etruscan cities. The coins of Populonia show the Etruscan name of the city, Pupluna — that is, Fufluna, "the city of Fufluns."[42]

CONCLUSION: THE PLACE OF WRITING IN ETRUSCAN RELIGION

Because writing was so important for the Etruscans, our knowledge of Etruscan religion depends to a large extent on Etruscan inscriptions and their contexts. There is still much to learn from these texts — ritual and funerary, votive, legal, and mythological, as recent studies have shown: the names of the gods and their contexts — whether they are mythological figures from Greek or Etruscan traditions or gods who receive cult in local sanctuaries. Sometimes, as in the case of Hercle, they are clearly both. We learn the names of the donors, the ritual formulas, and forms of votive gifts and of funerary dedications.

Writing defined and fixed the established channels of communication between gods and mortals. In a way, the signs of the gods were themselves a kind of writing that had to be deciphered by men.[43] After the 1985 exhibit on Etruscan texts at Perugia, *Scrivere Etrusco*, Massimo Pallottino remarked that we could well call the Etruscans, like the Hebrews, the "People of the Book." When Livy tells us that the Romans used to send their children to Etruria to learn letters in the fourth century BCE, as they later used to send them to Athens, we can assume that it was the children of aristocrats, the Roman oligarchy, who needed to learn the art of divination as part of their training, to be able to lead armies in the field and carry out religious rituals in peace. With the study of the Etruscan books of divination they received a technical training that might have been the ancient equivalent of going to MIT to study engineering.

11.19. *Bronze mirror with Athrpa, Turan, Atunis, Meliacr, and Atlenta. Ca. 320 BCE Berlin, Antiquarium. (After G. Zimmer, Spiegel in Antikenmuseum, Berlin, 1987, pl. 19.)*

There were characteristic styles for religious texts, some of which we can recognize in spite of the loss of Etruscan literature and the paucity of long, continuous texts. The solemnity of the style occasionally comes through even in the limited amount of written material that has come down to us.

In Etruscan art, moreover, a number of the longer texts echo the solemn rhythm characteristic of religious and legal documents, with their repeated symmetries, parallel clauses, and synonyms. When Laris Pulenas lists his titles and priesthoods, recording the ceremonies, sacraments, functions, and sacrifices at which he has officiated, their ritual order seems to determine the rhythm of the repeated *pul, pul, pul*—"first, then, then...." In the Pyrgi tablets a similar rhythm appears from the beginning: *ita tmia icac heramasva*, "This is the *tmia* and this is the *heramasva* ...," and later, *ilacve ... ilacve*, "since on the one hand ... since on the other hand." In calendars such as those on the Zagreb mummy wrappings or the Capua tile, which prescribe specific sacrifices, libations, and prayers to be offered to particular divinities at given dates, the repetitions are necessitated by their very nature. On the Perugia boundary stone, the patterns, symmetries, and other rhetorical devices of ritual language are reflected in the spacing of the words and lines of the inscription.[44]

Written texts—books, scrolls, and tablets—are frequently represented in Etruscan art, and the solemnity of the written style of religious and legal texts is also sometimes represented on the monuments themselves. One of the best examples of such a visual rendering of a document recording the ceremony is the mirror from Volaterrae with the symbolic ritual of the adoption of Hercle on the part of Uni (Fig. 11.8). This solemn moment is witnessed by an assembly of divinities, one of whom points to the tablet that records the ceremony and assures its legality, like the contracts and legal documents recorded on the Perugia *cippus* and *Tabula Cortonensis* (Figs. 11.12 and 11.13). This documentation of a divine rite of passage is paralleled by funerary scenes such as that of the Lasa holding out a scroll with the names of the dead heroes (Fig. 11.18), or of Laris Pulenas exhibiting his scroll on his sarcophagus (Fig. 11.7). An image similarly assuring the permanence of the destiny of an individual or a group may be the ritual gesture of the female divinity Athrpa (Atropos) hammering the nail of Fate on another mirror, as the two unfortunate couples, Turan and Atunis, Meliacr and Atlenta (Meleager and Atalanta), look on (Fig. 11.19).[45]

The importance of the written word is underlined by the appearance of the word for "writing," *ziχ*, on religious and legal documents. On the Capua tile, an individual whose name is lost has been responsible for the text, which he wrote down or ordered to be written, *ziχunce*. The Zagreb mummy wrappings have *ziχne*, as well as the phrase *ziχri cn*, "Let this be written down."[46] The epitaph of Laris Pulenas refers to the book on divination he has written, the *ziχ neθśrac*. The *cippus* from Perugia ends with the solemn ruling, *ceχa ziχuχe*, "as this sentence has been written down, prescribed"—the sentence has been written in stone. In the bronze tablet from Cortona, the *Tabula Cortonensis*, the verb *ziχ-* also refers to the contents of the document.

The luxurious writing implements buried with the dead indicated the importance of writing in the seventh century, an importance emphasized in the fourth century and later by specific references to books and writing in the documents themselves and by their representation in art. Religion, the art of divination, the stability of boundaries, the security of the society all depended upon the inviolability of the written word. Prophecies, which were crucial to the Etruscan system of religion and life, were often spoken, or otherwise indicated. Many were written down, like the prophecies of Tages and of Vegoia.[47] The act of writing itself was important and defined the character of rituals or sacred law and the very nature of the religion concerned.[48] Etruscan religion provides a striking example of the symbolic, religious significance of writing.

NOTES

1. Rix, in *ET*.
2. Further, Rix (*ET*) omits "graffiti," the *sigla* of one, two or three letters that abound on pottery and other objects from Etruscan archaeological sites but are usually discounted by philologists because they do not have recognizable words. Cf. de Grummond, Bare and Meilleur 2000.
3. Cristofani 1987, 127–131; Cornell 1991, 21. Greek inscriptions: Guarducci 1987, 34–87.
4. Colonna 1976, 7–24, esp. 18–22.
5. Cristofani 1979, 378–379.
6. Morandi 1982.
7. Pfiffig 1969, 12; Fiesel 1928; De Simone 1968–1970; Rix 1978–1984, 84.
8. Roncalli 1985; Rix 1985, 21–37; Christofani 1995.
9. Roncalli 1985, 17–64.
10. Van der Meer 1987; Maggiani 1982.
11. This was the case when the Etruscan princess Tanaquil, wife of Tarquin, read the signs of the bird's flight in different regions of the sky when they arrived in Rome and foresaw their future there. Indeed, her husband did become king and began the Etruscan dynasty at Rome as Tarquinius Priscus. For further discussions of the sky and its divisions, see the discussion by Ingrid Edlund-Berry below, Chap. 7.
12. Van der Meer 1987, 22–26; Weinstock 1946.
13. For the deities mentioned here and throughout this volume, the reader may refer to the fuller treatment by Simon in Chapter 4. See especially the glossary of gods (pp. 57–61) and Chart 1 (p. 46), which gives a list of selected Etruscan gods with conjectured identi-

fications of the counterparts in Greece and Rome. As noted earlier, Etruscan spellings were not standardized, and so minor variations in the names may appear, depending on which inscriptions are referenced. Here we try to observe the versions of the names used on the liver, some of which, however, are surely abbreviations.

14. Van der Meer 1987, 146.

15. Thanr: Cristofani 1995, 70, 119; Uni, *unialθi:* 118-119.

16. *Santuari d'Etruria* 153-154. Cver: Pfiffig 1969, 264-267, 284, "votive gift," or "boy" ("Geschenk," "Weihegabe," or "Knabe").

17. Pallottino 1975, 143.

18. Pyrgi tablets: CIE 6314-6316. Pallottino 1975, 170, with previous bibliography; *Die Göttin von Pyrgi,* 1981.

19. CIE 5430. Devoto 1936, 287; Heurgon 1957, 106-126; Heurgon 1961, 291-293; Pallottino 1984, 425, 441; Van der Meer 1987, 129-130, 172-173, 187, fig. 78; Morandi 1991, 156-167, no. 15, fig. 20 (drawing); Cataldi 1988: Beekes and van der Meer 1991, 57-59.

20. Heurgon 1969, 526-551; Carruba 1976, 163-173.

21. For mothers and children in ancient art, see Bonfante 1989, 85-106; Bonfante 1997b, 174-196. See also van der Meer 1995, 124-130. For reference to a statue of Juno nursing Hercules, see *Anthologia Palatina* 9.589.

22. Cristofani 1991a, 2-5. For such a group illustrated on a mirror in the Metropolitan Museum of Art, see Bonfante 1997a, 13.

23. Bonfante and Bonfante 2002, 166, source 48, fig. 32.

24. For the Roman equivalent, Silvanus *custos,* see Dorcey 1992, esp. 17-25, 28-32, 179. See also Collins Clinton, forthcoming. The epithet *custos* appears only in Rome and Italy.

25. Bonfante 1997a, no. 7.

26. De Simone 1987-1988, 346-351; Fabing 1988, 254-258; Van der Meer 1987, 61; Bonfante 1991, 835-844; Cristofani 1991b, 148, no. 36.

27. Roncalli 1985, 74-81.

28. Agostiniani and Nicosia 2000.

29. Manchester base: Turfa 1982, 183; Bonfante and Bonfante 2002, 175, source 61; Pallottino 1983, 611-614; Colonna 1987-1988, 345; ET, OA 3.9 (wrongly reads *luθs* as *lusθ*). On the cult of Hercle at Cerveteri, see Cristofani 1996, 39-54.

30. For the bronze statuette of Hercle in Toledo, *hercales mi:* de Grummond 1986, 20-21, fig. I-1; Cristofani 1996, 54. For the bronze club of Heracles with votive inscription to Hercle, from Cerveteri, see Cristofani 1996, 54, fig. 29, and 55-60; Moretti Sgubini 1999, 1-24. For votive inscriptions, see Schrimer 1998, 38-56. For Hercle in Etruscan art, see Bayet 1926; Uehlenbrock 1986; Schwarz 1990; Neils 1998, 6-21.

31. Torelli 1977, 398-458.

32. Bonfante and Bonfante 2002, sources 46-50. Early Greek inscriptions on statues: Guarducci, 1987, 46-48, nude bronze male figure, Mantiklos Apollo, ca. 700 BCE, Boston Museum of Fine Arts; 49-51, marble statue of *kore** from Delos, Nikandre, ca. 650 BCE.

33. Pallottino 1975, 143; De Puma, 1973, 159-170; de Grummond 1991. Pallottino includes couples made up of "a male god and an accompanying goddess, as in the case of Aita and Phersipnai, the infernal couple." I feel male-female couples are different in kind and in any case unequal: Bonfante 1981, 157-187 (= *Reflections,* 323-343).

34. Colonna 1976-1977, 45-62; Colonna 1994, 134-135; Bonfante 1997b, 174-196; de Grummond 2004; Renard 1964.

35. CIE 76; Bianchi Bandinelli 1982, 288-314.

36. Van der Meer 1995, 119-122 (Menerva), 122-124 (Fufluns); Bonfante 1993, 221-235.

37. Bonfante 1997a, no. 20; Cristofani 1993, 9-21.

38. Bonfante 1997a, no. 11; Dobrowolski 1991, 1213-1230; Kerenyi 1963, 127-128. Kerenyi points to the remarkable resemblance of the image of Prometheus to that of a Renaissance Christ taken down from the Cross.

39. Bonfante 1997a, no. 4. On *suθina,* see Fontaine 1995, 201-216; Briquel 1995.

40. Martelli 1987, no. 174B.

41. Bonfante 1997a, no. 15. See also Bonfante and Bonfante 2002, 22.

42. Tripp 1986, 203-204.

43. Much of the following is adapted from a section, "The Written Word," in Bonfante and Bonfante 2002, 114-116.

44. De Simone 1997, 235-237; ET; Cristofani 1995, 85-87, 125. On the Perugia *cippus,* see Roncalli 1985, 81; and Roncalli 1985b, 161-170. The *Tabula Cortonensis* gives us a new example of the verb "to write."

45. On the importance of writing in Etruscan art and society, see Roncalli 1985a; Roncalli 1976, 187-195. On the nail of Fate, see Aigner Foresti 1979, 144-149; Bonfante 1998, 53-65.

46. New reading: Roncalli 1985, 52 (instead of *zaχri,* in ThLE, s.v., TLE, 1).

47. De Grummond, below, Chap. 3.

48. Beard 1991, 35-58: "The simple fact, for example, that writing becomes used, even by a tiny minority, to define the calendar of rituals or sacred law inevitably changes the nature of the religion concerned"; and also her discussion of the primacy of writing and the "clear determining power of the written word over the spoken" (39). See also Corbier 1987, 27-60; Corbier 1991, 99-118.

BIBLIOGRAPHY

Agostiniani, L., and F. Nicosia. 2000. *Tabula Cortonensis.* Rome.

Aigner Foresti, L. 1979. "Zur Zeremonie der Nagelschlagung in Rom und in Etrurien." *AJAH* 4, 144-149.

Bayet, J. 1926. *Herclé: Étude critique des principaux monuments relatifs à l'Hercule étrusque.* Paris.

Beard, M. 1991. "Ancient Literacy and the Function of the Written Word in Roman Religion." In *Literacy in the Roman World. JRA* Suppl. 3, 35-58.

Beekes, R. S. P., and L. B. van der Meer. 1991. *De Etrusken Spreken.* Muiderberg.

Bianchi Bandinelli, R. 1982. "Marmora Etruriae," and "La kourotrophos Maffei del museo di Volterra." In *L'arte etrusca.* Rome; orig. publ. 1967, 1968. 288-314.

Bonfante, G., and L. Bonfante. 2002. *The Etruscan Language: An Introduction.* Manchester. Revised ed.

Bonfante, Larissa. 1981. "Etruscan Couples and Their Aristocratic

Society." *Women in Antiquity: Women's Studies* 8, 157-187. Reprinted in *Reflections of Women in Antiquity*, ed. Helene P. Foley. New York, 1981, 323-343.

———. 1989. "Iconografia delle madri: Etruria e Italia antica." In *Le donne in Etruria*, ed. Antonia Rallo. Rome. 85-106.

———. 1991. "Un bronzetto da Bolsena (?)." In *Miscellanea etrusca e italica in onore di M. Pallottino. ArchClass* 43, 835-844.

———. 1993. "Fufluns Pacha: The Etruscan Dionysos." In *Masks of Dionysos*, ed. Thomas Carpenter and Christopher Faraone. Oxford. 221-235.

———. 1997a. *Corpus Speculorum Etruscorum [CSE] USA* 3. New York, The Metropolitan Museum of Art. Rome.

———. 1997b. "Nursing Mothers in Classical Art." In *Naked Truths: Women, Sexuality and Gender in Classical Art and Archaeology*, ed. Ann O. Koloski-Ostrow and Claire L. Lyons. London. 174-196.

———. 1998. 'Il destino degli Etruschi.' In *Libertà o necessità? L'idea del destino nelle culture umane*, ed. A. Bongioanni and E. Comba. Turin. 53-65.

Briquel, D. 1995. "Note sur les vases portant l'inscription 'suthina' et réputés provenir de Nola." *REL* 97, 217-223.

Carruba, O. 1976. "Nuova lettura dell'iscrizione etrusca dei cippi di Tunisia." *Athenaeum* 54, 163-173.

Cataldi, M. 1988. *I sarcofagi etruschi delle famiglie Partunu, Curuna, e Pulena*. Rome.

Collins Clinton, J. Forthcoming. "Stone Sculpture." In *Catalogue of the Study Collection of the American Academy in Rome*.

Colonna, G. 1976. "Il sistema alfabetico." *L'etrusco arcaico: Atti del Colloquio*. Florence. 7-24.

———. 1976-1977. "La dea etrusca Cel e i santuari del Trasimeno." *Rivista storica dell'antichità* 6-7, 45-62.

———. 1987-1988. "Rivista di epigrafia etrusca," *StEtr* 55, 345 (no. 126).

———. 1993. "A proposito degli dèi del Fegato di Piacenza," *StEtr* 59, 1993 [1994], 123-139.

Corbier, M. 1987. "L'écriture dans l'espace public romain." In *L'Urbs*, ed. C. Pietri. Rome. 27-60.

———. 1991. "L'écriture en quête de lecteurs." In *Literacy in the Roman World. JRA* Suppl. 3, 99-118.

Cornell, T. 1991. "The Tyranny of the Evidence: A Discussion of the Possible Uses of Literacy in Etruria and Latium in the Archaic Age." In *Literacy in the Roman World. JRA* Suppl. 3, 7-33.

Cristofani, Mauro. 1979. "Recent Advances in Etruscan Epigraphy and Language." In *Italy before the Romans*, ed. D. Ridgway and F. R. Ridgway. London. 373-412.

———. 1987. "Appendice: Le iscrizioni del VII secolo a. C." In *Saggi di storia etrusca arcaica*. Rome. 127-131.

———. 1991a. "Chimereide." *Prospettiva* 61, 2-5.

———. 1991b. *Introduzione allo studio dell'etrusco*. Florence.

———. 1993. "Sul processo di antropomorfizzazione nel panteon etrusco," *Miscellanea etrusco-italica* 22, 9-21.

———. 1995. *Tabula Capuana*. Florence.

———. 1996. "Appendice: Ancora sulla kylix ceretana con dedica a *hercle* nel J. Paul Getty Museum." In *Due testi dell'Italia preromana*. Rome. 54-60.

de Grummond, N. T. 1986. "Rediscovery." In *Etruscan Life and Afterlife*, ed. L. Bonfante. Detroit. 18-46.

———. 1991. "Etruscan Twins and Mirror Images." *Bulletin of the Yale University Art Gallery*, 11-31.

———. 2004. "For the Mother and for the Daughter: Some Thoughts on Dedications from Etruria and Praeneste." ΧΑΡΙΣ, *Essays in Honor of Sara Immerwahr*, ed. A. P. Chapin. *Hesperia* Suppl. 33. Princeton. 351-370.

de Grummond, N. T., C. Bare, and A. Meilleur. 2000. "Etruscan Sigla ("Graffiti"): Prolegomena and Some Case Studies." *Archaeologia Transatlantica* 18, 25-38.

De Puma, R. D. 1973. "The Dioskouroi on Four Etruscan Mirrors in Midwestern Collections." *StEtr* 41, 159-170.

De Simone, C. 1968-1970. *Die griechischen Enthlehnungen im Etruskischen*. 2 vols. Wiesbaden.

———. 1987-1988. "Rivista di epigrafia etrusca." *StEtr* 55, 346-351.

———. 1997. "La radice etrusca *zich* - 'ritzen.'" In *Etrusca et Italica: Scritti in ricordo di Massimo Pallottino*. Pisa. 235-237.

Devoto, G. 1936. "Problemi dell'iscrizione di Pulena." *StEtr* 10, 277-287 (= 1967. "L'iscrizione di Pulena." *Scritti minori* II. Florence. 191-199).

Dobrowolski, W. 1991. "Il mito di Prometeo: Il limite tra il cielo e la terra nell'arte etrusca." *Miscellanea Pallottino, ArchClass* 43, 1213-1230.

Dorcey, P. F. 1992. *The Cult of Silvanus: A Study in Roman Folk Religion*. Leiden.

ET = H. Rix, *Etruskische Texte*, editio minor. 2 vols. Tübingen. 1991.

Fabing, Susannah. 1988. *The Gods Delight*. Cleveland.

Fiesel, Eva. 1928. *Namen des griechischen Mythos im Etruskischen*. Göttingen.

Fontaine, P. 1995. "A propos des inscriptions 'suthina' sur la vaisselle métallique étrusque." In *Vaisselle métallique, vaisselle céramique: Productions, usages et valeurs en Étrurie. REA* 97. Ed. J.-R. Jannot. 201-216.

Die Göttin von Pyrgi, 1981 = *Die Göttin von Pyrgi: Akten des Kolloquiums Tübingen 1979*. Ed. A. Neppi Modena and F. Prayon. Florence.

Guarducci, M. 1987. *Epigrafia greca dalle origini al tardo impero*. Rome.

———. 1961. *La vie quotidienne chez les Étrusques*. Paris.

———. 1969. *CRAI*. 526-551.

Heurgon, J. 1957. *REL* 25, 106-126.

Kerenyi, Karl. 1963. *Prometheus, Archetypal Image of Human Existence*. Bollingen Series 63. Princeton.

Maggiani, A. 1982. "Qualche osservazioni sul Fegato di Piacenza." *StEtr* 50, 53-88.

Martelli, M., ed. 1987. *La ceramica degli etruschi*. Novara.

Morandi, A. 1982. *Epigrafia italica*. Rome.

———. 1991. *Nuovi lineamenti di lingua etrusca*. Rome.

Moretti Sgubini, A. M. 1999. *Euphronios epoiesen: Un dono d'eccezione ad Ercole cerite*. Rome.

Neils, Jenifer. 1998. "Hercle in Cleveland." *Cleveland Studies in the History of Art* 3, 6-21.

Pallottino, Massimo. 1968. *Testimonia Linguae Etruscae* [TLE]. 2nd ed. Florence.

———. 1975. *The Etruscans*. Tr. J. Cremona, ed. D. Ridgway. Bloomington, IN.

———. 1982. "Iscrizione etrusca sulla basetta di bronzo del Museo di Manchester." *PBSR* 50, 193-195.

———. 1983. "Presentazione di due iscrizioni etrusche." *StEtr* 51 (1985), 609-614.

———. 1984. *Etruscologia*. 7th ed. Milan.

Pfiffig, A. 1969. *Die etruskische Sprache*. Graz.

Renard, M. 1964. "Hercule allaité par Junon." In *Hommages à Jean Bayet*, ed. M. Renard and R. Schilling. Brussels. 613-618.

Rix, Helmut. 1978-1984. "Das Eindringen griechischer Mythen in Etrurien nach Aussage der mythologischen Namen." *Schriften des Deutschen Archäologen-Verbandes* 4-7= 1981. Aufnahme. 96-106.

———. 1985. "Descrizioni di rituali in etrusco e in italico." In *L'etrusco e le lingue dell'Italia antica: Atti del Convegno della Società Italiana di Glottologia, Pisa 1984*, ed. A. Moreschini. 21-37.

———. 1991. "Etrusco *un, une, unu*, 'te, tibi, vos' e le preghiere dei rituali paralleli nel *liber linteus*." In *Miscellanea Pallottino*. 665-691.

Roncalli, F. 1983. "Etrusco *cver, cvera* = greco *agalma*." PP 38, 288-300.

———. 1985a. *Scrivere etrusco*. Milan.

———. 1985b. *StEtr* 53, 161-170.

Santuari d'Etruria = G. Colonna, ed., *Santuari d'Etruria*. Catalogue of exhibition in Arezzo. Milan. 1985.

Schrimer, B. 1998. "muluvanice/turuce." PP 48, 38-56.

Schwarz, S. J. 1990. "Hercle/Herakles." *LIMC* V, 196-253.

TLE = Pallottino 1968.

Torelli, M. 1977. "Il santuario greco a Gravisca." PP 32, 398-450.

Tripp, David. 1986. "Coinage." In *Etruscan Life and Afterlife*, ed. L. Bonfante. Detroit. 202-214.

Turfa, J. M. 1982. "The Etruscan and Italic Collection in the Manchester Museum." *PBSR* 50, 166-193.

Uehlenbrock, J. 1986. *Herakles: Passage of the Hero through 1000 Years of Classical Art*. New Rochelle, NY.

Van der Meer, L. B. 1987. *The Bronze Liver of Piacenza: Analysis of a Polytheistic Structure*. Amsterdam.

———. 1995. *Interpretatio Etrusca: Greek Myths on Etruscan Mirrors*. Amsterdam.

Weinstock, S. 1946. "Martianus Capella and the Cosmic System of the Etruscans." *JRS* 36, 101-129.

CHAPTER III

PROPHETS AND PRIESTS

Nancy Thomson de Grummond

For an Etruscan, the starting point of religion lay in the revelations of the prophets. After that, the continuing practice of religion was guided by inquiry into the will of the gods, properly revealed and interpreted by individuals with skills in divination. Here we shall make a distinction between these two different categories of communication of the will of the gods, using the words "prophet" and "prophecy" to refer to the traditions in which a particular individual made revelations that then became basic sacred scripture for the Etruscans. We will reserve the term "divination" for the multitude of examples in which a priest or other individual interpreted a message from the gods by consulting the previously revealed body of divine knowledge known as the *Etrusca disciplina*.*[1]

PROPHETS

We shall consider numerous references in Greek and Latin sources[2] to the utterances of Etruscan prophets, but unfortunately we do not have original Etruscan sources on this topic. As we consider these literary sources, we shall also look at evidence from the archaeological record that may help to confirm or expand ideas in the texts.

Tages

The central myth of Etruscan prophecy lies in the story of Tages, the wise child who sprang up from the freshly plowed earth and revealed in full the rules of the *Etrusca disciplina*. The form of the name "Tages" is Latin, employing the letter *g*, not used by the Etruscans. We may imagine that the prophet's name in Etruscan incorporated a hard *c* sound, a point to which we shall return. The most important sources for the myth are Cicero, ca. 44 BCE (*De div.* 2.23; Appendix B, Source no. II.3); Johannes Lydus, sixth century CE (*De ostentis* 2.6.B; Appendix B, Source no. II.5) and Verrius Flaccus (epitomized by Festus, second century CE, *De significatu verborum* 359.14, Lindsay, p. 492, v.6; Appendix B, Source no. II.2). These are a mixed lot, but all seem to have had access to antiquarian sources that may reflect original Etruscan writings. A number of other sources also make limited reference to the story.

Flaccus related that Tages was the son of Genius and grandson of Jupiter (i.e., the Roman equivalent of the Etruscan god Tinia). According to both Cicero and Lydus, Tages imparted his knowledge when a plowman cut a furrow in the ground and the child sprang up and started singing; Tages was like a newborn but had characteristics that evoked the wisdom of an old man. Cicero says the event took place at Tarquinii and was promptly attended by "all Etruria." Lydus tells us specifically that the plowman was none other than Tarchon, founder of the city. Flaccus noted that the child was responsible for teaching his message to the *duodecim populi*, the Twelve Peoples of Etruria. In Lydus' version, Tarchon took the child away and set him "in sacred places" to learn from him. A recurrent feature in the sources is that the teachings were written down and that the leaders or *lucumones** of Etruria were conduits for the transmission of the prophecy.

What were the teachings of Tages? Cicero says that they pertained to *haruspicina*, that is, the interpretation of the will of the gods through scrutiny of the inner organs of a sacrificed animal; elsewhere (*De div.* 2.38), Cicero says simply that the teachings pertained to the *disciplina* of the Etruscans. Other sources mention lightning and entrails (Arnobius, *Adv. nat.* 2.69); city foundations made with the plow (Macrobius, *Sat.* 5.19.13; Appendix B, Source no. IV.5); earthquakes (Lydus, *De ostentis* 54c); the spheres of habitation of the gods (Lactantius, *Comm. in Stat. Theb.* 4.516); and a remedy for mildew, i.e., agricultural lore (Columella, *De re*

III.1. Channel of the "shrine/ altar" emptying into the cavity in the bedrock, Building Beta, Pian di Civita, Tarquinii. (After Moretti Sgubini 2001, fig. 35.)

rustica 10.5, 337–347; Appendix B, Source no. IV.4). The writings derived from the revelation were sometimes referred to as *Libri Tagetici,* and these were described as containing *Libri haruspicini* and *Libri Acherontici* (on rituals pertaining to salvation and the Afterlife).

From archaeology we glean other evidence relative to the mythical child prophet. Excavations by the University of Milan at Pian di Civita, the city site of ancient Tarquinii, from 1982 to 1985 produced a quite remarkable find in an area identified by the excavators as sacred.[3] They discovered the skeleton of a child, 7–8 years old, buried around the end of the ninth century BCE by inhumation, a rite quite unusual at that time. The child, wearing a pendant or bulla around its neck, revealed a deformation of the bones that experts have associated with epilepsy. Near the body was a natural cavity in the earth (Fig. III.1), obviously used in a cult, since it was connected to a nearby altar by a drainage channel, presumably for blood and drink offerings from the altar.

There were many other signs of religious activity in the area, including strata of ashes indicating repeated acts of burning and segments of animal horns, sometimes in geometric shapes. Postdating the child burial were the scattered skeletal remains of other children, this time infants. In a pit nearby were found the remains of a bronze axe and a carefully folded shield and *lituus**/trumpet (Fig. III.2), all attributes of power and nobility. Quite apart from the disturbing question raised here about child sacrifice among the Etruscans, the find is very suggestive in regard to the founding myth of Etruscan prophecy. In antiquity epileptics were perceived to have special spiritual powers, manifested when they were under the effects of seizure, and the combination of this eccentric child with the cavity in the earth and the attributes of *lucumones* at Tarquinii provides a most suggestive backdrop for the myth of the wise child Tages.

Also from the archaeological record comes another type of evidence, namely, representations in art that may show the myth. A number of scarabs, mostly dating to the fourth century BCE, show a fascinating scene in which one or more figures stand over a being emerging from the ground. Sometimes only the head is shown, but at other times, more of the figure appears, as on an example of the fourth–third century BCE in the Villa Giulia (Fig. III.3)[4] that seems to show "Tarchon" bending over and listening to "Tages," the latter an amorphous figure, somewhat small in scale compared with the tall male figure. He raises his finger in a pointing gesture that is commonly used in Etruscan art by someone explaining a prophecy.[5]

An equally important supplement to the literary sources

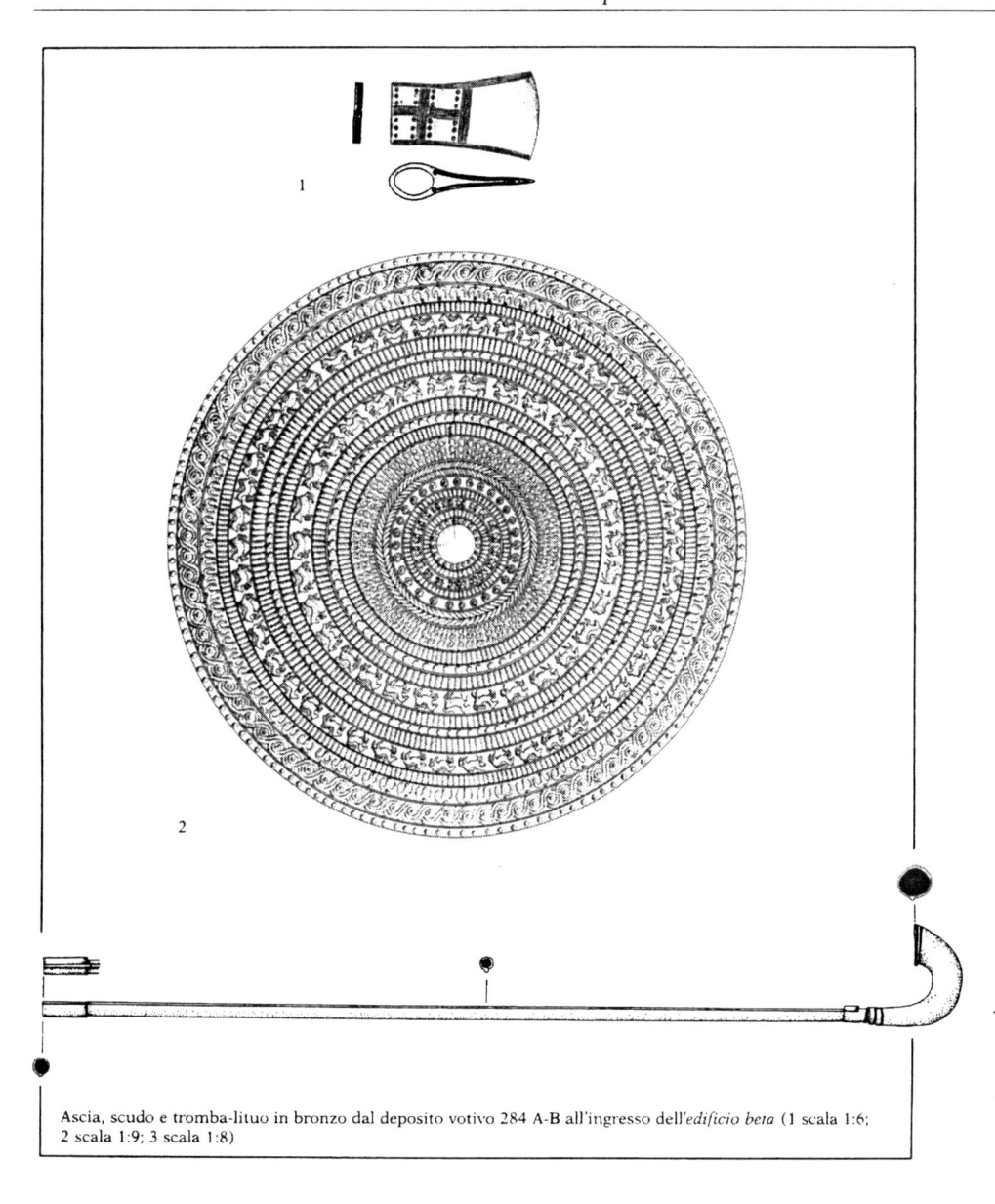

III.2. Votive bronze axe, shield, and lituus/*trumpet, found in front of Building Beta, Pian di Civita, Tarquinii. Early seventh century* BCE. *Tarquinia, Archaeological Museum. (After Bonghi Jovino and Chiaramonte Treré 1997, pl. 125.)*

Ascia, scudo e tromba-lituo in bronzo dal deposito votivo 284 A-B all'ingresso dell'*edificio beta* (1 scala 1:6; 2 scala 1:9; 3 scala 1:8)

is provided by the famous bronze mirror found in a tomb at Tuscania in 1898, dated to the third century BCE (Fig. III.4).[6] The identification of the figures has been thoroughly discussed since the seminal article by Pallottino in 1930, but scholars are far from final agreement on this subject. What is certain is that a youth labeled *pavatarχies*,[7] wearing a conical priest's cap, stands in a ritual pose with his left foot upon a rock and contemplates a liver. On the left, a bearded older man, with a similar conical hat laid back on his shoulder, assumes a position of listening and contemplating; he is labeled *avl tarχunus*.

No better explanation has been found than Pallottino's suggestion that we have here a version of the myth of Tages (*pava* may mean *puer* or child; *tarχies* could become Tages in Latin) instructing Tarchon (or perhaps his son, whose name would then be Avl) in *haruspicina*. The other figures present are somewhat difficult to account for. On the far right is a tall, bearded male, nude except for his boots and a mantle wrapped around his left arm; he holds a spear in his right hand. Labeled Veltune, he is often equated with the Etruscan god whom the Romans called Vertumnus (or Voltumna) and who was regarded as the principal deity of Etruria by Varro (*De lingua Latina* 5.46: Appendix B, Source no. VI.3). Since an overwhelming amount of evidence shows that Tinia was the chief Etruscan god (as noted, equivalent to Jupiter), some have argued that Veltune is simply another name for

III.3. Carnelian scarab with image of Tarchon and Tages (?). Fourth century BCE. Rome, Museo Etrusco di Villa Giulia (Photo: Courtesy of the Soprintendenza per i Beni Archeologici dell'Etruria Meridionale.)

III.4. Mirror with Pava Tarchies from Tuscania. Early third century BCE Florence, Archeological Museum. (After Torelli 1988, fig. 1.)

him; thus it is possible that we have here the god who was grandfather of Pava Tarchies.

As for the remaining figures, frustratingly little is clear. In the middle of the scene is a rather conspicuous lady labeled Ucernei, whose identity and reason for participation are quite unknown, while on the far left is a youth, nude except for his cloak; above him is the word *raΘlΘ*. The god Rath is named in inscriptions, but little is known about him, and the locative ending of the word on the mirror is puzzling.[8] It may identify him as a personification of the place where the prophesying of Tages took place.

Vegoia (Vecuvia)

Another highly important figure in Etruscan prophecy is the one called "Nymph Begoe" (or "Vegoia") in Latin texts. She is mentioned as the author or source of books on lightning that were kept in the Temple of Apollo (presumably on the Palatine; Servius, *Ad Aen*. 6.72) and is particularly recognized as a source for an account about the creation of the world. Her books are alluded to as *Libri Vegoici*. The thunder calendar attributed to the Roman savant Nigidius Figulus (surviving in a Greek translation; see Appendix A) may be derived from her prophecies. The Romanized expert on Etruscan lore, Tarquitius Priscus, a contemporary of Cicero, translated her books into Latin.

A precious scrap of prophecy exists in Latin, perhaps derived from the translations made by Tarquitius Priscus; the text pertains to the sanctity of boundaries and thus is preserved in the writing of field surveyors (see Appendix B, Source no. II.1).[9] Vegoia delivered her prophecy to a certain Arruns Veltymnus, sometimes equated with Arruns, an early prince of Clusium, though with little firm evidence. The name Veltymnus is remarkably similar to Veltune on the Etruscan mirror, and perhaps in this case it again refers to the principal Etruscan deity, Tinia (or Jupiter), indicating that Arruns had a special relationship with this god.

The prophecy in Latin does make specific reference to Jupiter. It begins with the origin of the sea and sky and relates how Jupiter had worked out boundaries in Etruria. For those who violated these boundaries, disastrous consequences were predicted, including storms, whirlwinds, drought, hail, and mildew. Similar spectacular effects of weather are part of the predictions in the Brontoscopic Calendar of Nigidius, for example, for June 3, "If in any way it should thunder, there will be a scorching and drying wind, such that not only grains but even the soft fruits will be parched through and through and shrivel up." Or again, from Oct. 3, "If it thunders, it signifies hurricanes and disturbances by which the trees will be overturned; there will be a great disruption in the affairs of common people." (See Appendix A.)

On the whole, the myth of the prophetess makes an interesting parallel to the story of Tages and Tarchon, with its combination of the instructor (Vegoia) and the disciple (Arruns) and with its reference to Veltune or Tinia, along with the connection with disasters of nature.

The writing down of the prophecy of Vegoia has been thought to date from the first century BCE (some five hundred years later than Arruns of Clusium), because it refers to the eighth *saeculum* or era of Etruscan history. The Etruscan doctrine of the periods of their sacred history is only dimly known and understood, but the eighth *saeculum* may be convincingly related to the last century of Etruscan civilization, when the Etruscans were being overrun by the Romans and a prophecy on boundaries might seem especially pertinent.

The figure known to the Romans as the Nymph Begoe has been identified in Etruscan art, twice on mirrors and once on a gold ring bezel. On a mirror from Vetulonia, ca. 300–275 BCE, a winged female figure appears, labeled Lasa Vecuvi(a), from which the translation to Latin of "Nymph Begoe" or "Vegoia" might easily have been made.[10] The figure appears in the exergue of the mirror, underneath an image of Tinia holding the thunderbolt, thus suggesting a connection between the two. On a mirror of unknown provenance in the Villa Giulia, of similar date, appears a winged figure in short chiton labeled Lasa Vecu. This time, however, the Lasa appears with Menrva (Fig. III.5). She seems to stand and listen, holding in her hand an object that is sometimes identified as a small lightning bolt, though more often as a plant. Either attribute would be acceptable for the prophetess who left a book on lightning but also had concern for boundaries, a matter of agrarian significance.

Finally, on the ring bezel, from Todi in Umbria (dated around the same time as the two preceding examples), the goddess is called Lasa Vecuvia, and is represented as a nude, nymphlike figure holding a mirror (Fig. III.6). From the numerous scenes of prophecy that appear on Etruscan mirrors, it may be conjectured that the mirror itself was an instrument of prophecy, as in the examples of *katoptromanteia* (conjuring with mirrors) attested in Greek and Roman ritual.[11] Rather like making predictions by gazing in a crystal ball or a vessel filled with liquid (*lekanomanteia*), one could discern the future by looking at a reflected but somewhat mysterious image in the shiny surface of the mirror. Several Etruscan mirrors show a female figure gazing intently into a mirror, seemingly not in the act of grooming but rather as a part of *katoptromanteia*. It may be hypothesized that Lasa Vecuvia prophesied on occasion by means of a mirror.

Cacu

Among the other scenes of prophecy on mirrors, the best known is that on the handsome grip mirror from Bolsena (Fig. III.7; ca. 300 BCE) that shows the long-haired, youthful Cacu in the act of playing his lyre and evidently singing an oracular message.[12] His pupil Artile sits at his feet and follows the prophecy with the aid of a booklike diptych containing an enigmatic script. On the right and on the left, soldiers approach, one with sword drawn, evidently in an ambush of the prophet. They are labeled as Avle Vipinas and Caile Vipinas, two brothers who are known from other sources, both Roman and Etruscan, as real historical figures, contemporary with the sixth-century kings of Rome. The same story appears on at least four ash urns coming from the territory of Clusium (Chiusi) dating to the second century BCE. All show the attempt to capture the prophet, but unfortunately we do not know the outcome of the situation.

The ambush to catch a seer is a well-known *topos* in Greek and Roman myth and legend, according to which you must seize the prophet to learn his secrets (cf. Silenus in Vergil, *Eclogue* 6; Proteus in Vergil, *Georgics* 4, and Picus and Faunus in Ovid, *Fasti* 2.385). Beyond this plausible hypothesis, there is little agreement. We do not know the subject of the prophecy, and though there are myths about Cacus in Latin literature (e.g., the brute of Vergil's *Aen.* 8.184–305), it is difficult to show how they may be related to the scene on the mirror. In the Roman versions, the threads of the myth have become so tangled that the fabric is no longer recognizable.

Other Prophetic Figures

A number of other little-known Etruscan figures appear in acts of prophecy or divination on Etruscan mirrors, both male and female. I have discussed these and the meager knowledge we have about them elsewhere.[13] There are also various figures from Greek mythology represented on mirrors as prophets or seers: Silenus, the seer Chalchas (Fig. III.8; represented in Etruria with wings and practicing divination with a liver), Orpheus, Teiresias. For most of these, evidence of scripture is lacking. Orpheus is an exception, since scenes of his head popping out of the ground with open mouth (the motif recalls Tages) include a tablet with writing upon it. These date around the same time as many of the other mirrors and gems with scenes of prophecy or divination, ca. 300 BCE. We have reviewed the principal evi-

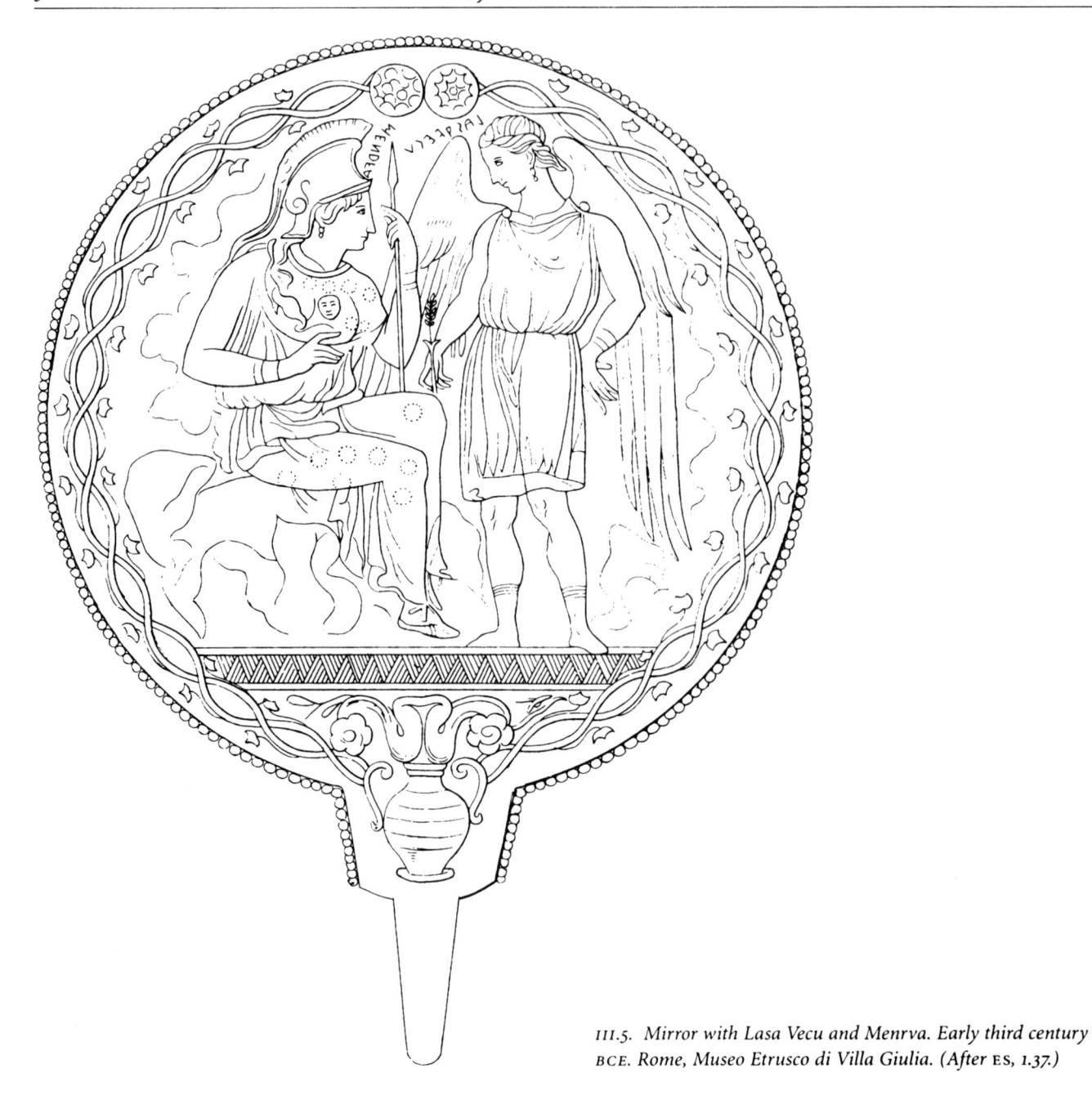

III.5. Mirror with Lasa Vecu and Menrva. Early third century BCE. Rome, Museo Etrusco di Villa Giulia. (After ES, 1.37.)

dence for prophets in Etruria, with particular attention to the major figures, one male and one female—Tages (Pava Tarchies) and Nymph Begoe (Lasa Vecuvia). Their books, the *Libri Tagetici* and the *Libri Vegoici,* constituted a significant portion of Etruscan scripture. Given the scrappy nature of the evidence, it is not safe to attempt much generalization, but it is clear that these writings and related Etruscan myth and legend included themes of creation and history, as well as references to the power of the chief god in connection with the forces of nature. The writings were preserved and interpreted by patriarchal figures such as Tarchon and the leaders of individual city-states (the *duodecim populi,* or Twelve Peoples).

Clearly the texts were thick with regulations on rituals and legal matters. One category of the books of Tages gave illumination concerning the Afterlife. Beyond that, the Etruscan ritual books focused on instructions concerning prognostication. Repeated references to thunder and lightning, haruspication, the flight of birds, unusual animals or plants, and other features of ritual make it clear that the chief

III.6. Gold ring bezel with Lasa Vecuvia from Todi. Early third century BCE. Rome, Museo Etrusco di Villa Giulia. (Photo: Courtesy of the Soprintendenza per i Beni Archeologici dell'Etruria Meridionale.)

III.7. Mirror with Cacu being seized by Avle Vipinas and Caile Vipinas. Ca. 300 BCE. London, British Museum. (After Bonfante 1990, fig. 18.)

III.8. Mirror with Chalchas as haruspex. Ca. 400 BCE. Vatican Museums. (After ES, 2.223.)

emphasis in the *Etrusca disciplina* lay in teaching divination, so that priests and others might assist in discerning the will of the gods.

PRIESTS

Discussions of Etruscan priests usually begin with the well-known *haruspices*,* the Etruscan diviners who served the Romans during the period of the Roman Republic and even sometimes during the Empire as well. Here we shall make a different kind of start and inquire whether it is possible to give a more general account of priesthood within Etruria. How do we define or recognize an Etruscan priest? Who served as priests and in what contexts? How did Etruscan priests resemble or differ from those of Greece and Rome? What were their duties?

The evidence is once again scanty, and barring spectacular new discoveries, we shall never be able to give very satisfactory answers to these questions or to come anywhere near the kind of responses provided in most of the chapters of *Pagan Priests, Religion and Power in the Ancient World* (1990), edited by Mary Beard and John North. They and their contributors make several points, however, that can illuminate our inquiry. The first has to do with the actual definition of "priest," which they provisionally relate to "the function of mediating between gods and men."[14] The mediation function, we shall see, is conspicuous in the surviving evidence about priests of Etruria. Also useful for our discussion is their generalization that the concept of such a mediator in ancient societies was very different from our own, beginning with the fact that the priest was not just a religious figure but often was a person of political or secular importance and duties; the separation of church and state was not an issue.[15] Another theme that recurs in Beard and North is the idea that priests would be marked out from ordinary people by some kind of distinctive, even paradoxical clothing, such as may be seen in modern priests, who may wear a skirt or turn their collar backwards, or nuns, who may wear medieval garments.[16]

Terminology

Was there an Etruscan word that would translate the Latin all-purpose term *sacerdos*? The most common word for priest in Etruscan was *cepen* (also *ceepena, cipen*; pl. perhaps *cepar*), a term that can already be found in the seventh century BCE.[17] The meaning of *cepen* was first suggested by a gloss from Varro (Servius, *Ad Aen.* 12.539), noting that the Sabine word for priest was *cupencus*, and it has been confirmed by its frequent occurrence in the *Liber Linteus* of Zagreb.[18]

Names for priestly office also may be learned from funerary inscriptions that list titles of the deceased in combination with *cepen* and other words. Four times *cepen* appears with another word whose root seems to refer to the activities of a magistrate[19] but may also be priestly: *maru* (occurring in Umbrian as *maron-*, the same word as Maro, the Latin cognomen of Vergil). This last term appears also in what seems to be a group plural form, *maruχva* or *marunuχva* (*TLE*, 194; *ET*, AT 1.61; *TLE*, 171; *ET*, AT 1.96.), which may be analogous to the Latin word *collegium*, used for a group of priests.[20] We also find *marunuχ spurana cepen* (*TLE*, 165; *ET*, AT 1.171), which makes a suggestive connection with the activity of the city-state (*spur*) and thus perhaps refers to a "public priest."

Yet another word for priest in general may be provided by *eisnev* (*TLE*, 195; *ET*, AT 1.1). A rare term, not nearly as common as *cepen*, it is found in an epitaph that seems to give a list of offices held and may be etymologically related to the Etruscan vocabulary of words referring to the gods (*ais-*, god, *aisna/eisna*, "pertaining to the gods").[21]

It has been recently argued that there is an Etruscan word for priestess, *hatrencu*, a term that occurs only in female graves and is limited in fact to the city of Vulci.[22] In the Hellenistic Tomb of the Inscriptions at Vulci were buried several women with the title but with different family names (*ET*, Vc 1.47, 49, 50, 55, 58), giving rise to the hypothesis that they were priestess members of a *collegium* that had a right to burial in a specific place. The finding of objects of considerable prestige in the tomb adds to the idea that these were elite women who belonged to a special caste.

Various other details emerge from close study of inscriptions. The famous funeral epitaph of L(a)ris Pulenas[23] gives a list of his achievements, including a phrase suggesting that he wrote a book on haruspication (*ziχ neθśrac*)[24] and referring to a rich life serving the gods Pacha (Fufluns), Catha, and (probably) Culśu. Elsewhere we have references to individuals as *marunuχ cepen* of Pacha (*TLE*, 137; *ET*, Ta 1.184) or as *maru* of both Pacha and Catha (*TLE*, 190; *ET*, AT 1.32). The evidence suggests that the Etruscans had a practice of naming individuals as being in charge of a particular cult. Roman religion is not lacking in parallels, but Beard has stressed that this is the basic pattern for the Greek priest (*hiereus*) or priestess, who attended only one deity and even only one sanctuary of that deity.[25]

From Latin texts comes information to confirm the idea of the individual or family serving a particular cult. When the Romans sacked Veii, and the youths came to carry away the statue of Juno, they feared to touch the statue because no one was *certae gentis sacerdos* (Livy 5.22.4; Appendix B, Source no. VI.5). We begin to think of a model like that in Rome of the families of the Potitii and Pinarii (Livy 1.7.12), who served the Roman altar of Hercules from earliest times (though once again the context could be Hellenic, since the god himself and King Evander, who established the cult, were Greek).

The idea of noble families handing down religious duties was certainly attested among the Etruscans, as we know from the sources regarding the *Etrusca disciplina*. In the story of Tages, Tarchon taught the other *principes* to use the *disciplina* in their own cities, and they in turn handed down the lore received from the child. Cicero (*Ad fam.* 6.6) referred to the idea that A. Caecina would learn about the *Etrusca disciplina* from his father. Claudius also noted the practice of families transmitting their knowledge (Tacitus, *Annales* 11.14), and earlier Cicero had talked about a decree of the second century (*De div.* 1.92; Appendix B, Source no. IV.8) in which the Senate had actually ordered that the noble families (of the individual Etruscan peoples?) should hand over six (or possibly ten) of their sons to study and preserve the *disciplina*.²⁶

It would help to know more about the priest of the Fanum Voltumnae, the central federal sanctuary of the Twelve Peoples.²⁷ Our references to the role are brief but suggestive. Livy (5.1.5) relates that at the time of the war with Veii, that is, the early fourth century, the Etruscans were voting for the *sacerdos* and declined to elect a wealthy, prominent leader from Veii who expected to receive the honor. In retaliation, he withdrew the performers in the games, most of whom were his own slaves. When the Veientines later made him king, the other Etruscan states, disgusted, refused to help Veii against the Romans.

It is of interest to learn that the priest was chosen by election and that he was a man of high political standing, though not a king (Livy speaks of this role as being offensive to contemporary Etruscans). From the well-known inscription from Spello, dated to the reign of Constantine (333–337 CE), used as evidence for the Fanum Voltumnae,²⁸ we also learn that the Etruscans elected the *sacerdos* annually. There is considerable evidence that games were an important part of the annual ceremonies, and it is likely that the priest was normally expected to contribute to these (though the Veii story stresses that their leader had provided entertainers before he was elected; maybe all candidates for the priesthood were supposed to contribute).

Dress and Attributes of Priests

For our question regarding how to recognize an Etruscan priest, we may turn especially to archaeological evidence. Scholars are unanimous in identifying a number of figures as priestly by their characteristic garb.²⁹ As we have already noted, Pava Tarchies and Avl Tarchunus, engaged in haruspication (Fig. III.4), wear the special hat with a peak on top, often shown as twisted. Pava Tarchies' wearing of his hat on his head actually indicates that he *is* a priest; likewise, the hat on the shoulder of Tarchunus is consistent with him being in the act of becoming one. Similar images of the hat, which seems to be the forerunner of the peaked *apex** worn by the Roman "flame priests" (*flamines**),³⁰ can be found in a number of representations in Etruscan art.³¹

To show the characteristic hat and other features of the costume of the *haruspex*, the favorite representative is the fourth-century bronze statuette of Vel Sveitus in the Vatican (*TLE*, 736; *ET*, Vs 3.7; Fig. III.9).³² It has an inscription:

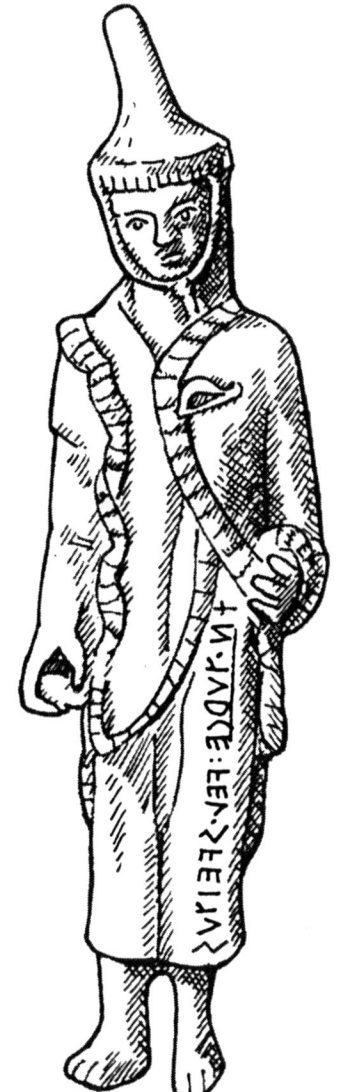

III.9. Bronze statuette of priest, dedicated by Vel Sveitus. Fourth century BCE. Vatican Museums. (After Pfiffig 1975, 48, fig. 6.)

tn turce vel sveitus, "Vel Sveitus gave this," perhaps referring to a priest who made this a votive offering to his deity. The peak of the hat is tall and slightly flattened at the top; it makes a smooth transition downward, broadening into a tightly fitted cap with a slight brim, which seems to be tied on with rather large straps around the chin. The cap is clearer in some other specimens, for example, the alabaster ash urn of Arnth Remzna in the University Museum, Philadelphia (third century BCE; Fig. III.10).³³ Here the gentleman has a thick roll over the forehead and ears, held by straps that come down in front of the ears and are tied in a complex loop ending in a three-pointed tip. This kind of head covering seems to be the counterpart of the Roman *galerus,** a close-fitting cap made from animal skin worn by priests of

III.10. Alabaster ash urn of Arnth Remzna. Late third century BCE. Philadelphia, University Museum. (Photo: University of Pennsylvania Museum, neg. #26517-9.)

various ranks, sometimes with the *apex* and sometimes with a knob.[34]

The Vel Sveitus figure has other intriguing elements to his dress, especially the mantle with a rough fringe all along its edges; this, too, relates to an animal skin (probably sheep). The mantle is fastened with a large fibula of a type that goes back to the Archaic period. For comparison we may look at a statuette of a priest said to be from the Siena area and dating to the third century BCE (Fig. III.11).[35] For the animal skin, this remarkable figure substitutes the *laena*, a mantle worn from front to back so that a loop of drapery hangs down in front. In addition, he wears the *apex* and *galerus,* thus combining elements that appear together in the famous images of the *flamines* on the Ara Pacis Augustae.[36] The *apex* is of a different type here, however, as noted by Maggiani, with a soft pileus-type cap rather than the sharp point of the *apex*.[37]

It is worth noting that all the images cited here show the priest as clean shaven. This may indicate not that the individuals had to be youths, like Pava Tarchies, but merely that the beard had to be shaved at the time of initiation into the priesthood. Avl Tarchunus, a priest in training, is still bearded.

One of the well-known attributes of the Etruscan priest is the magic wand known in Latin as the *lituus*,[38] the curved staff especially associated with religious activity in Roman literature and appearing in Etruscan archaeological contexts that support the oft-repeated association with augury. The basic texts of Cicero (*De div.* 2.80; Appendix B, Source no. IV.7), Livy (1.18.7), and Vergil (*Aeneid* 7.187) describe it as a curved stick without knots, used first in Rome by Romulus. Servius (*Ad Aen.* 7.187) adds the interesting details that the wand was considered royal, and that it was used in settling disputes. The Archaic usage of the staff and probable origin in Etruria are indicated by its presence on the plaque from Murlo with seated dignitaries (ca. 570 BCE)[39] and on an oft-reproduced sandstone *cippus** from Fiesole (second half of the sixth century BCE; Fig. III.12),[40] which shows a figure with rather unusual dress: he wears high boots and a tall hat from which the locks peek out at the bottom, and he seems to have something draped across his left arm. He holds the wand aloft in his right.

A handsome bronze model of a *lituus* comes from a burial, no doubt elite, at Caere, also dating to the sixth century (Fig. III.13).[41] The wand is 36 cm. high but very thin, suggesting that it either was attached to a wooden frame or was in fact not intended for usage except as insignia in the Afterlife of the priest or magistrate who would have been buried with it. There are numerous other representations of the *lituus* in Etruria, and the wand continues to appear in Roman representations, for example, of the god Jupiter, and as an instrument of priests on coins and gems.[42]

Without doubt, there were other ritual wands or staffs in Etruria, such as the bifurcated stick carried by priests represented on a black-figured amphora from Orvieto.[43] In this intriguing scene, four men seem to be involved in a ritual connected with a lightning bolt lodged upright in the

III.11. Bronze statuette of priest. Third century BCE. Göttingen, Archäologisches Institut der Universität. (Photo: Stephan Eckhart.)

III.12. Cippus with relief of a priest (?) with lituus. Second half of sixth century BCE. Berlin, Antikensammlung, Staatliche Museen zu Berlin. (Photo: Bildarchiv Preussischer Kulturbesitz/Art Resource, NY.)

ground. Their placement suggests that they formed a magic circle around it, perhaps in an act of rendering harmless the spot hit by the lightning. One priest standing next to the lightning bolt faces away from it and extends his right arm backward toward the bolt while he lifts in front of himself a wand with a bifurcation at the top.

There is one more reference to the attributes of Etruscan priests that cannot be omitted: the passage in Livy in which he describes the priests as marching to war (7.17.3–5; Appendix B, Source no. IV.10). The Tarquinians and (non-Etruscan) Faliscans routed the Romans in 356 BCE by a simple but remarkable strategy, arming their priests (*sacerdotes*) with torches and serpents, rushing down upon the Roman troops, and throwing them into a panic. The sight is recalled by the parade in the Tomb of the Typhon at Tarquinii, which probably features Etruscan priests or else performers dressed

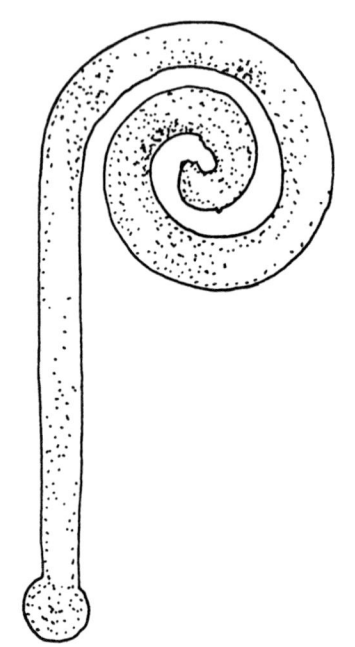

III.13. Bronze model of a lituus, *from Caere. Rome, Museo Etrusco di Villa Giulia. (After Pfiffig 1975, 48, fig. 5.)*

up as Underworld characters, with demonic faces and carrying serpents, torches, and *lituus*-shaped musical instruments (admittedly, they proceed at a more leisurely pace).[44]

Etruscan Priestesses

There is relatively little evidence for the appearance of Etruscan priestesses. A female figure on a sarcophagus in the British Museum, said to have come from the Tomb of the Triclinium at Tarquinii, has been referred to as a priestess of Fufluns (Bacchus); the hypothesis is not based on inscriptional evidence but rather on her appearance (Fig. III.14). She has the appropriate equipment for a Bacchant, or follower of Bacchus: a *thyrsos** and *kantharos.** In addition, a fawn is attending her, whom she seems to nurture by offering a drink, just as maenadic followers of Bacchus might have a small animal at hand for offering to the god.[45] Unfortunately, the date of the sarcophagus, probably third century BCE, is slightly too early to match with the famous description of the mania for Bacchus described by Livy that started in Etruria, spread to Rome, and led to the decree of the Roman Senate *de Bacchanalibus* (186 BCE; Livy 39.8.14; see Appendix B, Source no. VII.1).[46]

A group of five impressive stone sarcophagi for women's burials, also from Tarquinii and of the same date as the British Museum sarcophagus, may well show a number of priestesses. No comparable male sarcophagi have been reported from the tomb. These sarcophagi, discovered in the Tomba Bruschi in 1963, were not studied fully and put on display until 2004, when they were all shown at Viterbo in

III.14. Sarcophagus of a Bacchant. Third century BCE. London, British Museum. (After Pfiffig 1975, 28, fig. 1.)

an exhibition of materials from older excavations.[47] Each of the women wears a tall hat of some kind, and the hair seems to be arranged in a ritual way, with six major locks on each side of the head (like the *seni crines* of Roman brides and Vestal Virgins).[48] The clothing and jewelry are clearly indicative of elite status, and four of the ladies have an attribute that could imply some kind of special ritual activity. One holds a *kantharos*, two hold a sacrificial saucer (*patera**), and one holds a bird. It is tempting to relate this ensemble of sarcophagi to the group of burials in the Tomb of the Inscriptions at Vulci distinguished by the use of the term *hatrencu* and to hypothesize that those from the Tomba Bruschi may also relate to an agreement by which priestesses may be buried together.

Duties of the Priests

We turn now to the question of the duties of the priests of Etruria, a very difficult question indeed, and here at last we may consider more closely the *haruspices*. The name for *haruspex* in Etruscan, *netsvis*, is known from the bilingual inscription of a certain Larth Cafates, which is, to be sure, late and from outside Etruria proper (first century BCE, Pesaro; *TLE*, 697; *ET*, Um 1.7).[49] The word is etymologically related to that used to describe a book by Laris Pulenas, as noted above. But the interpretation of the inscription is complicated by the lack of a word-for-word translation: for the Etruscan we have *netsvis trutnvt frontac*, whereas in Latin we have *haruspex fulguriator*. It is exciting to see that we can learn another Etruscan name for a priest and that his duty has to do with interpreting lightning, but no one is sure exactly how to relate the one word *fulguriator* to the two *trutnvt frontac*. The second word sounds temptingly like the sound of thunder and in fact is like the Greek word for this phenomenon (*brontē*).[50] Perhaps Larth Cafates was one of those making use of the Brontoscopic Calendar of Nigidius Figulus, compiled around the same time (see Appendix A).

We have abundant references to the duties of the *haruspices* in Rome. The modern literature tends to show that we are comfortable, probably too much so, in our understanding of the *haruspices*. On the one hand, we know more about them than any other kind of Etruscan priestly functionaries, because the Romans mention them so frequently. On the other hand, they obviously were quite integrated into Roman culture, and it is all too easy to assume that evidence from Rome is transferable to Etruria.[51]

The literary evidence for *haruspices* in the Archaic period is meager,[52] though the passage from Livy (1.56.4) about the finding of the human head on the Capitoline, interpreted by *Etrusci vates*, has an authentic ring to it, especially since the seers were invited by the Etruscan king Tarquinius Superbus. The story of the old nobleman of Veii captured by the Romans and interpreting the omen of the overflow of the Alban Lake as portending the fall of Veii, told by both Cicero and Livy (*De div.* 1.44.100; Livy 5.15.4–11; Appendix B, Source nos. 11.10 and 11.11),[53] is absolutely believable, involving as it does a priest talking about how the water could be drained by a ritual act. Etruscan hydraulic skills were well known, and some of the most spectacular examples of the famous rock-cut channels known as *cuniculi* have been noted precisely around Veii.[54] While there is no specific reference to a *ritus Etruscus** connected with water control, it is likely enough that the Etruscan discipline contained instructions for this kind of problem associated with a very specific and fatal prophecy.

This incident occurred in connection with the fall of Veii in 396 BCE. MacBain argues, however, that the systematic interpretation of prodigies at Rome by the *haruspices* did not begin until the third century BCE, at the time when Etruria had been pacified by the Romans. He notes the persistence of the theme that these priests were of aristocratic birth and stresses that their presence in Rome was of considerable political significance.

THE NATURE OF OMENS

Among the many phenomena interpreted by Etruscan *haruspices* are listed lightning (numerous times), the sound of a trumpet in the sky, a sparrow with a grasshopper, the collapse of a rostrate column, a talking cow, oxen climbing stairs, and the birth of an androgyne (surprisingly numerous).[55] Undoubtedly the activity for which the *haruspices* were best known was the examining of entrails, in particular the liver. There is abundant evidence that the Etruscans themselves practiced the art, ranging from the representations of Pava Tarchies and Chalchas (Figs. III.4 and III.8) to the gem of Natis, which shows a colossal organ under interpretation (Fig. III.15),[56] to that quintessential monument of Etruscan culture, the Piacenza liver, discussed fully above by Larissa Bonfante (Fig. II.2 and pp. 10–11).[57] The study of entrails, of course, depended on the sacrifice of victims, and for the Romans at least, we know that the sacrifice often related to politics or war.[58]

Thunder and Lightning

In addition, we know that the *haruspices* employed a very rich lore of thunder and lightning, as can now be seen most vividly from Turfa's translation of the Brontoscopic Calendar (Appendix A). The sound of thunder could signal a wide

III.15. Carnelian scarab with image of a haruspex; inscription: natis. Fourth century BCE. Berlin, Antikensammlung, Staatliche Museen zu Berlin (Photo: Bildarchiv Preussischer Kulturbesitz/Art Resource, NY.)

III.16. Mirror with Menrva, Thesan, Tinia, and Thethis. Ca. 470 BCE. Vatican Museums. (After ES, 4.396.)

III.17. Mirror with Menrva. Third century BCE. Berlin, Antikenmuseums. (After CSE, Bundesrepublik Deutschland 4.24.)

variety of effects, good and bad, concerning the weather, crops, animals, disease, war, government, and social conflict. As for lightning, Pliny and Seneca provide us with extensive information (Appendix B, Source nos. VIII.1, VIII.2, VIII.4, and VIII.8), so that we learn there were supposedly nine gods who threw the sacred thunderbolt (*manubia*). Using various sources, we have identified six of these by their Roman names: Jupiter, Juno, Minerva, Vulcan, Mars, and Saturn.[59] Jupiter was said to be in control of three main types of bolts, and he often used his power in close consultation with group gods, such as the ones in the heavens of Martianus. The three types of bolts he might throw are (1) a benign bolt that served only to give warning; the god could decide on his own whether to send it; (2) a bolt that did both good and harm, for which he needed the approval of the Dii Consentes; and

III.18. Painting of Vel Saties, from the François Tomb, Vulci. Watercolor copy by C. Ruspi, Vatican Museums. Fourth century BCE. (After Buranelli 1992, 85.)

(3) a completely destructive bolt, for which he had to have permission from the Dii Involuti, perhaps the same as the Favores Opertanei of Martianus (Secret Gods of Favor).

The Etruscan belief in a wide variety of lightning bolts is reflected in the many different sizes and shapes of such bolts depicted with Tinia, the Etruscan Jupiter, in art. On a late Archaic mirror in the Vatican (ca. 470 BCE; Fig. III.16), he clutches two types, and seems to contemplate which one to hurl. The theme is Greek, showing the chief god entreated on the left by Thesan, the mother of Memnon, and on the right by Thethis (Thetis), the mother of Achilles.[60] Naturally, he has two very different kinds of bolts to determine the fate of the two heroes. It is disappointing that there is so little evidence from art of the usage of the bolt by other deities; in fact, only Menrva appears with the bolt, again on a number

III.19. Bronze handle of a pitcher (Schnabelkanne) with relief of Priest gazing upward. Fifth century BCE. Arezzo, Museo Archeologico Mecenate. (Photo: Soprintendenza Archeologica per la Toscana-Firenze.)

of mirrors. One splendid example shows the goddess carrying a huge combination spear/lightning bolt (Fig. III.17).[61]

Birds

Ranking in importance with the *disciplina* concerning entrails and thunder and lightning was the use of augury from birds. This is a topic still insufficiently investigated in Etruscan art and religion,[62] but it is certain that it was a fairly important form of divination. Dionysios of Halikarnassos refers to "Etruscan ornithoscopy" (τυρρηνική ορνιθοσκοπία) and Pliny notes (*HN* 10. 37) that there were types of birds *depicta in Etrusca disciplina* that could no longer be seen in his day; the passage has been taken to mean that there were illustrated bird books in the Etruscan sacred corpus.[63] Here he also refers to the observations about birds by Etruscan religious scholars such as Labeo and Nigidius, and in adjoining sections of the *Historia Naturalis* he makes observations about the omens from various birds: the crow has a persistent croak that is inauspicious (*HN* 10.30), and a gulping noise by a raven can be a very bad sign (*HN* 10. 33); the eagle owl, *bubo*, was the worst abomination (*HN* 30.34). Nigidius stated that the night owl (*noctua*) had nine cries (*HN* 10.39), though nothing is reported about the meaning of the various cries. He also noted a type of bird that broke eagles' eggs; again, we are not told the augural meaning, but the connection with Etruscan lore is evident.

Along with these citations we may mention the well-known passage in Livy (1.34.8-9; Appendix B, Source no. II.8) describing the omen of the eagle removing the cap of Tarquinius Priscus, then replacing it on the head of the king-to-be. The passage is noteworthy because it shows Roman recognition of the use of such a prodigy in an Etruscan political context. It gives evidence that Romans thought that it was not unusual for an Etruscan woman such as Tanaquil, Tarquin's wife, to be skilled in the interpretation of such a sign. A parallel image is provided by the famous painting at Vulci of the distinguished figure Vel Saties (Fig. III.18), in which the figure, surely a magistrate in his ceremonial garment, is involved in reading the omen supplied by one or more birds of the *picus* family.[64] The motif of the augur with his head turned up may be found in several other key representations, including an image on a *Schnabelkanne* (Fig. III.19), a type of pitcher known to be of ritual usage (see for example, the Chalchas mirror, Fig. III.8).[65]

Etruscan diviners, as we have seen, might serve as mediators to convey information from the gods transmitted by many different signs in nature, always with an eye on guides such as the various sacred texts we have mentioned. We have, however, no way of knowing if the Etruscans themselves were like the Romans in placing emphasis on the distinction between signs asked for (*impetrativa*) and signs that appeared voluntarily from the gods (*oblativa*; Servius *ad Aen.* 6.190). From the evidence we do have it is nevertheless possible to recognize this broad subdivision in divination. Thus the *impetrativa* embrace the signs of augury from birds and haruspication from entrails, while the *oblativa* include the occurrences of lightning and thunder and various prodigies; perhaps some omens of birds could also fall in this category.

NOTES

1. Cf. the discussion of the distinction (and similarities) between these two categories in Overholt 1989, 117-147 and Nissinen 2000, 108-109.

2. See below Appendix B, Sources, and my discussion of various authors who wrote about Etruscan religion in antiquity, above, pp. 1-4. The basic books for studying such sources are Buonamici 1939 and Thulin 1968.

3. Bonghi Jovino, 1986, esp. 84-85, 89-91, 99-101, 178-183.

4. Torelli 2000, 637 (no. 325) and pl. p. 529.

5. de Grummond, 2000, e.g., figs. 22-23.

6. The bibliography is considerable. See especially Pallottino 1979; Cristofani 1985, 4-20; de Grummond 2000, 30-32.

7. For the inscriptions on this mirror, see *ET*, AT S.11.

8. On Rath, see especially Colonna 1987, 431-435, 441.

9. Heurgon 1959; Harris 1971, 31-40.

10. In general on the meaning of Lasa and in particular on Lasa Vecuvia, see Rallo 1974, 32, 35-36; de Grummond 2000, 33-36.

11. See de Grummond 2000, 56-62; de Grummond 2002, 75-76.

12. See Small 1982 for a full review of the evidence. More recently, see Luschi 1991; de Grummond 2000, 32-33.

13. de Grummond 2000, passim.

14. Beard and North 1990, 8.

15. Beard and North 1990, 6-9.

16. Beard and North 1990, 41, 105, 202.

17. Basic review with list of inscriptions in Torelli 1986, 221; see also Pallottino 1975, 226; Pfiffig 1975, 44. Jannot (1998, 139) lists plurals of *cepenar* and *cepnar*, but these do not occur in *ET*.

18. See *ET*, vol. 1, 87, for indexing of *cepen* (15 occurrences in the LL; AT 1.108; AV 4.1; *cepar* in LL VII.19).

19. *TLE*, 133, 137, 165, 171; *ET*, Ta 1.34, 1.184, AT 1.171, AT 1.96.

20. Torelli 1986, 221; Pallottino 1975, 229; Pfiffig 1975, 44.

21. Pfiffig 1975, 44; Pallottino 1975, 225.

22. Torelli 1986, 222; Nielsen 1990; Haynes 2000, 285-286.

23. *TLE*, 131; *ET*, 1.17. Bonfante and Bonfante 2002, 149-151, is an excellent summary of the information to be obtained from the inscription.

24. For further discussion of words that have to do with haruspication, see below, p. 39.

25. Beard 1990, 45. Cf. Garland 1990, 77: "The most striking feature of Athenian priests and priestesses is their isolation."

26. Heurgon 1964, 230-231. See also Valerius Maximus 1.1 (Appendix B, Source no. IV.9), following Cicero closely, except that he seems to say that *Roman* boys were handed over to the Etruscans to study the discipline. He definitely uses ten for the number of youths, and some have corrected the reading in Cicero to be consistent with Valerius. Cf. p. 6, above, note 9.

27. The location is still unknown, but promising excavations have been undertaken in the "Fairgounds" (Campo della Fiera) on

the plain below the plateau of Orvieto, under the direction of Simonetta Stopponi and her collaborator Claudio Bizzarri. For earlier results in the Campo della Fiera, see Bruschetti 1999.

28. Pfiffig 1975, 70. One must always keep in mind that the edict does not actually name the Fanum Voltumnae, only Volsinii, where it was supposed to be located.

29. Maggiani 1984. Bonfante 2003, 53–54, 69, 75; Capdeville 1999, 114–115.

30. See Bonfante 1973, 587, 605.

31. Besides the ones discussed here, note the Tomba Golini "delle due Bighe": *Pittura etrusca a Orvieto*, 1982, fig. 18 (fourth century BCE; the deceased rides in his chariot); various ash urns from Chiusi: Jannot 1998, figs. 18, 78. It appears also on Etruscan coins of the Hellenistic period: Pfiffig 1975, 45, fig. 7.

32. Bonfante 2003, 53–54, fig. 137; Bonfante and Bonfante 2002, 165; Pfiffig 1975, 48–49; Jannot 1998, 137, pl. K.

33. Turfa 2005, 263–265.

34. Bonfante 1973, 607.

35. Four statuettes from the same source were published in the catalog of the Venice show, Torelli 2000, pl. pp. 278–279, 592–593, cat. nos. 152–155 (all now in Göttingen). The discussion in the text focuses on no. 153, but it is worth noting that two of these have the rough, skinlike mantle. Three of the four wear the *apex*, having in this case a rather conical shape.

36. Kleiner 1992, fig. 74.

37. Maggiani 1989, 1557–1558.

38. Thulin 1968, pt. III, 113–114; Pfiffig 1975, 48, 99; Torelli 1986, 220; Jannot 1998, 141–142.

39. Gantz 1971.

40. *Die Welt der Etrusker* 1988, 211 (no. B.9.5).

41. Pfiffig 1975, 99; de Grummond 1996, 360–362.

42. Relief from Chiusi: Jannot 1998, fig. 21. Bronze statuette from the *stips* of the Lapis Niger, Roman Forum, ca. 550 BCE: Torelli 2000, 591 (no. 146) Coins: Pfiffig 1977, 99. Julius Caesar is associated with the *lituus* on the Mettius denarius, Augustus (as Jupiter) carries the *lituus* on the Gemma Augustea, and there are various other Roman examples: Kleiner 1992, figs. 25, 47.

43. Massa-Parault 1999, 82–83 and fig. 1. Another ritual staff, covered with knots, appears in funerary scenes as part of the equipment of the deceased, for example, in scenes of the journey of the dead from the Vanth Group of vessels from Orvieto (Pfiffig 1975, 177, fig. 73a–b). Here the deceased is shown once lying in a wagon and holding the knotted staff and another time on foot, led by Charu, using the staff to support himself as he walks. The knotted staff also appears in the Tomb of the Jugglers, Tarquinii, held by an elderly man who walks along with a boy, probably also in a journey of the deceased (Steingräber 1986, pl. 90).

44. Steingräber 1986, 352.

45. Banti 1973, 241 and pl. 40b; Pfiffig 1975, 28 and fig. 1. For the fawn drinking, cf. another possible priestess in the museum of Barbarano Romano, and a male sarcophagus from Tarquinii: Cristofani 1978, fig. 165. I thank Larissa Bonfante for assisting with documentation of these items.

46. See also Beard, North, and Price 1998, vol. 2, 288–291, for the relevant passages from Livy and the surviving text of the senatorial decree.

47. Moretti Sgubini 2004, 188–198.

48. Bonfante 1973, 596, 612.

49. Torelli 1986, 221; Bonfante and Bonfante 2002, 69.

50. Bonfante and Bonfante 2002, 124, n. 29.

51. See esp. the salutary warnings of Jeffrey Tatum, in the Preface (above, p. xii). The *haruspices* were organized into a well-known *collegium* by the Romans, which reached the rather surprising size of sixty members. It is entirely possible that Etruscan city-states depended likewise on a large group of such seers, but so far the evidence is nonexistent. For a nuanced discussion, see Beard, North, and Price 1998, vol. 1, 19–20. For a general treatment of *haruspices* under the Romans, including the personal names of many priests, see Thulin 1968, III, 148–156.

52. Thulin 1968, pt. III, 131–132. See also MacBain 1982, 45, for an evaluation of the evidence.

53. Beard, North, and Price, 1998, vol. 1, 168–169. The story is another example of the theme of capturing the prophet to learn his secrets.

54. Barker and Rasmussen 1998, 197–198.

55. See Dumézil 1966, vol. 2, esp. 606–608. MacBain 1982, esp. the index of prodigies, 83–106, for a wide assortment.

56. Torelli 2000, 593 (no. 156, wrongly given as in Munich); *ET*, Vt G1.

57. Van der Meer 1987.

58. Beard, North, and Price 1998, vol. 1, 188, 326–327; vol. 2, 175–176.

59. Thulin 1968, I, 22–38. For a healthy skepticism concerning various contradictory scraps of information about which gods could throw lightning, see Capdeville 1989. He dismisses literary sources that suggest tantalizingly that the list of gods ought to include Auster (the West Wind), Hercules (Hercle), and Summanus (a Tinia of the Night).

60. Bloch and Minot 1986, 795, no. 33; (no. 33); *ES*, IV, pl. 396.

61. *ES*, III, pl. 246.

62. Interesting comments in Pairault-Massa 1985, 60–66, 78; Pfiffig 1975 has a short section, 150–152, and likewise Jannot 1998, 43–44; Dumézil 1970 ignores it. Basic for the study of the Roman tradition: Linderski 1986.

63. Heurgon 1964, 225–226. See recently McDonough 2003, 252.

64. Goidanich 1935.

65. Maggiani 1984, 144.

BIBLIOGRAPHY

Banti, L. 1973. *The Etruscan Cities and Their Culture*. Berkeley, CA.
Barker, G., and T. Rasmussen. 1998. *The Etruscans*. Oxford.
Beard, M. 1990. "Priesthood in the Roman Republic." In Beard and North 1990, 17–48.

Beard, M., and J. North. 1990. *Pagan Priests, Religion and Power in the Ancient World*. London.
Beard, M., J. North, and S. Price. 1998. *Religions of Rome*. 2 vols. Cambridge.

Bloch, R., and N. Minot. 1986. "Eos/Thesan." *LIMC* III, 789-797.

Bonfante, G., and L. Bonfante. 2002. *The Etruscan Language*. 2nd ed. Manchester.

Bonfante, L. 1973. "Roman Costumes: A Glossary and Some Etruscan Derivations." *ANRW* I.4, 584-614.

———. 2003. *Etruscan Dress*, new ed. Baltimore.

Bonghi Jovino, M., ed. 1986. *Gli etruschi di Tarquinia*. Modena.

Bonghi Jovino, M., and C. Chiaramonte Treré. 1997. *Tarquinia: Testimonianze archeologiche e ricostruzione storica: Scavi sistematici nell'abitato: Campagne 1982-1988*. Rome.

Bruschetti, P. 1999. "Indagini di scavo a Campo della Fiera presso Orvieto." *AnnFaina* 6, 159-181.

Buonamici, G. 1939. *Fonti di storia etrusca*. Florence.

Buranelli, F. 1992. *The Etruscans: Legacy of a Lost Civilization*. Ed. and tr. N. T. de Grummond. Memphis, TN.

Capdeville, G. 1989. "Les dieux fulgurants dans la doctrine étrusque." In *Secondo Congresso Internazionale Etrusco, Firenze, 26 maggio-2 giugno, 1985, Atti*. III, 1171-1190.

———. 1999. "Voltumna ed altri culti del territorio Volsiniese," *AnnFaina* 6, 109-135.

Colonna, G. 1987. "Note preliminari sui culti del Portonaccio a Veio," *Scienze dell'Antichità* 1, 431-441.

Christofani, M. 1978. *L'arte degli etruschi, produzione e consumo*. Turin.

———. 1985. "Il cosidetto specchio di Tarchon: Un recupero e una nuova lettura," *Prospettiva* 41, 4-20.

de Grummond, N. T. 1996. "Etruscan Italy Today." In *Etruscan Italy*, ed. J. Hall. Provo, UT. 336-365.

———. 2000. "Mirrors and Manteia: Themes of Prophecy on Etruscan Mirrors." In *Aspetti e problemi della produzione degli specchi figurati etruschi*, ed. M. D. Gentili. Rome. 27-67.

———. 2002. "Mirrors, Marriage and Mysteries." *JRA*, Suppl. 47, 63-85.

Dumézil, G. 1966. *Archaic Roman Religion*. 2 vols. Paris.

ES = *Etruskische Spiegel*, ed. E. Gerhard (vols. 1-4); A. Klügmann and G. Körte (vol. 5). Berlin. 1840-1897.

ET = H. Rix. 1991. *Etruskische Texte, editio minor*. 2. vol. Tübingen.

Les Étrusques et l'Europe. 1992. Catalogue of exhibition. Paris.

Gantz, T. N. 1971. "Divine Triads on an Archaic Frieze Plaque from Poggio Civitate (Murlo)." *StEtr* 39, 1-22.

Garland, R. 1990. "Priests and Power in Classical Athens." In *Pagan Priests, Religion and Power in the Ancient World*, ed. M. Beard and J. North. London. 73-91.

Goidanich, P. G. 1935. "Rapporto culturali e linguistici fra Roma e gli Italici: Del dipinto vulcente di Vel Saties e Arnza." *StEtr* 9, 107-118.

Harris, W. V. 1971. *Rome in Etruria and Umbria*. Oxford.

Haynes, S. 2000. *Etruscan Civilization: A Cultural History*. Los Angeles.

Heurgon, J. 1959. "The Date of Vegoia's Prophecy." *JRS* 49, 41-45.

———. 1964. *Daily Life of the Etruscans*. Tr. J. Kirkup. London.

Jannot, J.-R. 1998. *Devins, dieux et démons: Regards sur la religion de l'Étrurie antique*. Paris.

Kleiner, D. 1992. *Roman Sculpture*. New Haven.

Linderski, J. 1986. "The Augural Law." *ANRW* II.16.3, 2147-2312.

Luschi, L. 1991. "Cacu, Fauno e i venti." *StEtr* 57, 105-117.

MacBain, B. 1982. *Prodigy and Expiation: A Study in Religion and Politics in Republican Rome*. Brussels. Collection Latomus 177.

Maggiani, A. 1984. "Il pensiero scientifico e religioso." In *Gli etruschi: Una nuova immagine*, ed. M. Cristofani. Florence. 136-151.

———. 1989. "Immagini di aruspici." In *Secondo Congresso Internazionale Etrusco, Firenze 26 maggio-2 giugno 1985*. Vol. 3. Rome. 1557-1563.

Martianus Capella 1977 = *Martianus Capella and the Seven Liberal Arts*. Tr. W. H. Stahl and R. Johnson. New York.

Massa-Pairault, F. H. 1999. "Mito e miti nel territorio volsiniese." *AnnFaina* 6, 77-108.

McDonough, C. M. 2003. "The Swallows on Cleopatra's Ship." *CW* 96, 251-258.

Moretti Sgubini, A. M., ed. 2001. *Tarquinia etrusca, una nuova storia*. Rome.

———. 2004. *Scavo nello scavo, gli etruschi non visti*. Catalogue of exhibition. Viterbo.

Nielsen, M. 1990. "Sacerdotesse e associazioni cultuali femminili in Etruria: Testimonianze epigrafiche e iconografiche." *AnalRom* 19, 45-67.

Nissinen, M. 2000. "The Socioreligious Role of the Neo-Assyrian Prophets." In *Prophecy in Its Ancient Near Eastern Context: Mesopotamian, Biblical and Arabian Perspectives*, ed. M. Nissinen. Atlanta, GA. 89-114.

Overholt, T. W. 1989. *Channels of Prophecy: The Social Dynamics of Prophetic Activity*. Minneapolis.

Pairault-Massa, F.-H. 1985. "La divination en Etrurie: Le IVe siècle, periode critique." In *La divination dans le monde étrusco-italique*, Caesarodunum Suppl. no. 52, 56-115.

Pallottino, M. 1975. *The Etruscans*. Tr. J. Cremona, ed. D. Ridgway. Bloomington, IN.

———. 1979. "Uno specchio di Tuscania e la leggenda etrusca di Tarchon." In *Saggi di Antichità*. Vol. 2. Rome. 679-709.

Pfiffig, A. 1975. *Religio etrusca*. Graz.

Pittura etrusca a Orvieto, 1982 = *Pittura etrusca a Orvieto: Le tombe di Settecamini e degli Hescanas a un secolo dalla scoperta. Documenti e materiali*. Rome.

Rallo, A. 1974. *Lasa iconografia e esegesi*. Florence.

Small, J. P. 1982. *Cacus and Marsyas in Etrusco-Roman Legend*. Princeton.

Steingräber, S. 1986. *Etruscan Painting: Catalogue Raisonné of Etruscan Wall Paintings*. English ed., ed. D. and F. Ridgway. New York.

Thulin, C. O. 1968. *Die Etruskische Disciplin*. Repr. of I. *Die Blitzlehre* (1905); II. *Die Haruspicin* (1906); III. *Die Ritualbücher und zur Geschichte und Organisation der Haruspices* (1909). Darmstadt.

Torelli, M. 1986. "La religione." In *Rasenna: Storia e civiltà degli etruschi*, Milan. 159-240.

———. 2000. *Gli etruschi*. Catalogue of exhibition, Venice. Milan.

Turfa, J. M. 2005. *Catalogue of the Etruscan Gallery of the University of Pennsylvania Museum of Archaeology and Anthropology*. Philadelphia.

Van der Meer, L. B. 1987. *The Bronze Liver of Piacenza: Analysis of a Polytheistic Structure*. Amsterdam.

Die Welt der Etrusker. 1988. Catalogue of exhibition. Berlin.

CHAPTER IV

GODS IN HARMONY
The Etruscan Pantheon

Erika Simon

It is well known that the Etruscan religion was not monotheistic like the Jewish, Christian, and Islamic faiths but recognized many gods. The members of that pantheon lived in the sixteen regions of the Etruscan heaven, with which the priests, especially the *haruspices,** were well acquainted. The animals killed for the gods carried that heaven in small scale within them, on their livers. The highest god of this divine assembly, Tin or **Tinia**,[1] was restricted in his power in comparison with Yahweh or Allah. He was not the only wielder of the lightning bolt, because besides him some other gods used it.[2] Another difference was that Tinia, like the Greek Zeus but unlike Yahweh, had not created the world but was a relatively young god. In Etruscan art he may be represented as a beardless youth or as a bearded man, as in a bronze statuette in Heidelberg (Fig. IV.1).[3] Such statuettes of divinities were mostly votives; they have been studied in our generation especially by Giovanni Colonna, Emeline Richardson, Mauro Cristofani, and Martin Bentz.[4] A second great field for representations of gods are the Etruscan bronze mirrors. Here we will consult especially the old nineteenth-century compendium of Eduard Gerhard; the new *Corpus Speculorum Etruscorum,* still in process; and the *Guide,* edited by Nancy T. de Grummond.[5] Because of their inscriptions, the mirrors are especially useful. A third group of monuments in which gods appear are the architectural terracottas, a well-known phenomenon of Etruscan temples. These three groups represent the main bulk of material for our purpose, but there are also single monuments like vases, wall paintings, and ash urns.

For the characterization of Etruscan gods it is often necessary to look at their Greek and Roman counterparts — thus to look from Tinia to Zeus or Jupiter (see Chart 1, p. 46). We shall be interested here in the Etruscan core that remains in such comparisons. To find it, other areas aside from the visual arts must be examined and combined, such as linguistics, comparative studies of religion, observations of cult practices, and the topography of excavated Etruscan sanctuaries.

Helpful in keeping names of Greek, Italic, and Etruscan origin apart is the linguistic method. Beside genuinely Etruscan names like Tinia, **Turan**, and **Thesan**, there are names of Greek origin like **Aplu/Apulu** and **Aritimi/Artumes**. Still others, such as **Uni, Menerva, Nethuns**, are thought to come from the Latin or Italic names Juno, Minerva, Neptunus. In this category we are dealing not with subordinated gods but with important Etruscan cult deities. The opposite development, namely, that the Etruscan Uni later became the Latin Juno, is not possible, according to linguistic research, and the same seems to be true for Menerva and Nethuns. These deities and others must have been already worshiped by the Latins and their Italic neighbors before the Etruscans took them over. Thanks to Carlo De Simone, Ambrose J. Pfiffig, Gerhard Radke, Helmut Rix, and others, we now know much more than earlier generations about those important questions.[6]

In polytheistic religions, cults could wander; there was no conflict because of different faiths as we know from monotheism. The Etruscan pantheon, like the Roman one, had a special power to integrate gods from outside, which was strengthened by the tendency for harmony among the members, as we shall see in works of the visual arts.[7] Besides the gods, priests also could wander and take cults and cult practices with them. This leads clearly the other way round,

IV.1. *Bronze statuette of Tinia. Fifth century BCE. Heidelberg University, Antikenmuseum. (Photo: Archäologisches Institut der Universität Heidelberg, N.S. 867.)*

CHART 1. A Selected List of Etruscan Deities and Their Greek and Roman Comparisons

Listed below are some of the principal deities of the Etruscans within their spheres of influence. The spelling of their names varies in Etruscan inscriptions, and some of the major variants are supplied here, but it is not possible to include all of them. A word of caution is also in order regarding the equations with gods from Greece and Rome. Rarely is any Etruscan deity exactly equivalent to a Greek or Roman divinity, and it is best to think of these non-Etruscan mythological figures only as comparisons and in general to use Etruscan forms of the name to avoid making unwarranted assumptions.

Etruscan	Greek	Roman
"Olympian" Deities		
Aplu, Apulu	Apollon	Apollo
Artumes, Aritimi	Artemis	Diana
Fufluns, Pacha	Dionysos	Bacchus
Laran	Ares	Mars
Mariś	—	Genius?
Menrva, Menerva	Athena	Minerva
Nethuns	Poseidon	Neptunus
Sethlans	Hephaistos	Vulcanus
Tinia, Tin	Zeus	Jupiter
Turan	Aphrodite	Venus
Turms	Hermes	Mercurius
Turnu	Eros	Cupid, Amor
Uni	Hera	Juno
Vei	Ceres?	Demeter?
Cosmic Deities		
Catha, Kavtha, Cath	—	Solis filia
Cel	Gaia	Terra Mater
Culśanś	—	Janus
Thesan	Eos	Aurora
Tivr, Tiur	Selene?	Luna?
Usil	Helios	Sol
"Hero Gods"		
Hercle	Herakles	Hercules
Tinas Cliniiar (Cliniar), or Castur and Pultuce	Dioskouroi, or Kastor and Polydeukes	Dioscuri, or Castor and Pollux
Underworld Deities and Demons		
Aita, Calu	Hades	Pluto
Charu	—?	Charon
Phersipnei	Persephone	Proserpina

because the Latins and their Italic neighbors were strongly influenced by Etruscan rituals and priesthoods, as exemplified by Roman *haruspices* and augurs. Soothsaying by help of the livers of victims was an Etruscan custom inherited from Anatolia, as the clay models of livers from Hittite sites in the Museum of Ancient Anatolian Civilizations in Ankara suggest.[8]

Prophecy from the flight of the birds was in antiquity thought to be an invention of the Phrygians (Isidore of Seville, *Etymol.* 8.8.32), who had entered Anatolia in the late second millennium BCE. But recent excavations show that watching the birds for prophecy had already been practiced by the Hittites.[9] For Greeks and Romans the Hittites as well as the Trojans were "Phrygians."[10] In the newly discovered town of Sarissa, at modern Kuśaklı in northeast Turkey, two clay letters with cuneiform inscriptions were found, written by high Hittite officials, containing their observations of flying birds.[11] These are mentioned with their names, including eagles and falcons. In one case, the augurium of Sarissa is for the son of a lady of high status, while in the other case, it is for the king's daughter, because she had a bad dream. The writer did not make a detailed interpretation of their meaning, which was to be made by the addressee of the letter, a high official himself. Thus, soothsaying was "teamwork" for the Hittites, and the same is true for the Etruscans, as may be seen in images of the diviners such as Pava Tarchies and Cacu (Figs. III.4 and III.7).[12]

We know that among the Roman priesthoods the augurs had a high rank. After all, they used a practice that was more than one millennium old, coming to Rome from the late Hittite courts via Etruria. The early Romans who had taken over this practice must have felt the superiority of the Etruscans in this field, which was associated, as the Hittite letters show us, with the usage of writing. One high official wrote the record without interpreting it; another high official had to explain it. In Italy, of course, that record was not written in cuneiform but in letters that the Etruscans had learned from the Chalcidian Greeks at the Bay of Naples. Writing and religion in Etruria were closely tied, and this connection must have fascinated their Italian neighbors.

In earlier research, the topography of Etruscan sanctuaries was examined primarily through the writings of ancient authors such as Vitruvius, Dionysius of Halicarnassus, Livy, and Pliny the Elder. What excavations can contribute may be seen from the findings of Gravisca, Marzabotto, Pyrgi, Veii, and the Ara della Regina at Tarquinii,[13] to name only some examples. Thus the ongoing excavations of Pyrgi have shown that the ancient written sources about the main goddess of the sanctuary are far from being complete. They speak about Leukothea or Mater Matuta, but the main goddess was actually Uni, the Latin Juno, who could be also worshiped as Astarte, the great goddess of the Phoenicians. In addition, Tinia, the husband of Uni, is named in inscriptions from Pyrgi along with Thesan, the goddess of dawn, and **Śuri**-Apollo, the god of the south precinct.[14]

Neither Eos nor Aurora, the Greek and Roman pendants of Thesan, were cult deities, but she did receive cult. On a Classical mirror with name inscriptions from Tuscania in the Vatican (Fig. IV.2),[15] Thesan is grouped with the sun god **Usil** and the seated Nethuns, who is shown like the Greek god Poseidon holding a trident. The name Usil, which appears also on the bronze liver from Piacenza,[16] is written near the *nimbus** of the youth in the center. Mythical scenes on Etruscan mirrors can be taken from the Greek and/or Latin tradition or they can be genuinely Etruscan. The latter may be the case here, because Usil carries in his right hand a bow, which points to his equation with Apollo.[17] Now we know that this god in Homer is never equated with Helios, the Greek sun god, but that both Apollo and Helios are regularly equated in the Sibylline oracles. Some of these were known in fifth-century Rome and perhaps also in Etruria.[18] Thus the mirror from Tuscania (Fig. IV.2) may show an Etruscan myth of daybreak: Thesan, the goddess of dawn together with Usil rising from the sea and saying farewell to seated Nethuns. The close connection between dawn and sun—Thesan puts her arm on Usil's shoulder—is never shown in Greek art.

Another Etruscan myth of daybreak is represented in the Pyrgi terracotta antefixes* (Fig. IV.3). These I have discussed elsewhere, following Krauskopf's interpretation of the running youth as Usil (Fig. IV.3:A).[19] His cock-headed companion on another antefix type (Fig. IV.3:A) may be the personification of the morning dew, whose unknown name is perhaps hidden among the many Etruscan words we do not yet understand. The two stars in the hands of a running winged goddess in the same series (Fig. IV.3:D) may be the morning star and the evening star carried by Thesan.[20]

All the antefixes from Pyrgi (six types in all) have an Oriental flavor and thus go together with the inscriptions on the famous golden tablets from the sanctuary, in which the equivalent of Uni is the Phoenician goddess Astarte.[21] Her equation with a goddess of central Italy is much earlier attested by bronze statuettes from Satricum.[22] They were defined by Richardson as Orientalized Geometric and must represent the main deity of the sanctuary, Mater Matuta, in the shape of the great naked Phoenician goddess. The astral disc above her head is, according to Richardson, "perhaps borrowed from the Phoenician and Cypriote Astarte."[23]

Between these statuettes and the golden tablets from Pyrgi stands chronologically the large marble statuette from the Cannicella sanctuary of Orvieto, undoubtedly a real cult image (Fig. IV.4).[24] The naked goddess makes the same gesture as one of the bronze statuettes from Satricum, a gesture borrowed from Oriental prototypes.[25] Her sanctuary, however, was situated among graves. She was called Turan by J.-R. Jannot and others,[26] but this seems to me problematic. Inscriptions from the Cannicella cult place have the name of the goddess **Vei**, whom others rightly equate with the Greek Demeter.[27] She was, among the Olympians, the only deity who took care of the dead, who in Greece could even be called Demetreioi, "Demeter's property." The Cannicella

IV.2. Mirror with Nethuns, Usil, and Thesan. Fourth century BCE. Vatican Museums. (After ES, 1.76.)

goddess must be, like her, a mother deity who took the life she had borne back to her womb. Perhaps the mother goddess Cel Ati, Mother Earth, whose name is known from votives,[28] was very near to Vei or identical with her. In any case, sanctuaries among graves, as we know them from the Christian religion, are a typical central Italian custom in pagan antiquity. The Etruscan gods seem to have been nearer to the chthonic sphere than the Greek Olympians and the Roman pantheon.

Deities mighty in the realms of both the living and the dead are characteristic for Etruscan religion. This may be specially said about Apulu/Aplu, whose most powerful representation comes from the Portonaccio sanctuary at Veii (Fig. VIII.38).[29] In the *Iliad* (16.667–680) the god Apollo takes care of the body of fallen Sarpedon as well as the dead Hector (24.18–21). This may be due to his Oriental connections,[30] which were given up in Greek Apolline myths. Thus in the beginning of Euripides' *Alkestis*, Apollo leaves the house of his friend Admetos, whose wife is dying.

In Etruria, however, he was the god of Mount Soracte north of Rome, who is called in Latin sources Apollo Soranus and Dis Pater, god of the Underworld. In the *Aeneid* of Vergil (11.785) the Etruscan Arruns prays to him: *Summe deum, sancti custos Soractis Apollo*.[31] Colonna has convincingly identified Soranus with Śuri, who is known by many votive inscriptions from different regions of Etruria.[32] His connection with the Underworld may possibly be explained by the equation of Apulu with Usil, as he is represented on the mirror from Tuscania (Fig. IV.2). His forerunners, the Oriental sun gods, were connected not only with the daylight. For example, the Egyptian sun god Re went through the Underworld during the night.[33] Thus also the Etruscans

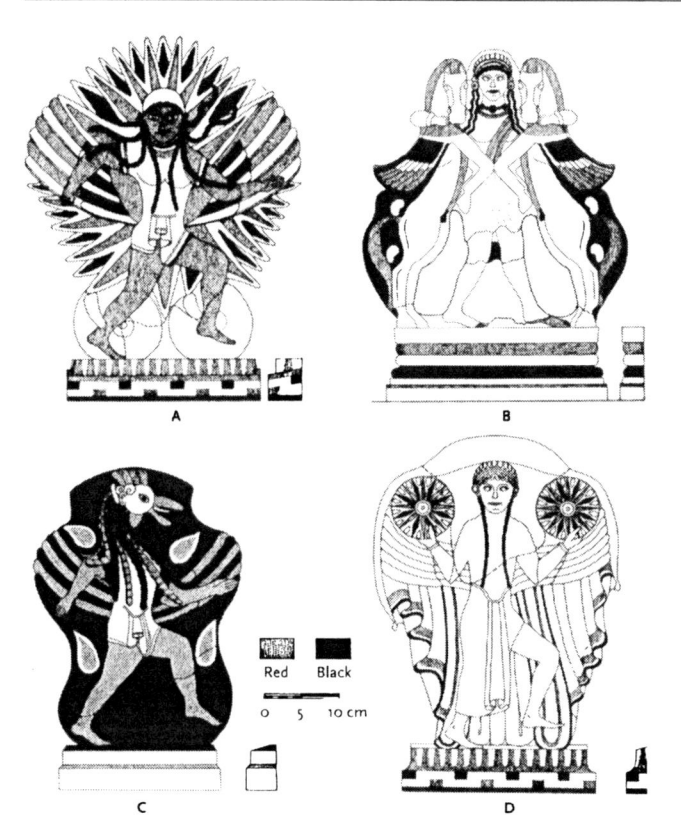

IV.3. *Terracotta antefixes with "Daybreak": Usil, a Mistress of Horses, a dew demon, and Thesan. Late sixth century BCE. Pyrgi, Antiquarium, and Rome, Museo Etrusco di Villa Giulia. (After Haynes 2000, fig. 153.)*

wished their dead to have light. They gave them amulets with astral symbols and painted the holy laurel grove of Apulu/Usil on the walls of their tombs.[34]

As shown elsewhere, those laurel groves were combined with the ivy of **Fufluns**, the Etruscan Dionysos, Apulu's very different brother.[35] In spite of this, Apollo and Dionysos were in Greece also *synnaoi*, that is, they shared the important Apolline sanctuaries in Delphi and Delos.[36] The Etruscans, who had close relations with Delphi, imitated the Greeks in this respect. On a mirror from a workshop in Vulci of the second quarter of the fourth century in Berlin (Fig. IV.5),[37] the Delphian festival Herois is represented in a typically Etruscan manner. That festival commemorated Dionysos descending to the Underworld in order to guide his mother Semele to heaven. The mirror shows Semla and Fufluns embracing, along with Apulu—who has a small piping satyr by his side—looking at them. The Delphian festival Herois can show that Dionysos was also mighty in the Underworld, and this was the reason why the Etruscans painted his ivy in their graves.

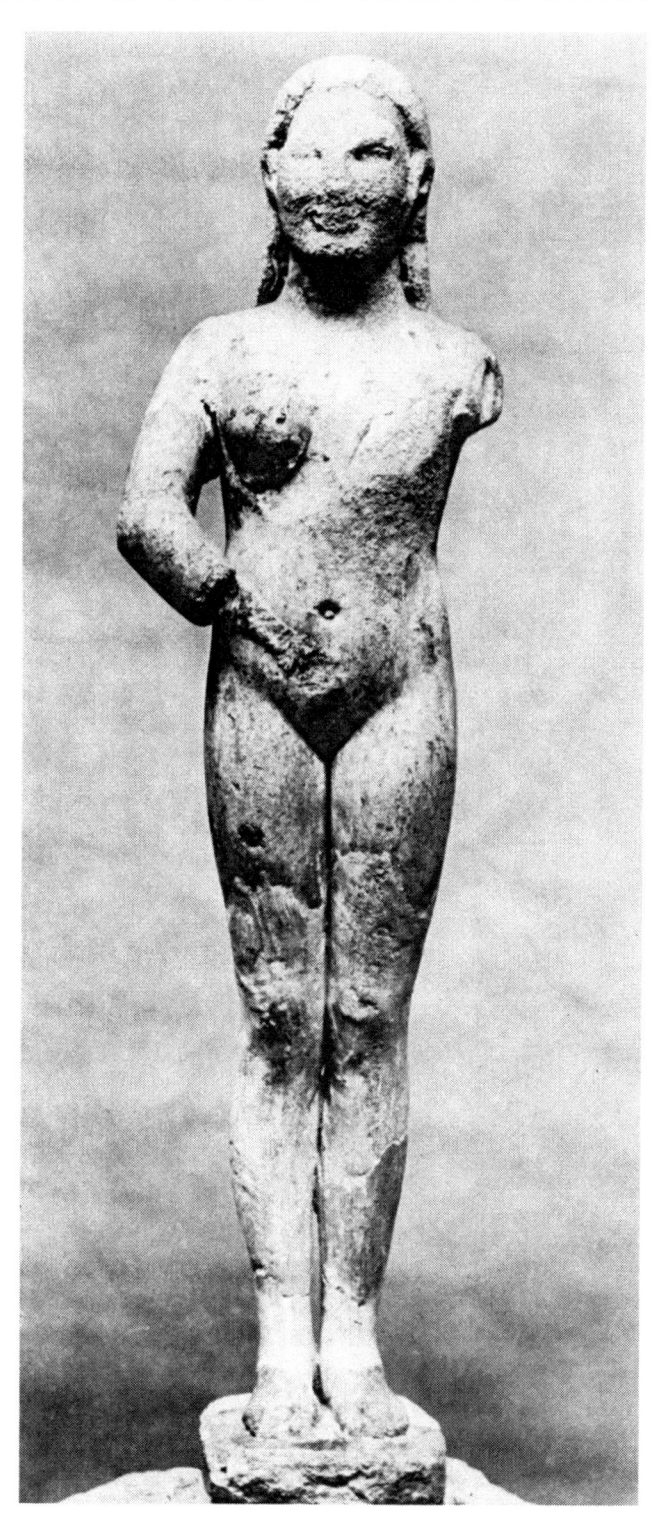

IV.4. *Naked goddess from Cannicella sanctuary. Late sixth century BCE. Orvieto, Museo Faina. (Photo: Felbermeyer. DAI 65.616 R.)*

IV.5. Mirror with Apulu, saytr, Fufluns, Semla. Fourth century BCE. Berlin. (After ES, 1.83.)

It was a great surprise when a Late Classical mirror was found in 1989 in the necropolis of Castel Viscardo near Orvieto (Fig. IV.6). It has the same composition as the mirror from Vulci, but some of the names are different.[38] Apulu in the center remained, but he is accompanied not by a satyr boy but by the winged god of love, who is called **Turnu**—child of Turan (Aphrodite)—and is playing with an *iynx*.*[39] The group on the right side is labeled Turan, also holding an *iynx*, and Atunis. The latter, in Greek Adonis, was the young lover of Aphrodite-Turan. His cult is attested in Gravisca from later Archaic times onward.[40]

The newly excavated mirror shows what is often forgotten, namely, that the type of a figure and the name need not be identical even though the compositions are very similar. Fufluns and Semla, son and mother, can be represented like Atunis and Turan, the beautiful boy and his divine lover. This "romantic" couple was an ideal theme for mirrors, of which we look only at one other (Fig. IV.7), not much later in date, in St. Petersburg.[41] Here not Turnu, but a very big goose and a winged goddess called Zipna are shown together with Turan and Atunis. The border is filled with winged boys and girls, attendants of Turan, among them **Alpan**, to whom we shall return later. Atunis was mortal like plants and flowers. His festival was in high summer, in July, a month that was

iv.6. Mirror with Apulu, Turnu (Eros), Atunis, Turan. Fourth century BCE. Orvieto, Museo Nazionale. (After Feruglio 1998, fig. 2.)

named after Turan in Etruria.⁴² Atunis had to leave her and go to the Underworld. It was through love for him that the great goddess fell under the laws of time and death.

There was another figure of the Etruscan pantheon belonging to life and Afterlife: **Turms**, the Greek Hermes.⁴³ Eric Hostetter has commented on a beautiful bronze handle from Spina with two Turms figures (Fig. iv.8), one connected with Tin and one with **Calu-Aita**.⁴⁴ We even have an inscription on a mirror naming the latter Turmś Aitaś, the "Hermes of Hades" (Fig. iv.9).⁴⁵ He accompanies a figure called Hinthial Teraśiaś—shadow of Teiresias—before Uthuze, that is Odysseus-Ulixes seated at the entrance to the Underworld. The scene is described in the Nekyia of the *Odyssey* (11.90–151) but without the presence of Hermes, who would correspond to Turms.⁴⁶ Whereas the Homeric Teiresias is an old man, Teraśiaś has a young, female face: he was in a part of his life a woman.⁴⁷ As far as we know, the old tradition of the double gender of the great Theban prophet was nowhere represented in Greek visual art.⁴⁸ The artist of this Vulci mirror has dared to show it.

The most beautiful representation of Turms is among the clay statues from Veii, though only his head is preserved.⁴⁹ Here he is surely the messenger of Tin, who has sent him to make peace between **Hercle** and Apulu. The expression of his smiling face shows that he will succeed in spite of all quarreling. If we look for other groupings of Etruscan deities in Archaic art, we find quite often scenes of saber-rattling, which will end in reconciliation. One of the most original Etruscan vase painters, the Paris Painter, depicted the scene of a quarrel between Hercle and Uni on a "Pontic" amphora in London (Fig. iv.10).⁵⁰ Uni is shown as Seispes or Sospita, as her Latin name was, wearing a goat skin over her head and a shield on her side.⁵¹ She brandishes a lance against Hercle, who threatens with his club. In Etruria he was not a hero as in Greece but a god from the beginning. That he belonged to the Etruscan pantheon is shown, for example, by his name on the liver from Piacenza (Fig. ii.2). In the Etruscan myth represented on this amphora, Hercle has intruded into Uni's sanctuary, perhaps to rob the precious cauldrons with *protomai** of snakes. They are dedications such as those that Hera received at Argos, Samos, and Olympia.⁵² The accompanying figures of the picture show that a reconciliation will grow from this mutual threatening. Behind Hercle stands his protectress Menerva, the Greek Athena, in the Early Archaic version of the unarmed goddess,⁵³ because an additional lance would be too much; behind Uni stands her husband Tin. The attribute in his left hand is not a scepter but an arrow-shaped lightning bolt. Tin, out of concern for a peaceful pantheon, grabs Uni by her arm.

On a bronze relief from a chariot in Perugia (Fig. iv.11) Tin has even thrown two bolts of lightning between Hercle and Uni, who has riled up the Amazons against Hercle.⁵⁴ The bolts here do not hurt anybody—they are the signals of divine will. With such a signal ends the *Odyssey* (24.539): Zeus throws a lightning bolt between the people of Ithaka and Odysseus to show he wishes an end of their enmities. The artist of the Late Archaic bronze relief in Perugia, one of the best Etruscan metal artists we know, has represented Tin with the peace-making lightning bolt in the sense of the end of the *Odyssey*. The Etruscans must have known that ending and liked it.

The figure in long dress and with *calcei repandi** behind the Amazons (Fig. iv.11) can be restored as Uni in the form of Juno Sospita, as on the amphora in London (Fig. iv.10). She and Hercle will be reconciled by the will of Tin. They will become such good friends that Hercle even shelters Uni against attacking satyrs, a beloved theme in Etruscan bronze art,⁵⁵ and Uni makes peace even with them. Otherwise we could not understand why her head, with the goat skin of

IV.7. Mirror with Turan and Atunis and her retinue. Fourth century BCE. St. Petersburg, Hermitage. (After ES, 4.322.)

Juno Sospita, is to be seen together with satyr heads on the terracotta roofs of many central Italian temples.[56]

Turan at peace with the other two rival goddesses in the Judgment of Paris is the astonishing theme of a mirror of the late fourth century in the Indiana University Art Museum (Fig. IV.12).[57] The winner Turan is the only seated goddess, whereas the losers Uni and Menrva approach her as if she were a bride visited by friends. That the judgment is certainly the background for this meeting is shown by Elcsntre (=Paris) standing on the left. The figure on the right side has the inscription Althaia, whom we know as Meleager's mother. She should not be taken as an error of this very able artist[58] but as an anti-theme to the peace within the family of the gods. In Althaia's family there is war between her son Meleager and his uncles, her brothers. She is on their side, and this will cause Meleager's death. On an Early Hellenistic mirror in Berlin we see him under the wings of the goddess of fate.[59]

To understand this mirror (Fig. II.19) we should remember that the Etruscans expressed the inexorability of human fate through the symbol of the hammering of nails. Every year they repeated this ritual in the **Nortia** sanctuary at Vol-

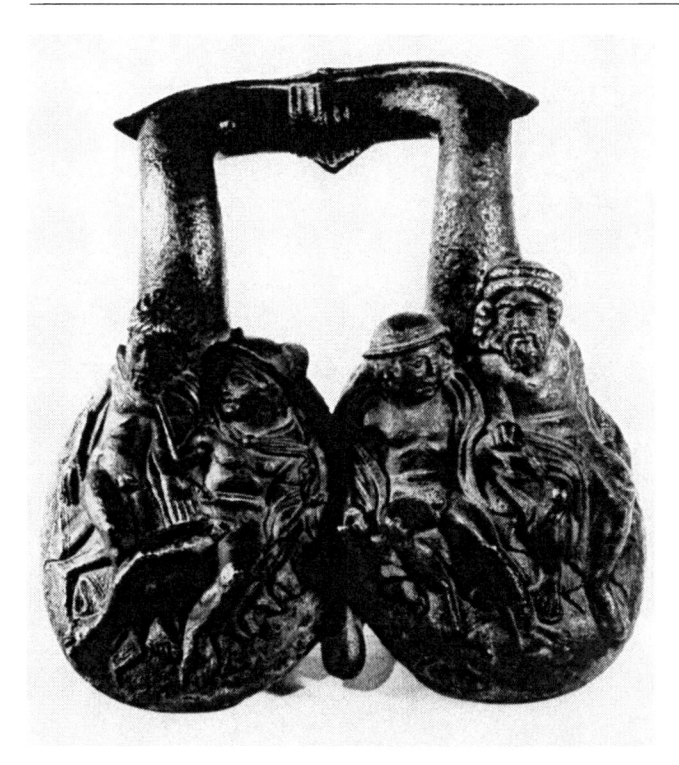

IV.8. Bronze handle with Turms of Tin and Turms of Calu. Fourth century BCE. Ferrara. (After Hostetter 1986, pl. 6a.)

IV.9. Mirror with Uthuze, Turmś Aitaś and Hinthial Terasiaś. Fourth century BCE. Vatican Museums. (After ES, 2.240.)

sinii, the capital of their league of Twelve Peoples. The nails that were hammered in formed the basis of their time reckoning (Livy 7.2.7; see Appendix B, Source no. V.1). In the center of the mirror stands a half-naked winged goddess who holds in her left hand a nail to be pounded in by the hammer in her right hand. The inscription identifies her as **Athrpa**, a name coming from Atropos, Greek goddess of fate, one of the three Moirai. On the right side of the picture are seated Meleager and Atalanta—both names written with Etruscan spelling—and on the other side, Turan and Atunis. Both of these loving pairs were involved with a fateful boar hunt; because of this there is a boar's head at the peak of the composition. Both pairs were separated by death; in Meleager's case, we heard, his own mother was guilty. In spite of the Greek protagonists, this is a purely Etruscan scene, which was never shown in this shape in Greece.

The wild boar like other wild animals belonged to the realm of deities, which occur in Etruscan art already in the seventh century BCE. There is a "mistress of animals" and also a "master of animals." We do not know their Etruscan names, but perhaps for the female deity we can use a name that was early imported from Greece: Aritimi or Artumes.[60] In Archaic Greek and Etruscan art she may be winged, holding two wild mammals or birds in her hands, a heraldic pic-

IV.10. Etruscan ("Pontic") amphora, Hercle (with Menerva) fights against Uni (with Tinia). Late sixth century BCE. London, British Museum. (After Hampe and Simon 1964, pl. 6.1.)

IV.11. Bronze relief from a chariot. Hercle (with Tinia) fights against Amazons (with Uni). Perugia, Museum. (Courtesy of E. Simon.)

ture that can appear repeated in the same composition. This is the case on two silver reliefs from an identical mold of the time around 600 BCE, now in the Vatican (Fig. IV.13).[61] The goddess is wingless here, but her arms are spread like wings to the shoulders of two young men on her sides. This is certainly not Helen with the Dioskouroi, as she was called by scholars, because two wolves are leaping up to her, defining her as mistress of wild animals. At the same time she is, like the Greek Artemis and the Latin Diana, a goddess of human assemblies: the Latin League met in Diana's grove near Aricia;[62] on the silver relief she shelters young men. Her connection with wolves instead of lions or panthers is typical for Italy.[63] A winged female bronze statuette of the later seventh century in Cortona,[64] which Emeline Richardson called Artumes, carries a bird on her head. With her hands, today empty, she may have held animals (wolves?).

The Etruscan name of the Dioskouroi was **Tinas Cliniar**, sons of Tin. Because one of them was mortal and the other was immortal, they were especially appropriate in tomb art, as perhaps in the Tomba del Barone in Tarquinii.[65] This grave is contemporary with the famous Oltos cup in the Archaeological Museum of Tarquinii, which has an Etruscan votive inscription for the divine twins;[66] Giovanni Colonna has shown that their hats are represented at Tarquinii in the Tomba del Letto Funebre.[67] Like Turms, they were great helpers in the transition from life to death. They must have been deeply venerated in Tarquinii and elsewhere until Late Hellenistic times, when they were represented again and again on mirrors, frequently at the door of transition.[68]

IV.12. Mirror with Judgment of Paris. Fourth century BCE. Bloomington, Indiana University Art Museum. (After CSE U.S.A. 1.4a.)

IV.13. Silver relief. Artumes as mistress of animals (wolves) and goddess of human assemblies. Seventh century BCE. Vatican Museums. (After Cristofani and Martelli 1983, pl. 115.)

The name of the Etruscan god of war was not **Mariś**, as earlier scholars thought, but **Laran** (Figs. IV.14 and IV.16).[69] He fights on a mirror from Populonia in Florence against the giant Celsclan, the son of the earth goddess **Cel**.[70] Laran wears a cuirass and is bearded, whereas in votive bronzes he is mostly beardless.[71] Instead of a sword as on the mirror, he brandishes a lance like his female pendant Menerva in a number of statuettes.[72] Because Laran appears just as a warrior, it is often unknown if the god himself is meant. This is also valid for the life-sized bronze statue of a warrior from Todi in the Vatican (Fig. IV.15), which according to F. Roncalli was made in Orvieto.[73] He has a votive inscription on his cuirass, held an iron lance in his left hand, and in his right a *patera** for libations.

Laran and Menerva appear together with their names inscribed on an early Hellenistic mirror (Fig. IV.14). Also present is Turan with other figures, among them two male babies.[74] This seems to be again an Etruscan myth, which in this case is shaped after a Greek—more exactly a Theban —prototype. Myths of Thebes were especially popular in Etruria, on vases of clay and bronze, on gems, mirrors, cinerary urns, and in architectural sculpture from Pyrgi to Talamone.[75]

In Thebes, according to Hesiod's *Theogony* (lines 933–937), Aphrodite and Ares, the pendants for Turan and Laran, were a wedded couple with three children: two demons of war and a daughter called Harmonia. This goddess, who became the wife of the Theban king Kadmos, personified peace and amiability. She does not appear with her Greek name Harmonia in Etruscan inscriptions, but there is Alpan, who may be her Etruscan equivalent, as Cheryl Sowder has

IV.14. Mirror with Leinth, Turan, Menrva, Laran, and two Mariś babies. Early third century BCE. Berlin, Antikensammlung. (After ES, 2.166.)

IV.15. Bronze statue of Mars from Todi. Fourth century BCE. Vatican Museums. (Photo: Schwanke. DAI Rome 81.237.)

noted.[76] We have seen her on the Atunis mirror in St. Petersburg (Fig. IV.7), and there are other mirrors with Alpan belonging to the realm of Turan.[77] The Theban myth of Harmonia, daughter of the war god and the goddess of love, must have appealed to the Etruscan mentality very much.

A Hellenistic sarcophagus from Tuscania may be placed into the same Theban context.[78] An old man and a young woman, both naked, are attacked by warriors at an altar. Behind it appear the deities of the sanctuary: Laran and Turan as a loving couple. The scene had been interpreted as a human sacrifice, whereas I have argued for Teiresias and his daughter Manto fleeing to the altar of Ares and Aphrodite during the capture of Thebes by the Epigonoi. The prophetess Manto was said to have later come to Italy, where her son founded Mantua.[79] In the divine couple behind the altar, the well-known groups of Mars and Venus in Roman art are anticipated.[80]

Another Etruscan parallel for a Roman deity is **Culśanś**,[81] the god with two faces like Janus. He is represented in an Early Hellenistic bronze statuette in Cortona (Fig. II.9).[82] The inscription on his left leg calls him a votive gift for Culśanś. His left arm is akimbo; the lost rodlike attribute in his right hand could have been a key, because Culśanś was connected with doors, and this statuette was found near a door of the town. His two faces are beardless, whereas terracotta double heads from Vulci[83] show the god bearded like the Roman Janus. As many other gods in Hellenistic Etruria, especially Tin, Culśanś may appear with or without a beard. The two-faced head of the statuette in Cortona (Fig. II.9) wears a helmetlike cap. It seems to be a *galerus*,* the sacral cap of the Roman *flamines*,* which consisted of the hide of an animal victim. It is known that the Romans imported this cap from Etruria like many other cult implements.[84] For certain sacral services, the *galerus* had an *apex*,* which is represented on the double head of Culśanś on coins of Volterra,[85] contemporary with the statuette in Cortona. This young god, after all, appears as a priest, small wonder since an important attribute of ancient priests and priestesses was the key with the power to open and shut a temple.[86]

As a god may become a priest, a priest in Etruria may also become a god or demon. On a well-known mirror from Vulci in the Vatican (Fig. III.8), a winged *haruspex* is shown studying a liver.[87] The inscription labels him **Chalchas**. Kalchas was the name of the Achaean seer in the Trojan War, who never had wings. The *haruspex* Chalchas, announcing the divine will from a liver, is thus shown as a superhuman being, a mediator between humans and gods. He may be compared with Turms, the messenger god with wings on head and/or shoes, who is quite different from the Roman Mercury. Turms could even split into twins (Fig. IV.8), to be a messenger of Tin as well as of Aita.

Others, such as the Dioskouroi, were real twins who helped especially at the door of transition between life and death. In Archaic representations, members of the pantheon like Uni and Hercle (Figs. IV.10 and IV.11) may be in conflict, but Tin with his messenger Turms promotes reconciliation. The lightning bolt in Tin's hand is less a weapon than a signal of his will. A special goddess of peace was Turan, the wife of the war god Laran. According to Theban mythology, which was always popular in Etruria, they were the parents of Harmonia, who in Etruscan was perhaps called Alpan. Thus over and over we find themes that create a picture of the Etruscan gods as seeking a balance in the universe, of striving for peace and harmony, a paradigm for men as well as gods.

A GLOSSARY OF ETRUSCAN GODS

The following survey presents the Etruscan gods in alphabetical order. The selection of the deities for inclusion emphasizes those for whom there is evidence of an actual cult and those that have been discussed or mentioned in the text above. As in the text, boldface type indicates that a god has an entry in the glossary. Only the briefest bibliography is given here (mostly articles in *LIMC*), to provide a portal to fuller bibliography elsewhere.

Aita

God of the Underworld (=Greek Hades). In tomb paintings he may be represented together with his consort Phersipnei (=Greek Persephone). They are mythological figures, whereas **Calu** is a genuine Etruscan Underworld god with a cult (see also **Śuri**). In tomb paintings Aita is shown with a wolf's cap, while his consort may have serpents in her hair. His messenger is **Turms** or Turmś Aitaś, "the Hermes of Hades" (Fig. IV.8). Krauskopf 1988a.

Alpan

Name of a special spirit, perhaps a **Lasa**, a servant of **Turan**. She may be represented with wings (Fig. IV.7) or without. She seems to symbolize harmony (see nn. 76–77). Lambrechts 1981.

Aplu/Apulu

Coming to Etruria from Greece via Latium, Aplu/Apulu (=Greek Apollon) remained a god from abroad, mainly the god of the Delphic oracle. His foreign character strengthened his authority. His best-known representation in art is the Veii Apollo (Fig. VIII.38). In cult, as Giovanni Colonna has shown, Aplu could be equated with **Śuri** (=Latin Soranus), who, like **Aita**, had the wolf as his attribute. In his "Greek" appearance, Aplu may have his attributes of bow, lyre, and laurel. He shared the sanctuary of Delphi with his brother Dionysos (**Fufluns**); see also **Usil** and Figure IV.2. A special Etruscan aspect is his friendship with **Uni**. Krauskopf 1984a.

Aritimi/Artumes

Her name is directly borrowed from Greek Artemis (Latin Diana), a hunting deity of Neolithic origin. Though in myth she is the sister of Aplu, the goddess was often venerated as a single figure. She was a mistress of animals—in Italy especially of wolves (Fig. IV.13)—and a goddess sheltering human assemblies (cf. Diana from Aricia). In Archaic art she often appears with wings. Krauskopf 1984b and Simon 1984b.

Athrpa

Goddess of fate (=Greek Atropos). See **Nortia**; see Fig. II.19.

Atunis

The name comes from Greek Adonis, the beautiful youth beloved by Aphrodite, Greek goddess of love. His cult, together with that of **Turan**, is attested at Gravisca, the harbor of Tarquinii (see n. 40). He is often represented with Turan on mirrors (Figs. IV.6–7). Servais-Soyez 1981 (unfortunately, in this article, Etruscan representations are mixed in with Greek ones).

Calu

God of the Underworld known from many inscriptions, because the dead "went to Calu." Representations of Calu under this name are unknown; if he appears in visual art, he is called **Aita**. Krauskopf 1988a.

Catha/Kavtha (and other spellings)

Goddess who shared cult with **Śuri** at Pyrgi. Etruscan inscriptions refer to her as "daughter," and she has been connected with a reference in Martianus Capella (Appendix B: Source no. III.4) to "the daughter of the Sun." Colonna 1992, 98–99; de Grummond 2004, 357–361.

Cel

Name of the earth goddess, as Colonna (1976–1977) has shown. Cel appears on the Piacenza liver and in votive inscriptions to Cel Ati, "mother earth" (see n. 28). No representations are certain (cf., however, **Vei**), but we do have a representation of Celsclan ("son of Cel," i.e., a Giant) on a mirror from Populonia in Florence (see n. 70).

Chalchas

A figure represented on an Etruscan mirror (Fig. III.8), shown as a winged *haruspex* reading a liver, obviously the Etruscan counterpart of a Greek priest and seer, Kalchas, in the *Iliad* (1.68–100, 2.300–332).

Charu(n)

Demon of death. His name is taken from the Greek ferryman of the souls, who is, however, an old man, not a demon.

Charu has an ugly face, and—unlike any depiction of Charon—animal's ears, and often wings. He appears in tomb paintings, on sarcophagi, on urns, and in other tomb art. Mavleev and Krauskopf 1986.

Cilens

Deity whose name is inscribed on the Piacenza liver in three different sections, once paired with Tin, perhaps to be equated with the Latin god of the night, Nocturnus. A terracotta relief from Bolsena shows Cilens, dressed in rich, ample female clothing, attending Mera (=Menerva). Unfortunately, the head is lacking. Camporeale 1986.

Culśanś

Double-faced god of the gates, whose name is connected with the Etruscan word for gates and doors (**Culśu**). Culśanś corresponds to the Roman god Janus, who also had two faces, looking east and west. Whereas Janus was bearded, Etruscan Culśanś may be a youth (Fig. 11.9). Krauskopf 1986a and Simon 1988.

Culśu

A demonic female guardian of the gate to the Underworld, represented with label only once, on the sarcophagus of Hasti Afunei from Chiusi (Fig. v.1). Culśu does not show a double face, as does Culśanś, whose name has the same root, very likely something to do with the word for "door." (Cf. Latin *ianua*.) She wears a short dress, crossed ribbons over the breast, and high boots like those of the female demon **Vanth** standing nearby. Culśu appears within a gate and carries a torch in one hand and what is probably a key in the other. Krauskopf 1986b.

Fufluns

Etruscan name for Dionysos. God of wine, ecstasy, and mysteries, brother of **Aplu**, with whom he shared the sanctuary at Delphi (Fig. IV.5). Another name for Fufluns was **Pacha** (Greek Bakchos). Like **Hercle**, Fufluns and his retinue of satyrs and maenads are beloved themes of Etruscan art. Cristofani 1986.

Hercle

Etruscan name for the Greek Herakles (Latin Hercules). His appearance in Archaic Etruscan art is strongly influenced by representations of the Cypriote (Phoenician) Melqarth. Hercle was not, like Herakles, a hero, but a god from the beginning. He had many sanctuaries in Etruria and Latium, where he was more an oracular god than in Greece. Hercle was popular and often represented in Etruscan art (Figs. II.8, II.15). **Uni** is sometimes his adversary (Figs. IV.10, IV.11), but **Tinia** reconciles them. Schwarz 1990.

Laran

God of war, counterpart of the Greek Ares and the Latin Mars. (The Etruscan equivalent of Mars was not **Mariś**, as earlier scholars thought.) On a mirror from Populonia, Laran is fighting against the giant Celsclan (**Cel**). Often represented as heavily armed; his consort is **Turan** (Fig. IV.14). Simon 1984a.

Lasa

Divine female servant (Fig. II.18) of **Turan**, alone or in a group of similar secondary goddesses, who all may have, like **Alpan**, individual names (Fig. IV.7). If they are winged, they sometimes look like female Erotes, but they may also be wingless. As love is connected with fate, Lasa may also appear as a fate goddess, thus on a mirror in London, British Museum 622. Lambrechts 1992a.

Leinth

Secondary figure represented on mirrors, sometimes male (a naked youth), sometimes female. Perhaps the name Leinth indicates a personification that relates more to a function than to an actual mythological being. Camporeale 1992a.

Letham

This deity (male or female?) appears in several votive inscriptions and was represented on a late Etruscan mirror in Como with the birth of **Menerva** from the head of **Tinia** (not preserved). Thus, if female, she may be a deity connected with birth, like **Ethausva** and **Thanr**, and thus a counterpart of Greek Eileithyia. Krauskopf 1992a.

Mariś

Pfiffig (1975, 249) has shown that this god is not identical with Mars, whose Etruscan name was **Laran**. On mirrors, the name Mariś is given to several babies (Fig. IV.14) together with an individual name: Mariśhalna, Mariśhusrnana, and Mariśisminthians. They could be the sons of **Turan** and **Laran**, educated by **Menerva**. Mariś may also be a youth, but his functions are not well known. Nancy de Grummond (forthcoming) argues that Mariś is equivalent to the Latin "Genius"; Cristofani 1992b.

Mean

Secondary divine female, winged or unwinged, known only from mirrors. Like the Greek Nike, she sometimes crowns a hero for victory. Lambrechts 1992b.

Menerva/Menrva

One of the most important goddesses, though her name is not genuine Etruscan (it comes from Latin Minerva) and though she does not appear on the Piacenza liver. The latter object relates to a north Etruscan pantheon, whereas Menerva is south Etruscan. She had important sanctuaries like the temple at Veii (Portonaccio) and at Lavinium (Pratica di Mare). From the votives found there we know that Menerva was, in spite of her warlike appearance (Fig. III.17), also a peaceful goddess who educated children (see also Fig. IV.14). Her Greek pendant Athena, born from the head of the highest god, had been a Bronze Age palace goddess, who educated the children of royal families like Erichthonios in Athens. Menerva often accompanies **Hercle**. Colonna 1984; Simon 1998c, 168–181.

Nethuns

The Piacenza liver and the *liber linteus* of Zagreb show that Nethuns, whose name comes from Latin Neptunus (Neptune), was an important Etruscan god. On mirrors he resembles the Greek Poseidon, bearded and holding a trident (Fig. IV.2). Like Poseidon, Nethuns has sway over the sea. Krauskopf 1994.

Nortia

Latin name for an Etruscan goddess whose name was perhaps Nurtia. Livy 7.3.7 (Appendix B, Source no. V.1) writes about the nails in the temple of this goddess at Volsinii (probably Orvieto). Each year a new nail was added by hammering. Nortia was a goddess perhaps related to **Menerva**, for in the Capitoline Temple in Rome, between the cellas* of Minerva and Jupiter, the same nailing ritual was observed. For Etruscans and Romans, hammering a nail was also a symbol of necessity and fate (see Horace, *Carm.* 1.35.17). Thus on a superb mirror (Fig. II.19), **Athrpa** is shown hammering a nail between two couples of lovers who will soon be separated by death. Camporeale 1992b.

Pacha

Cult name for **Fufluns** in later Etruria. The god is sometimes connected with **Catha**/Kavtha, a deity related to the sun god (**Usil**). Like the Greek Bakchos, Pacha was especially the god of the Dionysiac mysteries. These rituals came to Rome via Etruria (Livy 39.9; see Appendix B, Source no. VII.1) and were forbidden by the Senate; the *senatus consultum de Bacchanalibus* (186 BCE) is preserved.

Satre

Name of a deity on the Piacenza liver. He was formerly thought to be the same as the Latin Saturnus (Saturn), but Saturnus seems to be a genuine Roman god. The cult could have migrated to Etruria like the cults of **Menrva**, **Nethuns**, or **Uni**. But the names of Satre and Saturnus may sound similar by chance, like **Mariś** and Mars. As there is no known representation of Satre in visual art, this deity remains a riddle. Latte 1960, 132; Pfiffig 1975, 312.

Selvans

Votive inscriptions and the Piacenza liver show that Selvans (from Latin Silvanus) was a popular god in Etruria, a god of pastures and forests. There is, however, only one certain representation (Fig. IV.16): a bronze statuette, found together with a statuette of **Culśanś** in Cortona. Selvans wears high boots and the hide of a bear's head as his cap. He is a youth, whereas Silvanus is normally a bearded man. Jentel 1994.

Sethlans

Etruscan god corresponding to Greek Hephaistos. The name of the Roman god Volcanus/Vulcanus (Vulcan) seems to be of Etruscan origin (cf. Vulca, Vulci; *velχ-* on the Piacenza liver). Perhaps, like Fufluns, the god had various names. Sethlans, the mythological name, appears on mirrors. To the realm of this god belonged fire, metal, and forging. Small wonder that he was important in a metal-rich land like Etruria. Krauskopf 1988c.

Śuri

According to votive inscriptions, often to father Śuri, the god was well known in Etruria. The Etruscan name of Viterbo, Surrina, comes from him, similarly Mount Soracte, where Soranus (=Śuri, Latin Dis Pater) was venerated (see Vergil, *Aen.* 11.785). Giovanni Colonna has equated Śuri convincingly with **Aplu**, who in Etruria also had connections with the Underworld. Cherici 1994; Colonna 1992.

Thanr/Thanur

The goddess was venerated in Caere and Clusium, where vessels with votive inscriptions have been found. Like Ethausva, on mirrors she has the function of a birth goddess (especially at the birth of **Menrva**) and of a *kourotrophos.** Weber-Lehmann 1994.

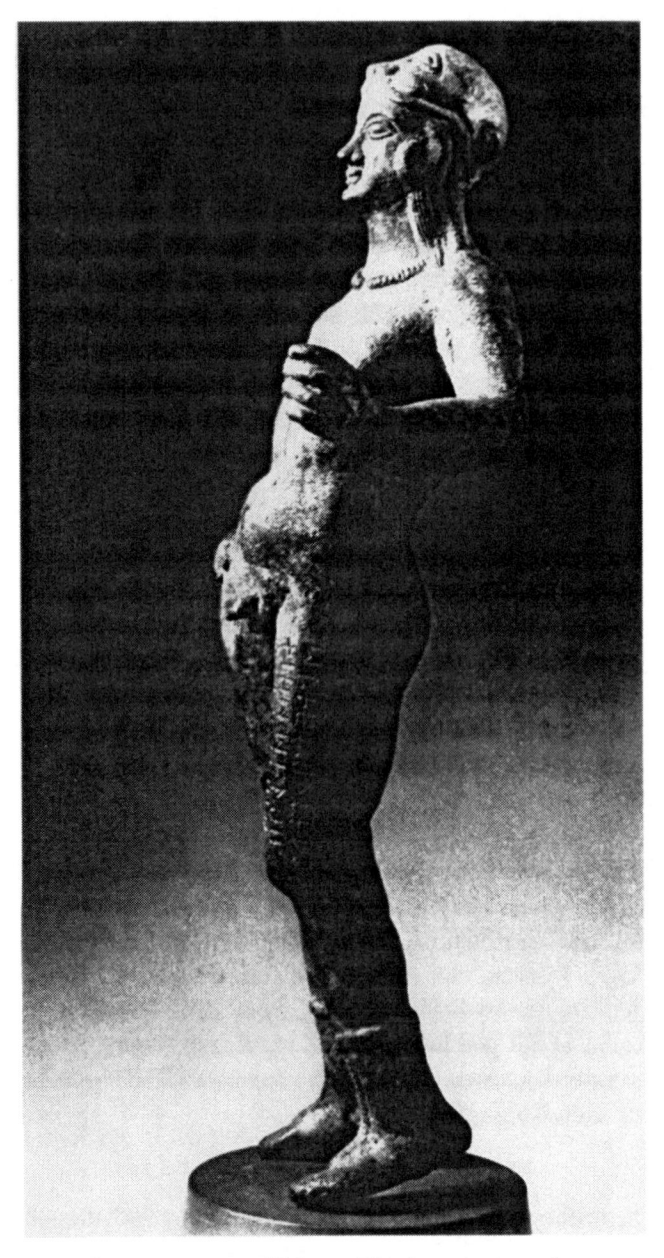

IV.16. *Bronze statuette of Selvans. Third century BCE. Cortona, Museo dell'Accademia Etrusca. (After Cristofani 1985, fig. 105.)*

Thesan

The goddess of the morning dawn (Greek Eos, Latin Aurora) was much beloved in ancient poetry. In Etruria Thesan was also a cult goddess, who received offerings together with the sun god **Usil** in the *liber linteus*. She was especially venerated at Caere and its harbor Pyrgi, where a singular series of "daybreak antefixes" was excavated (Fig. IV.3). Bloch and N. Minot 1984.

Tinas Cliniar

On the foot of the famous Oltos cup from Tarquinii is an Etruscan votive inscription for the Tinas Cliniiar, the sons of **Tinia**/Tin. The Greeks called them Dioskouroi, sons of Zeus, with the individual names Kastor and Polydeukes, while in Rome they were the Castores (Castor and Pollux). They were important gods in Etruscan mythology and cult. In the Tomba del Letto Funebre at Tarquinii, a *lectisternium** for them is painted, as Colonna has shown (Fig. V.15). There, their presence is symbolized by their pointed caps crowned with laurel. They are very commonly represented on late Etruscan mirrors. De Puma 1986; Steingräber 1985, pl. 110; Colonna 1996.

Tinia/Tin

Highest god in the Etruscan pantheon, counterpart of Zeus and Jupiter. His consort is **Uni**; his attribute is the lightning bolt (Fig. IV.1), which was used, however, also by a number of other Etruscan gods. In art he may be bearded or (typically Etruscan) a beardless youth. He is much concerned with harmony among the gods (Fig. IV.10). Camporeale 1997.

Turan

The goddess of love (= Greek Aphrodite, Roman Venus), along with **Uni** and **Menrva**, was one of the most important Etruscan goddesses. She had her festivals in summer—the Etruscan month Traneus (July) was named after her. In Archaic art and sometimes also later, she may be winged. Like **Tinia**, she likes harmony, even after her victory in the Judgment of Paris (Fig. IV.12). On mirrors she is often represented with **Atunis** (Figs. IV.6–7), whose festival was also in summer. Her son, as we know from a newly discovered mirror (Fig. IV.6), was called **Turnu** (Greek Eros); her servant is **Lasa** (also in the plural; see also **Alpan**). The peaceful Turan lives on in the Venus of the *Aeneid*: Vergil knew about Etruscan religion. Bloch and Minot 1984; Wlosok 1967.

Turms

The god whose Greek and Roman equivalents are Hermes and Mercury appears in Etruria only in mythological context. This is strange, as he was much venerated by the Greeks, mostly in the shape of a "herm" (a form that does not play a role in Etruria). Perhaps Turms had a special cult name that has not been identified up to now. The herald Turms was a mediator between gods and humans as well as between this world and the Underworld (**Aita**; **Calu**). In this function Turms may be called Turmś Aitaś (Fig. IV.9; see also Fig. IV.8). Harari 1997.

Turnu

Son of **Turan**, whom we know thanks to a newly excavated mirror (Feruglio 1998; Fig. IV.6; not in *LIMC*). Like the Greek Eros, he is represented as a winged boy. The name can now be given to other Erotes in Etruscan art. Krauskopf 1988b.

Uni

The Etruscans took the name of this most important goddess (Greek Hera, wife of Zeus) from the Latin/Faliscan Juno, who was much venerated in central Italy. The bilingual gold tablets found at Pyrgi have shown that Uni was equated there with the Phoenician goddess Astarte. This powerful astral deity was warlike; thus Uni was also often represented fighting, especially in the form of Juno Sospita (Fig. IV.10). But **Tinia**, her husband, does not like fights between Uni and **Hercle** (Figs. IV.10-11); they are reconciled on a famous mirror that shows Uni adopting Hercle by nursing him (Fig. II.8). In Greece, Astarte was more equivalent to Aphrodite; **Turan**, the Etruscan equivalent, was perhaps too peaceful to be Astarte's counterpart, whereas Uni was warlike. In Vergil the great Phoenician goddess from Carthage, Juno, is the divine enemy of Aeneas.

A typical Etruscan combination is Uni and **Aplu**. The votive inscription of Sostratos of Aegina, a dedication to Apollo, was found at the sanctuary of Uni at Gravisca; at Pyrgi the same combination between these two deities is found; and in Livy 5.21.1 the Roman general Camillus, before taking Veii, prays to Apollo Pythicus and Juno Regina. The relations between Uni and Aplu, which are not known in Greece, have perhaps astral reasons (**Usil**). Colonna and M. Michetti 1997; Simon 1984c, 167.

Usil

The sun god (Greek Helios, Latin Sol) known from representations and inscriptions. He is already represented on an Archaic mirror rising from the sea. As Krauskopf has shown he appears on the antefixes from Pyrgi (Fig. IV.3A). An important representation is on a mirror from Tuscania (Fig. IV.2) where Usil is grouped with seated **Nethuns** and accompanied by **Thesan**. Usil has a *nimbus* around his head and a bow in his raised right hand, and he is thus equated with Aplu. Later on, this equation would be normal but not in the fourth century BCE. There is no similar representation in Classical Greece, but in the Sibylline oracles, used by the Romans in questions of cult, Apollo and Helios were regularly equated. Krauskopf 1990.

Vanth

Female demon connected with death and the Underworld, who may be winged or wingless and may wear a short or long dress. Vanth sometimes holds snakes and is very stern, though not frightening like **Charu**. Generally she helps the dead, carrying a torch on their hard way to the Underworld. Weber-Lehmann 1998.

Vei

Inscriptions from the Cannicella sanctuary at Orvieto mention a goddess Vei, perhaps a name for the mother earth (**Cel**). It is possible that Vei, whom we do not know from mirrors or other monuments, is represented in the unusual marble image of a naked goddess found in that sanctuary (Fig. IV.4).

NOTES

[Editor's Note: At the end of this chapter is a glossary of Etruscan gods (pp. 57-61). The presence of a deity within the glossary is indicated in boldface type the first time it is mentioned in the text and in each glossary entry.]

1. Pfiffig 1975, 231-234; Richardson 1983, 249, 356-360; Simon 1984c, 164-165; Camporeale 1997.
2. Servius, *Ad Aen.* 1.4.2; Appendix B, Source no. VIII.7. Pliny, *NH* 2.138; see Appendix B, Source no. VIII.8.
3. Heidelberg, University, Antikenmuseum Inv. F 148. Hampe and Gropengiesser 1967, 56, pl. 22; Richardson 1983, 357, figs. 855 and 856; Camporeale 1997, no. 105.
4. Colonna 1970; Richardson 1983, 249-250, 333-364; Cristofani 1985, 227-287; Bentz 1992, 185-218. See the full review of votives by J. M. Turfa, below, Chap. VI.
5. De Grummond 1982; see also Bonfante 1986, Index 286, s.v. mirrors and *CSE*.
6. De Simone 1968; Pfiffig 1975; Radke 1979; Rix 1998.
7. See below, esp. Figs. IV.10-11.
8. Pfiffig 1975, 115-117.
9. I would like to thank warmly my Würzburg colleague Gernot Wilhelm, through whom I learned about those excavations before their publication. See Wilhelm 1998.
10. Priam, Paris, Ascanius, and other Trojans were represented in Classical Greek as well as in Roman art in Phrygian dress.
11. Wilhelm 1998 (cf. above, n. 9).
12. See N. T. de Grummond in this volume, above, Chap. III. During my stay at Florida State University in Tallahassee (January-April 1999) I learned much from Nancy de Grummond about such Etruscan problems, for which I am deeply grateful.
13. Generally, see *Santuari d'Etruria*. For convenient surveys, see Cristofani 1985b, ss. vv. Marzabotto, Gravisca, Veio; for recent excavations at the Ara della Regina, see Cataldi 1994; Bonghi Jovino 1997; for Pyrgi, see Colonna 1992, and below, Chap. VIII.

14. For Thesan, see Bloch 1986; for recently found inscriptions in Pyrgi: Colonna 1992, 92-97, and below, p. 139.

15. Vatican Museums Inv. 12645. Herbig 1965, 4, pl. 4; Fischer-Graf 1980, 2, no. 4 (north Etruscan); Simon 1984c, 162, after Gerhard, ES, 1.76; Krauskopf 1994; Jannot 1998, 168, fig. 93 (wrongly located in Villa Giulia); see also below, n. 17.

16. Richardson 1986, 222, fig. VII.13; Simon 1984c, 155, s.v. Cavtha/Cautha/Cath, must now be corrected, because it is clear that Cavtha is female rather than a male sun god: Cristofani 1992. For Cavtha, see also Colonna in this volume, below, pp. 139-140, 149; for Usil, see Krauskopf 1990; for the Piacenza liver, see the discussion, with bibliography by Bonfante in this volume, above, pp. 10-11.

17. Simon 1998a, 127, pl. 17; see also above, n. 15.

18. The first Roman temple which was erected according to Sibylline oracles (496 BCE) was the temple for Ceres: Simon 1998d, 45.

19. Krauskopf, 1991; Krauskopf 1997; Simon 1996, 73-76.

20. She was also interpreted as the goddess of night (Greek Nyx); for an alternate candidate for the deity of the night, see p. 58, s.v. Cilens. For Thesan, who is often shown running in art, see above, n. 14.

21. Turfa 1986, 76-78, and Richardson 1986, 222; Simon 1998d, 95, fig. 117.

22. Richardson 1983, 23, figs. 28 and 29; Simon 1998d, 153, figs. 192 and 193.

23. Richardson 1983, 23.

24. Orvieto, Museo Claudio Faina. Andrén 1967; Cristofani 1987, 27-39 and 41-45; Cordischi 1987; Colonna 1987; Bentz 1992, 23-24; Colonna 1997a.

25. For the gesture, see one of the Orientalizing statuettes from Satricum (above, n. 22); for the Etruscan character of the Cannicella "Venus," see Boehm 1990, 123.

26. Jannot 1998, 158, fig. 89.

27. Jannot 1998, 160. For the goddess Vei, see also Colonna 1997, 173-174.

28. For Cel, see Colonna 1976-1977; Colonna 1997, 174; Simon 1984c, 156.

29. Krauskopf 1984a, no. 12, and other Etruscan representations of this god; Pfiffig 1975, 251-255; Simon 1984c, 153-154; Simon 1998a; Jannot 1998, 154-155.

30. About Apollo's Oriental connections: Simon 1998c, 116-121.

31. "Most worshipful god, Apollo, guardian of blessed Soracte." Mount Soracte belonged to the Faliscan region; the language of the Faliscans was very near to Latin, but their culture was, as in Latin Praeneste, Etruscanized.

32. On earlier literature for Śuri, see Bentz 1992, 20. Recently, other Śuri inscriptions have turned up, even at the Ara della Regina (above, n. 13): Cataldi 1994, pl. 2; for Pyrgi, see StEtr 1989/1990, 313-314, nos. 21-23; Colonna 1992, 92-97 and esp. Colonna, below, p. 139.

33. Helck 1965.

34. Astral amulet: Cristofani and Martelli 1983, no. 92; Apolline laurel in tomb painting: Simon 1996, 63; see also below, n. 35.

35. For ivy connected with laurel in Etruscan tomb painting, see among others the Tomba del Triclinio in Tarquinii: Steingräber 1985, 360, no. 121; Brendel 1995, 270, fig. 184. The ivy is better preserved in the copies by Carlo Ruspi; see Blanck and Weber Lehmann 1987, 136-158. For Fufluns, see Cristofani 1986; Jannot 1998, 168-169.

36. That the temple in Delphi also belonged to Dionysos is well known. For the temple in Delos, see Simon 1998b, esp. 458-459.

37. Berlin Inv. Fr. 36 from Vulci. Herbig 1965, 6-7, fig. 2; Fischer-Graf 1980, 64-72, pl. 18 (according to her, from the same workshop as the mirror below, n. 45); de Grummond 1982, fig. 91; Simon 1984c, 158; Cristofani 1986, 537; Kossatz-Deissmann 1994, 723, no. 25; Brendel 1995, 362-363, fig. 281; Simon 1996, 64-66, fig. 8 (interpretation as Delphic festival Herois); LPRH 1997, 332-333 (F.-H. Massa-Pairault). The drawing in Gerhard, ES, pl. 83, remains valuable because the mirror is not well preserved.

38. Feruglio 1998, 301, fig. 2. For Turan, see Bloch and Minot 1984.

39. Feruglio 1998, 310-313; see also Paul-Zinserling 1994, 118-119; Boehr 1997.

40. Torelli 1997; Feruglio 1998.

41. St. Petersburg, Hermitage Inv. V 505. Herbig 1965, 25-27, fig. 9; Servias-Soyez 1981, 225, no. 17; de Grummond 1982, fig. 98; Brendel 1995, 364, fig. 282.

42. Pfiffig 1975, 94 (Traneus).

43. Pfiffig 1975, 239-241; Harari 1997.

44. Hostetter 1986, 20-27; Harari 1997, no. 115.

45. Vatican Museums Inv. 12687 from Vulci. Fischer-Graf 1980, 72-73, pl. 19 (same workshop as the mirror above, n. 37); de Grummond 1982, fig. 92; Harari 1997, no. 103; Zimmerman 1997, no. 6.

46. In the Nekyia tragedy Psychagogoi by Aeschylus, however, of which only fragments remain (TrGF III, pp. 370-374 Radt), Hermes played an important role.

47. Hesiod, frgs. 275-276, Merkelbach and West; Ovid, Meta. 3.316-333.

48. Perhaps the artist of the mirror was influenced by a mask of Teiresias in the Aeschylean Nekyia tragedy (above, n. 46).

49. Brendel 1995, 240, fig. 167; Harari 1997, no. 76. For the problems of the reconstruction of the temple roof, see Simon 1996, 71-73.

50. London, British Museum B57. Hampe and Simon 1964, 5, pl. 6.1; Hannestad 1974, 45, no. 11; Colonna 1997a, no. 67; Camporeale 1997, no. 81. Colonna identifies the god behind Uni as Nethuns, because of his tridentlike attribute. But the scepter or the lightning bolt of Tin may have this shape.

51. For Juno Sospita, see Richardson 1983, 360-361, figs. 864 and 865; Haeussler 1995, 24-26; Colonna 1997a, nos. 3-8 and 66-73; Simon 1998d, 96-99.

52. Cauldrons with griffin heads as votives for Hera: Simon 1998c, 41-43.

53. Menerva appears without weapons, for example on the Loeb tripods in Munich: Colonna 1984, no. 215; Brendel 1995, 162, fig. 108.

54. Perugia, from Castel S. Mariano. Hampe and Simon 1964, 11-17, pl. 21; Mavleev 1981, 661, no. 51; Höckmann (1982, 114-116, n. 593) tries to maintain the old Kyknos interpretation, but her argument that Amazons do not fight with lances is wrong; see the Amazons on the Euphronios krater* in Arezzo, compared by Hampe and Simon 1964, 12, fig. 2; Colonna (1997, no. 74) follows the interpretation of Hampe and Simon. Uni in our reconstruction drawing (Hampe and Simon 1964, 16, fig. 3) should be changed into the Sospita type (see Simon 1996, 17, fig. 1).

55. Herbig 1965, 14, pl. 18 (Mainz); Brendel 1995, 219-220, figs. 146 and 147 (Copenhagen).

56. Simon 1997, 1126, no. 169.

57. Bloomington, Indiana University Art Museum Inv. 74.23. Bonfante 1977, 149-167, pls. 21-23; Simon 1981; de Grummond 1982, 107, 155-156, figs. 50 and 51; *CSE USA* 1.4.

58. It is usual to assume that Althaia, the mother of Meleager, has nothing to do with the Judgment of Paris: Bonfante 1977, 152. I should like to thank Helmut Rix, who advised me that the name Althaia could be taken into the Etruscan language without change.

59. Berlin fr. 146, from Perugia. Herbig 1965, 20-21, pl. 7; Fischer-Graf 1980, 4, no. 30 (northern Etruscan); Simon 1986, no. 1; Brendel 1995, 366-367, fig. 284.

60. Krauskopf 1984b; Krauskopf 1998.

61. Cristofani and Martelli 1983, 285, no. 115, with literature. The two wolves at the sides of the goddess are not hunter's prey, as Cristofani thought, but alive.

62. Diana of Aricia: Simon 1986b.

63. For the importance of the wolf in Italy, see Richardson 1977, 91-101; Elliott 1995, 17-31; Simon 1996, 87-95.

64. Cortona 1571; Richardson 1983, 339, fig. 800. The whereabouts were not known at that time. Giovanni Colonna told me that in the meantime it has been learned that the statuette was found near Perugia.

65. Steingräber 1985, 293, no. 44; Simon 1996, 63, n. 33.

66. De Puma 1986.

67. Colonna 1996, 177-179; Steingräber 1985, 327-328, no. 82.

68. De Grummond 1991.

69. Pfiffig 1975, 309-311; Simon 1984a; Bentz 1992, 192-194.

70. Florence, Archaeological Museum, from Populonia. Simon 1984a, no. 17; Simon 1984c, 156.

71. Richardson 1983, 354-355; Simon 1984a, 499-500, nos. 7-12; Brendel 1995, 312-314, figs. 230-233.

72. Richardson 1983, 346-354; Colonna 1984, 1058-1059, nos. 109-120.

73. Vatican Museums, Inv. 13886. Roncalli 1973; Simon 1984a, 508-509, no. 1; Haynes 1985, no. 146; Cristofani 1985a, 292, no. 116; Bonfante 1986, 93, fig. IV-1; Brendel 1995, 317, fig. 237.

74. A second mirror with this theme in London has three babies: de Grummond 1982, fig. 102. On the Mariś babies, see also Simon 1984b, nos. 19 and 20; Colonna 1984, nos. 165 and 166; Simon 1996, 36-40, figs. 4 and 5.

75. Hampe and Simon 1964, 18-28; Krauskopf 1974; Freytag gen. Loeringhoff 1986; Krauskopf 1994, 735-736, nos. 7-11; gems, 741, no. 47; Pyrgi *antepagmentum,* and 741-742, nos. 46-53; Camporeale 1997, 407, no. 55.

76. In de Grummond 1982, 106-107.

77. The Hermitage mirror: above, n. 41; other Alpan representations: Lambrechts 1981, nos. 1-5; for the name, see also Feruglio 1998, 308.

78. Simon 1984a, no. 15.

79. Krauskopf 1992, 354-356. For the Tuscania sarcophagus, see no. 4. The source for Manto as mother of the founder of Mantua is Vergil, *Aeneid* 10.198-201, with the commentary of Servius.

80. Groups of Venus and Mars: Schmidt 1997, 225; interpretation: Simon 1984d, 556-558. Mars and Venus appear in such groups as parents of Concordia (Harmonia). They appear also as a married couple on a classicizing votive relief in Venice: Boehm 1999, pl. 6.

81. Krauskopf 1986; Simon 1996, 41-53.

82. Cortona, Museo Accademia Etrusca Inv. 1278. Cristofani 1984, 157; Cristofani 1985, 285-286, pl. 104; Krauskopf 1986a, no. 1; Bentz 1992, 188; Simon 1996, 46, pl. 13.1. A statuette of Selvans found with it (Fig. IV.16): Small 1994, 718, no. 1.

83. Rome, Villa Giulia. Krauskopf 1986, nos. 8a and b.

84. Hats of Etruscan priests with *apex*: Cristofani 1984, 151 (A. Maggiani).

85. Krauskopf 1986a, nos. 2-4.

86. For Etruscan priests, see above, n. 12, and this volume, pp. 33-38.

87. Vatican Museums Inv. 12240. Herbig 1965, 9, pl. 5; Fischer-Graf 1980, 42-44, pl. 10.3; Bonfante 1986, 248, fig. VIII.23.

BIBLIOGRAPHY

Andrén, A. 1967. "Il santuario della necropoli di Cannicella ad Orvieto," *StEtr* 35, 41-85.

Bentz, M. 1992. *Etruskische Votivbronzen des Hellenismus.* Biblioteca di Studi Etruschi 25. Florence.

Blanck, H., and C. Weber Lehmann. 1987. *Malerei der Etrusker in Zeichnungen des 19. Jahrhunderts.* Mainz.

Bloch, R., and N. Minot. 1984. "Turan." *LIMC* II, 169-176.

———. 1986. "Eos/Thesan." *LIMC* III, 789-797.

Boehm, S. 1990. *Die "Nackte Göttin": Zur Ikonographie und Deutung unbekleideter weiblicher Figuren in der frühgriechischen Kunst.* Mainz.

———. 1999. "Römische eklektische Weihreliefs nach griechischem Vorbild." *AntKunst* 42, 26-31.

Boehr, E. 1997. "A Rare Bird on Greek Vases: The Wryneck." In *Athenian Potters and Painters,* ed. J. H. Oakley, W. D. E. Coulson, and O. Palagia. Oxbow Monograph 67. Oxford. 109-123.

Bonfante, L. 1977. "The Judgment of Paris, the Toilette of Malavisch and a Mirror in the Indiana University Art Museum," *StEtr* 45, 149-167.

———, ed. 1986. *Etruscan Life and Afterlife.* Detroit.

Bonghi Jovino, M. 1997. "La phase archaïque de l'Ara della Regina à la lumière des recherches récentes." In *LPRH,* 69-95.

Brendel, O. J. 1995. *Etruscan Art,* 2nd ed., with bibliography by F. R. Serra Ridgway. New Haven.

Camporeale, G. 1986. "Cilens." *LIMC* III, 294-295.

———. 1992a. "Leinth." *LIMC* VI, 217-225.

———. 1992b. "Nortia." *LIMC* VI, 934-935.

———. 1997. "Tinia." *LIMC* 8, 400-421.

Cataldi, M. 1994. "Nuova testimonianza di culto sulla civita di Tarquinia." In *Tyrrhenoi philotechnoi: Atti della giornata di studio, Viterbo, 1990,* ed. M. Martelli. Rome. 61-69.

Cherici, A. 1994. "Suri." *LIMC* VII, 823-824.

Colonna, G. 1970. *Bronzi votivi umbro-sabellici a figura umana.* Vol. I. Florence.

———. 1976-1977. "La dea etrusca Cel e i santuari del Trasimeno." *Rivista storica dell'antichità* 6-7, 45-62.

———. 1984. "Menerva." *LIMC* II, 1050-1074.

———. 1987. "I culti del santuario della Cannicella." *AnnFaina* 3, 11-26.

———. 1992. "Altari e sacelli: L'area sud di Pyrgi dopo otto anni di ricerche." *RendPontAcc* 64, 63-115.

———. 1996. "Il dokanon, il culto dei Dioscuri e gli aspetti ellenizzanti della religione dei morti nell' Etruria tardo-arcaica." In *Scritti di antichità in memoria di Sandro Stucchi II (=StMisc 29)*. 165-184.

———. 1997. "Divinités peu connues du panthéon étrusque." In *LPRH*, 167-184.

Colonna, G., and M. Michetti. 1997. "Uni." *LIMC* VIII, 159-171.

Cordischi, D. 1987. "Identificazione della provenienza di marmi mediante la tecnica di risonanza di spin elettronico: Analisi dei frammenti della 'Venere' di Cannicella." *AnnFaina* 3, 41-45.

Cristofani, M., ed. 1984. *Gli Etruschi: Una nuova immagine*. Florence.

———. 1985. *I bronzi degli Etruschi*. Novara.

———. 1986. "Fufluns/Dionysos." *LIMC* III, 531-540.

———. 1987. "La 'Venere' della Cannicella." *AnnFaina* 3, 27-39.

———. 1992a. "Celeritas Solis Filia." In *Kotinos: Festschrift E. Simon*, ed. H. Froning, T. Hölscher, and H. Mielsch. Mainz, 347-349.

Cristofani, M. 1992b. "Mariś I." *LIMC* VI, 359-360.

Cristofani, M., and M. Martelli. 1983. *L'oro degli Etruschi*. Novara.

de Grummond, N. T., ed. 1982. *A Guide to Etruscan Mirrors*. Tallahassee, FL.

———. 1991. "Etruscan Twins and Mirror Images: The Dioskouroi at the Door," *Yale University Art Gallery Bulletin*, 10-31.

———. 2004. "For the Mother and for the Daughter: Some Thoughts on Dedications from Etruria and Praeneste," *ΧΑΡΙΣ, Studies in Honor of Sara A. Immerwahr*, ed. A. P. Chapin. Princeton. 351-370.

———. Forthcoming. "Mariś, the Etruscan Genius." In *Across Frontiers: Studies in Honour of David Ridgway and Francesca R. Serra Ridgway*, ed. I. Lemos et al. London, Accordia Research Institute.

De Puma, R. 1986. "Tinas Cliniar." *LIMC* III, 597-608.

De Simone. 1968. *Die griechischen Entlehnungen im Etruskischen*. Tübingen.

Elliott, J. 1995. "The Etruscan Wolfman in Myth and Ritual." *Etruscan Studies* 2, 17-31.

Emiliozzi, A., ed. 1997. *Carri da guerra e principi etruschi*. Catalogue of exhibition. Rome.

Feruglio, A. E. 1998. "Uno specchio della necropoli di Castel Viscardo, presso Orvieto, con Apollo, Turan e Atunis." In *Etrusca et Italica: Scritti in ricordo di Massimo Pallottino*. Pisa. 299-314.

Fischer-Graf, U. 1980. *Spiegelwerkstätten in Vulci*. Archaeologische Forschungen 8. Berlin.

Freytag gen. Loeringhoff, B. von. 1986. *Das Giebelrelief von Telamon und seine Stellung innerhalb der Ikonographie der "Sieben gegen Theben."* RM-EH 27. Mainz.

Haeussler, R. 1995. *Hera und Juno: Wandlungen und Beharrung einer Göttin*. Stuttgart.

Hampe R., and H. Gropengiesser 1967. *Werke der Kunst in Heidelberg*. Vol. 1. Berlin.

Hampe R., and E. Simon 1964. *Griechische Sagen in der frühen etruskischen Kunst*. Mainz.

Hannestad, L. 1974. *The Paris Painter*. Copenhagen.

Harari, M. 1997. "Turms." *LIMC* VIII, 98-111.

Haynes, S. 1985. *Etruscan Bronzes*. London.

———. 2000. *Etruscan Civilization: A Cultural History*. Los Angeles.

Helck, W. 1965. "Re." In *Götter und Mythen im Vorderen Orient*. W. Haussig, ed. Vol. 1. Stuttgart. 390.

Herbig, R. 1965. *Götter und Dämonen der Etrusker*, 2nd ed., ed. E. Simon. Mainz.

Höckmann, U. 1982. *Die Bronzen aus dem Fürstengrab von Castel San Mariano*. Munich.

Hostetter, E. 1986. *Bronzes from Spina* I. Mainz.

Jannot, J.-R. 1998. *Devins, dieux et démons: Regards sur la religion de l' Étrurie antique*. Paris.

Jentel, M.-O. 1994. "Selvans." *LIMC* VII, 718.

Kossatz-Deismann, A. 1994. "Semele." *LIMC* VII, 718-726.

Krauskopf, I. 1974. *Der thebanische Sagenkreis und andere Sagen in der etruskischen Kunst*. Mainz.

———. 1984a. "Apollon/Aplu." *LIMC* II, 335-363.

———. 1984b. "Artemis/Artumes." *LIMC* II, 774-792.

———. 1986a. "Culśanś." *LIMC* III, 306-308.

———. 1986b. "Culśu." *LIMC* III, 308-309.

———. 1988a. "Aita/Calu." *LIMC* IV, 394-399.

———. 1988b. "Eros (in Etruria)." *LIMC* IV, 1-12.

———. 1988c. "Sethlans." *LIMC* IV, 654-659.

———. 1990. "Helios/Usil." *LIMC* V Addenda, 1038-1047.

———. 1991. "Ex oriente Sol. Zu den orientalischen Wurzeln der etruskischen Sonnenikonographie." In *Miscellanea etrusca e italica in onore di M. Pallottino*. Rome. 1261-1283.

———. 1992a. "Letham." *LIMC* VI, 256.

———. 1992b. "Manto." *LIMC* VI, 354-356.

———. 1994a. "Nethuns." *LIMC* VII, 479-483.

———. 1994b. "Septem." *LIMC* VII, 730-748.

———. 1997. "Influences grecques et orientales sur les représentations de dieux étrusques." In *LPRH*, 25-36.

———. 1998. "Artemis." *AnnFaina* 5, 171-206.

Lambrechts, R. 1981. "Alpan." *LIMC* I, 573-576.

———. 1992a. "Lasa." *LIMC* VI, 217-225.

———. 1992b. "Mean." *LIMC* VI, 383-385.

Latte, K. 1960. *Römische Religionsgeschichte*. Munich.

LPRH = F. Gaultier and D. Briquel, eds., *Les Étrusques, les plus religieux des hommes: État de la recherche sur la religion étrusque*. Actes du colloque international Grand Palais. 17-18-19 novembre 1992. XII[er] Rencontres de l'École du Louvre. Paris.

Mavleev, E. "Amazones Etruscae." *LIMC* I, 654-662.

Mavleev, E., and I. Krauskopf. 1986. "Charu(n)." *LIMC* III, 225-236.

Nagy, H. 1988. *Votive Terracottas from La Vignaccia*. Rome.

Paul-Zinserling, V. 1994. *Der Jena-Maler und sein Umkreis*. Mainz.

Pfiffig, A. J. 1975. *Religio etrusca*. Graz.

Radke, G. 1979. *Die Götter Altitaliens*. 2nd ed. Münster.

Richardson, E. H. 1977. "The Wolf in the West." *Journal of the Walters Art Gallery* 36, 91-101.

———. 1983. *Etruscan Votive Bronzes: Geometric, Orientalizing, Archaic*. Mainz.

———. 1986. "An Archaeological Introduction to the Etruscan Language." In Bonfante 1986, 215-231.

Rix, H. 1998. "Teonimi etruschi e teonimi italici." *AnnFaina* 5, 207-229.

Roncalli, F. 1973. *Il Marte di Todi. MemPontAcc* 11.
Santuari d'Etruria = G. Colonna, ed., *Santuari d'Etruria*. Catalogue of exhibition in Arezzo. Milan. 1985.
Schmidt, E. 1997. "Venus." *LIMC* VIII, 192-230.
Schwarz, S. 1990. "Hercle/Herakles." *LIMC* V, 196-253.
Servais-Soyez, B. 1981. "Adonis." *LIMC* I, 222-229.
Simon, E. 1981. "Althaia." *LIMC* I, 579.
———. 1984a. "Ares/Laran." *LIMC* II, 498-505.
———. 1984b. "Artemis/Diana." *LIMC* II, 792-849.
———. 1984c. "Le divinità di culto." In Cristofani 1984, 152-167.
———. 1984d. "Ares/Mars." *LIMC* II, 505-559.
———. 1986. "Athrpa." *LIMC* III, 1-2.
———. 1990. "Ianus." *LIMC* V, 618-623.
———. 1996. *Schriften zur etruskischen und italischen Kunst und Religion*. Stuttgart.
———. 1997. "Silenoi." *LIMC* VIII, 1108-1133.
———. 1998a. "Apollo in Etruria." *AnnFaina* 5, 119-141.
———. 1998b. "Apollon und Dionysos." *In Memoria di Enrico Paribeni*, ed. G. Capecchi. 2 vols. Rome. 451-460.
———. 1998c. *Die Götter der Griechen*. 4th ed. Munich.
———. 1998d. *Die Götter der Römer*. 2nd ed. Munich.
Small, J. P. 1994. "Selvans." *LIMC* VII, 718.
Sowder, C. 1982. "Etruscan Mythological Figures." In de Grummond 1982, 100-128.
Steingräber, S. 1985. *Etruskische Wandmalerei*. Stuttgart.
Torelli, M. 1997. "Les Adoneis de Gravisca, archéologie d'une fête." In *LPRH*, 233-291.
Turfa, J. M. 1986. "International Contacts: Commerce, Trade and Foreign Affairs." In Bonfante 1986, 66-91.
Weber-Lehmann, C. 1994. "Thanr." *LIMC* VII, 908.
———. 1998. "Vanth." *LIMC* VIII, 173-183.
Wilhelm, G. 1998. "Zwei mittelhethitische Briefe aus dem Gebäude C in Kuśaklı." *Mitteilungen der Deutschen Orientgesellschaft* 130, 175-187.
Wlosok, A. 1967. *Die Göttin Venus in Vergils Aeneis*. Heidelberg.
Zimmerman, K. 1997. "Teiresias." *LIMC* VIII, 1189-1190.

CHAPTER V

THE GRAVE AND BEYOND IN ETRUSCAN RELIGION

Ingrid Krauskopf

About twenty years ago, Larissa Bonfante remarked that "Etruscan concepts of the Afterworld are not clear."[1] This statement still holds true today, if perhaps to a lesser degree, after many years of further intensive research.[2] One reason for this persisting lack of knowledge is obvious: we know that books about death, the grave, and the Afterlife existed in Etruria; they were known in Roman tradition as *Libri Acheruntici*. But we know almost nothing about their contents, except for one aspect: Servius (quoting Cornelius Labeo) and Arnobius (Appendix B, Source nos. IX.1 and IX.2) reveal that the Etruscans believed that certain animal sacrifices existed that could transform human souls into gods. These gods were known as *dii animales*, because they were transmuted souls and were assumed to be equivalent to the Penates, the elusive ancestral gods of the Roman household.[3]

Obviously, these texts include a good portion of Roman interpretation and cannot be taken at face value for Etruscan ideas of the sixth or fifth centuries BCE. We shall see, however, that these passages are by no means merely random fragments preserved by chance; on the contrary, they hand down to us a central element of Etruscan beliefs about life after death.

Another reason for our lack of knowledge lies in the basic human fact that everything having to do with death, burial, and the grave in general concerns emotional acts and customs. We cannot rationally analyze these acts and customs down to the most minute detail and thus create a logically coherent conception of the Afterlife and of the way to get there. A modern example could make the meaning clearer: almost no one would be able to explain the act of planting flowers on the graves of one's grandparents. Do we really believe that the dead can see the flowers? And why do we plant flowers and not, for instance, an apple tree? Most people would be extremely surprised when asked these questions and would not show the least interest even in looking for an explanation. The reasons they might give, in any case, would be many, in spite of the uniformity of this custom in some countries.

The nineteenth and twentieth centuries are, of course, not comparable to the time of the Etruscans. Traditional beliefs have now become a private matter and also somewhat superficial. Today, graves are memorials devoted to remembrance from the viewpoint of the living. For many people, this remembrance obviously has to be bound to a concrete place. Ritual needs of the deceased that have to be satisfied by the living to insure the dead soul's well-being in the hereafter are of no importance in our times. Nonetheless, the other side of the coin—the emotional needs of the mourners—would have been just as strong in antiquity as today.[4] Particularly in this respect, individual embellishments are possible, which—even in the case of strictly canonized rites—would be inexplicable without knowledge of the specific circumstances.

Thus we will never be able to fit every single grave gift or every picture painted on a tomb wall into the framework of a logically consistent and uniform conception of the Underworld and of the transition into that realm. It is not possible to avoid a certain degree of uncertainty in the interpretation of all the material excavations have provided. The simultaneous usage of cremation and inhumation shows that there was obviously leeway for individual preferences in Etruscan burial practices.[5] At different times and in different places, one or the other method of burial predominates; there are, however, exceptions observable everywhere.

Jean-Réné Jannot has shown that the themes of reliefs on the numerous Archaic urns, as well as on the relatively rare sarcophagi from Clusium (Chiusi) are basically identical and show the same burial rituals and the same concepts of life after death.[6] Much the same could apply for all of the Etruscan cemeteries. In no case can the different methods of burial be interpreted as evidence for divergent beliefs about the hereafter. Even if a synthesis of all those beliefs concerning death, burial, grave, and the netherworld was laid down in the *Libri Acheruntici* (by a time unknown to us, but probably not too early) as a part of the *Etrusca disciplina*,*[7] we are forced to interpret the archaeological sources without the help of texts, since they are not preserved to us. We may assume that the depictions used to decorate urns, sarcophagi, or the walls of the tomb chambers transform at least a part of the ideas held by the artists and their employers into a generally intelligible form. This is actually true, easily understandable particularly in the case of several representations dating to the later epochs, that is to say, to the Late Classical (fourth century BCE) and Hellenistic (third-first centuries BCE) periods, with which we should like to begin. After considering these relatively clear examples, we shall proceed to examine the more problematic earlier Etruscan material.

THE LATE CLASSICAL AND HELLENISTIC PERIODS

The Way

On the sarcophagus of Hasti Afunei,[8] originating from Chiusi, we see a half-open gate (Fig. v.1). A demoness is shown stepping out of the gateway. Her inscribed name, Culśu,[9] brings her into connection with it: she obviously opens, locks, and guards this gate, which possibly leads to the Realm of the Dead. Beside the gate, a second demoness, Vanth,[10] is waiting. At the opposite end of the relief, a third demoness, whose name is no longer legible, is coercing the deceased in the direction of the gate. Along the way stand a number of people, probably relatives of the deceased, but it remains uncertain whether they belong to the realm of the living or to that of the dead. Both of the persons immediately to the left of Hasti Afunei, and to whom she is apparently saying good-bye, are most probably living. We see, therefore: (1) There is a Realm of the Dead surrounded by walls and a gatekeeper.[11] (2) A journey to the Afterlife, accompanied by demons, begins at the moment of death. Gates and thresholds are important as passages or places of transition, and they must be guarded. This principle applies not only to the gate to the Realm of the Dead but to the door of the tomb as well, which also had to be guarded by demons, depicted, for instance, near the doors of the Tomb of the Aninas[12] (Fig. v.2) and the Tomb of the Caronti[13] (Figs. v.3 and v.4) at Tarquinii. (3) There are male and female demons who apparently have different functions, which we can only occasionally discover. By means of epithets, for example, the demon Charun can be divided into various beings, each of which probably has particular functions.[14] (4) The journey into the hereafter begins with the rites celebrated at burial among the living. This can be seen most clearly on the Hellenistic urns and sarcophagi that depict a funeral procession similar to the Roman *pompa funebris**; it depicts an event in the world of the living but already accompanied by demons.[15] The procession continues to the frontier where the living have to stay behind and at the end of which the gate to the Realm of the Dead comes into sight. On a sarcophagus from Tarquinii[16] and the fresco in Tomb 5636,[17] also from Tarquinii, two persons are waiting for the deceased outside that gate. More clearly than on Hasti Afunei's sarcophagus, we have the impression that they have come through the gate to welcome the new arrival.

Another conception of the journey to the Underworld diverges widely from the belief that it could be reached by land, inasmuch as it presupposes a sea voyage. Many funerary monuments decorated with sea monsters, and on which the deceased is sometimes portrayed as a rider, make reference to this idea.[18] The same is true of the stylized waves in some tombs, which can look back on a long tradition, beginning with the Tomb of the Lionesses.[19] Sometimes, most clearly on a sarcophagus in Chiusi[20] (Fig. v.5), it seems that the journey to the Afterlife has to be taken in a series of stages. There we see, on the right, the moment of death;[21] then, the deceased on horseback; and on the left, a sea monster waits to carry him further. Herbig rejects this simple explanation and describes the sarcophagus as an "atelier-pattern book" (*Werkstattmuster*) or as the "quite artless work of a bungler." Even a bungler, however, would have to make the figures he chiseled out of the stone at least minimally significant for or appropriate to the situation or assign them names. The assumption of a collection of "atelier-patterns" would merely question the necessity of *combining* a sea route and a land route. Originally, these may well have been two different concepts; it seems, however, not implausible, that in Etruria, where both versions were known, attempts would be undertaken to combine them. Exactly that, or so it seems

v.1. Sarcophagus of Hasti Afunei, with Culśu. From Chiusi. Second century BCE. Palermo. (Photo: Archäologisches Institut der Universität Heidelberg.)

to me, was undertaken on this humble sarcophagus, if in a somewhat naive manner of execution. The same concept may be seen on grave *stelai** from Felsina/Bologna dating about 400 BCE, where waves or sea monsters are combined with a journey by coach.[22]

What follows out of all this, in any case, is that for the Etruscans, the journey into the Underworld, and not only the destination, was of great importance. A detailed portrayal of many different persons on their way into the Underworld, which may have been based on literary sources, has survived in the Tomb of the Cardinal.[23] Unfortunately, it is in a poor state of preservation, and so the details of interpretation remain quite disputable. It apparently treats the different "routes" and the various types of accompaniment by different demons. It also shows the "prologue" or prelimi-

nary stage: the death of the various individuals, including the mother, the child, and men killed in a surprise or in combat—an ancient version of the medieval "danse macabre." For our purposes, it is important to note how very detailed and how very differently ideas about the passage into the hereafter could be imagined.

It is, however, inconceivable that the last journey was believed to be as harmless and as unproblematic as it is shown in many representations. What is depicted there is doubtless the ideal case. The quite frightening appearance of some demons can only partially be explained by the universal human fear of death, and—in spite of all promises of reunion—the pain of the surviving. Figures like Tuchulcha, with his birdlike beak (Fig. v.6), show that there were threats and dangers along the way,[24] which possibly not everyone mastered. Sup-

v.2. Tomb of the Aninas, with Charu and Vanth. Third century BCE. Tarquinii. (Photo: Schwanke. DAI Rome 82.565.)

porting rites might be helpful. Servius and Cornelius Labeo mentioned sacrifices that transform the dead into *dii animales*.[25] If we combine this information with the pictorial representations shown and discussed to this point, we could venture to say that certain sacrifices were necessary to insure that the dead reached their goal: the symposium with their ancestors and the gods of the Underworld, Aita and Phersipnei (Figs. v.7-8). A sacrifice of this type is probably shown in the Tomb of Orcus II and in a quite similar way on a Hellenistic urn from Volaterrae, now in the British Museum.[26]

The Destination

Which fate awaited the newly deceased behind the walls of the Underworld? Here, too, the pictorial representations come to our assistance: In the Tomb of Orcus I (Fig. v.9), we see a sort of banquet of the members of the *gens** in the presence of demons.[27] The same theme, integrated in a Greek Nekyia scene, evidently was represented in the Tomb of Orcus II, where only the table displaying the vessels, the *kylikeion*,* is preserved, with young demons as cup bearers[28] (Fig. v.10). Life after death, therefore, can be a banquet, as we

v.3. Tomb of the Caronti. Third century BCE. Tarquinii. (Photo: Schwanke. DAI Rome 81.4359.)

also see it in the Tomb of the Shields at Tarquinii[29] and even more clearly in the Golini Tomb I of Orvieto, where Eita and Phersipnai[30] take part. Here, as in the Golini Tomb II and the Tomb of the Hescanas,[31] newly deceased are just starting on their way into the Realm of the Dead; relatives who arrived earlier are waiting for them at the banquet. They do not go to meet them, as in some of the depictions we have seen earlier, but, in some way, the dead are taken into the society of their ancestors who died before them and now participate in an eternal banquet.

The numerous reclining figures on the lids of sarcophagi and urns from all around Etruria evidently allude to this symposium in the hereafter. Those who are depicted as not reaching the goal of the banquet because of their crimes or misdeeds are Greek heroes, for example, Theseus and Sisyphos.[32] The notion that misdemeanors would be punished in the Underworld is, as far as we know, among the Etruscan paintings reflected only in scenes of Greek origin, and the concept itself might be Greek.[33] We have no evidence at all that judgment and punishment in the hereafter were a native element of Etruscan religion.[34]

v.4. Tomb of the Caronti. Third century BCE. Tarquinii. (Photo: Schwanke. DAI Rome 81.4358.)

Messages Intended for the Living

The depiction of a *gens*, ancestors and newly deceased, in the Realm of the Dead serves as a kind of self-portrait of a clan, a message addressed to the living but discernible only during the few hours they spent in the tomb. More or less far-reaching political statements could also be combined with this self-portrayal (they were obviously disguised in the form of myths), most strikingly in the François Tomb at Vulci[35] (Fig. v.11). But messages of this type, addressed to the living and intended to influence the life on earth, are of less interest

v.5. Sarcophagus from Chiusi, with Journey to Underworld. Second century BCE. Chiusi, Museo Etrusco. (Alinari 37521.)

v.6. Tomb of Orcus II, with Tuchulcha. Fourth century BCE. Tarquinii. (After MonInst 8, 1870, pl. 15.)

v.7. Tomb of Orcus II, Aita and Phersipni. Fourth century BCE. Tarquinii. (Hirmer 754.1088.)

v.8. Tomb of Orcus II, Aita. Fourth century BCE. Tarquinii. (Photo: Schwanke. DAI Rome 82.635.)

for our topic, and for that reason, I would prefer to refrain from discussing the François Tomb in detail here.

Tomb or Underworld?

One phenomenon may, at first sight, seem to be incompatible with the relatively simple and presumably generally accepted view of Etruscan beliefs about the Underworld: some graves—in the late period, which we have treated up to this point—above all, the Tomb of Reliefs at Caere (Cerveteri),[36] are so lavishly furnished that the deceased would have everything he (or she) needed to continue life as if on earth. In the case of the Tomb of the Reliefs (Fig. v.12), this meant a fully equipped household. Similar evidence for a continuation of life in the tomb is plentiful in earlier times,[37] down to the house urns of the ninth and eighth centuries BCE.[38]

Ambros Pfiffig[39] tried to explain these contradictions—on the one hand, life as usual in the tomb; on the other, a Realm of the Dead, a long journey away—by postulating a dualism of the soul, that is to say, by dividing whatever part is supposed to survive the body's death in two. Just as living people are made up of body and soul, he argued, the soul itself is now supposed to consist of two elements: the "corpse-soul," bound more closely to the body in the grave or tomb, and the "I-" or "self-soul," more freely mobile, which could go into the Afterlife and could be heroized or deified. These souls would not continue to exist completely independently of one another but would remain bound to one another by a sort of "sharing."

Pfiffig's explanation is extremely complicated, hardly a basis for understanding a popular funeral rite, and conceivable only as a modern philosophical interpretation of a no

v.9. Tomb of Orcus I, Banqueting Scene. Fourth century BCE. Tarquinii. (Photo: Schwanke. DAI Rome 82.640.)

v.10. Tomb of Orcus II, Kylikeion. Fourth century BCE. Tarquinii. (Photo: Schwanke. DAI Rome 82.628.)

v.11. Painting in François Tomb, sacrifice of prisoners. From Vulci. Fourth century BCE. Rome, Villa Albani. (Istituto Centrale per il Catalogo e la Documentazione, NY E 8186.)

longer fully comprehensible custom or of an ancient, complex, elaborate system, as we find in the Egyptian religion. The belief that sacrifices offered at the grave comfort a dead soul in the grave or at least in a place where he can perceive them is widespread in early times. The idea of a faraway Realm of the Dead may well have superceded that of an Afterlife in the tomb. In most cases, people accept new ideas without necessarily wanting to abandon old ones. Of course, we do need to look for models that help us to explain such a striking juxtaposition of beliefs as we find in Etruria. It is unlikely, however, that we would come nearer the truth by setting up hypotheses that are too complicated to ever have found a place in ancient popular religion.[40]

THE ARCHAIC AND CLASSICAL PERIODS

Tomb, Underworld, and the Vestibulum Orci

In the search for such a model, it might be useful to go back a step and take a look at graves of the sixth and fifth centuries BCE. As late as the 1980s, scholars generally assumed that something must have happened between this phase and the subsequent Late Classical and Hellenistic periods, which resulted in a radical change of older beliefs. Before the Archaic and Classical periods there were cheerful symposia and dancing in the realm of the living or of the dead; after, there were sinister, melancholic gatherings in the Underworld, in the company of frightful, threatening demons.[41] Gradually, the conviction gained ground that the postulated change was not really so fundamental, and in fact perhaps did not take place at all.[42]

The discovery of the Tomb of the Blue Demons finally closed the supposed gap perfectly[43] (Fig. v.13). We learned

v.12. Tomb of the Reliefs, with Kerberos. Ca. 300 BCE. Caere. (Photo: Schwanke. DAI Rome 83.436.)

that death demons existed already at the end of the fifth century. Their representations had been developed even earlier on the basis of Greek models: Charon, the Greek ferryman of the dead;[44] Thanatos ("Death") on Attic white-ground *lekythoi**;[45] Eurynomos, a demon known from the fresco of Polygnotos at Delphi;[46] and the Erinyes (Furies).[47] These figures were noted particularly in Etruscan settlements of the Po Valley and in North Etruria[48] (cf. Fig. v.16) and immediately adapted to Etruscan needs.[49] Etruscan predecessors for these

v.13: a, b, and c. Tomb of the Blue Demons. Ca. 400 BCE. Tarquinii. (After Pittura etrusca, figs. 108, 109, 110.)

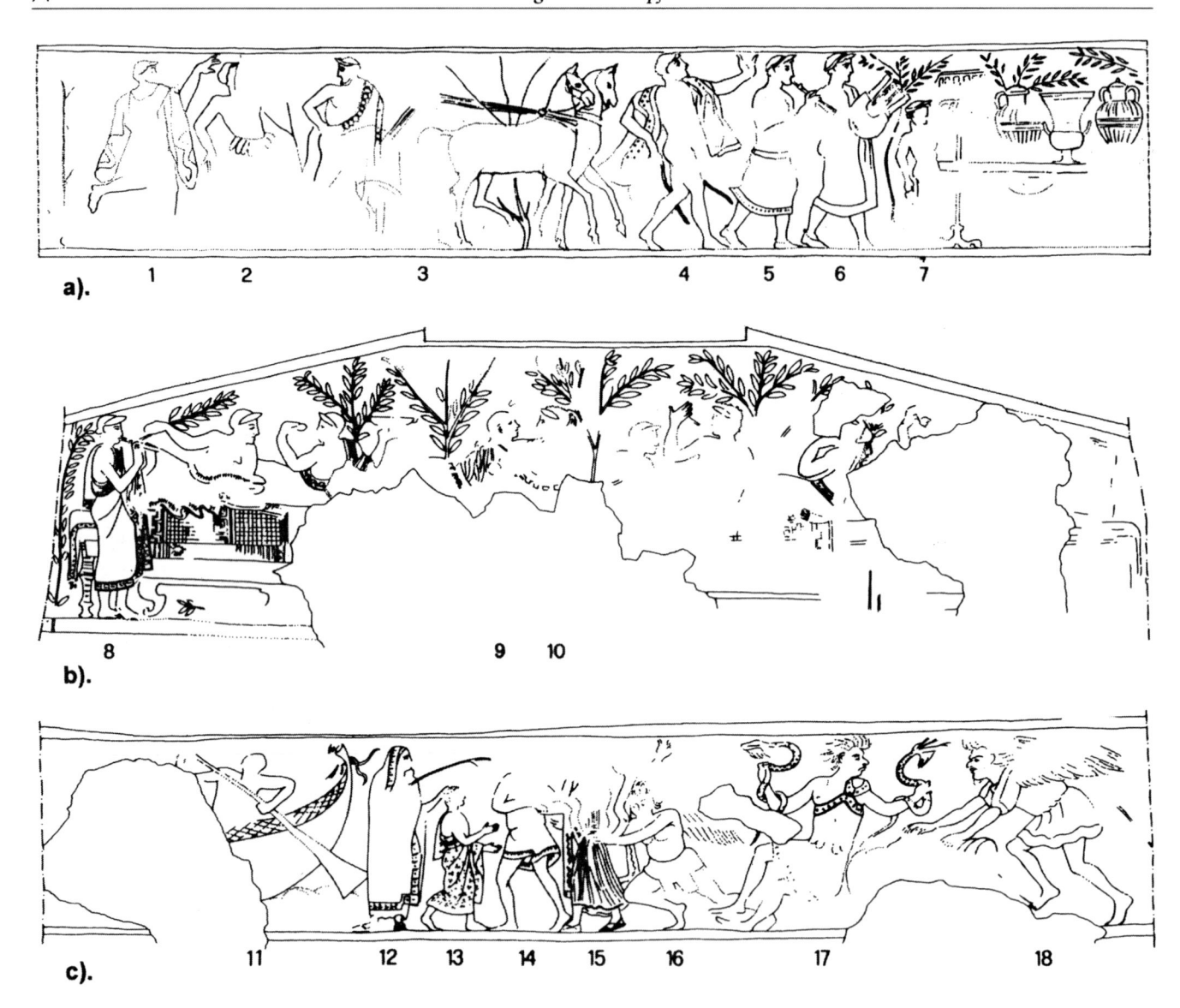

"hellenized" demons can be found in the sixth century, however, in creatures that combine a generally human shape with the heads of wolves or predatory birds[50] (Fig. v.14).

Further, in the Tomb of the Blue Demons, the journey to the Underworld and the welcome among the ancestors are depicted in a similar way (Fig. v.12c), as we had already seen them on Hellenistic sarcophagi and frescoes.[51] Francesco Roncalli[52] has convincingly shown that the scene takes place in a sort of antechamber to the Underworld, which is bounded on the one side by the dead souls' ferryman, Charun (? the figure is not well preserved), and on the other by a rock or cliff, which marks the threshold to the earthly world of the living, analogous to some Greek representations of the Nekyia. Demons have driven the dead into this antechamber and lead her to the ship that will take her to the final destination. Obviously, it is also possible to gain entrance to this anteroom from the other side, as the two figures on the left, who come to meet the newly deceased, show. If we replace the ship with the walls and gate of the Underworld, we have exactly the same scene as on the sarcophagus discussed above. The ship in the Tomb of the Blue Demons is seaworthy and not a mere skiff, like that of the Greek Charon. On Hellenistic sarcophagi and in tombs we have already seen allusions, in the sea monsters and stylized waves, to a sea that had to be crossed on the way to the Realm of the Dead. These can be traced back to the sixth century, with the waves to the

v.14. Black-figured vessel with Wolf god. Sixth century BCE. Rome, Museo Etrusco di Villa Giulia. (Photo: Courtesy of the Soprintendenza per i Beni Archeologici dell' Etruria Meridionale.)

Tomb of the Lionesses,[53] the riders on sea monsters to the Tomb of the Bulls[54] and the *nenfro** statues from Vulci.[55]

The man in the *biga** on the left wall of the Tomb of the Blue Demons, moving toward the *kylikeion* (Fig. v.12a) is an early forerunner of the processions known from Hellenistic urns and sarcophagi; comparable scenes are found also among the frescoes in the tombs of Orvieto.[56] In the fifth century, we encounter the same motif in other Tarquinian tombs,[57] on Felsinian grave *stelai*,[58] whereas the real *pompa funebris*, the *ekphora*,* that is, the transport of the corpse from the house to the burial place, seems to be represented only in the funerary monuments of Chiusi.[59] The symposium[60] depicted on the back wall is a key motif of earlier and subsequent funerary art. The context of both side walls suggests that the symposium depicted in the Tomb of the Blue Demons (Fig. v.12b) takes place in the Afterlife, as does that in the Tomb of Orcus I and all its descendants.

On the basis of these observations, we must take a second look at the numerous symposia in the Archaic and sub-Archaic tombs in Tarquinii. In the case of the frescoes, they are slightly earlier than those of the Tomb of the Blue Demons; from the Querciola Tomb I up to the Tomb of the Black Sow,[61] there is no concrete evidence that would forbid an analogous interpretation. Trees, which are abundant on the frescoes in Tarquinii,[62] also grow in the Underworld, as the Tomb of Orcus I[63] shows. A location in the Realm of the Dead is more problematic where tentlike constructions can be seen sheltering the symposium guests.[64] Such constructions could easily be explained as provisional shelters built for the burial rites, but they would be almost inexplicable in the Underworld. Localization in the Realm of the Dead can be excluded whenever doors are shown standing amid the symposium or the dance scenes.[65]

Doors[66] obviously have the same function as the ship in the Tomb of the Blue Demons and the city gates on the Hellenistic monuments. They mark the transition from an "antechamber" (in this case, the tomb) into the Afterlife. We have seen that such doors and thresholds can apparently open for a short time in the opposite direction as well, when the dead come to greet newcomers. This is also true of the doors in Tarquinian tombs: the deceased has to pass through them but under certain circumstances can return for a while not to the earth but to the tomb or to the anteroom of the Underworld, in Latin, *vestibulum Orci*.

A vestibule of this type is described by Vergil in the *Aeneid*:[67] monsters and spirits who can endanger living human beings, and even drive them into the Realm of the Dead, dwell there: War, Disease, Anxiety, Grief, Fear, Discord, Poverty, Hunger, and other figures. The spirits who have their abode here can exercise their powers above all on earth, which is why they live in an intermediate zone. In a more abstract manner, they have a function similar to that of the Etruscan demons: they conduct men into the Underworld. Of course we cannot equate Vergil's *vestibulum Orci* directly with the intermediate zone shown in the Tomb of the Blue Demons and on Hasti Afunei's sarcophagus. Related conceptions, however, probably form the basis for both of these representations.

If the hypotheses we have discussed so far are correct, then the question where the banquet is thought to take place is no longer so important. In many cases, the location was probably felt to be ambivalent.[68] The feast as depicted took place as part of the burial rites, and one hoped that the deceased—and all the others who were then still among the living—would be able to enjoy it further in the Afterlife. The symbol of a door, which is not quite as impenetrable as a wall, guarantees that the deceased could take part in the festivities celebrated to his (or her) benefit. Possibly the Etruscans also believed that the deceased needed a certain amount of time for the journey into the Underworld corresponding to the Roman *novendiale* (the nine days of display of the body) and remained in the grave for the duration of the funeral ceremonies.[69]

At the outset, I mentioned the uncertainty in regard to our understanding of many burial rites and customs. No attempt to explain the tomb frescoes of the fifth century can really succeed without taking this "uncertainty principle" into consideration. When it is employed, even singularities

v.15. Tomb of the Funeral Couch, Tarquinii, back wall. Watercolor copy in the Ny Carlsberg Museum. Ca. 460 BCE. (Photo: Archive of the Archäologisches Institut der Universität Heidelberg.)

like the hunting tent in the Tomb of the Hunter[70] become less problematic. This tent has been interpreted as having been set up to shelter the body laid out on the bier. The reason it was "decorated" with game hung up on it remained enigmatic. This fresco becomes more intelligible if we assume that the mourners wanted to surround the deceased, whom they believed to be present in the tomb as long as the body was lying in state, or also on other occasions, with the things he had appreciated in life. The ship in the Tomb of the Ship[71] or the scenes in the Tomb of Hunting and Fishing[72] could possibly be interpreted in this sense.

Sacrifices and Helping Gods

In the case of the hunting scenes, another aspect has been emphasized in recent scholarship: one sees in them an allusion to the sacrifices of animals, which Roman sources[73] have handed down to us. Taking into account the "uncertainty principle" that I postulated, this conjecture does not seem utterly impossible, but I find it improbable that such an extremely vague hint should be the sole purpose of the hunting scenes.[74] The real meaning of the hunt as a popular aristocratic pastime would hardly have let itself be so easily overshadowed. Nevertheless, the belief that blood was necessary to placate the anger of the dead on the one hand, and to strengthen and to protect their souls magically against the dangers of the transition to the Afterlife on the other, was a widespread ancient conception.[75] It probably forms the basis for the Etruscan sacrifices to the dead and becomes tangible in the blood-thirsty Phersu game,[76] in other dangerous games,[77] and, in mythical guise, in the sacrificing of the Trojans in the François Tomb and other monuments of funerary art.[78] The striking similarity to altars of the kingposts in the pediments in some Archaic tombs can best be explained as an allusion to those sacrifices,[79] in much the same way as can the impending death of Troilos in the Tomba dei Tori[80] and the animal-combat groups in the pediments.[81] These last can of course be more simply interpreted as a symbol of death, which suddenly overwhelms human beings. It will be prudent to formulate the argument very cautiously: kingposts and animal-combat groups may have been seen sometimes in this way, but there are also other possible interpretations, which may have been intended more frequently.

We might logically see the gods of the Underworld and the demons who lead the dead as the beneficiaries of the sacrifices under discussion. This view would fit well with the dedicatory inscription χarus, "of Charu(n)," found on a sixth-century vessel of unknown provenance (*ET*, OA 0.4).[82] But, as Giovanni Colonna[83] has demonstrated, other gods could also be invoked as companions on the last journey: Castur (Castor) and Pultuce (Pollux), who, as far as we know, did not have any such function in Greece. According to their myth, however, which had them constantly migrating between the Underworld and immortality, they were predestined to serve as guides in this zone of transition. The dedi-

v.16. Stone tomb figure from Chiusi. Ca. 600 BCE. Florence, Museo Archeologico. (Photo: Archive of the Archäologisches Institut der Universität Heidelberg.)

v.17. Grave stele with deceased escorted by demons. Fourth century BCE. Bologna, Museo Civico Archeologico. (Photo: Archive of the Archäologisches Institut der Universität Heidelberg.)

cation to the *tinas cliniiaras* ("sons of Tinia"; *ET*, Ta 3.2)[84] as well as the *lectisternium** in the Tomb of the Funeral Couch (Fig. v.15)[85] clearly point out this *interpretatio Etrusca* of the Greek divinities. Another god who, in complete contrast to his Greek nature, could play a role in the funerary cult is Apollo, as Erika Simon has shown.[86] On the other hand, the Dionysus/Bacchus worshipers among the Etruscans had apparently seen their god as a helpful guide and guard for their way to the desired destination in the Underworld in much the same manner as the Greeks did.

Mario Torelli attempted to ascribe the new emphasis given to the symposium in the Tarquinian tombs of the late sixth century to the introduction of Dionysian cults into Etruria, noting the moving of the symposium from the pediment to the main part of the rear wall, a change that allowed the representation of a larger number of participants.[87] But inasmuch as (1) the conception of a banquet in the Afterlife or in the tomb was an ancient Etruscan tradition and (2) the Greek symposium was, above all, a social phenomenon and not a religious one, the general attribution of the "new" symposia to the introduction of special Dionysian cults would probably be an overinterpretation. The Etruscans may have recalled Fufluns/Dionysos whenever satyrs are shown taking part in the symposium[88] or possibly also when a large, wine-filled *krater** (not a cinerary urn in the shape of a *krater*) stands in the midst of the rear wall;[89] a door is more frequently shown on this wall, symbolizing the passage into the Underworld and, at the same time, the deceased. A Dionysiac symbol in this particular location could indicate that the deceased was a follower of Fufluns/Dionysos, as the vases with dedications to *fufluns paχies* found in tombs at Vulci (*ET*, Vc 4.1–4) also indicate.[90]

To sum it all up: we could repeatedly confirm Greek influences, but these merely supplemented fundamental Etruscan beliefs, without completely transforming them. The conception of an Afterlife, which can be thought of as a banquet, and the idea of a journey into the Underworld, which was probably subdivided into a series of stages and was replete with dangers, most likely belong to the Etruscan substratum. The dangers had to be averted by means of sacrifices, which either the living had to bring on behalf of the dead or the deceased themselves could carry out in the tomb: this is probably the purpose of the small, altarlike objects found, for example, in the Tomb of the Five Chairs[91] and in the Campana Tomb[92] in Caere.

Giovanni Colonna and Stephan Steingräber have compiled any and all allusions found in Archaic tombs to places where the survivors could make sacrifices[93] and to venues for games (e.g., Grotta Porcina; Fig. VIII.12), for games[94] were also believed to fortify the dead for the journey into the Underworld. It would seem that these sacrifices and games not only secured a safe journey into the hereafter but also gave the souls of the dead the possibility to come back, under certain circumstances, to receive ritual honors and (as ancestors) to assist their descendants in one manner or another. This aspect may indicate what was meant by the *dii animales* of Roman tradition.

THE EARLIEST PHASE

Now that we have reviewed the evidence of the later periods of Etruscan culture, in which we find the clearest articulation of concepts of the Afterlife, we may examine briefly the earliest period of Etruscan culture and make several conjectures about the first manifestations of these concepts.

The terracotta statuettes from the Tomb of the Five Chairs at Caere and the sculptures in the Tomb of the Statues in Ceri[95] and in the "Pietrera" Tumulus at Vetulonia[96] could be interpreted as ancestors, whereas the so-called *xoanon** figures from Chiusi[97] (Fig. V.16), which are always feminine, and the statues from the Isis Tomb of Vulci[98] more probably depict a goddess or a demoness, an early form of Vanth (whose name has been discovered in a dedicatory inscription of the seventh century).[99] The famous urn from Montescudaio[100] can probably be seen as an early example of the Afterlife symposium. The Sardinian ship models in the tombs of Vetulonia,[101] the chariots found in some tombs, and the scene on the "Pietra Zannoni"[102] may already have been allusions to a journey into the Underworld. A chariot or a depiction of it can also be used to indicate the social status of the deceased, which does not necessarily conflict with this interpretation. The discussion could be extended to the Villanovan tombs with miniature chariots and boats that also "could be meant as a magical and symbolic instrument of the deceased's journey into the after life."[103]

All these early monuments could hardly have been understood on the basis of internal criteria alone. They can, however, with all due caution, be interpreted as early evidence for Etruscan beliefs about death and the Afterlife, some of which, in Greek "disguise," were retained into the later periods.

To close this chapter, I would like to return to the beginning of this paper concerning the difficulties of interpretation, and close with the words of Arnold van Gennep, taken from the English translation of his noted book *Les rites de passage*, one of the incunabula of anthropology and the history of religion: "Funeral rites are further complicated when within a single people there are several contradictory or different conceptions of the afterworld which may become intermingled with one another, so that their confusion is reflected in the rites."[104]

NOTES

1. Bonfante 1986, 268.

2. An extensive listing of publications since 1984 is included in the bibliography, which therefore contains not only the literature cited in the notes but all the studies concerning Etruscan funeral rites and eschatology since 1984 that were accessible to me. Publications of excavations of necropoleis or of single tombs are listed only when combined with discussion of rites or eschatological concepts, not when confined to the presentation of the material or to sociological aspects. Likewise, only a selection of studies concerning the types of architecture is given.

3. See esp. Briquel 1985 (1987), 267-277; Briquel 1997, 19, 128-135.

4. Generally on death, burial, and mourning: Humphreys and King 1981; Metcalf and Huntington 1991; Barley 1995; see also Burkert 1972, 60-69. For Greece: Kurtz and Boardman 1971; Vermeule 1979; Garland 1985; Sourvinou-Inwood 1995; Díez de Velasco 1995; Johnston 1999.

5. The best summary of types of burial and of tombs: *Dizionario*, 298-303, s.v. tomba (G. Nardi). Important considerations on the coexistence of inhumation and cremation at Tarquinii and the use of different types of vases in different Etruscan cities: de La Genière 1986 (1987). See also Coen 1991, 119-133; Izzet 1996; Bruni 1995; Prayon 1975a; Prayon 1989; Steingräber 1995.

6. Jannot 1984a, 406-419.

7. See above, n. 3. Generally on the *Etrusca disciplina*: Pfiffig 1975, 36-43, and the series dealing with ancient authors as sources for the *disciplina* in *Caesarodunum* Suppl. 61 (1991), Suppl. 63 (1993), Suppl. 64 (1995), Suppl. 65 (1996), and Suppl. 66 (1999).

8. Herbig 1952, 41, no. 76, pls. 55-57a; Colonna 1993a, 358-359, 364-365, pls. 21-23; Jannot 1993, pl. 9.1.

9. The root *culś* is also contained in Culśanś, the name of a double-faced god corresponding evidently to the Roman Janus; *culś* probably has the same meaning as the Latin *ianua*, door, gateway. For Culśanś and Culśu, see Simon, Chap. 4, glossary of gods.

10. The name Vanth is more frequent: it occurs seven times with pictures of female demons, but we are not yet certain whether it is a collective name for all female demons of death (ultimately derived from the name of an old divinity of death [see below, n. 47]) or if Vanth has special functions. If Vanth is the collective name, Culśu would mean "Vanth Culśu," "the Vanth of the gate." See Spinola 1987; Krauskopf 1987, 78-85; Scheffer 1991; Haynes 1993; Jannot 1997; Weber-Lehmann 1997.

11. There has been a long discussion on the interpretation of the arched door. Some see it as a city gate (most decidedly Jannot 1998, 81-82: "La cité des morts"; the mallet of Charun as instrument for opening and closing the bars of gates: Jannot 1993, 68-76). Others prefer to interpret it as the door of the tomb (most decidedly Scheffer 1994). Cypresses decorated with garlands growing on the sides of it (Scheffer 1994, 198, fig. 18.3) probably mean that the door of a tomb is intended. It is, however, difficult to identify the door as belonging to the tomb when the door has merlons (e.g., sarcophagus of Hasti Afunei) and a procession of men and demons is moving towards it, while others, evidently coming out of the gate, wait for the newly arriving person. But, of course, both doors, the gate of the Underworld and the door of the tomb, can be guarded by demons. The first door the deceased has to pass, the door to the tomb, might in its shape and its surroundings foreshadow the second one, the city gate of the Realm of the Dead.

Generally on the topography of the Underworld: Roncalli 1997.

12. *Etruscan Painting*, 282, no. 40, figs. 48-51, pls. 11-12.

13. *Etruscan Painting*, 300, no. 55, pls. 61-63. The T-shaped false doors that the Charuns flank are an old motif of the tombs of the late sixth and fifth centuries (see below, n. 66), resumed here.

14. For the four Charuns of the Tomba dei Caronti (*ET*, Ta 7.78-81), see Jannot 1993, 63-64. For Charun generally, see Mavleev 1986; Krauskopf 1987, 73-78; Jannot 1997, 139-145; Jannot 1993.

15. Sarcophagi and urns: Lambrechts 1959, 123-197; Weber 1978, 94-116; Moscati 1997; frescoes (Tomba Bruschi, Tomba del Cardinale, Tomba del Convento, Tomba del Tifone): Cristofani 1971, 27-32. Especially in German literature, the interpretation of the so-called *Beamtenaufzüge* as voyages to the Realm of the Dead has been contested (Höckmann 1982, 156-157; Schäfer 1989, 36), but the decisive argument is the presence of demons as Weber (1978, 110-113) correctly points out. It is not possible to separate the representations with demons from those without the demons.

16. Tarquinia, Museo Nazionale Archeologico, Inv. 1424: Herbig 1952, 60, no. 116, pl. 74c; Mavleev and Krauskopf 1986, 231, no. 71*; Jannot 1993, pl.10.2.

17. Tomb 5636: Colonna 1985a, 156, fig. 29; *Etruscan Painting*, 371, no. 165, pl. 180; Jannot 1993, pl. 10.1. See also Tomba Querciola II (Colonna 1985a, 154, fig. 25; *Etruscan Painting*, 339, no. 107, fig. 286).

18. Etruscan sea monsters: Boosen 1986. Riders: Boosen 1986, 161-162 (nos. 89-94), 179-182, 206 (no. 79), 220 (pl. 29).

19. Waves are to be found in the following tombs (with the numbers of the catalogue of *Etruscan Painting*, 259ff.): Tarquinii, Leonesse (no. 77), Triclinio (no. 121), 5513 (no. 162; see also Weber-Lehmann 1989, pl. 1a); Letto Funebre (no. 82), Scudi (no. 109), Bruschi (no. 48), Querciola II (no. 107), Tifone (no. 118); Blera, Grotta dipinta (no. 1); Bomarzo, Grotta dipinta (no. 2); Cerveteri, Tomba delle Onde Marine (no. 8); dei Sarcofagi (no. 10); del Triclinio (no. 11); Orvieto, Tomba degli Hescanas (no. 34); Populonia, Tomba del Corridietro (no. 35). The motive occurs also on sarcofagi (e.g., from Viterbo, locality of San Francesco-La Cipollara, Proietti 1977, 293, no. 24, pl. 43; Colonna 1985a, 161, fig. 41; Pairault Massa 1988, 82, pl. 15.2) and on other objects of funeral character (bronze *krater** from the Tomba dei Curunas of Tuscania (Moretti and Sgubini Moretti 1983, 28-29, pls. 21, 22, 25).

20. Chiusi, Museo Nazionale Archeologico Inv. 860: Herbig 1952, 18, no. 15, pl. 49; Boosen 1986, 189, no. 17, pl. 25; Colonna 1993a, 359-360.

21. The wounded warrior has a long, Gallic shield, and therefore G. Colonna proposes that originally a Galatomachia had been intended and changed into the more modern theme of the voyage to the Realm of the Dead. This seems plausible, but nevertheless the actual state of the sarcophagus gives, in a rather careless way, the sequence "fight, voyage by horse, sea monster," which can be understood as continuous.

22. E.g., a *stele** (Ducati 1910, 437, no. 164, pl. II; *Rasenna*, fig. 570) gives the sequence (from below) "lady with demon announcing the moment of the death, voyage by car, sea monsters"; another (Ducati 1910, 439, no. 168, pl. IV; Bonfante 1986, 117, fig. IV:30) "fight with a Gaul, voyage by car, sea monsters."

23. Morandi 1983, with rich parallels and bibliography for all the themes represented; *Etruscan Painting*, 297-299, no. 54, pls. 59-60, figs. 109-132.

24. For the dangers of the way, see Roncalli 1997, 41; Bonamici 1998. The common demons of death such as Charun and Vanth usually are more friendly, they accompany the deceased, and eventually they even defend them against threatening monsters and demons. Attributes such as swords and other arms may be explained in this way (Jannot 1997, 156; Jannot 1993, 68, 76, pl. 7.3). Pictures in which Charun or Vanth seem to attack the dying or dead persons are extremely rare; some are discussed in the still useful book of De Ruyt 1934, 89-91, 202. Vanth(?) seems to be aggressive especially on a *stamnos* from Vulci (Greifenhagen 1978, 70-71, no. 8, pl. 41) and has been interpreted as watching a prisoner (Peirithoos?) in the Underworld on a stamnos of the Funnel Group in the British Museum with a very aggressive Charun at the other side of the vase(F 486: Del Chiaro 1974, 41-42, no. 3, pls. 46-47; Mavleev 1986, 233, no. 102; Weber-Lehmann 1997, no. 11), but Marisa Bonamici (1998, 8, 10-11, 8, fig. 14) has shown that even the interpretation of these demons as malignant is not unequivocal. The most famous "victim," Laris Pulenas on his sarcophagus in Tarquinia (Herbig 1952, 59, no. 111, pl. 70a; Mavleev 1986, 233, no. 103; Jannot 1993, pl. 7.1; Roncalli 1996, 46, fig. 1), has been interpreted in a completely different and convincing way by F. Roncalli 1996 as crossing calmly the threshold of the Underworld, unworried by the flanking demons. This Roncalli sees as an allusion to the sacrifices held for Laris Pulenas in the figure of the young man with the knife (in the left part of the relief), and an allusion to the destiny of less happy individuals, in this case, Sisyphos—(in the right part). For the frescoes of the Tomba del Cardinale, see above, n. 23.

For Tuchulcha, see Krauskopf 1987, 72-73, pl. 13; Jannot 1993, 78-80, pl. 11.3; Harari 1997a. The only evidence for the name is the fresco in the Tomb of Orcus II, where the demon is watching over and threatening Theseus and Peirithoos. Demons with the same birdlike features occur in some vase paintings (e.g., volute *krater* Paris, Bibliothèque Nationale, Cabinet des Médailles Inv. 918 with Admetos and Alkestis: Krauskopf 1987, pl. 13b; Roncalli 1996, 56-57, fig. 11; Harari 1997a, 97-98, no. 2) and may be also named Tuchulcha. In the Tomb of Orcus, the menacing, frightening character Tuchulcha is evident and well justified; it should be studied to determine whether reasons for a similar menace can be found in other representations of the demon with the birdlike features. For the Alkestis *krater,* Roncalli (1996, 56-57; 1997, 43, 47) proposes the interpretation that one of the demons is making the way between the entrance of the Underworld and the final goal of the journey dangerous, just as a successor of the two demons is doing on the left side of the Tomba dei Demoni Azzurri (see below); the same could apply to the demon on the kalyx *krater* of the same painter at Trieste Museo Civico Inv. 2125 (Mavleev and Krauskopf 1986, and n. 85; Cristofani 1992, 98, pl. 37; the different gestures of the two demons are convincingly interpreted by Bonamici 1998, 8, fig. 8).

25. See above, n. 3.

26. Cristofani 1987a, 198, pl. 49; Roncalli 1997, 44-45, fig. 5. The urn: Scott Ryberg 1955, pl. 5.11; Felletti Maj 1977, pls. 7, 12a. The scene in the Tomb of Orcus has also been interpreted as Ulysses' sacrifice at the entrance to Hades, as his position (right next to the Greek Nekyia) might suggest (Weber-Lehmann 1995, 91). It is extremely difficult, however, to see Ulysses in the left figure with the wide cloak (Weber-Lemann's explanation for this divergence from his usual iconography is not convincing), and the small scale of the right figure (reconstruction Cristofani 1986 [1987] pl. 49, 12) is inappropriate for the supposed companion of Ulysses. For a possible allusion to the sacrifice on the sarcophagus of Laris Pulenas, see above, n. 24.

27. *Etruscan Painting,* 329-330, no. 93, figs. 244-250, with preceding bibliography. A good reconstruction of the original chamber: Torelli 1975, 45-56, pls. 6-7. A new inscription: Morandi and Colonna 1995.

28. *Kylikeion: Etruscan Painting,* pl. 132; Cristofani 1987a, pl. 52.19. The main part of the banquet scene (not preserved) must have been painted at the right wall of the so-called corridor, in continuation of the *kylikeion.* A mythological interpretation of it seems to be extremely difficult (hypothesis discussed by Weber-Lehmann 1995, 99-100). At first view, it is difficult to understand why the banquet is separated from the sacrifice, which has opened the way to the banquet, by Underworld scenes with the punishment of Theseus, Peirithoos, and Sisyphos (the best survey of the location of the scenes is Weber-Lehmann 1995, fig. 2.10). The distribution of the scenes is more intelligible if one combines the sacrifice with the arrival of the deceased in the Underworld, as supposed by Cristofani 1987, 199, pl. 51.16.

29. *Etruscan Painting,* 341-343, no. 109, pls. 145-149.

30. The direct participation of Eita and Phersipnai at the banquet of the *gens* in the Golini Tomb I is unparalleled and could eventually be influenced by Orphic-Pythagorean ideas emphasizing the intimacy of the *mystai* (initiates) and the gods of the Underworld in the common symposium (see Graf 1974, 98-103). The couple of the sovereigns of the Realm of the Dead may have been conceived, as their names are, under Greek influence with some originally Etruscan ingredients, e.g., the affinity of Aita to the wolves, which Hades did not share. The old Etruscan name of the ruler of the Underworld was probably Calu; Phersipnei may have been preceded by a single Vanth, eventually—but here we enter the region of complete hypothesis—a divinity of dying, i.e., the passage from life to death, but nothing points to the presumption that they were imagined as a couple. The existence of a great goddess of death in the archaic Etruscan religion, which had been postulated especially by A. Hus (1961, 545-548; 1976, 181), is difficult to prove. For Etruscan divinities of death: Pfiffig 1975, 319-323; Hostetter 1978, esp. 262-265; Krauskopf 1987, 61-68; Krauskopf 1988; Mavleev 1994.

31. For the three Orvietan tombs, see *Pittura Orvieto; Etruscan Painting,* 278-280, nos. 32-34, figs. 43-47, pl. 3-10; Pairault Massa 1985.

32. Theseus, Peirithoos, watched by Tuchulcha, and Sisyphos in the Tomb of Orcus II, and Sisyphos and Tantalos(?) in the François Tomb: *Etruscan Painting,* 331, figs. 254, 259, 261, pl. 131; *Etruscan Painting,* 379, fig. 408; Cristofani 1987a, 200, pls. 53-54; Tomba François 1987, 103, fig. 16; Roncalli 1997, 46-48, figs. 7-8; Manakidou 1994, 238, no. 86; Oakley 1994, 784-785, nos. 27-28; Weber-Lehmann 1994, 955, no. 39; Harari 1997a, 97, no. 1. For other eventual pictures of Peirithoos in Etruscan vase painting, see Manakidou 1994, 238-239, nos. 85, 88 (but for the stamnos London F 486, cf. the different interpretation Bonamici 1998, 10-11).

33. Graf 1974, 103-126.

34. The only possible representation of one of the Greek judges over the dead, Rhadamanthys, on an Etruscan mirror at Boston incorporates him in a context of Greek gods: De Puma 1993, 41-43, no. 21. pl. 21a, b, d; De Puma 1998. In the first half of the twentieth century there was a long discussion on punishment in the Etruscan Underworld, beginning with the book of Weege 1921 (esp. 24-56), who saw Orphic influence especially in supposed scenes of punishment, and the critique of van Essen 1927. From that time on, Weege's corpus of pretended punishment scenes has been more and more reduced until it is nonexistent. What remained may be classified as the dangers of the way (see n. 24), and of course, it is possible that those dangers may be caused not only by missing or false sacrifices and rites of passage but also by a misguided life. Because we lack any written sources, however, we know absolutely nothing about this point.

35. Pallottino 1987; Coarelli 1985; on the Tomba Giglioli, see Pairault Massa 1988 and generally Pairault Massa 1992. Considering our poor knowledge of Etruscan history, all these studies must remain highly hypothetical, but this does not mean that they should not be done.

36. Blanck and Proietti 1986.

37. E.g., the canopic urns from Chiusi: Gempeler; Colonna and von Hase 1984, 37; Maetzke 1989 (1993); Damgaard Andersen 1993, 37, fig. 44, 42-43, nos. 41-42, fig. 55.

38. Urns in the shape of a hut or a house, Orientalizing period: Buranelli 1985, 34-77; Coen 1991, 119-133; earlier: Bartoloni, Buranelli, D'Atri, and De Santis 1987, esp. 223-225; cf. also Damgaard Andersen 1993, 7-29.

39. Pfiffig 1975, 13-15, 162-167.

40. The contradiction between offerings in or upon the tomb and the belief in an Afterlife in a faraway world is nearly ubiquitous in antiquity; for Greece, see, e.g., Vermeule 1979, 48-56.

41. The discussion began with the studies of Weege and van Essen (see above, n. 34). A short summary can be found in Pensa 1977, 14-15; Manino 1980, esp. 59-61; Krauskopf 1987, 11-18.

42. Krauskopf 1987, passim.

43. Cataldi Dini 1986 (1987); Cataldi Dini in *Pittura etrusca,* 151-153, pls. 39-41; Krauskopf 1987, 105-107; Roncalli 1997, 37-44, figs. 1-4; Rendeli 1996, 12-25, figs. 6-10, 12, 14, 17, 20, 23, 24, 28.

44. Sourvinou-Inwood 1986; Sourvinou-Inwood 1987; Sourvinou-Inwood 1995, 303-361; Mugione 1995; Díez de Velasco 1995, 42-57.

45. Bažant 1994. The demon on the right in the Tomb of the Blue Demons (Fig. v.12c) is similar, even if far larger, to the Thanatos on the white-ground *lekythos* Louvre CA 1264 (Bažant 1994, 906, no. 27; Krauskopf 1987, pl. 7a; Díez de Velasco 1995, 57-60, fig. 2.24; Rendeli 1996, 20, fig. 23). Evidently the type was more widespread than one might assume: a demon very similar to the Etruscan one occurs in a painted tomb at Paestum, dating about 340-330 BCE: Gaudo tomb 2/1972 (Pontrandolfo-Rouveret 1992, 63, 264, fig. 2.3, 387). Thanatos and Hypnos carrying a corpse (Bažant 1994, 904-905, nos. 2-25) have parallels in Etruria, too, but only for a short period in the fifth century: Krauskopf 1987, 25-30, pls. 2a.b, 3.

46. Pausanias 10.28.7; Robertson 1988. Among the figures in the Tomb of the Blue Demons, the demon with the snakes, sitting on a rock, is the figure most likely influenced by the Eurynomos of Polygnotus' Nekyia, even if the latter has no snakes. Snakes appear in the hands of a related Etruscan demon on a *stele* from Felsina/Bologna, not sitting but also seen frontally, in the middle panel of the *stele,* isolated and surely not belonging to the group of demons escorting men, frequent on the *stelai* from Felsina. Therefore, this demon possibly belongs to the same category of demons as Eurynomos and the sitting demon of the Tomb of the Blue Demons (Ducati 1910, 449, no. 182, fig. 5; Krauskopf 1987, 44-45). The vase in the shape of a demon's head with black skin, made by the Attic potter Sotades and found at Spina (Krauskopf 1987, 40-44, pl. 4), may also represent Eurynomos; E. Paribeni (1986, 46-47, figs. 4-6) gives another, non-funerary interpretation, but whatever the head may have meant for Sotades, for the Etruscan owner it rather probably had a demonic aspect. At least vases like this one furnished the model for the Etruscan vase in the shape of Charun's head at Munich (Mavleev and Krauskopf 1986, 227, no. 29; Krauskopf 1987 pl. 4c-d; Elliot 1986, 41, 283, fig. 72, Donderer 1998, pl. 1).

47. Sarian 1986; Aellen 1994, 24-90, especially in relation to the Etruscan demonesses: von Freytag 1986, 136-162, 287-294. The Erinyes may have furnished the model already for the first type of Vanth (see the bibliography above, n. 10) in a long garment, but the demoness or goddess Vanth is certainly older, as the inscription on an *aryballos** of the second half of the seventh century (see below, n. 99) clearly proves. Weber-Lehmann 1997 stresses too much the Greek influence in the genesis of Vanth. Vanth originally was, as far as a demon of death can be that, a kind guide, like the Greek Hermes Psychopompos, and not an *interpretatio etrusca* of the Erinyes. She maintained this manner even when the West Greek "huntress" type of the Erinyes with a short chiton or skirt and crossed shoulder straps and boots was adopted for her. Only slowly, under the influence of those West Greek Furies, her character began to include less benevolent aspects.

48. Within that geographical and chronological horizon the Greek Hermes Psychopompos, too, entered Etruscan iconography and religion (Hostetter 1978; Krauskopf 1987, 45-60; Harari 1997b, 106-107). For the various types of demons on the *stelai* from Felsina, see Sassatelli 1984; Stucchi 1986; Krauskopf 1987, 35-45; Mastrocinque 1989 (1991); Morigi Govi and Sassateli 1993; Cerchiai 1995. For the *stelai,* see further Sassatelli 1989; Sassatelli 1993.

49. This applies to all the types, but the case of Charon and Charun (Sassatelli 1984; Krauskopf 1987, 38-44, 73-78) is especially interesting. Considering the Etruscan idea of a voyage to the beyond by sea, it is a little surprising that the Etruscans did not use the figure of the Greek ferryman more extensively. This might be caused by two factors: (1) Charon was a ferryman and no sailor and therefore not precisely the figure needed to substitute for the Etruscan sea monsters and (2) the Etruscans probably looked for a representable appearance for demons already existing in their concept of demonic powers, guiding the deceased to the gates of the Netherworld, and they found it, with some modifications, in Charon. It makes no great difference whether they imagined two or more completely different types of Charun—the ferryman with the oar and the guide of the overland route with the mallet or the torch (Jannot 1993, 60-61)—or used different attributes to characterize the actual function of Charun in the respective pictures. It is nevertheless important to realize that in the later Etruscan periods, Charun is not a single figure but a plurality. Whether he was originally one or many beings is not clear. The dedicatory inscription χarus on an Attic cup seems to point to a single demon, possibly even with an original Etruscan name (Louvre F 126, by Oltos: CVA Paris Louvre 10, France 17, III 1b, pls. 1.5-8 2.1; Briquel and Gaultier 1989-1990, 361-362, no. 78, pl. 66, with a critical commentary by M. Cristofani; Jannot 1993, 64-65, with summary of discussion; Colonna 1996, 183-184, fig. 21, connecting the name with the Greek Charon).

50. There are a considerable number of possible combinations; the inverse scheme, human head, including Gorgoneia, with animal's body, has also been used. Cf. Krauskopf 1987, 20-25, pls. 1b-d, 2c-d. For the demons with the heads of wolves or lions, see also Simon 1973; Richardson 1977; Prayon 1977; Elliott 1995. For late Etruscan reminiscences of these mixed creatures, see Simon 1997.

51. Above, nn. 16-17.

52. Roncalli 1997, 40-44. Less convincing is the interpretation of Rendeli (1996), who sees the *anagoghe* ("leading up") of Persephone (the woman on the right), who is met by Demeter (the woman on the left), and the boy Eubouleus, based on the resemblance of this group to that of the great Eleusinian relief. Rendeli's interpretation is not, however, very compelling: the figures on the relief are not walking, Eubouleus as a guide to the Netherworld should not be a boy, and the generally accepted interpretation of the goddess on the left as Demeter and the figure on the right as Persephone had to be reversed. In addition, the demons are the dominant figures in the painting, which seems improbable in the supposed presence of the queen of the Underworld and her mother. Rendeli himself (1966, 23) already mentioned the main problem with the interpretation:

we have absolutely no evidence for a *katabasis* (descent) of Demeter and Eubouleus in Classical Greek art, which usually represented the *anodos* (ascent) of Persephone. Even if a version of the myth including a *katabasis* of Demeter should have existed in Classical literature (Rendeli 1996, nn. 114-116; Harrison and Obbink 1986), it is hard to see how anybody could have recognized the Underworld as the place of the meeting in the Eleusinian relief. The only motive for such a locale is the supposed resemblance of the scene to the Etruscan fresco, and there, the only argument to identify the figures as the Eleusinian goddesses is the (not very strong) resemblance to the Greek relief, evidently a kind of circular reasoning.

53. Above, n. 19.

54. *Etruscan Painting*, pl. 165; Boosen 1986, 158, no. 78, pl. 23.33; Torelli 1997a, 144, fig. 126 (= Torelli 1997b, 80, fig. 38).

55. Hus 1961, 39, no. 5, pl. 21 (Rome, Villa Giulia; Boosen 1986, 158, no. 77, pl. 22.32); Hus 1961, 51, nos. VI-VII, pl. 8 (lost), 176-179; Bonfante 1986, 112, fig. IV.23. Hippocamp without rider: Comstock and Vermeule 1976, 252, no. 391. with illustration (= Boosen 1986, 138, no. 5).

56. Above, nn. 15 (sarcophagi) and 31 (Orvieto).

57. All of the same period of transition as the Tomb of the Blue Demons: Tomba Querciola I (*Etruscan Painting*, 338-339, no. 106, figs. 279-280; Adam 1993), where the chariot with the warrior, directly above the entrance, is inserted in a line of dancing figures moving to the banquet on the rear wall, as a newcomer is arriving at the place of the eternal banquet; the Tomb of Francesca Giustiniani (*Etruscan Painting*, 305, no. 65, pl. 70); and the Tomb of the Pygmies (*Etruscan Painting*, 333, no. 97, fig. 265, pl. 135), where riders are on the way to the eternal banquet. Problematic is the Tomb of the Warrior (*Etruscan Painting*, 313, no. 73, figs. 180-182), where the *biga* on the entrance wall is being used in acrobatic performances, and the action of the warriors on the right wall is not clear.

58. Ducati 1910, 582-606; Weber 1978, 74-93.

59. Jannot 1984a, 370-373. Generally on the reliefs from Chiusi, realistic scenes like the *prothesis*,* the *ekphora* and dances and games in honor of the deceased, seem to be preferred to more symbolic ones.

60. The term *symposium* is used here, because in the majority of the tombs, indeed only drinking vessels are represented. A meal may also have been imagined, as the preparations for a meal in the Golini Tomb I (see above, nn. 30 and 31, and *L'alimentazione* 1987, 107, 109, 112, 119-121, 168-169) clearly prove. Probably the symposium was the last part of a complete banquet. For banquets and symposia, see De Marinis 1961; Cristofani 1987, 123-132; Rathje 1994, 95-99; Small 1994, 85-94; Rathje 1995, 167-175. For Chiusi: Jannot 1984a, 362-368. For Archaic tombs of Tarquinii: Weber-Lehmann 1985; d'Agostino 1987, 215-219.

61. For these tombs, see Stopponi 1983, 62-65, with a list of all tombs with banqueting scenes at p. 64.

62. A range of interpretations exists for the trees in the frescoes: as elements marking the boundaries of the *templum*,* as the sacred place of the rituals of "passage" in the period immediately after death (Rouveret 1988), as sacred groves of Aplu/Apollo (Simon 1973, 28-38, with a list of tombs with laurel trees at p. 28), or as the trees of the Elysian Fields. Given that more than one hundred years separate the Tomb of the Bulls from the Tomb of Orcus, however, trees may have changed their meaning more than once.

63. *Etruscan Painting*, 330, fig. 244; Torelli 1975, pl. 7.

64. The most famous examples are the Tomb of the Lionesses and the Tomb of the Funeral Couch: Stopponi 1968, 60-62; Rouveret 1988, 203-204, with further bibliography; Jannot 1988, 59-65, with a reconstruction of a tent. For the tent in the Tomb of the Hunter, see below, n. 70.

65. Only once, in the Tomb of the Biclinium (*Etruscan Painting*, 288, no. 46, figs. 72-76), is the false door combined with a symposium; the false door is often combined with dances (*komos* in Torelli's terminology: Torelli 1997a, table on p. 127) that cannot be separated from the symposia, because the two scenes fuse very often in Tarquinian frescoes (see Torelli 1997a, table on p. 143).

66. The meaning of the painted or sculptured "false" doors is one of the most intensively discussed problems of Etruscan funerary art. For the arched doors of the Hellenistic period, see above, n. 11. For the T-shaped doors of earlier periods, see Staccioli 1980, 1-17; Jannot 1984b; D'Agostino 1987, 215, 217-218; Camporeale 1993, 186-187; Torelli 1997a, 127-131; Dobrowolski 1997, 133, with bibliography for both types of doors in n. 42. The T-shaped door is one of the oldest and most important motifs of Etruscan funerary art that is not connected directly with the banquet, dance, games, or voyage. It occurs in the following Tarquinian tombs, always in the middle of the rear wall and in the oldest tombs (the tombs of the Hut, Marchese, 6120, Jade Lions, and Labrouste); in the Tomb with Doors and Felines, there are three doors, one door on each wall; the door occurs as the only or main motif, among trees (the Tomb of the Mouse) and sometimes flanked by persons turning towards it (Augurs, Cardarelli, Bronze Door, Skull). Doors may be combined with dances or games: Olympiads, Inscriptions and Flagellation=1701 (both with three doors, one on each wall), Citheroid and 4255 (both with two doors on the rear wall, evidently destined for two persons buried there) and Biclinium (symposium). A *loculus** is framed as a T-shaped door in 3098; the motif of the door has a Hellenistic revival in the Tomb of the Charons at Tarquinii. Tombs at Chiusi with the false door: Colle Casuccini, Poggio al Moro (Camporeale 1993, pls. 1-2). *Stelai* of Felsina: Ducati 1910, 634-635 fig. 65; Sassatelli 1989, 935, no. 16, pl. 3b.

67. *Aeneid* 6.273-294.

68. The various models of interpretation (realistic, magic, and social) and the difficulties that result if one strictly uses only one of these models are discussed by d'Agostino 1988.

69. This concept has been elaborated very convincingly by Torelli 1997a, 126-127. There the tomb, too, in a slightly different sense, is interpreted as an intermediate room.

70. *Etruscan Painting*, 295, no. 51, figs. 100-104, pls. 52-53; Bonfante 1986, 158, fig. IV.90; Rouveret 1988, 212, fig. 49.2: "tend à créer autour du mort un lieu familier"; Roncalli 1987, 237. A different interpretation: Torelli 1997a, 131, 134, fig. 113.

71. Moretti 1961; *Etruscan Painting*, 327-328, no. 91, figs. 236-239, pls. 118-120; *Pittura etrusca*, 145, fig. 100, pl. 37, with further bibliography. Torelli (1997a, 134) sees in the ships on the left wall an allusion to the voyage of the deceased by sea, but a harbor scene with a cargo vessel and its crew seems to me too realistic scenery for a voyage to the beyond; it would be better compared with the warship on the *stele* of Vele Caicna from Felsina, likewise realistic (Ducati 1910, 369-372, no. 10 fig. 82; Bonino 1988, 76-77, fig. 7 with bibliography).

The case of the Tomb of the Ship I of Caere (*Etruscan Painting*, 262, no. 7, fig. 5), dating from the end of the seventh century, is different. The ship is represented in the middle of the rear wall, where usually the most important theme is placed.

72. *Etruscan Painting*, 293-294, no. 50, figs. 92-99, pl. 41-51; *Pittura etrusca*, 133-135, figs. 84-85, pls. 13-19, with further bibliography; Cerchiai 1987; Rouveret 1988, 208-209.

73. Above, p. 66.

74. Tombs with hunting scenes: Stopponi 1983, 68-77. For the funerary hunts: Jannot 1984a, 357-362; Roncalli 1990, 237; Adam 1993, 80-85. It cannot be excluded that in some cases, hunts were part of the funerary games (Jannot, Adam), but the other "aristocratic" aspect must also be taken into consideration in the hunting-scenes of the fifth century. The aristocratic aspect is certainly the only one in the fresco with the returning from the hunt in the Tomb of Hunting and Fishing (*Etruscan Painting*, pl. 50).

75. Dobrowolski (1997, 135, n. 46) and Blome (1986, 99) give references to the literature. Blome (1986, 101-102) insists that the living have an interest in blood for calming the *Trauerwut*, that is, the rage of the surviving relatives because of the loss. Blome cites Burkert 1972, 64-65, and Meuli 1946, 201-209 (= Meuli 1975, 924-932), but this is, of course only the other side of the coin and not a contradiction.

76. In the tombs of the Augurs and Olympiads (*Etruscan Painting*, pls. 20, 122; Bonfante 1986, 160, fig. IV-93). For the interpretation of these and other "Phersu" figures: Elliott 1986, 22-26; Blome 1986; Jannot 1993; Adam 1993, 85.

77. For these games: Jannot 1993, 307-309, 317-320; Adam 1993, passim. Other athletic games: Jannot 1984a, 340-355; Thuillier 1985; Jannot 1986 and various contributions in *Jeux* 1987, 159-222 and in *Spectacles*. For games of dexterity: d'Agostino 1993.

78. Bonfante 1986, 162, fig. IV-96; Camporeale 1981, 205-206, 211; Blanck 1985, 83-84; Roncalli in *Tomba François*, 85-89, fig. 3.

79. Roncalli 1990, 232-235, figs. 1 (Bulls), 2 (3098), 4 (Bacchants), 6 (Little Flowers), 9 (Deer Hunt).

80. Bonfante 1986, 236, fig. VIII-3; Cerchiai 1980, 25-39; for the *machaira*, see also Adam 1993, 93-94.

81. Jannot 1982, 124-130; Roncalli 1991, 236; Dobrowolski 1997, 135.

82. Above, n. 49.

83. Colonna 1996.

84. Colonna 1996, 174-175, fig. 15; see also Cristofani 1988-1989, 14-16.

85. Colonna 1996, 177-179, figs. 16-17; Roncalli 1990, 239-241, fig. 12; *Etruscan Painting*, pl. 110. For the tomb, see also Jannot 1988.

86. Simon 1973.

87. Torelli 1997a, 135, 138, with tables on pp. 127, 143; Torelli 1997b, 75-76.

88. For various observations on the tombs of Dionysos and the Silenoi, of Hunting and Fishing, of the Inscriptions and Number 1999, cf. Weber-Lehmann 1985, 27, 37-38, fig. 1 and pl. 11; pl. 20.1; pl. 21.1; Torelli 1997a, 135, 139-141, fig. 119 (= Torelli 1997b, 75-76, fig. 26).

89. Tombs of the Lionesses, of the Dead Man, of the Chariots. Normally the *krater* for the symposium is placed at the side, close to the *kylikeion*. Nevertheless, the "central" *kraters*, too, are thought to contain wine and not ashes, since in the Tomb of the Lionesses, a ladle hanging down near the *krater* and a jug on the floor (*Etruscan Painting*, pl. 97) and in the Tomba delle Bighe cupbearers (*Etruscan Painting*, 290, fig. 79) demonstrate the intended use of the *krater* (see also d'Agostino 1987, 217-218). Of course, the association with the vessel containing the ashes of the deceased is not impossible, but this is only an analogy and not a reality. *Kraters* as cinerary urns: Valenza Mele 1981, 113-118; de la Genière 1986 (1989), 271-282; Pontrandolfo 1995, 190-195.

90. Cristofani and Martelli 1978. For the cult of Fufluns, see further Colonna 1991; Cristofani 1995; Krauskopf forthcoming. For the "Orphic-Pythagorean" influences, which did exist but not in the manner supposed by Weege and others (above, n. 34), see Harari 1988 (with bibliography) and above, n. 30.

91. For the reconstruction of the tomb: Prayon 1974.

92. Prayon 1975a, 112-113, pl. 39.62; Colonna 1986, fig. 278; Colonna 1996, 166, fig. 2.

93. Colonna 1986, passim; Colonna 1993b; Colonna 1996, 165-171; Colonna and Di Paolo 1997, 160-167; Steingräber 1982, 103-116; Steingräber 1995, 74; Steingräber 1996. See also Rafanelli 1997; Zamarchi Grassi 1992, 121-138 (English summary by M. Torcellan Vallone in *EtrSt* 2, 1995, 126-129); Zamarchi Grassi 1998; Rastrelli 1998, 75-78. For the Cuccumella tomb at Vulci, see Sgubini Moretti 1994, 29-33.

94. Above, nn. 76 and 77.

95. Prayon 1975b, 165-179, pls. 41-46; Colonna and von Hase 1984, with a discussion of the other statues of "*maiores*" (Pietrera, Five Chairs) at 35-41, and a list of thrones in tombs at 55-59; Damgaard Andersen 1993, 45-49, figs. 56a-57d.

96. Hus 1961, 23-35, 98-134, 496-498, pls. 1-3, 17-18: goddess of death, with male demons? (see also above, n. 30); Damgaard Anderson 1993, 49-50, no. 45, fig. 59.

97. Hus 1961, 58-65, no. 1-17, 257-264, pls. 10-11, 29-32. Damgaard Anderson 1993, 50-52, nos. 46-47, fig. 60 interprets them as ancestors, too, but also notes that they have always been found at the entrance of the tombs. In my opinion, the placement at the entrance fits better with an interpretation of the *xoanon* figures as tomb guardians or demonic guides, like the later figures of Vanth and Charun at the doors of tombs. For a goddess in the tomb, cf. also the winged figurines in Damgaard Anderson 1993, 43, fig. 55b. Especially the busts from Chiusi, but sometimes also the Pietrera statues, have been interpreted as mourners or wailing women, perpetuating the ritual lamentation (e.g., Camporeale 1986, 289-290). That interpretation, however, is made difficult by their gestures, which are not unequivocal. Further, in the case of the Pietrera statues, men are present, and the Chiusi busts are apparently only single figures, not parts of a group, and in both cases their large size raises questions (some of the Chiusi busts measure more than 50 cm, the Pietrera statues are even taller).

98. Haynes 1965, 13-25, pls. 6-11; Cristofani 1985, 289, no. 111, pl. 217; Haynes 1991, 3-9, pls. 1-3; Roncalli 1998. It seems plausible to reconstruct the bronze bust from the Isis Tomb with a cylindrical lower part resembling that of the Chiusi statues, but it is impossible to combine the bust with the damaged alabaster stand, as proposed by Roncalli, since the latter is a companion piece to the alabaster "pyxis" from the same tomb and not only has identical measure-

ments but also shows the beginning of the flaring top of the "pyxis"; see Haynes 1991 and Bubenheimer-Erhart forthcoming.

99. *Aryballos* from Marsigliana d'Albegna, ca. 640–620 BCE: *ET*, AV 2.3; Colonna 1996, 182, with bibliography in n. 83; Weber-Lehmann 1997, 173.

100. Nicosia 1969, 369–401, pls. 93–98; Damgaard Andersen 1993, 30–32, no. 24, fig. 37; Bonfante 1986, 99, fig. IV.7; Torelli 1997a, 33, fig. 21.

101. Camporeale 1967, 138–140, pl. C.5; Lilliu 2000, 189–193, 195–196; F. LoSchiavo and M. Bonino in *Mache* 2000, 117–134 and 135–145. The concept of a Realm of the Dead beyond the sea usually has been traced back to the Greek idea of the Isles of the Blest. At least in the Archaic and Classical periods, however, the isles are imagined only as the mythic residence of a few heroes (for the discussion of a supposed voyage by sea in Minoan times, see Sourvinou-Inwood 1995, 45–49) and therefore an improbable model for the Etruscan Beyond. Frequently in ancient religions we find the idea of crossing a river or a lake but not the sea. In the Near East we have the immense mass of fresh water under the earth, the isle of Uta-napishti beyond the ocean, and the Waters of Death in the *Epic of Gilgamesh*, which may have furnished the model for the Greek Isles of the Blest (for the text telling the search for and the story of Uta-napishti, see George 1999, 75–95) but not for a general Realm of the Dead beyond the sea. For a first survey of Near Eastern concepts of death and beyond, see various articles in *Death in Mesopotamia* 1980; Kappler 1987, 47–116; and *Mort* 1982, 349–418; Chiodi 1994.

102. An initial list of models of chariots and chariots in tombs: Ducati 1943, 412–415, but see also Colonna 1980, 188, n. 39. An extensive catalogue of the chariots found in Italy and the problems involved: Carri 1997; Adam 1993, 88.

"Pietra Zannoni": Ducati 1910, 583–586, fig. 46; Meller Padovani 1977, 52–56, no. 25, figs. 45–47. A chariot is also represented on the *stele* of Via Tofane, second phase: Meller Padovani 1977, 44–45, no. 20, figs. 31–32. The tendency of the interpretation has been moved in the past decades to a more "realistic" meaning, an aristocratic parade: Colonna 1980, 188; Sassatelli 1988, 208; Cerchiai 1988, 232–233, fig. 57.1, who compares Assyrian friezes with the royal chariot (fig. 56.1; the whole frieze: Thureau-Dangin and Dunand 1936, Album pl. 49), but that comparison shows exactly the important difference between the two pictures: the Assyrian warrior, who does not hold the reins but a lance, is no taller than the horses and in no case could his head be higher than that of the person in the chariot. The excessive size of the man leading the horses on the *stele* of Zannoni, however, which nearly exceeds the frame and certainly is not attributable to a lack of skill of the sculptor, makes him the dominant figure; he cannot be a groom. Torelli (1986, 173) interpreted the chariot scene on the ivory pyxis from the Tomba della Pania at Chiusi in an eschatological sense; contra: Cristofani 1996, 8–9 (= *Scripta selecta* II 903).

103. Iaia 1999, 142 (English summary); 24–25.

104. Van Gennep 1960, 146.

BIBLIOGRAPHY

This bibliography includes some items not referred to in the text, but cited here to make it more useful for the study in general of the Etruscan Underworld.

Adam, A.-M. 1990. "Vegetation et paysage dans la peinture funérare étrusque." *Ktema* 15, 143–150.

———. 1993. "Les jeux, la chasse et la guerre: La tomba Querciola I de Tarquinia." In *Spectacles sportifs et scéniques dans le monde étrusque-italique: Actes de la table ronde Rome 1991*. Rome. 69–95.

Aellen, C. 1994. *A la recherche de l'ordre cosmique: Forme et fonction des personnifications dans la céramique italiote I*. Kilchberg.

Balty, J. C. 1985. "L'espace dans la peinture funéraire étrusque." *Académie Royale de Belgique: Bulletin de la Classe des Beaux-Arts* 67, 142–168.

Barley, N. 1995. *Dancing on the Grave: Encounters with Death*. London.

Bartoloni, G., F. Buranelli, V. D'Atri, and A. De Santis. 1987. *Le urne a capanna rinvenute in Italia*. Rome.

Batino, S. 1998. "Contributo alla costruzione di una ideologia funeraria etrusca arcaica: I corredi ceretani tra l'Orientalizzante recente e l'età arcaica." *Ostraka* 7, 7–38.

Bažant, J. "Thanatos." *LIMC* VII, 904–908.

Blanck, H. 1985. "Le pitture del "sarcofago del sacerdote" nel Museo Nazionale di Tarquinia" In *Ricerche di pittura ellenistica*. Quaderni dei *DialArch* 1. Rome. 79–84.

Blanck, H., and G. Proietti. 1986. *La Tomba dei Rilievi di Cerveteri*. Rome.

Blome, P. 1986. "Das Opfer des Phersu: Ein etruskischer Sündenbock." *RM* 93, 97–108.

Blumhofer, M. 1993. *Etruskische Cippi*. Cologne.

Bonamici, M. 1998. "Lo stamnos di Vienna 448: Una proposta di lettura." *Prospettiva* 89–90, 2–15.

Bonfante, L. 1986. *Etruscan Life and Afterlife*. Detroit.

———. 1996. "Etruscan Sexuality and Funerary Art." In *Sexuality in Ancient Art*, ed. N. B. Kampen. Cambridge. 155–169.

Bonfante, L., and N. de Grummond. 1989. "Wounded Souls: Etruscan Ghosts and Michelangelo's 'Slaves.'" *AnalRom* 17–18, 99–116.

Bonino, M. 1988. "L'attività navale in età protstorica." In *La formazione della città in Emilia Romagna*. Studi e documenti di Archeologia 4. Bologna. 69–78.

Boosen, M. 1986. *Etruskische Meeresmischwesen*. Rome.

Briguet, M.-F. 1988. *Le sarcophage des Époux de Cerveteri du Musée du Louvre*. Paris.

Briquel, D. 1985 (1987). "Regards étrusques sur l'au-delà." In *La mort, les morts et l'au-delà dans le monde romain: Actes du Colloque de Caen 20–22.11.1985*. Caen. 263–277.

———. 1997. *Chrétiens et haruspices*. Paris.

Briquel, D., and F. Gaultier. 1989–1990. "Rivista di epigrafia etrusca." *StEtr* 56, 361–362.

Brocato, P. 1995. "Sull' origine e lo sviluppo delle prime tombe a dado etrusche." *StEtr* 61, 57–93.

Bruni, S. 1995. "Rituali funerari dell'aristocrazia tarquiniese durante la prima fase orientalizzante." In *Miscellanea in memoria di Giuliano Cremonesi*. Pisa. 213–252.

Bubenheimer-Erhart, F. forthcoming. "Studien zum Isis-Grab von Vulci" (dissertation Heidelberg 2001).

Buranelli, F. 1985. *L'urna Calabresi di Cerveteri*. Rome.

Burkert, W. 1972. *Homo necans*. Berlin.

Camporeale, G. 1967. *La Tomba del Duce*. Florence.

———. 1981. "Achle." *LIMC* I, 200-214.

———. 1986. "Vita privata." In *Rasenna*, 241-308.

———. 1993. "Aperture tarquiniesi nella pittura tardoarcaica di Chiusi." In *La civiltà di Chiusi e del suo territorio. Atti del XVII convegno di studi etruschi ed italici Chianciano Terme. 28.5.-1.6.1989*. Florence. 183-192.

Carri 1997 = *Carri da guerra e principi etruschi*. Catalogue of exhibition Viterbo 24.5.1997-31.1.1998, ed. A. Emiliozzi. Rome.

Cataldi Dini, M. 1986 (1987). "La tomba dei Demoni Azzurri." In *Tarquinia: Ricerche, scavi e prospettive. Atti del Convegno Internazionale Milano 24.-25.6.1986*. Milan. 37-42.

Cerchiai, L. 1980. "La machaira di Achille: Alcune osservazioni a proposito della 'Tomba dei Tori.'" *AION* 2, 25-39.

———. 1987. "Sulle tombe 'del Tuffatore' e 'della Caccia e Pesca': Proposta di una lettura iconologica." *DialArch* ser. 3, 5.2, 113-123.

———. 1988. "Le stele villanoviane." *AION* 10, 227-238.

———. 1995. "Daimones e Caronte sulle stele felsinee." In *Caronte: Un obolo per l'aldilà* (=PP 50, fasc. 3-6). 376-394.

Cherici, A. 1994. "Due cippi chiusini inediti." *ArchCl* 46, 319-329.

Chiodi, S. M. 1994. "Le concezioni dell'oltretomba presso i Sumeri." *MemLinc* ser. 9, vol. 4, fasc. 5.

Coarelli, F. 1985. "Le pitture della Tomba Francois a Vulci. Una proposta di lettura." In *Ricerche di pittura ellenistica*. Quaderni dei *DialArch* 1. Rome. 43-69.

Coen, A. 1991. *Complessi tombali di Cerveteri con urne cinerarie tardo-orientalizzanti*. Florence.

Colonna, G. 1980. "Rapporti artistici tra il mondo paleoveneto e il mondo etrusco." In *Este e la civiltà paleoveneta a cento anni dalle prime scoperte: Atti del XI convegno di studi etruschi ed italici Este—Padova 27.6.-1.7.1976*. Florence. 177-190.

———. 1985a. "Per una cronologia della pittura etrusca di età ellenistica." In *Ricerche di pittura ellenistica*. Quaderni dei *DialArch* 1. Rome. 139-162.

———. 1985b. "Il culto dei morti." In *Civiltà degli Etruschi*, Catalogue of exhibition (Florence 1985), ed. M. Cristofani. Milan. 290-306.

———. 1986. "Urbanistica e architettura." In *Rasenna*, 371-530.

———. 1991. "Riflessioni sul dionismo in Etruria" In *Dionysos: Mito e mistero. Atti del Convegno Internazionale Comacchio 3.-5.11.1989*. Ferrara. 117-155.

———. 1993a. "I sarcofagi chiusini di età ellenistica." In *La civiltà di Chiusi e del suo territorio: Atti del XVII convegno di studi etruschi ed italici Chianciano Terme 28.5.-1.6.1989*. Florence. 337-374.

———. 1993b. "Strutture teatriformi in Etruria." In *Spectacles sportifs et scéniques dans le monde étrusque-italique: Actes de la table ronde Rome 1991*. Rome. 321-347.

———. 1996. "Il *dokanon*, il culto dei Dioscuri e gli aspetti ellenizzanti della religione dei morti nell' Etruria tardo-arcaica." In *Scritti di antichità in memoria di Sandro Stucchi II* (= *StMisc* 29). 165-184.

Colonna, G., and E. Di Paolo. 1997. "Il letto vuoto, la distribuzione del corredo e la "finestra" della Tomba Regolini-Galassi." In *Etrusca et Italica: Scritti in ricordo di Massimi Pallottino I*. Pisa. 131-168.

Colonna, G., and F.-W. von Hase. 1984. "Alle origini della statuaria etrusca: La tomba delle Statue presso Ceri." *StEtr* 52, 13-59.

Comstock, M. B., and C. C. Vermeule. 1976. *Sculpture in Stone: The Greek, Roman and Etruscan Collection of the Museum of Fine Arts Boston*. Boston.

Cristofani, M. 1971. *Le pitture della tomba del Tifone: Monumenti della pittura antica scoperti in Italia sez. I Tarquinii V*. Rome.

———. 1985. *I bronzi degli Etruschi*. Novara.

———. 1987a. "Pittura funeraria e celebrazione della morte: Il caso della Tomba dell' Orco." In *Tarquinia: Ricerche, scavi e prospettive. Atti del Convegno Internazionale Milano 24.-25.6.1986*. Milan. 191-202 (= *Scripta selecta*, 655-680).

———. 1987b. "Il banchetto in Etruria." In *L'alimentazione*. 123-132.

———. 1988-1989. "Dedica ai Dioscuri." *Prospettiva* 53-56, 14-16.

———. 1992. "La ceramografia etrusca fra età tardo-classica ed ellenismo." *StEtr* 58, 89-114.

———. 1995. "Mystai kai bakchoi: Riti di passagio nei krateri volterrani." *Prospettiva* 80, 2-14 (= *Scripta selecta*, 869-888).

———. 1996. "*Paideia, arete e metis*: A proposito delle pissidi della Pania." *Prospettiva* 83-84, 2-9 (= *Scripta selecta*, 889-903).

Cristofani, M., and M. Martelli. 1978. "Fufluns paχies: Sugli aspetti del culto di Bacco in Etruria." *StEtr* 46, 119-133.

d'Agostino, B. 1987. "L'immagine, la pittura e la tomba nell' Etruria arcaica." In *Images et société en Grèce ancienne: L'iconographie comme méthode d'analyse. Actes du Colloque international Lausanne 8.-11.2.1984*. Lausanne. 213-220 (= *Prospettiva* 32, 1983, 2-12).

———. 1988. "Le immagini e la società in Etruria arcaica." In *La parola, l'immagine, la tomba: Atti del Colloquio Internazionale di Capri*. *AION* 10, 217-225.

———. 1993. "La tomba della Scimmia: Per una lettura iconografica delle immagini etrusche." In *La civiltà di Chiusi e del suo territorio: Atti del XVII convegno di studi etruschi ed italici Chianciano Terme 28.5.-1.6.1989*. Florence. 193-202.

Damgaard Andersen, H. 1993. "The Etruscan Ancestral Cult: Its Origin and Development and the Importance of Anthropomorphization." *AnalRom* 21, 7-66.

Death in Mesopotamia 1980 = *Death in Mesopotamia. Papers Read at the XXVIᵉ Rencontre assyriologique internationale*, ed. Bendt Alster. Copenhagen.

de la Genière, J. 1986 (1987). "Rituali funebri e produzione di vasi." In *Tarquinia: Ricerche, scavi e prospettive. Atti del Convegno Internazionale Milano 24.-25.6.1986*. Milan. 203-208.

———. 1986 (1989). "Des usages du cratère." In *Grecs et Ibères au IVᵉ siècle av. J. Chr.: Commerce et iconographie. Actes de la Table ronde tenue à Bordeaux III 16.-18.12.1986*, ed. P. Rouillard and M.-C. Villanueva-Puig. Paris. 271-282.

Del Chiaro, M. 1974. *The Etruscan Funnel Group: A Tarquinian Red-Figured Fabric*. Florence.

De Marinis, S. 1961. *La tipologia del banchetto nell'arte etrusca arcaica*. Rome.

De Puma, R. D. 1993. *Corpus Speculorum Etruscorum USA 2: Boston and Cambridge*. Ames, IA.

———. 1998. "The Etruscan Rhadamanthys?" *EtrStud* 5, 37-52.

De Ruyt, F. 1934. *Charun, démon étrusque de la mort*. Brussels.

Díez de Velasco, F. 1995. *Los caminos de la muerte*. Madrid.
Dizionario = *Dizionario della civiltà etrusca*, ed. M. Cristofani. Florence. 1985.
Dobrowolski, W. 1997. "La tomba della Mercareccia e i problemi connessi." *StEtr* 63, 123-148.
Donderer, M. 1998. "Das etruskische Kopfgefäß in München als Bindeglied zwischen Phersu und Charu(n)." *NumAntC* 27, 105-127.
Drago Troccoli, L. 1997. "Le tombe 419 e 426 del sepolcreto di Grotta Gramiccia a Veio: Contributo alla conoscenza di strutture tombali e ideologia funeraria a Veio tra il VI e il V secolo a.C." In *Etrusca et Italica: Scritti in ricordo di Massimi Pallottino I*. Pisa. 239-280.
Ducati, P. 1910. "Le pietre funerarie felsinee." *MonAnt* 20, 357-728.
———. 1943. "Nuove stele funerarie felsinee." *MonAnt* 39, 373-446.
Elliott, J. A. 1986. "The Mask in Etruscan Religion, Ritual and Theater" (dissertation Florida State University, Tallahassee).
———. 1995. "The Etruscan Wolfman in Myth and Ritual." *EtrSt* 2, 17-33.
Etruscan Painting = S. Steingräber, *Etruscan Painting: Catalogue Raisonné of Etruscan Wall Paintings*, ed. D. Ridgway and F. R. S. Ridgway. New York. 1986.
Felletti Maj, B. M. 1977. *La tradizione italica nell'arte romana 1*. Rome.
Freytag gen. Löringhoff, B. von. 1986. *Das Giebelrelief von Telamon und seine Stellung innerhalb der Ikonographie der "Sieben gegen Theben,"* RM-EH 27. Mainz.
Garland, R. 1985. *The Greek Way of Death*. Ithaca, NY.
Gempeler, R. D. 1974. *Die etruskischen Kanopen*. Einsiedeln.
Gentili, M. D. 1994. *I sarcofagi in terracotta di età recente*. Rome.
George, A. 1999. *The Epic of Gilgamesh*. Harmondsworth.
Graf, F. 1974. *Eleusis und die orphische Dichtung Athens in vorhellenistischer Zeit*. Berlin.
Greifenhagen, A. 1978. "Zeichnungen nach etruskischen Vasen im Deutschen Archäologischen Institut, Rom." *RM* 85, 59-81.
Harari, M. 1988. "Les gardiens de paradis: Iconographie funéraire et iconographie mythologique dans la céramique étrusque à figures rouges tardive." *NumAntCl* 17, 169-193.
———. 1997a. "Tuchulcha." *LIMC* VIII, 97-98.
———. 1997b. "Turms." *LIMC* VIII, 78-111.
Harrison, G., and D. Obbink. 1986. "Vergil, Georgics I 36-39 and the Barcelona Alcestis (P. Barc. In. No. 168-161) 62-65: Demeter in the Underworld." *ZPE* 63, 75-81.
Haynes, S. 1965. "Zwei archaisch-etruskische Bildwerke aus dem 'Isis-Grab' von Vulci." In *AntP* 4. Berlin. 13-25.
———. 1991. "The Bronze Bust from the 'Isis-Tomb' Reconsidered." *StEtr* 57, 3-9.
———. 1993. "Thoughts on the Winged Female Figure in the Funerary Sculpture of Chiusi of the Classical Period." In *La civiltà di Chiusi e del suo territorio: Atti del XVII convegno di studi etruschi ed italici ChiancianoTerme 28.5.-1.6.1989*. Florence. 297-307.
Herbig, R. 1952. *Die jüngeretruskischen Steinsarkophage*. Berlin.
Höckmann, U. 1982. *Die Bronzen aus dem Fürstengrab von Castel San Mariano bei Perugia*. Munich.
Hostetter, E. 1978. "A Bronze Handle from Spina." *RM* 85, 257-281.
Humphreys, S. C., and H. King, eds. 1981. *Mortality and Immortality: The Anthropology and Archaeology of Death*. London.
Hus, A. 1961. *Recherches sur la statuaire en pierre étrusque archaique*. Paris.

———. 1976. *Les siècles d'or de l'histoire étrusque*. Collection Latomus 146. Brussels.
Iaia, C. 1999. *Simbolismo funerario e ideologia alle origini di una civiltà urbana: Forme rituali nelle sepolture "Villanoviane" a Tarquinia e Vulci e nel loro entroterra*. Florence.
Iozzo, M. 1995. "Un cippo chiusino in collezione privata." *StEtr* 61, 45-56.
Izzet, V. 1996. "Engraving the Boundaries: Exploring Space and Surface in Etruscan Funerary Architecture." In *Approaches to the Study of Ritual: Italy and the Ancient Mediterranean*, ed. John Wilkins. London. 55-72.
Jannot, J.-R. 1982. "La tombe de la Mercareccia à Tarquinia." *RBArch* 60, 101-135.
———. 1984a. *Les reliefs archaiques de Chiusi: Collection de l'École Francaise de Rome 71*.
———. 1984b. "Sur les fausses portes étrusques." *Latomus* 43, 273-283.
———. 1985 (1987). "Sur la représentation étrusque des morts." In *La mort, les morts et l' au-delà dans le monde romain: Actes du Colloque de Caen 20.-22.11.1985*. Caen. 279-291.
———. 1986. "La tombe clusienne de Poggio al Moro ou le programme des jeux clusiennes." *Ktema* 11, 189-197.
———. 1988. "À propos de la tombe du Lit Funèbre." In *Studia Tarquiniensia*. Rome. 53-67.
———. 1991. "Charon et Charun: À propos d'un démon funéraire étrusque." *CRAI*, 443-464.
———. 1993. "Phersu, Phersuna, Persona: À propos du masque étrusque." In *Spectacles sportifs et scéniques dans le monde étrusque-italique: Actes de la table ronde Rome 1991*. Rome. 281-320.
———. 1993. "Charun, Tuchulcha et les autres." *RM* 100, 59-81.
———. 1997. "Charu(n) et Vanth, divinités plurielles?" In *LPRH*, 139-166.
———. 1998. *Devins, dieux et démons: Regards sur la religion de l'Étrurie antique*. Paris.
Jeux 1987 = *Les jeux étrusco-italiques: Iconographie et idéologie. Contributions d'une table ronde organisée à l'ENS 21.3.1987*. In *Ktema* 11, 1986, 159-222.
Johnston, S. I. 1999. *Restless Dead: Encounters between the Living and the Dead in Ancient Greece*. Berkeley, CA.
Kappler, C., et al. 1987. *Apocalypses et voyages dans l'au-delà*. Paris.
Krauskopf, I. 1987. *Todesdämonen und Totengötter im vorhellenistischen Etrurien: Kontinuität und Wandel*. Florence.
———. 1988. "Hades/Aita, Calu." *LIMC* IV, 394-399.
———. Forthcoming. "Die Verehrer des Dionysos in Etrurien." In *Miscellanea di studi in memoria di Mauro Cristofani*.
Kurtz, D. C., and J. Boardman. 1971. *Greek Burial Customs*. London.
L'alimentazione 1987 = *L'alimentazione nel mondo antico: Gli Etruschi*. Rome.
Lambrechts, R. 1959. *Essai sur les magistratures des républiques étrusques*. Brussels.
Lilliu, G. 2000. "D'una navicella protosarda nello Heraion di Capo Colonna a Crotone." *RendLinc* ser. 9, 11, 181-216.
LPRH = F. Gaultier and D. Briquel, eds., *Les Étrusques, les plus religieux des hommes: État de la recherche sur la religion étrusque. Actes du colloque international Grand Palais 17-18-19 novembre 1992. XII^{er} Rencontres de l'École du Louvre*. Paris.

Mache 2000 = *Mache: La battaglia del Mare Sardonio: Studi e ricerche,* ed. P. Bernardini, P. G. Spanu, and R. Zucca. Cagliari.

Maetzke, G. 1993. "Tre canopi inediti da Sarteano." In *La civiltà di Chiusi e del suo territorio: Atti del XVII convegno di studi etruschi ed italici Chianciano Terme 28.5.-1.6.1989.* Florence. 133-148.

Maggiani, A. 1993. "Problemi della scultura funeraria a Chiusi." In *La civiltà di Chiusi e del suo territorio: Atti del XVII convegno di studi etruschi ed italici Chianciano Terme 28.5.-1.6.1989.* Florence. 149-169.

———. 1994. "Tombe con prospetto architettonico nelle necropoli rupestri d'Etruria." In *Tyrrhenoi philotechnoi: Atti della giornata di studio Viterbo 13.10.1990,* ed. Marina Martelli. Rome. 1994. 121-159.

———. 1997. "Reflexions sur la réligion étrusque "primitive": De l'époque villanovienne à l' époque archaique." In *LPRH,* 431-447.

———. 1997. "Variazioni sul tema della tomba a dado: La necropoli rupestre di Case Rocchi a Sorano." *RdA* 21, 38-43.

———. 1997. "Modello etico o antenato eroico? Sul motivo di Aiace suicida nelle stele felsinee." *StEtr* 63, 149-165.

Manakidou, E. 1994. "Perithoos." *LIMC* VII, 232-242.

Manino, L. 1980. "Semantica e struttura della figura demonica nel pittore orvietano della 'Vanth.'" *AnnFaina* 1, 59-72.

Markussen, E. P. 1993. *Painted Tombs in Etruria: A Catalogue.* AnalRom Suppl. 17. Rome.

Martelli, A., and L. Nasorri 1998. "La tomba dell'Iscrizione nella necropoli di Poggio Renzo." In *AION* n.s. 5, *Studi su Chiusi arcaica,* ed. Patrizia Gastaldi. 81-101.

Mastrocinque, A. 1991. "Giganti silenici in Grecia e in Etruria." In *Dionysos: Mito e mistero. Atti del Convegno Internazionale Comacchio 3.-5.11.1989.* Ferrara. 277-291.

Mavleev, E. 1994. "Phersipnai." *LIMC* VII, 329-332.

Mavleev, E., and I. Krauskopf. 1986. "Charon/Charu(n)." *LIMC* III, 225-236.

Meller Padovani, P. 1977. *Le stele villanoviane di Bologna.* Capo di Ponte.

Metcalf, P., and R. Huntington. 1991. *Celebrations of Death: The Anthropology of Mortuary Ritual.* 2nd ed. Cambridge.

Meuli, K. 1946. "Griechische Opferbräuche." In *Phyllobolia für Peter Von der Mühll zum 60. Geburtstag.* Basel. 201-209 (= *Gesammelte Schriften* II. Basel 1975. 924-932).

Minetti, A. 1998. "La tomba della Pania: Corredo e rituale funerario." In *AION* n.s. 5, *Studi su Chiusi arcaica,* ed. P. Gastaldi. 27-56.

Morandi, A. 1983. *Le pitture della tomba del Cardinale: Monumenti della pittura antica scoperti in Italia sez. I Tarquinii fasc. VI.* Rome.

Morandi, M., and G. Colonna. 1995. "La gens titolare della tomba tarquiniese dell'Orco." *StEtr* 61, 95-102.

Moretti, M. 1961. *La Tomba della Nave.* Milan.

Moretti, M., and A. M. Sgubini Moretti. 1983. *I Curunas di Tuscania.* Rome.

Moretti Sgubini, A. M. 1985 (1989). "Tomba a casa con portico nella necropoli di Pian di Mola a Tuscania." In *Atti del Secondo Congresso Internazionale Etrusco Firenze 26.5.-2.6.1985.* Rome. 321-335.

Morigi Govi, C., and G. Sassatelli. 1993. "Il sepolcreto etrusco del Polisportivo di Bologna: Nuove stele funerarie." *Ocnus* 1, 103-124.

Mort 1982 = *La mort, les morts dans les sociétés anciennes,* directed by G. Gnoli and J.-P. Vernant. Cambridge.

Moscati, P. 1997. "Un gruppo di urne volterrane con rappresentazione del 'viaggio agli inferi in carpentum.'" In *Etrusca et Italica: Scritti in ricordo di Massimo Pallottino* II. Pisa. 403-423.

Mugione, E. 1995. "Le raffigurazioni di Caronte in età greca." In *Caronte: Un obolo per l'aldilà* (= *PP* 50, fasc. 3-6). 357-375.

Murlo 1994 = *Murlo and the Etruscans: Art and Society in Ancient Etruria,* ed. R. D. De Puma and J. P. Small. Madison, Wisc.

Nicosia, F. 1969. "Il cinerario di Montescudaio." *StEtr* 37, 369-401.

Nielsen, M. 1989. "Women and Family in a Changing Society: A Quantitative Approach to Late Etruscan Burials." *AnalRom* 17-18, 53-98.

Oakley, J. 1994. "Sisyphos I." *LIMC* VII, 781-787.

Pairault Massa, F.-H. 1985. "Problemi di lettura della pittura funeraria di Orvieto." In *Ricerche di pittura ellenistica.* Quaderni dei *DialArch* 1. Rome. 19-42.

———. 1988. "La tombe Giglioli ou l'espoir déçu de Vel Pinie: Un tournant dans la société étrusque." In *Studia Tarquiniensia.* Rome. 69-100.

———. 1992. *Iconologia e politica nell'Italia antica: Roma, Lazio, Etruria dal VII al I secolo a.C.* Milan.

———. 1998. "Libri Acherontici—sacra Acheruntia: Culture grecque et Etrusca disciplina." *AnnFaina* 5, 83-103.

Pallottino, M. 1987. "Il fregio dei Vibenna e le sue implicazioni storiche." In *Tomba François,* 225-233.

Paolucci, G. 1988. "La diffusione dei tumuli nell'area chiusina e l'errata provenienza della seconda pisside della Pania." In *AION* n.s. 5, *Studi su Chiusi arcaica,* ed. P. Gastaldi. 11-26.

Paribeni, E. 1986. "Di alcuni chiaramenti e di un quiz non risolto." *NumAntCl* 15, 43-60.

Pensa, M. 1977. *Rappresentazioni dell'oltretomba nella ceramica apula.* Rome.

Pfiffig, A. 1975. *Religio Etrusca.* Graz.

Pittura etrusca = *Pittura etrusca al Museo di Villa Giulia.* Rome 1989.

Pittura Orvieto = *Pittura etrusca a Orvieto: Le tombe di Settecamini e degli Hescanas a un secolo della scoperta. Documenti e materiali.* Rome. 1982.

Pontrandolfo, A. 1995. "Simposio e élites sociali nel mondo etrusco e italico." In *In vino veritas,* ed. O. Murray and M. Tecusan. London. 176-195.

Pontrandolfo, A., and A. Rouveret. 1992. *Le tombe dipinte di Paestum.* Modena.

Prayon, F. 1974. "Zum ursprünglichen Aussehen und zur Deutung des Kultraumes in der Tomba delle Cinque Sedie bei Cerveteri." *MarWPr,* 1-15.

———. 1975a. *Frühetruskische Grab- und Hausarchitektur.* RM-EH 22. Heidelberg.

———. 1975b. "Zur Datierung der drei frühetruskischen Sitzstatuetten aus Cerveteri." *RM* 82, 165-179.

———. 1977. "Todesdämonen und die Troilossage in der frühetruskischen Kunst." *RM* 84, 181-197.

———. 1989. "L'architettura funeraria etrusca: La situazione attuale delle ricerche e problemi aperti." In *Atti del Secondo Congresso Internazionale Etrusco Firenze 26.5.-2.6.1985.* Rome. 441-449.

Proietti, G. 1977. "Rivista di epigrafia etrusca." *StEtr* 45, 293, no. 24.

Rafanelli, S. 1997. "Altare su podio a gradini: Nota su un cippo funerario dell' "Antiquarium" di Vulci." *RdA* 21, 33-37.

Rasenna = *Rasenna: Storia e civiltà degli Etruschi*, ed. G. Pugliese Carratelli, M. Pallottino, et al. Milan. 1986.

Rastrelli, A. 1998. "La necropli di Poggio Gaiella." In *AION* n.s. 5, *Studi su Chiusi arcaica*, ed. P. Gastaldi. 57-79.

Rathje, A. 1994. "Banquet and Ideology: Some Considerations about Banqueting at Poggio Civitate." In *Murlo* 1994, 95-99.

———. 1995. "Il banchetto in Italia Centrale: Quale stile di vita?" In *In vino veritas*, ed. O. Murray and M. Tecusan. London. 167-175.

Rendeli, M. 1996. "Anagoghe." *Prospettiva* 83-84, 10-29.

Richardson, E. H. 1977. "The Wolf in the West." *JWalt* 36 (= *Essays in Honor of Dorothy Kent Hill*, ed. D. m. Buitron et al.), 91-101.

Riva, C. 1998 (1999). "Funerary Ritual, Cultural Identity and Memory in Orientalising South Etruria." In *Proceedings of the XVth International Congress of Classical Archaeology, Amsterdam, July 12-17, 1998*. Amsterdam. 331-335.

Robertson, M. 1988. "Eurynomos." *LIMC* IV, 109.

Roncalli, F. 1990. "La definizione pittorica dello spazio tombale nella 'età della crisi.' " In *Crise et transformation des sociétés archaiques de l'Italie antique au Ve siècle av. J.-C.: Actes de la table ronde organisée par l'École Francaise de Rome et l'Unité de recherches étrusco-italiques associée au CNRS, Rome 19-21 novembre 1987*. Rome. 229-243.

———. 1990 (1994). "Cultura religiosa, strumenti e pratiche cultuali nel santuario di Cannicella a Orvieto." In *Tyrrhenoi philotechnoi: Atti della giornata di studio Viterbo 13.10.1990*, ed. Marina Martelli. Rome. 99-118.

———. 1996. "Laris Pulenas and Sisyphos: Mortals, Heroes and Demons in the Etruscan Underworld." *EtrStud* 3, 45-64.

———. 1997. "Iconographie funéraire et topographie de l'au-delà en Étrurie." In *LPRH* 37-54.

———. 1998. "Una immagine femminile di culto dalla 'Tomba d'Iside' di Vulci." *AnnFaina* 5, 15-39.

Rouveret, A. 1988. "Espace sacré/espace pictural: Une hypothèse sur quelques peintures archaiques de Tarquinia." In *La parola, l'immagine, la tomba: Atti del Colloquio Internazionale di Capri*, *AION* 10, 203-216.

Sarian, H. 1986. "Erinys." *LIMC* III, 825-843.

Sassatelli, G. 1984. "Una nuova stele felsinea." In *Culture figurative e materiali tra Emilia e Marche: Studi in memoria di Mario Zuffa*, ed. P. Delbianco. Rimini. 107-137.

———. 1988. "Topografia e 'sistemazione monumentale' delle necropoli felsinee." In *La formazione della città preromana in Emilia Romagna: Atti del convegno di studi Bologna/Marzabotto 7-8.12.1985*. 197-255.

———. 1989. "Problemi cronologici delle stele felsinee alla luce dei rispettivi corredi tombali." In *Atti del Secondo Congresso Internazionale Etrusco Firenze 26.5.-2.6.1985*. Rome 1989. 927-949.

———. 1991 (1993). "Rappresentazioni di giochi atletici in monumemti funerari d' area padana." In *Spectacles*, 45-67.

Schäfer, T. 1989. *Imperii Insignia: Sella curulis and fasces*, *RM-EH* 29. Mainz.

Scheffer, C. 1988 (1991). "Harbingers of Death? The Female Demon in Late Etruscan Funerary Art." In *Munuscula Romana: Papers Read at a Conference in Lund (1.-2.10.1988) in Celebration of the Re-opening of the Swedish Institute in Rome*, ed. A.-M. Leander Touati, E. Rystedt, and O. Wikander. Stockholm. 51-63.

———. 1994. "The Arched Door in Late Etruscan Funerary Art." In *Murlo* 1994, 196-210.

Scott Ryberg, I. 1955. *Rites of the State Religion in Roman Art*, *MAAR* 22.

Scripta selecta = M. Cristofani, *Scripta selecta: Trenta anni di studi archeologici sull'Italia preromana* II. Pisa. 2001.

Sgubini Moretti, A. M. 1994. "Ricerche archeologiche a Vulci: 1985-1990." In *Tyrrhenoi philotechnoi: Atti della giornata di studio Viterbo 13.10.1990*, ed. Marina Martelli. Rome. 9-46.

Simon, E. 1973. "Die Tomba dei Tori und der etruskische Apollonkult." *JdI* 88, 27-42.

———. 1997. "Sentiment religieux et vision de la mort chez les Étrusques dans les derniers siècles de leur histoire." In *LPRH*, 449-457.

Small, J. P. "Eat, Drink, and Be Merry: Etruscan Banquets." In *Murlo* 1994, 85-94.

Sourvinou-Inwood, C. 1986. "Charon I." *LIMC* III, 210-225.

———. 1987. "Images grecques de la mort: représentations, imaginaire, histoire." *AION* 9, 145-158.

———. 1995. "Reading" Greek Death: To the End of the Classical Period. Oxford.

Spectacles = *Spectacles sportifs et scéniques dans le monde étrusque-italique: Actes de la table ronde Rome 1991*. Rome. 1993.

Spinola, G. 1987. "Vanth: Osservazioni iconografiche." *RdA* 11, 56-67.

Staccioli, R. A. 1980. "Le finte porte dipinte nelle tombe arcaiche etrusche." *Quaderni dell'Istituto di Archeologia e Storia Antica, Libera Università Abbruzzese degli Studi "G. d'Annunzio," Chieti* 1, 1-17.

Steingräber, S. 1982. "Überlegungen zu etruskischen Altären." In *Miscellanea Archaeologica Tobias Dohrn dedicata*. Rome. 103-116.

———. 1992 (1997). "Le culte des morts et les monuments de pierre des nécropoles étrusques." In *LPRH*, 97-116.

———. 1995. "Funerary Architecture in Chiusi." *EtrSt* 2, 53-83 (= "L'architettura funeraria chiusina." In *La civiltà di Chiusi e del suo territorio: Atti del XVII convegno di studi etruschi ed italici Chianciano Terme 28.5.-1.6.1989*. Florence. 1993. 171-182).

———. 1996. "New Discoveries and Research in Southern Etruscan Rock Tombs." *EtrStud* 3, 75-104.

Stopponi, S. 1968. "Parapetasmata etrusche." *BdA* 53, 60-62.

———. 1983. *La Tomba della "Scrofa Nera."* Rome.

Stucchi, S. 1986. "Il motivo del *prosbainein* su una nuova stele di Bologna." *RendLinc*, ser. 8, 40, 99-102.

Thuillier, J. P. 1985. *Les jeux athlétiques dans la civilisation étrusque*. *BEFAR* 256. Rome.

———. 1997. "Un relief archaique inédit de Chiusi." *RA*. 243-260.

Thureau-Dangin, F., and M. Dunand. 1936. *Til-Barsip*. Paris.

Tomba François = *La Tomba François di Vulci*, Catalogue of exhibition, Vatican Museums, 20.3.-17.5.1987, ed. F. Buranelli. Rome. 1987.

Torelli, M. 1975. *Elogia Tarquiniensia*. Florence.

———. 1985. "Ideologia e rappresentazione nelle tombe tarquiniesi dell'Orco I e II." In *Ricerche di pittura ellenistica*. Quaderni dei *DialArch* 1. Rome. 7-17.

———. 1986. "La religione." In *Rasenna*, 159-237.

———. 1997a. *Il rango, il rito e l'immagine:Alle origini della rappresentazione storica romana*. Milan.

———. 1997b. "Limina Averni: Realtà e rappresentazione nella pittura tarquiniese arcaica." *Ostraka* 6, 1997, 63-93 (= Torelli 1997a, 122-151, with minor corrections).

Valenza Mele, N. 1981. "La necropoli cumana di VI e V A.C. o la crisi di una aristocrazia." In *Nouvelle contribution à l'étude de la société et de la colonisation Eubéennes: Cahiers du centre Jean Bérard* 6. Naples. 97-130.

van Essen, C. C. 1927. *Did Orphic Influence on Etruscan Tomb Paintings Exist? Studies in Etruscan Tomb Paintings* 1. Amsterdam.

van Gennep, A. 1960. *The Rites of Passage*, tr. M. B. Vizedom and G. L. Caffee, Chicago.

Vermeule, E. 1979. *Aspects of Death in Early Greek Art and Poetry*. Berkeley, CA.

Walberg, C. 1986. "The Tomb of the Baron Reconsidered." *StEtr* 54, 51-59.

Weber, W. 1978. *Die Darstellungen einer Wagenfahrt auf römischen Sarkophagen und Loculusplatten des 3. und 4. Jahrhunderts n. Chr.* Rome.

Weber-Lehmann, C. 1985. "Spätarchaische Gelagebilder in Tarquinia." *RM* 92, 19-44.

———. 1989. "Beobachtungen zur Tomba 5513 in Tarquinia." In *Atti del Secondo Congresso Internazionale Etrusco Firenze 26.5.-2.6.1985*, 2. Rome. 733-740.

———. 1994. "Theseus/These." *LIMC* VII, 951-955.

———. 1995. "Polyphem in der Unterwelt? Zur Tomba dell'Orco II in Tarquinia." *RM* 102, 71-100.

———. 1997. "Die sogenannte Vanth von Tuscania: Seirene anasyromene." *JdI* 112, 191-246.

Weege, F. 1921. *Etruskische Malerei*. Halle.

Zamarchi Grassi, P., ed. 1992. *La Cortona dei Principes*. Catalogue of exhibition, Cortona, Palazzo Casali 1992. Cortona.

———. 1998. "Un edificio per il culto funerario: Nuovi dati sul tumulo II del Sodo a Cortona." *RdA* 22, 19-26.

CHAPTER VI

VOTIVE OFFERINGS IN ETRUSCAN RELIGION

Jean MacIntosh Turfa

Votive religion touches upon basic human needs and the innermost prayers of all, from rulers to slaves. The material remnants of Etruscan votives, after two millennia in Tuscan soil, represent only a tiny fraction of all the ceremony, belief, and sacrifice that went into their dedication. In 1981, Comella was able to count 161 deposits of the fourth to first century BCE in Etruria and Latium, and in 1985, the exhibition *Santuari d'Etruria* considered nearly 80 sanctuary sites of all periods.[1] By now the number of significant votive deposits of all periods exceeds 200. Unfortunately, most were either exposed and dispersed long ago or occur in areas like Tarquinii or Vulci, where the subsequent history of a rich metropolis has written over the earlier traces.

In our efforts to interpret votive gifts, our understanding is easily colored by modern beliefs; we expect that acts of kindness and proselytizing will most please the divine, but, from the archaeological evidence, it appears as though the gods of the Mediterranean wanted *things*. As Barker and Rasmussen put it, "No-one approached the gods empty-handed."[2] In fact, it is not so much the gifts but the activity, the public ceremony of a majority of worshipers, that defines ancient votive religion. A survey of major votive deposits within Etruria, followed by possible interpretations of votive offerings in their artistic and religious contexts, is offered here to augment the analysis of Etruscan religion. The survey is prefaced by a general description of Mediterranean votive practices, including votive offerings of other cultures.

The origins of Etruscan votive religion are to be sought in protohistoric Italy. Excavation at Tarquinii Pian di Civita has shown that votive offerings were made at sacred places during the Protovillanovan and Villanovan periods, as will be discussed below. A continuity of preference for certain types of objects characterizes the earliest days to the latest, and by the time foreign sanctuaries were established in Italy (as at Greek colonies or at Graviscae), votive cult had been flourishing in Etruria for centuries. When, near the end of the fourth century, healing requests escalated dramatically, these were not attached to Greek Asklepios but to native gods like Vei, Uni, Turan, and Menerva. It appears that these functions had already been the province of Italian (Etruscan and Italic) gods and that models of body parts simply became popular as urban populations rose and, with them, industrial production of terracottas. The terracotta anatomical models depicted a number of types and organs not found in Greek sanctuaries, with regional styles of medical illustration distinguishing the coroplastic industries of different Etruscan/Latin cities, again, a token of a longstanding native tradition.

It is no wonder, if Etruscans had been presenting their native gods with gifts for centuries, that when they learnt to inscribe them, the formulae of dedication showed an easy familiarity. For instance, votaries addressed *cel ati* (Mother Cel), as in the set of five bronze figurines from a deposit at Castiglione del Lago, which all proclaim *mi cels atial celθi* (*ET*, Co 4.1–5).[3]

A bronze bird from Volaterrae announces that Fel Supri gave him "to Grandmother Cel" (*clz tatanus*; *ET*, Vt 4.5).[4] The inscriptions demonstrate that votives were the material tokens of a very lengthy public—and personal—process, which today must be interpreted with reference to Greek and Roman literary and epigraphic documentation.

THE CLASSICAL VOW

The public act of dedicating an offering was the core of a personal ritual, to judge from ancient terminology. Ample similarities in the record of Etruscan and Latin deposits are grounds for extrapolating from known Roman terms.[5] *Votum** represents a formal vow, made publicly, and couched in somewhat legalistic language. The Roman prayer was accompanied with a promise: *do ut des*, "I am giving so that you will give." A suppliant might inscribe the promise on a tablet and tie it to the knee of a statue; if the god fulfilled the bargain, a public offering was made. There was a formal succession of events: proclamation and inscription of the vow, fulfillment of the god's implied promise, and public recognition of this with the display of the promised offering. Extra promises made on the battlefield, in shipwreck, or in childbirth presumably occasioned a single, public trip to make a thank offering. On the level of the city, a general might vow a temple worthy of victory in battle, as attributed to Themistokles and Gelon at the battles of Salamis and Himera in 480, or the temple dedicated to Bellona Victrix by Appius Claudius Caecus in 296.[6] The Pyrgi plaques might be our one Etruscan token of such an event, possibly the erection of a temple by the *mlk 'l Kysry* ("ruler of Caere") after Astarte "supported him [in his reign]."[7]

As Pfiffig and others have indicated,[8] we seek in vain for certainty in Latin terms such as *stips*, which contained coins; or *favissae*,* underground vaults or cisterns, yet now often used of any pit or trench in which votives were buried; or *mundus*,* a special hole in the earth through which offerings were passed to the chthonic gods. Greek terminology includes *bothros** for a formal offering pit and *anathemata* for objects, specifically, statues, "set up" in sanctuaries, emphasizing the aspect of public display of the gifts. Since none of the terms is strictly Etruscan, it is safer to eschew them. Often, votives in considerable numbers have been found lying in spread fill, atop or around altars, as at Lavinium, Tredici Altari.[9] (In some cases, worshipers must have crunched old votives underfoot as they walked in a *temenos*.*)

Roman inscriptions show formulae for votive dedications that illustrate the public oath and the timing of the gift, as a thank offering and proof that the request had been fulfilled. Common phrases or acronyms include *v(otum) s(olvit)* ("[he] fulfilled the vows"); *v(otum) s(olvit) l(aetus) l(ibens) m(erito)* ("[he] fulfilled the vows willingly, deservedly"); *v(otum) p(osuit) l(ibens) m(erito)* ("[he] completed the vows willingly, deservedly"). This condition of donation of the votive after the request had been granted fits not only human nature but the evidence of the ancient *tabella votiva* recorded in verse in Book 6 of the *Palatine Anthology*.[10] While not Etruscan, these verses do illustrate general conditions of vows, as well as the ephemeral or perishable nature of many offerings.

> To Glaukos, Nereus, and Melikertes . . . and to the Samothracian gods, do I, Lucillius, saved from the deep, offer these locks clipped from my head, for I have nothing else (Lucian 6.164).

> The head-kerchief and water-blue veil of Ampharete rest on thy head, Eileithyia; for them she vowed to thee when she prayed thee to keep dreadful death far away from her in her labor (Nicias 6.270).

> The two oxen are mine and they helped to grow the corn. Be kind, Demeter, and receive them, though they be of dough and not from the herd. Grant that my real oxen may live, and fill my fields with sheaves . . . for the years of thy husbandman . . . are already four-score and four. He never reaped rich Corinthian harvests, but never tasted bitter poverty . . . (Macedonius 6.40).

> Once more, Eileithyia, come at Lykainis' call, easing thus the pangs of labor. This, my Queen, she bestows on thee for a girl, but may thy perfumed temple afterwards receive from her something else for a boy (Callimachus 6.146).

Vertumnus, in Propertius' elegy (Propertius 4.2; Appendix B, Source no. VI.1), says that he is given the first fruits and that "here the grafter pays his vows with a wreath of orchard stuff, when his pear tree has lent an unwilling stock of apples." His allusions to being clothed like people of various occupations probably refer to gifts left by members of these trades: silk of Kos, toga, sickle, arms, reaper's basket, birding twig, fishing rod, peddler's tunic, shepherd's crook, baskets of roses, or vegetables. As yet, there are no offerings to Vertumnus/Voltumna inscribed in Etruscan. Extant inscriptions are generally terse, as in a second-century bronze figurine from Montalcino, which proclaims: θa: cencnei: θuplθaś / l. calzniś śuvluśi zana menaχe ("Thana Cencnei: of Thufltha. Of Larth Calzni for Suvlu the offering was made.").[11]

Modern Christian votives placed in churches in Europe and the Mediterranean are generally thank offerings, too.[12] Their inscribed acronyms proclaim *v.f.g.* or *v.r.g.*: "*voto fatto grazie*" and "*voto ricevuto grazie*" ("Vow made, thanks." "Vow received, thanks."). A tantalizing hint of lost archaeological treasure are the shrines of Malta and shops of Cyprus, where votive images of wax are displayed. Many ancient *vota*

VI.1. Bronze Chimaera statue from Arezzo, inscribed tinścvil. *Fourth century* BCE. *Florence, Museo Archeologico Nazionale Inv. 69 750. (Photo: Florence, Museo Archeologico.)*

or *tabellae votivae* commemorated the ending of something, such as a dangerous voyage or a lifetime of work, when writing, fishing, or medical equipment was left at the sanctuary upon the retirement of a scribe, a fisherman, or a doctor. Other occasions were passage to puberty, offering of a prize just won, victory in or survival of war, illness, childbirth, or a good harvest.[13]

SITES AND TYPES OF OFFERINGS

Votive offerings, tokens of individual vows, appear in urban and rural, extramural or extraurban, spring-, lake-, mountain-, cave-, and seashore-oriented sites, as well as state and private cults, thus all the categories of sacred places recognized by Edlund (1987a). Nearly all cultic gods received individuals' gifts. Even after the abandonment of shrine and city, as at Pyrgi, Graviscae, and Veii, votive rites continued in ruined cult buildings, even when there were no cult functionaries on hand to care for the offerings.[14]

A sacred place may have incorporated pits, a temple or less formal cult building, an altar, enclosure wall, or natural landmark such as a spring or cave. A single one of these features was sufficient to occasion the placement of offerings by multiple visitors. Few objects were considered inappropriate for dedication, although mirrors are among the few deliberate omissions.[15] Admitting differences of style and economics, nearly all the Etruscan offerings have counterparts in the well-documented Greek cults.

Cult equipment may be differentiated from private offerings, because the majority of votives almost certainly were never used again. Donors sometimes gave useful metalware,

VI.2. Bronze statuette, small boy, from the region of Lake Trasimene, inscribed fereś tec sanśl cver. *Third century* BCE. *Vatican Museums. (Photo, DAI Rome f1 254.)*

like the fifth-century bronze incense shovel in New York, which proclaims *mi selvansel: smucinθiunaitula*.[16] Many vases may have been personal items brought for celebration and deliberately left behind. At Greek sanctuaries, anything used in the course of a ceremony became sacred and could not be removed from the *temenos*.[17]

Many familiar bronze sculptures today viewed as emblems of Etruscan culture were created or deposited as votive objects, and thus they were the products of a commercial, as well as an ideological, system, for instance:

- Fig. VI.1. The fourth-century Chimaera of Arezzo, discovered in 1553, and probably part of a large group, had been inscribed in the wax before casting, *tinścvil*, "gift of Tin[ia]."[18]
- The over-life-sized *Arringatore* ("Orator"), found in 1566, probably came from a sanctuary of the god Tece near Trasimene; his cloak, inscribed in letters of the first century BCE, notes that he was given in honor of Aule Meteli.[19]
- Statuettes of chubby little boys, dedicated to Tec Sanś (Fig. VI.2) and Thufltha, are offerings of the Hellenistic period, the type known from Trasimene, Tarquinii, Vulci, Cortona and Caere.[20]
- The so-called Mars of Todi (Fig. IV.15) is a votive. Its inscription in the Umbrian language (*ahal trutitis donum dede*) takes it into the realm of Italic cult.[21]

VI.3. *Bronze statuette, female offrant with bunch of flowers. Late fifth century BCE. London, British Museum. (By permission, Trustees of the British Museum.)*

VI.4. *Bronze figurine, female offrant. Third century BCE. Florence, Museo Archeologico Nazionale Inv. 554 (Photo: Sopintendenza Archeologica per la Toscana-Firenze.)*

- Figs. VI.3 and 5. Figurines portray gods, worshipers, and priests, such as the Plowman from Arezzo (Fig. VII.2)[22] and the dedication by Vel Sveitus (Fig. III.9); the janiform dedication of Velia Cvinti to Culśanś (Fig. II.9);[23] and the figurine of Apulu, given to Spulare Aritimi by Fasti Riufri, on behalf of her son.[24]
- Uninscribed bronzes such as the graceful ladies now in the British Museum (Fig. VI.3), a refined female offrant in Florence (Fig. VI.4) and a wreathed male with *patera** in the British Museum (Fig. VI.5),[25] though bereft of provenance, must have been offered at Etruscan shrines.

Famous names appear among the dedicators of the sixth century BCE, evoking images of the heyday of Etruscan foreign trade with the anchor dedicated (in Greek) by Sostratos at Graviscae,[26] or vases placed at Veii by the Vipenas brothers from the era of the *condottieri*.[27] The offerings of generations of the Tulumnes (Tolumnii) family[28] and large monuments like the *Elogia tarquiniensia*[29] are part of a continuum with Roman votive worship, for which Roman authors acknowledged Etruscan inspiration.

BACKGROUND: VOTIVE RELIGION IN ITALIC, GREEK, AND LEVANTINE/PUNIC CULTS

A review of other cultures shows how much Etruscan votive religion was part of a general Mediterranean phenomenon, as well as where it differed.

VI.5. *Bronze figurine, male offrant. Second century* BCE *London, British Museum. (By permission, Trustees of the British Museum.)*

Italic and Related Cults

In the large Sant'Omobono deposit in Rome, precursor to the famous temples of Mater Matuta and Fortuna, in addition to vases and valuables were the bones of sacrifices, meals with the remains of food (mainly legumes and grain), or both, a reminder of a bounty of first fruits, homemade treats, and perhaps communal meals, now vanished.[30] This is paralleled in other Latin sites and suggestive of the public and participatory aspect of votive rites.[31]

The Venetic peoples evinced a distinctive character, in a preference for the use of bronze for figurines and cut-out plaques depicting human organs such as eyes and limbs.[32] Special designs have been recognized for the Adriatic territory, for instance, an Archaic anatomical votive in a composite style, a leg with architectural molding, and a bird finial.[33]

Southern Italic votive religion reflects the proximity of Greek settlements in its use of Greek vase types and terracotta figurines, but even in the late period (fourth–second century BCE), strong similarities to contemporary Etruria remain, in the form of terracotta statues and anatomical models, as at the Belvedere of Lucera.[34]

Greece and East Greek Deposits

Greek votive tradition was rooted in its own Bronze Age practices. Hägg has pointed out the ideological continuity of votives made of foil or in miniature and deposited in Aegean caves with the sculptural array dedicated during the Classical period.[35] Snodgrass and Simon have commented on a dramatic increase in votive offerings at many Ionian and mainland sanctuaries during the later eighth and seventh centuries,[36] when the varied aspects of Greek life were reflected in offerings, as if the identity of the donor was relevant to the gift. These comprise jewelry, combs, mirrors, arms and armor, fishing and weaving equipment, musical instruments, and magical and symbolic offerings. The majority of votives were ceramics obtained on site, which has suggested to some that the cult's hierarchy had some tangible interest in manufacture and exchange of votives.[37]

In the Samian Heraion, the offerings of the common man or sailor often appear, with wooden boat models and "naturalia" of seashells, minerals, or rare animal bones, from hippo teeth to leopard skins;[38] similar things fill the treasuries of Medieval cathedrals. The find of a small votive deposit of coral in a vase at Graviscae may have significance within the gardens of Adonis.[39]

Terracotta figurines were common votives from the end of the seventh century through the Hellenistic period; many in Greek sanctuaries are more carefully executed than those found in Etruscan or Levantine cults.[40] Etruria has yet to provide examples of votive display in houses, as known for Greece and Rome, although occasionally figurines found in residential districts have been attributed to domestic cult. Dedications were often inscribed and displayed for centuries or protected by their home cities in treasuries at Greek international and panhellenic sanctuaries. (Might there have been treasuries at Lucus Feroniae or the Fanum Voltumnae?)[41]

Trophies of war or adventure, such as the chest that saved Kypselos or ships taken in naval battles, were favored by the politically inclined Greek elite.[42] Graphic examples are the helmets taken from Etruscan marines at the battle of Cumae, inscribed in Olympia by "Hieron and the Syracusans."[43] Still earlier Etruscan arms and armor have been identified in many Greek sanctuaries. Villanovan crested helmets, a sword, greaves, spears, and many shields in Delphi, Olympia, and Samos were almost certainly trophies of Greek colonialist aggression.[44] Fibulae probably represent offerings of pilgrims or merchants from Italy, donations of their clothing or native costume.[45] The phenomenon of Greek dedication of bucchero pottery may be explained as fascination with an alien fabric.[46]

Many sanctuaries were peopled with monumental sculpture like the *korai** of the Athenian Acropolis or Kleobis and Biton at Delphi. Greek dedicants were more inclined than Etruscans to offer stone monumental sculpture and relief plaques.[47] The presence of (fragmentary) Vulcian tripods on the Athenian Acropolis might stem from an official presentation.[48] In the seventh–sixth century, Greek sanctuaries received Phoenician silver bowls, bronze griffin cauldrons, tridacna shell cosmetic compacts, and bronze hand mirrors.[49] All these goods are well known in Etruria—in tombs—yet seldom seen in votive contexts.

Levantine, Punic Cults

In the Levant, Cyprus, and Punic regions, vanished elements such as incense, music, musicians and dance were indispensable parts of the cult. Dedications of personal belongings, valuables, and statues appeared beside small terracottas of execrable aesthetic quality, such as the *dea Syria gravida* from Archaic Dor.[50] A Bronze Age tradition of gilded or silver flesh on bronze votive figures was continued for centuries.[51] Phoenico-Punic votives were inscribed with the exact purpose of the dedication, in stock phrases that signal the votive act, for example, "because she has heard his prayer."[52] The offering of the "best loved" in the *tophet* (infant sacrifice shrine) was not accompanied by more than a token vase, amulet, or small animal, and the ritual has no archaeological correlate in Etruria.[53]

CHRONOLOGICAL SURVEY OF MAJOR ETRUSCAN VOTIVE CONTEXTS

Funerary Cult

Funerary cult in Etruria and Latium offers some of the earliest indications of votive ritual. The grave goods of Villanovan burials might be considered offerings to the deceased, the ancestors, or the gods of the Underworld: they are not always personal belongings, and they had to be given by survivors. The use of a separate niche for goods in a Villanovan *tomba a pozzo* (tomb in a well) burial symbolically places the offerings beyond the hands of the deceased, as does their condition: they were not cremated with the body.[54] The use of miniatures and models such as hut urns not in human scale extends the donor's intentions to a realm beyond the physical.

Certain gifts were selected with regard to the identity of the deceased: a knife for men, weaving implements for women. Weaving would become a favored association of famous women in the Latin sanctuaries of Archaic times and beyond, as shown in the dedication by Tanaquil of her weaving tools and wool in the temple of Semo Sancus on the Quirinal (seen by Varro) and possibly in the second-century bronze statuette, probably from Nemi, as suggested by Haynes.[55]

Miniature razors and arrowheads of sheet bronze interred with men foreshadow the transfer of symbolic votives to sanctuaries. The most telling votive objects may be the impasto figurines found in rare Latin graves, as at Osteria dell'Osa (Gabii).[56] The standing figure extends a right hand in what has been interpreted as an act of worship. The scale of the figure is appropriate to the hut urn and miniature vessels and led Bietti Sestieri to interpret them as images of the deceased in ritual pose. Another buried at San Lorenzo Vecchio holds a tiny bowl on his hand.[57]

In Osa grave 126, cult activity is shown by an amphora deliberately broken and miniature vases carefully placed on the mouth of the *dolio* (large jar) and on the upper surface of the grave's fill. This would have been a public act, witnessed by those present. The act of giving and, with the breaking of the amphora, of dedicating, altering seemingly mundane objects exclusively for deposition, constitutes votive ritual. The funerary version of a *votum* is an implied covenant with the ancestors.[58]

One purpose of some Villanovan *ripostigli* (hoards) was probably votive, especially when they were buried in vases or trenches at some distance outside the village.[59] Tools, utensils, arms, ornaments, or ingots could have indicated a donor's occupation. (The value inherent even in scrap bronze would make any hoard a worthy gift.)

Survey of Representative Etruscan Votive Deposits

Tarquinii

Pian di Civita This site illustrates an urban cult of long-standing tradition extending into the Roman period.[60] Protovillanovan structures were erected near a natural cavity in bedrock (Fig. III.1). Burnt material, containing sherds and worked bits of deer antler, has been interpreted as a votive deposit laid down in the cavity and in an adjacent *fossa*.*

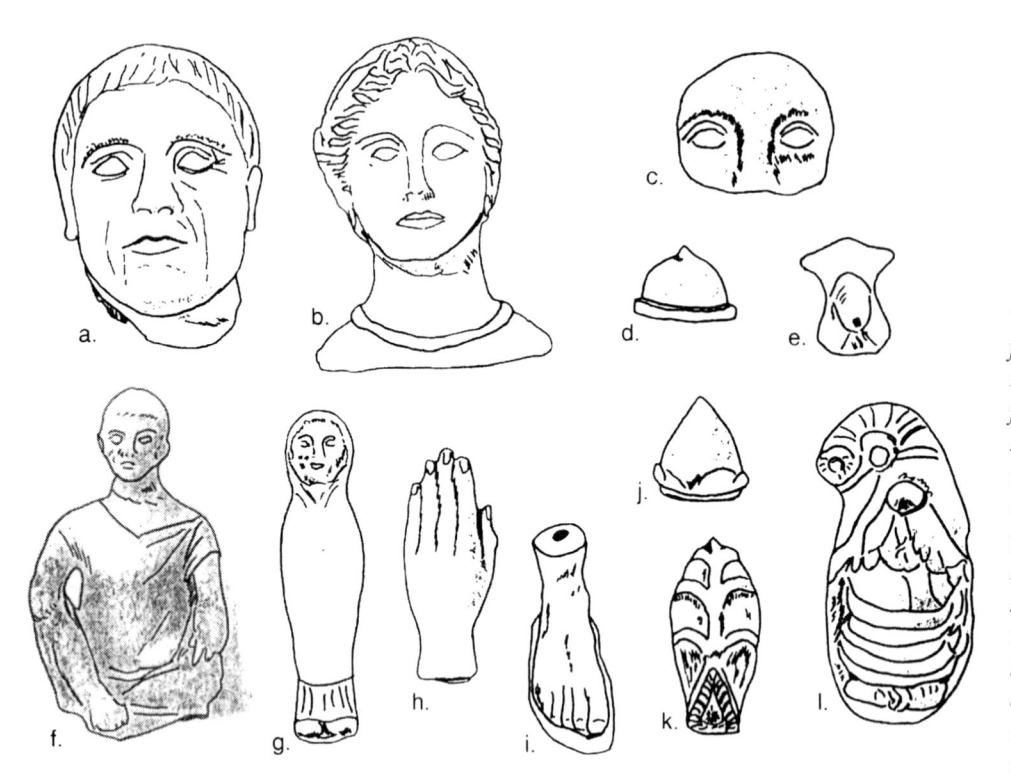

VI.6. *Votive terracotta types, from deposit of the Ara della Regina, Tarquinii. Fourth to first century BCE. Tarquinia, Museo Nazionale. Top row: (a) male "portrait" head, (b) female bust, (c) face plaque, (d) breast, (e) male genitals. Bottom row: (f) crouching child statuette, (g) swaddled infant, (h) hand, (i) foot, (j) human heart, (k) uterus (multiparous cervix), (l) polyvisceral plaque. (Drawing by author after objects in Comella 1982, plates, passim.)*

From the ninth century on, constant ritual activity focused on the cavity, with the unusual burial of an epileptic boy who died of an aneurism after a life of seeing and hearing things that others could not. During the course of the eighth century, offerings continued amid thatched structures. Burials of infants with cranial deformities may represent the "offering" of *prodigia*,* on analogy with Roman state rituals of supplication for healthy offspring.

A special votive deposit was made early in the seventh century when a pit was stacked with three bronze emblems: an old-fashioned axe, with at least part of its wooden handle attached; the sheet armor of a round shield folded into quarters and stacked atop the axe; and above it, a *lituus**/trumpet originally 1.5 m long (Fig. III.2) but folded into three segments so that it could never be used again. The excavators interpret this offering as representing the civic, military and religious authority of a *grande personaggio*. The axe is of a type identified by G. Carancini as sacrificial, developed in the tenth century and paralleled in eighth century hoards from central Italy.[61] The careful folding of the objects must have been a dramatic labor: dismantling the shield's wooden backing, perhaps breaking the axe handle, and bending shield and *lituus* over a board or rock. The *fossa* of the bronzes, and a second votive deposit of the seventh century, held vases as well, and these offerings were to continue for centuries.

Ara della Regina By the fifth century, the Pian di Civita site was marked by a city crossroads and the nearby building of the Ara della Regina. This sanctuary illustrates votive conditions of the fourth–first century BCE, performed in the general vicinity of the temple and monuments like the *Elogia tarquiniensia*. A votive deposit excavated in the 1960s produced over a thousand objects placed within a large *fossa*, perhaps segregated by type (Fig. VI.6).[62]

A spear point bears a dedication to Artumes, but in addition to pottery and lamps, most items are of a healing character: terracotta anatomical models and statues of the third-second century BCE. Coins, too, began to appear, in a trend parallel to their increasing frequency in the hands of consumers. There are statues and heads of men, women, boys, and swaddled babies; male and female half-heads and busts; and a full array of moldmade anatomical models: facial masks, arms, hands, fingers, legs, feet (adult, child, and sandaled), parts of torsos, female breasts, male and female genitals, and internal organs, including gravid uteri, hearts, and polyvisceral plaques.

One adult leg and knee model was inscribed before it was

fired, showing that the process of votive dedication could be a prolonged affair and perhaps controlled by cult authorities, since many days must elapse between a client's order and the firing and finishing of a terracotta. Of course, if a suppliant made his *votum* in the format of a promise, there would have been plenty of time between vow, cure, and the day of thank offering for a terracotta to be produced. The inscription says *alce:vel:tiples:*, according to Colonna, "Vel Tiples dedicated," the name an Etruscan version of Diphilos, indicating a Greek formerly of the servile class.[63]

Other dedicated objects include terracotta animals, animal parts and fruit, and bronze figurines. Animal bones indicate sacrifice, and pottery and lamps imply meals and nighttime rituals. Some of the heads and statues are fine works of art, even if it is "popular" art, such as the near-life-sized head that probably came from a statue modeled freehand in the style of the second century BCE.[64]

Brolio

A tradition of aristocratic cults at home in the country is represented in the find in 1863 of a deposit of at least forty-six bronze artifacts of the seventh–sixth century BCE at Brolio in Val di Chiana. These had been buried in a swamp, where excavation in the 1930s uncovered more bronzes and traces of wood interpreted as a palisade. Romualdi was able to restore the deposit on paper long after its dispersal.[65] In addition to the well-known statuettes, actually finials of furniture in the Orientalizing tradition, there were figurines of warriors, votaries, wild animals (deer, hare), griffin cauldrons and other vessels (cups, basins, ladles) appropriate to banquet or libation ritual. There were also tools, arms and personal ornaments, and pieces of bronze, perhaps *aes rude*.*

The character of these votives, a rare analogy for the contents of the princely tombs, recalls visits of local nobles to a rural shrine. The emblems of their lifestyles link them to war, the hunt, and the symposium. Such personal possessions put their mark on this sacred place, as if it were their home or the home of a fellow aristocrat whom they honor with their princely gifts.

Graviscae

The sanctuary at the Tarquinian port of Graviscae fits a very different model.[66] It seems to have been founded by foreigners—Greeks—and continued by the native Etruscan population. Continuously undergoing a long series of remodeling campaigns, the seashore agglomeration of cult rooms and courtyards was used from the early sixth century until ca. 270 BCE, when the settlement ceased to exist and the shrine was mostly dismantled. Votives were still brought here after the buildings were gone, to judge from the style of the anatomical terracottas deposited in a courtyard. Although its Archaic donations express the concerns of merchants and adventurers, the cult ultimately showed aspects of fertility and healing.

Inscriptions of various periods identify three goddesses, Aphrodite-Turan, Hera-Uni, and Demeter-Vei, the earliest donations made by Greeks (some famous), the later ones by Etruscans.[67] Building β held dedications to Demeter/Vei, about a thousand lamps and plowshares, analogous to offerings common in Greek Demeter cults. After the fifth-century nativization of these cults, dedications to Uni and Vei continued, including terracotta figurines portraying two seated goddesses, possibly Demeter and Kore. Two inscribed vases name Apollo; the famous stone anchor model of Sostratos specifies, in Greek, Aeginetan Apollo. While many dedicants were evidently foreign merchants or affluent natives, including women, some seem to have had humbler origins or occupations, perhaps prostitution, yet were still literate.[68]

Other goods in a separate deposit of 580–480 BCE include a bronze nuragic (Sardinian) boat model, stones from abroad, and a dish containing mural painters' pigments. While many or most votives may have been heaped up in courtyards, stacked on tables, or buried in pits or wells, some, on the evidence of large stone bases, were kept on view for generations.

When, in the fourth century, the cult shrank to a small courtyard, worshipers offered anatomical models from the workshops that produced for the city cults. Many models of gravid uteri, in fact the largest category of anatomical votives in Graviscae, were cast into the water of a cistern near Building α. In Courtyard I of Building γ, bronzes, figurines, and anatomical models (ears, hands, feet, hearts, breasts, external and internal female genitals) were found lying symmetrically along the NW–SE walls. In Room G, terracottas lay parallel to the walls, uteri on the north side and center, and broken heads, statues, figurines and aedicula models along the south and west sides. Such multiple examples of the same types placed in the same or adjacent deposits may indicate contemporaneous dedications, all supplied from the same manufacturer, perhaps on the occasion of a festival. Lamps are evocative of the nighttime mass rituals of the Demeter cult; grain and bones of a piglet in an early cist (Courtyard A) may show affinities with the Thesmophoria of Athens or similar Greek rituals. In room M, only models of uteri and swaddled babies were found, one of the few associations of these organs with their desired product.

VI.7. Bronze figurine of boar from deposit at Fonte Veneziana, Arezzo. Late sixth–early fifth century BCE. Florence, Museo Archeologico Nazionale. (Photo: Sopintendenza Archeologica per la Toscana-Firenze.)

Punta della Vipera

Near the sea north of Punicum, a shrine was excavated in 1964, with a temple built in the late sixth century and completely refurbished in the fourth, no doubt the result of the predations of Dionysios of Syracuse.[69] Votives range from the sixth to second century BCE, including inscriptions naming Menerva, along with pottery, terracotta figurines, and anatomical models. A fourth-century altar has been interpreted as a *mundus* with two interconnecting channels communicating with the earth.

Model uteri include the "deflated type," with appendage (this is a congenital malformation, a vestigial second uterus), and there is one possible example of pathology, a pair of breasts, one of which is swollen, with lesions around the nipple. A long sixth-century inscription on a lead sheet has been interpreted as a *votum* (Fig. II.4), although no god's name is recognized in it.[70]

Veii: Portonaccio

Another example of a major city cult, perhaps political in nature, was at the Portonaccio site of Veii, an extramural shrine featuring elaborate waterworks and a large pool.[71] Offerings illustrate aspects of military, healing, and perhaps purification rites of a cult of Menerva, Turan, and possibly Aritimi, as indicated by inscribed dedications. Votives were deposited continuously from the seventh century (before

VI.8. Bronze figurine of female, from deposit at Fonte Veneziana, Arezzo. Late sixth–early fifth century BCE. Florence, Museo Archeologico Nazionale. (Photo: Sopintendenza Archeologica per la Toscana-Firenze.)

there was a temple) until the demise of the city in 396 BCE and thereafter as well.

Pottery, including miniatures, was the most common offering, and terracotta sculpture also seems to have been popular, including standard, moldmade types and fine statuary like the Testa Malavolta.[72] Votive heads show the beginning of this tradition in the early fifth century, following models set by architectural terracottas.[73] The Portonaccio attracted famous worshipers. Fine bucchero vases of the first half of the sixth century bear dedications by Avile Vipiennas (*mini muluv[en]ece avile vipiennas* ["Avile Vipiennas dedicated me."]). A member of the Tulumnes family, a relation of the king Tolumnius of Livy's story of 428 BCE, dedicated

VI.9. Votive bronze head, female, from deposit at Fonte Veneziana, Arezzo. Late sixth–early fifth century BCE. Florence, Museo Archeologico Nazionale. (Photo: Sopintendenza Archeologica per la Toscana-Firenze.)

VI.10. Bronze figurine of nude, elongated youth, from deposit at Fonte Veneziana, Arezzo. Late sixth–early fifth century BCE. Florence, Museo Archeologico Nazionale. (Photo: Sopintendenza Archeologica per la Toscana-Firenze.)

a jug to Menerva in the fourth century.[74] The rich series of votives shows the double names of important families, inscribed in the same formulae as gifts made from one aristocrat to another.

Arretium: Fonte Veneziana and Monti Falterona

Two sanctuaries illustrative of the differences between north and south, coast and interior, are the Fonte Veneziana and Monti Falterona at Arretium (Arezzo).

Fonte Veneziana   The Fonte Veneziana deposit (Figs. VI.7–10), at a gate shrine, comprising bronzes of 530–480 BCE, was associated in 1869 with a round masonry construction that may have been a votive pit. Bocci was able to reconstruct the original inventory in Florence: about two hundred male and female bronze figurines, some originally decorated (in Levantine style?) with gold foil.[75] There were also anatomical plaques (eyes, limbs, busts), ceramics, and a large amount of *aes rude*. The images of *korai* wearing the *tutulus*, *kouroi*,* and domestic animals are the gifts of citizens as opposed to the aristocratic emblems of war and hunt at Brolio.

Monti Falterona   The deposit at Falterona (Laghetto Ciliegeta), discovered in 1838 and revisited in 1972, is indicative of mountain sanctuaries. Offerings of the sixth to third century BCE were thrown into the lake and dramatize both military and healing requests.[76] Fortuna and Giovannoni reassembled 1,000 pieces of *aes rude*, 2,000 arrowheads, fragmentary terracottas, vases, and 620 bronzes including *kouroi*, *korai*, draped worshippers, domestic animals, and anatomical models. This list includes a very fine bearded male head and an armored male figure now in the British Museum

VI.11. *Votive bronze head, bearded man, from votive deposit at Falterona. Late fifth century BCE. London, British Museum. (By permission, Trustees of the British Museum.)*

(Figs. VI.11–12).[77] The Falterona worshipers may be seen as affluent, some military, many able to purchase pretty statuettes from the same workshop, but not people who favored cities and coinage.

Volsinii (Orvieto): Cannicella shrine

A funerary setting—the Cannicella necropolis of Orvieto—provides another votive sanctuary with distinctive structures (spring, basins, altar, and roofed chapel with an unusual nude female statue), epigraphic documents, and standard offerings.[78] It was visited throughout the life of the necropolis: mid sixth to first century BCE (thus long after Orvieto/Volsinii was abandoned ca. 264). A plaque associated with the third century altar reads θval veal—"Vei who is going to reveal," according to van der Meer.[79] The votives are a standard accumulation of bronzes, personal belongings, pottery, coins, terracotta figurines, and two anatomicals: male genitals and a heart. All the votives were very battered, even those found near the altar, as if all had been repositioned, perhaps more than once before the site was abandoned.

VI.12. *Votive bronze statuette, warrior, from deposit at Falterona. Late fifth century BCE. London, British Museum. (By permission, Trustees of the British Museum.)*

Sovana

Bianchi Bandinelli noted the discovery of a sanctuary with altar and *favissa* in the Sovana necropolis, where there were votives common also in Hellenistic healing deposits: model heads, limbs, viscera, and a uterus. Figurines at Sovana portray a nude goddess, a patron of fertility, perhaps the same as the lady of the Cannicella.[80]

Marzabotto: Santuario Fontile

Short lived though the extramural Marzabotto Santuario Fontile was (essentially just the fifth century), it has provided an interesting array of votives.[81] The cult received locally cast bronzes, especially figures standing with arms extended in worship, a model leg and foot, fibulae, and bronze vessels made in Vulci, in addition to local pottery and an Attic black-figured *kylix.** An inscribed basin rim names Tiur. Several stone *cippus** bases that once held figurines were scattered around the building; they are characteristic of the Bologna sanctuaries but are less common in other regions.

Caere (Cerveteri): Pyrgi

The cult of Uni/Eileithyia/Astarte at Pyrgi offers the closest parallel yet to any of the Greek international sanctuaries. The gold plaques of Thefarie Velianas (Fig. II.6) mark the one sure instance of a public *votum* by a city or its erstwhile ruler, comparable to the dedication of a temple after a battle. The Punic formula is paralleled by the Etruscan version "because Astarte has supported him by her hand," a thank offering for a wish granted as much by Punic marines as by the Punic goddess, conflated with Uni as Unialastres.[82]

Votive objects were buried in one of the wells, apparently when the sanctuary was dismantled, but most of the terracottas had been placed in the vicinity of the dilapidated temples after their abandonment. These are a diverse selection of at least three hundred statues and organs in the style of the second–first century BCE. Wells also held pottery and wood from furniture and ships' tackle. A menagerie of animal bones indicates exotic sacrifices; Iberian painted vases may have held honey from Ibero-Punic Spain, while a hoard of nine silver Greek tetradrachms is a hint of the international wealth for which Pyrgi was famous. Two bronze plaques and two Spurinas bowls name Uni, Tinia, and Thesan as recipients of sixth–fifth century *vota*. One plaque shows a woman, Thanachvil Catharnai, as maker of the *votum*.

Veii: Campetti

A large extramural shrine at Veii named Campetti and excavated in the 1930s and 1960s incorporated a *bothros* and small cave, although today these cannot be traced, according to Vagnetti's exhaustive study.[83] Two buildings of several rooms within a *temenos* wall evoke the character of South Italian and Sicilian Demeter or chthonic shrines. The goddess at Campetti is identified as Ceres, on a Roman jug of the third century BCE.

Of approximately three thousand *ex votos*, most are terracotta heads and figurines of the sixth–second century, including some of the earliest votive heads. Of two hundred fifth-century figurines, just four are male (warriors). Among the others are several *kourotrophoi*,* types favored by Italic cults. Later terracottas depict animals, fruit, soldiers with rectangular and oval shields, and the famous Aeneas group.[84] A *pocolom* (cup) inscribed *L. Tolonio. Ded. Menerva/ Crere L. Tolonio D.*, from one of the citizens transferred after Roman conquest, bears the name of the fifth-century rogue king, also named in a sixth-century dedication at Veii Portonaccio. Is the tradition represented one of family piety or just of a family accustomed to inscribe dedications more than most?

Vulci

Porta Nord Vulci has provided several large votive deposits, such as the rural shrine at Tessennano.[85] At the Porta Nord site, the deposit includes terracotta statues of gods, worshipers, children, swaddled babies, heads and janiform busts, figurines, and model arms and breasts.[86] There are also models of temples and other buildings. The shrine was frequented during the third century BCE to the second century CE. In about 80 BCE, relatively fresh votives were layered with clean dirt in a deep, elliptical trench at the edge of a little *temenos* just outside the city wall.

Fontanile di Legnisina The extraurban sanctuary at Fontanile di Legnisina was just outside a city gate, near an altar in an area of little rock outcrops and a spring. A deposit was placed in a small cave during the fourth and third centuries, with inscriptions naming Uni and Vei. The hand-sized votives came from the same urban workshops as those of the other Vulcian sanctuaries. Noteworthy are the bronzes of the fifth–fourth century: a female with pomegranate and egg, a togate man, a Hercle, and a simple male offrant of the later fourth century dedicated to Uni: *ecn:turce:pivepatrus:unial-huinθnaias*.[87]

Suggestive of either cost saving or some especially significant possession or event is a female figure originally the finial of a candelabrum, now converted to a simple figurine.[88] Three little *nenfro** bases show how many bronzes must originally have been displayed standing. Anatomical models include a large number of uteri of several distinctive types. Some are rendered like vases on stands.[89] One expects a somewhat provincial rendering in the countryside, as at Ghiaccio Forte,[90] but since more sophisticated products were available in Vulci, this "vessel" style must have been a deliberate choice of the worshiper. It does indicate eloquently, albeit in schematic fashion, the vessel-like character of the uterus. Other uterine models are types common at Tarquinii, showing a triangular, sectioned cervix (Fig. VI.6k), and schematized fibroid tumors. Of five examples of a deflated uterus, clearly indicating its recently emptied condition, two were inscribed prior to firing: "*vei*."[91]

The Legnisina uteri are among the rare inscribed anatomicals; Vei is a logical protector for wombs and childbirth. The others are the man's knee from the Tarquinii Civita deposit (*alce:vel:tiples* ["Vel Tiples gave (it)."]), and a third-century heart at Lavinium inscribed in Latin (?) to Menerva

VI.13. The type of the capite velato offrant, *drawings after votive terracottas found in the Tiber at Rome: (left) figurine of draped youth, (top) votive head of youth, (bottom) half-head of youth, all Hellenistic/Late Republican period. (Drawings by author, after* Tevere, *pls. 45, 73, 85.)*

by a certain Senenia.[92] A sporadic find in the vicinity of Veii's Campetti sites was a knee, but its dedication was fragmentary.[93] Such models illustrate the close relationship between cults and artisans: incised before firing, the models could not be changed and must have been commissioned in advance. It was in the third century that the *haruspices*,* according to Pliny (*HN* 10.71.186) began officially to include hearts in their readings of victims' entrails, and this may have stimulated interest in this organ in the popular imagination.[94]

Caere: Manganello

A single-cella* temple above the valley of the Manganello stream at Caere was excavated by Mengarelli in 1926.[95] A large votive deposit of the fourth–second century is today known only from a sample said to be representative, including pottery, weaving equipment, *arulae*,* terracotta figurines (enthroned goddesses), statues, and anatomical models. Heads include veiled types often associated with Roman rites (performed *capite velato**; Fig. VI.13), and the common bareheaded Etruscan version. They offer a rare confirmation of identity in votive images, since veiled heads must represent a worshiper rather than a god. The male Manganello head

VI.14. Votive terracotta male head, from sanctuary on the Manganello stream, Caere. First century BCE. Rome, Museo di Villa Giulia. (DAI Rome fo 426.)

(Fig. VI.14), with its asymmetrical stiffness, has often been proposed as an example of a stroke victim.[96]

CONCLUSIONS
Votive Ritual

What can votive deposits reveal about Etruscan popular religion? First, how Etruscan was votive ritual? Riva and Stoddart view the emporia sanctuaries—Graviscae, Pyrgi, Punta della Vipera—as representing the symbolic boundaries of Etruscan civilization.[97] Such sanctuaries would have prompted emulation of foreign customs, perhaps including votive ritual. We know, in the case of the Graviscae dedications, that a number of local women frequented the shrines after Greek observance waned.

Yet votive ritual was practiced by Italian natives long before any of the "metic" settlements were founded. The finds at Tarquinii Civita place religious ritual securely in Protovillanovan and Villanovan times. The early use of anatomical votives, among the bronzes of Arretium, Marzabotto, and Falterona, precedes the anatomical phenomenon in Greece, by a century or more, and speaks to the independence of Italian cults.

The question of regional preferences for materials, bronze in the North and terracotta in the South, cannot be resolved without more confidence in our sampling. It might be an ecological effect, the result of differential access to materials. Some northern deposits did contain terracottas. Might southern or later, highly trafficked shrines have practiced melting down metals, as in the Greek sanctuaries? Without the Athenian Asklepieion inventories, for instance, we would not have guessed the large amounts of metal gifts converted to bullion by temple administrators. In 384 BCE, the raiders of Pyrgi took a thousand talents of silver, probably in the form of bullion.[98]

The Nature of Votives

Casting goods into a lake or well effectively takes them out of circulation yet preserves them intact, whereas valuables are more likely to be dispersed or looted from land or urban shrines. Poor men must have brought gifts of wood, wax, cloth, or food.[99] *Naturalia*, favorites at the Samian Heraion, are less common in Etruscan shrines. Perhaps for Etruscans veneration of the place makes its natural products like stones and shells less prized when handled by men. The repertoire of objects specially designed for votive dedication does seem to have increased over time, for instance, the quantities of terracotta anatomical models usually eclipse all but pottery in later deposits. We cannot know if this was a strategy to prevent looting or merely a consequence of the growth of a large, affluent middle class (see below).

Vases were probably the most common votives, but unless they were inscribed, we cannot be sure that they were gifts and not the sanctified equivalent of picnic plates. Important people, such as Avile Vipiennas, dedicated mere pottery, albeit bucchero, yet one might have expected the *condottiere* to bring armor or statuary. He may have done both, but perhaps the vase, a footed chalice, was marked because it functioned in a libation or other public ceremony. It is very neatly incised: are we to imagine this was the handwriting of Avile, or was it written by a scribe during or after the ritual?

Gran-Aymerich, in his analysis of vases related to sanctuaries,[100] notes that the preferred fabrics were dark impasto, bucchero, and imitations of Greek painted imports. Impasto and bucchero represented a tradition rooted in prehistoric Italy and must have seemed conservatively appropriate to Etruscan consumers. Shapes are usually those of the banquet, as well as cups, *oinochoai,** and *phialai** for libations, although many *aryballoi** and *balsamarii** were dedicated for their contents. A few were exclusively votive designs, like mesomphalic *phialai,* globular *aryballoi* too big for personal use, and footless *askoi,** which continued a Villanovan tradition. At the Portonaccio of Veii, Avile's pedestal cup is unusual, as is a bucchero casket (for *sortes**?) inscribed *laris velkasnas [mini muluvenike] menervas.*[101] Veii in fact shows the highest percentage of inscribed vases: three-quarters are bucchero.

There are few complete omissions in the Etruscan votive repertoire. Valuable Orientalizing and Archaic imports such as cauldrons, silver bowls, or ivories are rare, as are amber carvings (which do appear at Rome, Sant'Omobono). Small terracotta altars (*arulae*), common in Sicilian deposits, appear only occasionally in Etruria, more often in Latium and Falerii.[102] Symbolic miniatures, seen in Greece and at Tivoli, are not Etruscan, presumably because the real cakes and winnowing trays they depict were not used in Etruscan mysteries.[103] Full busts in terracotta, characteristic of the Punic sphere, Sicily, and South Italy, are less common in Etruscan shrines, in spite of a Late Villanovan–Orientalizing tradition of schematic bronze busts in tombs.[104]

Further to terracottas, the *protomai** so common in Greek cults were not routinely produced in Etruria, yet cults of Vei/Ceres abound.[105] Perhaps the Vei cult is so old that its votive types were formalized before East Greek *protomai* began to circulate at the end of the sixth century. Nor do the relief plaques (*typoi* in Greek inventories)[106] or *stelai** favored by Greek cults occur. Since the architectural revetment industry at Veii, which manufactured relief frieze plaques, probably developed the votive head, we may assume that Etruscans, unlike the Lokrians, did not wish to see images of themselves enacting cult scenes. Yet individual, generic figures of worshipers in bronze or terracotta were common. Mirrors, important offerings in Greece, are so far completely lacking, except for a funerary offering: a silver mirror shown hanging from a tree in the Tomb of Hunting and Fishing.[107]

In bronzes and figurines, only a few designs were reserved for votive use. The so-called *Ombra della sera* types known for Volaterrae and the North seem to have been favorites at Latin Nemi, perhaps brought by Etruscan pilgrims?[108] Whom do all the "normal" figures represent? Some must be gods—the janiform figures cannot be human, and others shown enthroned, such as the *kourotrophoi,* are divine.[109] Men depicted *capite velato* must be worshipers (Fig. VI.13).[110] Swaddled infants in terracotta do not occur outside votive contexts and can represent only mortal children, although

Fridh-Haneson has proposed that their oddly mature faces were intended to evoke the identity of reborn, adult initiates of an Orphic cult.[111]

Anatomical votives, on the other hand, must depict mere mortals, and so too the heads and half-heads (Fig. VI.15) that were rendered in the same scale and style as body parts. The mortality of other statue types is expressed, as at Veii, Rome, Nemi and Capua, in their exposed abdominal organs, and by analogy, statues available in identical types but without exposed viscera ought to be mortals as well. The style of the teardrop incisions of some statues matches that of a class of polyvisceral plaques associated with Veii.[112]

What of the purpose of votives? Some inscriptions suggest that protection of a child (*clen ceχa*) was requested, while the names of Vipiennas and Velianas carry the connotation of political or military favors received. Finds of actual trophies such as armor are rare in Etruria, although a set of fifth-century greaves inscribed in a Volsinian sanctuary did turn up in the tomb of the Roman who probably sacked it.[113] The hundreds of swaddled babies and gravid human uteri at many Hellenistic shrines can have commemorated only birth or conception of a child. While many gifts are ambiguous, the anatomical votives must acknowledge healing by gods. The dearth of images of diseased organs is consonant with the use of anatomicals as post facto gifts.[114] Many earlier offerings probably also rendered thanks for healing. I note that in the Brontoscopic Calendar of Nigidius Figulus, a high percentage of *ostenta** (over 80 of 360) relate to the health or disease of humans and animals.[115]

By the time terracotta anatomical models (Figs. VI.6, VI.16) became widespread, urban centers with large populations and sophisticated infrastructure were the rule, and politics may have influenced the healing cults,[116] although sanctuaries of Asklepios, known at Rome (Tiber Island) and Fregellae, are not well attested in Etruria proper. It seems Etruscans did not usually add Asklepios to the repertoire because they already had, for centuries, been supplicating native goddesses such as Vei and Menerva.

Something seems to have influenced the Etruscan and Italic populations, in the Early Hellenistic period, to prefer the pseudo-realism of anatomical models to the prettiness of figurines or reliefs. Etruscan medical knowledge was highly developed, albeit different from Greek traditions. Several major cities had idiosyncratic traditions of medical illustration: a Tarquinian artist modeled an obliquely sectioned, multiparous uterus, while a Veientine coroplast saw a different surgical section.[117] The deliberate display of anatomical knowledge in the Manchester Museum's uterus model,

VI.15. Votive terracotta, female head. Fourth century BCE. London, British Museum. (By permission, Trustees of the British Museum.)

which slightly resembles the coroplastic types of Veii and Rome, must have been specially commissioned. It probably represents a postmortem C-section to save an infant whose mother died in labor.[118] What made the family give an offering if the mother had died? They would have known that infants thus rescued were at great risk, physically, and perhaps metaphysically,[119] and so might there have been *vota* made on their behalf for protection by a kourotrophic goddess?

The independent creation of "anatomical illustrations" in several cities at about the same time shows that artists could witness medical or funeral procedures and that they worked in close association with the healing cults. The men and women who purchased anatomical models or other terracottas, while perhaps donating cash or produce to the sanctuary, were probably not offering personal belongings or cult equipment (in Greece, *instrumenta* were the prerogative of priests). These donors represent a class affluent enough to purchase gifts, yet confident enough to retain their personal valuables. Might they fit some of the classes of the Brontoscopic Calendar? Did the freed persons (*lautni*) or the affluent servile class criticized by Greeks[120] find terracottas

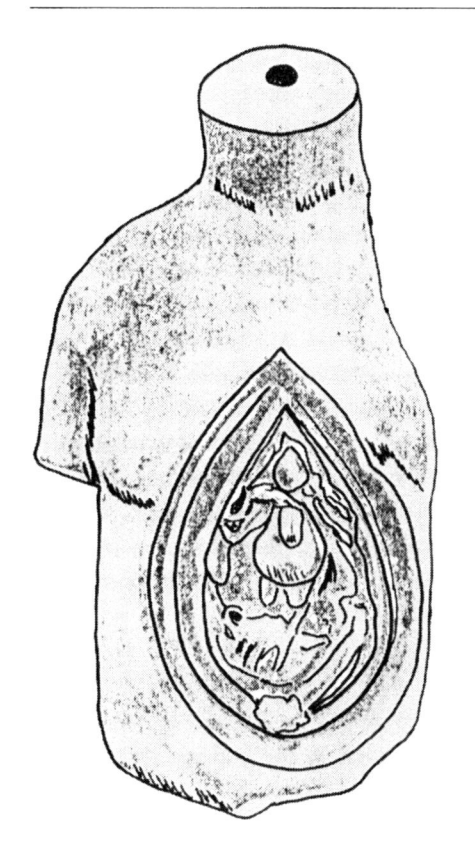

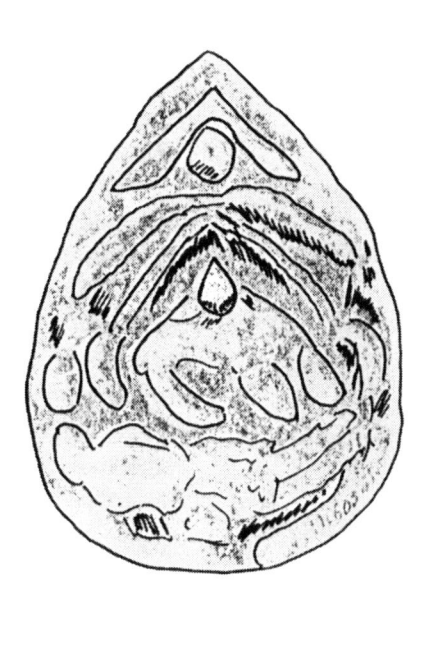

VI.16. Votive terracotta statues and figurines showing incision and internal organs. (Left) torso, drawing by author after Holländer 1912, 200, fig. 111, 205, fig. 117, also Tevere, pl. 96, no. 581; (right) polyvisceral plaque type found in Latium, Veii sphere. (Drawing by author after Tevere, pl. 98, no. 584.)

more appropriate offerings than other signs of wealth? Such goods express human needs without revealing the identity of the suppliant.[121] Of course, the autonomous "outsider" class of the calendar, "the women," constituted the best market for such offerings. Etruscan women did not offer their hand mirrors, and the numbers of uteri and female heads in many deposits are quite high.[122] Many Etruscan head types were made with customized earrings, presumably to appeal to female consumers.[123]

Potter and Wells have analyzed the medical aspects of nearly 8,400 terracottas from the trench at Ponte di Nona near Rome.[124] While the ratios of different body parts varied from those in Etruscan sanctuaries (which show more internal organs), general epidemiological data apply. In rural or preindustrial populations, walking and working are of prime importance, and healing of hands and feet is commonly sought. The external genitals, usually male, are concentrated in urban areas, and some scholars suggest that venereal diseases were more common in densely populated centers. It is possible that votives were also offered for the onset of delayed puberty, as Reilly has suggested for "naked and limbless" Greek terracottas previously classified as dolls.[125] The shrines whose votives came from big-city workshops (Caere, Pyrgi, Tarquinii, Vulci, Veii) are the only ones that received polyvisceral plaques or statues with exposed organs. Might this reflect formal education or greater access to organized medicine? We are left to wonder whether hypochondria was a facet of Etruscan urban life.

What is the rationale behind the sculptural portrayal of human organs? Arms, legs, hands, and feet were occasionally modeled even in the Geometric period in Greece and Italy, but the medically motivated portrayal of organs is a later phenomenon. The terracotta versions first appeared in the late fourth century, apparently subsequent to the use of body parts in Greek Asklepieia. Greek depiction of internal organs does not seem to have been common, although some references appear in the Athens inventories.[126] There seems to have been no Greek tradition of polyvisceral plaques. Bronze plaques in the deposits of Arretium and Marzabotto have been dated on stylistic grounds to the fifth century, and some Venetic plaques are distinctly older than Greek anatomical sculpture.[127]

Certainly the anatomical tradition burgeoned in Italy, but what did internal organs mean as a visual symbol? By the fourth century, images of *haruspices* holding sheep livers would have been familiar to worshipers attending traditional sacrifices. There were even models of exposed sheep livers, as preserved in the fourth-century terracotta from the deposit

VI.17. *Votive bronze figurine of male holding sheep's liver, inscribed by Arnth Alitle Pumpus, from Paterno di Vallombrosa, Arezzo. Third century BCE. Florence, Museo Archeologico Nazionale. (Photo: Florence, Museo Archeologico.)*

at Falerii Scasato or the more complex Piacenza model (cf. the discussion by Larissa Bonfante in Chapter 2).[128] Etruscan augury was familiar to Roman authors for its practice of extispicy, excision of the victim's entrails for scrutiny. *Haruspices* are portrayed on urns and in statuettes as holding the liver in a special orientation (Fig. VI.17). The liver (and later the heart, according to Pliny) was seen as a virtual model of the universe.[129] The anatomical votives approximate actual human size, in marked contrast to most other votive sculptures. A votary carrying his red-painted heart or multicolored viscera plaque to the altar would have resembled the *haruspex*, about to perform his divination, or a votive figurine, such as that of Arnth Alitle Pumpus from the territory of Arretium, who proclaims: "*eit viscri ture arnth alitle pumpus.*"[130] (Since Pumpus is not costumed as a *haruspex*, might he be the donor of the sheep whence "these *viscri*" came, and this bronze his token of the more valuable gift of a victim?)

Perhaps models were viewed as metaphors of the human suppliant as sacrificial victim, a vulnerable, natural creature. The map to a human life's unfolding might be perceived as written in the person's bodily configuration and health. In the Etruscan universe, as in many societies, ill health or deformity may have been a sign that moral status is likewise imperiled. The sacrificing of *prodigia* might have derived from this belief. The placement of offerings, presumably part of a public ceremony, might be instructive for the interpretation of the objects, but none have been found in completely undisturbed contexts. At Graviscae, some terracottas of the late period seem to have been aligned to the walls of the dilapidated rooms and segregated by types. It is evident that half-heads and organ models had to be propped up or set on flat surfaces, and so we must assume that most votives were heaped up and never examined again. Metal or terracotta statues and polyvisceral plaques are unwieldy and must have required special care even to erect them at the time of dedication.

The Recipients of Votives

Which gods received votive offerings? While figures of worshipers were inscribed, even at the expense of their appearance, images displaying divine attributes were less often marked. Tinia's thunderbolt and Menerva's armor are easily read, but in other cases it is difficult to match a divine name with an image. Many sanctuaries show the practice that Alroth has termed "visiting gods,"[131] although we cannot be sure in Etruria if there was a single, formal dedication of a sanctuary; it seems more likely that the place was sacred and gods accrued to it. Inscriptions are our only sure indication of divine recipients. But of thousands known, only five anatomical models are inscribed: two to Menerva and two to Vei. (The fifth does not name a god.)

The gods to whom objects have been inscribed tend to be protectors, healers, feeders, and comforters. Perhaps even warrior figurines were offered for these activities or perhaps warriors just did not inscribe the gifts to their patron gods. Many deposits lack inscriptions; votives at Lucus Feroniae, for instance, are presumed to have been offered to the eponymous goddess. Major dedications were inscribed for Tinia, Uni, Menerva, Turan, Vei, Catha, Culśanś, Cel Ati, Tec Sanś/Tecvm, and Selvans.[132] In Rome, Silvanus had no female offrants, but many women in Etruria inscribed gifts to him.[133] Other gods are Thufltha, to whom a Hellenistic middle class offered bronze utensils and statuettes, Fufluns, and Artumes, but the only dedications to Aplu are Greek, like the Sostratos anchor. Further, there are the Tinas Cliniar,[134] Atunis, and Hercle.[135] Tiur received some offerings, such as a basin at Orvieto Cannicella and a sixth-century bronze crescent from Acquasanta di Chianciano.[136] Inscriptions on votives are thus far lacking for some gods, for instance, Usil, Cilens, and Nethuns. While this may be indicative of radically different cults, arguments from negative evidence are especially precarious with archaeological materials.[137] The Cannicella and Sovana necropolis shrines received the same kinds of offerings to the same gods as the sanctuaries of the living. The Cortona lamp, designed in a local foundry for funerary use, was later dedicated with a plaque to Tinia (*tinścvil*) by the Muśni family at Fratta.[138]

To summarize, in early Etruria, the nonperishable votives were given by aristocrats as if they were part of the princely gift-giving process of mortals (cf. Brolio, Falterona). Gradually, as urbanization accelerated and more people acquired wealth, common citizens, too, gave gifts of metal and ceramics (Arretium, Marzabotto), alongside powerful worshipers (Veii Portonaccio), and they increasingly, yet tersely, inscribed these gifts. In later Etruria (Tarquinii, Ara della Regina, Veii Campetti, Vulci various, Caere Manganello), the nonperishable and inscribed objects were probably given by self-sustaining urban families, gentry, women with family and health concerns, and perhaps the affluent common and servile classes. We cannot see the offerings of the common man, because truly poor people probably never had the wherewithal to obtain manufactured votives. Even the best biological analyses cannot tell us about the donors of cloth, wood, or bread, or a mother's most prized possession. With all the variety of visible offerings and recorded vows, we still are left to confront the universality of human need and gratitude that shaped the lengthy process of vowed promise, hopeful purchase, happy outcome, and generous offering that were the votive experience for thousands of Etruscans.

NOTES

1. See the ongoing *Corpus delle stipi votivi in Italia*, published as volumes of Bretschneider's *Archaeologica* series, such as Comella 1981 and 1986. For an extensive table of anatomical votive types indexed by site, see Fenelli 1975. For references on individual sanctuary sites, see Edlund 1987a. For more background, see also Lowe 1978. Early works on votives include Maule and Smith 1959; Bonghi Jovino 1976; *Santuari d'Etruria*; and *Civiltà degli Etruschi*. Subsequent finds of votive deposits are published in the monographs cited below and in excavation journals.

2. Barker and Rasmussen 1998, 224.

3. Fourth century BCE: van der Meer 1987, 72-73, figs. 32, 33. See Colonna 1976-1977; cf. Haynes 1985, 294, no. 132.

4. Second century BCE: van der Meer 1987, 73; after the translation of G. Colonna, "Fel Supri dedicated (?) on behalf of Vipinei (daughter) of Ulchni to Grandmother Cel." See *Santuari d'Etruria*, 34, 49, no. 1.17.

5. *OCD*, 3rd ed., 1996, 1612-1613, s.v. votive offerings (I. Malkin); and *RE* Suppl. 14 (1974), 964-973, s.v. Votum, (W. Eisenhut); see also *OLD* (1982) s.v. *mundus, stips, favissa*; Hackens 1963; *Tevere*, 25-28.

6. Plutarch, *Themistocles* 22; Diodorus Siculus 11.26.7 (Gelon); Livy 9.43.25 (Appius Claudius Caecus).

7. See for background, including find spots of inscribed votives, Ridgway 1990. See also G. Colonna in this volume, below, pp. 155-156. On the Pyrgi tablets, see the discussion by Bonfante and Bonfante 2002, 64-68.

8. Pfiffig 1975, 83-88.

9. *Lavinium II*, 11, fig. 4, 26-27, figs. 21-22, 29, fig. 24, 68, fig. 70; also *Enea nel Lazio*, 188-190, figs.; *Tevere*, 29-31. Most such finds are deposits of the Hellenistic period containing terracottas of little value to ancient looters. For images of other types of offerings involving libations, burning, and altars, see Thuillier 1991.

10. The quotations that follow are from Paton 1960, 382-383, 444-445, 318-319, and 374-375 respectively.

11. *TLE*, 447; the text here follows the amended reading by Rix in *ET*, As 3.4 and As 6.1; Cristofani 1985, 182-183, 276, no. 78. Van der Meer (1987, 96-107, 102, figs. 53-54) noted that, although Thufltha may be a deity of punishment and the Underworld in texts such as the Zagreb linen and Piacenza liver, the votives indicate a more complex identity for this god.

12. Modern plaques add material well-being, symbolized by cars and houses, as in tin plaques sold in Athens today. Many modern votives are already collectors' items; I am grateful to Stella Miller-Collett and Alice Donohue for sharing theirs with me. See Inturrisi 1989, who recommends Italian plaques as displayed in San Crisogono in Trastevere.

13. See *Anthologia Palatina* 6; ancient authors cited above, n. 10; and, e.g., Hesiod, *Works and Days* 659.

14. Edlund-Berry 1994, 20-24. See Barker and Rasmussen 1998, 277. The Portonaccio sanctuary of Veii was used well after 396, and some dedications are in Latin; the Cannicella continued for more than a century after Orvieto/Volsinii was destroyed in 264; and the Scasato deposit at Falerii was used into the first century BCE, although Falerii had been conquered/relocated in 241 BCE.

15. See Nijboer 1998, 244-264, with reference to the votive deposit at Satricum.

16. New York, Metropolitan Museum of Art, from the Bastis Collection: Haynes 1985, 183, 283-284, no. 104, dated ca. 475-450 BCE; *ET*, OA 4.1. Also van der Meer 1987, 63, 60, fig. 24. Colonna (1978) proposed the reading "I belong to Selvans Smucinthiunaitule." He noted that the Etruscan name of this utensil was *persie*, source of the Latin instrument, the *persillum*. (Note the iconography of a nude girl and pomegranate, which we might not have associated with Selvans, god of boundaries, flocks, and healing.) On cult equipment, see Pfiffig 1975, 94-101, 80-81. A ladle at Pyrgi was inscribed to Farthan: *Santuari d'Etruria*, 32, no. 1.12. Standard bronze vessels for libation or sacrificial meals would have resembled a simple banquet service: basin, jug such as a *Schnabelkanne* or S-handle *oinochoe*,* ladle or small jug, strainer, cup or *phiale*,* as *Santuari d'Etruria*, 31-32.

17. Aleshire (1989, 44) has even indicated entries on the invento-

ries of the Athens Asklepieion noting "lumps," which may be things that fell to the ground inside the boundary and then were considered dedicated—the place conferring sanctity on the thing. See also Aleshire 1991; useful background is offered by Dillon 1997.

18. TLE, 663; ET, Ar 3.2; Santuari d'Etruria, 172-174, no. 10.1. Cristofani 1985, 228-231, 295-297, no. 121, ca. 400-350 BCE. Small bronzes were also present in this deposit excavated at Arezzo's Porta Laurentina under Medici jurisdiction. See Haynes 1985, 76, 302, no. 156, who identifies it as the work of an Aretine artist; Brendel 1995, 327. On the formula tinścvil, see van der Meer 1987, 37, and Bonfante and Bonfante 2002, 147-148, source 26.

19. TLE, 651 (ET, Pe 3.3), found at Pila near Perugia. Cristofani 1985, 242-246, 300, no. 129. As Haynes notes (1985, 244, 322-323, no. 200), the interpretation of the full inscription remains controversial, since it may have been funerary. The date was established at 100-80 BCE on evidence of the portrait style and Etruscan letter forms. See Brendel 1995, 430-432; Bonfante and Bonfante 2002, 182-183, source 56.

20. Cristofani 1985, 238, 299, no. 126 (200-150 BCE); 240-241, 299-300, nos. 127, 128 (200-150 BCE) = Haynes 1985, 238, 319, no. 192; Santuari d'Etruria, 37-38, 49 no. 1.24. Dedication to Tec Śanś: TLE, 624, ET, Co 3.8; to Selvans: TLE, 148, ET, Ta 3.7; to Thuflthas: TLE, 652, ET, Co 3.6.

One must wonder why, if the child or image was now in the care of the god, it still needed the bulla amulet worn on the neck. The winged horses of the Ara della Regina columen,* however, also wear bullae, and they presumably are immortal. Note bullae worn by Apollo, a goddess, and a horse/Bucephalus in bronze figurines: Cristofani 1985, 206-207, 284, nos. 100-101; 164, 271, no. 56; and 166-167, 272, no. 59. See Palmer 1996 and Warden 1983.

21. Haynes 1985, 208, 299, no. 146; Cristofani 1985, 222-223, 292, no. 116 (ca. 400 BCE).

22. Cristofani 1985, 166, 270, no. 54 (430-400 BCE), there identified as a farmer, although he is surely a priest. Rasenna, fig. 30; Civiltà degli Etruschi, 139-140, no. 6.3.

23. TLE, 640; ET, Co 3.4. Cristofani 1985, 209, 285-286, no. 104; also from Cortona is Velia's dedication to Selvans: Cristofani 1985, 212, 286, no. 105.

24. TLE, 737; ET, OB 3.2. Cristofani 1985, 206, 284, no. 100; Rasenna, fig. 124.

25. British Museum: Haynes 1985, 199, 293, no. 129; 198, 292-293, no. 128, both dated 425-400 BCE. Cristofani 1985, 161-162, 270, nos. 52, 51. Dress as well as attitude and attributes may distinguish the images of worshipers from their gods: both these figures are barefoot, their hair fastened up beneath a half-diadem. The so-called, and probably misnamed, Fogg Turan, however, wears shoes and a wreath, perhaps markers of a different cult, such as a pilgrimage shrine, symbolized by her traveling costume. See Florence: Cristofani 1985, 274, no. 170; also Cristofani 1985, 162, 270, no. 53, probably from Populonia, ca. 460-430 BCE.

26. Cf. Torelli 1982 and Cristofani 1996, 49-57.

27. TLE, 35; ET, Ve 3.11. See Cornell 1995, 135, 143-146, for background. Also F. Boitani in Buranelli 1987, 234, no. 93; Grande Roma, 19-20, no. 12. Civiltà degli Etruschi, 277-279, no. 10.19. (TLE, 942; ET, Vc 3.9, which has the name avles vpinas, is discussed by Buranelli 1987, 234-235, no. 94.)

28. TLE, 36; ET, Ve 3.6. mine mulvanice karcuna tulumnes. On the fourth-century inscription L. Tolonio(s) ded(et) Menerva, see Santuari d'Etruria, 107, no. 5.1.F.4.

29. Torelli 1975; see Cornell 1978 (review of Torelli 1975).

30. Coarelli 1988, 205-328; Fayer 1982, chap. 4 (197-220), passim. Grande Roma, 111-130 (on Sant'Omobono deposit), also color plates, and passim for other Latin deposits. On politics at Sant'Omobono, cf. Smith 1997.

31. E.g., Melis and Quilici Gigli 1983. For later deposits, see Gatti Lo Guzzo 1978; Tevere; also Ponte di Nona (here, below, nn. 110, 124). On the Lapis Niger deposit in the Roman forum, see Cristofani 1985, 246-247; on social and political aspects of Latin sanctuaries such as Nemi, see Blagg 1985 and Lowe 1978. For a good selection of votives from one deposit (Rome, Via Prenestina), see Guzzo, Moscati, and Susini 1994, 168 (photo) and cat. nos. 643-663.

32. E.g., Maioli and Mastrocinque 1992.

33. Gualandi 1974, 42, fig. 2 (fig. 1 illustrates a likely parallel, from the Bologna, Villa Cassarini deposit).

34. For instance, D'Ercole 1990. For background on votives of other Italian ethnics, see Prosdocimi 1989.

35. For the Geometric formation of panhellenic sanctuaries, see Morgan 1997, also Morgan 1993; Morgan 1994. For bibliography on Greek sanctuaries, see Ostby 1993 and de Polignac 1995, 155-187.

36. Snodgrass 1989-1990 and Snodgrass 1980, 52-63; also Simon 1997, with earlier references.

37. How was the exchange effected? Since for the seventh and sixth centuries, most people did not have access to coinage, how did they obtain, at some distance from home, a little terracotta figurine or miniature vase to place at an altar or tack on a wall? Were they expected to bring something of greater value, such as metal, cloth, or food, the surplus "worth" to be considered a donation and the votive merely a token thereof? What could a family have carried to Olympia, for instance, in addition to their journey's food and shelter, which could have been a worthy offering? Evidence of metalworking on site at Olympia and elsewhere may represent exchange as well as production of offerings. Etruria presents some relevant analogies, since coinage became common there even later. Recent studies suggest that smelting/casting of metal was also practiced in Etruscan/Latin sanctuaries: see Nijboer 1998. The presence of large numbers of terracottas manufactured from the same molds or workshops at sites like Kirrha, the staging port for Delphi, suggests seasonal production or supply from factory to sanctuary, and thus the sanctuary as the "retail" supplier of votives. (For illustration, see Luce 1992; cf. Uhlenbrock 1985.)

38. Kyrieleis 1993.

39. Torelli 1997.

40. See, e.g., Iacobone 1988. Dedication of figurines in large quantities is attested at Delphi, Olympia, the Argive Heraion, Perachora, Corinth, and the Theban Ptoion, among others. Cf. the Etruscan figurines from Caere: Nagy 1988; Nagy 1994.

41. For the proposed sites of these sanctuaries, see Pfiffig 1975, 51, 69-71, 309; Edlund 1987a, 85-87, with full references; Sgubini Moretti and Bordenache Battaglia 1975, 110-154.

42. References to such votives, occasionally alluded to by historians, are scattered throughout the account of Pausanias, especially for Delphi and Olympia; they were also famous on Rhodes, Samos, and Ephesus.

43. See Civiltà degli Etruschi, 256-257.

44. Herrmann 1983; in addition to shields, helmets, and horse tack, there were also large vessels of Orientalizing type, similar to those of the "princely tombs" — perhaps official offerings from rulers of Etruscan cities?

45. Von Hase 1997, with earlier bibliography; also Gras 1985, 651-701, and passim.

46. MacIntosh 1974; Gras 1985, 676-679. Some examples found in the Corinthian Potters' Quarter were associated with the potters' domestic and roadside shrines.

47. See van Straten 1981.

48. Tripods: Kunze 1951-1953. A fifth-century Vulcian incense burner is attested by the find of one of its figurine legs in Olympia, near the Altis, where it must have been dedicated: see Haynes 1985, 189, 288-289, no. 118.

49. See Strøm 1992, with earlier bibliography.

50. See Stern 1986. A shipwrecked cargo of rather shabby female figurines found off Shave Zion, Israel, has been identified as commercial shipment from a seaport factory to sanctuaries along the coast: Linder 1973. See also the deposit at Kharayeb, which produced 1,100 terracottas of the fourth through first centuries BCE: Chéhab 1951-1952; Chéhab 1953-1954.

51. E.g., a bronze Ptah figure with gold foil on the face, from Cadiz (eighth-seventh century BCE): Martín Ruiz 1995, 50. For others from the Levant, and references, see Falsone 1992, 80-81 and color pl. 11a. On Phoenician/Punic religion, see Lipinski 1992; Clifford 1990; Lancel 1995, 193-215. See also entries in *Religio Phoenicia*.

52. A convenient reference is Vance 1994, with votive inscriptions passim; see esp. 12-13 "Baalshillem," and 118, the Astarte from El Carambolo (Seville).

53. Brown 1991, 21-75; also Day 1989. Offerings of *prodigia* cited in the Roman annals noted by Livy and the finds of infant skeletons at Tarquinii Civita reflect a different practice, not the sacrifices of the common man made en masse in a springtime, nocturnal festival.

54. Bartoloni 1989, 77-81; illustrated with tomb groups from Veii, Quattro Fontanili (201, fig. 7.13, and 202, fig. 7.14, with full references).

55. Haynes 1985, 240-241, 320-321, no. 196; Haynes 1989.

56. Bietti Sestieri, De Santis, and Regina 1989-1990, 65-88; and Bietti Sestieri 1992: chaps. 6-8 and passim. See another analysis in Smith 1996. The relative homogeneity of the material culture of Etruria and Latium during the Late Villanovan and Orientalizing periods makes it appropriate to cite Latian evidence here, in the absence of Etruscan burials of figurines: by the time of Orientalizing showpieces such as the Olmo Bello and Montescudaio urn, such figures do emerge. See Torelli 1986, 164-166; also Maggiani 1997; Tuck 1994; Damgaard Andersen 1993.

57. San Lorenzo Vecchio: *Civiltà del Lazio Primitivo* 1976, 82-83, pls. 6D, 7g. Also Bietti Sestieri 1992, 56, 59, fig. 3.13. The attitude of the statuettes from the Tomba delle Cinque Sedie at Caere (*Rasenna*, fig. 462) surely derives from this type of image.

58. In Classical sanctuaries, the conspicuous—to modern eyes, disfiguring—inscribing of objects may have been analogous to the breaking of funerary goods. It certainly occurred from the earliest epigraphic periods, as seen in the Mantiklos Apollo, for instance. Osteria dell'Osa also held a discreet, later, votive deposit (periods III-IV) of over sixty vessels, including miniatures, perhaps the remnant of a communal offering ceremony (Bietti Sestieri 1992, 85).

Different evidence for funerary, votive cult was found in the Valle Trebba necropolis of Spina, in the form of Attic vases with Greek inscriptions naming Hermes, Dionysos and Apollo: see *Civiltà degli Etruschi*, 186-187.

59. Bartoloni 1989, 32-33. Is it possible, on analogy to the theories of de Polignac 1995 for early Greek sanctuaries, such as the Argive Heraion, that some Villanovan hoards marked community boundaries with a gift to their divine patron? The literature on early Greek sanctuaries and city territory is summarized critically by Sourvinou-Inwood 1993.

60. Bonghi Jovino and Chiaramonte Treré 1987, 81-202; Bonghi Jovino and Chiaramonte Treré 1997.

61. Bonghi Jovino and Chiaramonte Treré 1987, 67-68, nn. 29-30, 34-35. For further discussion of the burial, the boy with the aneurism, and the cult of "Tages," see N. de Grummond in this volume, above, pp. 27-30. Yet if this was the site of the "Tages" apparition, the preserved votives do not reflect any difference in the type or importance of this cult.

62. Dimensions of the *fossa*: 20 x 14.5 m. Comella 1982. See also Bonghi Jovino 1997. Also *Santuari d'Etruria*, 70-78; Bonghi Jovino and Chiaramonte Treré 1987, 355-376.

63. G. Colonna, REE in StEtr 34 (1966), 321-322, pl. 51; Comella 1982, 112, 115, no. D9Fr.I. Other instances of foreign worshipers integrated into Etruscan cults are the inscriptions of Larth Telicles and Rutile Hipukrates of the seventh century BCE = TLE, 761, 155 (Tarquinii); ET, OA 2.2 and Ta 6.1.

64. Bonghi Jovino 1976, pl. 21, fig. 3; Pallottino 1975, pl. 77.

65. Romualdi 1981; *Santuari d'Etruria*, 162-164, no. 9.2; Cristofani 1985, 247-250, 78-87, nos. 2.2-2.21.

66. *Santuari d'Etruria*, 141-144; *Civiltà degli Etruschi*, 181-186, no. 7.1. Torelli 1977; Torelli 1997; Moretti et al. 1970; Pianu 1991. The location and types of the terracottas have been studied and discussed by Comella 1978, 89-95.

67. Early pieces include two armed Aphrodite statuettes in bronze and an imported griffin cauldron. Painted vases inscribed in Ionian Greek of the sixth century feature names that also appear on votives at Naukratis. One cup was inscribed *Here anetheke Paktyes* ["Paktyes dedicated (this) to Hera."], thus commemorating a visit from a Lydian, presumably a relation of that Paktyes who was treasurer of Kroisos.

68. Torelli 1977, 422, 428-429.

69. *Santuari d'Etruria*, 149-154, no. 8.1.

70. TLE, 878; ET, Cr 4.10; *Santuari d'Etruria*, 153-154, no. 8.1.c.1. The formula *muluvenice* is characteristic of sanctuary dedications (the numerals read MMMCCC or 3300).

71. *Santuari d'Etruria*, 99-109.

72. See also the group of Menerva and Hercle: Colonna 1987.

73. Cf. Veii (Campetti) votive head, *Civiltà degli Etruschi* 279, no. 10.23.1.

74. "L. Tolonio[s] ded[et] Menerva," *Santuari d'Etruria*, 105, 107, no. 5.1.F.4; F. Coarelli in *Roma Medio Repubblicana*, 334-335, no. 484.

75. *Santuari d'Etruria*, 174-179, no. 10.2; Bocci 1980, with earlier bibliography; Bocci 1984. Also illustrated in Cristofani 1985, 250-253, and Richardson 1983, 111-112.

76. Fortuna and Giovannoni 1975. Illustrated Cristofani 1985, 98-107, 253-257, nos. 4.1-4.10; *Civiltà degli Etruschi*, 284-287, no. 10.30.

77. Haynes 1985, 182, 283, no. 103; 207, 209, 297-298, nos. 143, 145.

78. Andrén 1967; Andrén 1984, 30-33; *Santuari d'Etruria*, 116-121, no. 6.1; Pfiffig 1975, 65-68.

79. *TLE*, 905; *ET*, Vs 8.2. *Santuari d'Etruria*, 120-121, no. 6.1.D; van der Meer 1987, 112-114; G. Colonna, REE in *StEtr* 34 (1966), 310-312; Colonna 1967, 548.

80. Bianchi Bandinelli 1929, 36-37, 126-127, pl. 30.

81. *Santuari d'Etruria*, 113-115, no. 5.4; Cristofani 1985, 258-259. See for background, Gualandi 1974 and 1970.

82. See also G. Colonna, in this volume, below, pp. 155-156. *Civiltà degli Etruschi* 255, 259, no. 9.18. Site reports in *NSc* 1959, 143-263; 1970 Suppl. 2; and 1988-1989. Also Colonna 1984-1985. For background, see *Santuari d'Etruria*, 127-141, and above, n. 7; also Pfiffig 1975, 64-65. For the inscriptions, see Bonfante and Bonfante 2002, 64-68; Bartoloni 1970.

83. Vagnetti 1971; see review by Martelli (1972). Comella and Stefani 1990; see also Torelli and Pohl 1973.

84. Pfiffig 1975, 355-357, fig. 140; Vagnetti 1971, 88, no. N1, pl. 48.

85. Tessennano, recognized in the nineteenth century near the village of Canino and excavated in the 1950s, had a small structure, now lost, and ceramics spread over this rural site. Pottery of the sixth century BCE to fifth century CE (much of the second-third century CE) is punctuated by 567 terracotta figurines of humans and animals, statues of swaddled babies, heads, model arms, legs, breasts, uteri, and a distinctive group of polyvisceral models displayed as if heaped within a latticelike frame, more resembling the organs of sacrificed animals placed in baskets than emblems of human medicine. The terracottas are stylistic types of the third-second century BCE. There were also 14 small bronzes, 94 coins, and a Latin inscription *Marti*, the only identification of the god venerated here. Although rural, Tessennano seems as sophisticated as the urban shrines, with a large number of coins and anatomical models. See Costantini 1995.

86. Pautasso 1994.

87. Massabò 1985; Colonna 1988; Massabò and Ricciardi 1988; Massabò 1988-1989; and Ricciardi 1988-1989. On the altar at Fontanile di Legnisina, see the discussion by Colonna in Chapter VIII.

88. First half of the third century: *NSc* 1988-1989, 156-157, no. 37.

89. At Falerii, similar stands correspond to vases made in the decades around 300 BCE: Ricciardi 1988-1989, 172-180, figs. 38-43.

90. Del Chiaro 1976, 27-28, pl. 11, nos. 38-40; *Santuari d'Etruria*, 157-159, for background. Cf. Turfa 1994, 239, n. 75.

91. This type is known from several examples in Caeretan sanctuaries (Manganello, Pyrgi, Punta della Vipera: *Santuari d'Etruria*, 153, no. 8.1.B.13; Turfa 1994, 227, fig. 20.2.H). I suggest that it was understood as depicting a uterus from which the infant had just been extracted. The organ still shows the ridges of third stage labor contractions, but it is not convex like the usual types: in life this configuration results from either rigor mortis or is temporarily visible in a live, healthy C-section.

92. sen⟨ ⟩nia. menrva. me⟨ ⟩ isa. Fenelli 1984, 336, fig. 11.

93. Ambrosetti 1954, fig. 5.

94. Incidentally, the presentation of this organ in the polyvisceral plaques of Caeretan design seems to fit Pliny's description of it at *NH* 11.69.181. See Turfa 1994, 226, 235, n. 26.

95. Mengarelli 1935. *Santuari d'Etruria*, 38-41, no. 1.26.

96. *Santuari d'Etruria*, 39, 49, no. 1.26.A.6; *Rasenna*, fig. 596. A few handmade or retouched heads seem to render a sort of Italian folk style, although, following Mengarelli, they might have been understood as expressing the characteristics of severe physical and mental handicap: eyes that are too small or other abnormalities of the skull speak to a profound congenital deformity. (I am indebted to Dr. Deborah Goldberg for discussion of juvenile anomalies.) Might this be reminiscent of the burial of real *prodigia* at Tarquinii Civita? (Other seeming primitivisms or deformities are merely the result of shoddy manufacture, the attempt to retouch a mold or cast that was damaged before firing. See Turfa forthcoming, text discussing fig. 13.)

97. Riva and Stoddart 1996.

98. 37,000 kg, by Greek weight standards, is a large figure to derive from the culling of individual offerings, since it would take 1.5 million tetradrachms to produce this weight of bullion. The find of nine silver tetradrachms associated with Temple A (*Santuari d'Etruria*, 139-140, no. 7.1.O) is sometimes interpreted as part of the city treasury and does represent complex commercial ties (Athens, Syracuse, Messana, Leontinoi), if not Greek pilgrims of the fifth century. Clearly much of the precious metals at rich shrines must have been in the form of bullion or monumental art objects.

99. Terracottas were not the gifts of poor persons either; their clay and labor may have come cheap, but they represent a lengthy process of curing, handling, firing, and consumption of expensive fuel. Except for members of a coroplast's family, customers would have had to purchase them with currency or surplus.

100. Gran-Aymerich 1997.

101. "Laris Velkasnas (dedicated me) to Menerva." Gran-Aymerich 1997, 126-127, fig. 6c; Colonna, REE in *StEtr* 51 (1983), 237-239.

102. For Greek/Italiote material, see van der Meijden 1993. For Latian deposits, see F. Coarelli in *Roma Medio Repubblicana*, 72-99, pls. 16-21.

103. For examples of model food and miniature trays, see Bookidis 1993, 56, fig. 3.6. For Italic examples, see *Grande Roma*, 68-69, no. 3.6 (Capitoline deposit), 212-213 (Valvisciolo), and 238-239, no. 9.6.45 (Satricum).

104. Cristofani 1985, 214-215, 288-289, nos. 107, 109. Cf. the famous bust from Ariccia and related sculptures: A. Z. Gallina in *Roma Medio Repubblicana*, 321-324, nos. 473-474, pls. 62-65. Cf. *Rasenna*, fig. 597, from Caere.

105. The first Greek-style female *protome* has been found at Pyrgi's southern shrine, as indicated by Colonna in this volume, below, p. 139. For background, references, and comparisons, see Uhlenbrock 1988.

106. I thank Björn Forsén for the gift of his invaluable book (Forsén 1996). See Aleshire 1989, 37-100, for identification of Greek terms with artifact types. Almost three-quarters of the dedications in the Athenian Asklepieion were model body parts, coins, or *typoi* (plaques with clothed images of worshipers). For more references on the Greek healing cults, see Chaniotis 1998. A fragmentary Lokri-type plaque was found at Graviscae: Torelli 1977, 411, fig. 9. For illustration of the variety of Lokrian plaques, see Pruckner 1968; Zancani Montuoro 1994-1995 (reprints of collected articles).

107. *Anthologia Palatina* 6.1, the dedication of Lais, the aged courtesan, supposedly recorded by Plato. Greek examples from sanctuary deposits (Hera): *Perachora* I, 105-106, 140-143, 180 = pls. 34 (figs. 3-5), 44 (fig. 12), 46, 80 (figs. 3, 9-14). See de Grummond 1982, 170, 172-173, fig. 110. For the painted funerary offering, Stein-

gräber 1985, 293-294, fig. 93 (first chamber, rear wall). An Archaic bronze figurine of a young woman carrying a mirror was probably a votive: *Enea nel Lazio,* 180, no. D19; *Grande Roma,* 187, no. 1.

108. See Terrosi Zanco 1961; other illustrations in Haynes 1985, 122, 243, 322, no. 199 (third century BCE); Cristofani 1985, 172-173, 273-274 (no. 66), 178-180, 275 (nos. 73-75), 184, 276 (no. 79); *Rasenna,* figs. 130-131. They represent men, women, *haruspices,* youths both clothed and nude, and some with leaf crowns. Why the distorted shape? By analogy to the rare finds of wooden statuettes from Palma di Montechiaro and Roman Gaul, might they reflect a wooden origin? Some bronzes in the Arretium Fonte Veneziana deposit (e.g., Cristofani 1985, 96, 253, no. 3.22, 500-470 BCE) already show distinctive attenuation of body and limbs (cf. Colonna 1970, passim). The consensus is that the later *"ombre"* stem from an Italian tradition of abstract art, a substrate that survived for centuries as a reservoir of images. Certainly Greek artisans did not participate in this trend. Or are the images even more abstract; like the nearly contemporary stick figures in the Tomba del'Orco, might they represent the *hinthial* (soul) or the ancestors seen in the Iron Age Latin funerary terracottas?

109. See Bonfante 1989.

110. If the few veiled heads in Etruscan deposits are not the gifts of Italic ethnics, the custom does point to strong commercial ties between Etruscan and Italic sanctuaries. At Ponte di Nona, a single, unveiled male head among the local offerings might be an Etruscan pilgrim's gift. See Potter 1989, 58-59, figs. 53-53a, discussed p. 52. I am grateful to the late Dr. Potter for sharing this information and his analysis with me in 1981 before the final publication of this deposit.

111. Fridh-Haneson 1987.

112. Turfa 1994, 225, nn. 14-15. Others show an oval incision more like the Tarquinian-Caeretan versions of polyvisceral display. Cf. *Tevere,* pl. 96, nos. 581-582; cf. with polyvisceral plaques: pl. 98, nos. 584, 586.

113. I am indebted to Professor Colonna for this reference: Colonna forthcoming. Another instance of the Roman plundering of Volsinii is a pair of statue bases (fragmentary) inscribed in the sanctuary of Mater Matuta and Fortuna Virilis (Sant'Omobono) by the *triumphator* M. Fulvius Flaccus: M. Torelli in *Roma Medio Repubblicana,* 103-104, no. 89. A possibly related phenomenon, discussed with full background references, is Flower 1998.

114. E.g., a female head in the "Minerva Medica" deposit with hair regrown: D. R. Ricciotti in *Roma Medio Repubblicana,* 168-169, no. 230, pl. 39; knee or elbow with bumps: Gatti Lo Guzzo 1978, 139, nos. 8-9, pl. 52.

115. An even greater number, about 180, predict food supplies, famine being the greatest worry for agricultural societies, with disease recognized as attendant upon hunger. See the calendar, Appendix A, under July 16, Feb. 11, or Aug. 7.

116. See Edlund 1987b.

117. Turfa 1986 and 1994.

118. Since Roman law of the Archaic period (attributed to Numa) required a family to attempt fetal salvage before the mother could be buried, this might represent some sort of proof that it had been accomplished. See Turfa 1994, 232.

119. Physical dangers are apparent even today: brain damage or breathing troubles could result, or there could be need for a wet nurse. Metaphysical conditions are suggested by the Etruscan preoccupation with boundaries of space and time: just as precise age is recorded by funerary epitaphs, might untimely birth, whether late or early, or the loss of the mother be interpreted as evidence of a moral failure?

120. For social background of the *lautni* and *eterau* ("client," "serf"), see Torelli 1987, 87-95; Heurgon 1964, 62-64 and 70-73.

121. The presence of curse tablets such as those found in Greek sanctuaries supports suspicions that personal belongings left in a public place might make the donor vulnerable to witchcraft; cf. Faraone 1991 and Versnel 1991.

122. In fourth-third century Athenian inventories, women's dedications were sometimes twice as frequent as men's; although all heads and feet were male, all other body parts were female. See Aleshire 1989, 110.

123. Again we see the hand of the revetment industry, which also produced antefixes* with the same applied earrings. See Andrén 1955-1956.

124. Potter and Wells 1985; Potter 1989.

125. Reilly 1997.

126. Turfa 1994, 232. Two terracotta plaques said to be from Kos cannot be authenticated. The Corinth Asklepieion shows the only serious use of terracotta anatomicals, logical in this ceramic capital (Roebuck 1951).

127. The finished upper end of the bronze leg from Marzabotto (*Santuari d'Etruria,* 114-115, no. 5.4.B.6), like the bird finial on the Adria leg (see above, n. 33), shows that these were designed as anatomical models and not allusions to walking or serving.

128. *Santuari d'Etruria,* 30-31, no. 1.8. Van der Meer 1987, 153-154, fig. 71; 157-164 on the practice of haruspicy. Cf. Guittard 1997.

129. Van der Meer 1987, 3-18, 147-164. "Human" livers only appear in polyvisceral groups and are especially recognizable in the Caeretan design, less so in types from Vulci and Veii. Hearts and uteri are the only viscera commonly modeled in isolation, and they match Caeretan style. Turfa 1994, 226.

130. "Arnth Alitle Pumpus gave these *viscri.*" *Santuari d'Etruria,* 31, no. 1.9; Dohrn 1968, 11, pl. 22, no. 3, there dated on stylistic grounds to the late third or first half of the second century BCE.

131. Alroth 1989, 65-66.

132. Van der Meer 1987, 144 and passim: this work is of course limited to gods also associated with the Piacenza liver inscriptions; other references are Pfiffig 1975, 231-366; Torelli 1977, 208-210; also Colonna 1997.

133. Van der Meer 1987, 58-66. See Colonna 1966.

134. On the sixth-century Oltos cup from Tarquinii, see *TLE,* 156; *ET,* Ta 3.2; *Rasenna,* fig. 247; V. Olivotto in Bonghi Jovino 1986, 51-52, no. 19.

135. As, for instance, on the Manchester bronze base: Turfa 1982, 183, no. 72, pl. 22e; Pallottino 1982; M. Pallottino, REE in *StEtr* 51 (1983), 609-614. Also G. Colonna, REE in *StEtr* 55 (1987-1988), 345, no. 126.

136. *Santuari d'Etruria,* 29, no. 1.4. See van der Meer 1987, 133-135.

137. For instance, although no votive inscriptions to Letham have yet been identified, this deity is named several times on the Capua tile as a recipient of offerings, and other gods, too, appear as objects of worship in the Zagreb *liber linteus,* Capua tile, and/or the

Piacenza model liver. Cf. van der Meer 1987, 136-141, and 39-40 (Nethuns) and 95 (Cilens).

138. *Santuari d'Etruria*, 160, fig. 19; Haynes 1985, 193, 290-291, no. 122, cast ca. 450-400 BCE, with the inscription riveted onto the side during the Hellenistic period. Bruschetti et al. 1996, 17-20, figs. 1-6, 9-11; del Francia, Bruschetti, and Grassi-Zamarchi 1988 (*ET*, Co 3.1).

BIBLIOGRAPHY AND ABBREVIATIONS

Aleshire, S. B. 1989. *The Athenian Asklepieion: The People, Their Dedications, and the Inventories*. Amsterdam.

———. 1991. *Asklepios at Athens: Epigraphy and Prosopography Essays on the Athenian Healing Cults*. Amsterdam.

Alroth, B. 1989. *Greek Gods and Figurines: Aspects of the Anthropomorphic Dedications*. Boreas. Uppsala Studies in Ancient Mediterranean and Near Eastern Civilizations 18. Uppsala.

Ambrosetti, C. 1954. "Veio. (Località 'Campetti.') Iscrizione votiva." *NSc* 1954, 5.

Andrén, A. 1955-1956. "Una matrice fittile etrusca." *StEtr* 24, 207-219.

———. 1967. "Il santuario della necropoli di Cannicella ad Orvieto." *StEtr* 35, 41-85.

———. 1984. *Orvieto*. Gothenburg.

Barker, G., and T. Rasmussen 1998. *The Etruscans*. Oxford.

Bartoloni, G. 1970. "Pyrgi: Le terrecotte votive." In *Pyrgi: Scavi del santuario etrusco*. *NSc* 1970 Suppl. 2. 552-577.

———. 1989. *La cultura villanoviana*. Rome.

Bianchi Bandinelli, R. 1929. *Sovana*. Florence.

Bietti Sestieri, A. M. 1992. *The Iron Age Community of Osteria dell'Osa: A Study of Socio-Political Development in Central Tyrrhenian Italy*. Cambridge.

Bietti Sestieri, A. M., A. De Santis, and A. La Regina. 1989-1990. "Elementi di tipo cultuale e doni personali nella necropoli laziale di Osteria dell'Osa." *Scienze dell'Antichità* 3-4, 65-88.

Blagg, T. F. C. 1985. "Cult Practice and Its Social Context in the Religious Sanctuaries of Latium and Southern Etruria: The Sanctuary of Diana at Nemi." In *Papers in Italian Archaeology*, vol. 4, ed. C. Malone and S. Stoddart. BAR-IS 246. 33-50.

Bocci Paccini, P. 1980. "La stipe della Fonte Veneziana ad Arezzo." *StEtr* 48, 73-91.

———. 1984. "Alcuni bronzetti arcaici della 'Fonte Veneziana.'" In *Studi di Antichità in Onore di Guglielmo Maetzke*. Florence. 119-123.

Bonfante, G., and L. Bonfante. 2002. *The Etruscan Language: An Introduction*. 2nd ed. Manchester.

Bonfante, L. 1989. "Iconografia delle madri: Etruria e Italia antica." In *Le donne in Etruria*, ed. A. Rallo. Rome. 85-119.

Bonghi Jovino, M. 1976. *Depositi votivi d'Etruria*. Milan.

———, ed. 1986. *Gli Etruschi di Tarquinia*. Catalogue of exhibition. Modena.

———. 1997. "La phase archaïque de l'Ara della Regina à la lumiére des recherches récentes." In *LPRH*, 69-95.

Bonghi Jovino, M., and C. Chiaramonte Treré, eds. 1987. *Tarquinia: Ricerche, scavi e prospettive*. Catalogue of exhibition [1986]. Milan.

Bonghi Jovino, M., and C. Chiaramonte Treré, eds. 1997. *Tarquinia: Testimonianze archeologiche e ricostruzione storica*. Rome.

Bookidis, N. 1993. "Ritual Dining at Corinth." In *Greek Sanctuaries, New Approaches*. 45-61.

Brendel, O. J. 1995. *Etruscan Art*. New Haven.

Brown, S. 1991. *Late Carthaginian Child Sacrifice*. Sheffield.

Bruschetti, P., et al., 1996. *Il Museo dell'Accademia Etrusca di Cortona*. 2nd ed. Cortona.

Buranelli, F., ed. 1987. *La Tomba François di Vulci*. Rome.

Chaniotis, A. 1998. Review of Forsén 1996. *Bryn Mawr Classical Review* 98.2.10. Retrieved January 30, 2005, from http://ccat.sas.upenn.edu/bmcr

Chéhab, M. H. 1951-1952. *Les Terres cuites de Kharayeb: Bulletin du Musée de Beyrouth* 10. Paris.

———. 1953-1954. *Les Terres cuites de Kharayeb: Bulletin du Musée de Beyrouth* 11. Paris.

Civiltà degli Etruschi = M. Cristofani, ed. *Civiltà degli Etruschi*. Catalogue of exhibition. Milan. 1985.

Civiltà del Lazio Primitivo. Catalogue of exhibition. Rome. 1976.

Clifford, R. J. 1990. "Phoenician Religion." *BASOR* 279, 55-64.

Coarelli, F. 1988. *Il Foro Boario* III. Rome.

Colonna, G. 1966. "Selvans sanchuneta," *StEtr* 34, 165-172.

———. 1967. "Ager Tarquiniensis: Norchia," in REE. *StEtr* 35, 547-548.

———. 1970. *Bronzi votivi umbro-sabellici a figura umana. I.- Periodo "Arcaico."* Florence.

———. 1976-1977. "La dea etrusca Cel e i santuari del Trasimeno." *RivStorAnt* 6-7, 45-62.

———. 1978. "Originis incertae." REE. *StEtr* 46, 379-381 (no. 140).

———. 1984-1985. "Novità sui culti di Pyrgi." *RendPontAcc* 57, 57-88.

———. 1987. "Il maestro dell'Ercole e della Minerva: Nuova luce sull'attività dell'officina veiente." *OpRom* 16, 7-41.

———. 1988. "Una nuova dedica alla etrusca Uni," *BdA* ser. 6, vol. 73, 23-26.

———. 1997. "Divinités peu connues du panthéon étrusque." In *LPRH*, 167-184.

———. forthcoming. "Volsinio capto: Sulle tracce dei donari asportati da Orvieto nel 264 a.C." In *Mélanges A. Magdelain*.

Comella, A. 1978. *Il materiale votivo tardo di Gravisca*. Archaeologica 6. Rome.

———. 1981. "Tipologia e diffusione dei complessi votive in Italia in epoca medio e tardo repubblicana: Contributo alla storia dell'artigianato antico." *MÉFRA* 93, 717-803.

———. 1982. *Il deposito votivo presso l'Ara della Regina*. Archaeologica 22. Rome.

———. 1986. *I materiali votivi di Falerii*. Rome.

Comella, A., and G. Stefani. 1990. *Materiali votivi del Santuario di Campetti a Veio: Scavi 1947 e 1969*. Archaeologia 84. Rome.

Cornell, T. J. 1978. "*Principes* of Tarquinia." Review of Torelli 1975. *JRS* 68, 167-173.

———. 1995. *The Beginnings of Rome*. London.
Costantini, S. 1995. *Il deposito votivo del santuario campestre di Tessennano*. Archaeologica 112. Rome.
Cristofani, M. 1985. *I Bronzi degli Etruschi*. Novara.
———. 1996. *Etruschi e altre genti nell'Italia preromana: Mobilità in età arcaica*. Rome.
Damgaard Andersen, H. 1993. "The Etruscan Ancestor Cult: Its Origin and Development and the Importance of Anthropomorphization." *AnalRom* 21, 7-66.
Day, J. 1989. *Moloch: A God of Human Sacrifice in the Old Testament*. Cambridge.
De Grummond, N. T., ed. 1982. *A Guide to Etruscan Mirrors*. Tallahassee, FL.
Del Chiaro, M. A. 1976. *Etruscan Ghiaccio Forte*. Santa Barbara, CA.
Del Francia, P. R., P. Bruschetti, and P. Grassi-Zamarchi eds. 1988. *Nuove letture del lampadario etrusco*. Catalogue of exhibition. Cortona.
De Polignac, F. 1995. Tr. Janet Lloyd. *Cults, Territory, and the Origins of the Greek City-State*. Chicago.
D'Ercole, M. C. 1990. *La stipe votiva del Belvedere a Lucera*. Archaeologica 80. Rome.
Dillon, M. 1997. *Pilgrims and Pilgrimage in Ancient Greece*. London.
Dohrn, T. 1968. *Der Arringatore*. Berlin.
Edlund, I. E. M. 1987a. *The Gods and the Place*. Skrifter utgivna av Svenska Institutet i Rom 43. Stockholm.
———. 1987b. "*Mens Sana in Corpore Sano*: Healing Cults as a Political Factor in Etruscan Religion." In *Gifts to the Gods*, eds. T. Linders and G. Nordquist. Symposium, Gifts to the Gods, Uppsala, 1985 = Boreas 15. Uppsala. 51-56.
Edlund-Berry, I. E. M. 1994. "Ritual Destruction of Cities and Sanctuaries: The 'Un-founding' of the Archaic Monumental Building at Poggio Civitate (Murlo)." In *Murlo and the Etruscans*, ed. R. D. De Puma and J. P. Small. Madison, WI. 16-28.
Enea nel Lazio = *Enea nel Lazio, archeologia e mito*. 1980. Catalogue of exhibition. Rome.
ET = H. Rix. 1991. *Etruskische Texte: Editio Minor*. 2 vols. Tübingen.
Falsone, G. 1992. "Bronzes." In *Dictionnaire de la civilisation phénicienne et punique*, ed. E. Lipinski. Brepols. 80-81.
Faraone, C. A. 1991. "The Agonistic Context of Early Greek Binding Spells." In *Magika Hiera: Ancient Greek Magic and Religion*, ed. C. A. Faraone and D. Obbink. Oxford. 3-32.
Fayer, C. 1982. *Aspetti di vita quotidiana nella Roma arcaica*. Rome.
Fenelli, M. 1975. "Contributo per lo studio del votivo anatomico: I votivi anatomici di Lavinio." *ArchCl* 27, 206-252.
———. 1984. "Lavinium." *Archeologia Laziale* 6, 325-344.
Flower, H. 1998. "The Significance of an Inscribed Breastplate Captured at Falerii in 241 B.C." *JRA* 11, 224-232.
Forsén, B. 1996. *Griechische Gliederweihungen*. Papers and Monographs of the Finnish Institute at Athens, 4. Helsinki.
Fortuna, A. M., and F. Giovannoni. 1975. *Il lago degli idoli*. Florence.
Fridh-Haneson, B.-M. 1987. "Votive Terracottas from Italy, Types and Problems." In *Gifts to the Gods*. Symposium, Gifts to the Gods, Uppsala, 1985 = Boreas 15. Uppsala. 66-75.
Gatti Lo Guzzo, L. 1978. *Il deposito votivo dell'Esquilino detto di Minerva Medica*. StMat 17. Florence.
Goold, G. P., ed. and tr. 1990. *Propertius, Elegies*. (Loeb Classical Library.) Cambridge, MA.

Gran-Aymerich, J. 1997. "Les vases céramiques et la place du bucchero dans les dépôts votifs et les sanctuaires." In *LPRH*, 117-136.
Grande Roma = *La grande Roma dei Tarquini*. 1990. Catalogue of exhibition. Rome. 1990.
Gras, M. 1985. *Trafics tyrrheniens archaïques*. BEFAR 258. Rome.
Greek Sanctuaries, New Approaches = N. Marinatos and R. Hägg, eds. 1993. *Greek Sanctuaries, New Approaches*. New York.
Gualandi, G. 1970. "[Marzabotto.] Il santuario fontile a nord della città." *StEtr* 38, 217-223.
———. 1974. "Santuari e stipi votive dell'Etruria Padana." *StEtr* 42, 37-68.
Guittard, C. 1997. "Questions sur la divination étrusque: Les formules dans la tradition latine." In *LPRH*, 399-412.
Guzzo, P. G., S. Moscati, and G. Susini, eds. 1994. *Antiche genti d'Italia*. Rimini.
Hackens, T. 1963. "Favisae." *Études Étrusco-italiques*. Louvain. 71-99.
Haynes, S. 1985. *Etruscan Bronzes*. London.
———. 1989. "*Muliebris certaminis laus*: Bronze Documents of a Changing Ethos." *Secondo Congresso Internazionale Etrusco (1985), Atti* 3. Rome. 1395-1405.
Herrmann, H. V. 1983. "Altitalisches und etruskisches in Olympia." *ASAtene* 61, 271-294.
Heurgon, J. 1964. *Daily Life of the Etruscans*. Tr. J. Kirkup. London.
Holländer, E. 1912. *Plastik und Medizin*. Stuttgart.
Iacobone, C. 1988. *Le stipi votive di Taranto*. Archaeologica 78. Rome.
Inturrisi, L. 1989. "Votive Figures for Collectors." *New York Times*, Sunday 2/19/1989, sec. 5, p. 12.
Kunze, E. 1951-1953. "Etruskische Bronzen in Griechenland." In *Studies Presented to David M. Robinson*, ed. G. E. Mylonas. St. Louis, MO. 1.736-746.
Kyrieleis, H. 1993. "The Heraion at Samos." In *Greek Sanctuaries, New Approaches*. 125-153.
Lancel, S. 1995. *Carthage: A History*, tr. A. Neville. Original ed. 1992. Oxford.
Lavinium II = F. Castagnoli, L. Cozza, M. Fenelli, et al., 1975. *Lavinium II: Le tredici altari*. Rome.
Linder, E. 1973. "A Cargo of Phoenico-Punic Figurines." *Archaeology* 26, 182-187.
Lipinski, E. 1992. "Offrandes." In *Dictionnaire de la civilisation phénicienne et punique*, ed. E. Lipinski. Brepols. 330.
Lowe, C. 1978. "The Historical Significance of Early Latin Votive Deposits (up to the 4th Century B.C.)." In *Papers in Italian Archaeology I. The Lancaster Seminar*. Part ii, ed. H. McK. Blake, T. W. Potter, and D. B. Whitehouse. BAR Suppl. ser. 41, 1.141-151.
LPRH = F. Gaultier and D. Briquel, eds., *Les Étrusques, les plus religieux des hommes: État de la recherche sur la religion étrusque*. Actes du colloque international Grand Palais 17-18-19 novembre 1992. XII[er] Rencontres de l'École du Louvre. Paris.
Luce, J.-M. 1992. "Les terres cuites de Kirrha." In *Delphes: Centenaire de la "Grande Fouille" Réalisé par l'École Française d'Athénes (1892-1903)*, ed. J.-F. Bommelaer. Leiden. 263-275.
MacIntosh, J. 1974. "Excavation at Corinth, 1973. Appendix I. Etruscan Bucchero Pottery Imports in Corinth." *Hesperia* 43, 34-45.
Maggiani, A. 1997. "Réflexions sur la religion étrusque 'primitive': De l'époque villanovienne à l'époque archaïque." In *LPRH*, 431-447.

Maioli, M. G., and A. Mastrocinque. 1992. *La stipe di Villa di Villa e i culti degli antichi Veneti*. Archaeologica 102. Rome.

Martelli, M. 1972. Review of Vagnetti 1971. *StEtr* 40, 574-577.

Martín Ruiz, J. A. 1995. *Catálogo documental de los Fenicios en Andalucía*. Junta de Andalucía.

Massabò, B. 1985. "Contributo alla conoscenza topografica di Vulci: Le aree sacre di Fontanile di Legnisina e di Polledrara." *BdA* ser. 6, vol. 70.1, 17-24.

———. 1988-1989. "III. CANINO (Viterbo): Il santuario etrusco di Fontanile di Legnisina a Vulci: Relazione delle campagne di scavo 1985 e 1986: Il tempio." *NSc* 42-43, 103-135.

Massabò, B., and L. Ricciardi. 1988. "Il tempio, l'altare e il deposito votivo." *BdA* ser. 6, vol. 73, 27-42.

Maule, Q. F., and H. R. W. Smith. 1959. *Votive Religion at Caere: Prolegomena*. University of California Publications in Classical Archaeology 4.1. Berkeley, CA.

Melis, F., and S. Quilici Gigli. 1983. "Votivi e luoghi di culto nella campagna di Velletri." *ArchCl* 35, 1-44.

Mengarelli, R. 1935. "Il tempio del Manganello a Caere." *StEtr* 9, 83-94.

Moretti, M. 1970. "Gravisca (Tarquinia): Scavi nella città etrusca e romana. Campagne 1969 e 1970." *NSc* 1, 195-299.

Morgan, C. 1993. "The Origins of Pan-Hellenism." In *Greek Sanctuaries, New Approaches*, 18-44.

———. 1994. "The Evolution of a Sacred 'Landscape': Isthmia, Perachora, and the Early Corinthian State." In *Placing the Gods: Sanctuaries and Sacred Space in Ancient Greece*, ed. S. E. Alcock and R. Osborne. Oxford. 105-142.

———. 1997. "The Archaeology of Sanctuaries in Early Iron Age and Archaic *Ethne*: A Preliminary View." In *The Development of the Polis in Archaic Greece*, ed. L. G. Mitchell and P. J. Rhodes. London. 168-198.

Nagy, H. 1988. *Votive Terracottas from the "Vignaccia," Cerveteri, in the Lowie Museum of Anthropology*. Archaeologica 75. Rome.

———. 1994. "Divinities in the Context of Sacrifice and Cult on Caeretan Votive Terracottas." In *Murlo and the Etruscans*, ed. R. D. De Puma and J. P. Small. Madison, WI. 211-223.

Nijboer, A. J. 1998. *From Household Production to Workshops*. Groningen.

Ostby, E. 1993. "Twenty-five Years of Research on Greek Sanctuaries: A Bibliography." In *Greek Sanctuaries, New Approaches*, 192-227.

Pallottino, M. 1975. *The Etruscans*. Bloomington, IN.

———. 1982. "Iscrizione etrusca sulla basetta di bronzo del Museo di Manchester." *PBSR* 50, 193-195.

Palmer, R. E. 1996. "Locket Gold, Lizard Green." In *Etruscan Italy*, ed. J. Hall. Provo, UT. 17-27.

Paton, W. R., ed. and tr. 1960. *The Greek Anthology*, vol I. (Loeb Classical Library.) Boston.

Pautasso, A. 1994. *Il deposito votivo presso la Porta Nord a Vulci*. Archaeologica 107. Rome.

Perachora I = H. Payne et al. *Perachora* I. Oxford. 1940.

Pfiffig, A. 1975. *Religio etrusca*. Graz.

Pianu, G. 1991. "Gli altari di Gravisca." In *L'Espace sacrificiel*, ed. R. Étienne and M.-T. Le Dinahet. Paris. 193-199.

Potter, T. W. 1989. *Una stipe votiva da Ponte di Nona: Lavori e studi di archeologia* 13. Rome.

Potter, T. W., and C. Wells. 1985. "A Republican Healing-Sanctuary at Ponte di Nona near Rome and the Classical Tradition of Votive Medicine." *Journal of the British Archaeological Association* 138, 23-47.

Prosdocimi, A. L. 1989. "La religione degli Italici." In *Italia omnium terrarum parens*, ed. C. Ampolo et al. Milan. 477-545.

Pruckner, H. 1968. *Die Lokrischen Tonreliefs: Beitrag zur Kunstgeschichte von Lokroi Epizephyrioi*. Mainz am Rhein.

Rasenna = G. Pugliese Carratelli, M. Pallottino, et al., eds. 1986. *Rasenna: Storia e civiltà degli Etruschi*. Milan.

REE = *Rivista di Epigrafia Etrusca*, appearing continuously in *StEtr*.

Reilly, J. 1997. "Naked and Limbless: Learning about the Feminine Body in Ancient Athens." In *Naked Truths: Women, Sexuality and Gender in Classical Art and Archaeology*, ed. O. Koloski-Ostrow and C. L. Lyons. New York. 154-173.

Religio Phoenicia = *Religio Phoenicia: Acta coloquii Namurcensis habiti diebus 14 e 15 mensis Decembris anni 1984*, ed. C. Bonnet, E. Lipinski, and P. Marchetti. Namur. 1986. Studia Phoenicia 4.

Ricciardi, L. 1988-1989. "L'altare monumentale e il deposito votivo." *NSc* 42-43, 137-209.

Richardson, E. H. 1983. *Etruscan Votive Bronzes: Geometric, Orientalizing, Archaic*. Mainz.

Ridgway, F. R. S. 1990. "Etruscans, Greeks, Carthaginians: The Sanctuary at Pyrgi." In *Greek Colonists and Native Populations*, ed. J.-P. Descoeudres. Oxford. 511-530.

Riva, C., and S. Stoddart. 1996. "Ritual Landscapes in Archaic Etruria." In *Approaches to the Study of Ritual*, ed. J. B. Wilkins. Accordia Specialist Studies on the Mediterranean 2. London. 91-109.

Roebuck, C. 1951. *The Asklepieion and Lerna. Corinth XIV*. Princeton.

Roma Medio Repubblicana = *Roma Medio Repubblicana: Aspetti culturali di Roma e del Lazio nei secoli IV e III a.C. 1983*. Catalogue of exhibition. Rome. 1973.

Romualdi, A. 1981. *Catalogo del deposito di Brolio in Val di Chiana*. Rome.

Santuari d'Etruria = G. Colonna, ed., *Santuari d'Etruria*. Catalogue of exhibition in Arezzo. Milan. 1985.

Sgubini Moretti, A. M., and G. Bordenache Battaglia. 1975. "Materiali archeologici scoperti a Lucus Feroniae." In *Nuove scoperte e acquisizioni nell'Etruria meridionale*, ed. M. Moretti. Rome. 93-175.

Simon, C. G. 1997. "The Archaeology of Cult in Geometric Greece: Ionic Temples, Altars, and Dedications." In *New Light on a Dark Age*, ed. S. Langdon. Columbia, MO. 125-143.

Smith, C. 1996. "Dead Dogs and Rattles: Time, Space and Ritual Sacrifice in Iron Age Latium." In *Approaches to the Study of Ritual*, ed. J. B. Wilkins. Accordia Specialist Studies on the Mediterranean 2. London. 73-89.

———. 1997. "Servius Tullius, Cleisthenes and the Emergence of the Polis." In *The Development of the Polis in Archaic Greece*, ed. L. G. Mitchell and P. J. Rhodes. London. 208-216.

Snodgrass, A. 1980. *Archaic Greece: The Age of Experiment*. London.

———. 1989-1990. "The Economics of Dedication at Greek Sanctuaries." *Atti del Convegno Internazionale ANATHEMA. Scienze dell'Antichità* 3-4, 287-294.

Sourvinou-Inwood, C. 1993. "Early Sanctuaries, the Eighth Century and Ritual Space: Fragments of a Discourse." In *Greek Sanctuaries, New Approaches*, 1-17.

Steingräber, S. 1985. *Catalogue Raisonné of Etruscan Wall Paintings:*

Etruscan Painting, ed. D. Ridgway and F. R. S. Ridgway. New York.
Stern, E. 1986. "Two *Favissae* from Tel Dor, Israel." In *Religio Phoenicia*, 277-287.
Strøm, I. 1992. "Evidence from the Sanctuaries." In *Greece between East and West*, ed. G. Kopcke and I. Tokumaru. Mainz. 46-59.
Terrosi Zanco, O. 1961. "Ex-voto allungati dell'Italia centrale." *StEtr* 29, 423-459.
Tevere = P. Pensabene et al. *Terrecotte votive dal Tevere*. StMisc 25. Rome. 1980.
Thuillier, J. P. 1991. "Autels d'Etrurie." In *L'Espace sacrificiel*, ed. R. Étienne and M.-T. Le Dinahet. Paris. 243-247.
TLE = M. Pallottino. 1968. *Testimonia Linguae Etruscae*. 2nd ed. Florence.
Torelli, M. 1975. *Elogia Tarquiniensia*. StMat 15. Florence.
———. 1977. "Il santuario greco di Gravisca." *PP* 32, 398-458.
———. 1982. "Per la definizione del commercio greco-orientale: Il caso di Gravisca." *PP* 37, 304-325.
———. 1986. "La religione." In *Rasenna*, 159-237.
———. 1987. *La società etrusca*. Rome.
———. 1997. "Les Adonies de Gravisca: Archéologie d'une fête." In *LPRH*, 233-291.
Torelli, M., and I. Pohl 1973. "Veio: Scoperta di un piccolo santuario etrusco in località Campetti." *NSc* 1973, 40-258.
Tuck, A. S. 1994. "The Etruscan Seated Banquet: Villanovan Ritual and Etruscan Iconography." *AJA* 98, 617-628.
Turfa, J. M. 1982. "The Etruscan and Italic Collection in the Manchester Museum." *PBSR* 50, 166-193.
———. 1986. "21. Anatomical Votive Terracottas from Etruscan and Italic Sanctuaries." In *Italian Iron Age Artefacts in the British Museum*, ed. J. Swaddling. London. 205-213.
———. 1994. "Anatomical Votives and Italian Medical Traditions." In *Murlo and the Etruscans*, ed. R. D. De Puma and J. P. Small. Madison, WI. 224-240.
———. Forthcoming. "Figurines Are Bought and Sold, but not Art: The Sanctuary of Demeter and Kore on Acrocorinth, and Corinthian Terracottas in the West." In *Art and Myth in the Colonial World*, ed. G. Tsetskhladze and C. Morgan. Papers of symposium, Royal Holloway College, 1997.
Uhlenbrock, J. 1985. "Terracotta Figurines from the Demeter Sanctuary at Cyrene: Models for Trade." In *Cyrenaica in Antiquity*, ed. G. Barker, J. Lloyd, and J. Reynolds. BAR-IS 236. Oxford. 297-304.
———. 1988. *The Terracotta Protomai from Gela*. Rome.
Vagnetti, L. 1971. *Il deposito votivo di Campetti a Veio*. StMat 11. Florence.
Vance, D. R. 1994. "Literary Sources for the History of Palestine and Syria: The Phoenician Inscriptions, Parts I and II." *BiblArch* 57, 2-19, 110-120.
Van der Meer, L. B. 1987. *The Bronze Liver of Piacenza*. Amsterdam.
Van der Meijden, H. 1993. *Terrakotta-Arulae aus Sizilien und Unteritalien*. Amsterdam.
Van Straten, F. T. 1981. "Gifts for the Gods." In *Faith, Hope and Worship*, ed. H. S. Versnel. Leiden. 65-151.
Versnel, H. S. 1991. "Beyond Cursing: The Appeal to Justice in Judicial Prayers." In *Magika Hiera: Ancient Greek Magic and Religion*, ed. C. A. Faraone and D. Obbink. Oxford. 60-106.
von Hase, F.-W. 1997. "Présences étrusques et italiques dans les sanctuaires grecs (VIIIᵉ-VIIᵉ siècle av. J.-C.)." In *LPRH*, 293-323.
Warden, P. G. 1983. "Bullae, Roman Custom and Italic Tradition." *OpRom* 14, 69-75.
Zancani Montuoro, P. 1994-1995. "I pinakes di Locri." *ASMG* ser. 3, vol. 3, 151-261.

CHAPTER VII

RITUAL SPACE AND BOUNDARIES IN ETRUSCAN RELIGION

Ingrid E. M. Edlund-Berry

It remains now for us to speak of the Tyrrhenians. For they, excelling in vigor, in ancient times possessed much land and founded many noteworthy cities.
Diodorus Siculus 5.40

The Greek historian Diodorus Siculus is one of the many ancient Greek and Latin authors who supply a wealth of observations about the Etruscan presence in Italy and the geography of the region known as Tyrrhenia or Etruria.[1] Depending on the type of text and the author's objectives, the tone of the narrative may range from statements of historical facts and mythological foundation stories to accounts of Etruscan lifestyle and society. With the additional help of the material remains from the Etruscan period and an awareness of the physical space of the area between the Arno and the Tiber primarily, it is also possible to supplement these written sources to identify a distinct pattern in the Etruscan definitions of ritual space and boundaries as experienced in many aspects of Etruscan life, but primarily in the sphere of Etruscan religion.

DEFINITION OF SPACE AND BOUNDARIES

To appreciate the Etruscan concept of space, it is important to acknowledge the physical configuration of Etruria (Fig. VII.1).[2] While the wide open spaces of southern Italy or Sicily provide a sense of infinity, the Tuscan landscape presents a variety of smaller units, where valleys and rivers, fields and pastures alternate with wooded hills and high mountains. Depending on the area, one community would look out over an inviting set of rolling hills, continuing down into the plains along the Tyrrhenian shores, while others further inland were enclosed by steep mountain sides that provided protection but that also discouraged interaction with the inhabitants in the next valley over.

All these spaces were part of the daily experience of the Etruscans. From the earliest evidence of human habitation in Etruria we find that some spaces were set aside for living, other spaces for burials, and yet others for the worship of deities. Within all these aspects of Etruscan activity, some spaces may be called ritual because of a religious act that took place there, such as a sacrifice or a procession, and such a place may be synonymous with, or exist parallel to, a space that is sacred in and by itself. Such ritual and sacred spaces exist in contrast to those that were designated for secular activities, independent of divine intervention or involvement.[3]

Any space, whether sacred or secular, was defined by its shape and boundaries. In a landscape like that of Tuscany, these spaces are most commonly defined by the natural setting, the presence of rivers and lakes, narrow valleys, caves, and groves. The terms for such spaces and boundaries are usually known from the Latin vocabulary (*templum,** *auguraculum,** *limes,** *limitatio,** *pomerium**)[4] but exist also in the limited Etruscan nomenclature preserved in inscriptions or referred to in Latin texts ("boundaries," *tular,**[5] and perhaps also "surveyor's pole," *groma/gruma*).[6] As with customs and traditions, more often than not there would have been no need to mark the boundaries of such spaces in any particular way since their existence was well known to the local

VII.1. Etruscan landscape near Tarquinii; view from the temple of the Ara della Regina. (Photo: Ingrid Edlund-Berry.)

inhabitants. The Latin texts indicate, however, that spaces and boundaries could be defined in some particular fashion,[7] such as by a plowed furrow (Fig. VII.2), and were thus made recognizable to any passerby. At other times a boundary was marked by especially designed boundary stones, inscribed in Etruscan with a form of the word *tular* translated as "boundaries" (Fig. VII.3).[8]

As always, it is difficult to separate the original Etruscan traditions[9] from their distinctly Roman counterparts in the historical and literary tradition. According to the so-called prophecy of Vegoia, the division of land and the establishment of boundaries was the result of Jupiter's (i.e., Tinia's) interaction with humans.[10] The reason for his action was to create order and to prevent human greed for land from upsetting the established balance of ownership.

In the specific case of boundaries, the Roman author Frontinus, best known for his treatise on aqueducts, quotes the polyhistor Varro as saying that boundaries were part of the Etruscan science or *Etrusca disciplina** since the division of the world according to the cardinal points of north, south, east, and west was designed by Etruscan priests, the *haruspices*.*[11]

As can be expected, boundaries, natural as well as artificial, needed to be under the protection of a deity. As will be discussed later, any number of deities could be entrusted with this task, but the names Tul, as inscribed on the bronze model of a sheep's liver known as the Piacenza liver (Fig. II.2),[12] and Selvans (or Selans)[13] stand out. While there is no

VII.2. Bronze statuette with priest and oxen from Arezzo. Early fourth century BCE. Rome, Museo Etrusco di Villa Giulia. (Photo: Soprintendenza per i Beni Archeologici dell'Etruria Meridionale.)

known anthropomorphic representation of Tul, the statuette of Selvans from Cortona (Fig. IV.16) illustrates this boundary deity as a young man, parallel to the companion piece depicting the two-faced Culśanś, like the Roman Janus a guardian of gates (Fig. II.9). Selvans is usually equated with the Roman Silvanus, god of the woods or of wooded spaces defined by tree boundaries, rather than with Terminus, the abstract Roman boundary deity known from the Capitoline hill in Rome.[14] According to the accounts by the historians Livy and Dionysios of Halikarnassos of the selection of the

VII.3. Stone boundary cippus, *with inscription* tular larna, *"boundaries of the Larna family." Second century* BCE. *Bettona, Museo Civico. (Photo: Soprintendenza per i Beni Archeologici dell'Umbria.)*

proper location for the future temple to the triad Jupiter, Juno, and Minerva, Terminus refused to give up his rights to occupy the hill, and special arrangements had to be made to incorporate his space into the new temple.[15]

APPEARANCE OF RITUAL SPACE IN HEAVEN AND ON EARTH

In addition to the patchwork of the Tuscan landscape with its manifold divisions based on hills and valleys, plains and mountain peaks, there are two main examples of Etruscan perceptions of space and boundaries related to the deities. The first is the bronze liver found near Piacenza in northern Italy (Fig. 11.2), inscribed with names of Etruscan deities arranged in cells or irregular wedges of different sizes, separated by incised lines. There are sixteen cells along the edge of the upper side of the liver, forming a continuous band around the center, which is divided up into a total of twenty-four more segments. The underside of the liver has two additional inscribed names, separated by a line.[16]

The second example is a set of Latin texts that describe a division of the sky into sixteen regions. In addition to brief references by Cicero[17] and Pliny,[18] the Late Roman author Martianus Capella provides a long description of the Etruscan system of dividing the sky into sixteen regions, each inhabited by one or more deities.[19]

Despite both the liver and the texts including names of deities that are otherwise undocumented or less well known than those of the established Etrusco-Roman pantheon, there are immediate similarities in the configuration of spaces. Most importantly, the sixteen divisions around the edge of the liver correspond to the sixteen regions or houses described in the texts. It is possible to correlate at least some of the deities (Jupiter, Liber, and Juno) assigned to a division on the liver with those of the regions in the texts.[20]

Complex as the Piacenza liver and the descriptions of the regions of the sky are, these testimonia stand out as examples of an Etruscan belief system about spaces and boundaries that are the key for our understanding of much of the Etruscan worldview. What they both illustrate is an absolute need for defining spaces as contiguous entities, related to each other by a common border, but also separate from each other because of the very same border and because of the deity in charge of each space. Regardless of the nature of each specific space, each gains its identity and strength by being part of a pattern, a design of molecules, with infinite possibilities for expansion.

Furthermore, these contiguous spaces, as indicated on the liver and in the sixteen regions, not only extended horizontally on earth or in heaven but provided vertical links between heaven and earth, and between earth and the Underworld. In heaven the orientation of the regions was guided by the spatial directions: north, south, east, and west. On earth, these celestial spaces corresponded with a variety of spaces: first, the delimited, inaugurated spaces, *templum* or *auguraculum*, from which the sky was observed; second, the *temenos*,* or enclosed space around a sanctuary, including features such as altars and temples; and third, features in nature such as mountaintops, rivers, lakes, and groves.[21] As shown by the texts that describe the taking of auspices from such areas on earth, the orientation of their layout and the direction from which the celestial signs arrived were all tied to the division of the skies into the sixteen regions. The most famous of these instances is the contest between Romulus and Remus for the right to become the sole founder of Rome,[22] but, as Cicero points out, this tradition was rooted in Etruscan principles.[23]

Comparable to the compass orientation of the celestial sixteen regions is the orientation of the known Etruscan temples. Unlike Greek temples, which were usually oriented with the entrance towards the east, the Etruscan temples as a rule faced south to southeast or southwest.[24] According to the analysis by Prayon, there is a direct correlation between the types of deities worshiped in the temples and their orientation.[25] In the Archaic period, there existed a concentration of temples dedicated to female deities oriented towards the southwest, whereas a few temples dedicated to male deities faced toward the southeast.

In addition to the compass orientation, we should also take into account the location of sanctuaries in relation to their surroundings, whether urban or rural. As evidence from recent excavations such as those in the area of Monte Falterona and Monte Giovi in northern Etruria shows, it is important to relate the orientation of any type of building, but sanctuaries in particular, to the layout of the land and to certain features in nature that connected sites, linking natural elements such as mountaintops to each other.[26] At other sites, the configuration of hilltops and means of access may have determined the orientation of a temple or other building such as the complexes at Murlo or Acquarossa.[27] The layout of the *auguraculum* and temples at the Etruscan site of Marzabotto[28] and later the Roman colony at Cosa further illustrates that the tradition of respecting the features of the landscape was carried into Roman times.[29]

The connection between the heavens, the earth, and the Underworld is further expressed by terms referring to "openings" in the earth, such as a pit dug in the earth for offerings of fruits, known as *mundus*.*[30] In the setting of the Etruscan landscape, such openings were reflected in natural formations such as the lakes formed by extinct volcanic craters[31] or in caves set in the hill slopes.[32] Hot springs and sulphur fumes emanating from fissures in the ground were further indications of links between the earth and the Underworld, and as such they were venerated with votive offerings from the earliest times in the prehistory of ancient Italy. Among the most famous of these sulphurous smelling sites is the sanctuary of Apollo on Mount Soracte in the Faliscan territory of Etruria, where the priests known as Hirpi underwent an act of purification by fire each year in honor of the god.[33] Sites with sulphur springs appear all over Italy and not only in Etruria, and many were connected with the cult of the goddess Mephitis as a healing deity.[34] Whether or not sulphuric, many spring sanctuaries have been documented through place names and finds of votive deposits, with a concentration to the west of Lake Bracciano in southern Etruria.[35] As witnessed by the many health spas in modern Tuscany based on water cures, the tradition of places with healing waters still continues.[36]

CROSSING OF BOUNDARIES

While boundaries serve to separate spaces, they also invite the crossing over from one space to another. Such a crossing between the celestial space and the space on earth was defined in the Latin term of *religio*,* or binding, which is another way of marking a contiguous vertical boundary or "tie" between heaven and earth.[37] The link between above and below provided strength and security, and a focal point, in Eliade's terminology, an *axis mundi,* which served as a corner stone for the stable world, for *cosmos*.[38]

The interaction between heaven and earth required a language of communication. Mountaintops, such as those of Mount Soracte and Monte Falterona, provided a sense of proximity to the skies, and the ancient texts indicate that the language of interaction was usually dramatic. Depending on their role and the circumstances of their intervention, the deities in the skies would communicate with the humans on earth by signs such as thunder and lightning.[39] The sending and acceptance of signs were performed with birds as messengers, and it was the task of the priests, *haruspices* and others, to interpret these signs through augury.[40] The humans, in turn, sought the attention of the deities by using prayers and sacrifices and by observing the celestial signs from assigned spaces (*templum, auguraculum*).

In the same way as the sun and the moon, lightness and darkness, rain and snow, provided the interaction between the celestial space and earth, the boundaries of time were also expressed in the Etruscan calendar. As documented in religious texts such as those preserved on the Zagreb mummy wrapping (Fig. 11.1)[41] and on the so-called Capua tile (Fig. 11.3),[42] the indications of segments of time in days, months, and parts of the year suggest that the Etruscans were as meticulous in their time management as they were in establishing the order of the universe through appropriate boundaries defining different kinds of spaces.[43] The months were divided into units equivalent to the Roman Kalends, Nones, and Ides,[44] and the days were numbered from one through twenty-nine (or thirty), as shown in the Zagreb mummy wrapping and other texts.[45] According to Servius, the late

Roman commentator of Vergil, the Etruscan day began at twelve noon.[46] The months from March through October can be identified with their respective Etruscan names, but other names suggest that the calendars were local and that the nomenclature varied from city to city (Appendix B, Source no. III.8).[47]

Many of the time boundaries may have been perceived of as abstract entities, such as the *saeculum,* or generation,[48] which, according to the late Roman grammarian Censorinus, was calculated on the basis of the number of years lived by the last person born at the end of the previous timespan.[49] Other markers of time were more concrete and included the nail that, according to Livy, was hammered yearly into the temple wall of the Capitoline temple in Rome by the *praetor maximus* on the Ides of September.[50] As in so many instances of Early Roman practices, this event was part of an Etruscan tradition, documented also from the temple of Nortia at Volsinii.[51]

BOUNDARIES ON EARTH

Once a carefully defined system of compartmentalization, or spaces and boundaries, had been established, and an effective system of interaction set up between the upper (the heavens), middle (the earth), and lower spheres (the Underworld) of the *axis mundi,* the Etruscans devoted their energy to setting up and defining the boundaries of their daily life. The different aspects of life pertained to governing their cities, cultivating their fields, establishing trade contacts, honoring their dead, and appeasing the deities.

Boundaries of Landscape

By utilizing as much as possible the boundaries provided by nature to separate the different spheres of their lives, the Etruscans were keen observers of the surrounding landscape, following in the footsteps of their predecessors in time and space.[52] In the cases where it was considered essential to supplement the natural boundaries by artificial ones, they used a plowed furrow or a boundary stone, thereby providing a precedent for the Romans, who continued the tradition of establishing boundaries for cities as well as for fields.

Although the Greek geographer Strabo states that of all Etruscan cities, Populonia was the only one located directly on the sea,[53] the shoreline in antiquity indicates that such inland cities as Caere or Tarquinii were close to the sea and thus able to control the sea trade with Greeks and Carthaginians.[54] The natural barrier for Etruria was instead the Apennine mountain range, which effectively separated the western and the eastern shores of the Italian peninsula with only a few mountain passes to provide communication between the inhabitants on either side.[55]

The Hills and Rivers as Boundaries for Cities

As shown by the location of urban settlements, the Etruscans (and in many cases their Iron Age ancestors) took full advantage of the landscape. The natural space that became most important in establishing settlements was the hill, often separated from neighboring hills by rivers. The hill provided a defined space for habitation, further reinforced by the city wall, which, according to Servius limited the approach to the city through three city gates.[56] As a result, the outline of the natural boundary between the space above and the space below also became a useful tool in designating areas for the living, for the deities, and for the dead. Only when viewing the steep hill from below, or by finding that a nearby hill is separated by water, does an inhabitant of an area, or a visitor, friend or foe appreciate the pattern of boundaries—vertical, as well as horizontal. These urban habitation spaces would not necessarily have needed any further protection. Political as well as religious concerns, however, seem to have led to the building of defensive walls as well as the construction of ritual spaces intended for strengthening the boundaries and for facilitating their crossing.

This phenomenon of marking the boundaries of settlements also explains the location of the many extramural and extraurban sanctuaries (for example, at Veii or Civita Castellana), which are located along the line of a city hill and along the roads leading into a city.[57] Depending on the precise location of such sanctuaries in relation to the city and the roads, they may have been more closely related to protecting the city or to facilitating the journey to and from the city. Many of these sanctuaries include temples and altars and a *temenos,* whereas others preserve only the findspot for an offering of coins, miniature vases, or other votives.[58] Because of their location, these sanctuaries served two main functions, those of determining the boundaries between life and death and between political territories, as will be discussed below.

Boundaries between Life and Death

On earth, the most important division of space seems to have been that between the world of the living and the world of the dead. Usually, the cities located on hills were separated from the extraurban burial areas by rivers, such as at Veii, Tarquinii, and Caere.[59]

The rivers separating the urban hills from the burial hills could be crossed by bridges and roads leading from the

VII.4. View of Orvieto. (Photo: Simonetta Stopponi.)

space of the living to the space of the dead. Once such a river boundary was crossed, the road would take the traveler to the city of the dead, passing by cemeteries or individual tombs and occasionally sanctuaries located along the way. Depending on the specific location and the layout of such cemeteries, they can be perceived as extramural or extraurban sanctuaries or as funerary sanctuaries. As shown by the monumental Montetosto sanctuary located next to a tumulus tomb on the road between Pyrgi and Caere, the funerary context here required an architectural layout that in other locations indicates gatherings of a political and religious nature.[60]

Once within a funerary space, the roads led to tombs laid out in a pattern similar to that of the houses of the living, with a carefully designed layout of streets, as shown at Caere and Orvieto (Figs. VII.4-5) in particular.[61] As part of the concerns of the community, the family members would have good reason to frequent these tombs not only for burials but also for ceremonies related to the cult of the dead, including meals at the grave.[62] The link between the immediate survivors and the dead was further made by depictions of ancestors who may have been represented in the tombs.[63] As the survivors entered a family tomb, they may have made use of the tomb furniture carved in the tufa,* or they may have placed images of the deceased there, as has been suggested to explain the group of terracotta statuettes in the Tomb of the Five Chairs at Caere.[64]

The Fields and Their Boundaries

In addition to city hills and burial hills, the fields for agriculture and grazing were an important part of the Etruscan landscape. The size of the fields was determined by the layout of the land and perhaps identified by sighting from a central point, a centuriation system that the Romans used so successfully in the third century BCE layout of colonies such as Cosa in the former Etruscan territory.[65] Since most of the farm sites are known from field surveys rather than from excavation, we can only estimate the size of the Etruscan farms compared to their Roman successors.[66] According to Vegoia's prophecy, it was the god Jupiter who deter-

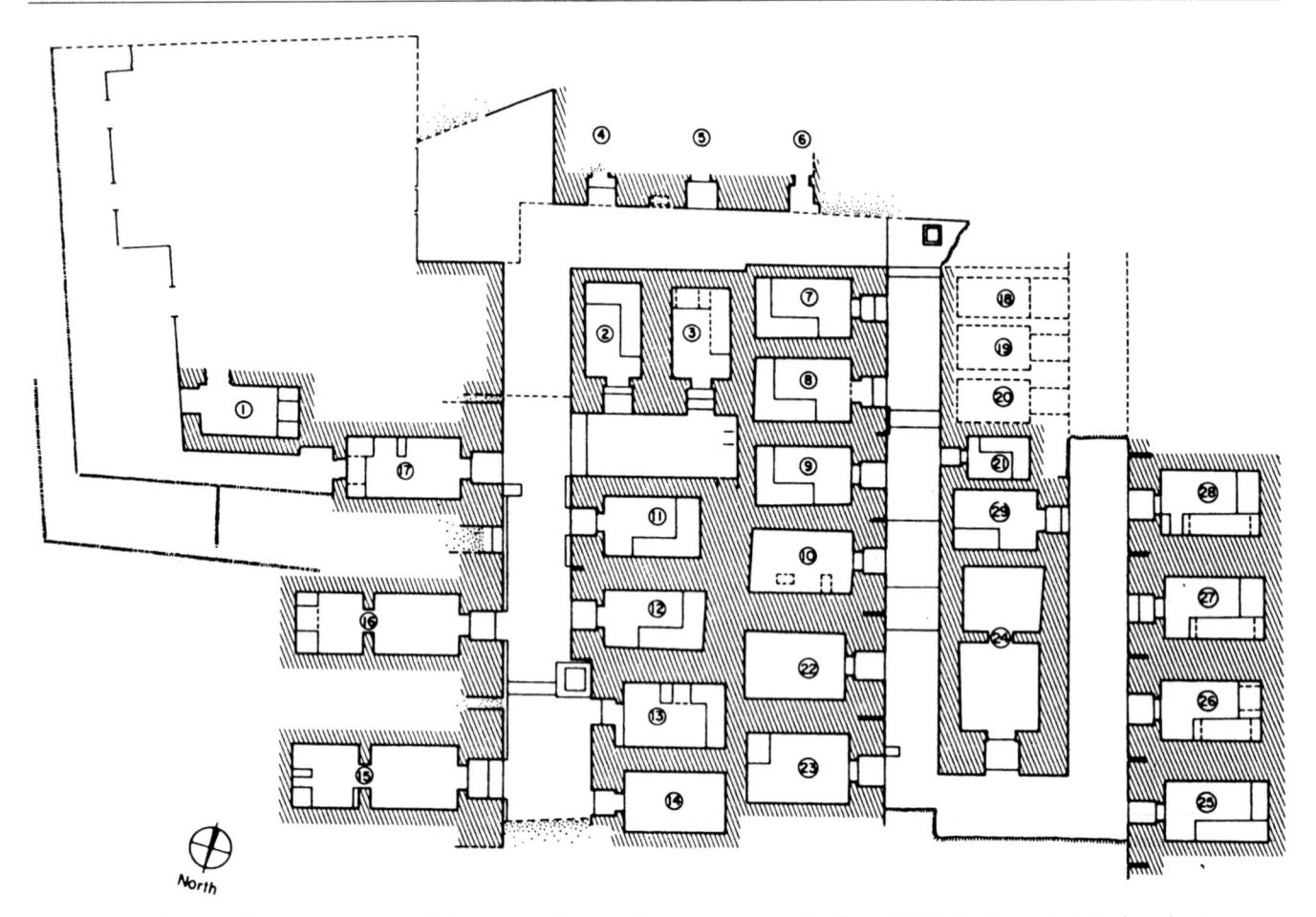

VII.5. *Plan of necropolis of Crocefisso del Tufo, Orvieto. Late sixth century BCE. (After D. and F. R. Ridgway,* Italy before the Romans, *London, 1979, 361, fig. 2.)*

mined the measuring and divisions of fields.[67] As mentioned earlier, another god who was in charge of overseeing the boundaries (*tular*) of sanctuaries, cemeteries, or territories was Selvans.[68]

Although no direct parallel exists in the preserved evidence of the Etruscan calendar, comparisons with later Roman practices such as the purification of the boundaries, known as the Ambarvalia festival in late May, suggest that the divine protection of the fields, whether by Jupiter or by Selvans or some other deity, formed part of the agricultural cycle of the year.[69]

Roads as Communication Tools and as Boundaries

As can be expected, boundary stones reinforced the division of territory marked by roads.[70] Furthermore, the roads that connected smaller settlements with the urban centers provided linear means of access that could serve as trade routes across the plains.[71] Depending on the region, such roads were cut into the tufa, as seen at the necropolis at Caere or at Tuscania, or as defensible "ridgeways" along the mountain ridges, as documented, for example, in the Chianti area[72] and in the Mugello north of Florence.[73]

Cities and Their Territories

Although there are many factors such as location, trade pattern, language, and artistic traditions that indicate the independence of each major Etruscan city in relation to its neighbors, the ancient texts are remarkably silent about identifying the division of Etruria into cities and territories.[74] In addition to isolated statements such as those of Servius,[75] and the historical accounts by Livy and others about the alliances and conflicts among the Etruscan cities, different criteria for analyzing the components of the Etruscan land and peoples must be used. As suggested by Banti,[76] it is the culture, defined as types of burials and pottery, that helps identify one city from another, but these cultural spheres of

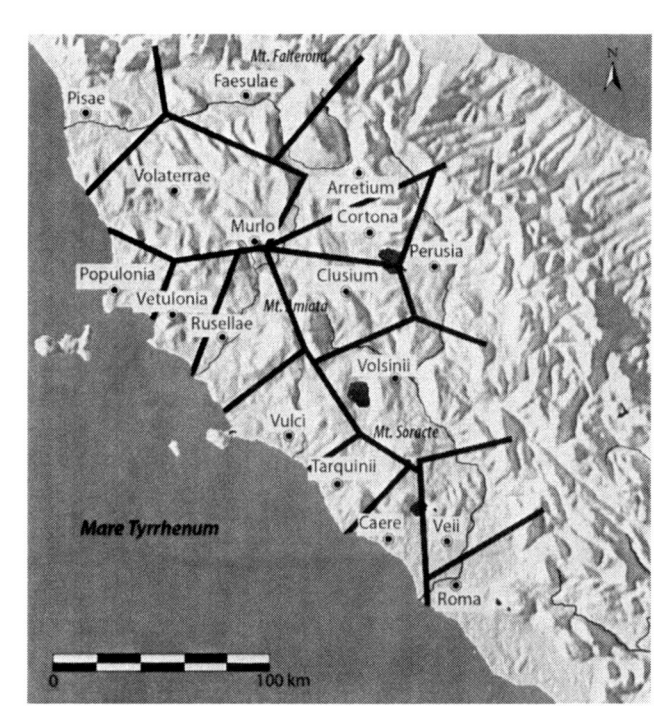

VII.6. *Etruscan territories. (Prepared by Alys Thompson and Chris Williams in collaboration with Ingrid Edlund-Berry and John L. Berry.)*

influence should not be seen as synonymous with political boundaries.

Surveys and topographical studies in recent years have provided more evidence for analyzing the location of cities and surrounding communities, both in terms of projecting a pattern of artificial boundaries by means of the so-called Thiessen polygons (Fig. VII.6)[77] and by studying the natural boundaries. For the purposes of correlating the ancient beliefs in boundary deities with the terrain, it is the presence of small streams and major rivers such as the Ombrone or the Fiora that provides evidence for the natural boundaries for the territory belonging to each urban center,[78] reinforced by the mountain ranges and lakes that provided reference points within the landscape.[79]

Political Boundaries

The cities came to define the political spheres within the setting of these natural boundaries. Although the extent of each city's power may surface only sporadically and incompletely in the historical sources,[80] there are other ways of measuring the boundaries that defined the major cities and that separated them from their neighbors. As can be expected, such boundaries were closely tied to the presence of sanctuaries that directly or indirectly reinforced both the natural and the political boundaries.

The boundaries of life and death were often defined by doors, open or closed.[81] Similarly, the boundaries of a city, whether marked by a wall, boundary stones, a natural hill, or by an invisible *pomerium*, provided a defined space for the sacred and secular activities within a city community.[82] Sanctuaries or sacred spaces could appear within the city proper, but with limitations such as those suggested by the Roman architect Vitruvius, who specified that certain cults should be practiced outside the city limits. In his account of the location of temples, Vitruvius specifies that the shrines of Venus, Volcanus, Mars, and Ceres should be confined to an extramural or extraurban location.[83] The same practice may well have governed other extramural or extraurban locations, as seen in the cluster of sanctuaries at Falerii (Civita Castellana) and at other sites.[84]

If then, the immediate area of the city nucleus was defined by a variety of boundaries, each protected by a sanctuary, the transition to the surrounding territory required special attention. Depending on the location of the city, and its control of the immediate countryside, the political boundaries could be provided by *cippi** marked with *tular*, as seen at Poggio di Firenze southeast of Florence[85] or at Campaccio southeast of Cortona.[86]

Although the countryside of Etruria has been explored to a lesser extent than other parts of Italy, evidence of roads, tombs, small settlements, and sanctuaries helps determine the population density around each city.[87] If we estimate the average distance for a one-day journey back and forth to market centers, and assume that the cities served also as such centers, the distribution of major cities suggests that there were points where two market territories met or overlapped, such as at Arretium and Cortona, Cortona and Clusium, Vulci and Tarquinii, Tarquinii and Caere, Caere and Veii, and Veii and Rome (Fig. VII.7, inner circles). Based on a two-day journey, Arretium and Clusium, Clusium and Volsinii, Pisae and Volaterrae, and Populonia and Rusellae have contiguous (or almost contiguous) or overlapping borders (corresponding to the outer circles, Fig. VII.7).

By focusing on the boundaries between cities, whether identified as rivers or as manmade, the political conflicts between cities such as Rome and Veii fall into the pattern of neighborly rivalry, perhaps mainly economical, which ultimately was resolved by military conflict.[88] At other times, the location of sanctuaries, identified individually as "rural" because of their location,[89] takes on a political meaning, as seen for example in the string of sanctuaries in the Tolfa moun-

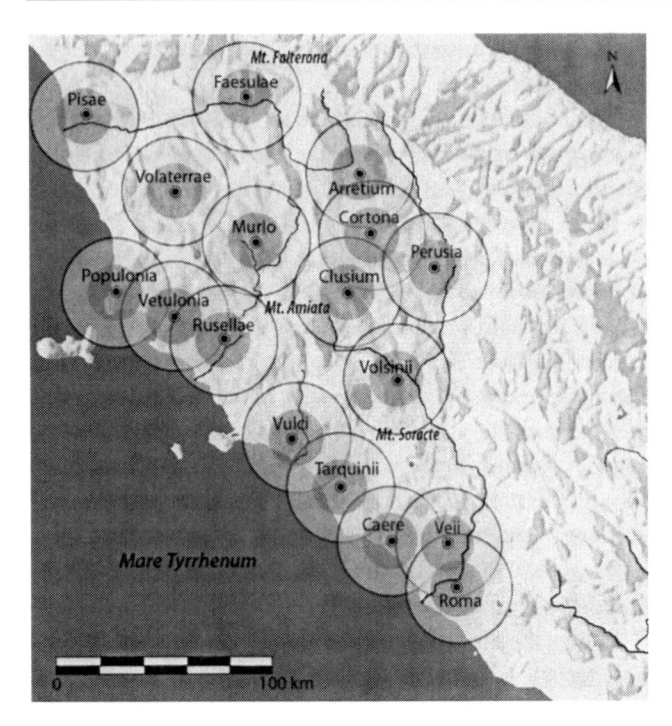

VII.7. Map indicating travel to nearest Etruscan centers. (Prepared by Alys Thompson and Chris Williams in collaboration with Ingrid Edlund-Berry and John L. Berry.)

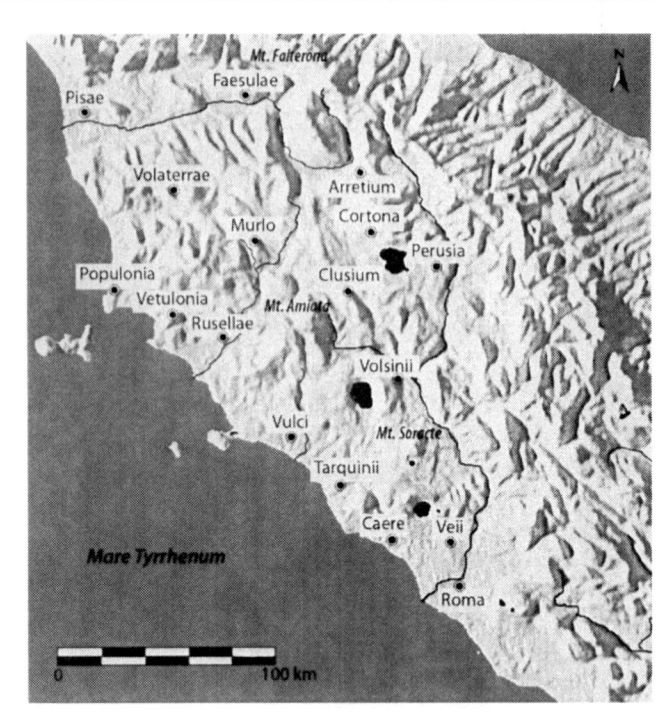

VII.8. Map of major cities and mountains of Etruria. (Prepared by Alys Thompson and Chris Williams in collaboration with Ingrid Edlund-Berry.)

tains, which provide a religious, hence also political, boundary between the two powerful cities of Caere and Tarquinii.[90]

Political Confederations and Their Sanctuaries

The purpose of the political and economic boundaries, reinforced by sanctuaries, was to identify and protect the interests of each city. But in Etruria, as also in the Greek and Roman lands, groups of cities were united in coalitions (leagues, federations) for the purpose of mutual benefit and support.[91] The presence of such coalitions in Etruria is well documented in the ancient sources, primarily Livy and epigraphical texts. The details of their activities, however, let alone the location for their meetings, have given rise to much debate and many differences in interpretation.[92]

The coalition of Etruscan cities that is best known through the historical texts centers around meetings held at the Fanum Voltumnae, the shrine of Voltumna.[93] The number of peoples included in the coalitions seems to have varied between twelve and fifteen, and there is no unified agreement as to the names of their cities. Of those mentioned, Pisae and Faesulae are located north of the Arno; Volaterrae, Arretium, Cortona, Perusia, and Clusium in the inland of northern Etruria; Populonia, Vetulonia, and Rusellae closer to the coast; and Volsinii, Vulci, Tarquinii, Caere, and Veii in southern Etruria (Fig. VII.8).[94]

The location of this coalition is usually identified as Volsinii (modern Orvieto), based on a late Roman inscription from Spello, but many other sites have also been suggested.[95] Since no archaeological site at this point can be identified with any degree of certainty as the sanctuary of Voltumna, several possibilities exist for defining a likely location for such a place. If we work under the assumption that a coalition of any number of Etruscan cities would meet within the territory of the city that at any given time was the most powerful, Veii would qualify for the time period 434–389 BCE, when, according to Livy, this city and Falerii summoned the assistance of the Twelve Cities against Rome.[96] At other times, inscriptions referring to the Chief of the Etruscan people (*zilath mechl rasnal* or *praetor Etruriae*) suggest that Tarquinii in particular held a leading position in the coalition since chiefs were appointed from this city.[97]

The existence of a coalition of twelve (or fifteen) Etruscan cities meeting at the Shrine of Voltumna at Volsinii is based on historical references that cover a great span of up to nine hundred years (fifth century BCE–fourth century CE).[98] It is therefore important to recognize the obvious fact that although coalitions of Etruscan cities seem to have existed that at some point met at a Shrine of Voltumna and at the town of Volsinii, there is little evidence that allows us to identify once and for all the location of the meeting place.

By looking at other sanctuaries in ancient Italy that served as gathering places for neighboring cities, we find that at least in Latium, such sites reflected a connection with nature, such as Mons Albanus (Monte Cavo),[99] Lake Nemi with the Grove of Diana,[100] and the Grove of Ferentina, probably located near the Lake of Turnus below Castelgandolfo.[101] In addition to their significance as sanctuaries in nature, it has also been suggested that the location of these sanctuaries coincided with the boundaries of the communities they served, including Rome.[102]

By using the sanctuaries in Latium as a model, it is thus possible to suggest that the location of the Shrine of Voltumna should be sought either at the boundaries between Etruscan cities or at some central point in nature that did not interfere with any known political territory. We can seek such a sanctuary and meeting place near Veii if we assume that Livy's reference to the Shrine of Voltumna in the conflict between Rome and Veii in the late fifth century BCE applies to a border sanctuary between these two cities, or at least to one within the domain of Veii as the dominant city at the time.[103] Since other texts referring to the meetings do not include references to Voltumna per se, we may assume that the coalition could meet at any appropriate point within the territory of the city in charge of the coalition. There may have been several or many sanctuaries to Voltumna as a boundary deity that have not been identified as such or that were shared also with other deities for which epigraphical and votive evidence provides an identification.[104] Which of these shrines were chosen for the meetings would then depend on the configuration of the coalition each time it met.

On the other hand, if we assume that no single Etruscan city consistently had the leadership of the coalition of Etruscan cities, we should consider that each city, with its surrounding territory and boundaries, was an equal partner and that the only acceptable meeting place would be in politically neutral territory. Because of the location of the twelve (or fifteen) cities within the overall boundaries of Etruria, marked to the east by the river Tiber, there is no suitable area that is equidistant to all the members. By excluding Pisae and Faesulae as border cities to the north of the river Arno, the remaining cities fit into two reasonably neat clusters, a northern one, consisting of Volaterrae, Arretium, Cortona, Perusia, Clusium, Rusellae, Populonia, and Vetulonia, and a southern one, consisting of Volsinii (Orvieto), Vulci, Tarquinii, Caere, and Veii. The central point for these two clusters falls to the north/northeast of Sovana, south of Monte Amiata, an impressive mountaintop that dominates the surrounding area (Fig. VII.8), much like Mons Albanus (Monte Cavo) in Latium.

On the basis of a central location in nature, Monte Amiata is a good candidate for a meeting point for the Etruscan coalition. In addition to forming a commanding landmark, it is also between the territories of Clusium and Rusellae and may have served as a natural boundary, whether or not marked with any boundary stones or a sanctuary.[105]

Obviously, so far no site or building connected with the deity of Voltumna has been identified on Monte Amiata or further south in the area of Saturnia. Since there is no indication that the Latin term *fanum** (sanctuary, shrine) necessarily implied any architectural structures such as a temple or meeting hall or even an unroofed enclosure,[106] we cannot immediately assume that material remains are going to provide the identification of the meeting place for the Etruscan coalition of cities.

In addition to the texts that refer to a coalition for all or most of the major cities in Etruria, there is evidence that individual cities could support each other in smaller groups.[107] One example of such a coalition is the alliance of five major northern Etruscan cities, namely, Clusium, Arretium, Volaterrae, Vetulonia, and Rusellae (Fig. VII.8). According to Dionysios of Halikarnassos, these cities formed an alliance with the Latins in their struggles against the Etruscan king in Rome, Tarquinius Priscus, who according to tradition ruled 616–579 BCE.[108] Although no meeting place or name of a protecting deity such as Voltumna is mentioned for this coalition, the location of the five cities and their boundaries, calculated as Thiessen polygons, indicates that the central point, equidistant to all five, falls between the Crevole and Ombrone rivers, at the site near Murlo known as Poggio Civitate (Fig. VII.6).[109]

Poggio Civitate (Fig. VII.9) is the local name of a hill located by the Crevole, a tributary to the Ombrone, some twenty-five km to the south of Siena. The hill is dominated by two building complexes, one from the Orientalizing period that, following a disastrous destruction by fire ca. 600 BCE, was replaced by a monumental Archaic building. Seen in isolation, the square complex with rooms surrounding an open courtyard does not at first sight meet the criteria of a sanctuary or temple. In the context of spaces and boundaries, however, the organization of the rooms provides the contrast between open and closed, unroofed and roofed spaces, to which access is provided by narrow doorways.

Once within the building, smaller rooms provided protected spaces for assemblies or banquets, as shown on the terracotta plaques that decorated the building, whereas the large courtyard, fully enclosed by the surrounding rooms, provided space for activities such as the horse races also depicted on the plaques. The immediate boundary of the build-

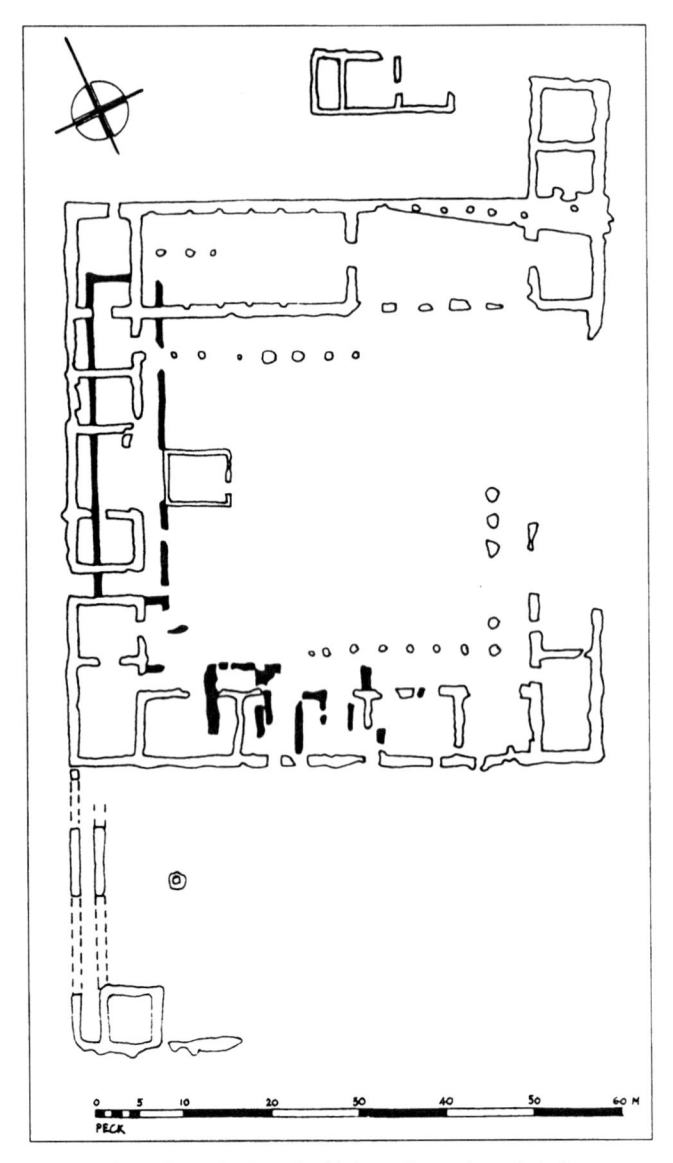

VII.9. *Plan of Murlo, Poggio Civitate. Seventh and sixth century BCE. (After S. Stopponi, ed.,* Case e Palazzi d'Etruria, *Milan, 1985, fig. 3.2.)*

VII.10. *Terracotta statue of male figure from Poggio Civitate. Ca. 570 BCE. Murlo, Museum. (Photo: Soprintendenza Archeologica per la Toscana.)*

ing, beyond the rooms and courtyard, is formed by the hill proper. As depicted in the plaques, this hill is crossed and the building approached by carriage. Once within sight of the building, the visitors' view was guided by the roof decoration, including *akroteria** of animals and well over twenty seated and standing figures providing the vertical connection between heaven and earth (Fig. VII.10).[110]

These statues may represent those very deities, male and female, who protected the building and provided the link with the celestial regions but who also guarded the political, and hence religious, boundaries on earth. In its central position, the monumental building provided a meeting place in a location at the very center of the area controlled by the framework of a coalition of cities. In this way, the blocks of territorial spaces, or territories, were tied to Poggio Civitate as its spatial, hence religious and political, center, much in the same way as the compartments of the Piacenza liver or the celestial sixteen regions defined by Martianus Capella provided a unified whole, under the protection of deities.

Deities in Charge of Boundaries

As mentioned throughout the previous discussion, both the boundaries and the areas defined by boundaries were considered to be under divine protection. While the wealth of sanctuaries and votive offerings connected with boundaries indicates the Etruscan involvement with boundary deities and their sacred spaces, only a few of these deities can be identified by name.

As the chief god, Tin/Tinia controlled mountaintops and thus defined the vertical boundaries between the heavens and the earth. Examples of his sphere of power appear as place names (e.g., Monte Giovi) and in the presence of the major Etruscan temple in Rome dedicated to Jupiter, Juno, and Minerva, located on the Capitoline hill.[111]

Selvans or Silvanus, as discussed above, presided over sacred boundaries.[112] As a nature goddess and protectress of groves, Artumes (Latin Diana) may also have guarded the boundaries, both those in nature and those established by the peoples of Etruria.[113] If indeed the coalition of Etruscan cities gathered at the Shrine of Voltumna, this deity, whether male or female, whether or not related to Vertumnus (according to Varro, the "chief deity of Etruria"),[114] represented the focal point where boundaries met, either those protected by one dominant city or those that provided a neutral gathering place for a number of cities.

Other boundary deities were undoubtedly acknowledged by the Etruscans. Because of the alignment of spaces on the Piacenza liver, the names that are written along the outside border may include such boundary deities.[115] Likewise, the deities worshiped in extramural or extraurban temples, at small roadside sanctuaries, or at river crossings may take on the role as protective boundary deities in addition to their other functions.

CONCLUSION

Whether or not known to us by name, the deities of boundaries were as important in the Etruscan pantheon as was the Etruscan belief that all matters were in divine hands. By creating a system of boundaries with spatial contiguity, the Etruscans were able to control fully the natural landscape with the addition of artificial boundaries such as roads and boundary stones, where nothing existed in a vacuum. Whether or not part of a numerological system in units of twelve, sixteen, or more, the network of sacred spaces and boundaries in the skies as on earth ensured the stability of the society and its belief systems.[116]

This tightly knit pattern in Etruscan life was broken when the boundaries were trespassed or just crossed by outsiders. The Etruscan principle of gathering to conduct political and religious business at a central point (the Shrine of Voltumna or somewhere else) stood in sharp contrast to the Roman system of forming alliances with one Etruscan city at a time.[117] Without its carefully designed pattern of spaces, the Etruscan world of religion, and therefore life, was shattered.[118] What was inherited by the Romans were the vertical links between heaven and earth, expressed by *religio* and to some degree by the respect for boundaries,[119] but, on the whole, Rome viewed itself as the center of a wheel, from which the spokes emerged. The abstract powers or *numina** were isolated from each other and did not exist side by side, as did the deities in the spaces on the Piacenza liver. But, in spite of Roman political supremacy in Italy and the Mediterranean, the Romans were the first to acknowledge the strength of the Etruscan influence on Roman religious traditions. Throughout Roman history *Etrusca disciplina* and *ritus Etruscus** thus became coupled with the highest symbol of military success as a Roman general was crowned with the golden Etruscan crown (*corona ex auro Etrusca*) in the triumphal procession through the city of Rome.[120]

NOTES

1. Müller and Deecke 1877, 65–124; Dennis 1848, introduction; Buonamici 1939; Aversa 1995.

2. The variety of the Etruscan landscape has inspired writers and artists of all periods. For a recent evaluation of the geology and topography, appropriately prefaced with a quote from D. H. Lawrence, *Etruscan Places*, see Barker and Rasmussen 1998, 1–42.

3. For definitions of sacred and secular places, see Edlund 1987, 30–38.

4. Briquel 1987, 171–190; Edlund 1987, 37–38.

5. Lambrechts 1970; De Simone 1987–1988; Colonna 1988; Zifferero 1995, 333.

6. Thulin 1968, 26.

7. See, for example, Varro, *De lingua Latina* 5.143 and Servius, *Ad Aen.* 4.212; Briquel 1987 (collection of ancient sources pp. 188–190); Edlund-Berry 1994, 18.

8. See Lambrechts 1970, *TLE*, 2nd ed., s.v.; Colonna 1988; Morandi 1987–1988; for illustrations, see also *Rasenna*, figs. 39, 71, and 245–246.

9. Here, as in the following discussion, the term "Etruscan" refers to the Etruscan culture as a political entity, separate from the Roman, as distinct from "Tuscanicus" used as a synonym for "old" and "antiquated" by Vitruvius in particular (see Edlund-Berry 1997).

10. See the text of the prophecy, Appendix B: Sources, no. II.1, and the discussion by de Grummond in this volume, above, pp. 30–31.

11. *De limitibus* F22, 10–11.

12. Van der Meer 1987, 107–108.

13. Small 1994.

14. See, e.g., Simon 1990, 201–202; Simon in this volume, above,

p. 59; and Chiadini 1995. In contrast, however, Dorcey (1992, 10-11) states that "the origin and meaning of Selvans is unknown."

15. Livy 1.55.2-4; Dionysios of Halikarnassos 3.69.3-6; see also Piccaluga 1974.

16. See van der Meer 1987 and Jannot 1998, 34-37. The liver is discussed in greater detail by Bonfante in this volume, above, pp. 10-11.

17. *De div.* 2.18.42. See the text of Cicero, Appendix B, Source no. III.3.

18. *HN* 2.55.143. See the text of Pliny, Appendix B, Source no. III.1.

19. *De nuptiis Mercurii et Philologiae* 1.45-61. See the text of Martianus, Appendix B, Source no. III.4.

20. Maggiani and Simon 1984, 139-141; Prayon 1997, 357-358.

21. In my opinion, the physical landscape is the best indicator of how the Etruscans and their predecessors selected places for living, burial, and worship. As pointed out by Riva and Stoddart 1996, 106, there seems to have been a difference between northern and southern Etruria in that in the north the landscape played a greater role than in the south in determining areas of liminality or points of transition between life and death, city and country, sacred and secular. For an example of the use of a lake (Lake Trasimene) as a *templum*, see Colonna 1976-1977.

22. Cicero, *De div.* 1.48.107; Livy 1.5.

23. Cicero, *De div.* 2.38.80.

24. For the characteristic features of an Etruscan temple, see Colonna in *Santuari d'Etruria*, 60. For a discussion of the orientation of temples, see Aveni and Romano 1994.

25. Prayon 1991 and 1997.

26. See Warden, Thomas, and Galloway 1999, 231 and fig. 1.

27. The importance of access has been studied by Meyers 2003.

28. Sassatelli 1989-1990, 604-606, fig. 1.

29. Brown 1980, 16-17, 51-52.

30. See, e.g., Ovid, *Fasti* 4.821-824. Plutarch, *Life of Romulus* 11 (Appendix B, Source no. IV.3); Macrobius, *Sat.* 1.16.18.

31. Lake Trasimene, Lake Bolsena, Lago di Mezzano, Lago di Vico, Lago di Bracciano; Barker and Rasmussen 1998, 16-19.

32. Many of these caves have been used as sanctuaries or as burial places since prehistoric times; see, e.g., Edlund 1987, 49-51; Guidi 1989-1990; Whitehouse 1992; Whitehouse 1995.

33. Jones 1963, 126; Edlund 1987, 46-47.

34. For the function of water and sulphur in the healing cults, see Edlund-Berry 1999 and Edlund-Berry forthcoming.

35. Gasperini 1988, 29, fig. 1. Chellini 2002.

36. De Lorenzo 1979.

37. *KlPauly* 4, 1376-1377 (K. Ziegler).

38. Eliade 1959, 29-32, 36-37.

39. Cicero, *De div.* 1.41.92 (Appendix B, Source no. IV.8); Seneca, *QN* 2.32.2, 2.40-41 (Appendix B, Source nos. VIII.1-3 and VIII.2); Nigidius Figulus, *Diarium Tonitruale* (tr. J. M. Turfa), for which, see Appendix A. Thulin 1968, 13-128; Jannot 1998, 40-43.

40. See, e.g., Livy 1.34; Ovid, *Fasti* 4.810-817. The depiction of Vel Saties and a young boy, Arnza, holding a bird on a leash, is usually interpreted as an example of augury (see, e.g., Jannot 1998, 43). Recently, the scene has also been interpreted as a genre scene of a child with his pet bird (Weber-Lehmann 1998). See the discussion by de Grummond in this volume, above, p. 42.

41. *Scrivere etrusco* 1985, 17-64 (F. Roncalli).

42. *Scrivere etrusco* 1985, 65-73 (M. Guldan); Cristofani 1995.

43. See, e.g., Edlund-Berry 1992; Cristofani 1995, 59-66.

44. The Etruscan equivalent of Kalends is *ilacve* or *ilucve*, as recorded in the Pyrgi plaques and the Capua tile. The Nones correspond with Etruscan *saiuzie* in the Capua tile, and the Ides correspond with *ituna* in the Capua tile, or *itus/itis* (according to Varro and Macrobius; Edlund-Berry 1992).

45. Edlund-Berry 1992, 331.

46. Servius, *Ad Aen.* 5.738 (Appendix B, Source no. III.9).

47. Edlund-Berry 1992, 331-332.

48. Hall 1985, 2567-2569.

49. *De die natali* 17.5-6. See the text of Censorinus, Appendix B, Source no. III.6.

50. Livy 7.3.5-7.

51. Livy 7.3.5-7. See the text of Livy, Appendix B, Source no. V.1. It has been suggested that this temple may correspond to the site of Pozzarello at Bolsena, but the evidence is not conclusive (*Santuari d'Etruria*, 84-85).

52. Barker and Rasmussen 1998, 10-42.

53. Strabo 5.2.6.

54. Cristofani 1983.

55. Potter 1987, 15-18; Barker and Rasmussen 1998, 22-25.

56. Servius, *Ad Aen.* 1.422.

57. Edlund 1987, 64-66, 73-75.

58. Edlund 1987, 64, 80; Jannot 1998, 101-104.

59. See, e.g., Banti 1973, 16-17; Barker and Rasmussen 1998, 149-158.

60. Edlund 1987, 70-71.

61. *Città etrusche* 1973, 158 (Caere) and 272 (Orvieto).

62. Bonfante 1986, 233-234.

63. Bartoloni 2000, 167-168.

64. Colonna and von Hase 1986, 40.

65. See, e.g., Brown 1980; Barker and Rasmussen 1998, 262-265.

66. Barker and Rasmussen 1998, 268-273.

67. *Gromatici Veteres*, I, p. 350. See Appendix B, Source no. II.1.

68. Above, nn. 13-14.

69. See Scullard 1981, 124-125. A reference in Columella 10.338-347 mentions the head of an Arcadian donkey being used by the Etruscan soothsayer Tages to ward off Rubigo, the deity of mildew, at the edge of the field. See Appendix B, Source no. IV.4. I thank Nancy de Grummond for drawing my attention to this passage.

70. Colonna 1988, 26-28, discusses a boundary stone found alongside a road southeast of Cortona. Cf. below, n. 86.

71. See, e.g., Barker and Rasmussen 1998, 172-173.

72. Stopani 1991, 35-36.

73. Warden, Thomas, and Galloway 1999, 233.

74. See, e.g., Banti 1973, 16-17; Barker and Rasmussen 1998, 100.

75. Servius, *Ad. Aen.* 10.172, 183. Scullard 1967, 231-236.

76. Banti 1973.

77. Renfrew 1991, 159. I thank John L. Berry, Alys Thompson, and Chris Williams for their valuable contributions to the study of Etruscan cities and their territories.

78. Zifferero 1995.

79. Edlund 1984, 46-47 (Mount Soracte); Prayon 1997, 366, fig. 7 (Lake Trasimene).

80. Buonamici 1939, 37-63.

81. Scheffer 1994; Torelli 1997, 69.

82. Briquel 1987, 171-190; Edlund 1987, 37-38.

83. *De architectura* 1.7.1. Appendix B, Source no. V.2.
84. Edlund 1987, 80.
85. Colonna 1988, 17–19, fig. 1.
86. Colonna 1988, 26–28, fig. 2.
87. See, for example, *Caere* 1990.
88. Livy 5.18–22.
89. Edlund 1987, 42; Jannot 1998, 101–104.
90. *Caere* 1990; Zifferero 1995.
91. Seen as a focal point that combined political and religious concerns, the term "political sanctuary" can be applied to those places that are mentioned in the ancient texts in connection with political actions. When it comes to other such meeting places that have been documented archaeologically, however, the definition of a political sanctuary becomes much more complex and controversial. Although in one sense all sanctuaries are "political" in that they involve the citizens of a community, the problem of nomenclature becomes severe when the architectural form of a structure does not immediately identify it as a sanctuary with a designated space or set of artifacts implying worship of deities.
92. Edlund 1987, 85–86.
93. The literature on this sanctuary is vast; see *AnnFaina* 1985. The most recent discussion is that of a conference on La Lega Etrusca, held at Chiusi, October 9, 1999. The speakers included Francesco Roncalli ("I santuari Federali") and Giovanni Colonna ("Porsenna, la lega etrusca e il Lazio"). The proceedings of the conference are forthcoming.
94. Müller and Deecke 1877, 319–333.
95. Edlund 1987, 86. The ongoing excavations at Campo Della Fiera, just outside Orvieto, conducted by Simonetta Stopponi, may ultimately clarify the problem.
96. Edlund 1987, 85, n. 193.
97. Rosenberg 1913, 51–71; but see also G. Camporeale in *AnnFaina* 1985, 34.
98. Edlund 1987, 85–86.
99. Finocchi 1980.
100. Ghini 1993; *Nemi* 2000.
101. Colonna 1985.
102. For the relation of these sanctuaries to the assemblies of the Latins, see, e.g., Ampolo 1981; Colonna 1985; Colonna 1991; Ghini 1995.
103. Edlund 1987, 86.
104. For the identification of Etruscan deities, see Jannot 1998, 179–191.
105. Edlund 1987, 47. For the location of Monte Amiata, see also Torelli 1992; Cambi 1996; Barker and Rasmussen 1998, 12. I am grateful to John L. Berry for exploring the Tuscan landscape with me and for his insightful observations.
106. For the etymology of the word, see Varro, *De lingua Latina* 6.54 and Festus (ed. Lindsay), 78.
107. Rosenberg 1913, 51–71.
108. Dionysios of Halikarnassos 3.51.
109. Edlund-Berry 1987, 87–92; Edlund-Berry 1991. Meyers 2003.
110. As pointed out by Rowland 2001, the discussion of the function of the building complex and architectural decoration at Poggio Civitate has focused on concepts that have little or no foundation in the primary sources for Etruscan history and culture.
111. Camporeale 1997.
112. Above, nn. 13–14.
113. Krauskopf 1984.
114. Varro, *De lingua Latina* 5.46; Small 1997; Harari 1997.
115. For the names recorded on the liver, see van der Meer 1987.
116. As an example of this system of order we can also look at Etruscan architecture where a detail such as the Etruscan round had its definite place on a base (or a crown) on tombs, podia, or altars, for which see Shoe 1965.
117. Harris 1971.
118. Cf. Simon 1997.
119. Briquel 1987.
120. Pliny, *HN* 33.4.11.

BIBLIOGRAPHY

Ampolo, C. 1981. "Ricerche sulla lega Latina." *ParPass* 36, 219–233.

AnnFaina 1985 = "Volsinii e la dodecapoli etrusca, relazioni e interventi nel convegno del 1983." In *Annali della fondazione per il museo "Claudio Faina,"* II. Orvieto.

Aveni, A., and G. Romano. 1994. "Orientation and Etruscan Ritual." *Antiquity* 68, 260, 545–563.

Aversa, A. D. 1995. *L'Etruria e gli Etruschi negli autori classici*. Brescia.

Banti, L. 1973. *Etruscan Cities and Their Culture*. Berkeley, CA.

Barker, G., and T. Rasmussen. 1998. *The Etruscans*. Oxford.

Bartoloni, G., ed. 2000. "La tomba." In *Principi etruschi*, 163–171. Bologna.

Bonfante, L., ed. 1986. *Etruscan Life and Afterlife*. Detroit.

Briquel, D. 1987. "I riti di fondazione." In *Tarquinia: Ricerche, scavi e prospettive*, ed. M. Bonghi Jovino and C. Chiaramonte Treré. Milan. 171–190.

Brown, F. E. 1980. *Cosa: The Making of a Roman Town*. Ann Arbor, MI.

Buonamici, G. 1939. *Fonti di storia Etrusca*. Florence.

Caere 1990 = A. Maffei and F. Nastasi, eds., *Caere e il suo territorio da Agylla a Centumcellae*. Rome.

Cambi, F., ed. 1996. *Carta archeologica della provincia di Siena*. Siena.

Camporeale, G. 1997. "Tinia." *LIMC* VIII, 400–421.

Chiadini, G. 1995. "Selvans." *StEtr* 61, 161–180.

Città etrusche 1973 = F. Boitani et al., *Le città etrusche*. Verona.

Colonna, G. 1976–1977. "La dea etrusca CEL e i santuari del Trasimeno." *Rivista storica dell'Antichità* 6–7, 45–62.

———. 1985. "Il lucus Ferentinae ritrovato?" *Archeologia Laziale* 7, 40–43.

———. 1988. "Il lessico istituzionale etrusco e la formazione delle città, specialmente in Emilia Romagna." In *La formazione della città preromana in Emilia Romagna*, 15–36. Bologna.

———. 1991. "Acqua Acetosa Laurentina, l'Ager Romanus Antiquus e i santuari del I miglio." In *Scienze dell'Antichità Storia Archeologia Antropologia* 5, 209–232.

Colonna, G., and F.-W. von Hase. 1986. "Alle origini della statuaria etrusca: La tomba delle statue presso Ceri." *StEtr* 52: 13-59.

Cristofani, M. 1983. *Gli Etruschi del mare*. Milan.

———. 1995. *Tabula Capuana*. Florence.

De Lorenzo, G. 1979. *La terapia con le acque minerali*. Pordenone.

Dennis, G. 1848. *The Cities and Cemeteries of Etruria*. London.

De Simone, C. 1987-1988. "Volsinii (*Bolsena*) (?)," *StEtr* 55, 346-351.

Dorcey, P. T. 1992. *The Cult of Silvanus*. Leiden.

Edlund, I. E. M. 1987. *The Gods and the Place*. Stockholm.

Edlund-Berry, I. E. M. 1991. "Power and Religion: How Social Change Affected the Emergence and Collapse of Power Structures in Central Italy." In *Papers of the Fourth Conference of Italian Archaeology*, ed. E. Herring, R. Whitehouse, and J. Wilkins. London. II, 161-172. London.

———. 1992. "Etruscans at Work and Play: Evidence for an Etruscan Calendar." In *Kotinos: Festschrift für Erika Simon*, ed. H. Froning et al. Mainz. 330-338.

———. 1994. "Ritual Destruction of Cities and Sanctuaries: The 'Unfounding' of the Archaic Monumental Building at Poggio Civitate (Murlo)." In *Murlo and the Etruscans*, ed. R. D. De Puma and J. P. Small. Madison, WI. 16-28.

———. 1997. "'Etruscheria' in Vitruvius and Strabo." In *Ultra terminum vagary: Scritti in onore di Carl Nylander*, ed. Börje Magnusson et al. Rome. 77-79.

———. 1999. "Disciplina Medica: Form and Function of Healing Sanctuaries in Central Italy." Paper given at the conference on "Italian Sanctuaries: New Perspectives," held at the British School in Rome, May 28, 1999 and "Sulphur Fumes and Medicine Bottles in Sicilian Sanctuaries." Paper given at Keramik i Kontext, the Second Nordic Vase Colloquium held in Helsinki, Finland, June 11-13, 1999.

———. Forthcoming. "Hot, Cold, or Smelly: The Power of Sacred Water in Roman Religion, 400-100 B.C." In *Religion in Republican Italy*, ed. C. E. Schultz and P. B. Harvey, Jr. Cambridge.

Eliade, M. 1959. *The Sacred and the Profane*. New York.

Finocchi, P. 1980. "Il 'templum' di Iuppiter Latiaris sul mons Albanus." *Archeologia Laziale* 2, 156-158.

Gasperini, L. 1988. "Gli Etruschi e le sorgenti termali." In *Etruria meridionale: Conoscenza, conservazione, fruizione*. Rome. 27-35.

Ghini, G. 1995. "La ripresa delle indagini al santuario di Diana a Nemi." *Archeologia Laziale* 11, 277-289.

———. 1995. "Il santuario di Diana a Nemi (RM): Nuove richerche." In *Settlement and Economy in Italy 1500 B.C.-A.D. 1500*, ed. N. Christie. Oxford. 143-154.

Guidi, A. 1989-1990. "Alcune osservazioni sulla problematica delle offerte nella preistoria dell'Italia centrale." *Scienze dell'Antichità Storia Archeologia Antropologia* 3-4, 403-414.

Hall, J. F., III. 1985. "The *Saeculum Novum* of Augustus and its Etruscan Antecedents." In *ANRW*, vol. II.16.3, 2564-2589.

Harari, M. 1997. "Voltumna." *LIMC* VIII, 281-282.

Harris, W. V. 1971. *Rome in Etruria and Umbria*. Oxford.

Jannot, J.-R. 1998. *Devins, dieux et démons*. Paris.

Jones, G. D. B. 1963. "Capena and ager Capenas." *BSR* 31, 100-158.

Krauskopf, I. 1984. "Artumes." *LIMC* II, 774-792.

Lambrechts, R. 1970. *Les inscriptions avec le mot 'tular' et le bornage étrusques*. Florence.

LPRH = F. Gaultier and D. Briquel, eds., *Les Étrusques, les plus religieux des hommes: État de la recherche sur la religion étrusque. Actes du colloque international Grand Palais 17-18-19 novembre 1992. XII^{er} Rencontres de l'École du Louvre*. Paris.

Maggiani, A., and E. Simon 1984. "Il pensiero scientifico e religioso." In *Etruschi: Una nuova imagine*, ed. M. Cristofani. Florence. 136-167.

Meyers, G. 2003. *Etrusco-Italic Monumental Architectural Space from the Iron Age to the Archaic Period: An Examination of Approach and Access*. Unpublished dissertation. The University of Texas at Austin. Austin, TX.

Morandi, A. 1987-1988. "Cortona e la questione dei confini etruschi." *Annuario dell'Accademia Etrusca di Cortona* 23, 7-37.

Müller, K. O., and W. Deecke. 1877. *Die Etrusker*. Stuttgart.

Nemi 2000 = J. R. Brandt et al., eds., *Nemi—Status quo: Recent Research at Nemi and the Sanctuary of Diana*. Rome.

Piccaluga, G. 1974. *Terminus*. Rome.

Potter, T. W. 1987. *Roman Italy*. London.

Prayon, F. 1991. "*Deorum sedes*. Sull'orientamento dei templi etrusco-italici." In *Miscellanea etrusca e italica in onore di M. Pallottino*. Rome (= *ArchCl* 43). 1285-1295.

———. 1997. "Sur l'orientation des édifices culturels." In *LPRH*, 357-371.

Rasenna = M. Pallottino et al., *Rasenna*. Milan. 1986.

Renfrew, C. 1991. *Archaeology*. London.

Riva, C., and S. Stoddart. 1996. "Ritual Landscapes in Archaic Etruria." In *Approaches to the Study of Ritual: Italy and the Ancient Mediterranean*, ed. J. B. Wilkens. London. 91-109.

Rosenberg, A. 1913. *Der Staat der alten Italiker*. Berlin.

Rowland, I. D. 2001. "Etruscan Secrets." *New York Review of Books* 48:11, 12-17.

Santuari d'Etruria = G. Colonna, ed., *Santuari d'Etruria*. Catalogue of exhibition in Arezzo. Milan. 1985.

Sassatelli, G. 1989-1990. "Culti e riti in Etruria padana: Qualche considerazione." *Scienze dell'Antichità Storia Archeologia Antropologia* 3-4, 599-617.

Scheffer, C. 1994. "The Arched Door in Late Etruscan Funerary Art." In *Murlo and the Etruscans*, ed. R. D. De Puma and J. P. Small. Madison, WI. 196-210.

Scrivere etrusco 1985 = F. Roncalli, *Scrivere etrusco*. Milan.

Scullard, H. H. 1967. *The Etruscan Cities and Rome*. London.

———. 1981. *Festivals and Ceremonies of the Roman Republic*. Ithaca, NY.

Shoe, L. T. 1965. *Etruscan and Republican Roman Mouldings*. Rome.

Simon, E. 1990. *Die Götter der Römer*. Munich.

———. 1997. "Sentiment religieux et vision de la mort chez les Étrusques dans les derniers siècles de leur histoire." In *LPRH*, 449-457.

Small, J. P. 1994. "Selvans." *LIMC* VII, 718.

———. 1994. "Vertumnus." *LIMC* VIII, 235.

Stopani, R. 1991. "Ipotesi sulla viabilità etrusca e romana nel Chianti." In *Gli etruschi nel Chianti: Il Chianti, Storia, arte, cultura, territorio* 15. Radda in Chianti. 35-47.

Thulin, C. O. 1968. *Die etruskische Disciplin* III, *Die Ritualbücher*. Darmstadt. (Repr. of Göteborg 1909.)

Torelli, M. 1992. *Atlante dei siti archeologici della Toscana*. Foglio 129 Santa Fiora, 511-532. Entry by M. Menichetti. Rome.

———. 1997. "Limina Averni: Realtà e rappresentazione nella pittura tarquiniese arcaica." *Ostraka* 6.1, 63–86.

Van der Meer, L. B. 1987. *The Bronze Liver of Piacenza.* Amsterdam.

Warden, P. G., M. L. Thomas, and J. Galloway. 1999. "The Etruscan Settlement of Poggio Colla (1995–98 Excavations)." *JRA* 12, 231–246.

Weber-Lehmann, C. 1998. "Die Auspizien des Vel Saties: ein Kinderspiel." In *Proceedings of the XVth International Congress of Classical Archaeology, Amsterdam, July 12–17, 1998*, ed. R. F. Docter and E. M. Moormann, 449–453. Amsterdam.

Whitehouse, R. D. 1992. *Underground Religion: Cult and Culture in Prehistoric Italy.* London.

———. 1995. "From Secret Society to State Religion: Ritual and Social Organization in Prehistoric and Protohistoric Italy." In *Settlement and Economy in Italy 1500 B.C. to A.D. 1500*, ed. N. Christie. Oxford. 83–88.

Zifferero, A. 1995. "Economia, divinità, frontiera: Sul ruolo di alcuni santuari di confine in Etruria meridionale." *Ostraka* 4, 333–350.

CHAPTER VIII

SACRED ARCHITECTURE AND THE RELIGION OF THE ETRUSCANS

Giovanni Colonna

This chapter offers a panoramic survey, obviously brief, of the sacred architecture of the Etruscans, intended to bring out what it can teach us about the religion of that people. By sacred architecture I mean all the manifestations of the art of building that have a cultic scope, both in places and contexts specifically sacred (i.e., sanctuaries)[1] and elsewhere. I shall not be able to give a truly exhaustive account, for the material is too vast and rich in its ramifications, especially as regards the funerary aspects, so important in Etruria. I shall attempt, however, to put the problems in focus, referring to recent, even the very latest discoveries. Obviously I shall have much to say of the sanctuary at Pyrgi (Figs. VIII.1–2), not only because I am and have been its excavator, up until 1980 by the side of Massimo Pallottino, and later as the sole responsible director; but because, considering the celebrated early discoveries and the no less remarkable ones of the last fifteen years, the site appears indisputably to be the main sanctuary of Etruria, revealing on the shore of the Tyrrhenian Sea a concentration of sacred architecture that does not have a comparison in the West, except in a few great sanctuaries of Sicily and Magna Graecia.[2]

Pyrgi provides exemplars of the four major categories of Etruscan sacred architecture: altars, precincts, shrines, and temples. We shall review these, and particularly the first three, in considerable detail, as they provide much information about Etruscan cult practice, sometimes unknown from other sites in Etruria. But of course we shall collect comparisons from all other Etruscan sanctuaries, including those of the Po valley and Campania and sometimes also those of Latium. Since we shall make such frequent reference to Pyrgi, it will be helpful to have in mind the chronology that has been developed for the sacred areas there, showing activity ranging from around the middle of the sixth century to the war with Hannibal (218–201 BCE) and as late as the first century BCE. Of particular importance was the momentous event that drastically affected the life of the sanctuary, the sack of it by Dionysios of Syracuse in 384 BCE (main source: Diodorus Siculus 15.14.3–4).

ALTARS

To follow an ideal "historical" thread from the earliest material to the latest, in terms of typology, the discourse must begin with the altars. In regard to these it must be said that the relevant list of cases, already rather complex,[3] has been enriched in recent years thanks to the excavation of the South Area of the sanctuary of Pyrgi (Fig. VIII.2), with a type new for Etruria and rare elsewhere: the altar of rough stones or "unworked rubble altar" of the "amorphous" variety.[4] These are lens-shaped mounds of broken stones, mostly calcareous, of small to medium size, drawn from river beds that are not nearby. The mounds are no more than 30 cm high and have a plan that is subcircular or elliptical, with the greatest diameter surpassing in one case 2 m.

The two largest and most evident examples are located along the eastern limit of the sacred area, the perimeter of which was not actually marked with a precinct wall, in contrast to the well-known North Area brought to light during the 1950s, '60s and '70s. These are the features *Zeta* and *Iota* (Figs. VIII.3–4), the identity of which as altars is assured for *Zeta* by the adjacent "sacrificial *fossa*,"* *Omicron*, containing animal bones and votive offerings (perhaps a *magmen*-

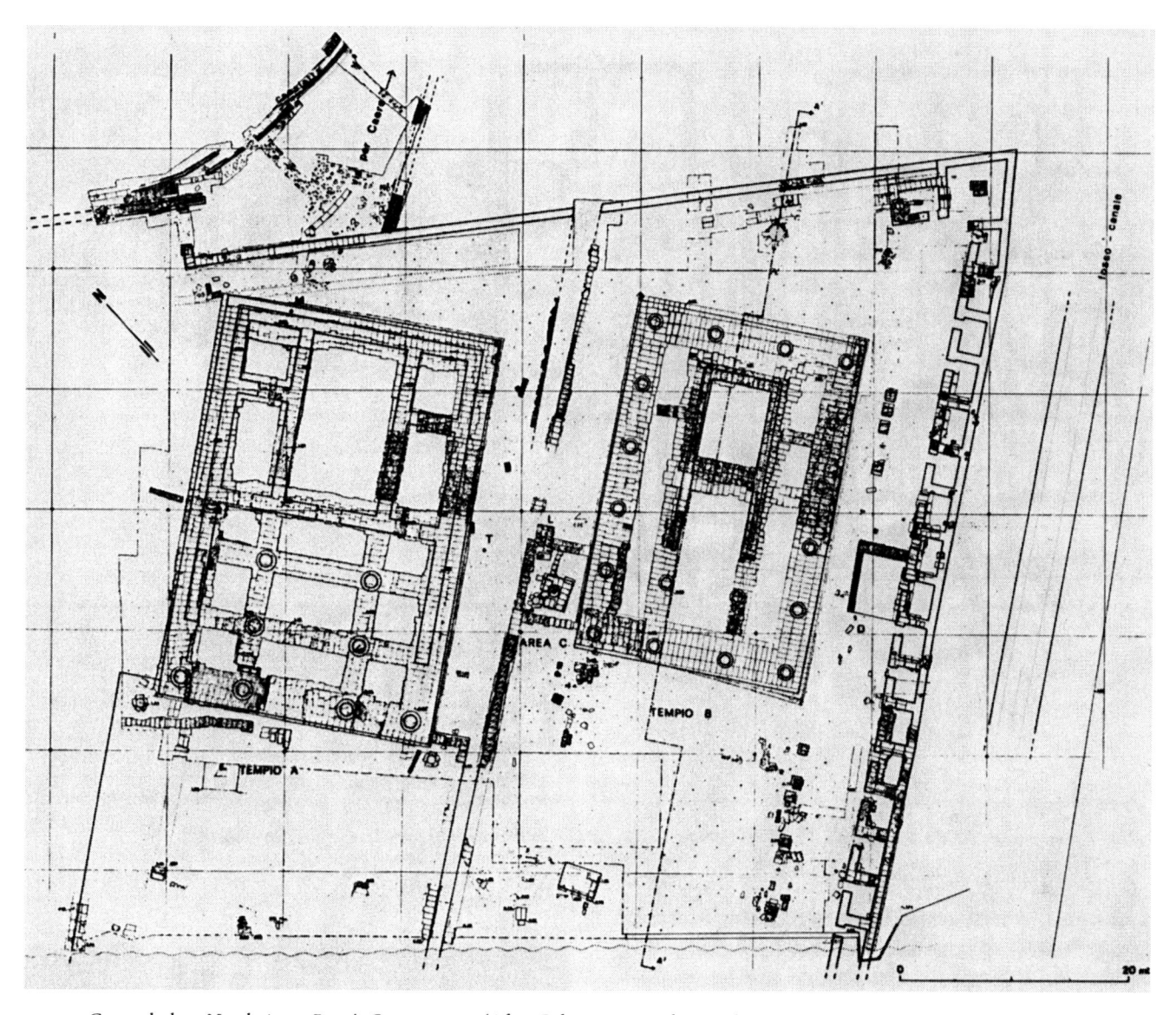

VIII.1. General plan, North Area, Pyrgi. Ca. 450 BCE. (After Colonna 1986, pl. XXII.)

tarium* in the sense of Varro, *De lingua Latina* 5.112), and for *Iota* by the contiguous block of tufo* set at ground level and pierced by a vertical quadrangular conduit, at least 2 m deep (Fig. VIII.4). A boulder of sandstone was found over the opening, concealing and protecting it, apparently identical to the Roman *lapis manalis* ("stone of flowing water"), if it was primarily intended to block up the so-called *ostium Orci* ("the mouth of hell": Paulus ex Festo, p. 115 Lindsay). In any case, the conduit had the same function as those in the cylindrical altar of Area C of the Pyrgi sanctuary (see below), in the altar at Punta della Vipera near S. Marinella and in the Volsinian altars sacred to Tinia, as well as the one contiguous to the altar of Menerva in the Portonaccio sanctuary at Veii (a better comparison because it, too, was at ground level)—that is, to conduct into the subsoil the blood of sacrificed victims or other possible liquid offerings that were poured into it.[5]

A third altar of rough stones, *Nu*, not as large and not as well preserved as *Zeta* and *Iota*, is found more toward the interior of the sacred area, along the way that gave access to the oldest shrine of all, *Beta*. In contrast to the other mounds of rubble, this was finished off on the surface by a circular slab of sandstone, originally 1.2 m in diameter (only a segment of it survives), functioning as a "table of sacrifice," as in some representations of altars of stones on Attic red-figured vases.[6] In this case, its presence is confirmed by a ring of dark

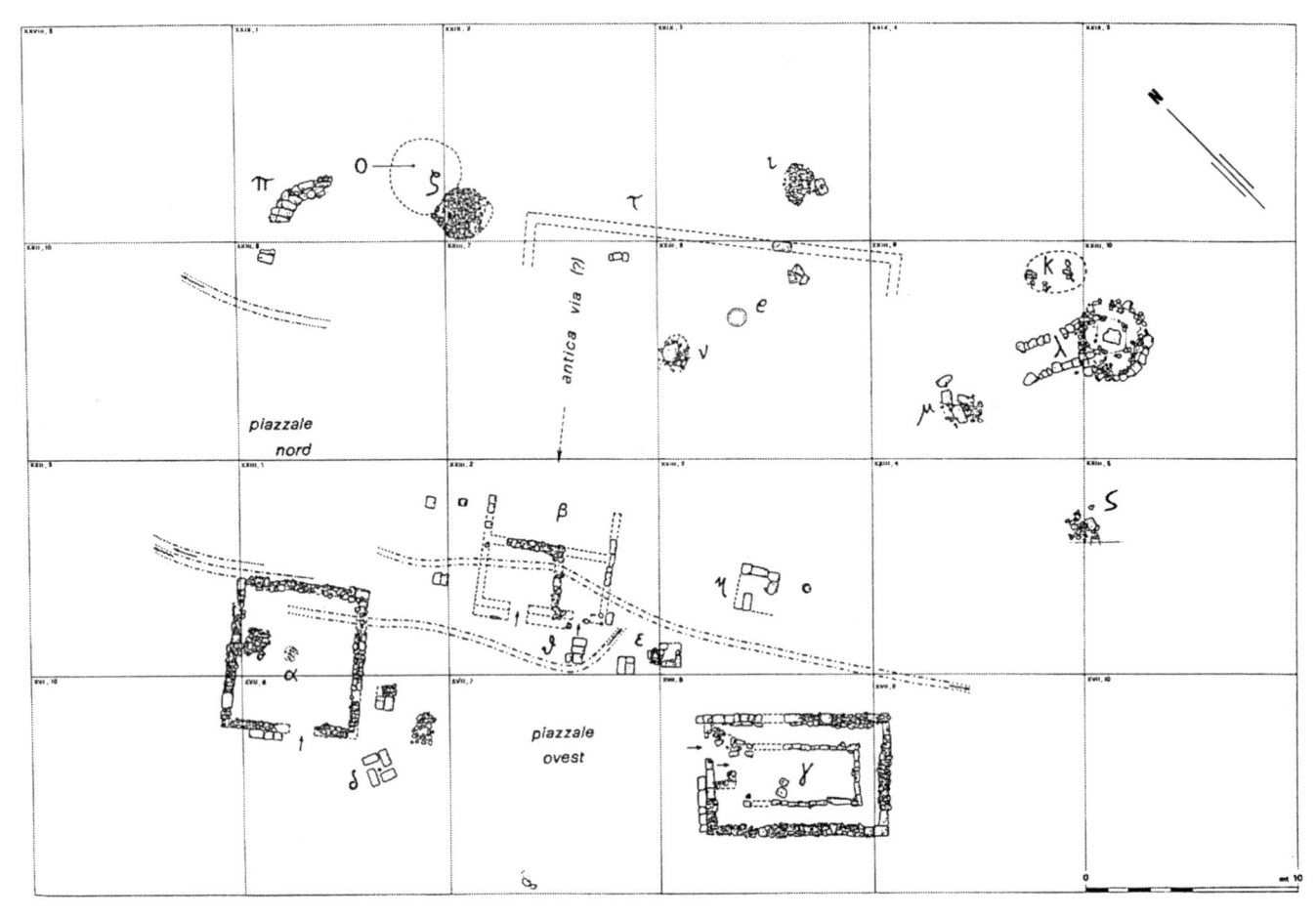

VIII.2. General plan, South Area (1998), Pyrgi. Ca. 350 BCE. (Università di Roma La Sapienza, Pyrgi Excavations.)

earth with ashes and animal bones surrounding it. Similar disks or "wheels" of stone have been found: one at the center of the shrine of Poggio Casetta at Bolsena and others out of position at the sanctuary of Pieve a Sòcana in the Casentino (Fig. VIII.5), at Poggio della Melonta near Orvieto, and most recently in the locality of Fùcoli near Chianciano, which has yielded such extraordinary discoveries, well displayed in the local museum just inaugurated.[7] The upper surface of the slabs at Sòcana and at Melonta bear an inscription with the name not of the divinity but of the donor, which in the past has led to the erroneous idea that these were offerings.[8] Instead, they are "ground altars," either not supported or raised on one or two layers of stones, dedicated, along with the sacrifices that took place on them, to a deity at once chthonic and solar, of which I shall soon say more.

A fourth altar of stones in the South Area at Pyrgi, smaller than the others (ca. 90 cm in diameter), is inside of the shrine Alpha (Fig. VIII.6), the latest of the three shrines brought to light, constructed around the middle of the fourth century BCE and covered with a roof furnished with at least one

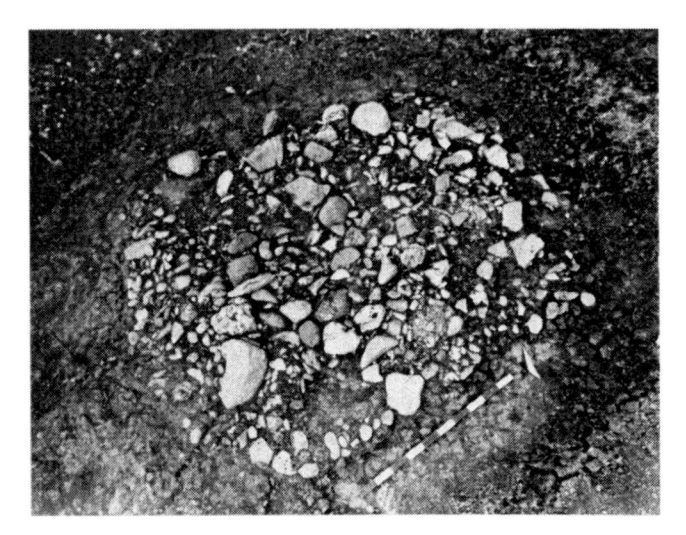

VIII.3. Altar Zeta, Pyrgi. 480–470 BCE. (Università di Roma La Sapienza, Pyrgi Excavations.)

VIII.4. *Altar Iota, Pyrgi. After 480–470 BCE. (Università di Roma La Sapienza, Pyrgi Excavations.)*

VIII.5. *Altar stone, Pieve a Sòcana. Early fifth century BCE. (Photo: Soprintendenza Alle Antichità-Firenze.)*

tile with an *opaion* (skylight) of horseshoe shape. The position of the altar very near the north wall of the shrine, on the side of the building off axis from the entrance, makes it very unlikely that this was an altar with fire, in contrast to the smaller circular *eschara* (hearth) placed almost at the center of the room, sufficient in itself to necessitate one or more roof openings.

The prominence of the cult of the altar within the entire sector is nevertheless proven by the fact that the altar continued to be frequented, as shown by the votive offerings, and remained in use under the open sky, even after the roof of *Alpha* collapsed, around 270 BCE, as a result of the general decline suffered by the sanctuary. The same continuation of devotional practices, at least to the end of the third century BCE, was otherwise verified in particular by the presence of coins of the Roman Prow series in the peripheral altar *Zeta*, adjacent to the contiguous *fossa Omicron*.

As for the chronology, all four secure examples, fortu-

nately, are datable. For the altar of shrine *Alpha*, it has already been stated that it goes back to the middle of the fourth century BCE when the shrine was constructed. *Zeta* and *Iota* are stratigraphically later than the enlargement of the sacred area that took place ca. 480–470 BCE. *Nu*, on the other hand, the only altar furnished with a sacrificial surface in the form of a stone slab (circular in shape), is placed in the first phase of activity in the area, which began around the middle of the sixth century BCE.

An exceptional discovery, made in the fall of 1998, now allows a precise dating of 510–500 BCE. I refer to *Rho*, a cylindrical *bothros** dug into the yellow clay of the original rise of the land and filled with more than forty painted vases, exclusively Greek and in great part Attic black figure. Included as the latest material were twelve "Floral Band Cups" and some *lekythoi** of the Phanyllis Group (Fig. VIII.7). In the amphora placed in the middle were a silver necklace, with the largest bead in the shape of a tortoise, and an amber pendant with a miniature inscription, almost illegible; both objects imply a female divinity.

Located just 2 m east of the altar, *Rho* is probably to be understood as a sumptuous offering buried at the occasion of its foundation. Nearby on the top of the east rise have been found some sheets of bronze in the form of leaves, pierced at the base to be bound into a bundle, like those found in the deposit *Kappa* (Fig. VIII.8), of which I will speak shortly. These sheets may be interpreted as cleromantic *sortes** (*sors*), precisely in the form of leaves (cf. Vergil, *Aeneid* 3.445–450). This leads to the consideration that the altar was sacred to an oracular divinity, certainly the same to whom was dedicated the deposit cited.[9]

The altars described, still unknown at the time of my *Santuari d'Etruria* (1985) and of Edlund's book on extraur-

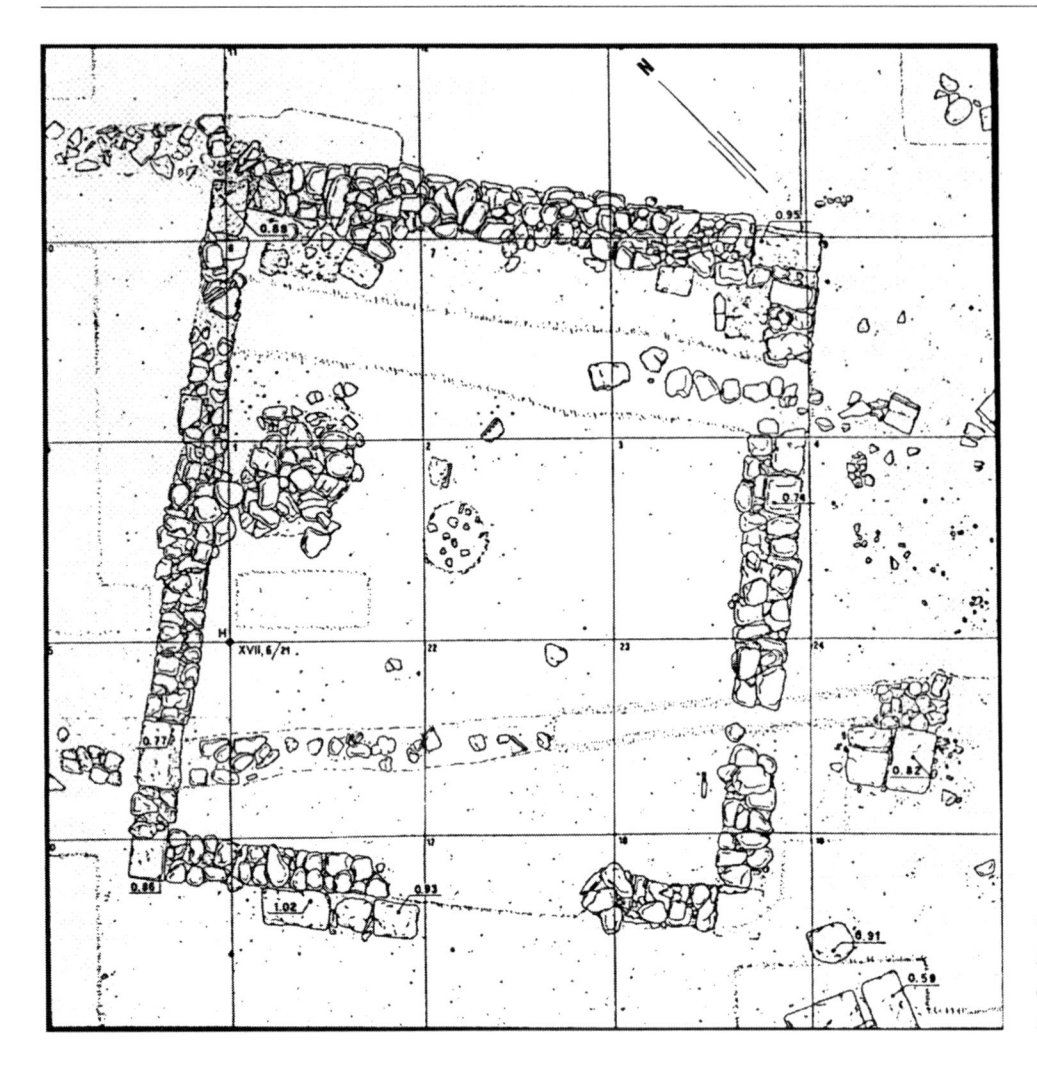

VIII.6. Plan, Shrine Alpha, *Pyrgi. Ca. 350 BCE. (Università di Roma La Sapienza, Pyrgi Excavations.)*

ban and rural sanctuaries (1987), have no comparisons that I know of in Etruria, except for the "wheels" found generally out of position in sanctuaries of inner Etruria, nor in the rest of ancient Italy. Nevertheless, these can be related to the tradition, remaining alive in the full Imperial age even for the most solemn and official occasions (Tacitus, *Hist.* 4.53), of altars of clods of grassy turf. Varro traced this tradition back to religion before Numa, when for the Romans there existed neither temples nor divine images. In that remote and mythicized age they would have had recourse to only *temporaria de caespite altaria* ("temporary sod altars") for cult activity, as well as humble "Samian" or clay pots.[10] For the clods, if one substitutes rocks without any particular arrangement, the altars then become lasting and defy time, surviving down to our age, provided that the sacred areas have been excavated with due attention and above all in a thorough manner.

The examples from Pyrgi are all the more interesting in that they do not go back, as do the few brought to light in Greece, to the Geometric or Early Archaic period.[11] Rather they belong to the Late Archaic and Classical periods, showing a phenomenon of conservatism worthy of the greatest attention. It is probable that this type of altar was favored in our case by the strongly symbolic value attributed in the Etruscan iconographic lexicon to boulders and rocks, as allusions to the threshold that separates the world of the living from that of the dead.[12] Particularly significant in this regard are the representations on the sarcophagus of Laris Pulenas (Fig. 11.7) and on that of Torre San Severo (Fig. VIII.9), where the sacrifice of Polyxena takes place next to what seems to be a true and proper altar of stones, upon which the shade of Achilles places his foot.

That ideological factors and conservatism were operative is shown by an equal number of other altars, of a different type and "normal," so to speak, which we find in the same South Area of Pyrgi, probably consecrated to the same di-

VIII.7. Greek pottery found in Pit Rho (including "Floral Band" Cups and lekythos of the Phanyllis Group), Pyrgi. Late sixth century BCE. (Università di Roma La Sapienza, Pyrgi Excavations.)

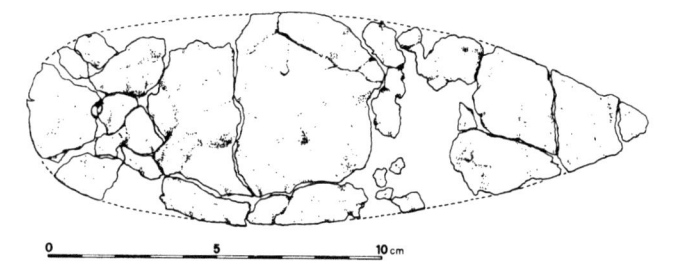

VIII.8. Bronze sheet in shape of leaf, prophetic sors, from deposit Kappa, Pyrgi. 480–470 BCE. (Università di Roma La Sapienza, Pyrgi Excavations.)

VIII.9. Relief from sarcophagus from Torre San Severo, Achilles standing with foot on rustic altar. Mid fourth century BCE. Orvieto, Museo Claudio Faina. (DAI Rome 69.2434.)

vinities, even if the rituals are presumed to be of another character. I refer to the altars *Theta* and *Epsilon* (see Fig. VIII.2), placed in the service of the shrines *Beta* and *Gamma* and belonging respectively to the first and second phase of the sanctuary; and also to the altar *Delta* (Fig. VIII.10), also of the second phase, demolished when the shrine *Alpha* rose there in the area immediately adjacent, during the successive phase. They are altars that, as far as can be judged from the surviving footing of the foundations (or in the case of *Epsilon*, from the remains of the first course of the elevation), were constructed in *opus quadratum** of blocks of red tufo in the form of a parallelepiped tending toward a cube ("simple, built altars with a short rectangular plan," in the terminology of Rupp).[13] There was attached, on the northwest side of altar *Epsilon*, a small *cista** of slabs of stone, found uncovered, which functioned as a *bothros*, and perhaps at the same time as a low *prothysis* (altar base).[14] When it was uncovered, it still contained two miniature vessels related to libations (an unpainted *krateriskos** and an Attic *oinochoe** of late black figure); in the surrounding area was discovered a foundation offering of a parallelepiped ingot of lead.

A fourth constructed altar, *Lambda,* was found at the south margin of the sacred area, thus in a position not unlike that of the rubble altars *Zeta* and *Iota,* but corresponding with a wide depression in the terrain. Perhaps to compensate for this situation, but certainly not only for that reason, the altar, of which remains only the rectangular footing for a foundation of compacted chips of tufo, had been placed on a podium of a circular form and almost 4 m in diameter. A wide ramp (Fig. VIII.11) joined the altar to facilitate access, one might say for the sacrificial animals rather than for those making the sacrifice. This structure was stripped of the altar and of the mural facing of the podium at the time of the reworking of the entire south flank of the sanctuary, which occurred in the aftermath of the Syracusan sack of Pyrgi, around the middle of the fourth century BCE. It retains only the ring of the foundation with the interior earthen nucleus, containing a dense concentration of offerings of rough lead, in the form of parallelepiped ingots in three different sizes, the smallest similar to that recorded in relation to the first course of the altar *Epsilon.*

We have no parallels either in the sanctuaries of Pyrgi or in the others of Etruria and the Greek world, but the structure of *Lambda* strongly recalls the so-called Altar of Grotta Porcina, in a cemetery context near Blera, of the first half of the sixth century BCE (Fig. VIII.12).[15] The latter was in reality the rock-cut base of an altar, or alternatively of one or more *cippi** (in the form of an obelisk?), sculptured on the sides of the drum and on the access "ramp" with a majestic procession of quadrupeds. It was located in the center of an area shaped like a theater, with risers cut out of the rock. Its proximity to the colossal tumulus that has given its name to the place leads one to think that the whole complex functioned for a funerary cult, suited for the ancestors of the members of the aristocratic *gens** that owned the tumulus. The typological resemblance to a similar monument within the framework of the Pyrgi sanctuary probably signifies appropriation in the community of Caere of architectonic forms that arose to satisfy the needs of a *gens* for "visibility" but then came to be put to use for civic religion, taking a new significance (in this case, as I am about to relate, connected to the cult of the gods of the Afterlife).

In fact, fortunately we know not only the date of altar *Lambda* at Pyrgi but also the divinities to whom it was con-

VIII.10. Altar Delta, Pyrgi. 480–470 BCE. (Università di Roma La Sapienza, Pyrgi Excavations.)

VIII.11. Altar Lambda, Pyrgi. 480–470 BCE. (Università di Roma La Sapienza, Pyrgi Excavations.)

secrated. The open space surrounding the monument contained the remains of some offerings deposited in the bare earth, the most notable of which was the feature *Kappa* (Fig. VIII.2), excavated in 1994. It consists of three groups of offerings, deposited in shallow pits separated by a few stones and covered over by a single mound of earth, a sort of small tumulus, pulled over the top of the deposit. Around the

VIII.12. Altar of Grotta Porcina, Blera. First half of fourth century BCE. (Photo: Giovanni Colonna.)

middle of the fourth century, the whole south flank of the sanctuary was reworked, as noted previously, reusing earth and materials for the construction of an open court on the opposite (i.e., north) side of the area. The offerings, of a quite varied nature, in contrast to those in the formerly noted deposit *Rho*, include crude lumps of bronze (*aes rude**), worked bronzes, a bundle of probable *sortes* in sheets of iron and bronze in the shape of a leaf (Fig. VIII.8), terracottas (two molded *protomai** of a Magna Graecia type and of a female deity), glass vases, small *alabastra**, and especially fictile objects, of both Attic (red figure) and in lesser quantity, Etruscan wares.

The most easily datable vases M. P. Baglione assigned to the decade 480–470 BCE: a janiform *kantharos** attributed to the Syriskos Painter and a colonnette *krater** with the drinking Herakles served by a satyr, attributed to the Tyskiewicz Painter.[16] The dating may be extended to the altar on the podium *Lambda*, which belongs therefore to the second phase of the sanctuary. The *krater* bears on the underside of the foot the Etruscan inscription *mi fuflunusra*,[17] in which the adjective *fuflunusra*, or "Fuflunian," is to be understood probably as an epithet of a masculine divinity. This is a divinity to whom a second and even more important inscription from the same deposit—placed on the foot of an Attic *kylix** (the rest is lost)—gives the name of Śuri, associating it with that of the goddess Cav(a)tha, omitting a connective: *mi śuris cavaθas*, "I am of Śuri (and) of Cavatha."

The names of the gods Śuri and Cav(a)tha, both already noted in other sanctuaries but up until recently often misunderstood, reappear separately in numerous inscriptions on vases found at many points in the South Area.[18] Given the absence, now well confirmed, of different gods' names,[19] there can be no doubt that reference here is to the two gods who were titulars of the cult in that area. Added to the explicit references are obviously epithets, which for the god are Apa, "Father," and perhaps Lapse, given on two small bronze plaques probably once attached to offerings.[20] For the goddess we might think of the name Ecile, painted on the bottom of the foot of a late, local black-glazed cup, through a phonetic sequence *Eicle>*Ecle>Ecile, to the Greek Αἴγλη, "The Shining One,"[21] a name borne by, among others, a wife or daughter of Helios. This name is all the more suitable for Cavtha, given that a plant with a similar name (καυταμ, known also as the Millefolia or Achillea), is called *Solis oculus* ("Eye of the Sun") in a gloss of Dioskorides. Since Śuri, whose name appears at Orvieto in the variant Śur (*ET*, Vs 0.6), is certainly identical to the Soranus of the Faliscans, and through him not only to Apollo but also to Dis Pater of the Romans and to the Greek Hades, his female companion has a great likelihood of being a hypostasis of Persephone/Proserpina.

Dis Pater and Proserpina were venerated together in Rome near the Comitium, in relation to a *mundus** going back to the origins of the city, and at the Tarentum of the Campus Martius, where the *Ludi saeculares* were celebrated throughout Imperial times, with nocturnal rituals at *arae temporales*,[22] perhaps at the beginning not unlike those of rubble in the South Area of Pyrgi.[23] The verification of the identity proposed for Cavtha comes from the epithet śeχ, "Daughter" (clearly a calc of the Greek appellative Kore), given to the goddess in an Orvietan dedication of the mid fifth century BCE.[24] Also instructive is the later dedication of a bronze cone to "Espi, mother of Ca(v)tha," or, which is equivalent, to "Espi, the mother (and) Ca(v)tha," published by Larissa Bonfante.[25] In this inscription Espi can only be an appellative, up to now unknown, of Vei/Demeter.

The solar connotations of Cavtha are not so surprising, first because of the belief that the sun of night shone in Hades, as attested by Pindar and Aristophanes.[26] In addition, already in the *Odyssey* (24.12), not only are the gates of Hades called the "Gates of Helios" but it is Kirke, the daughter of Helios, who teaches Odysseus precisely how to descend to the dead. To this we can add the chthonic character assumed by Sol in central Italy, revealed by the most ancient epithet of Indiges accepted at Rome and at Lavinium, which made him the mythical ancestor of the Latins.[27] Even at Pyrgi, the most notable cults of the Roman colony were, to judge from inscriptions, those of Sol Juvans and of Pater Pyrgensis.[28] The identification of the goddess with Hekate, recently proposed,[29] is less convincing, given that although indeed the Underworld connection is retained, it does not rely on specific attributes made known by excavations, and it does not take into account either the pairing with Śuri or the epithet of "Daughter."

Continuing with the theme of the altar, in the South Area at Pyrgi the shrine *Gamma*, of which I will speak shortly, had an altar inside but of a type quite different from that of the shrine *Alpha*, although equally rudimentary: there were two awkwardly squared ashlar blocks of tufo, placed one beside the other in the cella,* on the right, each provided with a large cuplike depression carved in the upper face with a little channel for the run-off of liquid (Fig. VIII.13). This is a simplified version, one might say, of the *mensae* ("tables") for libations and blood offerings appropriate for the Etruscan cult of ancestors, whether domestic or funerary. Examples appear in the Campana Tomb (Fig. VIII.14) and the Tomb of Five Chairs at Caere, on some *fossa* tombs in the territory

VIII.13. *Shrine* Gamma, *Pyrgi. Ca. 450 BCE. (Università di Roma La Sapienza, Pyrgi Excavations.)*

of Bolsena (the largest one with a *mensa* of stone, set up in the shelter of the *stele** grave marker and, significantly, bearing a dedication to Farth(ans), "The Progenitor"), on the so-called fictile hearths of the tombs of the territory of Vulci, and on the so-called incense burners and presentation pieces of bronze of the Orientalizing tombs.[30] The only Etruscan temple in which excavators reported finding blocks with the cup depression is the temple of the Belvedere at Orvieto (see below, p. 160), although in this case the blocks were out of position. Not by chance has this temple yielded also dedications on pottery to Śur(i) and to Apa, to which later was added Tinia Calusna or a Tinia related to the Underworld deity Calu.

Returning to the altars on a podium, *Lambda* of the South Area at Pyrgi has no comparison in the realm of sanctuaries, as noted, because of the circular form of the base and the access ramp. The comparison does not extend to the principle of placement on an appropriate raised platform that isolates it from the surrounding area. Functionally similar, in fact, are podiums B and D of the acropolis sanctuary at Marzabotto (Fig. VIII.15).[31] Both have a square plan, provided with access stairs, and are completely independent of temples A and C along their sides. (The altars for these temples are to be considered lost or may be conjectured to have been lost in the collapse of the terrain in front of them.) Podium D, richly endowed with moldings in cut stone, seemingly had on its surface of more than 80 sq m not only one or two altars but also donations and perhaps a cult image. In other words, it was a sort of tiny raised *temenos*,* whose squared plan formally assimilated that of a *templum minus** or *templum in terra*,*[32] in contrast to the one found at Monteguragazza in the last century.[33] Podium B, much smaller (17 sq m) and unadorned, extends considerably into the subsoil, enclosing a well inside in the center, some 6.5 m deep. It has been correctly recognized that it is a special type of "altar" for chthonic and catachthonic deities, functioning also as a foundation pit, which was a *mundus*.[34]

Constructed when the nearby temples did not yet exist, to judge from obvious structural evidence, Podium B is probably to be considered the first cult installation rising on the city acropolis. Because all the Etruscan cities of the Po River area, according to the tradition preserved by Aulus Caecina, were dedicated by the *oikist** Tarchon to the god the Romans called Dis Pater, there can be no doubt that the *mundus* of podium B is sacred to this very god. The Etruscans of the Po area called him not Śuri but Mantus, as can be seen from Servius (*ad Aen.* 10.199) and from the very name of the "capital" Mantua/Mantova, the native city of Vergil. That we are talking about a homologue of Śuri is now proven by an Archaic dedication to the god *manθ*,[35] found in a *bothros* in a sanctuary at Pontecagnano (Via Verdi), which has also yielded three Greek dedications on pottery to Apollo, published some time ago.

In fact, whether at Pyrgi or Arezzo, at Falerii or Mount Soracte, the contemporary *interpretatio Graeca* of Śuri/Soranus was that he was Apollo himself, as is shown by literary and epigraphical sources. Evidence of the first order is provided by the oracular capabilities of the indigenous god, attested by the *sortes* with his name found near Viterbo and at Arezzo; he is probably more the Underworld Apollo of Cumae than the god of Delphi.[36]

Other altars on a podium, high and of quadrangular form and endowed with a complex set of moldings, arose at Vignanello (Faliscan territory) and at the Patturelli site

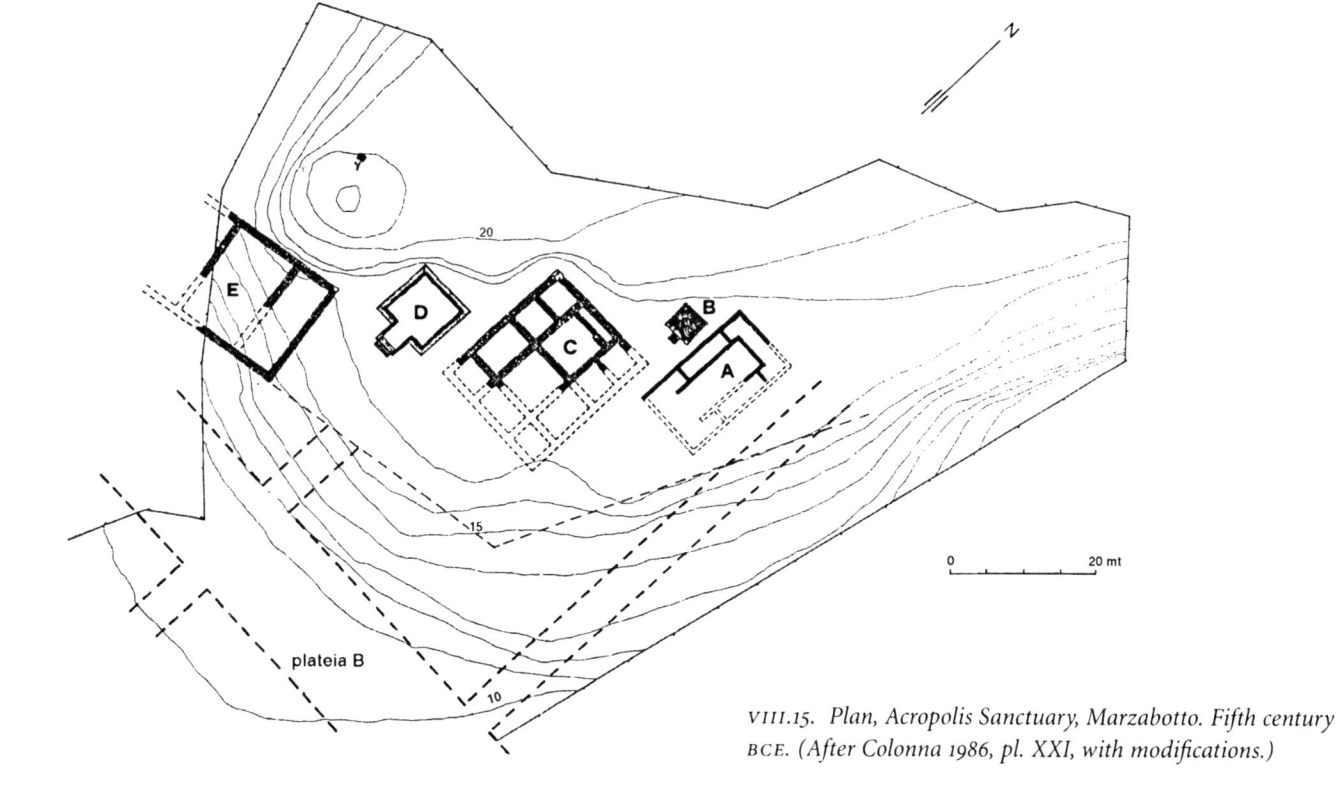

VIII.14. Rock altar, Campana Tomb, Caere. Mid seventh century BCE. (After Prayon, 1975, pl. 62:2.)

VIII.15. Plan, Acropolis Sanctuary, Marzabotto. Fifth century BCE. (After Colonna 1986, pl. XXI, with modifications.)

VIII.16. Structure added to the Tumulus of Melone del Sodo II, Cortona. Mid sixth century BCE. (Photo: Giovanni Colonna.)

at Capua, in isolated spots just outside the city walls. They were probably built in relation to the contiguous necropolis (and we know that the altar at Capua was sacred to a funerary goddess similar to Venus Libitina).[37] The type of altar on a platform, like podiums B and D at Marzabotto, also had great prestige in funerary architecture. At the tumulus of the Melone del Sodo II at Cortona, with its 64 m diameter one of the greatest tumuli existing in Etruria, the discovery of a projecting body, of exceptional monumentality and decorative refinement (Fig. VIII.16), has raised anew the question of the cultic significance that such furnishings, functional to reach the top surface of the tumulus, could assume. This is a terrace of 5 m × 6.5 m, 2 m high, with ten steps leading to it.[38] The terrace and stairs are bordered by parapets surmounted by six great palmette *akroteria** with double volutes and decorated at the bottom edge with the two sculptural groups of a lioness wrestling with a warrior who stabs her with his sword.

Datable in the second quarter of the sixth century, the monument is surely inspired by the great Greco-Oriental altars such as that at Capo Monodendri near Miletos. The absence of the remains of an altar or of *cippi* at first sight renders problematic the supposed cultic function, as in the case of the terrace reconstructed at the portico of the tomb in the form of a house at Pian di Mola, Tuscania (Fig. VIII.17),[39] and of the terrace carved at the corners with colossal heads of a lion and a ram on a tomb with three chambers in the necropolis of Castro at the Crocifisso del Tufo.[40] Never-

VIII.17. Tomb at Pian di Mola, Tuscania. Sixth century BCE. (After Sgubini Moretti 1989, fig. 7.)

theless, the presence of *cippi* on the surface of the tumulus and, in the case of the tomb at Tuscania, on the ridge beam of the gabled roofs, makes it likely that cult activities (prayers, libations) could take place just in sight of and not in direct contact with the markers of the deceased, probably by using appropriate cavities in the pavement. Their poor state of preservation does not allow us to verify their existence. The direct contact with *cippi* did regularly take place on the crowning terraces of the rock-cut façade tombs of the fourth–third century BCE at Norchia (Fig. VIII.18), Castel d'Asso, Sovana, and other sites, where the *cippi* are or

VIII.18. Terrace of rock-cut tomb, Norchia. Late fourth–early third century BCE. (Photo: Giovanni Colonna.)

were fixed into the top floor. Monumental *cippi* of altarlike form are probably the two cylindrical monoliths, splendidly molded and carved with friezes of a Late Orientalizing style, found at Bologna in Via Fondazza, in what seems to be a small cemetery sanctuary (Fig. VIII.19).[41]

The altars on a podium mentioned so far are obviously different from those altars — at times likewise furnished with moldings and of considerable mass — such as, for example, that of Pieve a Sòcana.[42] The latter were not spatially isolated with respect to the remaining sacred area, nor were they out of line in relationship to the temple. These were altars on which one sacrificed while standing on the ground and thus at a low point with respect to the temple (Vitruvius, *De architectura* 4.9) but in a position so that the person making the sacrifice could see its façade and possibly as well the door of the cella in which the cult image was found. These altars are relatively unproblematic and need no further discussion.[43]

PRECINCTS

Further consideration is due to the type of altar inside a precinct specifically related to it, which seems to have been, at least in Etruria, the logical precedent of the altar on a podium. The smallest example (but quite clear) is the altar of the fifth–fourth century BCE at Fontanile di Legnisina on the outskirts of Vulci, which lay inside a narrow rectangular precinct (Fig. VIII.20). It was next to a monumental temple with a triple cella, as in the case of the podiums B and D at Marzabotto.[44] Its back wall was nearly joined to the cliff, but also on that side it was closed off by a high wall of orthostates. The entrance was probably on the short side on the south, where the molding of the base seems to be lacking, though it is present on the two other sides exposed to view.

VIII.19. Monolithic cippus of Via Fondazza, Bologna. Ca. 600 BCE. (Photo: Soprintendenza ai Beni Archeologici dell'Emilia Romagna.)

The evident intention to make the altar "secret" leads one to believe that of the two divinities mentioned in the exvotos — Uni and Vei — it was the latter, commonly assimilated to Demeter, the goddess of the Mysteries, who was the mistress of this minimal precinct. But the temple was dedicated to Uni, venerated here as Huinthnaia, perhaps with an allusion to the copious spring that has given its name to the place and constitutes the most characteristic element.[45] We are not acquainted with an altar for the temple here because the area in front of it appears to have been devastated. All this leaves aside the unique nature of the votive deposit,[46] which was favored by the availability of a site more or less predestined, the space between the altar precinct and the cliff.[47]

I began drawing attention to such precincts in the 1960s, when I started excavating the structure in the monumental sanctuary at Pyrgi, which we call Area C.[48] It is near where

VIII.20. Plan, sanctuary of Fontanile di Legnisina, Vulci. Fifth–fourth century BCE. (After Massabò and L. Ricciardi 1988, pl. I.)

the famous inscribed gold tablets were found, mentioning the cult of an Uni assimilated to the Phoenician Astarte (see the discussion above, pp. 13–14). This was in fact in origin none other than a precinct enclosing a well for water and two monolithic altars (Fig. VIII.21). One was cylindrical and pierced by a vertical channel on the axis, already mentioned in regard to the analogous feature in altar *Iota* of the South Area. The other was instead of rectangular form, conserved only as far as the great rock of *peperino*,* irregularly trapezoidal, which functioned as their base.

The enclosure was constructed at the same time as the contiguous temple B, for a probably double cult since there were two altars. The large plaque of bronze (Fig. VIII.22) found along with the gold tablets (Fig. II.6) mentions an Uni Chia and a Tina called Atalena Śea, as well as Thvariena and Spuriaze.[49] The cult was independent of the temple's cult of Uni assimilated to Astarte, even if also closely related. This is proved by the direct contact between the two structures, which was different than at Marzabotto and at Fontanile di Legnisina, where the temple and the podium or the precinct remained separated from each other. The same thing happened at Narce to the precincts with altars, *bothroi*, and *cippi*, filled with votive offerings. These were arranged, at the distance of only an *ambitus*,* along one of the long sides of a monumental temple, which has not yet been excavated. The temple is set at the foot of one of the hills of Narce, in the locality that bears the name Le Ròte ("The Mill-wheels"), perhaps not accidentally (Fig. VIII.23).[50]

Sacred Architecture

VIII.21. Area C, sacred precinct, Pyrgi. Ca. 510 BCE. (Courtesy of Università di Roma La Sapienza, Pyrgi Excavations.)

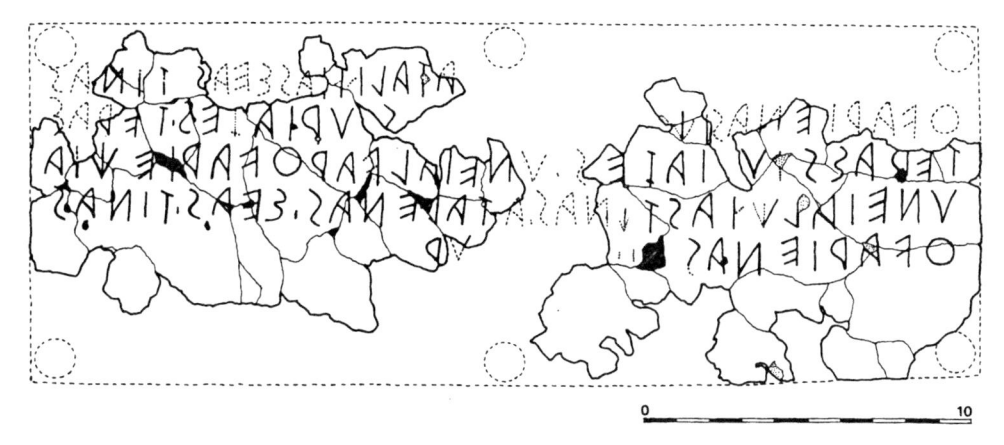

VIII.22. Bronze plaque, found in Area C, Pyrgi. Ca. 510 BCE. (Courtesy of Università di Roma La Sapienza, Pyrgi Excavations.)

At the Civita of Tarquinii the complex brought to light by the University of Milan in a fully urban area consists almost exclusively of an agglomeration of such precincts set around a natural cleft in the rock, the focus of cult, as far as can be told, since the end of the Bronze Age.[51] In this case, the only altar so far identified lay inside a building, of which I will soon say more. The Late Archaic sanctuary at Montetosto along the Pyrgi-Caere road, only partially excavated,[52] is in substance a unique large precinct with a square plan of 54 m on a side, divided internally on at least three sides by rooms of various shapes and sizes and including one or more altars in the central court. It was erected around 530–520 BCE, perhaps for the "heroic" cult commemorating the Phokaians stoned after the battle of the Sardinian Sea. The

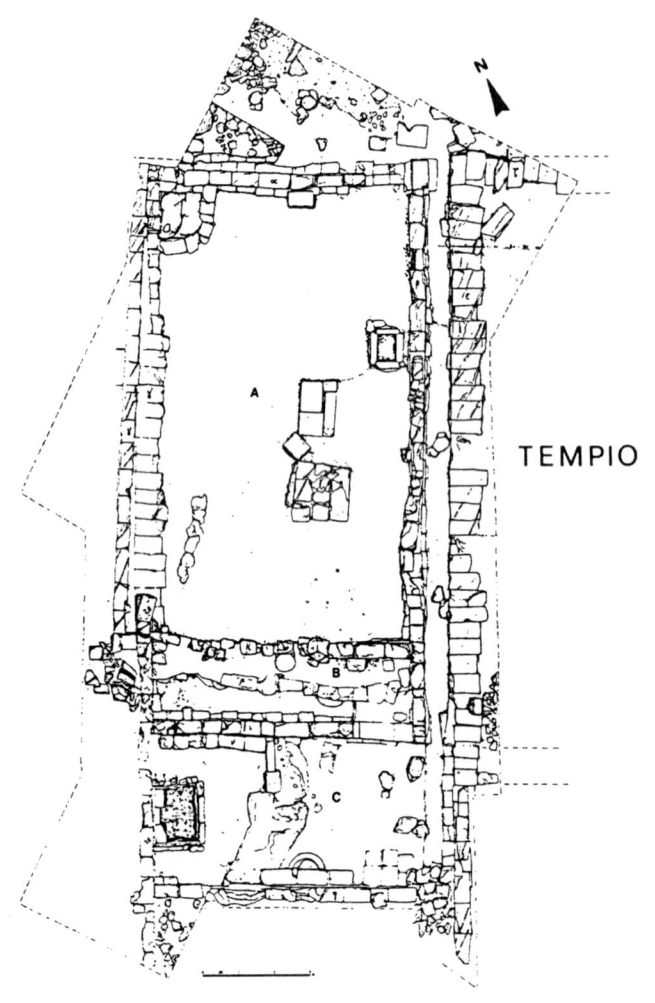

VIII.23. Precincts at Le Ròte sanctuary, Narce. Fifth–third centuries BCE. (After M. A. De Lucia Brolli, BollArch 3, 1990, 66 fig. 8.)

building complex, whose terracotta decoration was replaced many times in successive centuries, was apparently inspired by forms once customary for palatial architecture, now appropriated by the city. A form extremely simplified of the same typology is displayed in the third century BCE by the sanctuary of the Pozzarello at Bolsena, consisting only of a precinct of 37.5 m × 43.6 m, with an angular porch at one of the corners, an altar of the hourglass type, a great well, two stone repositories, and other features.[53] The sanctuary was sacred to a goddess assimilated in Roman times to Ceres, but its boundaries were under the protection of Selvans (ET, Vs 4.8).

*Sacellum** is the one Latin word that would probably describe architectural structures as diverse as the precincts of Pyrgi (Area C), Monteguragazza, Narce, and Tarquinii, those reduced to the smallest possible area at Fontanile di Legnisina or, in contrast, grown gigantic at Montetosto and at Pozzarello, as well as the podiums, typologically later, of Marzabotto, Vignanello, and Capua. *Sacellum* is a technical term misunderstood already in the time of Cicero by Trebatius (who derived it from *sacra cella,** an etymology rightly refuted by Gellius 7.12.5). In fact, with this diminutive of the substantive adjective *sacrum*, equivalent to the Greek ἱερόν, "sanctuary" (though in Latin of the historic period the word was no longer used in that sense; it was replaced by *fanum,** *templum,** and even *delubrum*),[54] were designated the "places without a roof, sacred to the gods" (*loca dis sacrata sine tecto;* Festus, p. 422 Lindsay) or a "little place with an altar consecrated to a god" (*locus parvus, deo sacratus cum ara;* Trebatius, in Gellius 7.12.5).[55]

To these definitions, which well suit the precincts and the podiums in question, if we leave aside the dimensions, one can add the *consaeptum sacellum** ("fenced sanctuary") adjacent to the Ara Maxima of Hercules in the Forum Boarium. In the Roman world, this sanctuary was the oldest and the most venerated of such structures open to the sky.[56] Their "invention" was attributed to the mythical progenitor and civilizer Phoroneus (Varro, *De gente populi romani,* fr. 13 Fr.), the same to whom was ascribed the invention of fire (Pausanias 2.19.5), preliminary to that of sacrifice. In the Italic world this kind of structure, remaining far more central in religious architecture than in Etruria and Latium, was given the name of *sakaraklúm,* or "place where sacred acts are made,"[57] used by extension in the sense of "sanctuary," in opposition to *fíísnú,* "temple" or "shrine," set inside.[58]

SHRINES

In the reconstruction that Varro traced of the historical development of Roman religion, the shrine, or *aedes,** makes its appearance with Numa.[59] At that time it was a place to accommodate not the cult image but a direct antecedent, which was in fact the nonanthropomorphic fetish, most commonly a stripped stake of wood. (The cult image was introduced only at the end of the reign of Tarquinius Priscus, with the fictile statue of Capitoline Jupiter commissioned to the Etruscan Vulca.)[60] At Rusellae, excavations have revealed a large precinct of mud bricks of the mid seventh century BCE (ca. 26 × 7.5 m), oriented toward the east. Inside, the precinct accommodates a small building of square plan, constructed with mud bricks, and inside that, a circular room (diam. 4.5 m).[61] The room imitates, as did the Roman Temple of Vesta, primitive huts of wood and boughs (but perhaps, in

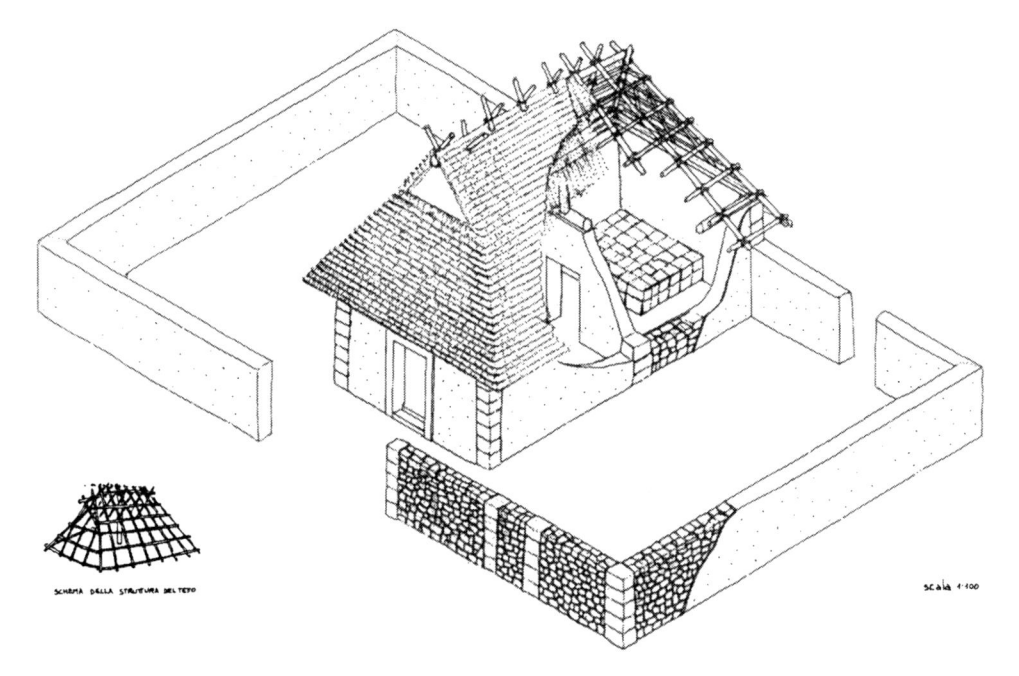

VIII.24. Building Beta *of Pian di Civita, Tarquinii. Seventh century* BCE. *(After M. Bonghi Jovino, in* Roma, Romolo, Rema e la fondazione della città, *ed. A. Carandini and R. Cappelli, Rome, 2000, 267.)*

consideration of the circular antechambers of the great contemporary Caeretan tombs, it is better to speak of the oldest form of the *atrium**).

As far as we can tell, the shrine/temple of the time of Numa already had a well-developed rectangular plan. Its chief characteristic (exemplified throughout antiquity by the *aedes* of Jupiter Feretrius on the Capitoline, built by Ancus Martius on a *templum* founded by Romulus)[62] was its complete inaccessibility to the faithful, owing to the absence of an open *pronaos** and of a peristyle, the small dimensions, and the covering with a complete testudinate* roof (i.e., with four pitches, initially certainly of thatch). Basically we are talking about the kind of shrine we would define as "*oikos** type," given the more or less "domestic" aspect, but subject as time passed to decoration with sophisticated terracotta revetments, as first shown by the temple at Piazza d'Armi at Veii.

The oldest example, dated to the first half of the seventh century by the exceptional foundation offering found before it (a shield, an axe, and a *lituus**/trumpet of bronze; Fig. III.2), is now the building *Beta* of the complex investigated at the Civita of Tarquinii by the University of Milan (Fig. VIII.24). The building, precisely oriented, measures 6.50 × 11 m and is divided in two axial rooms, the inner containing a great constructed altar, which was leaning against the rear wall and linked to the sacral cleft by a channel (Fig. III.1). The type and placement of the altar, together with the "pier-and-rubble" construction[63] used for the walls, are probably

VIII.25. Terracotta antefix from temple of Piazza d'Armi. Early sixth century BCE. *Veii. (Photo: Soprintendenza per i Beni Archeologici dell'Etruria Meridionale.)*

inspired from Near Eastern (Phoenician) features, until now unknown elsewhere in Etruria.[64] At about the mid seventh century, the building was surrounded by a precinct of 15.70 × 25 m, aligned to its rear wall, with an arrangement similar, apart from the dimensions, to that shown much later by the sanctuary of Poggio Casetta at Bolsena[65] and in part by that of the Cannicella at Orvieto.

VIII.26. Shrine of Grasceta dei Cavallari, Monti della Tolfa. Third century BCE. (DAI Rome 79.1952.)

At the beginning of the sixth century the temple of Piazza d'Armi at Veii shows an *oikos* plan of larger size (8.07 × 15.35 m), with internal supports, probably a pair, dividing the interior. The roof had a gable at least on the façade and was decorated with antefixes* (Fig. VIII.25) and molded terracotta plaques.[66] Many sacred buildings share this typology in Etruria, in Latium, and in the Italic world, where it lasted longer, becoming combined at times, as we have seen for Etruria at the Civita of Tarquinii and at Poggio Casetta of Bolsena, with the precinct typical of the *sakaraklúm*. An example is the sanctuary of S. Giovanni in Galdo in Samnium, in which the squared shrine, set in the back of a porticoed precinct, has a podium but remains inaccessible.[67] In Etruria a similar disposition, with its shrine on a podium but here also lacking access stairs, may be found in the rural precinct of Grasceta dei Cavallari on Monti della Tolfa (Fig. VIII.26),[68] on the boundary between Tarquinii and Caere. In this case, perhaps the shrine, dating to the third century BCE, was surrounded not by a portico but by a series of small square altars, comparable to those in the North Area at Pyrgi, which faced the so-called building of the 20 cells.[69] An even better example might be those altars that presumably existed in the *hortus* ("garden") of Ceres, mentioned in the Oscan tablets from Agnone.[70]

But the most varied and instructive example of shrines of a relatively advanced period, contemporary with the manifestations of grand temple architecture, is provided for Etruria once again by the South Area at Pyrgi (Fig. VIII.2), whose numerous and disparate altars are illustrated above. In truth, one could cite also the sanctuary at Gravisca, a coastal city and a port whose emporium aspect, tied up with the intense Greek traffic, was overwhelming. All concerns of an architectural or urbanistic character developed later and took always second place, with the result that the almost wild agglomeration of structures was strictly functional. In the South Area at Pyrgi (Fig. VIII.2) we have instead a clearly organized space, with three shrines in chronological succession: *Beta* (530–520 BCE), *Gamma* (mid fifth century), and *Alpha* (mid fourth century). Of these, *Beta* was the first to be demolished, at the same time as the construction of *Alpha* and the creation of the north open court, the main gutter of which traversed the area of the destroyed shrine.

All lack a podium and are constructed with walls of stone rubble reinforced here and there with blocks of tufo, or in the case of *Beta*, with external walls in blocks (later carried away, for the most part) and with internal walls of rubble. The tile roofs were fitted with a partial figured decoration, of decreasing complexity from *Beta* (*akroteria* and antefixes), to *Gamma* (only antefixes), down to *Alpha* (total disappearance of decoration). Elements common to all were the entrance with a simple door, which opened on the façade but was off center from the axis of the building, evidently to maintain secrecy inside, and the presence of a bench placed against the façade on the exterior for the repose of the faithful, composed of a single line of blocks of tufo. In addition, *Gamma* and *Alpha* held, as noted, interior altars, these also off center; in the first was the type with the cup depression, in the second, that of rough stones. The plans of the buildings, each very different from the others, notwithstanding the rather similar dimensions (*Beta*: 32 sq m; *Gamma*: 49 sq m; *Alpha*: 44 sq m), have no precise parallels among other known shrines.

Beta, the smallest and the oldest,[71] has an oblong plan, with two little cellas of unequal size and a portico *in antis** standing behind, which does not communicate with the cellas. Excavators discovered a pair of gold earrings, hooked together, in the tufaceous beaten earth paving the left cella. Interpreted as a foundation offering, this find confirms that that cella, larger than the other, was sacred to a female divinity, to be identified certainly with Cavtha, considering all the evidence of the altars and inscriptions. The other cella, in whose beaten earth was found a small *olpe** with only the neck painted and of Ionic type, suitable for making a libation on the altar *Theta* standing in front, will have been the cella of Śuri. The two gods seem to have been venerated in separate cellas but under the same roof, decorated on the ridge pole and on the slopes with *akroteria* in the form of huge, extremely original *rampant* torsoes of Acheloos (Fig. VIII.27) and of poorly preserved animal figures. There were also the usual antefixes with female heads without *nimbus** in an Ionianizing style, in this case surely representing Nymphs.

The overall aspect of the building recalls, apart from the posterior location of the *pronaos* and the decoration of the roof, that of a well-known votive model from a Roman site of the territory of Velletri, which also has two cellas and dates

VIII.27. Terracotta akroterion *with torso of Achelous, South Area, Pyrgi. Late sixth century* BCE. *(Università di Roma La Sapienza, Pyrgi Excavations.)*

VIII.28. *Votive model of shrine from Velletri. Late sixth century* BCE. *Rome, Museo Etrusco di Villa Giulia. (Photo: Soprintendenza per i Beni Archeologici dell'Etruria Meridionale.)*

to the Late Archaic (Fig. VIII.28).[72] One may propose as the point of its original location the sanctuary, also seemingly for a pair of divinities, located slightly farther along the Via Appia in the locality with the significant name of Soleluna.[73]

At the Cannicella cemetery of Orvieto, a large shrine with an almost square plan (first decades of the fifth century BCE) occupied the central sector of the terrace of the sanctuary and embraced two cellas of slightly unequal width; it lacked a *pronaos* and was constructed with walls in "pier-and-rubble" masonry.[74] The terracotta decoration included female-head antefixes with *nimbus* and *akroteria* with volutes, one of which represented perhaps the cruel sacrifice of Polyxena.[75] In the late fifth century, appliqués with busts of the couple Hades and Persephone were added (Fig. VIII.29)[76] and perhaps also of the pair Demeter and Kore, which can explain the two cellas.[77]

The shrine *Gamma* is an *oikos* with elongated rectangular plan (5.7 m × 8.7 m), with a narrow entrance off axis and an ample cella that repeats the plan of the perimeter walls (Fig. VIII.13). The cella is delimited by a thin socle of random stones, including half of a stone anchor stock, such that one imagines a lightweight superstructure of wood or wattle, similar to what must be postulated for the shrine existing at the back of the court at Murlo (Fig. VII.9). The two blocks of stone with cup depressions, mentioned earlier, were found on the ground in this *adyton** or *penus,** recalling the *penus Vestae*, which was "the most internal place, fenced by mats" (*locus intimus tegetibus saeptus*: Festus, p. 296 Lindsay). In 1997 a trial trench dug behind the building on its axis brought to light a large parallelepiped ingot of lead, set up vertically in the earth, evidently both as a planimetric refer-

VIII.29. *Terracotta appliqué of Hades and Persephone, from the shrine at the Cannicella cemetery, Orvieto. Late fifth century BCE. (After* Santuari d'Etruria, *119.)*

VIII.30. *Antefix from shrine Gamma, South Area. Pyrgi. Ca. 450 BCE. (Università di Roma La Sapienza, Pyrgi Excavations.)*

ence for the projected construction and also as a foundation offering. It was surely addressed, as in the cases of the altar *Epsilon* standing in front and the altar *Lambda,* to the god of the Underworld, lord of the riches of the subsoil. The roof was decorated with antefixes of the lady's head with *nimbus* (Fig. VIII.30) and of the Gorgon, of types presumably Campanian, not attested elsewhere in Etruria. It seems that in the middle of the fifth century, the cult of Śuri, disassociated from that of Cavtha, was transferred to this shrine, which must have been the location of the table of silver of "Apollo" that was carried away by Dionysios the Elder during the Syracusan sack in 384 BCE (Aelian, *Var. hist.* 1.20).

The rectangular plan recalls that of the most ancient shrines, such as the building *Beta* of the Civita at Tarquinii and that of the Piazza d'Armi at Veii, both mentioned above, the one adjacent to the so-called *regia** of Acquarossa,[78] and the one that preceded the famous temple of Juno Curites in the locality of Celle beneath the acropolis at Falerii, which was very small but contained an exceptional life-sized image carved in tufo, of which only the head survives.[79] In Latium one can cite the shrine of the eastern sanctuary at Gabii and the one that preceded the first peripteral temple of Mater Matuta at Satricum.[80] The plan is linked directly to the type of noble house of the Orientalizing period imitated in the tombs at Caere such as the Campana Tomb of Monte Abatone (Fig. VIII.31).[81] Cellas equally long and narrow were found on monumental temples of Tuscanic type and also on many of those with only cella and *pronaos,* beginning with the oldest temple at the Ara della Regina at Tarquinii, recently identified.[82]

The shrine *Alpha* at Pyrgi has a quadrangular plan (6.3 m × 7 m), with entrance on the short side facing the sea (Fig. VIII.6). Its construction coincided with the demolition of the altar *Delta,* oriented differently (Fig. VIII.10), whose functions seem to have been continued by the altar in rough stones that was set inside the building, as mentioned above. The dedications on pottery, found inside or nearby, mention only the goddess Cav(a)tha,[83] who was summoned by the many pieces of jewelry (a very appropriate offering for the *pulchra Proserpina* ["lovely Proserpina"]; Vergil, *Aeneid* 6.142). It seems evident that much later, the goddess, left as the only inhabitant of *Beta* after the transfer of Śuri to *Gamma,* which was expressly constructed for him, received a shrine all to herself, when *Beta* was demolished as a consequence of the Syracusan sack. The absence of all roof decoration, including antefixes, probably means that there was a complete "camouflaging" of the building, when it was made to look like a normal house. The plan, almost squared, finds

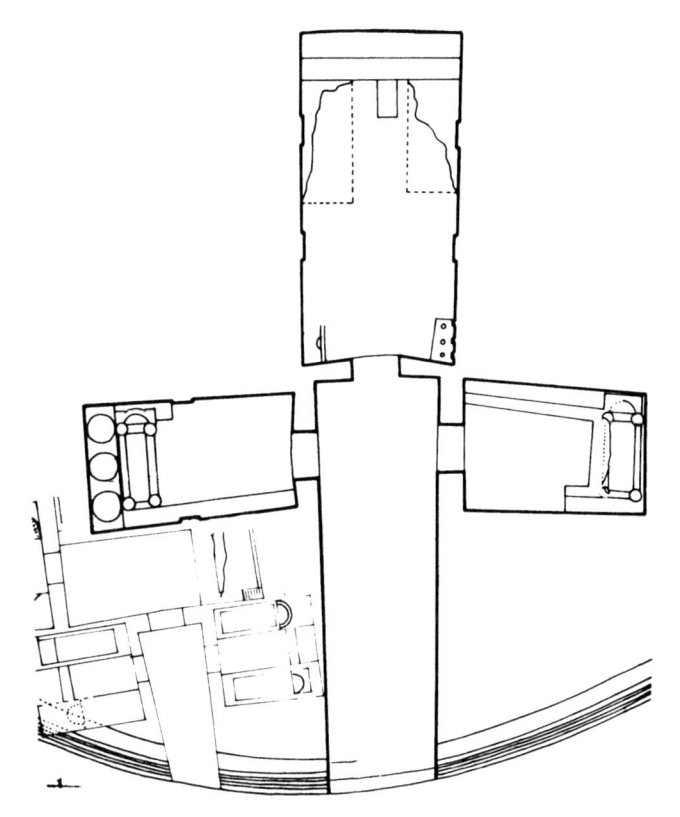

VIII.31. Plan, Campana Tomb, Monte Abatone, Caere. Mid seventh century BCE. (Photo: Soprintendenza per i Beni Archeologici dell'Etruria Meridionale.)

parallels in the little shrine in the court at Murlo, in the shrine of Menerva at the east corner of the Portonaccio sanctuary at Veii (Fig. VIII.37),[84] and in the shrines, already noted, at the Cannicella at Orvieto and at Poggio Casetta at Bolsena.

A different category of shrine has a more markedly domestic character, built this way also because it was foreseen that it would be opened for frequent visitation. This type has inside benches placed at right angles, evidently for the consumption of common meals during celebrations or other activities. Examples are the smaller shrine of the rural sanctuary of Grasceta dei Cavallari[85] and the one at the head of the Archaic bridge of San Giovenale (Fig. VIII.32), whose sacral relevance is testified by the inscriptions found on vessels there, including a dedication to L[?urs] Larunita.[86]

Of this type were in all probability the "private" shrines constructed by the great aristocratic families near their tumulus tombs, secure and consistent remains that have been discovered only recently. I refer to the shrines of the end of the seventh century whose foundations have been discovered at Vulci near the tumulus of the Cuccumelletta, having a rectangular plan, with vestibule[87] and to another of the first

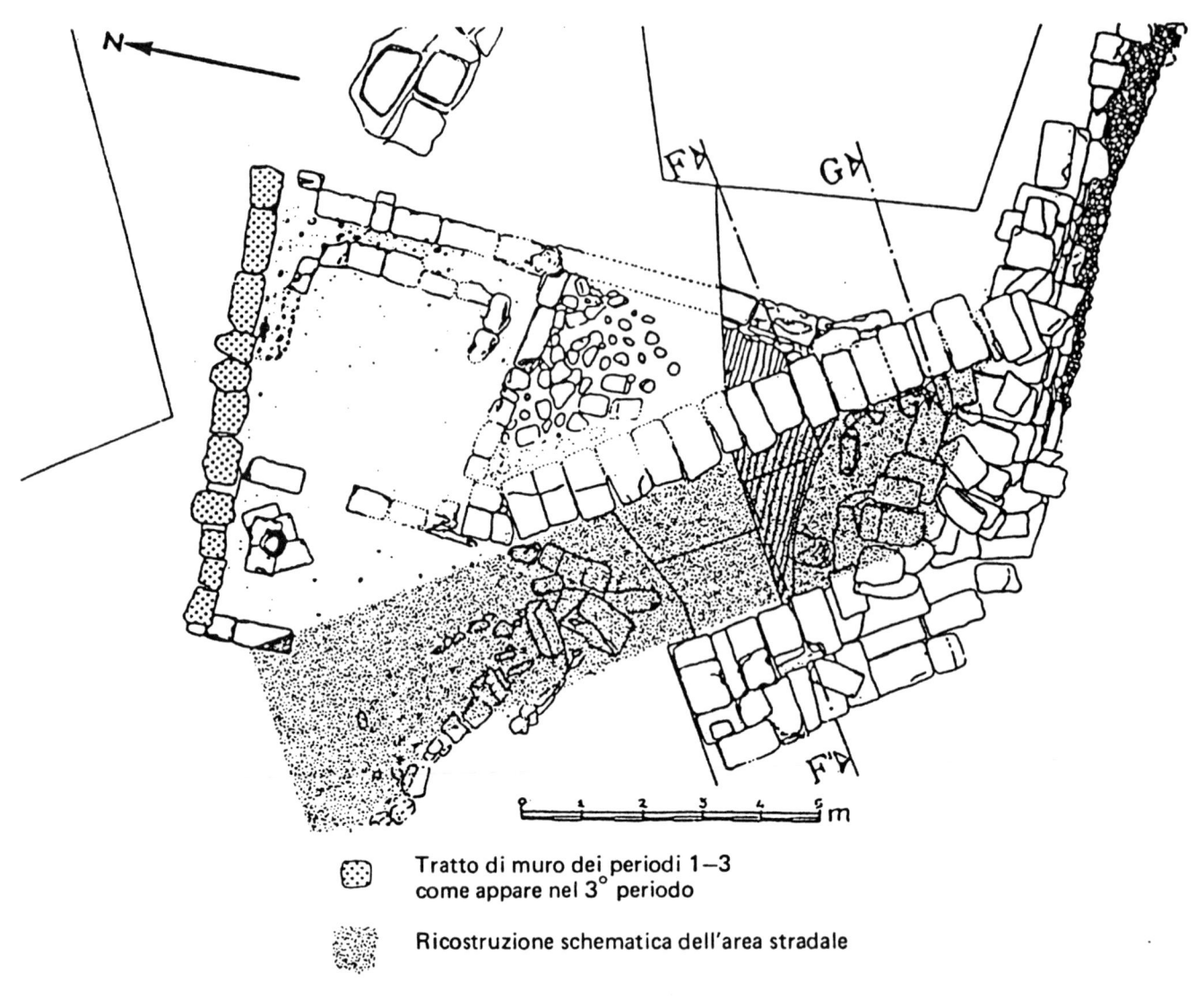

VIII.32. Plan, shrine at the bridge, S. Giovenale. Sixth century BCE. (After Forsberg 1984, fig. 37.)

half of the sixth century attested by the architectural terracottas found near the tumuli of the Ara del Tufo at Tuscania.[88] Distant successors of these Archaic funerary shrines are the rooms, with or without benches and often with porticoes, of the rock-cut façade tombs at San Giuliano, Norchia, Castel d'Asso, Falerii, and Corchiano[89] and also of the subterranean tombs of the two-story type, as at Tarquinii (in the Mercareccia, Tappezzeria, and Caronti Tombs) and at Caere (in the Torlonia Tomb).[90] The laying out of the dead did not take place in these shrines or ceremonial rooms, as is often asserted. That was a ceremony closely connected with the home and was disposed in the relevant vestibule, in a courtyard in front, in the shelter of porticoes, or under appropriate coverings. Instead, the funerary banquets with the connected games and blood sacrifices were held near the tombs, and for these banquets, monumental altars were created in the Archaic period, like the circular one of Grotta Porcina (Fig. VIII.12) and the one at the Cuccumella of Vulci, which was of the type with *antae*.*[91]

TEMPLES

It remains to speak, very briefly, of the *aedes* with a more complex and articulated plan, normally monumental in dimensions, construction technique, and decoration, of which the most notable representative example is the temple of Tuscanic type described by Vitruvius (*De architectura* 4.6.6; 4.7.1–5; see Appendix B, Source no. v.3), concerning which

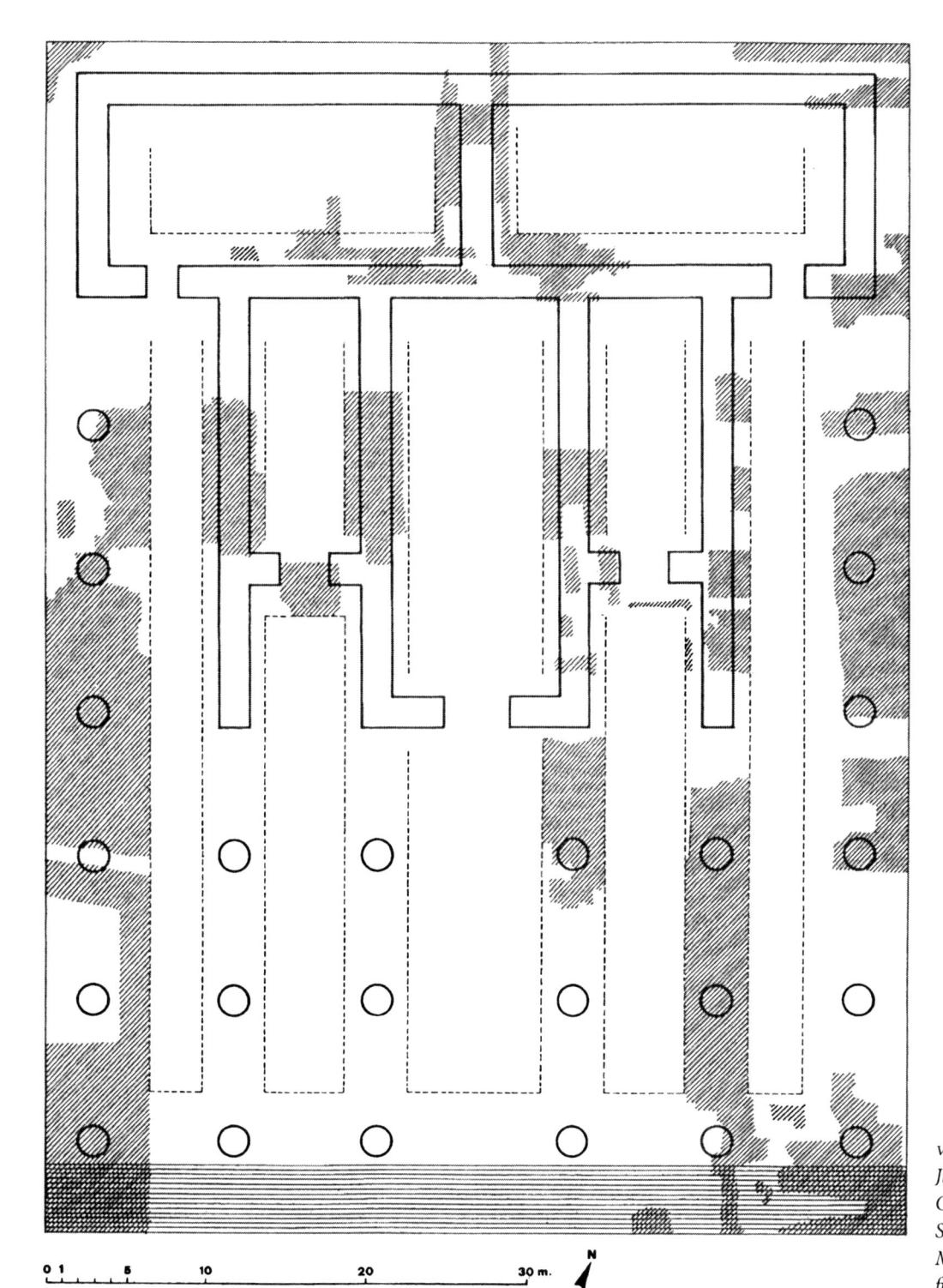

VIII.33. *Plan, temple of Jupiter Optimus Maximus, Capitoline Hill, Rome. Sixth century BCE. (After Mura Sommella 1998, fig. 6.)*

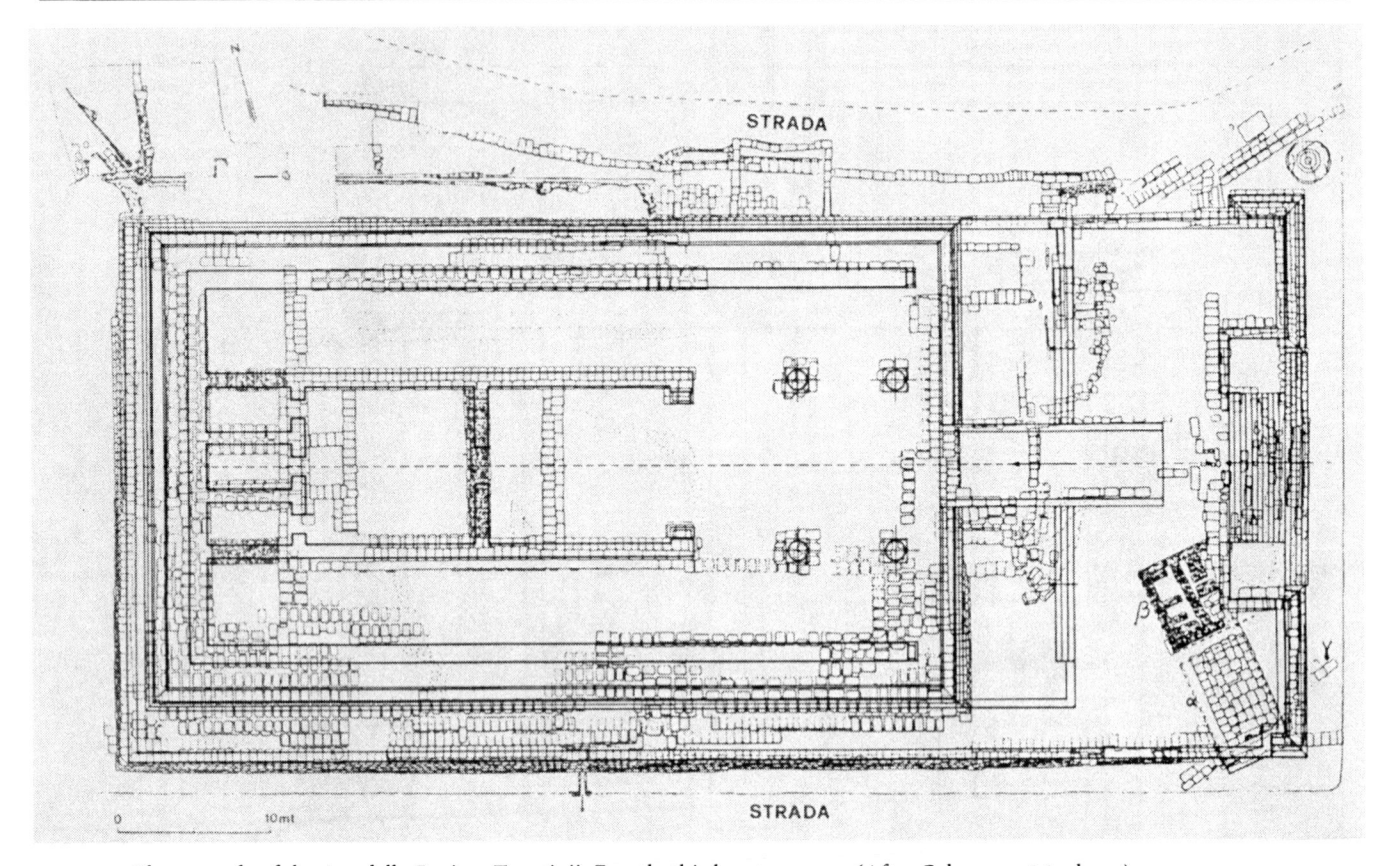

VIII.34. Plan, temple of the Ara della Regina, Tarquinii. Fourth-third century BCE. (After Colonna 1986, pl. 29.)

an imposing literature now exists.[92] The appearance of this and other new types of sacred architecture is linked by Varro — with a connection that does not seem to be based solely on chronological order — to the introduction of anthropomorphic cult images, according to him occurring more than 170 years after the foundation of the city of Rome, that is, around 580 BCE.[93] From that moment the cella, holding the image and covered with the traditional testudinate roof, clearly now with only three pitches, would have been distinct from the *pronaos,* which was no longer provided with an entrance door but was left completely open. The *pronaos,* covered by a gabled roof with a front opening and well lighted, became quite accessible and attractive to the faithful, the very place *ubi religio administraretur* ("where religion must have been performed"; Varro, *Ant. rerum divinarum* 2.147–148 Cardauns).[94]

In truth, in temple architecture there was a turning point around 580 BCE, documented by archaeology, in which occurred the introduction both of a *pronaos* with *antae* considerably prolonging the lateral walls of the cella, and of a podium, which raised the building above the surrounding area, giving a unique access marked by an axial staircase. At Rome this happened with the transposition to the temple of the plan of the "grand house," with at least three chambers and a wider vestibule, often having columns inside: that is the Late Orientalizing house type, known in architecture mainly from Caeretan tombs such as those of the Capitals, Shields and Chairs, Giuseppe Moretti, and Greek Vases.[95] The result was the Tuscanic temple, a square or almost squared building showing a tidy division in halves, with the *pars antica** in front serving the function of a columned vestibule and enclosed within walls (*antae*), prolonging the lateral walls of the *pars postica.** This rear part was occupied either by three cellas provided with entrance doors or by a central cella and two lateral *alae** ("wings") directly connected to the *pronaos*. This last alternative considerably enlarged the space useful for cultic performances, display, and the storage of gifts, archives, and so on.

For the ancients, the prototype of such monumental buildings was the Capitoline temple, made more majestic by the exceptional addition in front and at the sides of a peristyle and on the back, as it appears from the last investigations, of a sort of two-room *posticum** (Fig. VIII.33).[96] Initiated by Tarquinius Priscus (in the years 584–579 BCE) on an area "exaugurated" from the preexisting cults by the destruction of many altars and shrines, it was finished by Tarquinius Superbus (534–510 BCE) and dedicated by a consul of the first year of the Republic (509 BCE). The temple, raised on a podium of 54 × 74 m, housed a divine triad (Jupiter, Juno, and Minerva), but this was not always the case for such temples, in Etruria as at Rome: in fact, only the central cella always housed a divinity (or, as in the temple of Castores in the Forum, several divinities), the others having often merely practical functions (as treasuries, annexes, *sacraria*,* or other types of rooms). Until the excavation of the gigantic foundations of the Capitoline temple verifies the dating handed down by the annalists, the little Servian temple of Mater Matuta at S. Omobono in Rome remains for us the first evidence of a Tuscanic temple. This rose on a square podium, 10.30 m on a side, clearly inspired by the plan of a *templum minus*,[97] 1.70 m high (575–560 BCE), enlarged about 530, when the building received the famous group of Hercules and Minerva as central *akroterion*.[98]

In the more traditionalist Etruria, the plan of the new kind of temple resulted initially from the adding of the *pronaos* to a building of the ancient *oikos* type, as is documented by the small rural temple at Punta della Vipera near S. Marinella, sacred to Menerva.[99] To this example we can now add also the first phase of the Ara della Regina, the colossal chief city temple of Tarquinii, datable around 560–550 BCE on the basis of the stratigraphic data and the few scraps of fictile revetment.[100] The temple, probably already at that time sacred to Artumes, a goddess whose cult was propagated in the West by the Phokaian Greeks, had imposing dimensions (12 × 27 m, on an enormous podium, lacking moldings and measuring 31.5 × 55 m), with a cella and a deep *pronaos in antis* without columns (Fig. VIII.34). At the end of the sixth century, it was greatly enlarged, occupying almost the entire surface of the podium. Two very long *alae* and a second, outer *pronaos*, much wider than the first, having four interior columns, were then added to it, according to the model of the Tuscanic temple.

Temple B at Pyrgi (Fig. VIII.35), sacred to Uni-Astarte, built around 510 BCE thanks to King Thefarie Velianas, was the first Etruscan example of a great peripteral temple. It had an almost square cella, a deep, *prostyle** pronaos with unmolded *antae* and a peristyle of 4 × 6 columns, with a contracted rear portico; walls and columns were of tufo covered by a white plaster. This kind of building, of a clear Greco-Campanian kind, already known in Latium at Satricum and, with regard to the peristyle only, in the Capitoline temple,[101] probably was the rare temple type, referred to

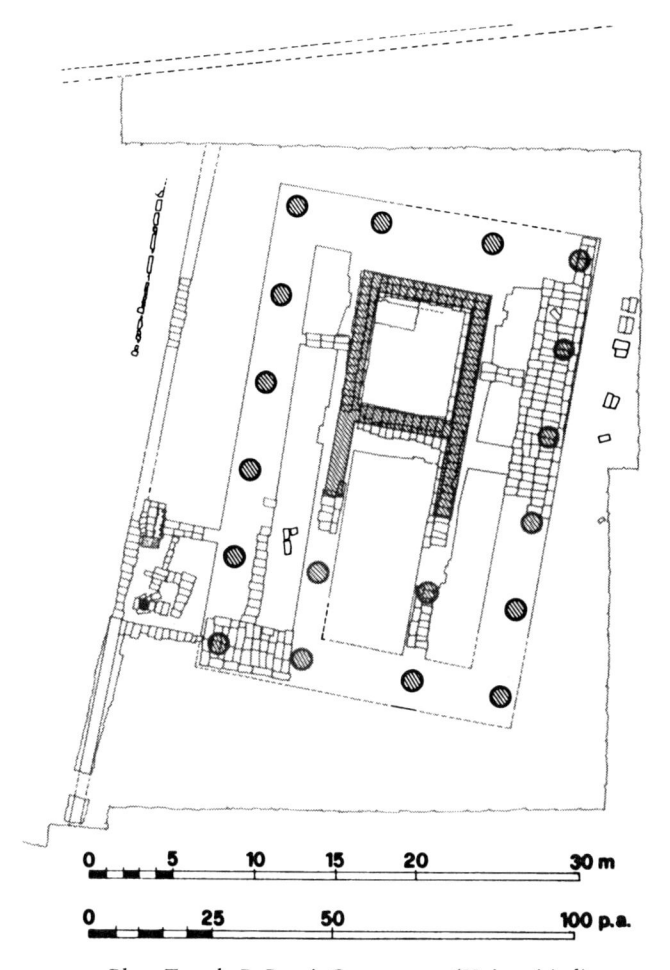

VIII.35. *Plan, Temple B, Pyrgi. Ca. 510 BCE. (Università di Roma La Sapienza, Pyrgi Excavations.)*

by Vitruvius (3.3.5) with the Greek name *araeostylos*, "with columns standing far apart." It had gables decorated *Tuscanico more* ("in the Tuscan fashion") but did not conform to the *Tuscanicae dispositiones* ("the arrangements of the Tuscan order"), especially in the plan and in the proportions of the columns.[102]

Not much later, to judge from the terracottas published in 1997,[103] is the so-called Great Temple of Vulci, located on what was surely the principal artery of the city, not far from the west gate (Fig. VIII.36). This great urban temple, measuring 24.6 × 36.4 m and perhaps sacred to Menerva,[104] pursued the tradition of Temple B of Pyrgi, having a single *prostyle* cella of 10 × 15 m within a peristyle of 4 × 6 stone columns. Its huge podium, 2.40 m high, was dressed, perhaps only at the beginning of the fourth century, by a molded facing in *nenfro*,* extended to revet the front terrace with its large flight of steps. The same temple plan and dimensions appeared in the temple revealed by geophysical prospection at Marzabotto

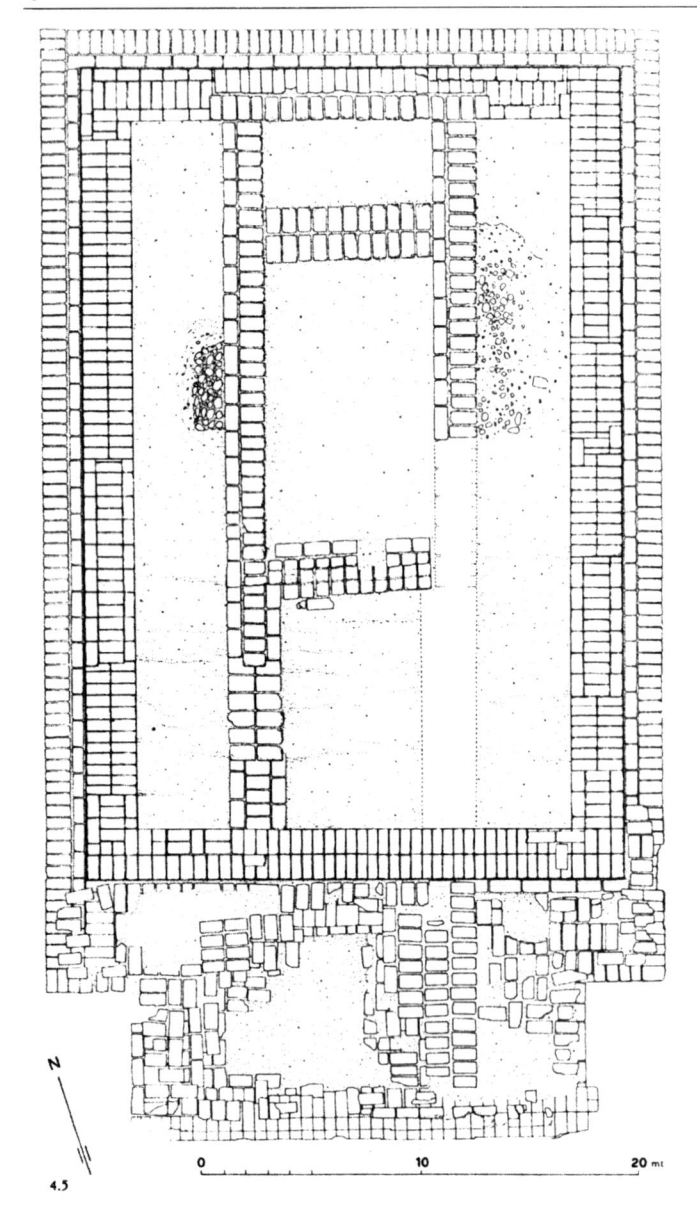

VIII.36. Plan of the Great Temple, Vulci. Early fifth-fourth century BCE. (After Santuari d'Etruria, fig. 4.5.)

within the town[105] and also in temple A of the acropolis, as shown by the recent excavations.[106]

The other monumental temples of the fifth century BCE in Etruria are all of the Tuscanic type. At the head, and not only in terms of the chronology, is the temple at the Portonaccio of Veii (Figs. VIII.37–40), a building exactly square like that of S. Omobono but greater (18.5 m on a side) and much more highly ornamented, with three cellas (for Aplu, Tina, and Hercle?) and an oblong *pronaos* with two columns only in the front, internally decorated with terracotta painted plaques featuring narrative mythological friezes.[107] The stone columns had capitals of Etruscan Doric style, with hawk's beak molding, *echinus,** and *abacus.** The roof and its beams shone with polychrome terracotta (Fig. VIII.38),[108] including antefixes with heads of Medusa, Acheloos, Satyrs, and Maenads, as well as the *akroteria* of Apollo (Fig. VIII.39), Herakles, Leto(?) (Fig. VIII.40), and other figures. These *akroteria* can be ascribed to the same artists whom Tarquinius Superbus commissioned for the colossal *quadriga** of the Capitoline temple. In fact, unique to this temple in all the panorama of Etruscan sanctuaries, and weakly imitated by the Gigantomachy of the later temple of Satricum,[109] is the extensive usage of *akroteria* in the form of over-life-sized statues of divine or heroic personages, displayed along the ridge beam and reciprocally connected in a complex figurative program. Certainly the authorities who commissioned the works intended to convey content and messages of great importance, but unfortunately for us, these remain in large part obscure.

The second temple at Pyrgi, A,[110] sacred to the goddess Thesan, corresponding to the Latin Mater Matuta, was built on the flank of the first around 470–460 BCE, as was proved by the pottery found within the packing of the foundation. The building, 24 × 34.4 m, was built according to the Tuscan scheme but having in the *pronaos* three rows of columns, the first extending to the entire façade and all founded on a regular grid of walls (Fig. VIII.41). It is exactly the adaptation of the Tuscan scheme in the temple of Castor and Pollux in the Forum at Rome, which was similar also in its measurements and dedicated in 484 BCE.[111]

But at Pyrgi we have the first occurrence of an innovation clearly showing off the hierarchy existing between the cellas: those on the sides are now shortened by the cutting of a small inner chamber, reserved evidently for the storage of the most precious furnishings and *donaria,* beginning with gold and silver, coined or not (the Greek silver coins, residual from the sack of 384 BCE, were unearthed in the area behind).[112] The columns and external walls were of tufo, while the interior walls seem to have been of mud bricks, plastered and decorated with paintings. Of the terracotta decorations, the best preserved are from the pediment on the back of the building, well visible from the road from Caere and for this reason no less sumptuous than those of the façade facing the sea.

The central relief (Fig. VIII.42), now almost completely reconstituted from numerous fragments, is the most important we have from an Archaic Tuscan temple. It measures 1.4 × 1.2 m and it covered over the projecting end of the central beam of the gabled roof. The six figures in high relief, at three-fourths life size, are involved in episodes of the saga of

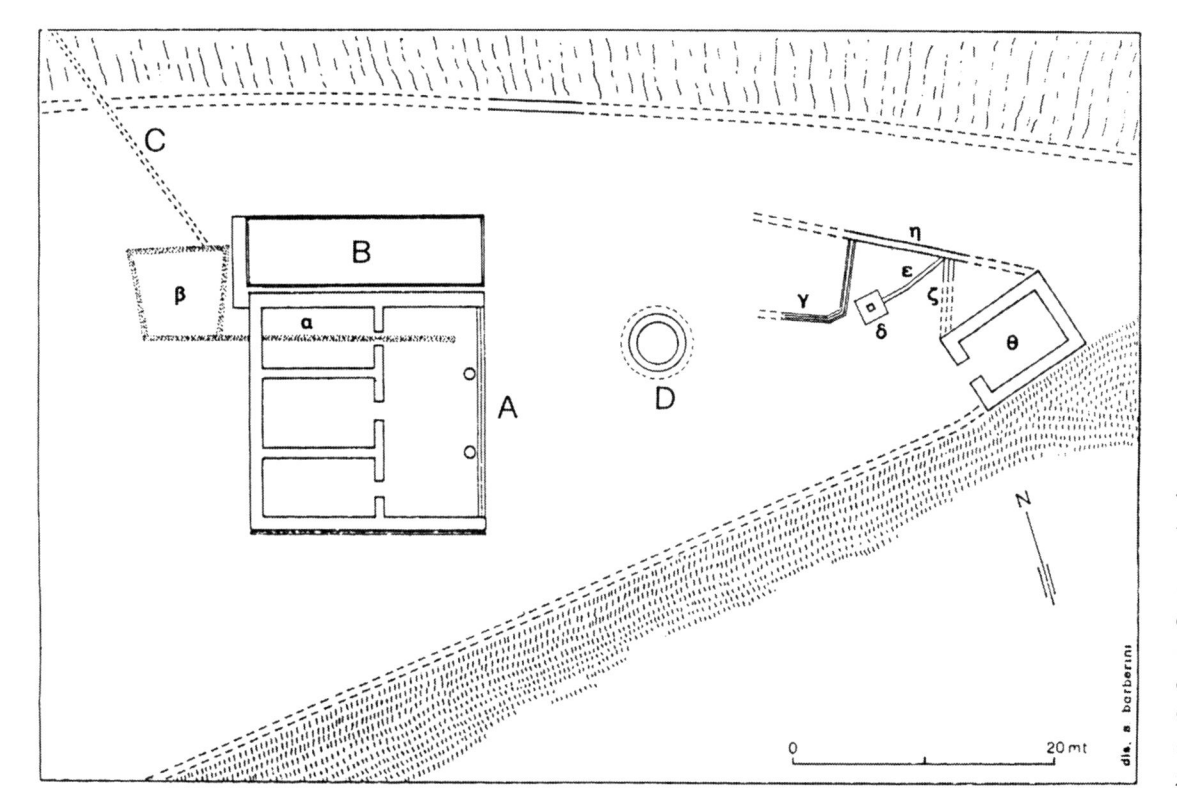

VIII.37. Plan, temple and sanctuary of the Portonaccio, Veii: temple (A), pool (B), cistern (D) altar (δ) and shrine of Menerva (θ) Ca. 500 BCE. (After Colonna 2002, fig. 9.)

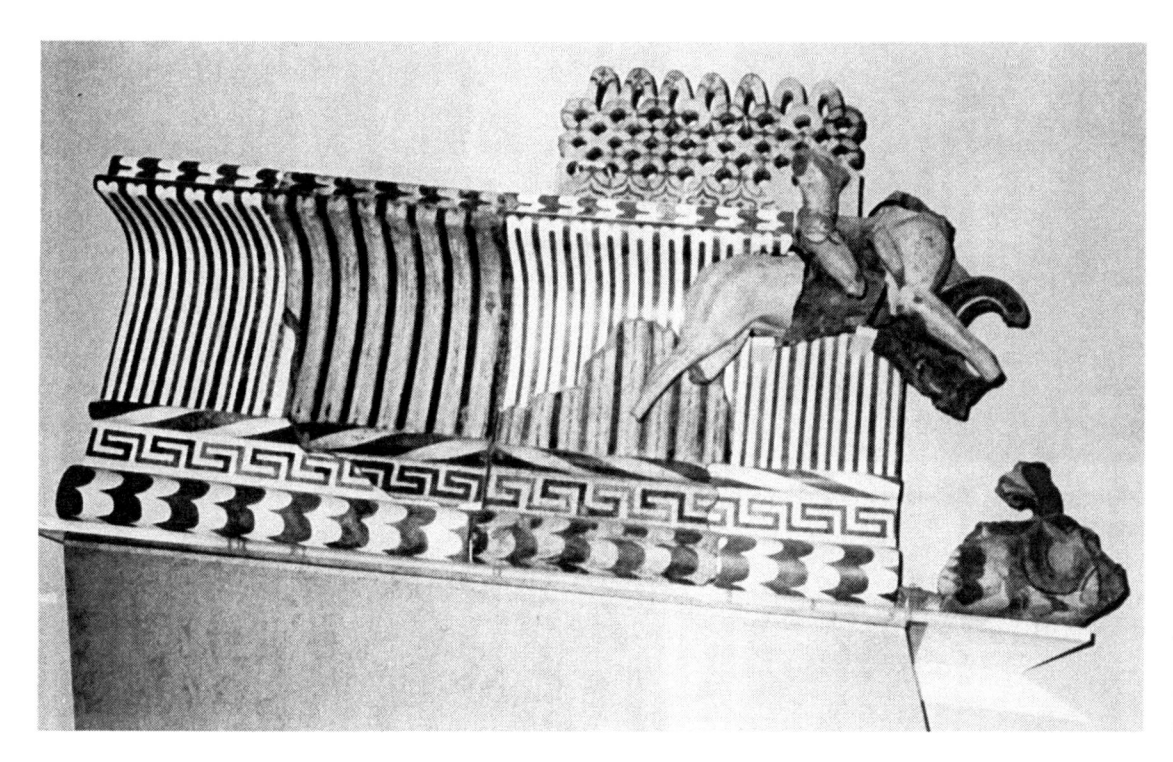

VIII.38. Pedimental sima *from the Portonaccio temple, Veii. Reconstruction by Claudia Carlucci. Ca. 500 BCE. (Photo: Giovanni Colonna.)*

VIII.39. Akroterion *of Aplu from the Portonaccio temple, Veii. Ca. 500 BCE. (DAI Rome 57.896.)*

VIII.40. Akroterion *of Leto (?) from the Portonaccio temple, Veii. Ca. 500 BCE. (DAI Rome 73-1557.)*

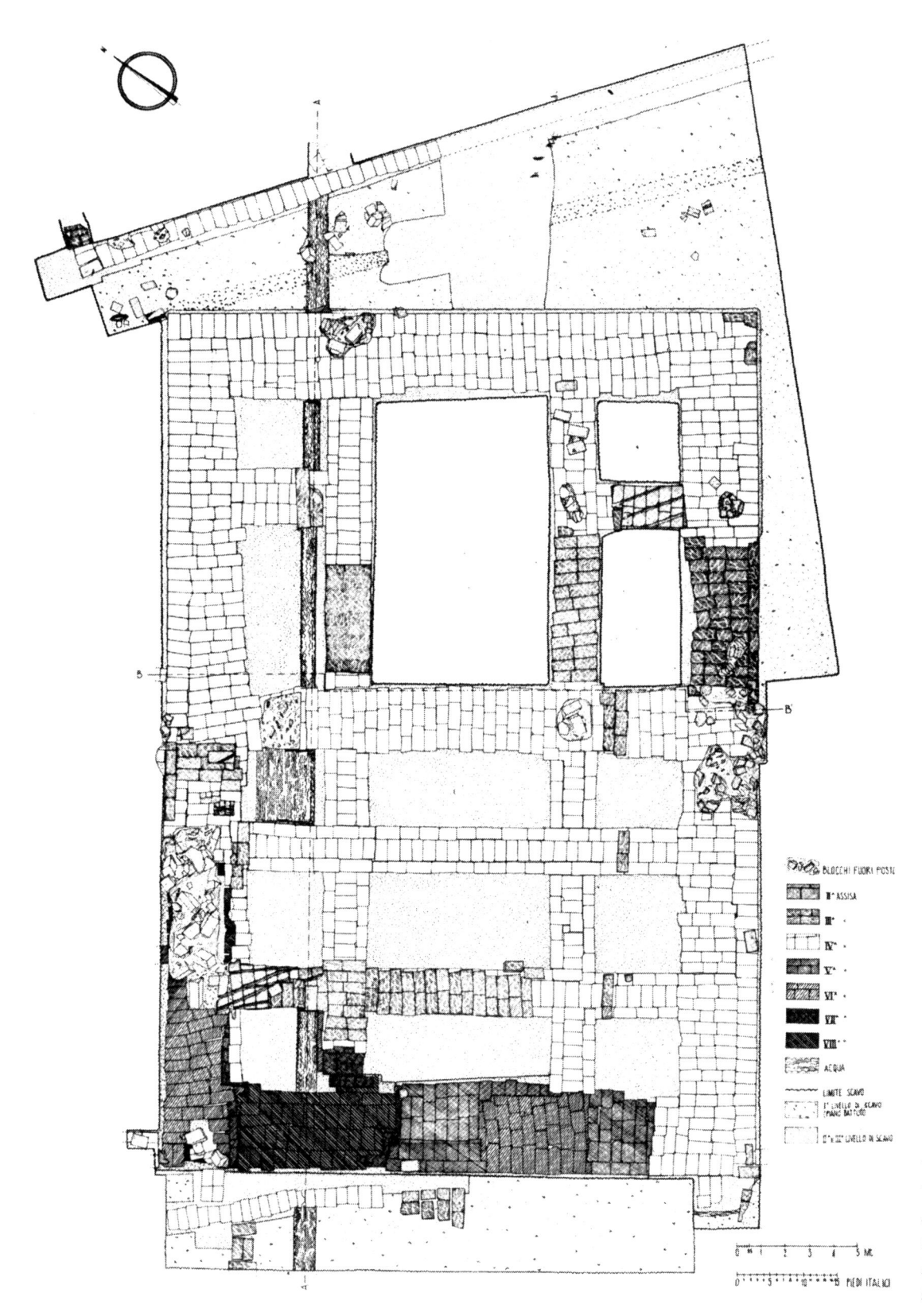

VIII.41. Plan,
Temple A, Pyrgi.
470–460 BCE.
(Università di Roma
La Sapienza, Pyrgi
Excavations.)

VIII.42. Columen sculpture of the Seven against Thebes from Temple A, Pyrgi. 470–460 BCE. (Università di Roma La Sapienza, Pyrgi Excavations.)

the Seven against Thebes: Zeus hurls lightning against Kapaneus and Athena registers disapproval as Tydeus bites Melanippos on the back of the head.

Temples similar to the bipartite plan of the lateral cellas and to the grid pattern of the foundations to temple A of Pyrgi, but with the normal two rows of columns in the *pronaos*, are that of Hercle, recently excavated at Caere in locality S. Antonio,[113] and the larger temple of the acropolis of Marzabotto, C, flanked by the already mentioned altar podium D (Fig. VIII.15). In this case, a service room was also cut in the back of the central cella, but it was very narrow, perhaps better explained as a large base for multiple images. Strangely enough, the temple was decorated, as far as we know, only with painted eaves tiles and palmette antefixes, similar to ones found in the habitation area, not earlier than the second quarter of the fifth century. The complete absence of a figural program provides a measure of the practical mentality of the authorities of that provincial site.

The numerous temples at Orvieto present a very different case, and they have yielded rich terracotta decorations. The only one whose plan we know is that at the Belvedere (Fig. VIII.43),[114] on the extreme northwest of the cliff, the seat of a cult of Tinia as an Underworld god. It rose on sloping terrain, with a quadrangular court in front, quite large, recalling the ancient tradition of precincts with altars inside. The building had a Tuscan plan (16.9 × 21.91 m), with a double file of columns in the *pronaos*, the location of which is certain because each column was provided with a footing of masonry isolated from the rest of the foundation. Of the terracotta decoration, little has survived from the time of the building during the first half of the fifth century BCE, but a quite notable series of figures in high relief has been identified as decoration added to the rear of the temple (cf. again Pyrgi A) in the first half of the fourth century.

Another version of the Tuscan temple was adopted in the fifth century in the Legnisina sanctuary at Vulci, already mentioned (Fig. VIII.20),[115] and in temple E at Marzabotto, probably the latest of the three standing there (Fig. VIII.15). In this case, the *pars postica* occupied only a third or slightly more of the length of the building, leaving the other two-thirds to a doubled *pronaos*, with a row of two columns separating the outer from the inner space. This is the model elaborated upon at Ardea in Latium, where it occurs in all the three great temples of the city but with isolated foun-

TEMPIO DEL BELVEDERE - ORVIETO

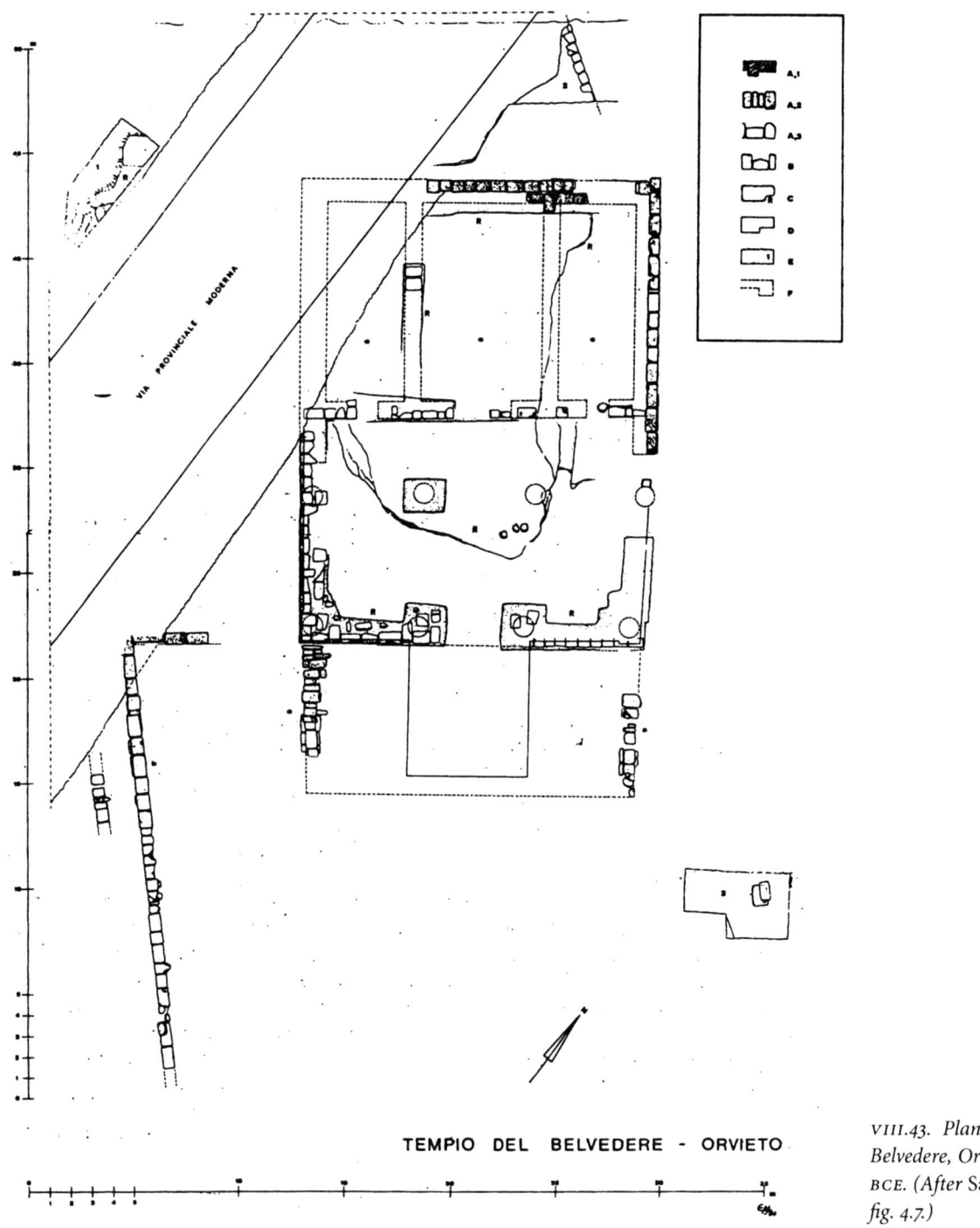

VIII.43. Plan, Temple at the Belvedere, Orvieto. Fifth century BCE. (After Santuari d'Etruria, fig. 4.7.)

dations for the columns.[116] It emphasizes the special function and importance that the *pronaos* had inside this type of temple, comparable to that of the *atrium* in the old Roman house.

The greatest temple ever built in Etruria, symbol of the role of leadership attained by Tarquinii after the fall of Veii and the entrance of Caere into the Roman orbit, was the fourth-century Ara della Regina (Fig. VIII.34).[117] At that time, the temple was entirely rebuilt and enlarged, with a *posticum* of two chambers at the back, almost a quotation of the Capitoline temple, and with a spectacular terrace in front, which prolonged the podium to a length of 77 m. The

VIII.44. Terracotta sculpture of winged horses, from temple of the Ara della Regina, Tarquinii. Ca. 350 BCE. Tarquinia, Museo Archeologico Nazionale. (Photo: Soprintendenza per i Beni Archeologici dell'Etruria Meridionale.)

terrace, functioning also as a tribune towards the square in front of it, had two levels, with a large central staircase and a ramp to go up to the temple. At one corner there were an altar and a precinct, differently oriented, which duplicated Archaic structures once existing at a lower level. The columns and the *antae*, some 9 m high, were of an Italian-Ionic order; the podium had a facing molded at the bottom; and the terrace was bordered by a molded balustrade. The building, constructed before the middle of the fourth century, underwent an extensive reworking inside, perhaps at the same time as a partial renovation of the fictile revetments in the first half of the third century BCE.

In both phases, the cella featured three small chambers at the back, suggesting a cult for a triad or at least for a single divinity present in three different hypostases. This feature might fit well with Artumes, whose name is the only one to appear on the few votive objects found in the excavation. Among the terracottas are the handsome winged horses of a chariot in high relief, now in the Tarquinia museum (Fig. VIII.44), which, to judge from their findspot and the size and shape of the supporting plaque (1.14 × 1.24 m), covered the

VIII.45. Terracotta pedimental sculpture of the Seven against Thebes, from the temple at Talamone. Second century BCE. (After B. von Freytag gen. Löringhoff, Das Giebelrelief von Telamon, Mainz 1986, Suppl. 1.)

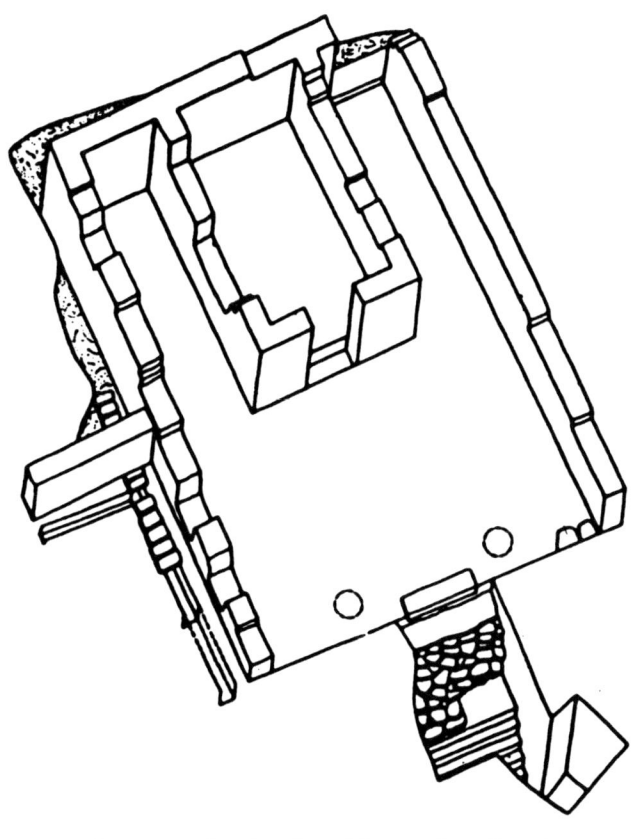

VIII.46. Reconstruction drawing of the temple at Faesulae. Fourth–third century BCE. (After Colonna 1986, pl. XXXIV.)

left mutule* of the pedimental area of the temple, whereas the extant goddess should belong to the right mutule.

In the second half of the fourth century may be placed the construction of a temple of Tuscan type, on the acropolis of the coastal *oppidum** of Talamone, along the border between Vulci and Rusellae. It probably had *alae*, with a columned *pronaos* and lateral walls extending to the façade.[118] A broad terrace somewhat lower than the temple was in front of it. In the first half of the second century, after the tremendous battle of Talamone of 225 BCE, which resulted in the final removal of the Gallic threat to central Italy, the temple was remodeled with a "closed" pediment of Roman inspiration, the first that occurred in Etruria, in which the figures are placed in high relief all across the triangular space rather than being confined to the *columen** and mutules, as until then was normal. A narrative scene was represented here, strongly symbolic and propagandistic, of the tragic conclusion of the Seven against Thebes (Fig. VIII.45).

A temple that is small but precious due to its excellent state of preservation was erected at Faesulae (Fiesole) at the beginning of the third century BCE, in a glen beneath the acropolis within the city walls (Fig. VIII.46).[119] The temple, covered over during a major rebuilding program of the period of Sulla, retains a significant portion of the elevation, with the cella walls of stone, once plastered over and painted red. The plan is that of the Tuscan temple with *alae*, closed on the sides by walls that extended to the façade, framing two columns. Votive offerings found in the area include anatomi-

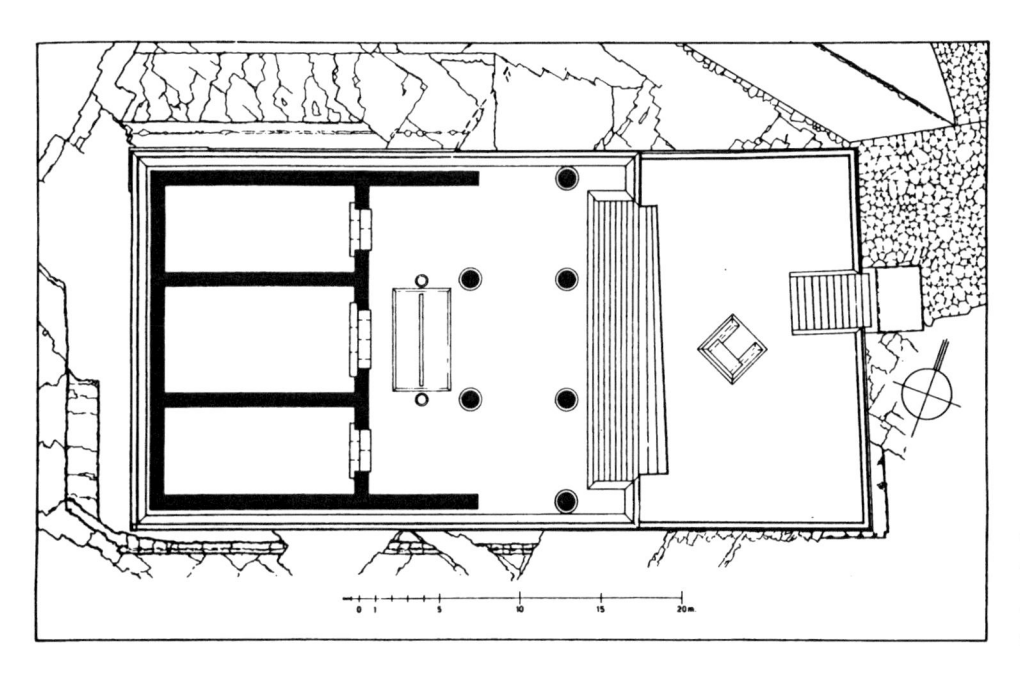

VIII.47. Plan, Capitolium, Cosa. Third century BCE. (After F. E. Brown, Cosa, II, The Temples of the Arx, Rome, 1960, fig. 60.)

cal parts and an owl, suggesting that the temple may have been dedicated to Menerva as a goddess of healing.

A greater temple of canonical Tuscan type was erected in the second half of the third century on the acropolis at Volaterrae, a city that retained and even increased its prosperity under the *pax Romana*.[120] The *pronaos*, the only surviving part, was entirely open, with three rows of columns, as in the temple of the Castores at the Roman Forum, in Pyrgi A, and in the temple of the acropolis of Signia (rebuilt in the second century BCE),[121] each column resting on a proper square foundation, as in the Archaic temple of Orvieto-Belvedere. Later, around the mid second century, a second temple was built at the side, in a totally different plan, inspired by Hellenistic temple architecture. This was probably also the case for the temple recently excavated on the acropolis of Populonia[122] and oriented, as results from recent investigations indicate, in the direction opposite to that of the first, at northeast, quite unusual for an Etruscan temple.[123] This fact can be explained only by a radical rearrangement and new planning of the area, not previously noticed.

However strange, temples of Tuscan type were erected in the second and first century BCE more frequently in the Roman and Latin colonies, as at Cosa (Fig. VIII.47) and Luni, and also farther away, as in the Samnite federal sanctuary of Pietrabbondante, than in the Etruscan cities. This is not surprising, because the *Tuscanicae dispositiones*, as Vitruvius and the monuments largely testify, would soon become a universal feature of the Roman world.

NOTES

1. See *Santuari d'Etruria*.
2. Colonna 2000. For the South Area, see also Baglione 2000.
3. Steingräber 1982; Thuillier 1991.
4. Rupp 1991b. For Pyrgi, see Colonna 1992, 75-78.
5. Area C, Punta della Vipera and Volsinian altars: Colonna 1966, 91-95 (Pfiffig 1986 excludes blood offerings, which is unjustified). Portonaccio: Colonna 2002, 141-142, 149-150. See also below, n. 36, for the fictile apparatus found in the acropolis sanctuary at Volaterrae, probably better to explain as a *mundus*.
6. Rupp 1991a.
7. Poggio Casetta: *Santuari d'Etruria*, 23, fig. 1; Tamburini 1999, 100-101. Sòcana: *Santuari d'Etruria*, 164-168. Melonta: Rosi Bonci 1990. Fùcoli: *Atti Chiusi-Chianciano* 1993, 465, pl.3b, 481-482.
8. *Santuari d'Etruria*, 168 (G. Colonna).
9. Colonna 2000, 273.
10. *Ant. rerum divinarum*, I, fr. 38 Cardauns; for Samian vases, see Onorati 1992, 226-231. These pots correspond to what is now called "impasto," as can be deduced from the passages, seemingly also Varronian, in Isidore, *Etym.* 14.6.31 and 20.4.3. The *samii* would have been the oldest fictile vases, invented on Samos, before those in "Red Ware," whose invention, at least in the circle of coroplastics, was attributed by Pliny, *NH* 35.152, to the Sikyonian Butades, perhaps again following Varro.
11. We do know that in the peripheral zones of that country, altars of such stones remained in use down to the Imperial age; note the case of Pharai in Achaia: Pausanias 7.22.5.
12. Roncalli 1996; Roncalli 1997.
13. Rupp 1991b.
14. Colonna 1992, 72, figs. 12-14.
15. Colonna 1993, 331-337.
16. Baglione 2000, 339-351.
17. Colonna 1997.
18. Colonna 2001a, 418-421, with references to Maras 2001. See also de Grummond 2004, 359-361, 365-367, who brings out the lunar connections of Cavatha.

19. Except for that of Menerva, probably in function of *Pronaia* (Colonna 2001a, 421-422; Colonna 2002), and also that of Hercle.
20. Now Maras 2001, 396-397, nos. 63-64; Colonna 2001a, 419-420.
21. Now better interpreted as a variant of the name Cilens, related to Śuri (Colonna 2001a, 420-421).
22. "Temporary altars"; see La Rocca 1984, 43-46; Coarelli 1997, 87-90.
23. The numismatic evidence proves that in Imperial times they were of normal form, even if removable (but certainly not of wood, as La Rocca thinks).
24. Maggiani 1997, 23, 42-45. As of the time of this writing, we have at Pyrgi, too, a fifth-century dedication to "Cavatha the Daughter," still unpublished.
25. Bonfante 1994. Cf. Colonna 1996b, 368-369, n. 59. De Grummond 2004, 357, reads Esti instead of Espi.
26. Quoted by Rohde 1970, 541, n. 1.
27. Torelli 1984, 175-179.
28. Colonna 1992, 114-115.
29. Maggiani 1997, 46-47.
30. Colonna 1996a, 165-166, figs. 1-4, with references. For the "*presentatoi*," see also Torelli 1997, 586-597 (with the dubious theory of a derivation from the Latial "*calefattoi*").
31. Vitali, Brizzolara, and Lippolis 2001, 28-35, 255-257 (podium B), 45-53 (podium D).
32. Torelli 1966; for the etymology, Cipriano 1983.
33. Edlund 1987, 83-85.
34. A more modest example was perhaps the *fossa* linked to the surface by a great tube of terracotta and filled with earth, grain, and burned bones, together with ritual vases and three loom weights, found in the acropolis sanctuary of Volaterrae (Bonamici 1999, 32-36, fig. 10). Note that the same sanctuary has also yielded two cups with the word *munθ* inscribed before firing (Bonamici 1999, 36, fig. 11).
35. Colonna 1999.

36. Colonna 1996b, 373-375.
37. Coarelli 1995.
38. Zamarchi Grassi 1992, 121-131; Zamarchi Grassi 2000.
39. Sgubini Moretti 1989.
40. Colonna 1986, 448-449.
41. Ortalli and Bermond Montanari 1986.
42. Steingräber 1982, 108-109, pl. 4.
43. I limit myself to recalling that in the monumental sanctuary at Pyrgi (North Area) lies the altar of temple B, reduced to foundations only, under a blanket of sand from the shore, while that of temple A was completely destroyed by the sea.
44. Massabò and Ricciardi 1988, 30-36.
45. Colonna 1988; Ricciardi 2003.
46. For votive offerings found at the site, see the discussion by Turfa, pp. 101-102, above.
47. It is sufficient to cite, in comparison, the Portonaccio temple at Veii, where the celebrated discoveries of 1916 took place right between the wall of the precinct and the foot of the overlying cliff. A similar precinct, but bipartite inside and occupied by more foundations of small altars (?), can probably be recognized in the squared structure *Beta* on the terrace of the temple of the Ara della Regina at Tarquinii (*Santuari d'Etruria*, 71-72).
48. Colonna 1966, 87-95.
49. Colonna 2000, 298-303.
50. De Lucia Brolli and Benedettini 1996.
51. *Tarquinia* 2001, 21-44.
52. Colonna 1985.
53. Tamburini 1999, 101-106; Acconcia 2000.
54. Cf. Castagnoli 1984, 3-6.
55. *Santuari d'Etruria*, 23.
56. Coarelli 1988, 71-73.
57. Franchi de Bellis 1988, 44-47, 103-105.
58. The *sacellum*, in the sense used in modern languages (cf. Italian *sacello*) and also in that presupposed in Latin by the fantasized etymology of Trebatius is something else entirely. This is true even if it arose, so to speak, from the precinct in which initially it was only an accessory, as is well shown by the great precinct in unbaked brick at Rusellae (see below).
59. Varro calls *delubrum* (in Nonius, 792 L) the oldest form of an *aedes*, with an ambiguous term valid both for the building and for the surrounding area *ubi aqua currit*, according to the etymology of the antiquarian L. Cincius (Servius, *ad Aen.* 2.225), and even for the type of fetish most commonly accommodated in it, the stripped stake (Paulus ex Festus, p. 64 Lindsay).
60. Colonna 1981, 46-48.
61. *Santuari d'Etruria*, 53-57 (P. Bocci Pacini). Bocci Pacini 1998.
62. Colonna 1984, 401, n. 21; Carandini and Cappelli 2000, 327-328.
63. Pritchard 1983, 522-523.
64. Bonghi Jovino 1999.
65. See above, n. 7.
66. *Santuari d'Etruria*, 53, 58-59; Colonna 1986, 433.
67. See, most recently, Coarelli 1996, 8-9.
68. Colonna 1986, 506.
69. Colonna 1984-1985, 61-62; Colonna 1989a, 281-283.
70. Bonfante 1990, 53-57.

71. Colonna 2000, 267-268, 272.
72. Staccioli 1968, 41-43, no. 32.
73. Melis and Qulici Gigli 1983, 9-18.
74. Roncalli 1987, 53-55. Note the well at the entrance of the greater cella, closed by a rough stone that recalls the arrangement near the altar Iota of Pyrgi (South Area).
75. Stopponi 1991.
76. *Santuari d'Etruria*, 119, nos. 9-10.
77. Prayon 1993, 417, pl. 1.
78. Torelli 1983, 485-487; *Santuari d'Etruria*, 53.
79. *Santuari d'Etruria*, 111 (basement *Alpha*).
80. Colonna 1984, 400-401, figs. 1, 6.
81. Prayon 1975, 18, 64-68, pl. 85, nos. 11-19, 87, nos. 9-11; Colonna 1981, 55-56, fig. 7.
82. Bonghi Jovino 1997.
83. The sigla *anχ* incised underneath a *skyphos* probably refers to the sacral function of the vessel; cf. the *vasa anclabria* used in the cult of the priests according to Festus, p. 10 Lindsay (for a different interpretation, see now Colonna 2001a, 419).
84. Colonna 2002, 149. A third example is perhaps that of the spring goddess Ana in the Valle Zuccara sanctuary at Caere (Nardi 1988, 105-106), decorated with Nymph antefixes (Nardi 1989, 67, fig. 34).
85. See above, n. 68.
86. Forsberg 1984; Colonna and Backe Forsberg 1999, 67-76.
87. Sgubini Moretti 1994, 23-24.
88. Sgubini Moretti and Ricciardi 1993.
89. Colonna Di Paolo 1978, 11-12; Colonna 1990, 120-122, 127-135.
90. Colonna 1993, 337-343. In the poorer tombs of Fondo Scataglini the upper rooms also seem in fact to have been used for burials (Serra Ridgway 1997, 143-147, 175).
91. Sgubini Moretti 1994, 36-37.
92. For references, see *Santuari d'Etruria*, 60-66, and Belelli Marchesini 1997 (a very accurate and reliable contribution). For the architectural terracottas, see Strazzulla 1997, 711-714.
93. Colonna 1981, 47-48.
94. Colonna 1981, 49.
95. Prayon 1975, 23-27, 70-74, pl. 85, nos. 36-37, 42-44, 47, and pl. 87, nos. 18-23.
96. Mura Sommella 1998.
97. See above, n. 32.
98. Colonna 1991.
99. *Santuari d'Etruria*, 149-153 (S. Stopponi).
100. Bonghi Jovino 1997.
101. Colonna 2000, 276, 279, 283-293.
102. Colonna 1989, 181-183.
103. Moretti Sgubini 1997.
104. Pandolfini 1997.
105. Verger and Kermorvant 1994. The excavations pursued since 2002 by the University of Bologna under the direction of Giuseppe Sassatelli have confirmed the results of the prospection.
106. Vitali, Brizzolara, and Lipollis 2001, 231-141. I believe that the temple was the first built on the acropolis, beside the earlier podium B.
107. *Veio, Cerveteri, Vulci* 2001, 40-43, 57-64.
108. The figure shows the reconstruction of a corner of the pedi-

mental *sima** with the related small *akroteria*, created by Claudia Carlucci at the Exposition "Veio, Cerveteri, Vulci," at Rome, 2001.

109. Lulof 1996.
110. Colonna 2000, 309-335.
111. Nielsen and Poulsen 1992, 61-79.
112. *Santuari d'Etruria*, 139-141.
113. *Veio, Cerveteri, Vulci* 2001, 143-145; Colonna 2001b, 160. Recent excavations have shown that the isolated footings of the *pronaos* belong to a fourth-century reconstruction.
114. *Santuari d'Etruria*, 80-83 (S. Stopponi).
115. Massabò and Ricciardi 1988, 27-29.
116. Colonna 1984, 409-411.
117. *Santuari d'Etruria*, 70-78; *Tarquinia* 2001, 45-49, 69-72.
118. Ciampoltrini 1997, with bibliography.
119. *Santuari d'Etruria*, 93-95 (G. Maetzke).
120. *Santuari d'Etruria*, 96-97 (G. Colonna).
121. Cifarelli 2003.
122. Bonamici 1997, 331.
123. Prayon 1991. But see now temple E of the acropolis at Marzabotto (Fig. VIII.15).

BIBLIOGRAPHY

Acconcia, V. 2000. *Il santuario del Pozzarello a Bolsena (Scavi Gabrici 1904)*. Rome.

Atti Chiusi-Chianciano 1993 = *La civiltà di Chiusi e del suo territorio*. Atti del XVII Convegno di Studi Etruschi e Italici a Chiusi-Chianciano 1989. Florence.

Baglione, M. P. 2000. "I rinvenimenti di ceramica attica dal santuario dell'area Sud." *Scienze dell'antichità* 10, 337-382.

Belelli Marchesini, B. 1997. "Tempio: Etruria." In *EAA*, Suppl. 2, vol. 5, 628-638.

Bocci Pacini, P. 1998. "L'insediamento orientalizzante nella valle del Foro." In *Roselle, Guida al parco archeologico*, ed. F. Nicosia and G. Poggesi. Siena. 87-88.

Bonamici, M. 1997. "Un affresco di I stile dal santuario dell'acropoli." In *Aspetti della cultura di Volterra etrusca fra l'età del Ferro e l'età ellenistica*, ed. G. Maetzke. Atti del XIX convegno di Studi Etruschi e Italici a Volterra 1995. Florence. 315-332.

———. 1999. "Santuario dell'acropoli: Testimonianze sulle pratiche di culto." In *Laboratorio universitario volterrano: Quaderno 2*. 29-41.

Bonfante L. 1990. *Reading the Past: Etruscan*. London.

———. 1994. "Originis incertae," in REE, *StEtr* 59, 269-270, no. 26.

Bonghi Jovino, M. 1997. "La phase archaïque de l'Ara della Regina à la lumière des découvertes récentes." In LPRH, 69-92.

———. 1999. "*Tantum ratio sacrorum gerebatur*: L'edificio Beta di Tarquinia in epoca orientalizzante e alto-arcaica." In *Koiná: Miscellanea di studi archeologici in onore di Piero Orlandini*, ed. M. Castaldi. Milan. 87-103.

Carandini, A., and R. Cappelli, 2000. *Roma: Romolo, Remo e la fondazione della città*. Catalogue of exhibition in Rome. Milan.

Castagnoli, F. 1984. "Il tempio romano: questioni di terminologia e di tipologia." *PBSR* 52, 3-20.

Ciampoltrini, G. 1997. "Talamone." In *EAA*, Suppl. 2, vol. 5, 517-519.

Cifarelli, F. M. 2003. *Il tempio di Giunone Moneta sull'acropoli di Segni*. Rome.

Cipriano, P. 1983. *Templum*. Rome.

Coarelli F. 1988. *Il Foro Boario*. Rome.

———. 1995. "Il santuario del Fondo Patturelli a Capua." In *L'incidenza dell'antico: studi in memoria di Ettore Lepore*, vol. 1. Naples. 371-387.

———. 1996. "*Legio linteata*. L'iniziazione militare nel Sannio." In *La Tavola di Agnone nel contesto italico*. Atti del convegno di Agnone 1994. Florence. 3-16.

———. 1997. *Il Campo Marzio*. Rome.

Colonna, G. 1966. "Nuovi elementi per la storia del santuario di Pyrgi." *ArchClass* 18, 82-108.

———. 1981. "Tarquinio Prisco e il tempio di Giove Capitolino." *PP* 32, fasc. 196-198, 41-59.

———. 1984. "I templi del Lazio fino al V secolo compreso." *Archeologia Laziale* 6, Rome. 396-411.

———. 1984-1985. "Novità sui culti di Pyrgi." *RendPontAcc* 57, 57-88.

———. 1985. "Il santuario di Montetosto." In *Case e palazzi d'Etruria*. Catalogue of exhibition in Siena. Milan. 192-196.

———. 1986. "Urbanistica e architettura." In *Rasenna: Storia e civiltà degli Etruschi*, ed. G. Pugliese Carratelli. Milan. 371-530.

———. 1988. "Una nuova dedica alla etrusca Uni." *BdA* 48, 23-26.

———. 1989a. "Il tempio B." In *Pyrgi: Scavi del santuario etrusco (1969-1971)*. (Suppl. 2 to *NSc* 42-43.) 171-183.

———. 1989b. "La piazza a sud del tempio B." In *Pyrgi: Scavi del santuario etrusco (1969-1971)*. (Suppl. 2 to *NSc* 42-43.) 280-290.

———. 1990. "Corchiano, Narce e il problema di *Fescennium*." In *La civiltà dei Falisci*. Atti del XV Convegno di Studi Etruschi e Italici a Civita Castellana 1987. Florence. 127-135.

———. 1991. "Le due fasi del tempio arcaico di S. Omobono." In *Stips votiva: Papers Presented to C. M. Stibbe*, ed. M. Gnade. Amsterdam. 51-55.

———. 1992. "Altari e sacelli: l'area Sud di Pyrgi dopo otto anni di ricerche." *RendPontAcc* 64, 63-115.

———. 1993. "Strutture teatriformi in Etruria." In *Spectacles sportifs et scéniques dans le monde étrusco-italique*. Actes de la table ronde de Rome 1991. Rome. 321-347.

———. 1996a. "Il *dokanon*, il culto dei Dioscuri e gli aspetti ellenizzanti della religione dei morti nell'Etruria tardo-arcaica." In *Scritti di antichità in memoria di Sandro Stucchi*, ed. L. Bacchielli and M. Nonanno Aravantinos. Studi Miscellanei 29. Rome. 165-184.

———. 1996b. "L'Apollo di Pyrgi." In *Magna Grecia, Etruschi, Fenici*. Atti del XXXIII convegno di studi sulla Magna Grecia, Taranto 1993. Naples. 345-375.

———. 1997. "L'iscrizione del cratere di Pyrgi con Eracle bevitore." In Maggiani 1997, 94-98.

———. 1999. "Pontecagnano," in REE, *StEtr* 63, 405-407, no. 33.

———. 2000. "Il santuario di Pyrgi dalle origini mitistoriche agli altorilievi frontonali dei Sette e di Leucotea." *Scienze dell'Antichità* 10, 251-336.

———. 2001a. "Pyrgi," in REE, *StEtr* 64, 413-422.

———. 2001b. "Divinazione e culto di Rath/Apollo a Caere (a proposito del santuario in loc. S. Antonio)." *ArchClass* 52, 151-173.

———. 2002. "Le vicende e l'interpretazione dello scavo." In *Il santuario di Portonaccio a Veio, 1. Gli scavi di Massimo Pallottino nella zona dell'altare (1939-1940)* (*MonAntLinc*, ser. misc. 6.3). 133-159.

Colonna, G., and Backe Forsberg, Y. 1999. "Le iscrizioni del 'sacello' del ponte di San Giovenale." *OpRom* 24, 63-81.

Colonna Di Paolo, E. 1978. *Necropoli rupestri del Viterbese*. Novara.

de Grummond, N. T. 2004. "For the Mother and for the Daughter: Some Thoughts on Dedications from Etruria and Praeneste." In *ΧΑΡΙΣ: Essays in Honor of Sara A. Immerwahr*, ed. A. P. Chapin. *Hesperia* Suppl. 33, 351-370.

De Lucia Brolli, M. A., and M. G. Benedettini. 1996. "Narce (Com. di Nazzano Romano)." *StEtr* 61, 432-435.

Edlund, I. E. M. 1987. *The Gods and the Place*. Stockholm.

ET = H. Rix. 1991. *Etruskische Texte: Editio Minor*. 2 vols. Tübingen.

Étienne, R., and Le Dinahet, M.-T., eds. 1991. *L'espace sacrificiel dans les civilisations méditerranéennes de l'antiquité*, Paris.

Forsberg, S. 1984. "Il complesso del ponte sul Fosso Pietrisco." In *San Giovenale: Materiali e problemi*. Atti del simposio di Roma 1983. Stockholm. 73-75.

Franchi de Bellis, A. 1988. *Il cippo abellano*. Urbino.

La Rocca, E. 1984. *La riva a mezzaluna: Culti, agoni, monumenti funerari presso il Tevere nel Campo Marzio occidentale*. Rome.

Lulof, P. S. 1996. *The Ridge-pole Statues from the Late Archaic Temple at Satricum*. Amsterdam.

LPRH = F. Gaultier and D. Briquel, eds., *Les Étrusques, les plus religieux des hommes: État de la recherche sur la religion étrusque. Actes du colloque international Grand Palais 17-18-19 novembre 1992. XII^{er} Rencontres de l'École du Louvre*. Paris.

Maggiani, A. 1997. *Vasi attici figurati con dediche a divinità etrusche* (Suppl. to *RdA*, 18). Roma.

Maras, D. F. 2001. "Pyrgi. Iscrizioni e sigle etrusche." *StEtr* 64, 375-409, nos. 36-90.

Massabò, B., and L. Ricciardi. 1988. "Il tempio, l'altare e il deposito votivo." *BdA* ser. 6, 73, 27-42.

Melis, F., and Quilici Gigli, S. 1983. "Votivi e luoghi di culto nella campagna di Velletri." *ArchClass* 35, 1-44.

Mura Sommella, A. 1998. "Le recenti scoperte sul Campidoglio e la fondazione del tempio di Giove Capitolino." *RendPontAcc* 70, 57-79.

Nardi, G. 1988. "L'area sacra di Valle Zuccara." In *Caere I, Il parco archeologico*, ed. M. Cristofani and G. Nardi. Rome. 103-106.

———. 1989. "Appunti sui santuari urbani." In *Miscellanea ceretana* I. Rome. 51-68.

Nielsen, I., and Poulsen, B. 1992. "The First Temple." In *The Temple of Castor and Pollux*, vol. 1, Rome. 87-117.

Onorati, M. T. 1992. "I Samiarii." In *La necropoli di Praeneste: Periodi arcaico e medio-repubblicano*. Atti del II convegno di Palestrina, 1990. Palestrina. 206-231.

Ortalli, J., and G. Bermond Montanari. 1986. "Il complesso monumentale protofelsineo di via Fondazza a Bologna." *StEtr* 54, 15-45.

Pandolfini, M. 1997. "Il frammento di antepagmentum iscritto da Vulci." In *Deliciae fictiles* II. Amsterdam. 165-166.

Pfiffig, A. J. 1986. "Über eine Besonderheit des etruskischen Götterkults." In *Festschrift Gerhard Radke*, ed. R. Altheim-Stiehl and M. Rosenbach. Münster. 186-192.

Prayon, F. 1975. *Frühetruskische Grab- und Hausarchitektur*. Heidelberg.

———. 1991. "*Deorum sedes*: Sull'orientamento dei templi etrusco-italici." *ArchClass* 43, 1285-1295.

———. 1993. "Il culto delle acque in Etruria." In *Atti Chiusi-Chianciano 1993*. 413-420.

Pritchard, J. B. 1983. "Sarepta and Phoenician Culture in the West." In *Atti del I convegno internazionale di studi fenici e punici*, vol. 2. Rome 1979. 521-525.

Ricciardi, L. 2003. "Il deposito votivo del santuario del Fontanile di Legnisina di Vulci." In *L'acqua degli Dei*. Catalogue of exhibition in Chianciano Terme. Montepulciano.

Rohde, E. 1970. *Psiche: Culto delle anime e fede nell'immortalità presso i Greci*, 1-2. Bari.

Roncalli, F. 1987. "Le strutture del santuario e le tecniche edilizie." *AnnFaina* 3, 47-60.

———. 1996. "Laris Pulenas and Sisyphus: Mortals, Heroes and Demons in the Etruscan Underworld." *Etruscan Studies* 3, 45-64.

———. 1997. "Iconographie funéraire et topographie de l'au-delà en Étrurie." In *LPRH*, 37-54.

Rosi Bonci, L. 1990. "Un disco di pietra con iscrizione arcaica da Monte Melonta (comune di S. Venanzo)." *AnnFaina* 4, 227-230.

Rupp, D. W. 1991a. "Blazing Altars: The Depiction of Altars in Attic Vase Painting." In Étienne and Le Dinahet 1991, 56-60.

———. 1991b. "The Altars of Southern Greece: A Typological Analysis." In Étienne and Le Dinahet 1991, 303-306.

Santuari d'Etruria = G. Colonna, ed., *Santuari d'Etruria*. Catalogue of exhibition in Arezzo. Milan. 1985.

Serra Ridgway, F. R. 1997. "Le tombe: Strutture e tipologia" and "Osservazioni conclusive." In *Lo scavo nel fondo Scataglini a Tarquinia*, vol. 1, R. E. Linington and F. R. Serra Ridgway. Milan. 133-147, 173-178.

Sgubini Moretti, A. 1989. "Tomba a casa con portico nella necropoli di Pian di Mola a Tuscania." In *Atti del II congresso internazionale etrusco, Firenze 1985*, I. Rome. 321-335.

———. 1994. "Ricerche archeologiche a Vulci: 1985-1990." In *Tyrrhenoi philotechnoi*. Atti della giornata di studio a Viterbo 1990, ed. M. Martelli. Pisa. 9-49.

———. 1997. "Il Tempio Grande di Vulci: Le terrecotte architettoniche di fase arcaica." In *Deliciae fictiles*, II. Amsterdam. 151-164.

Sgubini Moretti, A., and L. Ricciardi. 1993. "Le terrecotte architettoniche di Tuscania." In *Deliciae fictiles*. Proceedings of the first international conference, Rome 1990. Stockholm. 163-181.

Staccioli, R. A. 1968. *Modelli di edifici etrusco-italici: I modelli votivi*. Florence.

Steingräber, S. 1982. "Überlegungen zu etruskischen Altären." In *Miscellanea archaeologica Tobias Dohrn dedicata*. Rome. 10-116.

Stopponi, S. 1991. "Un acroterio dal santuario di Cannicella a Orvieto." *ArchClass* 43, 110-1161.

Strazzulla, M. J. 1997. "Terrecotte architettoniche." In *EAA*, Suppl. 2, vol. 5, 70-719.

Tamburini, P. 1999. *Un museo e il suo territorio: Il Museo territoriale del lago di Bolsena, 1. Dalle origini al periodo etrusco*, Bolsena.

Tarquinia 2001 = *Tarquinia etrusca: Una nuova storia.* Catalogue of exhibition in Tarquinia. Rome.

Thuillier, J.-P. 1991. "Autels d'Étrurie." In Étienne and Le Dinahet 1991. 243-247.

Torelli, M. 1966. "Un *templum augurale* d'età repubblicana a Bantia." *RendAccLinc* 21, 1-23.

———. 1983. "Polis e 'palazzo.'" In *Architecture et société de l'archaïsme grec à la fin de la république romaine.* Actes du colloque international de Rome 1980. Paris. 471-499.

———. 1984. *Lavinio e Roma.* Rome.

———. 1997. "*Secespita, praefericulum.* Archeologia di due strumenti sacrificali romani." In *Etrusca et Italica: Scritti in ricordo di Massimo Pallottino,* vol. 2. Pisa. 576-598.

Veio, Cerveteri, Vulci 2001 = *Veio, Cerveteri, Vulci: Città etrusche a confronto.* Catalogue of exhibition in Roma. Rome.

Verger, S., and A. Kermorvant. 1994. "Nouvelles données et hypothèses sur la topographie de la ville étrusque de Marzabotto." *MÉFRA* 106, 1077-1094.

Vitali, D., A. M. Brizzolara, and E. Lippolis. 2001. *L'acropoli della città etrusca di Marzabotto.* Imola.

Zamarchi Grassi, P., ed. 1992. *La Cortona dei principes.* Catalogue of exhibition in Cortona. Cortona.

———. 2000. "Il tumulo II del Sodo di Cortona." In *Principi etruschi tra Mediterraneo ed Europa.* Catalogue of exhibition in Bologna. Venice. 140-142.

GLOSSARY

abacus — in architecture, a flat, square stone at the top of a column, the uppermost member of the capital.

adyton — the inner or most holy room of a temple, often separated from the *cella** proper and accessible only to authorized persons.

aedes — "building for habitation, a house" (Lat.), used to refer to the dwelling of a god, hence a shrine or temple containing the cult image of the god.

aes rude — "rough bronze" (Lat.), lumps of bronze that served as currency before bronze was shaped into coins; often used in votive offerings. Its usage continued when coins were not available.

akroterion (pl. *akroteria*) — statuary or ornamentation placed on the high (Gk. *akron*) part of a temple or other building, either on the ridgepole of the roof or on one of the three points on the triangular pediment.

ala (pl. *alae*) — "wing" (Lat.). In architecture, refers to the rooms on the side (left or right) of the central vessel of a temple or house.

alabastron (pl. *alabastra*) — small perfume bottle, originally made of alabaster but later of clay; the form is like an elongated teardrop, rounded at the bottom. It may be used in a votive or funerary context.

ambitus — "circuit" (Lat.), an open space left around a house for the purpose of allowing circulation.

anta (pl. *antae*) — in architecture, a pilaster or post projecting slightly from the lateral walls of the *cella*,* at the front or back of a temple. If columns are placed between the *antae*, they are referred to as *in antis*.

antefix — decoration made of terracotta, attached to the end of a cover tile at the edge of the roof; conceals the open hole that would be present otherwise.

apex — "peak" (Lat.), in particular of a priest's hat. The Roman *flamen** wore a cap (*galerus**) with a rod sticking up at the top, wound around with wool. The term is sometimes used by extension for the entire hat.

arula (pl. *arulae*) — "little altar" (Lat.), a word used to refer to miniature or portable altars. Models of altars were sometimes used as votive offerings.

aryballos (pl. *aryballoi*) — small globular ceramic vessel with a narrow mouth on top, for precious oils or perfume; often used in a votive or funerary context.

askos (pl. *askoi*) — small, broad ceramic vessel for pouring, normally wider than it is high, with two openings. On one end there is a spout and, on the other end, a larger opening for insertion of ingredients; found in funerary and votive contexts.

atrium — entrance court or front hall of a Roman house; often open to the sky in the center.

auguraculum — "little place for augury" (Lat.), applied to the citadel of Rome as a place where augury (i.e., the observation of birds) took place and by extension to other sites.

balsamarius (pl. *balsamarii*) — a small jar originally intended for ointment made from the balsam tree; may be found in a votive context.

biga — chariot with two wheels drawn by two horses.

bothros (pl. *bothroi*) — "pit or hole in the ground" (Gk.), applied to a pit dug for the deposit of religious offerings.

calcei repandi — "turned-up boots" (Lat.), the characteristic laced boots with pointed, upturned toes, worn by the goddess Juno Sospita of Lanuvium. The fashion originates with the Etruscans and appears on numerous monuments, ca. 550 to 475 BCE, as actual dress; later preserved in the dress of goddesses and probably priestesses.

capite velato — "with veiled head" (Lat.), used to refer to the practice of pulling the mantle over the head to conform to ritual requirements.

cella — "chamber, cell" (Lat.), the enclosed central room of a temple, referred to in Greek as *naos*. See also the term *sacellum.**

cippus (pl. *cippi*) — "post, pillar" (Lat.), upright stone marker, placed on a monument or directly in the ground to indicate a tomb or boundary line.

cista — "chest, box" (Lat.). May be used to refer to (1) a cist in the ground lined with stone, for burial or other ritual purpose, or (2) a cylindrical bronze cosmetic chest such as those used in burials at ancient Praeneste.

columen — "top, summit" (Lat.), the highest part of a

Roman or Etruscan temple, the central ridge beam; a plaque may decorate the end of the ridge beam.

consaeptum sacellum—see *sacellum*.*

delubrum—"temple, shrine, sanctuary" (Lat.). Generic term for a religious area.

echinus—dish-shaped block of a Doric capital, with a convex profile; located underneath the *abacus*.*

ekphora—"act of carrying out" (Gk.), especially of a corpse for burial; refers to a funeral procession to the tomb.

Etrusca disciplina—"Etruscan discipline" (Lat.), a scientific system embracing the teachings of Tages and others about the relationship between men and gods and the rituals used for communication, written down in a series of authoritative books. The word order in Latin is almost always with the adjective first, in contrast with the normal Latin word order of noun first and adjective second.

Etruscus ritus—see *ritus Etruscus*.*

fanum—"sanctuary, temple" (Lat.), or area consecrated to a particular deity. Best known among the Etruscans was the Fanum Voltumnae, the sanctuary dedicated to the principal god of the Etruscans where the league of Twelve Peoples met periodically.

favissa (pl. *favissae*)—underground repository for sacred objects no longer to be used.

flamen (pl. *flamines*)—Roman priest assigned to the cults of individual deities: three "major" (Jupiter, Mars, Quirinus) and twelve "minor" gods.

fossa—"ditch" (Lat.), dug for a ritual or military purpose.

galerus (also *galerum*)—a helmetlike cap made of undressed animal skin, worn by Roman priests. It often had an *apex** on top of it.

gens—"family" (Lat.), especially in the extended sense of a clan or race; a group of individuals bound together by blood and by mutual customs and rituals.

haruspex (pl. *haruspices*)—"soothsayer or diviner" (Lat.), especially one who foretells the future or determines the will of the gods by consulting the entrails of animals.

haruspicina—"art of divination" (Lat.). The art or science of foretelling the future or divining the will of the gods by means of consulting animal entrails.

in antis—see *anta*.*

iynx—"wryneck" (Gk.), a bird able to twist its neck in a unique way, leading to the belief that it related to a magic ritual that could cast a spell of love; by extension, a love toy with wheel and string that could twist and cast a spell.

kantharos—ceramic "drinking cup" (Gk.), generally large and with two vertical handles.

kore (pl. *korai*)—"maiden" (Gk.), a designation given to a series of marble statues of young females found on the Acropolis in Athens dating to the Archaic period. Their pose and elaborate dress are formulaic.

kouros (pl. *kouroi*)—"boy, youth" (Gk.), a designation given to a series of marble statues of boys or young men, found at various sites in Greece and Italy and dating to the Archaic period. They are nude and have a formulaic pose with arms down by the side, fists clenched, and left foot stepping forward.

kourotrophos (pl. *kourotrophoi*)—"child-nourishing" (Gk.), a term applied to female figures in sculpture who carry or nurse children.

krater—ceramic "mixing bowl" (Gk.), a large vessel with a wide mouth, having two handles, used for mixing wine, water, and other ingredients of drink. The variants include the volute *krater* (handles have a scroll or volute shape), column or colonette *krater* (handles shaped like columns or little columns), and kalyx *krater* (handles encircle the bowl of the *krater* like the calyx of a flower).

krateriskos—small *krater*.*

kylikeion—a sideboard or stand for display of vessels for a banquet, including *kylikes*,* from which the name comes.

kylix (pl. *kylikes*)—ceramic "drinking cup" (Gk.) set on a tall foot, with a wide, low bowl and two horizontal handles.

lectisternium—a Roman ritual feast of the gods, in which images of the gods were placed on couches and food set out on tables before them.

lekythos (pl. *lekythoi*)—slender ceramic jug with a narrow neck and one handle, used to contain oil for an offering to the gods or the dead.

limes (pl. *limites*)—"boundary" (Lat.) of a field or of a territory.

limitatio—the act of fixing or determining *limites*, that is, boundaries.

lituus—ceremonial staff of a Roman priest or augur, curved and free of knots. The Latin word may originate with the Etruscans, who used the staff or wand before the Romans did. The term is also used to refer to a curved war trumpet.

loculus—"little place" (Lat.), a niche in the wall for containing the remains of the dead; also, a coffin.

lucumo (pl. *lucumones*)—Latin word for an Etruscan "prince" or "king"; probably a translation of the Etruscan *lauχume*.

magmentarium—place set aside for making sacrifices in

addition to ones made directly at an altar or other sacred central spot.

mundus — Latin term with multiple meanings, probably sometimes overlapping: (1) the universe or cosmos, (2) the adornment of a woman and/or the instruments of adornment (*mundus muliebris*), (3) a pit for offerings made at the center point of a new colony, and (4) a gateway to the Underworld.

mutule — in Etruscan architecture, a side beam running parallel to the main ridge beam (*columen**) of a temple. Its end projects in the triangular pediment and may be covered over with a decorative plaque.

naos — see *cella*.*

nenfro — a type of *tufa,** found especially around Vulci. A dense stone, it takes carving well and is often used for sculpture and for moldings in architecture.

nimbus — an aura or halo around the head. On terracotta antefixes, the shell running around the head and framing it may be referred to as a *nimbus*.

numen (pl. *numina*) — divine will or power of the gods (Lat.).

oikist — city-founder; leader in the foundation of a colony.

oikos — "house" (Gk.). The term is used to refer to a simple rectangular building serving as a shrine, lacking the *pronaos** and columns that help to distinguish a building as a temple.

oinochoe (pl. *oinochoai*) — one-handled pitcher for pouring water or wine.

olpe — small pitcher with one handle, the top of which rises above the rim of the pitcher.

oppidum — "town or settlement" (Lat.); often refers to a fortified hilltop town.

opus quadratum — masonry cut in large, regular squared blocks and laid in courses of equal height.

ostentum (pl. *ostenta*) — a prodigy or portent of something about to happen.

pars antica — the front half of a temple.

pars postica — the rear half of a temple.

patera — saucer-shaped vessel for pouring a libation to the gods or for receiving a libation; in Greek, a *phiale*.*

penus — a storeroom or repository for provisions; also the innermost chamber of a temple, especially of Vesta.

peperino — a type of *tufa** originating in the Alban Hills and used in Roman construction from the second century BCE into the Late Roman Empire.

phiale (pl. *phialai*) — see *patera*.*

pomerium — the sacred boundary of a city, characterized as an open space within and outside the city walls, left free of buildings. It sets the limits for the taking of auspices for the city.

pompa funebris — "funeral procession" (Lat.).

posticum — back part of a building; cf. *pars postica*.*

prodigium (pl. *prodigia*) — "prodigy, portent, omen" (Lat.).

pronaos — the front porch of a temple, standing in front of the *naos* (= *cella**).

prostyle — having columns in the front porch of the temple.

prothesis — laying out of the dead for mourning.

protome (pl. *protomai*) — a head of an animal or human "cut off in front" (Gk.), used as a decorative motif on a vessel or as a votive offering.

quadriga — chariot drawn by four horses.

regia — a royal residence or court, in particular that of Rome in the time of the king Numa; later used as a sacred site for priestly purposes.

ritus Etruscus — the "Etruscan ritual" (Lat.), in particular that used for founding and laying out a city, with a *mundus** and a *pomerium** delineating the city boundaries.

sacellum — "little sanctuary" (Lat.), a generic name for a broad range of outdoor shrines and open-air altars that do not qualify as temples. A *consaeptum sacellum* was such a sanctuary with a fence around the precinct. In antiquity, the term was falsely derived from *sacra cella*, for it really had nothing to do with the roofed building of a cella.

sacra cella — see *sacellum*.*

sacrarium (pl. *sacraria*) — "sacristy, chapel" (Lat.). A term used to designate a sacred repository.

sima — the terracotta or marble gutter for draining water from the roof of a building, in an Etruscan temple often featuring elaborate moldings.

sors (pl. *sortes*) — "lot, share" (Lat.). In religion, the *sors* was an object drawn to find out one's future.

stele (pl. *stelai*) — a slab of stone set up in a public place as an act of commemoration.

temenos — a precinct of land marked off from common use and dedicated to a god; sacred enclosed area in which stood a temple (or more than one temple).

templum — in Roman religion, an open, clear, broad space marked out in the air or on the earth (*templum in terra*) for the taking of observations for augury. The *templum minus* ("lesser *templum*") was a structure on the ground, small in size and with a square plan. The word *templum* was used by extension for a sanctuary, shrine, or temple.

templum in terra — see *templum*.*

templum minus — see *templum*.*

testudinate roof — a roof sloping downward and outward on

all four sides of the building so as to resemble the shell of a tortoise (Lat. *testudo*).

thyrsos—sacred wand of Dionysos (Fufluns), brandished at revels; it was adorned with a globe of ivy leaves on the top.

tufa (*tufo*)—porous stone, in Etruria, normally a volcanic stone, light in weight, featuring ashes, cinders, and other deposits in varying degrees of compaction. Cf. *nenfro** and *peperino*.*

tufo—see *tufa*.*

tular—"boundaries" (Etr.).

votum—"vow" (Lat.), solemn promise made to a deity; may also refer to an offering made with the vow.

xoanon—"image made of wood" (Gk.), wooden sculpture of a god of a type produced in ancient Greece and Italy from an early period. These have mostly vanished but are known to have had a blocklike shape reflecting the trunk or branch from which the image was carved.

APPENDIX A

THE ETRUSCAN BRONTOSCOPIC CALENDAR

Jean MacIntosh Turfa

PART I

THE ETRUSCAN BRONTOSCOPIC CALENDAR
AND ANCIENT AUTHORS

The Calendar's Text

The Greek translation of *De ostentis* (*On Omens*) 27–38, (Εφημερος Βροντοσκοπια) by John the Lydian (Johannes Lydus) is the only surviving text of an Etruscan divinatory calendar previously published in Latin by P. Nigidius Figulus (fr. 83 Swoboda), an admired contemporary of Cicero. It represents the longest coherent Etruscan document extant, albeit not in its original language. No trace of the Etruscan original has yet been found, but Lydus implied that it was of great antiquity, having been a part of the Etruscan *disciplina* dictated by the legendary Tages.

The Etruscan version of the calendar (subsequent to the presumed original Etruscan document of the eighth–early seventh century BCE) was probably monumental in form, such as a set of plaques in bronze or terracotta (as the Capua "tile"; ET, *Tabula Capuana*), or it may have been duplicated on *libri lintei*, such as the Zagreb "mummy binding" (ET, *Liber Linteus*), for use by individual priests. No city or sanctuary has been exclusively linked to it, but a likely candidate was Tarquinii, where Tages is said to have dictated the *Etrusca disciplina*.* According to Lydus (*De ostentis* 38), Figulus noted that the version he translated and published was appropriate only to the region of Rome. There is, however, no significant climatic or geographic difference between the region/latitude of Rome and that of the major Etruscan cities. While the original calendar must have been cryptic in style, and some Byzantinisms are evident (e.g., "the queenly city," meaning Rome, at June 29, or οἱ δῆμοι, "common people,"

which in Byzantium meant "factions"), hints of Etruscan syntax resemble phrases in cultic documents like the Zagreb *liber linteus*. Expressions such as "feathered ones" (τα πτηνα) are close to the meaning of archaic Italic texts such as the Umbrian *Iguvine Tables*.

Etruscan calendrical literature is known from ancient authors and epigraphical finds (see Edlund-Berry 1992). From Classical authors we know the names of some months, while the Capua "tile" and Zagreb linen text describe religious rituals to be observed in calendar order, with dates given by month and day.

Organized in twelve "lunar" months, beginning in June, the calendar functioned as a reference table for priests interpreting the phenomenon of "thunder." Embedded in it is a wealth of social, agricultural, religious, and medical information. The stratified society of the calendar is comprised of urban factions that include "powerful men," nobles, a "band of youth," common people, women, and a servile class, alternately fomenting rebellion and stricken by plagues. Mention is made of a king, war, onslaughts of various noxious and "harmless" diseases, and a wide array of meteorological conditions. Many crops are cited, usually in relation to predicted abundance or dearth; these include barley and wheat, fruit and nuts. Herds, flocks, wild birds, and fish of both river and sea are also noted.

The text from which my English translation has been made is the edition of I. Bekker in *Corpus Scriptorum Historiae Byzantinae: Johannes Lydus.* Ed. B. G. Niebhuhr. Bonn. 1837. (This includes a modern translation from Greek into Latin, but readers are advised to refer only to the Greek text.) A complete study of the Brontoscopic Calendar by this author is in progress.

For references on calendars, related texts, see:

Edlund-Berry, I. E. M. 1992. "Etruscans at Work and Play: Evidence for an Etruscan Calendar." In *Kotinos: Festschrift für Erika Simon*. Mainz. 330–338.

Cristofani, M. 1995. *Tabula Capuana: Un calendario festivo di età arcaica*. Biblioteca di "Studi Etruschi." 29. Florence.

Johannes Lydus

Johannes Lydus or Lydos ("John the Lydian"), born in Philadelphia in Lydia (490 CE), received an excellent classical education and came to Constantinople in 511, where, after studying philosophy (especially Neoplatonism), he received an appointment to the Praetorian prefecture. The next forty years were spent in civil service, where one of his distinctions was his ability to translate Latin documents. His palace career finished with the prestigious appointment to teach in the Imperial school (ca. 543). He retired in 551 but continued to write, and he died in Constantinople in 560 CE.

In the history of Byzantium, Lydus is best known for his *On the Magistracies*, a complete historical discussion of Roman bureaucracy from its origins to his own day. In addition to strongly political remarks about his contemporaries, he stressed the continuity of ancient developments with his own day. (Lost works include panegyrics on contemporary figures, as well as history and poetry.)

In the field of ancient religion, Lydus' two other works, both antiquarian, are of great importance. *De mensibus*, on the Roman calendar and holidays, includes some pagan festivals still celebrated under Justinian. *De ostentis* (*On Omens*) offers an antiquarian survey of classical and related divination, including the texts of some otherwise lost ancient works, most notably, the *Brontoscopic Calendar* of Publius Nigidius Figulus. *De ostentis* further covers astrology and divination by thunder, lightning, and earthquake. Although eloquent in denouncing public figures (like John of Cappadocia) in his work on contemporary bureaucracy, Lydus offers no criticism of ancient paganism and little indication that Christian belief influenced his writing. The high rank in palace bureaucracy, which must have guaranteed him access to libraries and archives, is additional circumstantial evidence for scholars' confidence in the authenticity of the ancient works preserved in Lydus' treatises.

Texts:

Wünsch, R., ed. 1898. *De mensibus*. Leipzig.

Wachsmuth, C., ed. 1897. *Liber de ostentis*. Leipzig.

References on Lydus (each includes bibliography):

Baldwin, B. 1991. "John Lydos." In *The Oxford Dictionary of Byzantium*, vol. 2. Ed. A. P. Kazhdan. Oxford. 1061–1062.

Tinnefeld, F. 1999. "Lydos [3] Iohannes Lydos." In *Der Neue Pauly*, 7, 550–551.

Jones, A. H. M., J. R. Martindale, and J. Morris, eds. 1980. *The Prosopography of the Later Roman Empire* 2, 612–615.

Maas, M. 1992. *John Lydus and the Roman Past*. New York.

Publius Nigidius Figulus

P. Nigidius Figulus, senator, statesman, grammarian, occultist, and natural historian (or encyclopedist), is known only in the last twenty years of his life, in large part because he was an admired friend of Cicero (who called him "most learned in all fields and most reverent" [*omnium doctissimo et sanctissimo*] in the letter sent to him in exile in 46 BCE—*Ad fam.* 4.13.3). He must have been born ca. 100 BCE, to a family of plebeian background, probably in Perusia, where Nigidii are attested in epitaphs since the second century BCE. Etruscan "roots" clearly informed his scholarship, even though his political career was purely Roman.

His friendship with Cicero began around 63, when he participated in the anti-Catilinarian crusade (Cicero, *Pro Sulla* 42). He held the post of praetor in 58 BCE, when he was among the "most friendly and most sharp-witted citizens" (*amicissimos et acerrimos cives*) who supported Cicero (*Epistula ad Quintum fratrem* 1.2.16). During the Civil War, he fought with the Optimates for Pompey and was at Pharsalos (cf. Cicero *Ad Atticum* 7.24). As Figulus, *cui cura deos secretaque caeli nosse fuit . . .* ("whose concern it was to know the gods and the secrets of heaven"), he is given a speech in Lucan's *De bello civili* 1.639–672, in which he prophesies, noting that "peace will come with a tyrant" (1.670). The inevitable exile followed in 46, where he died a year later, as Cicero was preparing a speech on his behalf.

Whether or not Figulus was the subject of a Suetonian biography (see Della Casa 1962, 17–36), his fame was further transmitted in Suetonius' reference to his predicting the Civil War and the birth of Augustus (*Divus Augustus* 94.5), noting that this event was common knowledge (*nota ac vulgata res est*). Figulus' place in Cicero's *Timaeus* is understood as a memorial tribute, perhaps crafted from some of the text composed for the undelivered speech to Caesar.

Figulus was a prolific writer, whose *Commentarii grammatici* led to his frequently being compared with contemporary Varro (Gellius, *NA* 19.14; Servius, *Ad Aen.* 10.175). A tradition that Figulus revived Pythagoreanism is not supported by his surviving scholarship, fragments of which have been preserved or noted by Pliny, Gellius, the scholiasts, and Byzantine authors. The *cognomen* Figulus was explained by the scholiast on Lucan (1.639) and by Augustine (*De civitate dei* 5.3): on the issue of twins, Figulus supposedly defended horoscopes by demonstrating that in a revolving universe, no two beings can have the same identity or fate, just as two ink splashes on a potter's turntable are always distinct from each other. (The possibility of a completely different and Etruscan source of his *cognomen* remains open.)

Titles are known for a number of Figulus' religious/natural historical works, all in Latin:

De diis (*On the Gods*): probably consulted by Cicero for his own *De natura deorum*; cf. Macrobius, *Saturnalia* 3.4.6.
De hominum natura (*On the Nature of Men*)
De animalibus (*On Animals*)
De ventis (*On Winds*): contained meteorological, astronomical, and astrological data.
Sphaera Graecanica and *Sphaera Barbarica* (*The Dome of the Sky, Greek* and *Near Eastern*): discussed names of constellations, astrology, and horoscopes.
De extis (*On Divination by Organs* [of sacrificed animals])
De augurio privato (*On Private Divination*)
De somniis (*On Dreams*): partially preserved in Lydus, *De ostentis* 45.
Diarium tonitruale (*Brontoscopic Calendar*): said to be a translation or adaptation of part of the books of Tages; see the English translation in this volume.

Figulus' erudition clearly earned him the respect of his contemporaries and presumably furthered the career that his political convictions ultimately ruined. He was one of the most successful (or best documented) of the men who left Etruria to seek their futures in Late Republican Rome. Ancient scholars seem not to have questioned the authenticity or validity of his research, and the praise of Cicero, that scathing critic of diviners, registers as particularly sincere about a colleague whose personal ethics were as admirable as his arcane studies.

Text:

Swoboda, A., ed. 1889. *Publius Nigidius Figulus, Operum Reliquiae*. Prague.

Another edition of Swoboda is:

Hakkert, A. M. 1964. *Publius Nigidius Figulus, Operum Reliquiae*. Amsterdam.

References on Nigidius Figulus:

Schmidt, P. L. 2000. "Nigidius Figulus, P.," *Der Neue Pauly* 8, 890–891.

Liuzzi, D. 1983. *Nigidio Figulo, astrologo e mago: Testimonianze e frammenti*. Lecce. (Includes Italian translation of Lydus' text.)

Della Casa, A. 1962. *Nigidio Figulo*. Rome. (See review by H. Thesleff. 1965. *Gnomon* 37, 44–48.)

Legrand, L. 1931. *Publius Nigidius Figulus*. Paris. (Superceded by references above.)

The role of Etruscan *literati* in Late Republican religion and politics is now recognized as extensive. See:

Hall, J. F. 1996. "From Tarquins to Caesars: Etruscan Governance at Rome." In *Etruscan Italy*, ed. J. H. Hall. Provo, UT. 149–189.

Macfarlane, J. T. 1996. "*Tyrrhena Regum Progenies*: Etruscan Literary Figures from Horace to Ovid." In *Etruscan Italy*, ed. J. H. Hall. Provo, UT. 241–265.

Rawson, E. 1985. *Intellectual Life in the Late Roman Republic*. Baltimore. 309–312.

PART II

DIARIUM TONITRUALE

Johannes Lydus, *De Ostentis* §§ 27–38
ΕΦΗΜΕΡΟΣ ΒΡΟΝΤΟΣΚΟΠΙΑ
ΤΟΠΙΚΗ ΠΡΟΣ ΤΗΝ ΣΕΛΗΝΗΝ
ΚΑΤΑ ΤΟΝ ΡΩΜΑΙΟΝ ΦΙΓΟΥΛΟΝ
ΕΚ ΤΩΝ ΤΑΓΗΤΟΣ
ΚΑΘ' ΕΡΜΗΝΕΙΑΝ ΠΡΟΣ ΛΕΞΙΝ

Εἰ ἐπὶ πάσαις ⟨ταῖς⟩ τῆς διοσημείας παραδόσεσι τὴν σελήνην φαίνονται λαβόντες οἱ ἀρχαῖοι (ὑπ' αὐτὴν γὰρ τά τε βροντῶν τά τε κεραυνῶν ἐκδέδοται σημεῖα), καλῶς ἄν τις ἄρα καὶ τὸν σελήνης οἶκον ἐπιλέξαιτο, ὥστε ἀπὸ τοῦ καρκίνου καὶ ἐνταῦθα τὴν ἐφήμερον ἀπὸ τῆς σεληνιακῆς νουμηνίας κατὰ τοὺς σεληνιακοὺς μῆνας ληψόμεθα τῶν βροντῶν ἐπίσκεψιν· ἐξ ἧς τὰς τοπικάς, ἐφ' ὧν ῥήγνυνται χωρίων αἱ βρονταί, παρατηρήσεις οἱ Θοῦσκοι παρέδοσαν.

ΜΗΝΙ ΙΟΥΝΙΩ

Σελ. α. ἐὰν βροντήσῃ, τῶν καρπῶν εὐφορία ἔσται, ἐξῃρημένων κριθῶν· νοσήματα δὲ ἐπισφαλῆ τοῖς σώμασιν ἐπισκήψει.

β. ἐὰν βροντήσῃ, ταῖς μὲς ὠδινούσαις ἀπαλλαγὴ μᾶλλον ῥᾳδία, τοῖς δὲ θρέμμασι φθορά, ἰχθύων γε μὴν ἀφθονία ἔσται.

γ. ἐὰν βροντήσῃ, καύσων ἔσται ξηρότατος, ὥστε μὴ τοὺς ξηροὺς μόνους ἀλλὰ καὶ τοὺς ὑγροὺς καρποὺς διαφρυγέντας ἀπακαυθῆναι.

δ. ἐὰν βροντήσῃ, νεφελώδης καὶ ὑετώδης ὁ ἀὴρ ἔσται, ὡς ἐκ σηπτικῆς ὑγρότητος φθαρῆναι τοὺς καρπούς.

ε. ἐὰν βροντήσῃ, ἀπαίσιον τοῖς ἀγροῖς· οἱ δὲ χωρίοις ἢ πολίχναις ἐφεστῶτες ταραχθήσονται.

ς. ἐὰν βροντήσῃ, ἀκμάσασι τοῖς καρποῖς ἐντεχθήσεταί τι θηρίον τὸ βλάπτον αὐτούς.

ζ. ἐὰν βροντήσῃ, νοσήματα μὲν ἐνσκήψει, ἀλλ' οὐ πολλοὶ ἐξ αὐτῶν τεθνήξονται· καὶ οἱ μὲν ξηροὶ καρποὶ ἐπιτεύξονται, οἱ δὲ ὑγροὶ ξηρανθήσονται.

η. ἐὰν βροντήσῃ, ἐπομβρίαν καὶ φθορὰυ σίτον δηλοῖ.

θ. ἐὰν βροντήσῃ, φθορὰ τοῖς θρέμμασιν ἔσται ἐξ ἐπιδρομῆς λύκων.

ι. ἐὰν βροντήσῃ, θάνατος μὲν ἔσται συχνός, εὐθηνία. δὲ ὅμως.

ια. ἐὰν βροντήσῃ, καύματα μὲν ἀβλαβῆ, τὰ δὲ πολιτικὰ ἐν εὐφροσύνῃ ἔσται.

ιβ. ἐὰν βροντήσῃ, ὁμοίως ὡς ἐπὶ τῇ πρὸ ταύτης.

ιγ. ἐὰν βροντήσῃ, δυνάστου πτῶσιν ἀπειλεῖ.

ιδ. ἐὰν βροντήσῃ, καυσῶδες μὲν τὸ περιέχον ἔσται, εὐφορία δὲ τῶν καρπῶν καὶ εὔροια τῶν ποταμίων οὐχ ἥκιστα ἰχθύων. τὰ σώματά γε μὴν ἐξασθενήσει.

ιε. ἐὰν βροντήσῃ, τὰ μὲν πτηνὰ λυμανθήσεται τῷ θέρει, οἱ δὲ ἰχθύες φθαρήσονται.

ις. ἐὰν βροντήσῃ, οὐκ ἐλάττωσιν μόνον τῶν ἐπιτηδείων ἀλλὰ καὶ πόλεμον ἀπειλεῖ, ἀνὴρ δέ τις εὐτυχὴς ἀφανισθήσεται.

ιζ. ἐὰν βροντήσῃ, καύματα ἔσται καὶ μυῶν καὶ ἀσφαλάκων καὶ ἀκρίδων φορά· εὐθηνίαν δὲ ὅμως καὶ φόνους τῷ δήμῳ φέρει.

ιη. ἐὰν βροντήσῃ, φθορὰν τῶν καρπῶν ἀπειλεῖ.

ιθ. ἐὰν βροντήσῃ, τὰ λυμαινόμενα τοῖς καρποῖς θηρία φθαρήσεται.

κ. ἐὰν βροντήσῃ, διχόνοιαν ἀπειλεῖ τῷ δήμῳ.

κα. ἐὰν βροντήσῃ, ἐλάττωσιν μὲν οἴνου, ἐπίδοσιν δὲ τῶν ἄλλων καρπῶν δηλοῖ καὶ ἀφθονίαν ἰχθύων.

κβ. ἐὰν βροντήσῃ, ἐπίφθορον ἔσται τὸ καῦμα.

κγ. ἐὰν βροντήσῃ, εὐφροσύνην καὶ κακῶν ἀπαλλαγὴν καὶ νόσων ἀφανισμὸν δηλοῖ.

κδ. ἐὰν βροντήσῃ, εὐθηνίαν δηλοῖ.

κε. ἐὰν βροντήσῃ, πόλεμοι καὶ μυρία ἔσονται κακά.

κς. ἐὰν βροντήσῃ, ὁ χειμὼν τοῖς καρποῖς ἐπιβλαβὴς ἔσται.

κζ. ἐὰν βροντήσῃ, κίνδυνος στρατιωτικὸς τοῖς κρατοῦσιν ἔσται.

κη. ἐὰν βροντήσῃ, εὐετηρία ἔσται τῶν καρπῶν.

κθ. ἐὰν βροντήσῃ, τὰ τῆς βασιλίδος πόλεως ἔσται κρείττονα.

λ. ἐὰν βροντήσῃ, πρὸς βραχὺ θάνατος ἔσται συχνός.

ΙΟΥΛΙΟΣ

α. Ἐπὶ τῆς σεληνιακῆς νουμηνίας ἐὰν βροντήσῃ, εὐθηνία μὲν ἔσται, τῶν δὲ θρεμμάτων πτῶσις.

β. ἐὰν βροντήσῃ, καλὸν τῷ φθινοπώρῳ.

γ. ἐὰν βροντήσῃ, χειμῶνα βαρὺν σημαίωει.

δ. ἐὰν βροντήσῃ, ἀέριοι ἔσονται ταραχαί, ὡς ἐξ αὐτῶν σπάνιν γενέσθαι.

ε. ἐὰν βροντήσῃ, εὐθηνία μὲν σίτου, ἄρχοντος δὲ ἀγαθοῦ πτῶσις ἔσται.

ς. ἐὰν βροντήσῃ, νόσους θανατηφόρους ταῖς δουλικαῖς τύχαις ἀπειλεῖ.

ζ. ἐὰν βροντήσῃ, κατομβρία ἔσται βλαβερὰ τοῖς σπορίμοις.

η. ἐὰν βροντήσῃ, εἰρήνην μὲν τοῖς κοινοῖς, ὄλεθρον δὲ τοῖς βοσκήμασι καὶ βῆχα ξηρὸν ἐνσκῆψαι δηλοῖ.

θ. ἐὰν βροντήσῃ, ἐποψίαν θεῶν καὶ ἀγαθῶν πολλῶν πρόσοδον δηλοῖ.

ι. ἐὰν βροντήσῃ, σωτηριώδη ἔσται τὰ ποτάμια ὕδατα.

ια. ἐὰν βροντήσῃ, καῦμα σημαίνει καὶ ὄμβρον βίαιον καὶ σπάνιν σίτου.

ιβ. ἐὰν βροντήσῃ, ψῦχος τῷ θέρει ἔσται ἀδόκητον, δι' οὗ φθαρήσεται τὰ ἐπιτήδεια.

ιγ. ἐὰν βροντήσῃ, ἑρπετὰ φανεῖται βλαβερώτατα.

ιδ. ἐὰν βροντήσῃ, εἰς ἕνα τὴν πάντων δύναμιν ἐλθεῖν φράζει· οὗτος δὲ ἔσται τοῖς πράγμασιν ἀδικώτατος.

ιε. ἐὰν βροντήσῃ, διχόνοια ἔσται τοῦ δήμου καὶ τοῦ σίτου ἔνδεια.

ις. ἐὰν βροντήσῃ, πόλεμον ὁ τῆς ἀνατολῆς βασιλεὺς ἐκδεχέσθω καὶ νόσον ἀπὸ ξηροῦ καύματος.

ιζ. ἐὰν βροντήσῃ, διαδοχὴν μεγάλου ἄρχοντος δηλοῖ.

ιη. ἐὰν βροντήσῃ, ἔνδειαν καρπῶν ἐξ ἐπομβρίας ἀπειλεῖ.

ιθ. ἐὰν βροντήσῃ, πόλεμον δηλοῖ καὶ ἀπώλειαν δυνατῶν· ἀφθονία δὲ ἔσται τῶν ξηρῶν καρπῶν.

κ. ἐὰν βροντήσῃ, αὐχμὸν νοσώδη ἀπειλεῖ.

κα. ἐὰν βροντήσῃ, διχόνοια ἔσται τοῖς ὑπηκόοις, ἀλλ' οὐκ εἰς μακράν.

κβ. ἐὰν βροντήσῃ, ἀγαθὰ μὲν τοῖς κοινοῖς πράγμασι, νόσους δὲ τοῖς σώμασι περὶ τὴν κεφαλὴν σημαίνει.

κγ. ἐὰν βροντήσῃ, ἡ διχόνοια τοῦ δήμου παυθήσεται.

κδ. ἐὰν βροντήσῃ, δυνατοῦ ἀνθρώπου δηλοῖ δυνατὸν ἀτύχημα.

κε. ἐὰν βροντήσῃ, τῇ νεολαίᾳ κάκωσις καὶ τοῖς καρποῖς μετ' αὐτῆς, νοσώδης δὲ ὁ καιρὸς ἔσται.

κς. ἐὰν βροντήσῃ, ἀπὸ μεγάλης εὐθηνίας ἔνδεια ἔσται.

κζ. ἐὰν βροντήσῃ, ἐκβρασμὸν τοῖς σώμασιν ἀπειλεῖ.

κη. ἐὰν βροντήσῃ, ἔνδεια ὑδάτων καὶ ὄχλος ἑρπετῶν ἐπιβλαβῶν ἔσται.

κθ. ἐὰν βροντήσῃ, εὐετηρίαν δηλοῖ.

λ. ἐὰν βροντήσῃ, οἱ ἄνθρωποι ἐκ ποινηλασίας ἐπὶ τὰ χείριστα τῶν πταισμάτων ὀλισθήσουσιν.

ΑΥΓΟΥΣΤΟΣ

α. Ἐὰν βροντήσῃ, καὶ τὰ τῆς πολιτείας ἠρέμα πως καλλίονα καὶ εὐθηνία ἔσται.

β. ἐὰν βροντήσῃ, νόσους ἅμα καὶ ἔνδειαν τῶν ἐπιτηδείων ἀπειλεῖ.

γ. ἐὰν βροντήσῃ, δίκας καὶ λέσχας τῷ δήμῳ ἀπειλεῖ.

δ. ἐὰν βροντήσῃ, ἔνδεια τροφῶν λογικοῖς ἅμα καὶ ἀλόγοις ἔσται.

ε. ἐὰν βροντήσῃ, τὰς γυναῖκας συνετωτέρας δηλοῖ.

ς. ἐὰν βροντήσῃ, μέλιτος μὲν ἀφθονία ἔσται, ὕδατος δὲ καὶ τῶν λοιπῶν τροφίμων λεῖψις.

ζ. ἐὰν βροντήσῃ, ἀνέμους τραχεῖς καὶ νόσους ὁμοῦ σημαίνει.

η. ἐὰν βροντήσῃ, νόσον ἀκίνδυνον τοῖς τετραπόδοις ἀπειλεῖ.

θ. ἐὰν βροντήσῃ, ὑγίειαν μὲν ἀνθρώποις ὡς ἐκ τοῦ πλείονος ἐπαγγέλλεται.

ι. ἐὰν βροντήσῃ, λύπας καὶ μοχθηρίας τῷ πλήθει ἀπειλαῖ.

ια. ἐὰν βροντήσῃ, εὐετηρία μὲν ἔσται, πτῶσις δὲ ἑρπετῶν καὶ βλάβη τοῖς ἀνθρώποις.

ιβ. ἐὰν βροντήσῃ, χόρτου καὶ βαλάνου ἀφθονία ἔσται, τῇ δὲ πρώτῃ ἡλικίᾳ κάκωσις.

ιγ. ἐὰν βροντήσῃ, ὄλεθρος ἔσται τοῖς σώμασι λογικῶν τε καὶ ἀλόγων.

ιδ. ἐὰν βροντήσῃ, πόλεμον μὲν τοῖς κοινοῖς, ἀφθονίαν δὲ τοῖς καρποῖς δηλοῖ.

ιε. ἐὰν βροντήσῃ, ἐπὶ τὸ χεῖρον τὰ πράγματα.

ις. ἐὰν βροντήσῃ, εἰρήνην βαθεῖαν ἐπαγγέλλεται.

ιζ. ἐὰν βροντήσῃ, οἱ χείρους τῶν ἀνθρώπων στυγνάσουσιν.

ιη. ἐὰν βροντήσῃ, πόλεμον ἐμφύλιον ἀπειλεῖ.

ιθ. ἐὰν βροντήσῃ, φόνους αἱ γυναῖκες καὶ τὸ δουλικὸν τολμήσει.

κ. ἐὰν βροντήσῃ, ὄλεθρον βοῶν καὶ ταραχὰς τοῖς πράγμασιν ἀπειλεῖ.

κα. ἐὰν βροντήσῃ, εὐθηνίαν ἅμα καὶ διχόνοιαν τῷ δήμῳ δηλοῖ.

κβ. ἐὰν βροντήσῃ, καλὰ μετρίως τὰ πράγματα ἀνὰ πάντα τὸν ἐνιαυτόν.

κγ. ἐὰν βροντήσῃ, κεραυνὸν πεσεῖσθαι δηλοῖ καὶ φόνους ἀπειλεῖ.

κδ. ἐὰν βροντήσῃ, ἀπώλειαν εὐγενῶν νέων ἀπειλεῖ.

κε. ἐὰν βροντήσῃ, χειμῶνα καὶ σπάνιν ὀπωρῶν ἔσεσθαι προλέγει.

κς. ἐὰν βροντήσῃ, πόλεμον σημαίνει.

κζ. ἐὰν βροντήσῃ, πολέμους ἅμα καὶ δόλους ἀπειλεῖ.

κη. ἐὰν βροντήσῃ, εὐθηνίαν μὲν τῶν καρπῶν, φθορὰν δὲ τῶν βοῶν σημαίνει.

κθ. ἐὰν βροντήσῃ, οὐδεμίαν ἐναλλαγὴν σημαίνει.

λ. ἐὰν βροντήσῃ, νόσους τῇ πόλει, ἐφ' ἧς ῥαγήσεται, ἀπειλεῖ.

ΣΕΠΤΕΜΒΡΙΟΣ

α. Ἐὰν βροντήσῃ, εὐετηρίαν ἅμα καὶ εὐφροσύνην δηλοῖ.

β. ἐὰν βροντήσῃ, διχόνοια τῷ δήμῳ ἔσται.

γ. ἐὰν βροντήσῃ, κατομβρίαν καὶ πόλεμον δηλοῖ.

δ. ἐὰν βροντήσῃ, δυνατοῦ πτῶσιν παὶ πολέμου παρασκευὴν δηλοῖ.

ε. ἐὰν βροντήσῃ, κριθῆς μὲν ἀφθονίαν, σίτου δὲ ἐλάττωσιν δηλοῖ.

ς. ἐὰν βροντήσῃ, δύναμις ἔσται ταῖς γυναιξὶ κρείττων ἢ κατ' αὐτάς.

ζ. ἐὰν βροντήσῃ, νόσον καὶ πτῶσιν τῷ δουλικῷ ἐξ αὐτῆς ἀπειλεῖ.

η. ἐὰν βροντήσῃ, τοὺς μάλιστα δυνατοὺς τοῦ πολιτεύματος σκολιὰ ἐννοεῖν, ἀποτεύξεσθαι δὲ τῶν νοουμένων κατηγορεῖ.

θ. ἐὰν βροντήσῃ, ἄνεμον πνεῦσαι ἐπίνοσον ἀπειλεῖ.

ι. ἐὰν βροντήσῃ, ἔρις ἔσται τῷ τόπῳ ἐφ' οὗ ῥαγήσεται πρὸς ἕτερον οὐκ ἄλογος.

ια. ἐὰν βροντήσῃ, οἱ ὑπεξούσιοι τῶν εὐγενῶν σκέψονταί τι καινὸν ἐν τοῖς κοινοῖς.

ιβ. ἐὰν βροντήσῃ, ἔπομβρον τὸν τοῦ ἀμητοῦ καιρὸν καὶ λιμὸν ἔσεσθαι λέγει.

ιγ. ἐὰν βροντήσῃ, λιμὸν βαρὺν ἀπειλεῖ.

ιδ. ἐὰν βροντήσῃ, νόσους ἀπειλεῖ.

ιε. ἐὰν βροντήσῃ, κατομβρίαν μὲν δηλοῖ, εὐθηνίαν δὲ ὅμως.

ις. ἐὰν βροντήσῃ, ὁ σπόρος πολύς, ἄκαρπος δὲ δηλοῦται.

ιζ. εἰ βροντήσῃ, ἔνδειαν τῶν ἀναγκαίων ἀπειλεῖ.

ιη. εἰ βροντήσῃ, λιμὸν ἅμα καὶ πολέμους σημαίνει.

ιθ. εἰ βροντήσῃ, ὁ μὲν δεωδρώδης καρπὸς ἐπιτεύξεται, νόσοι δὲ καὶ στάσεις δημοτικαὶ ἔσονται.

κ. εἰ βροντήσῃ, ἀπώλειαν κλεινοῦ ἀνθρώπου καὶ πόλεμον ἀπειλεῖ.

κα. εἰ βροντήσῃ, λύπας καὶ ζημίας τῷ δήμῳ ἀπειλεῖ.

κβ. εἰ βροντήσῃ, εὐθηνίαν μέν, χειμῶνα δὲ βαρὺν καὶ ὑγρὸν σημαίνει.

κγ. εἰ βροντήσῃ, τὸν χειμῶνα τοῦ ἔτους ἐνδεᾶ προλέγει.

κδ. εἰ βροντήσῃ, λειψυδρίαν ἀπειλεῖ. τῶν δὲ ἀκροδρύων εὐφορία ἔσται, περὶ τὸ φθινόπωρον θυέλλαις διαφθαρήσεται.

κε. εἰ βροντήσῃ, ἐκ διχονοίας τοῦ πολιτεύματος

τύραννος ἀναστήσεται, καὶ αὐτὸς θὲν ἀπολεῖται, ζημίαις δὲ ἀφορήτοις οἱ δυνατοὶ ὑποστήσονται.

κς. εἰ βροντήσῃ, ὁ κακὸς δυνάστης βουλῇ θεοῦ πεσεῖται.

κζ. εἰ βροντήσῃ, δυνατοὶ πρὸς ἑαυτοὺς διενεχθήσονται καὶ ἀλλήλους διαβολοῦσιν.

κη. εἰ βροντήσῃ, σημεῖα ἔσται πραγμάτων μεγάλων μηνυτικά. εὐλαβητέον δὲ μὴ καὶ πῦρ ἐπομβρήσῃ ἐνιαχοῦ.

κθ. εἰ βροντήσῃ, αὐχμὸν ἐπιβλαβῆ ἀπειλεῖ.

λ. εἰ βροντήσῃ, ἀπὸ χειρόνων ἐπὶ τὰ κρείττω τὰ κοινά.

ΟΚΤΩΒΡΙΟΣ

α. Εἰ βροντήσῃ, κακὸν τύραννον τοῖς πράγμασιν ἀπειλεῖ.

β. εἰ βροντήσῃ, εὐθηνία μὲν ἔσται, φθορὰ δὲ τῶν χερσαίων μυῶν.

γ. εἰ βροντήσῃ, θυέλλας καὶ ταραχὰς δηλοῖ, δι' ὧν τὰ μὲν δένδρα φθαρήσεται· μεγάλων δὲ ζαλῶν ἔσται τοῖς κοινοῖς μήνυμα.

δ. εἰ βροντήσῃ, οἱ ἐλάττους ⟨τὰ⟩ τῶν κρειττόνων καθέξουσιν, ὑγιεινὸν δὲ ἔσται τὸ τοῦ ἀέρος κατάστημα.

ε. εἰ βροντήσῃ, πάντων ἐπιδόσεις τῶν ἀναγκαίων, ἐξῃρημένου σίτου.

ς. εἰ βροντήσῃ, ἡ ὄψις μὲν εὐθηνίας, ἀμητὸς δὲ ἐλάττων, καὶ τὸ φθινόπωρον ἐγγὺς ἄκαρπον.

ζ. εἰ βροντήσῃ, ὄσπρια μὲν ἄφθονα, οἶνος δὲ ἐλάττων ἔσται.

η. εἰ βροντήσῃ, σεισμὸν μετὰ μυκήματος προσδοκητέον.

θ. εἰ βροντήσῃ, ὄλεθρον θηρίοις ἀπειλεῖ.

ι. εἰ βροντήσῃ, ἀνδρὸς ἐπαινουμένου πτῶσιν δηλοῖ.

ια. εἰ βροντήσῃ, ἀλληλανεμίαν ἐπισφαλῆ ταῖς βοτάναις δηλοῖ.

ιβ. εἰ βροντήσῃ, εὐθηνία μὲν ἔσται, σκηπτοὶ δὲ ἐκθλιβήσονται.

ιγ. εἰ βροντήσῃ, καλὰ τὰ συναλλάγματα, καὶ εὐθηνία πρὸς αὐτοῖς· ὁ δὲ ἐπὶ τῇ πολιτείᾳ βαρὺς οὐκ ἐπὶ πλέον ἰσχύσει.

ιδ. εἰ βροντήσῃ, πόλεμον καὶ φθορὰν βοσκημάτων ἀπειλεῖ.

ιε. εἰ βροντήσῃ, σπάνις ἔσται πνεύματος ξηροῦ καὶ καυστικοῦ ἐμπίπτοντος τοῖς καρποῖς.

ις. εἰ βροντήσῃ, ἐξασθενήσουσιν οὕτως ἄνθρωποι, ὡς ἄγνωστοι εἶναι δοκεῖν.

ιζ. εἰ βροντήσῃ, πλουσίου ἀνδρὸς καὶ εὐγενῶν εὐτυχήματα.

ιη. εἰ βροντήσῃ, ἐπείσακτον εὐθηνίαν δηλοῖ.

ιθ. εἰ βροντήσῃ, δυνάστου πτῶσιν ἢ βασιλέως ἐκβολὴν ἀπειλεῖ, διχόνοιάν τε τῷ δήμῳ καὶ ἀφθονίαν δηλοῖ.

κ. εἰ βροντήσῃ, ἕλκη ξένα ἀπειλεῖ, τῷ δὲ πλήθει ἐκ διχονοίας ἐσχάτην ἀτυχίαν.

κα. εἰ βροντήσῃ, νόσοι βηχώδεις ἔσονται καὶ στηθῶν κακώσεις.

κβ. εἰ βροντήσῃ, μοχθηρίας τῷ δήμῳ καὶ νόσους ποικίλας ἀπειλεῖ.

κγ. εἰ βροντήσῃ, ὁ δῆμος εὐφρανθήσεται παραδόξως.

κδ. εἰ βροντήσῃ, ἐκ διχονοίας τῶν κρατούντων ὁ δῆμος περιέσται.

κε. εἰ βροντήσῃ, βαρεῖα ἔσται ἀπὸ τῶν κακῶν δειλία.

κς. εἰ βροντήσῃ, αὐξηθήσεται μὲν τὰ θηρία, λιμώξει δὲ ὕως.

κζ. εἰ βροντήσῃ, ἐπομβρίαν δηλοῖ.

κη. εἰ βροντήσῃ, ἔνδεια ἔσται τῶν ἀναγκαίων.

κθ. εἰ βροντήσῃ, ἐπίνοσος ὁ ἐνιαυτός.

λ. εἰ βροντήσῃ, οὐκ εὐθηνίαν μόνον ἀλλὰ καὶ ἐλάττωσιν τῶν πολεμίων καὶ εὐφροσύνην τοῖς πράγμασι δηλοῖ.

ΝΟΕΜΒΡΙΟΣ

α. Εἰ βροντήσῃ, διχόνοιαν δηλοῖ τῇ πόλει.

β. εἰ βροντήσῃ, εὐθηνίαν προλέγει.

γ. εἰ βροντήσῃ, πράγματα ἀναφύεται, δι' ὧν οἱ ἐλάττους περιέσονται τῶν μειζόνων.

δ. εἰ βροντήσῃ, κρείττων ὁ σῖτος.

ε. εἰ βροντήσῃ, ζάλην τοῖς πράγμασι δηλοῖ, αἰσθητοῖς τε καὶ ἀλόγοις νόσον.

ς. εἰ βροντήσῃ, σκώληκες τῷ σίτῳ λυμανοῦνται.

ζ. εἰ βροντήσῃ, τοῖς ὑπὸ τὴν δύσιν ἀνθρώποις τε καὶ ἀλόγοις νόσοι.

η. εἰ βροντήσῃ, ἀδδηφαγίας ἔσεσθαι δεῖ διὰ νόσους ἀπειλουμένας.

θ. εἰ βροντήσῃ, δημοτῶν ἀνασκολοπισμοὶ ἔσονται, ἀλλὰ μὴν καὶ ἀφθονία τῶν ἐπιτηδείων.

ι. εἰ βροντήσῃ, πέρας ἔχει τὰ κακῶς βουλευθέντα τοῖς κρατοῦσιν, ἄνεμος δὲ καυσώδης τοῖς δένδροις λυμαίνεται.

ια. εἰ βροντήσῃ, εὐχαριστείτωσαν ἄνθρωποι τῷ θεῷ· ἄνεμος γὰρ ἐξ ἀνατολῶν ῥεύσει.

ιβ. εἰ βροντήσῃ, ἐνύπνια τοῖς ἀνθρώποις πλείονα δόξει.

ιγ. εἰ βροντήσῃ, ἐπικερδῆ μὲν τὸν καιρόν, λοιμικὸν δὲ ἀπειλεῖ, ἕλμισι δὲ ἐντοσθίοις κακοῖ τὰ σώματα.

ιδ. εἰ βροντήσῃ, ἑρπετὰ τοῖς ἀνθρώποις ἠρέμα πως λυμαίνεται.

ιε. εἰ βροντήσῃ, ὁ μὲν ἰχθὺς ἀφθονώτατος, λοιμώξει δὲ τὰ ἔνυδρα θηρία, καὶ τὰ κοινὰ δῆθεν καλλίονα.

ις. εἰ βροντήσῃ, ἀκρίδες καὶ μυῶν ἀρουραίων γένεσις, τῷ δὲ βασιλεῖ κίνδυνος, καὶ σίτου ἀφθονία ἔσται.

ιζ. εἰ βροντήσῃ, νομὴν ἄφθονον τοῖς κτήνεσι δηλοῖ.

ιη. εἰ βροντήσῃ, πόλεμον δηλοῖ καὶ τοῖς ἀστειοτέροις λύπας.

ιθ. εἰ βροντήσῃ, γυναικῶν εὐπραγίας.

κ. εἰ βροντήσῃ, λιμὸν ἀλλ' οὐκ εἰς μακρὰν δηλοῖ.

κα. εἰ βροντήσῃ, οἱ μύες φθαρήσονται, εὐθηνία δὲ οὐ σίτου μόνον ἀλλὰ καὶ νομῆς, καὶ ἰχθύων πλῆθος.

κβ. εἰ βροντήσῃ, εὐετηρίαν δηλοῖ.

κγ. εἰ βροντήσῃ, ἄνεμος νοσώδης πνεύσει.

κδ. εἰ βροντήσῃ, φρούριον τῇ πολιτείᾳ χρηστὸν ὑπὸ πολεμίοις τελέσει.

κε. εἰ βροντήσῃ, πόλεμος ἐπικίνδυνος ἔσται· καὶ ἄνεμος νοσώδης πνεύσει.

κϛ. εἰ βροντήσῃ, πόλεμον ἐμφύλιον καὶ πτῶσιν πολλῶν δηλοῖ· ὄμβροι τε ἔσονται λοιμώδεις.

κζ. εἰ βροντήσῃ, τὰ αὐτὰ ἀπειλεῖ.

κη. εἰ βροντήσῃ, τῆς συγκλήτου πολλοὶ ἀθυμίᾳ φθαρήσονται.

κθ. εἰ βροντήσῃ, οἱ μὲν χείρους κάλλιον πράξουσιν, αἱ δὲ ἐσόμεναι ὀπῶραι φθαρήσονται.

λ. εἰ βροντήσῃ, θεοφιλέστερον οἱ ἄνθρωποι ζήσονται· καὶ εἰκότως σύμμετρα τὰ κακά.

ΔΕΚΕΜΒΡΙΟΣ

α. Εἰ βροντήσῃ, εὐετηρίαν μεθ' ὁμονοίας δηλοῖ.

β. εἰ βροντήσῃ, ἀφθονία ἰχδύων καὶ καρπῶν διαφερόντως.

γ. εἰ βροντήσῃ, τοῖς θρέμμασιν ἄνθρωποι καταχρήσονται δι' ἔνδειαν ἰχθύων.

δ. εἰ βροντήσῃ, βαρὺς ἔσται χειμών, εὐθηνία δὲ ὅμως.

ε. εἰ βροντήσῃ, νόσους ψωρώδεις ἀπειλεῖ.

ϛ. εἰ βροντήσῃ, αἰσίους ὀνείρους οἱ ἄνθρωποι ἐνυπνιασθήσονται, οἳ κακὸν πέρας ἕξουσιν.

ζ. εἰ βροντήσῃ, τὸ αὐτὸ δηλοῖ πᾶσιν.

η. εἰ βροντήσῃ, νότος ἐπικρατήσει· ἐξ οὗ εὐθηνία μὲν καρπῶν ἔσται, ὄλεθρος δὲ θρεμμάτων.

θ. εἰ βροντήσῃ, κλεινοῦ ἀνδρὸς πτῶσις ἔσται.

ι. εἰ βροντήσῃ, φθορὰν ἀνθρώποις ἐκ νοσημάτων ἀπειλεῖ, οἱ δὲ ἰχθύες ἐπιδώσουσιν.

ια. εἰ βροντήσῃ, καυσώδης ἡ θερινὴ ἔσται τροπή, καὶ ἀφθονία ἐπείσακτος.

ιβ. εἰ βροντήσῃ, ἐκ γαστρορροίας νόσους ἀπειλεῖ.

ιγ. εἰ βροντήσῃ, εὐθηνίαν, νόσους δὲ ἀπειλεῖ.

ιδ. εἰ βροντήσῃ, ἐμφύλιον ἅμα πόλεμον καὶ εὐθηνίαν δηλοῖ.

ιε. εἰ βροντήσῃ, πολλοὶ ἐπὶ πόλεμον πορεύσονται, ὀλίγοι δὲ ἀναστρέψουσιν.

ιϛ. εἰ βροντήσῃ, καινοπρεπῆ πράγματα ἐπὶ τῆς πολιτείας.

ιζ. εἰ βροντήσῃ, ἀκρίδας φύσεσθαι λεπτὰς ἀπειλεῖ, εὐθηνίαν δὲ ὅμως.

ιη. εἰ βροντήσῃ, πόλεμος ἔσται βαρύς.

ιθ. εἰ βροντήσῃ, ἐπίτασιν τοῦ πολέμου ἀπειλεῖ.

κ. εἰ βροντήσῃ, ἔνδειαν τῶν ἀναγκαίων λέγει.

κα. εἰ βροντήσῃ, ἄνεμον θερμὸν καὶ νοσοποιὸν ῥεῦσαι ἀπειλεῖ.

κβ. εἰ βροντήσῃ, καυσῶδες ἔσται τὸ θέρος καὶ πολύκαρπον.

κγ. εἰ βροντήσῃ, ἀνθρώποις νόσον δηλοῖ, ἀλλ' ἀκίνδυνον.

κδ. εἰ βροντήσῃ, ἐμφυλίους πολέμους τῇ πόλει καὶ ὄλεθρον τοῖς ὑλαίοις θηρίοις ἀπειλεῖ.

κε. εἰ βροντήσῃ, ἐκστρατείας κίνησις ἐπὶ πόλεμον, ἀλλ' εὐτυχήσει.

κϛ. εἰ βροντήσῃ, νόσους τοῖς θεράπουσιν ἀπειλεῖ.

κζ. εἰ βροντήσῃ, ὁ βασιλεὺς πολλοὺς ὠφελήσει.

κη. εἰ βροντήσῃ, ἀκρίδων γένεσις.

κθ. εἰ βροντήσῃ, ἰσχνότητα τοῖς σώμασιν ὑγιεινὴν δηλοῖ.

λ. εἰ βροντήσῃ, ἀνταρσίαν κατὰ τῆς βασιλείας δηλοῖ καὶ εἰκότως πόλεμον.

ΙΑΝΟΥΑΡΙΟΣ

α. Εἰ βροντήσῃ, ἐλαφρὸς ἄνεμος ῥεύσει, ἀλλ' ἀκίνδυνος.

β. εἰ βροντήσῃ, ἀδόκητος ἔσται πόλεμος.

γ. εἰ βροντήσῃ, μετὰ νίκην ἧτταν τοῖς ἐν πολέμῳ φράζει· εὐθηνία δὲ ἔσται.

δ. εἰ βροντήσῃ, ὁμονοήσει ὁ δῆμος πρὸς εἰρήνην.

ε. εἰ βροντήσῃ, ὑγίειαν τοῖς κτήνεσι σημαίνει.

ϛ. εἰ βροντήσῃ, βηχώδη νόσον ἀπειλεῖ, ἀφθονίαν δὲ ἰχθύων καὶ καρπῶν δηλοῖ.

ζ. εἰ βροντήσῃ, δουλομαχία ἔσται καὶ νόσος συχνή.

η. εἰ βροντήσῃ, ὁ δυνάστης τῆς πολιτείας πρὸς τοῦ δήμου κινδυνεύσει.

θ. εἰ βροντήσῃ, ὁ τῆς ἀνατολῆς βασιλεὺς κινδυνεύσει.

ι. εἰ βροντήσῃ, ἀνέμου κίνησιν σφοδρὰν καὶ σίτου μὲν εὐφορίαν τῶν δ' ἄλλων καρπῶν ἀφορίαν δηλοῖ.

ια. εἰ βροντήσῃ, λιμὸν σημαίνει καὶ μέχρις ἀλόγων.

ιβ. εἰ βροντήσῃ, οἱ ἄνθρωποι τὰς ὄψεις νοσήσουσιν, ἔσται δὲ πολὺς χόρτος καὶ ἰχθύων ἐπίδοσις.

ιγ. εἰ βροντήσῃ, νόσους ἀπειλεῖ.

ιδ. εἰ βροντήσῃ, σπάνιν καὶ μυῶν γένεσιν καὶ ὄλεθρον τετραπόδων ἀπειλεῖ.

ιε. εἰ βροντήσῃ, στάσιν δουλικὴν καὶ τιμωρίαν αὐτοῖς καὶ εὐθηνίαν καρπῶν.

ιϛ. εἰ βροντήσῃ, ὁ δῆμος ὑπὸ τοῦ βασιλέως ταραχθήσεται.

ιζ. εἰ βροντήσῃ, νόσους ἀκινδύνους ἀπειλεῖ.

ιη. εἰ βροντήσῃ, πράγματα ἐκδειματοῦντα τὸν δῆμον ἀναστήσεται.

ιθ. εἰ βροντήσῃ, καὶ ὁ βασιλεὺς νικήσει καὶ ὁ δῆμος τὴν κρείττονα ἕξει τάξιν.

κ. εἰ βροντήσῃ, εὐθηνία μὲν ἐπείσακτος ἔσται, βηχώδης δὲ νόσος ἐνοχλήσει τοῖς σώμασιν.

κα. εἰ βροντήσῃ, ὁ βασιλεὺς πολλοῖς ἐπιβουλεύσας τέλος ἐπιβουλεύεται.

κβ. εἰ βροντήσῃ, εὐθηνία μὲν ἔσται, μυῶν δὲ καὶ ἐλάφων πλῆθος.

κγ. εἰ βροντήσῃ, εὐταξίαν τῇ πόλει δηλοῖ.

κδ. εἰ βροντήσῃ, νόσον μετὰ ἐνδείας δηλοῖ.

κε. εἰ βροντήσῃ, δουλομαχία ἔσται.

κς. εἰ βροντήσῃ, πολλοὶ πρὸς τοῦ κρατοῦντος ἀναιρεθήσονται, τέλος δὲ καὶ αὐτός.

κζ. εἰ βροντήσῃ, νόσους ἀκινδύνους δηλοῖ.

κη. εἰ βροντήσῃ, οἱ μὲν ἐνάλιοι ἰχθύες ἐπιδώσουσι, τὰ δὲ θρέμματα φθαρήσεται.

κθ. εἰ βροντήσῃ, λοιμικὸν καὶ νοσῶδες ἐπὶ πᾶσι τὸ τοῦ ἀέρος κατάστημα.

λ. εἰ βροντήσῃ, θάνατον συχνὸν ἀπειλεῖ.

ΦΕΒΡΟΥΑΡΙΟΣ

α. Εἰ βροντήσῃ, πόλεμον καὶ πτῶσιν ἀνδρῶν εὐπόρων ἀπειλεῖ.

β. εἰ βροντήσῃ, ὁ μὲν σῖτος ἐλάττων, ἡ δὲ κριθὴ κρείττων, καὶ θηρίων μὲν αὔξησις, φθίσις δὲ ἀνθρώπων ἔσται.

γ. εἰ βροντήσῃ, ἐμφύλοις ἔσται στάσις.

δ. εἰ βροντήσῃ, οἱ ἄνθρωποι οὐ προσώποις μόνον ἀλλὰ καὶ διανοίαις αὐταῖς ταραχθήσονται.

ε. εἰ βροντήσῃ, ἄμητος πολὺς καὶ ἀνθρώπων ἀπώλεια ἔσται.

ς. εἰ βροντήσῃ, φθορὰ τῶν ξηρῶν καρπῶν, καὶ διαφερόντως τῶν κριθῶν.

ζ. εἰ βροντήσῃ, φθορὰν οὐκ εἰς μακρὰν ἀνθρώποις ἀπειλεῖ.

η. εἰ βροντήσῃ, πρᾶγμα μέγιστον ἀναφύσεται τῇ πολιτείᾳ, καὶ οἱ μὲν ἰχθύες ἐπιδώσουσι, τὰ δὲ θηρία φθαρήσεται.

θ. εἰ βροντήσῃ, ἐλάττων ἡ κριθή.

ι. εἰ βροντήσῃ, τὰ θηρία τοῖς ἀνθρώποις λυμανεῖται.

ια. εἰ βροντήσῃ, εὐτοκία γυναικῶν.

ιβ. εἰ βροντήσῃ, θάνατον συχνὸν ἀπειλεῖ καὶ ἀνέμους ἀήθεις.

ιγ. εἰ βροντήσῃ, εὐθηνία μὲν ἔσται, στάσις δὲ ὅμως πολιτική.

ιδ. εἰ βροντήσῃ, ἀποβολὴν τέκνων καὶ ἔφοδον ἑρπετῶν ἐπιβλαβῆ ἀπειλεῖ.

ιε. εἰ βροντήσῃ, λοιμικὸς ἀὴρ ἔσται, θηρίων τε καὶ μυῶν γένεσος.

ις. εἰ βροντήσῃ, τῷ μὲν δήμῳ αἴσιον, τοῖς δὲ δυνατοῖς ἐκ διχονοίας κακόν.

ιζ. εἰ βροντήσῃ, θέρος ἔσται ἀφθονώτατον.

ιη. εἰ βροντήσῃ, ἄνεμον βαρὺν καὶ φλυκταινῶν ἀνάστημα τοῖς σώμασιν ἀπειλεῖ.

ιθ. εἰ βροντήσῃ, ἑρπετῶν καὶ ἑλμίνθων πρὸς αὐτοῖς ὄχλος ἔσται.

κ. εἰ βροντήσῃ, καλοὺς ἀέρας δηλοῖ.

κα. εἰ βροντήσῃ, εὐθηνίαν δηλοῖ.

κβ. εἰ βροντήσῃ, ἐπίνοσος ὁ ἀήρ, ἀλλ᾽ οὐ φθαρτικὸς ἔσται.

κγ. εἰ βροντήσῃ, ἀνθρώποις μὲν δυσμορφίαν, ὀρνέοις δὲ φθορὰν ἀπειλεῖ.

κδ. εἰ βροντήσῃ, ὑγίειαν μὲν ἀνθρώποις, ἰχθύσι δὲ καὶ ἑρπετοῖς ὄλεθρον ἀπειλεῖ.

κε. εἰ βροντήσῃ, τοῖς τρυφῶσιν ἐναντίον· πόλεμοι γὰρ ἔσονται, καὶ ζάλη βαρεῖα.

κς. εἰ βροντήσῃ, αὐχμὸν καὶ λειψυδρίαν καὶ ψώρωσιν τοῖς σώμασιν ἀπειλεῖ.

κζ. εἰ βροντήσῃ, στάσιν τῷ δήμῳ δηλοῖ.

κη. εἰ βροντήσῃ, εὐθηνίαν μέν, ἄνεμον δὲ νοσοποιὸν ῥεῦσαι μαντεύεται.

κθ. εἰ βροντήσῃ, πόλεμον καὶ εὐθηνίαν δηλοῖ.

λ. εἰ βροντήσῃ, ἀγαθὰ σημαίνει μετὰ μακρᾶς τινος τοῦ δήμου διχοστασίας.

ΜΑΡΤΙΟΣ

α. Εἰ βροντήσῃ, ἅπαν τὸ ἔτος ἀψιμαχίαι καὶ διχόνοιαι ἔσονται.

β. εἰ βροντήσῃ, παύσεται τὰ προαπειλούμενα.

γ. εἰ βροντήσῃ, κακοδαιμονία μετὰ ἐνδείας τοῖς πράγμασιν.

δ. εἰ βροντήσῃ, εὐθηνία ἀφθονωτάτη ἔσται.

ε. εἰ βροντήσῃ, εὐήλιον τὸ ἔαρ καὶ εὔκαρπον τὸ θέρος ἔσται.

ς. εἰ βροντήσῃ, ὅμοια τοῖς πρὸ ταύτης.

ζ. εἰ βροντήσῃ, ἄνεμος βαρὺς ἀναστήσεται, ὁ δὲ κρατῶν τὰ πράγματα κινήσει.

η. εἰ βροντήσῃ, βροχὰς σημαίνει.

θ. εἰ βροντήσῃ, φθορὰν μὲν ἀνθρώπων, γένεσιν δὲ θηρίων ἀπειλεῖ.

ι. εἰ βροντήσῃ, φθορὰ τοῖς τετραπόδοις.

ια. εἰ βροντήσῃ, κατομβρίαν καὶ ἀκρίδων γένεσιν δηλοῖ.

ιβ. εἰ βροντήσῃ, δυνατὸς τοῦ πολιτεύματος ἢ στρατηγὸς

κινδυνεύσει, διὸ μάχαι συρραγήσονται, καὶ τὰ θηρία τοῖς ἀνθρώποις ἐπέλθῃ.

ιγ. εἰ βροντήσῃ, εὐθηνία ἔσται, τὰ δὲ θηρία φθαρήσεται, καὶ οἱ ἰχθύες ἐπιδώσουσι· καὶ ἑρπετὰ τοῖς οἰκήμασιν ἐνοχλήσει, οὐ μὴν βλάψει.

ιδ. εἰ βροντήσῃ, εὐθηνίαν μὲν σημαίνει, θάνατον δὲ ἀνθρώπων καὶ γένεσιν θηρίων ἀπειλεῖ.

ιε. εἰ βροντήσῃ, καύματα σημαίνει καὶ λειψυδρίαν καὶ μυῶν ὄχλον καὶ ἰχθύων πολύν.

ις. εἰ βροντήσῃ, ὑγιεινὸν μὲν τὸ ἔτος, ἀλλ' ἐνδεὲς τῶν ἐπιτηδείων.

ιζ. εἰ βροντήσῃ, πρᾶγμα παράδοξον τῷ δήμῳ συμβήσεται, συχνὴ δὲ φθορὰ ἀνθρώποις τε καὶ θηρίοις τετράποσιν.

ιη. εἰ βροντήσῃ, κατομβρίαν καὶ νόσον καὶ ἀκρίδων γένεσιν καὶ ἐγγὺς ἀκαρπίαν δηλοῖ.

ιθ. εἰ βροντήσῃ, αὐχμὸς ξηρότατος καὶ φθοροποιός.

κ. εἰ βροντήσῃ, εὐπορώτερον οἱ ἄνθρωποι ἅμα καὶ ἀφθονώτερον ζήσονται.

κα. εἰ βροντήσῃ, εὐθηνίαν μετὰ πολέμους καὶ φθορώδεις αὐχμοὺς δηλοῖ.

κβ. εἰ βροντήσῃ, φθορὰν μὲν ὀρνέων, ἐπίδοσιν δὲ τῶν ἐπιτηδείων.

κγ. εἰ βροντήσῃ, στάσεις δηλοῖ.

κδ. εἰ βροντήσῃ, εὐθηνίαν σημαίνει.

κε. εἰ βροντήσῃ, καινὰ πράγματα τῷ δήμῳ ἀνὰ φύεται.

κς. εἰ βροντήσῃ, κτῆσιν ἐπεισάκτων ἀνδραπόδων δηλοῖ.

κζ. εἰ βροντήσῃ, ἐπείσακτον εὐθηνίαν δηλοῖ.

κη. εἰ βροντήσῃ, ἀφθονία ἰχθύων θαλαττίων ἔσται.

κθ. εἰ βροντήσῃ, αἱ γυναῖκες τῆς κρείττονος δόξης ἀνθέξονται.

λ. εἰ βροντήσῃ, δυνατός τις τῆς βασιλείας ἐγκρατὴς ἔσται, δι' οὗ εὐφροσύνη.

ΑΠΡΙΛΙΟΣ

α. Εἰ βροντήσῃ, ἐμφύλιον στάσιν καὶ ἀποπτώσεις οὐσιῶν ἀπειλεῖ.

β. εἰ βροντήσῃ, δίκης σημεῖον, ἐσθλοῖς ἐσθλὰ φερούσης καὶ φαύλοις φαῦλα.

γ. εἰ βροντήσῃ, κέρδη ἐξ ἐπεισάκτου εὐθηνίας δηλοῖ.

δ. εἰ βροντήσῃ, ὀργὴν τῶν κρειττόνων ἀπειλεῖ τοῖς ἀξίοις.

ε. εἰ βροντήσῃ, αὐχμὸν μὲν τῷ ἦρι, ὑγιεινὸν δὲ τὸν ἐνιαυτὸν σημαίνει.

ς. εἰ βροντήσῃ, πόλεμοι ἐμφύλιοι ἀναστήσονται.

ζ. εἰ βροντήσῃ, ἀγαθὰ πάντα καὶ ἄφθονον εὐετηρίαν δηλοῖ.

η. εἰ βροντήσῃ, κατομβρίαν δηλοῖ ἐπίνοσον.

θ. εἰ βροντήσῃ, νίκην τῇ βασιλείᾳ δηλοῖ καὶ τοῖς δυνατοῖς εὐφροσύνην.

ι. εἰ βροντήσῃ, ἀνδρῶν ἀγαθῶν προκοπαὶ ἔσονται.

ια. εἰ βροντήσῃ, τὰ αὐτὰ σημαίνει.

ιβ. εἰ βροντήσῃ, βροχὰς καὶ εὐθηνίας καὶ φθορὰν ἰχθύων δηλοῖ.

ιγ. εἰ βροντήσῃ, ἀνθρώποις καὶ κτήνεσι φθορὰν ἀπειλεῖ.

ιδ. εἰ βροντήσῃ, ὑγίειαν καὶ εὐθηνίαν δηλοῖ.

ιε. εἰ βροντήσῃ, λοιμὸν σημαίνει.

ις. εἰ βροντήσῃ, εὐθηνίαν μέν, μυῶν δὲ ἀρουραίων γένεσιν δηλοῖ.

ιζ. εἰ βροντήσῃ, ἀφθονίαν τῶν ἐπιτηδείων σημαίνει.

ιη. εἰ βροντήσῃ, διχόνοιαν καὶ ἀνδρῶν ἀστοχίαν σημαίνει.

ιθ. εἰ βροντήσῃ, δυνατὸς ἀνὴρ τῆς πολιτείας οὐσίας ἅμα καὶ δόξης ἀφαιρεθήσεται.

κ. εἰ βροντήσῃ, θεοχολωσίαν σημαίνει.

κα. εἰ βροντήσῃ, τοῖς μὲν καρποῖς δεξιόν, τῇ δὲ πολιτείᾳ πόλεμον σημαίνει.

κβ. εἰ βροντήσῃ, φθορὰ τῶν μυῶν ἔσται.

κγ. εἰ βροντήσῃ, βροχὴν ὠφέλιμον τοῖς σπορίμοις δηλοῖ.

κδ. εἰ βροντήσῃ, διχόνοια ἔσται τῶν δυνατῶν, τὰ δὲ σκέμματα αὐτῶν ἀναφανήσεται.

κε. εἰ βροντήσῃ, εἰρήνη ἀνὰ πάντα τὸν ἐνιαυτόν.

κς. εἰ βροντήσῃ, ἐλπίδα καρπῶν μεγάλην καὶ ἀμήτων σπάνιν δηλοῖ.

κζ. εἰ βροντήσῃ, διοσημεία παράδοξος ὀφθήσεται.

κη. εἰ βροντήσῃ, ὅπλοις ὁ δῆμος ἀναζώσεται.

κθ. εἰ βροντήσῃ, ἐπικρατήσει ὁ ζέφυρος.

λ. εἰ βροντήσῃ, πραγμάτων καλῶν ἐπομβρία.

ΜΑΙΟΣ

α. Εἰ βροντήσῃ, φυγὴν τῷ δήμῳ καὶ ἀτιμίαν δηλοῖ.

β. εἰ βροντήσῃ, λιμὸν ἀπειλεῖ.

γ. εἰ βροντήσῃ, ἐπείσακτον εὐθηνίαν δηλοῖ.

δ. εἰ βροντήσῃ, εὔκρατος ἀήρ, καὶ οἱ καρποὶ εὐθηνοὶ ἔσονται.

ε. εἰ βροντήσῃ, ἐναλλαγὴ τῶν λυπηρῶν τοῖς πράγμασιν ἔσται, καὶ πλείων ὁ σῖτος ἤπερ ἡ κριθή· τὰ δὲ ὄσπρια φθαρήσεται.

ς. εἰ βροντήσῃ, θᾶττον ἀκμάσαι τοὺς καρποὺς καὶ φθαρῆναι δηλοῖ.

ζ. εἰ βροντήσῃ, ὀρνέων καὶ ἰχθύων ἀφθονία ἔσται.

η. εἰ βροντήσῃ, ἀπαίσιον τῷ δήμῳ.

θ. εἰ βροντήσῃ, λοιμὸν σημαίνει, ἀλλὰ μετρίως ἐπικίνδυνον.

ι. εἰ βροντήσῃ, ταραχὰς κατομβρίας καὶ ὑπερχύσεις

ποταμῶν ἐπιβλαβεῖς δηλοῖ, σαυρῶν τε καὶ ἑρπετῶν πλῆθος.

ια. εἰ βροντήσῃ, εὐθηνίαν κατά τε τὴν γῆν κατά τε τὴν θάλασσαν ἐλπιστέον.

ιβ. εἰ βροντήσῃ, φθορὰ ἰχθύων ἔσται.

ιγ. εἰ βροντήσῃ, ἐπίδοσιν ποταμίων ὑδάτων δηλοῖ, νόσους δὲ τοῖς ἀνθρώποις.

ιδ. εἰ βροντήσῃ, ἀνατολικὸς ἔσται πόλεμος καὶ φθορὰ πολλή.

ιε. εἰ βροντήσῃ, εὐθηνίαν δηλοῖ.

ις. εἰ βροντήσῃ, εὔχεσθαι δεῖ διὰ τὰ ἀπειλούμενα.

ιζ. εἰ βροντήσῃ, ὑετὸν σημαίνει.

ιη. εἰ βροντήσῃ, στάσιν καὶ ἐξ αὐτῆς πόλεμον καὶ ἔνδειαν τῶν ἐπιτηδείων.

ιθ. εἰ βροντήσῃ, εὐνοίᾳ τοῦ δήμου ἀνήρ τις εἰς ἄκρον εὐδαιμονίας ἀρθήσεται.

κ. εἰ βροντήσῃ, τοῖς μὲν περὶ τὴν ἀνατολὴν εὐθηνία, τοῖς δὲ ἐπὶ δύσιν οὐχ οὕτως.

κα. εἰ βροντήσῃ, εὐχῶν δεῖ διὰ τὰ ἀπειλούμενα.

κβ. εἰ βροντήσῃ, κατομβρίαν καὶ φθορὰν τῶν θαλαττίων ἰχθύων σημαίνει.

κγ. εἰ βροντήσῃ, εὐομβρίαν καρποφόρον δηλοῖ.

κδ. εἰ βροντήσῃ, μεγάλα κακά, ὡς ἐξ ἀθυμίας λειποθυμῆσαι τοὺς ὑπηκόους.

κε. εἰ βροντήσῃ, ἀνάπαυλαν καὶ ὕφεσιν τῶν κακῶν ἐλπιστέον.

κς. εἰ βροντήσῃ, καλὸν τοῖς περὶ γεωργίαν ἔχουσιν.

κζ. εἰ βροντήσῃ, διοσημεία ἔσται καὶ κομήτης ἐξαφθήσεται.

κη. εἰ βροντήσῃ, ὡσαύτως ἔσται.

κθ. εἰ βροντήσῃ, πόλεμον ἀρκτῷον σημαίνει, ἀλλ' ἀκίνδυνον τοῖς πράγμασιν.

λ. εἰ βροντήσῃ, τὰ φυτὰ τῷ ἀνέμῳ συντριβήσεται. Ταύτην τὴν ἐφήμερον βροντοσκοπίαν ὁ Νιγίδιος οὐ καθολικὴν ἀλλὰ μόνης εἶναι τῆς Ῥώμης ἔκρινεν.

BRONTOSCOPIC CALENDAR

Arrangement according to the lunar month
By the Roman Figulus
From the sayings of Tages
Account translated word for word

27. Supposing that publicly, in all augural teaching, the ancients assumed the moon to be a reference point (for under this heading they classified both thunder- and lightning-signs), one likewise may correctly select the phase of the moon as a factor for reckoning, so that, beginning with Cancer, we shall make observations of thunder day by day, beginning with the first day of the lunar month, and following lunar months. From this [study] the Etruscans transmitted local observations with regard to the regions that are struck from the sky by thunder.

IN THE MONTH OF JUNE

Full Moon.[1] 1. If in any way it should thunder, there will be an abundance of fruits, with the exception of barley; but dangerous diseases will be inflicted upon bodies.

2. If in any way it should thunder, women in labor will have an easy delivery, but there will be abortion of cattle, yet there will be an abundance of fish.

3. If in any way it should thunder, there will be a scorching and drying wind, such that not only grains but even the soft fruits will be parched through and through and shrivel up.

4. If in any way it should thunder, the air will be cloudy and rainy, so that out of a moldy dampness the fruit crops will rot.

5. If in any way it should thunder, ill-omened for the countryside. Those responsible for villages or towns will be thrown into a state of disorder.

6. If in any way it should thunder, just as the crops are maturing, some sort of wild pest that has sunk deep into them will waste them.

7. If in any way it should thunder, diseases will infect [men], but not many shall die. And while the cereal crops shall be successful, the soft fruits shall dry up.

8. If in any way it should thunder, it indicates wet weather and ruin of the grain.

9. If in any way it should thunder, there will be a loss of flocks through being overrun by wolves.

10. If in any way it should thunder, there will be frequent death, yet prosperity.

11. If in any way it should thunder, there will be days of heat, burning but harmless; there will be glad festivities in state affairs.

12. If in any way it should thunder, the same thing as on the preceding day.

13. If in any way it should thunder, it announces the fall of a ruler.

14. If in any way it should thunder, the atmosphere shall be burning hot, but there will be abundant harvest and good flow, not the poorest, of the river fish. Bodies, nevertheless, shall be utterly weak.

15. If in any way it should thunder, the feathered creatures shall be injured during the summer, and also the fishes shall perish.

16. If in any way it should thunder, it threatens not only dearth of the necessities of life but also war, while a prosperous man shall disappear from public life.

17. If in any way it should thunder, there shall be days of burning heat and destruction by mice, blind mice, and locusts. Still, it brings abundance and at the same time murders to the people.

18. If in any way it should thunder, it threatens destruction to the crops.[2]

19. If in any way it should thunder, pests destructive to the crops shall perish.

20. If in any way it should thunder, it threatens discord for the community.

21. If in any way it should thunder, it means there will be a dearth of wine, but an increase in the other crops, and an abundance of fish.

22. If in any way it should thunder, the hot weather will be especially ruinous.

23. If in any way it should thunder, it announces good cheer, a putting aside of ills, and an end to disease.

24. If in any way it should thunder, it announces plenty.

25. If in any way it should thunder, there will be wars and countless ills.

26. If in any way it should thunder, the winter will be especially harmful to the crops.

27. If in any way it should thunder, there is danger from the army for the men in power.

28. If in any way it should thunder, there will be a good harvest for the crops.

29. If in any way it should thunder, the affairs of the ruling city[3] will be improved.

30. If in any way it should thunder, in a short time there shall be frequent death.

JULY

28. 1. Upon the new moon, if in any way it should thunder, there shall be plenty, yet there shall be ruin[4] of the flocks.

2. If in any way it should thunder, the late autumn will be good.

3. If in any way it should thunder, it signals a heavy winter.

4. If in any way it should thunder, the airs will be turbulent, so that of them will be born scarcity.

5. If in any way it should thunder, there will be an abundance of grain, yet it is the downfall of a virtuous ruler.

6. If in any way it should thunder, it threatens death-bearing diseases to the fortunes of slaves.

7. If in any way it should thunder, there will be rains harmful to the grain fields.

8. If in any way it should thunder, it signifies peace for the community, but ruin for the cattle herds, and a dry cough shall infect.

9. If in any way it should thunder, it foretells a vision of the gods and the advancement of many good men.

10. If in any way it should thunder, there will be lifesaving river waters.

11. If in any way it should thunder, it signals hot weather and stormy rain and a scarcity of grain.

12. If in any way it should thunder, there will be unexpected cold in the summer, because of which the necessities of life will be spoiled.

13. If in any way it should thunder, there will appear the most poisonous reptiles.

14. If in any way it should thunder, it shows one man will come to power over many. But this man is most unjust in state affairs.

15. If in any way it should thunder, there will be dissension among the common people and a scarcity of grain.

16. If in any way it should thunder, the king of the East . . . will be overcome [by?] war . . .[5] and disease will be received from dry hot weather.

17. If in any way it should thunder, it signifies the succession of a great ruler.

18. If in any way it should thunder, it threatens a dearth of crops due to rainy weather.

19. If in any way it should thunder, it signifies war and the destruction of the powerful. On the other hand, there will be a plenty of cereals.

20. If in any way it should thunder, it threatens an unhealthy drought.

21. If in any way it should thunder, there will be disagreement among the subjects, but not for long.

22. If in any way it should thunder, it signals good things for the affairs of state, but for the bodies, diseases around the head.

23. If in any way it should thunder, the dissension of the common people will come to an end.

24. If in any way it should thunder, it shows the possible misfortune of a powerful man.

25. If in any way it should thunder, it will go badly for a band of youth and also for the crops along with them. It will be a disease-bearing time.

26. If in any way it should thunder, after great plenty there will be famine.

27. If in any way it should thunder, it threatens subcutaneous eruptions to [men's] bodies.

28. If in any way it should thunder, there will be a dearth of water and a plague of poisonous reptiles.

29. If in any way it should thunder, it signifies a good harvest.

30. If in any way it should thunder, men bent on vengeance shall slip into the worst kind of treachery.

AUGUST

29. 1. If in any way it should thunder, the affairs of the state will be slightly better, and there will be plenty.

2. If in any way it should thunder, it threatens both diseases and at the same time a dearth of the necessities of life.

3. If in any way it should thunder, it threatens both [public] trials and debates among the common people.

4. If in any way it should thunder, there will be a dearth of foodstuffs for both humans and dumb animals.

5. If in any way it should thunder, it signifies that the women are the more sagacious.

6. If in any way it should thunder, there will be an abundance of honey, yet a lack of both water and the other foodstuffs.

7. If in any way it should thunder, it signals harsh winds and diseases at the same time.

8. If in any way it should thunder, it threatens harmless disease to the four-footed.

9. If in any way it should thunder, it proclaims good health for men for a full year.

10. If in any way it should thunder, it threatens pains/suffering and wretchedness for the greater part of the people.

11. If in any way it should thunder, there will be a good harvest, yet the downfall of reptiles and harm to men.

12. If in any way it should thunder, there will be an abundance of cattle fodder and of acorns, but in the first ripening season, it will go badly.

13. If in any way it should thunder, there will be plague upon the bodies of both humans and dumb animals.

14. If in any way it should thunder, it signals war for all the people, yet an abundance of crops.

15. If in any way it should thunder, affairs will change for the worse.

16. If in any way it should thunder, it promises a deep peace.

17. If in any way it should thunder, the men of lowly degree shall be gloomy.

18. If in any way it should thunder, it threatens civil war.

19. If in any way it should thunder, the women and the servile class will dare to commit murders.

20. If in any way it should thunder, it threatens a plague on the cattle and disorder in the affairs of state.

21. If in any way it should thunder, it threatens at once prosperity and discord among the commons.

22. If in any way it should thunder, affairs will be moderately good for an entire year.

23. If in any way it should thunder, it signifies that the lightning bolt shall fall, and warns of slaughter.

24. If in any way it should thunder, it threatens the loss of well-born youths.

25. If in any way it should thunder, it foretells that during a stormy winter there will be a shortage of tree fruits.

26. If in any way it should thunder, it signals war.

27. If in any way it should thunder, it threatens at once wars and treachery.

28. If in any way it should thunder, it signals both an abundance of crops and a loss by death of cattle.

29. If in any way it should thunder, it signals no sort of reversal.

30. If in any way it should thunder, it threatens diseases in the city over which it [the thunder] is cast down.

SEPTEMBER

30. 1. If in any way it should thunder, it signifies both a good harvest and good cheer.

2. If in any way it should thunder, there will be discord among the common people.

3. If in any way it should thunder, it signifies heavy rains and war.

4. If in any way it should thunder, it signifies the downfall of a powerful man and preparation for war.

5. If in any way it should thunder, it signifies an abundance of barley but a decrease in wheat.

6. If in any way it should thunder, there shall be power among the women greater than [what is] appropriate to their nature.

7. If in any way it should thunder, it threatens a disease and out of it, a disaster for the servile class.

8. If in any way it should thunder, it indicates that those especially powerful will consider crooked dealings in government, but they will not achieve their aims.[6]

9. If in any way it should thunder, it threatens that a disease-bearing wind will blow.

10. If in any way it should thunder, there will be strife in the area in which the thunder is let loose; for another place [it is] not inapplicable.

11. If in any way it should thunder, the underlings of the well born will foment revolution in the state.

12. If in any way it should thunder, it says that the time of harvest shall be very rainy and there shall be famine.

13. If in any way it should thunder, it threatens grave famine.

14. If in any way it should thunder, it threatens diseases.

15. If in any way it should thunder, it signifies a wet spell, but at the same time, prosperity.

16. If in any way it should thunder, it is made known that there will be good sprouting, but [the plants will be] fruitless.

17. If it thunders, it threatens a lack of the necessities.

18. If it thunders, it signals both famine and wars.

19. If it thunders, the fruits of the trees will be successful, but there will be diseases and sedition among the commons.

20. If it thunders, it threatens the destruction of a famous man and war.

21. If it thunders, it threatens ills and losses for the people.

22. If it thunders, it signals prosperity yet a heavy and wet winter.

23. If it thunders, it foretells a time of need during the winter of the year.

24. If it thunders, it threatens a drought. There will be an abundant harvest of the nut trees; around late autumn though, they will be destroyed by storms.

25. If it thunders, out of civil unrest a tyrant shall be raised up, and he will be undone, but the powerful will be destroyed utterly with insufferable penalties.

26. If it thunders, a corrupt ruler will be felled by divine decision.

27. If it thunders, powerful men will work hatred toward themselves and shall take sides against each other.

28. If it thunders, there will be signs revealing great things. Beware lest it pour rain upon the fire of joyful elation.

29. If it thunders, it threatens a severe drought.

30. If it thunders, affairs of state [shall change] from worse to better.

OCTOBER

31. 1. If it thunders, it threatens a corrupt tyrant over the affairs of state.

2. If it thunders, there will be prosperity but the destruction of the mice of dry land.

3. If it thunders, it signifies hurricanes and disturbances by which the trees will be overturned; there will be a great disruption in the affairs of common people.

4. If it thunders, the lower classes will have the upper hand over their betters, and the mildness of the air will be healthy.

5. If it thunders, there will be a surplus of all the necessities except grain.

6. If it thunders, appearance of future abundance, yet harvest will be less plentiful and autumn practically empty of fruit.

7. If it thunders, pulses will be plentiful but wine less.

8. If it thunders, an earthquake with roaring sound is to be expected.

9. If it thunders, it threatens destruction to wild beasts.

10. If it thunders, it signifies the downfall of a praiseworthy man.

11. If it thunders, it signifies a strange sort of wind will be of service to the pastures.

12. If it thunders, there will be prosperity, but wind squalls will oppress.

13. If it thunders, covenants/commerce will be good, and prosperity in addition. He who controls the government with heavy hand will not be strong for very long.

14. If it thunders, it threatens war and the loss of flocks to death.

15. If it thunders, there will be scarcity from a dry and searing wind falling upon the crops.

16. If it thunders, men will be weakened in such a manner that they will seem to be unrecognizable.

17. If it thunders, good fortune for a rich man and for men [who are] well born.

18. If it thunders, it signifies a plentiful grain supply brought in from foreign lands.

19. If it thunders, it warns of the downfall of a ruler or the overthrow of a king, but it warns of both discord among the common people and abundance.

20. If it thunders, it warns there will be a festering wound, and for the many, extreme suffering out of the discord.

21. If it thunders, there will be coughing sicknesses and oppression of the heart.

22. If it thunders, it threatens bad conditions and spotted diseases for the people.

23. If it thunders, the people will be of marvelously good cheer.

24. If it thunders, out of the discord of those in power, the common people will oppress [others].

25. If it thunders, there will be heavy misery resulting from misfortunes.

26. If it thunders, there will be an increase of animals, but at the same time they will suffer thirst.

27. If it thunders, it signifies heavy rains.

28. If it thunders, there will be a dearth of the necessities.

29. If it thunders, a year of serious disease.

30. If it thunders, it signifies not merely prosperity, but even fewer enemies, and good cheer for the state.

NOVEMBER

32. 1. If it thunders, it signifies discord for the city.

2. If it thunders, it foretells prosperity.

3. If it thunders, situations will pertain through which the lower classes will oppress [their] betters.

4. If it thunders, grain will be better.

5. If it thunders, it signifies storm for the state, and disease for humans and dumb animals alike.

6. If it thunders, borers will ruin the grain.

7. If it thunders, for those who are in the West, both humans and dumb beasts, diseases.

8. If it thunders, it says gluttony shall come about from menacing diseases.

9. If it thunders, the common people will be led into misery, but [there will be] an abundance of daily provisions.

10. If it thunders, for those in power, it makes an end to their perverted plans. A parching wind will wrack the trees.

11. If it thunders, men shall give blessings to the god, for the wind shall blow out of the East.

12. If it thunders, it indicates insomnia for some time for men.

13. If it thunders, a wealthy yet sickly period threatens, tormenting bodies with internal worms.

14. If it thunders, poisonous snakes shall somehow be gently undone by the men.

15. If it thunders, the fish will be especially plentiful, but it shall plague the water-bound beasts. The commonwealth rather better.

16. If it thunders, the creation of locusts and field voles, to the king, danger, and there will be an abundance of grain.

17. If it thunders, it signifies plentiful fodder for the flocks.

18. If it thunders, it signifies war and woes for city folk.

19. If it thunders, welfare of women.

20. If it thunders, it signifies famine not of long duration.

21. If it thunders, the mice shall perish; an abundance not merely of grain but also of pasturage, and a plenty of fishes.

22. If it thunders, it signifies a year of well-being.

23. If it thunders, disease-bearing wind will blow.

24. If it thunders, the watch-post shall complete for the state good service against enemy tricks.

25. If it thunders, there will be a very dangerous war.

26. If it thunders, it signifies a civil war and the death of many.

27. If it thunders, it threatens the same.

28. If it thunders, many of the councilmen of the wealthier rank shall be ruined utterly by cowardice.

29. If it thunders, the lower classes will do better, but the hoped-for fruit harvest shall be destroyed.

30. If it thunders, the mortals shall live in a condition more favored by the gods. Naturally, evils [will come] in due proportion.

DECEMBER

33. 1. If it thunders, it signifies a year of well-being corresponding to concord.

2. If it thunders, a plenty of fish and especially of fruits.

3. If it thunders, men will excessively consume their flocks because of a dearth of fish.

4. If it thunders, winter will be heavy, yet [there will be] abundance as well.

5. If it thunders, it threatens mangy diseases.

6. If it thunders, the men shall be visited with visions of the faces of the gods, they shall experience a bad outcome.

7. If it thunders, it signifies the same for all.

8. If it thunders, virulent disease; out of it, though, will be an abundance of crops, but a plague on the flocks.

9. If it thunders, there will be the downfall of a famous man.

10. If it thunders, it threatens slaughter for men from diseases, but the fish shall be abundant.

11. If it thunders, heat-bearing shall be the summer season, and plenty imported from foreign lands.

12. If it thunders, it threatens diseases from diarrhea.

13. If it thunders, plenty, yet diseases it threatens.

14. If it thunders, it signifies at the same time civil war and abundance.

15. If it thunders, many will set out for war, but few shall return.

16. If it thunders, newfangled affairs for the state.

17. If it thunders, it threatens that small locusts shall be born, yet there will still be plenty.

18. If it thunders, there shall be a heavy war.

19. If it thunders, it threatens prolongation of war.

20. If it thunders, it tells a lack of the necessities.

21. If it thunders, it threatens a hot and disease-making wind will blow.

22. If it thunders, the summer will be hot but plentiful in crops.

23. If it thunders, it signifies a disease for men but a harmless one.

24. If it thunders, it threatens civil wars for the city and a plague on the beasts of the woods.

25. If it thunders, a movement of troops to war, but it will turn out well.

26. If it thunders, it threatens diseases for the slaves.

27. If it thunders, the king will help many.

28. If it thunders, the hatching of locusts.

29. If it thunders, it signifies the most healthful leanness for the bodies.

30. If it thunders, it signifies a rebellion against the kingdom and, reasonably, war.

JANUARY

34. 1. If it thunders, a fast wind will blow, but not dangerous.

2. If it thunders, there will be unlooked-for war.

3. If it thunders, it shows after victory, loss for those in the war. Still, there will be plenty.

4. If it thunders, the common people will agree to make peace.

5. If it thunders, it signals health for the flocks.

6. If it thunders, it threatens a coughing sickness but signifies an abundance of fish and of fruits.

7. If it thunders, there will be a slave revolt and recurring illness.

8. If it thunders, the ruler of the state shall be in danger from the people.

9. If it thunders, the king of the East shall be in danger.

10. If it thunders, it signifies rapid movement of wind, and a plenty of grain, but a dearth of other crops.

11. If it thunders, it signals famine [reaching] just up to dumb animals.

12. If it thunders, men shall be damaged in their faces, but there will be much fodder [for horses/cattle], and a plenty of fish.

13. If it thunders, it threatens diseases.

14. If it thunders, it threatens need, and the creation/appearance of mice, and the slaughter of four-footed creatures.

15. If it thunders, servile revolt, and punishment for them, and abundance of crops.

16. If it thunders, the people shall be oppressed by the king.

17. If it thunders, it threatens nondangerous diseases.

18. If it thunders, affairs circulating abroad shall make the people rise up.

19. If it thunders, when the king will have victory, then the common people will have the upper hand/stronger position.

20. If it thunders, there will be abundance of imported goods, but a coughing disease will afflict bodies.

21. If it thunders, the king hated by many shall be the object of a final plot.

22. If it thunders, there will be plenty, but also there will be an abundance of mice and of deer.

23. If it thunders, it signifies good order for the city.

24. If it thunders, it signifies disease following want.

25. If it thunders, there will be unrest among the slaves.

26. If it thunders, many shall be cut down by a man in power, but in the end he himself [will be killed].

27. If it thunders, it signifies nonthreatening diseases.

28. If it thunders, the fish of the sea shall be plentiful, but yet the flocks will be ruined by death.

29. If it thunders, the condition of the air oppressive, and disease-bearing for all.

30. If it thunders, it threatens plentiful death.

FEBRUARY

35. 1. If it thunders, it threatens war and the ruin of wealthy men.

2. If it thunders, wheat in less supply, but barley better, and an increase in livestock, but there will be a wasting away of humans.

3. If it thunders, there will be civil unrest.

4. If it thunders, men shall be troubled not only in visage but also in their very minds.

5. If it thunders, there will be a large harvest, a destruction for men.

6. If it thunders, destruction of grain supplies and especially barley.

7. If it thunders, it threatens destruction though not for long to humans.

8. If it thunders, the greatest affair will inflame the state, and also fish will increase and yet dangerous wild beasts shall perish.

9. If it thunders, worse the barley.

10. If it thunders, the wild beasts shall undo the humans.

11. If it thunders, good deliveries [in childbirth] for women.

12. If it thunders, it threatens frequent death and unseasonable winds.

13. If it thunders, there will be plenty, yet at the same time, political unrest.

14. If it thunders, it threatens loss of progeny and an onslaught of poisonous reptiles.

15. If it thunders, the air shall carry plague, creation of both wild beasts and mice.

16. If it thunders, to the people, [it will be] auspicious, but of the powerful ones, bad [will come] out of discord.

17. If it thunders, summer will be most fruitful.

18. If it thunders, it threatens a heavy wind and eruption of pustules on bodies.

19. If it thunders, there will be a throng of reptiles and, in addition, of worms.

20. If it thunders, it signifies fine breezes.

21. If it thunders, it signifies abundance.

22. If it thunders, the air will be disease-carrying but not lethal.

23. If it thunders, it threatens deformity for men but destruction for birds.

24. If it thunders, it threatens good health for men but destruction for both fish and reptiles.

25. If it thunders, to those living luxuriously, a reversal. There will be wars and a heavy storm.

26. If it thunders, it threatens hot weather, and a lack of water, and scabs on bodies.

27. If it thunders, it signifies unrest among the commons.

28. If it thunders, it prophesies abundance, yet at the same time, a disease-giving wind will blow.

29. If it thunders, it signifies war and abundance.

30. If it thunders, it signifies good things with long duration after great divisions of the people.

MARCH

36. 1. If it thunders, for the entire year there will be strife and disagreements.

2. If it thunders, it shall end the threatening affairs.

3. If it thunders, for the state, discord following famine.

4. If it thunders, there will be boundless prosperity.

5. If it thunders, the spring will be sunny and the summer fruitful.

6. If it thunders, the same and even better.

7. If it thunders, a heavy wind will arise, which shall move the affairs of powerful men.

8. If it thunders, it signals rains.

9. If it thunders, it threatens ruin of man and creation of wild beasts.

10. If it thunders, destruction to the four-footed.

11. If it thunders, it signifies heavy rain and the creation of locusts.

12. If it thunders, a powerful man in politics or a general is endangered; on his behalf, battles will be waged, and the wild beasts shall fall upon man.

13. If it thunders, there will be plenty, but the wild beasts shall be destroyed, and the fish shall increase; and reptiles will trouble habitations but will not be harmful.

14. If it thunders, it signals prosperity but threatens a death of men and birth of wild beasts.

15. If it thunders, it signals hot spells and drought and a great throng of mice and fish.

16. If it thunders, healthful [will be] the year, yet lacking in necessities.

17. If it thunders, something unexpected will befall the people; ruin upon ruin for men and four-footed beasts.

18. If it thunders, it signifies a period of severe rain, and disease, and the birth of locusts, barrenness [of crops] near at hand.

19. If it thunders, a very dry summer and destructive.

20. If it thunders, man will live with better behavior at the same time as more prosperously.

21. If it thunders, it signifies prosperity after wars and hot spells causing destruction.

22. If it thunders, destruction of birds, but a plenty of daily supplies.

23. If it thunders, it signifies discord.

24. If it thunders, it signifies prosperity.

25. If it thunders, new affairs are given birth among the people.

26. If it thunders, it announces [the] acquisition of imported slaves.[7]

27. If it thunders, it signifies abundance imported from abroad.

28. If it thunders, there will be a plenty of marine fish.

29. If it thunders, the women shall obtain the better reputation.

30. If it thunders, there will be some powerful, self-possessed man of the kingdom, through whom [will come] good cheer.

APRIL

37. 1. If it thunders, it threatens civil discord and the downfalls of fortunes.

2. If it thunders, sign of justice, bearing prosperity to good men, and paltry things to evil men.

3. If it thunders, it signifies profit out of a grain supply brought from abroad.

4. If it thunders, anger it threatens of those more powerful against the upright.

5. If it thunders, it signals a hot summer early [in the season] but a healthful year.

6. If it thunders, civil wars will arise.

7. If it thunders, it signifies all good things and a prosperous season.

8. If it thunders, it signifies heavy rains bearing disease.

9. If it thunders, it signifies victory for the kingdom and good cheer for the powerful ones.

10. If it thunders, of upright men there will be advances.

11. If it thunders, it signals the same things.

12. If it thunders, rains and prosperity and ruin of fish it signifies.

13. If it thunders, for men and for cattle destruction it threatens.

14. If it thunders, good health and prosperity it signifies.

15. If it thunders, it signals a plague.

16. If it thunders, it signifies abundance but at the same time the birth of field voles.

17. If it thunders, it signals a plenty of daily supplies.

18. If it thunders, it signals discord and thoughtlessness of men.

19. If it thunders, a powerful man in the state shall be deprived at once of both reputation and property.

20. If it thunders, it signals divine anger.

21. If it thunders, it signifies good fortune for the crops, yet war for the state.

22. If it thunders, it will be the destruction of the flies.

23. If it thunders, it signifies a rain helpful for the sprouting time.

24. If it thunders, there will be discord among those in power, but their plans will be exposed.

25. If it thunders, peace during the entire year.

26. If it thunders, it signifies great hope of fruits and scarcity of harvests.

27. If it thunders, omens from the sky incredibly shall be revealed.

28. If it thunders, by shields the people shall be saved.

29. If it thunders, zephyrus will prevail.

30. If it thunders, a shower of good things.

MAY

38. 1. If it thunders, it signifies flight for the common people and loss of honor.

2. If it thunders, it threatens need.

3. If it thunders, it signifies abundance imported from abroad.

4. If it thunders, the air will be mild, and the crops will be plentiful.

5. If it thunders, there will be an interchange of hardships in political affairs, and wheat more plentiful than barley. The pulses, however, will be ruined.

6. If it thunders, it signifies that crops will ripen in haste and will be ruined.

7. If it thunders, there will be abundance of birds and fish.

8. If it thunders, ill-omened for the common people.

9. If it thunders, it signals plague, but not exceptionally life-threatening.

10. If it thunders, it announces storms, heavy rain, heavy floods of the rivers, a throng of lizards and of reptiles.

11. If it thunders, abundance to be hoped for both on land and sea.

12. If it thunders, there will be destruction of fish.

13. If it thunders, it signals an increase in river waters, but diseases for men.

14. If it thunders, there will be eastern war and great want.

15. If it thunders, it signifies abundance.

16. If it thunders, atonement must be made on account of terrible news.

17. If it thunders, it signifies rainy weather.

18. If it thunders, discord and out of it war and a lack of daily supplies.

19. If it thunders, through goodwill of the city, some man shall be exalted to the height of good fortune.

20. If it thunders, for those in the East, prosperity, but for those in the West, not the same.

21. If it thunders, atonement must be made on account of terrible news.

22. If it thunders, it signals heavy rains and destruction of marine fish.

23. If it thunders, it signifies a good and fruitful rain.

24. If it thunders, great evils such that those hearkening [to them] shall pass away from grief.

25. If it thunders, a hoped-for resting place and slackening of evils.

26. If it thunders, good for those working upon the tilled land.

27. If it thunders, there shall be prodigies, and a comet shall shine forth.

28. If it thunders, it shall be the same.

29. If it thunders, it signals northern war, but not dangerous for commerce.

30. If it thunders, the sprouting crops will be chilled by the winds.

"This brontoscopic almanac Nigidius claimed was not universal, but was only for Rome."[8]

NOTES

1. Byzantine: Monday (cf. Dio Cassius 37.18); meaning, "start with the first full moon in Cancer."

2. "Crops" translates καρπῶν—"of fruits" or "soft fruits," but may have been applied generically throughout, except where distinction is made between these and ξύλινα καρπά—"hard tree fruits," i.e., nuts.

3. "Queenly" = royal city, said only of Rome or Constantinople.

4. "Ruin" or "a falling" (πτῶσις) of the flocks: the connotation of falling-down, or -away, might have described a particular disease condition.

5. Damaged manuscript.

6. Text not clear here.

7. The connotation is of foreign prisoners of war sold as slaves.

8. The quotation marks at the end of the calendar indicate that Lydus is speaking here.

APPENDIX B

SELECTED LATIN AND GREEK LITERARY SOURCES ON ETRUSCAN RELIGION

Edited by Nancy Thomson de Grummond

Most of the Latin and Greek sources presented here have been taken from the editions of the texts used in the electronic bases of classical texts in the *Thesaurus Linguae Latinae* and the *Thesaurus Linguae Grecae*. The few exceptions are duly noted, almost all taken from C. O. Thulin, *Die Etruskische Disciplin,* Parts 1–3, Darmstadt, 1968, repr. of texts of 1905, 1906, and 1909.[1] The renditions into English are credited to their respective translators; if a credit is not given for a translation, it was made by the editor of this appendix.

I am grateful to Francis Cairns for assistance with the usage of *TLL* and *TLG*. Alexis Christensen contributed greatly in the selection of texts and translations.

The following outline indicates the way in which the texts are arranged:

I. General	191
II. Prophets, Priests, Prophecies, and Omens	191
III. Cosmos, Space, and Time	198
IV. The *Etrusca disciplina*	202
V. Etruscan Temples, Shrines, and Tombs	205
VI. Statues and Gods	208
VII. Rituals	212
VIII. Thunder and Lightning	213
IX. Demons and Spirits	217

I. GENERAL

I.1. Livy 5.1.6.

... gens itaque ante omnes alias eo magis dedita religionibus quod excelleret arte colendi eas.

... a people more than any others dedicated to religion, the more as they excelled in practicing it.

I.2. Arnobius, *Adv. nat.* 7.26

... genetrix et mater superstitionis Etruria

... Etruria, the begetter and mother of superstition.

II. PROPHETS, PRIESTS, PROPHECIES, AND OMENS

II.1. Prophecy of Vegoia

Idem Vegoiae Arrunti Veltymno. Scias mare ex aethera remotum. Cum autem Juppiter terram Aetruriae sibi vindicavit, constituit iussitque metiri campos signarique agros. Sciens hominum avaritiam vel terrenum cupidinem, terminis omnia scita esse voluit. Quos quandoque quis ob avaritiam prope novissimi octavi saeculi data sibi homines malo dolo violabunt contingentque atque movebunt. Sed qui contigerit moveritque, possessionem promovendo suam, alterius minuendo, ob hoc scelus damnabitur a diis. Si servi faciant, dominio mutabuntur in deterius. Sed si conscientia dominica fiet, caelerius dominus extirpabitur, gensque eius omnis interiet. Motores autem pessimis morbis et vulneribus efficientur membrisque suis debililabuntur. Tum etiam terra a tempestatibus vel turbinibus plerumque labe movebitur, fructus saepe ledentur decutienturque imbribus atque grandine, caniculis interient, robigine occidentur. Multae dissensiones in populo. Fieri haec scitote, cum talia scelera committuntur. Propterea neque fallax neque bilinguis sis. Disciplinam pone in corde tuo.

(Source of text: *Die Schriften der Römischen Feldmesser,* ed. K. Lachmann Vol. 1, Berlin 1848, 350–351.)

(Prophecy) of Vegoia, to Arruns Veltymnus: "Know that the sea was separated from the sky. But when Jupiter claimed the land of Aetruria for himself, he established and ordered that the fields be measured and the croplands delimited. Knowing the greed of men and their lust for land, he wanted everything proper concerning boundaries. And at some time, around the end of the eighth *saeculum*, someone will violate them on account of greed by means of evil trickery and will touch them and move them [. . .]. But whoever shall have touched and moved them, increasing his own property and diminishing that of another, on account of this crime he will be damned by the gods. If slaves should do it, there will be a change for the worse in status. But if the deed is done with the master's consent, very quickly the master will be uprooted and all of his family will perish. The ones who move [the boundaries] will be afflicted by the worst diseases and wounds, and they will feel a weakness in their limbs. Then also the earth will be moved by storms and whirl winds with frequent destruction, crops often will be injured and will be knocked down by rain and hail, they will perish in the summer heat, they will be felled by mildew. There will be much dissension among people. Know that these things will be done when such crimes are committed. Wherefore be not false or double-tongued. Keep this teaching in your heart."

II.2. Festus, *De significatu verborum* 359.14

Tages nomine, Genii filius, nepos Jovis, puer dicitur discipulinam haruspicii dedisse duodecim populis Etruriae (Thulin 1, 3).

A boy named Tages, the son of Genius, grandson of Jupiter, is said to have given the discipline of divination to the Twelve Peoples of Etruria.

II.3. Cicero, *De divinatione* 2.50-51.23.

Tages quidam dicitur in agro Tarquiniensi, cum terra araretur et sulcus altius esset impressus, extitisse repente et eum adfatus esse, qui arabat. Is autem Tages, ut in libris est Etruscorum, puerili specie dicitur visus, sed senili fuisse prudentia. Eius adspectu cum obstipuisset bubulcus clamoremque maiorem cum admiratione edidisset, concursum esse factum, totamque brevi tempore in eum locum Etruriam convenisse; tum illum plura locutum multis audientibus, qui omnia verba eius exceperint litterisque mandarint; omnem autem orationem fuisse eam, qua haruspicinae disciplina contineretur; eam postea crevisse rebus novis cognoscendis et ad eadem illa principia referendis. Haec accepimus ab ipsis, haec scripta conservant, hunc fontem habent disciplinae.

It is said that, once upon a time, in the countryside of Tarquinii, while the earth was being plowed, a rather deep furrow was dug and suddenly Tages sprang forth and spoke to the man plowing. Now this Tages, according to the books of the Etruscans, is said to have had the appearance of a child, but the wisdom of an elder. When the rustic had gaped at his appearance and had raised a great cry in astonishment, a crowd gathered and in a short time, all Etruria assembled at that place. Then he said many things to his numerous listeners, who received all of his words and entrusted them to writing. His whole address was about what is comprised by the discipline of soothsaying. Later, as new things were learned and made to refer to those same principles, the discipline grew. We received these things from (the Etruscans) themselves, they preserve these writings, they hold them (as) the source for the discipline.

II.4. Ovid, *Metamorphoses* 15.553-559.

Haut aliter stupuit, quam cum Tyrrhenus arator
fatalem glaebam mediis adspexit in arvis
sponte sua primum nulloque agitante moveri,
sumere mox hominis terraeque amittere formam
oraque venturis aperire recentia fatis:
indigenae dixere Tagen, qui primus Etruscam
edocuit gentem casus aperire futuros.

He [Virbius] was no less astonished than the Tyrrhenian plowman when he observed in the middle of his fields a clod, a thing of fate, moving first of its own accord and with no one stirring it, and then assuming the shape of a man and losing the form of earth. It opened its new-made mouth (to tell) of things fated in the future. The natives called him Tages, the one who first taught the Etruscan people how to open up the events of the future.

II.5. Johannes Lydus, *De ostentis* 2.6.B

Τάρχων, ταύτῃ τὴν προσηγορίαν, ἀνὴρ γ[έγονε μὲν] θυοσκόπος, ὡς αὐτὸς ἐπὶ τῆς γραφῆς εἰσενήνεκται, εἷς [τῶν ὑπὸ] Τυρρηνοῦ τοῦ Λυδοῦ διδαχθέντων. καὶ γὰρ δὴ τοῖς Θούσκ[ων γράμμα]σι ταῦτα δηλοῦται,

οὔπω τηνικαῦτα τοῖς τόποις ἐκείνοις Εὐάνδρου τοῦ
Ἀρκάδος ἐπιφανέντος. ἦν δὲ ἀλλοῖός τις ὁ τῶν γραμμάτων
τύπος, καὶ οὐδὲ ὅλως καθημαξευμένος ἡμῖν· ἡ γὰρ ἂν
τῶν ἀπορρήτων τε καὶ ἀναγκαιοτέρων οὐδὲν ἔμεινεν
ἄχρι τοῦ παρόντος λανθάνον. φησὶ τοίνυν ὁ Τάρχων
ἐπὶ τοῦ συγγράμματος, ὅπερ εἶναί τινες Τάγητος
ὑποπτεύουσιν, ἐπειδήπερ ἐκεῖ κατά τινα διαλογικὴν
ὁμιλίαν ἐρωτᾷ μὲν δῆθεν ὁ Τάρχων, ἀποκρίνεται δὲ
ὁ Τάγης ὡς προσκαρτερῶν ἑκάστοτε τοῖς ἱεροῖς, ὡς
[τυχὸν] συμβέβηκεν αὐτῷ κατά τινα χρόνον ἀροτριῶντι
θαυμάσιόν τι, οἶον οὐδὲ ἀκήκοέ τις ἐν τῷ παντὶ χρόνῳ
γενόμενον· ἀνεδόθη γὰρ <ἐκ> τοῦ αὔλακος παιδίον, ἄρτι
μὲν τεχθῆναι δοκοῦν, ὀδόντων δὲ καὶ τῶν ἄλλων τῶν
ἐν ἡλικίᾳ γνωρισμάτων ἀπροσδεές· ἦν δὲ ἄρα τὸ παιδίον
ὁ Τάγης, ὃν δὴ καὶ χθόνιον Ἑ[ρμῆν] εἶναι τοῖς Ἕλλησιν
ἔδοξεν, ὥς που καὶ Πρόκλος φησὶν ὁ διάδοχος.
τοῦτο δὲ ἀλληγορικῶς παρὰ τὸν ἱερατικὸν παρακεκά-
λυπται νόμον, ἐπεὶ οὐ προφανῶς ὁ περὶ θειοτέρων
πραγμάτων λόγος διὰ τοὺς ἀνιέρους, ἀλλὰ νῦν μὲν
μυθικῶς νῦν δὲ παραβολικῶς παραδέδοται· ἀντὶ γὰρ τοῦ
εἰπεῖν ψυχὴν τελειοτάτην καὶ τῶν οἰκείων ἐνεργειῶν
ἀπροσδεῆ ἐπὶ τὴν ὕλην ἐλθεῖν, βρέφος ἀρτιγενὲς ἐκ τοῦ
αὔλακος ἀναδοθῆναί φησι. Τάρχων δὲ ὁ πρεσβύτερος
(γέγονε γὰρ δὴ καὶ νεώτερος, ἐπὶ τῶν Αἰνείου στρατευσά-
μενος χρόνων) τὸ παιδίον ἀναλαβὼν καὶ τοῖς ἱεροῖς
ἐναποθέμενος τόποις ἠξίου τι παρ' [αὐτοῦ] τῶν ἀπορρήτων μαθεῖν. τοῦ δὲ αἰτουμένου τυχὼν βι[βλίον] ἐκ τῶν
εἰρημένων συνέγραψεν, ἐν ᾧ πυνθάνεται μὲν ὁ Τάρχων
τῇ τῶν Ἰταλῶν ταύτῃ τῇ συνήθει φωνῇ, ἀποκρίνεται δὲ ὁ
Τάγης γράμμασιν ἀρχαίοις τε καὶ οὐ σφόδρα γνωρίμοις
ἡμῖν γε ἐμμένων τῶν ἀποκρίσεων. πλὴν ἀλλ' ὅσον μοι
γέγονε δυνατόν, ἔκ τε τῶν Θούσκων ἔκ τε τῶν ἄλλων ὅσοι
τούτους ἡρμήνευσαν, Καπίτωνός τέ φημι καὶ Φοντηίου,
καὶ Ἀπουληίου Βικελλίου τε καὶ Λαβεῶνος καὶ Φιγούλου,
Πλινίου τε τοῦ φυσικοῦ, πειράσομαι ταῦτα πρὸς ὑμᾶς
διελθεῖν.

Tarchon ... was an haruspex, as he notes in his writing, one of those instructed by the Lydian Tyrrhenus. In fact, that is clear from the writing of the Tuscans, since Evander the Arcadian had not yet appeared in those places. It was thus a very different form of writing, not at all common among us; if it were not [different], certain mysterious and most necessary things would not remain hidden in any way. Thus Tarchon says in his writing, which some suppose is by Tages (because there, as in a type of dialogue Tarchon asks questions and Tages answers, like those who always attend to sacrifices), that one time, while he was working the land, there happened to him a marvelous thing, which no one ever at any time had perceived as happening: from the furrow was brought forth a child who seemed to be a newborn but not lacking teeth and other signs of mature age. This child, then, was Tages, the one who according to the Greeks is Chthonic Hermes, as is told in one place by Proclus Diadochus. This is veiled in an allegorical mode according to the priestly customs, because the discourse on divine things was not transmitted openly by profane means but in the form now of myths, now of parables. Thus, instead of saying that the most perfect soul, not lacking in any faculties, came to be matter, it says that the newborn baby was brought forth from the furrow. Thus Tarchon the Elder (for there was a Younger, who carried on war at the time of Aeneas) took up the child and placed it in sacred places, thinking to learn from it something about hidden matters. Having obtained what he had asked for, he composed a book about the things said, in which Tarchon inquires in the common language of the Italians, then Tages answers, keeping to the ancient letters, not very understandable for us. I am preserving as much as possible from the Tuscans and from others who translated them, such as Capito and Fonteius, Apuleius Vicellius, Labeo, Figulus, and Pliny the natural philosopher; I shall attempt to report these things to you.

II.6. Ovid, *Fasti* 4.812–818.

... ambigitur moenia ponat uter.
nil opus est, dixit, certamine, Romulus, ullo;
  magna fides avium est: experiamur aves.
res placet: alter init nemorosi saxa Palati;
  alter Aventinum mane cacumen init.
sex Remus, hic volucres bis sex videt ordine; pacto
  statur, et arbitrium Romulus urbis habet.

There was some doubt as to which one should found the walls; Romulus said, "There is no need for any contest. We have great faith in birds. Let us try the birds." The proposal was approved. One went to the rocks of the Palatine covered with groves; the other approached the peak of the Aventine at dawn. Remus saw six birds, and (Romulus) saw twice six, in order. They stood by their pact, and Romulus kept the direction of the city.

II.7. Livy 2.7.1–3.

Ita cum pugnatum esset, tantus terror Tarquinium atque Etruscos incessit ut omissa inrita re nocte ambo exercitus, Veiens Tarquiniensisque, suas quisque abirent domos.

Adiciunt miracula huic pugnae: silentio proximae noctis ex silva Arsia ingentem editam vocem; Silvani vocem eam creditam; haec dicta: uno plus Tuscorum cecidisse in acie; vincere bello Romanum. Ita certe inde abiere, Romani ut uictores, Etrusci pro uictis; nam postquam inluxit nec quisquam hostium in conspectu erat, P. Valerius consul spolia legit triumphansque inde Romam rediit.

And so when they had fought, so great a terror overcame Tarquin and the Etruscans that they gave up, though the battle was undecided, and by night both armies, Veientine and Tarquinian, went off each to their own homes. They report a prodigy for this battle; in the silence of the following night, from the Arsian forest came forth a mighty voice, believed to be the voice of Silvanus. This is what it said: "One more Tuscan fell in the battle line; the Roman wins the war." And so then indeed went away the Romans as victors, the Etruscans as conquered. For after the light appeared, the consul P. Valerius gathered the spoils and in triumph returned to Rome.

II.8. Livy 1.34.3–10.

Lucumoni contra, omnium heredi bonorum, cum divitiae iam animos facerent, auxit ducta in matrimonium Tanaquil, summo loco nata et quae haud facile iis in quibus nata erat humiliora sineret ea quo innupsisset. Spernentibus Etruscis Lucumonem exsule advena ortum, ferre indignitatem non potuit, oblitaque ingenitae erga patriam caritatis dummodo virum honoratum videret, consilium migrandi ab Tarquiniis cepit. Roma est ad id potissima visa: in novo populo, ubi omnis repentina atque ex virtute nobilitas sit, futurum locum forti ac strenuo viro; regnasse Tatium Sabinum, arcessitum in regnum Numam a Curibus, et Ancum Sabina matre ortum nobilemque una imagine Numae esse. Facile persuadet ut cupido honorum et cui Tarquinii materna tantum patria esset. Sublatis itaque rebus amigrant Romam. Ad ianiculum forte ventum erat; ibi ei carpento sedenti cum uxore aquila suspensis demissa leviter alis pilleum aufert, superque carpentum cum magno clangore volitans rursus velut ministerio diuinitus missa capiti apte reponit; inde sublimis abiit. Accepisse id augurium laeta dicitur Tanaquil, perita ut volgo Etrusci caelestium prodigiorum mulier. Excelsa et alta sperare complexa virum iubet: eam alitem ea regione caeli et eius dei nuntiam venisse; circa summum culmen hominis auspicium fecisse; leuasse humano superpositum capiti decus ut divinitus eidem redderet. Has spes cogitationesque secum portantes urbem ingressi sunt.

The self-confidence implanted in the bosom of Lucumo by his wealth was heightened by his marriage with Tanaquil, who was a woman of the most exalted birth, and not of a character lightly to endure a humbler rank in her new environment than she had enjoyed in the condition to which she had been born. The Etruscans looked with disdain on Lucumo, the son of a banished man and a stranger. She could not endure this indignity, and forgetting the love she owed her native land, if she could only see her husband honoured, she formed the project of emigrating from Tarquinii. Rome appeared to be the most suitable place for her purpose; amongst a new people, where all rank was of sudden growth and founded on worth, there would be room for a brave and strenuous man; the City had been ruled by Tatius the Sabine, it had summoned Numa to the sovereignty from Cures, even Ancus was the son of a Sabine mother, and could point to no noble ancestor but Numa. She had no trouble in persuading a man who was eager for distinction, to whom Tarquinii was only his mother's birthplace. They therefore gathered their possessions together and removed to Rome. They had come, as it happened, as far as Janiculum, when, as they were sitting in their covered wagon, an eagle poised on its wings gently descended upon them and plucked off Lucumo's cap, after which, rising noisily above the car and again stooping, as if sent from heaven for that service, it deftly replaced the cap upon his head, and departed on high. This augury was joyfully accepted, it is said, by Tanaquil, who was a woman skilled in celestial prodigies, as was the case with most Etruscans. Embracing her husband, she bade him expect transcendent greatness: such was the meaning of that bird, appearing from that quarter of the sky, and bringing tidings from that god; the highest part of the man had been concerned in the omen; the eagle had removed the adornment placed upon a mortal's head that it might restore it with the divine approbation. Such were their hopes and their reflections as they entered the City.

> (Translation reprinted by permission of the publishers and the Trustees of the Loeb Classical Library from *Livy in Fourteen Volumes,* Loeb Classical Library, Vol. 1, translated by B. O. Foster, Cambridge, MA: Harvard University Press, 1919, pp. 123, 125, 127. The Loeb Classical Library © is a registered trademark of the President and Fellows of Harvard College.)

II.9. Livy 1.39.1–4.

Eo tempore in regia prodigium visu eventuque mirabile fuit. puero dormienti, cui Servio Tullio fuit nomen, caput arsisse ferunt multorum in conspectu; plurimo igitur clamore inde ad tantae rei miraculum orto excitos reges, et cum quidam familiarium aquam ad restinguendum ferret, ab regina retentum, sedatoque eam tumultu moveri uetuisse puerum donec sua sponte experrectus esset; mox cum somno et flammam abisse. Tum abducto in secretum uiro Tanaquil viden tu puerum hunc, inquit, quem tam humili cultu educamus? Scire licet hunc lumen quondam rebus nostris dubiis futurum praesidiumque regiae adflictae; proinde materiam ingentis publice privatimque decoris omni indulgentia nostra nutriamus. Inde puerum liberum loco coeptum haberi erudirique artibus quibus ingenia ad magnae fortunae cultum excitantur. Evenit facile quod dis cordi esset : juvenis evasit vere indolis regiae nec, cum quaereretur gener Tarquinio, quisquam Romanae juventutis ulla arte conferri potuit, filiamque ei suam rex despondit.

At this time there happened in the house of the king a portent which was remarkable alike in its manifestation and in its outcome. The story is that while a child named Servius Tullius lay sleeping, his head burst into flames in the sight of many. The general outcry which so great a miracle called forth brought the king and queen to the place. One of the servants fetched water to quench the fire, but was checked by the queen, who stilled the uproar and commanded that the boy should not be disturbed until he awoke of himself. Soon afterwards sleep left him, and with it disappeared the flames. Then taking her husband aside, Tanaquil said: "Do you see this child whom we are bringing up in so humble a fashion? Be assured he will one day be a lamp to our dubious fortunes, and a protector of the royal house in the day of its distress. Let us therefore rear with all solicitude one who will lend high renown to the state and to our family." It is said that from that moment the boy began to be looked upon as a son, and to be trained in the studies by which men are inspired to bear themselves greatly. It was a thing easily accomplished, being the will of Heaven. The youth turned out to be of a truly royal nature, and when Tarquinius sought a son-in-law there was no other young Roman who could be at all compared to Servius; and the king accordingly betrothed his daughter to him.

(Translation reprinted by permission of the publishers and the Trustees of the Loeb Classical Library from *Livy in Fourteen Volumes,* Loeb Classical Library, Vol. 1, translated by B. O. Foster, Cambridge, MA: Harvard University Press, 1919, p. 139. The Loeb Classical Library © is a registered trademark of the President and Fellows of Harvard College.)

II.10. Cicero, *De divinatione* 1.44.100.

Quid, quod in annalibus habemus Veienti bello, cum lacus Albanus praeter modum crevisset, Veientem quendam ad nos hominem nobilem perfugisse, eumque dixisse ex fatis, quae Veientes scripta haberent, Veios capi non posse, dum lacus is redundaret, et, si lacus emissus lapsu et cursu suo ad mare profluxisset, perniciosum populo Romano; sin autem ita esset eductus, ut ad mare pervenire non posset, tum salutare nostris fore? Ex quo illa admirabilis a maioribus Albanae aquae facta deductio est. Cum autem Veientes bello fessi legatos ad senatum misissent, tum ex iis quidam dixisse dicitur non omnia illum transfugam ausum esse senatui dicere; in isdem enim fatis scriptum Veientes habere fore ut brevi a Gallis Roma caperetur, quod quidem sexennio post Veios captos factum esse videmus.

And what do you say of the following story which we find in our annals? During the Veientian War, when Lake Albanus had overflowed its banks, a certain nobleman of Veii deserted to us and said that, according to the prophecies of the Veientian books, their city could not be taken while the lake was at flood, and that if its waters were permitted to overflow and take their own course to the sea the result would be disastrous to the Roman people; on the other hand, if the waters were drained off in such a way that they did not reach the sea the result would be to our advantage. In consequence of this announcement our forefathers dug that marvellous canal to drain off the waters from the Alban lake. Later when the Veientians had grown weary of the war and had sent ambassadors to the Senate to treat for peace, one of them is reported to have said that the deserter had not dared to tell the whole of the prophecy contained in the Veientian books, for those books, he said, also foretold the early capture of Rome by the Gauls. And this, as we know, did occur six years after the fall of Veii.

(Translation reprinted by permission of the publishers and the Trustees of the Loeb Classical Library from Cicero, *De senectute, De amicitia, De divinatione,* Loeb Classical Library, Vol. 20, translated by W. A. Falcmer, Cambridge, MA: Harvard University Press, 1922, p. 331. The Loeb Classical Library © is a registered trademark of the President and Fellows of Harvard College.)

II.11. Livy 5.15.4-12.

Prodigia interim multa nuntiari, quorum pleraque et quia singuli auctores erant parum credita spretaque, et quia, hostibus Etruscis, per quos ea procurarent haruspices non erant: in unum omnium curae versae sunt quod lacus in Albano nemore, sine ullis caelestibus aquis causave qua alia quae rem miraculo eximeret, in altitudinem insolitam crevit. Quidnam eo di portenderent prodigio missi sciscitatum oratores ad Delphicum oraculum. Sed propior interpres fatis oblatus senior quidam Veiens, qui inter cavillantes in stationibus ac custodiis milites Romanos Etruscosque vaticinantis in modum cecinit priusquam ex lacu Albano aqua emissa foret nunquam potiturum Veiis Romanum. Quod primo velut temere iactum sperni, agitari deinde sermonibus coeptum est donec unus ex statione Romana percontatus proximum oppidanorum, iam per longinquitatem belli commercio sermonum facto, quisnam is esset qui per ambages de lacu Albano jaceret, postquam audivit haruspicem esse, uir haud intacti religione animi, causatus de privati portenti procuratione si operae illi esset consulere velle, ad conloquium vatem elicuit. Cumque progressi ambo a suis longius essent inermes sine ullo metu, praevalens juvenis Romanus senem infirmum in conspectu omnium raptum nequiquam tumultuantibus Etruscis ad suos transtulit. Qui cum perductus ad imperatorem, inde Romam ad senatum missus esset, sciscitantibus quidnam id esset quod de lacu Albano docuisset, respondit profecto iratos deos Veienti populo illo fuisse die quo sibi eam mentem obiecissent ut excidium patriae fatale proderet. Itaque quae tum cecinerit divino spiritu instinctus, ea se nec ut indicta sint revocare posse, et tacendo forsitan quae di immortales volgari velint haud minus quam celanda effando nefas contrahi. Sic igitur libris fatalibus, sic disciplina Etrusca traditum esse, [ut] quando aqua Albana abundasset, tum si eam Romanus rite emisisset uictoriam de Veientibus dari; antequam id fiat deos moenia Veientium desertouros non esse. Exsequebatur inde quae sollemnis derivatio esset; sed auctorem levem nec satis fidum super tanta re patres rati decrevere legatos sortesque oraculi Pythici exspectandas.

Meanwhile many portents were reported, most of which, because they had only one witness each to vouch for them, obtained no credence and were slighted; and besides, when the Etruscans, whose services they employed to avert evil omens, were at war with them, they had no soothsayers. One thing occasioned universal anxiety, namely that the lake in the Alban Wood, without any rains or other cause to make it less than a miracle, rose to an unwonted height. To inquire what the gods could possibly foretell by that prodigy, envoys were sent to the Delphic oracle. But a nearer interpreter of the fates presented himself, an old man of Veii, who, while the Roman and Etruscan soldiers were scoffing at one another as they stood guard at outposts, declared in a prophetic strain that until the water should be drawn off from the Alban Lake the Romans never could take Veii. At first they made light of this idle taunt; then they began to talk it over; presently one of the Roman outpost inquired of the townsman nearest him (for owing to the long continuance of the war they had now got into the way of conversing together) who that man was who threw out mysterious hints regarding the Alban Lake. When he heard that he was a soothsayer, being himself not without a touch of superstition, he alleged a desire to consult him about the averting of a domestic portent, if he could spare the time, and so enticed the seer to a conference. And when they had walked a little way apart from the friends of both, unarmed and fearing nothing, the stalwart young Roman laid hold of the feeble old man in the sight of them all, and despite an unavailing hubbub raised by the Etruscans, bore him off to his own fellows. There they had him before the general, who sent him on to Rome, to the senate. When the Fathers questioned him what it was he had meant about the Alban Lake, he answered that the gods must surely have been incensed at the people of Veii on the day when they had put it into his mind to reveal the destruction destined to befall his native city; and so what he had uttered under divine inspiration he could not now unsay and recall; and perhaps in concealing what the immortal gods wished to be published, guilt was incurred no less than by disclosing what should be hid. Thus then it was written in the books of fate, thus handed down in the lore of the Etruscans, that when the Alban water should overflow, if then the Romans should duly draw it off, they would be given the victory over the Veientes; until that should come to pass, the gods would not abandon the walls of Veii. He then went on to explain the appointed method of draining it. But the senators, making slight account of his authority, as not sufficiently trustworthy in so grave a matter, determined to wait for their deputies with the response of the Pythian oracle.

(Translation reprinted by permission of the publishers and the Trustees of the Loeb Classical Library from *Livy in Fourteen Volumes,* Loeb Classical Library, Vol. 3, translated by B. O. Foster, Cambridge, MA:

Harvard University Press, 1924, pp. 53, 55. The Loeb Classical Library © is a registered trademark of the President and Fellows of Harvard College.)

II.12. Ovid, *Metamorphoses* 15.565-621.

Aut sua fluminea cum vidit Cipus in unda
cornua (vidit enim) falsamque in imagine credens
esse fidem, digitis ad frontem saepe relatis,
quae vidit, tetigit, nec jam sua lumina damnans
restitit, ut victor domito remeabat ab hoste,
ad caelumque oculos et eodem bracchia tollensj
quicquid, ait, superi, monstro portenditur isto,
seu laetum est, patriae laetum populoque Quirini,
sive minax, mihi sit. Viridique e caespite factas
placat odoratis herbosas ignibus aras
vinaque dat pateris mactatarumque bidentum,
quid sibi significent, trepidantia consulit exta;
quae simul adspexit Tyrrhenae gentis haruspex,
magna quidem rerum molimina vidit in illis,
non manifesta tamen; cum vero sustulit acre
a pecudis fibris ad Cipi cornua lumen,
rex, ait, o! salve! tibi enim, tibi, Cipe, tuisque
hic locus et Latiae parebunt cornibus arces.
tu modo rumpe moras portasque intrare patentes
adpropera! sic fata jubent; namque urbe receptus
rex eris et sceptro tutus potiere perenni.
Rettulit ille pedem torvamque a moenibus urbis
avertens faciem, procul, a! procul omnia, dixit,
talia di pellant! multoque ego iustius aevum
exul agam, quam me videant Capitolia regem.
Dixit et extemplo populumque gravemque senatum
convocat, ante tamen pacali cornua lauro
velat et aggeribus factis a milite forti
insistit priscosque deos e more precatus,
est, ait, hic unus, quem vos nisi pellitis urbe,
rex erit: is qui sit, signo, non nomine dicam:
cornua fronte gerit! quem vobis indicat augur,
si Romam intrarit, famularia iura daturum.
Ille quidem potuit portas inrumpere apertas,
sed nos obstitimus, quamvis conjunctior illo
nemo mihi est: vos urbe virum prohibete, Quirites,
vel, si dignus erit, gravibus vincite catenis
aut finite metum fatalis morte tyranni!
Qualia succinctis, ubi trux insibilat eurus,
murmura pinetis fiunt, aut qualia fluctus
aequorei faciunt, siquis procul audiat illos,
tale sonat populus; sed per confusa frementis
verba tamen vulgi vox eminet una, quis ille est?
et spectant frontes praedictaque cornua quaerunt.
Rursus ad hos Cipus, quem poscitis, inquit, habetis
et dempta capiti populo prohibente corona
exhibuit gemino praesignia tempora cornu.
Demisere oculos omnes gemitumque dedere
atque illud meritis clarum (quis credere possit?)
inviti videre caput: nec honore carere
ulterius passi festam inposuere coronam;
at proceres, quoniam muros intrare vetaris,
ruris honorati tantum tibi, Cipe, dedere,
quantum depresso subiectis bobus aratro
conplecti posses ad finem lucis ab ortu.
Cornuaque aeratis miram referentia formam
postibus insculpunt, longum mansura per aevum.

No less amazed was Cipus when in a clear stream he saw horns springing from his head. For he saw them and, thinking that he was deceived by the reflection, lifting his hands again and again to his forehead, he touched what he saw; nor did he fight against the portent, blaming his own eyes, but as a victor returning from the conquered foe, he raised his eyes and arms to the heavens and cried, "O ye gods, whatever is portended by this monstrous thing, if it be fortunate, let the good fortune befall my country and the people of Quirinus; but if it threatens ill, may the ill be mine." Then, making an altar of green turf, he appeased the gods with a fragrant burnt offering, made a libation of wine, and consulted the quivering entrails of the slaughtered victims as to what they might mean for him. When the Etruscan seer inspected these he saw the signs of great enterprises there, but not yet clearly visible. But when he raised his keen eyes from the sheep's entrails to the horn of Cipus, he cried, "All hail, O king! For to thee, to thee, Cipus, and to thy horns shall this place and Latium's citadels bow down. Only delay not and make speed to enter the open gates! Such is fate's command; for received within the city, shalt thou be king and wield the sceptre in safe and endless sway." He started back, and keeping his gaze stubbornly turned from the city's walls, he said, "Far, oh, far from me may the gods keep such a fate. Better far is it that I should spend my days exiled from home than that the Capitol should see me king." He spoke and straightway called a joint assembly of the people and the reverend senate. But first he hid his horns with a wreath of peaceful laurel; then, standing on a mound raised by the brave soldiery and praying to the ancient gods according to the rite, he said, "There is one here who will be king unless you drive him from your city. Who he is, not by his name but by a sign I will disclose to you; he wears horns upon his brow! The augur declares that if once he enters Rome he will reduce you to the rank of slaves. He might have forced his way through your gates, for they stand open; but I withstood him, though no one is more closely bound to him than I. Do you, Quirites, keep him from your city, or if he deserves it, bind him with heavy fetters, or end your fear of the hated tyrant by his death!" At this such a murmur arose among the people as comes from a thick pine-grove when the boisterous wind whistles through them, or as the waves of the sea makes heard from afar. But, midst the confused words of the murmuring throng, one cry rose clear: "Who is the man?" They looked at each other's forehead, and sought to find the horns that had been spoken of. Then Cipus spoke again and said: "Him whom you seek you have"; and removing his wreath from his head, while the people sought to stay him, he showed to them his temples marked with the two horns. All cast down their eyes and groaned aloud, and (who could believe it?) reluctantly looked upon that deservedly illustrious head. Then, not suffering him further to stand dishonored, they replaced upon his head the festal wreath. But the senate, since you might not come within the walls, gave you, Cipus, as much land as you could enclose with a yoke of oxen and a plow from dawn till the close of day. And the horns in all their wondrous beauty they engraved upon the bronze pillars of the gates, there to remain through all the ages.

> (Translation reprinted by permission of the publishers and the Trustees of the Loeb Classical Library from Ovid, *Metamorphoses* 2, Loeb Classical Library, Vol. 4, translated by F. J. Miller, Cambridge, MA: Harvard University Press, 1916, pp. 405, 407, 409. The Loeb Classical Library © is a registered trademark of the President and Fellows of Harvard College.)

II.13. Suetonius, *Augustus* 97.

Sub idem tempus ictu fulminis ex inscriptione statuae eius prima nominis littera effluxit; responsum est, centum solos dies posthac victurum, quem numerum C littera notaret, futurumque ut inter deos referretur, quod aesar, id est reliqua pars e Caesaris nomine, Etrusca lingua deus vocaretur.

Around that same time, from a bolt of lightning the first letter on the inscription on his statue [i.e., of Augustus] melted off; the response [of the priests] was that 100 days after this — which the number "C" indicates — it was going to come about that he would be carried among the gods, because *aesar*, the part of the word remaining from the name Caesar, meant "god" in the Etruscan language.

II.14. Dio Cassius 56.29.

καὶ κεραυνὸς ἐς εἰκόνα αὐτοῦ τῷ Καπιτωλίῳ ἑστῶσαν ἐμπεσὼν τὸ γράμμα τὸ πρῶτον τοῦ ὀνόματος τοῦ Καίσαρος ἠφάνισεν· ὅθεν οἱ μάντεις ἑκατοστῇ μετὰ τοῦτο αὐτὸν ἡμέρᾳ θείας τινὸς μαίρας μεταλήψεσθαι ἔφασαν, τεκμαιρόμενοι ὅτι τό τε στοιχεῖον ἐκεῖνο τὸν τῶν ἑκατὸν ἀριθμὸν παρὰ τοῖς Λατίνοις καὶ τὸ λοιπὸν πᾶν ὄνομα θεὸν παρὰ τοῖς Τυρσηνοῖς νοεῖ.

And a thunderbolt, falling upon the image [of Augustus] on the Capitolium, blotted out the first letter of the name of Caesar. From this the soothsayers prophesied that on the hundredth day after this one he would partake of a certain divine destiny, judging from the fact that the letter "C" is the number 100 among the Romans, and the rest of the word means "god" among the Tyrsenians.

III. COSMOS, SPACE, AND TIME

III.1. Pliny, *Historia Naturalis* 2.55.143.

In sedecim partes caelum in eo spectu divisere Tusci. Prima est a septemtrionibus ad aequinoctialem exortum, secunda ad meridiem, tertia ad aequinoctialem occasum, quarta obtinet quod est reliquum ab occasu ad septemtriones. Has iterum in quaternas divisere partes, ex quibus octo ab exortu sinistras, totidem e contrario appellavere dextras.

In making these observations the Tuscans divided the heaven into sixteen parts: the first quarter is from the North to the equinoctial sunrise [East], the second to the South, the third to the equinoctial sunset [West], and the fourth occupies the remaining space extending from West to North; these quarters are divided into four parts each, of which they called the eight starting from the East the left-hand regions and the eight opposite ones the right-hand.

> (Translation reprinted by permission of the publishers and the Trustees of the Loeb Classical Library from Pliny the Elder, *Natural History,* Loeb Classical Library, Vol. 1, translated by H. Rackham, Cambridge, MA: Harvard University Press, 1938, p. 281. The Loeb Classical Library © is a registered

trademark of the President and Fellows of Harvard College.)

III.2. Servius, *Ad Aen.* 8.427.

Toto caelo, id est ab omni parte caeli: nam dicunt physici de sedecim partibus caeli jaci fulmina . . . ergo hoc dicit: faciebant fulmen in eorum similitudinem, quae Juppiter jacit toto caelo, hoc est de diversis partibus caeli, scilicet sedecim.

"From the whole sky," that is, from every part of the sky; for the natural philosophers say that lightning is thrown from sixteen parts of the sky. . . . Therefore this means: they were making lightning in their own likeness, which Jupiter throws from the whole sky, that is from the different parts of the sky, meaning sixteen.

III.3. Cicero, *De divinatione* 2.18.42.

Caelum in sedecim partis diviserunt Etrusci. Facile id quidem fuit, quattuor, quas nos habemus, duplicare, post idem iterum facere, ut ex eo dicerent, fulmen qua ex parte venisset. Primum id quid interest? deinde quid significat? Nonne perspicuum est ex prima admiratione hominum, quod tonitrua jactusque fulminum extimuissent, credidisse ea efficere rerum omnium praepotentem Jovem? Itaque in nostris commentariis scriptum habemus: Jove tonante, fulgurante comitia populi habere nefas.

The Etruscans divided the sky into sixteen parts. Of course it was easy enough for them to double the four parts into which we divide it and then double that total and tell from which one of those divisions a bolt of lightning had come. In the first place, what difference does its location make? And, in the second place, what does it foretell? It is perfectly evident that, out of the wonder and fear excited in primitive man by lightning and thunderbolts, sprang his belief that those phenomena were caused by omnipotent Jove. And so we find it recorded in our augural annals: When Jove thunders or lightens it is impious to hold an election.

(Translation reprinted by permission of the publishers and the Trustees of the Loeb Classical Library from Cicero, *De senectute, De amicitia, De divinatione*, Loeb Classical Library, Vol. 20, translated by W. A. Falconer, Cambridge, MA: Harvard University Press, 1922, p. 417. The Loeb Classical Library © is a registered trademark of the President and Fellows of Harvard College.)

III.4. Martianus Capella, *De nuptiis Mercurii et Philologiae* 1.45-61.

Nam in sedecim discerni dicitur caelum omne regiones in quarum prima sedes habere memorantur post ipsum Jovem dii Consentes Penates, Salus ac Lares, Janus, Favores opertanei Nocturnusque. In secunda itidem mansitabant praeter domum Jovis, quae ibi quoque sublimis est, ut est in omnibus praediatus, Quirinus Mars, Lars Militaris; Juno etiam ibi domicilium possidebat, Fons etiam, Lymphae diique Novensiles. Sed de tertia regione unum placuit corrogari. Nam Jovis secundani et Jovis Opulentiae Minervaeque domus illic sunt constitutae; sed omnes circa ipsum Jovem fuerant in praesenti. Discordiam vero ac Seditionem quis ad sacras nuptias corrogaret, praesertimque cum ipsi Philologiae fuerunt semper inimicae? De eadem igitur regione solus Pluton, quod patruus sponsi est, convocatur. Tunc Lynsa silvestris, Mulciber, Lar Caelestis nec non etiam militaris Favorque ex quarta regione venerunt. Corrogantur ex proxima transcursis domibus conjugum regum Ceres, Tellurus Terraeque pater Vulcanus et Genius. Vos quoque, Jovis filii, Pales et Favor cum Celeritate, Solis filia, ex sexta poscemini; nam Mars Quirinus et Genius superius postulati. Sic etiam Liber ac secundanus Pales vocantur ex septima. Fraudem quippe ex eadem post longam deliberationem placuit adhiberi, quod crebro ipsi Cyllenio fuerit obsecuta. Octava vero transcurritur, quoniam ex eadem cuncti superius corrogati, solusque ex illa Veris Fructus adhibetur. Junonis vero Hospitae Genius accitus ex nona. Neptune autem, Lar Omnium cunctalis, ac Neverita tuque Conse ex decima convenistis. Venit ex altera Fortuna et Valetudo Favorque pastor, Manibus refutatis, quippe ii in conspectu Jovis non poterant advenire. Ex duodecima Sancus tantummodo devocatur. Fata vero ex altera postulantur; ceteri quippe illic dii Manium demorati. Bis septena Saturnus eiusque caelestis Juno consequenter acciti. Veiovis ac dii publici ter quino ex limite convocantur. Ex ultima regione Nocturnus Janitoresque terrestres similiter advocati. Ex cunctis igitur caeli regionibus advocatis deis ceteri, quos Azonos vocant, ipso commonente Cyllenio convocantur.

(Source of text: *Martianus Capella*, ed. A. Dick, Stuttgart, 1978, 27-28.)

For in sixteen regions, it is said, the whole sky is divided, in the first of which, it is recorded, after Jupiter himself, the Dii Consentes and the Penates, Salus and the

Lares, Janus, the Favores Opertanei, and Nocturnus have an abode.

In the second, in like manner there dwelled—besides the house of Jupiter, which there, too, is very lofty, as he is well endowed in all things—Quirinus Mars, Lars Militaris. Juno also had a house there, Fons also, the Lymphae, and the Dii Novensiles.

But from the third region it was decided to invite one god. For the houses of Jupiter Secundanus and Jupiter of Opulentia and of Minerva were established there. But all had been present around Jupiter himself. Who would invite Discordia and Seditio to the sacred marriage, especially since they were always enemies to Philologia? Therefore from the same region only Pluto was summoned, because he was the uncle of the groom.

Then Lynsa Silvestris, Mulciber, Lars Caelestis, and likewise Lars Militaris and Favor came from the fourth region.

From the next, as the homes of the royal spouses were traversed, Ceres, Tellurus and the father of Terra, Vulcan, and Genius were invited.

You, too, sons of Jupiter, Pales, and Favor with Celeritas, daughter of Sol, are requested from the sixth region. For Mars Quirinus and Genius were asked above.

Thus also Liber and Secundanus Pales are called from the seventh region. From the same after long deliberation it was decided to include Fraus, because she had frequently complied with the Cyllenian himself.

The eighth is passed through, because from it all had already been invited, and only Veris Fructus is included from this region.

The Genius of Juno Hospita is summoned from the ninth.

But Neptune, Lar Omnium Cunctalis, and Neverita, and you, too, Consus, were called from the tenth.

From the next come Fortuna and Valetudo and Favor Pastor, with the Manes turned away, because indeed they were not able to come into the sight of Jupiter.

From the twelfth only Sancus is called.

From the next the Fata are requested; but others, the Dii Manes, tarry there.

From the twice-seven region Saturn and his Caelestis Juno are consequently summoned.

Veiovis and the Dii Publici are called from the thrice-five boundary.

From the last region Nocturnus and the Janitores Terrestris similarly are summoned.

Therefore when all the gods had been summoned from the regions of the sky, those whom they called the Azoni were invited at the urging of the Cyllenian himself.

III.5. *Suda, Lexikon*, s.v. Τυρρηνία:

ἱστορίαν δὲ παρ' αὐτοῖς ἔμπειρος ἀνὴρ συνεγράψατο· ἔφη γὰρ τὸν δημιουργὸν τῶν πάντων θεὸν ιβ χιλιάδας ἐνιαυτῶν τοῖς πᾶσιν αὐτοῦ φιλοτιμήσασθαι κτίσμασι, καὶ ταύτας διαθεῖναι τοῖς ιβ λεγομένοις οἴκοις· καὶ τῇ μὲν α χιλιάδι ποιῆσαι τὸν οὐρανὸν καὶ τὴν γῆν· τῇ δὲ β ποιῆσαι τὸ στερέωμα τοῦτο τὸ φαινόμενον, καλέσας αὐτὸ οὐρανόν, τῇ γ τὴν θάλασσαν καὶ τὰ ὕδατα τὰ ἐν τῇ γῇ πάντα, τῇ δ τοὺς φωστῆρας τοὺς μεγάλους, ἥλιον καὶ σελήνην καὶ τοὺς ἀστέρας, τῇ ε πᾶσαν ψυχὴν πετεινῶν καὶ ἑρπετῶν καὶ τετράπαδα, ἐν τῷ ἀέρι καὶ ἐν τῇ γῇ καὶ τοῖς ὕδασι, τῇ ς τὸν ἄνθρωπον. φαίνεται οὖν τὰς μὲν πρώτας ἕξ χιλιάδας πρὸ τῆς τοῦ ἀνθρώπου διαπλάσεως παρεληλυθέναι· τὰς δὲ λοιπὰς ἕξ χιλιάδας διαμένειν τὸ γένος τῶν ἀνθρώπων. ὡς εἶναι τὸν πάντα χρόνον μέχρι τῆς συντελείας χιλιάδας ιβ.

Tyrrhenia.
A knowledgeable man among them composed a mythology, for he said that the demiurge who created all things strove on behalf of his creations for twelve periods of one thousand years each and that he distributed those periods according to the twelve so-called Houses.

In the first period of one thousand years, he made the heaven and the earth.

In the second, he made this firmament manifest, calling it heaven.

In the third, he made the sea and all the waters in the earth.

In the fourth, he made the great lights: the sun, the moon, the stars.

In the fifth, he gave life to all the birds, the creatures that crawl, and those that go on all fours, in the air, on the land, and in the water.

In the sixth, he made man.

Thus it appears that the first six periods of one thousand years passed before the forming of man and that during the remaining six, the race of humans endured, since it existed during the whole time until the end of the twelfth period.

III.6. Censorinus, *De die natali* 17.5–6.

In una quaque civitate quae sint naturalia saecula, rituales Etruscorum libri videntur docere, in quis scriptum esse fertur initia sic poni saeculorum: quo die urbes atque civitates constituerentur, de iis, qui eo die nati essent, eum, qui diutissime vixisset, die mortis suae primi saeculi modulum finire, eoque die qui essent reliqui in civitate, de his rursum eius mortem, qui longissimam egisset aetatem, finem esse saeculi secundi. Sic deinceps tempus reliquorum terminari. Sed ea quod ignorarent homines, portenta mitti divinitus, quibus admonerentur unum quodque saeculum esse finitum. Haec portenta Etrusci pro haruspicii disciplinaeque suae peritia diligenter observata in libros rettulerunt. Quare in Tuscis historiis quae octavo eorum saeculo scriptae sunt, ut Varro testatur, et quot numero saecula ei genti data sint, et transactorum singula quanta fuerint quibusve ostentis eorum exitus designati sint, continetur. Itaque scriptum est quattuor prima saecula annorum fuisse centenum, quintum centum viginti trium, sextum undeviginti et centum, septimum totidem, octavum tum demum agi, nonum et decimum superesse, quibus transactis finem fore nominis etrusci.

(Source of text: *Censorini De die natali liber*, ed. N. Sallmann, Leipzig, 1983, 34.)

In each single city the ritual books of the Etruscans seem to teach what the natural *saecula* [divisions] of time are; it is said that in them is written what the beginnings of the *saecula* are: of those who were born on the day on which a city or state was founded, the one who lived the longest would set the end measure of the first *saeculum* on the day of his death; and of those who remained in the state on that day, again the death of the one who lived the longest age would be the end of the second *saeculum*. Thus in a series the time of the remaining ages would end. But since men would not know these things, portents were sent from the gods by which they were advised that each one *saeculum* was finished. These portents, diligently observed, the Etruscans recorded into their books for the sake of skill in divination and their teaching. Therefore in the Tuscan histories that were written in their eighth *saeculum*, as Varro witnesses, are recorded how many *saecula* have been given to that nation and how many have been accomplished one by one, and by what portents their conclusions were indicated. And thus it is written that the first four *saecula* were of one hundred years, the fifth was of one hundred and twenty-three, the sixth of one hundred and nineteen, the seventh the same, the eighth was going on at that time, and the ninth and tenth were still to come; when they were accomplished there would be an end of the Etruscan name.

III.7. Plutarch, *Life of Sulla* 7.3–6.

τὸ δὲ πάντων μέγιστον, ἐξ ἀνεφέλου καὶ διαίθρου τοῦ περιέχοντος ἤχησε φωνὴ σάλπιγγος ὀξὺν ἀποτείνουσα καὶ θρηνώδη φθόγγον, ὥστε πάντας ἔκφρονας γενέσθαι καὶ καταπτῆξαι διὰ τὸ μέγεθος. Τυρρηνῶν δὲ οἱ λόγιοι μεταβολὴν ἑτέρου γένους ἀπεφαίνοντο καὶ μετακόσμησιν ἀποσημαίνειν τὸ τέρας. εἶναι μὲν γὰρ ὀκτὼ τὰ σύμπαντα γένη, διαφέροντα τοῖς βίοις καὶ τοῖς ἤθεσιν ἀλλήλων, ἑκάστῳ δὲ ἀφωρίσθαι χρόνων ἀριθμὸν ὑπὸ τοῦ θεοῦ συμπεραινόμενον ἐνιαυτοῦ μεγάλου περιόδῳ. καὶ ὅταν αὕτη σχῇ τέλος, ἑτέρας ἐνισταμένης κινεῖσθαί τι σημεῖον ἐκ γῆς ἢ οὐρανοῦ θαυμάσιον, ὡς δῆλον εἶναι τοῖς πεφροντικόσι τὰ τοιαῦτα καὶ μεμαθηκόσιν εὐθὺς ὅτι καὶ τρόποις ἄλλοις καὶ βίοις ἄνθρωποι χρώμενοι γεγόνασι, καὶ θεοῖς ἧττον ἢ μᾶλλον τῶν προτέρων μέλοντες. τά τε γὰρ ἄλλα φασὶν ἐν τῇ τῶν γενῶν ἀμείψει λαμβάνειν μεγάλας καινοτομίας, καὶ τὴν μαντικὴν ποτὲ μὲν αὔξεσθαι τῇ τιμῇ καὶ κατατυγχάνειν ταῖς προαγορεύσεσι, καθαρὰ καὶ φανερὰ σημεῖα τοῦ δαιμονίου προπέμποντος, αὖθις δ' ἐν ἑτέρῳ γένει ταπεινὰ πράττειν, αὐτοσχέδιον οὖσαν τὰ πολλὰ καὶ δι' ἀμυδρῶν καὶ σκοτεινῶν ὀργάνων τοῦ μέλλοντος πτομένην. ταῦτα μὲν οὖν οἱ λογιώτατοι Τυρρηνῶν καὶ πλέον τι τῶν ἄλλων εἰδέναι δοκοῦντες ἐμυθολόγουν.

Most important of all, out of a cloudless and clear air there rang out the voice of a trumpet, prolonging a shrill and dismal note, so that all were amazed and terrified at its loudness. The Tuscan [lit. "Tyrrhenian"] wise men declared that the prodigy foretokened a change of conditions and the advent of a new age. For according to them there are eight ages in all, differing from one another in the lives and customs of men, and to each of these God has appointed a definite number of times and seasons, which is completed by the circuit of a great year. And whenever this circuit has run out, and another begins, some wonderful sign is sent from earth or heaven, so that it is at once clear to those who have studied such subjects and are versed in them, that men of other habits and modes of life have come into the world, who are either more or less of concern to the gods than their predecessors were. All things, they say, undergo great changes, as one age succeeds another, and especially the art of divination; at one period it rises in esteem and is successful in its predictions, because manifest and genuine signs are sent forth from the Deity; and again, in another age, it is in small repute, being off-hand, for the most part, and seeking to grasp the future by means of faint and blind senses. Such at any rate, was the tale told by the wisest of the Tuscans [lit. "Tyrrhenians"], who were thought to know much more about it than the rest.

> (Translation reprinted by permission of the publishers and the Trustees of the Loeb Classical Library from *Plutarch's Lives, Alcibiades and Coriolanus, Lysander and Sulla*, Loeb Classical Library, Vol. 4, translated by B. Perrin, Cambridge, MA: Harvard University Press, 1968, pp. 347, 349. The Loeb Classical Library © is a registered trademark of the President and Fellows of Harvard College.)

III.8. *Liber Glossarum.*

Aclus Tuscorum lingua Junis mensis dicitur.... Ampiles Tuscorum lingua Maius mensis dicitur.... Cabreas Tuscorum lingua Aprilis mensis.... Celius Tuscorum lingua September mensis dicitur.... [H]ermius Tuscorum lingua Augustus mensis dicitur.... Traneus Tuscorum lingua Iulius mensis dicitur.... Velcitanus Tuscorum lingua Martis mensis dicitur.... Xosfer Tuscorum lingua October mensis dicitur.

> (Source: TLE 801, 805, 818, 824, 836, 854, 856, 858.)

In the language of the Tuscans, the month of June is called Aclus.... In the language of the Tuscans, the month of May is called Ampiles.... In the language of the Tuscans, the month of April is called Cabreas.... In the language of the Tuscans, the month of September is called Celius.... In the language of the Tuscans, the month of August is called Hermius.... In the language of the Tuscans, the month of July is called Traneus.... In the language of the Tuscans, the month of March is called Velcitanus.... In the language of the Tuscans, the month of October is called Xosfer.

III.9. Servius, *Ad Aen.* 5.738.

Dies secundum Aegyptios inchoat ab occasu solis, secundum Persas ab ortu solis, secundum Etruscos et Athenienses a sexta hora diei, secundum Romanos a media nocte.

> (*Servianorum in Vergilii carmina commentariorum*, Oxford, 1965, vol. 3, 573.)

According to the Egyptians, the day begins at the setting of the sun; according to the Persians, at the rising of the sun; according to the Etruscans and the Athenians, at the sixth hour of the day; according to the Romans, at midnight.

IV. THE *ETRUSCA DISCIPLINA*

IV.1. Festus 285.

Rituales nominantur Etruscorum libri, in quibus perscribtum est, quo ritu condantur urbes, arae, aedes sacrentur, qua sanctitate muri, quo jure portae, quomodo tribus, curiae, centuriae distribuantur, exercitus constituant[ur], ordinentur, ceteraque eiusmodi ad bellum ac pacem pertinentia.

> (Source of text: Thulin I, 8).

[Those] books of the Etruscans are called *ritual* in which it is prescribed by what rite cities are founded [and] altars and temples are consecrated, with what sanctity walls, with what rule gates, in what manner tribes, councils, and centuries are divided, armies constituted, and other things of this type pertaining to war and peace.

IV.2. Varro, *De lingua Latina* 5.143.

Oppida condebant in Latio Etrusco ritu multi, id est junctis bobus, tauro et vacca interiore aratro circumagebant sulcum. Hoc faciebant religionis causa die auspicato, ut fossa et muro essent muniti. Terram unde exsculpserant fossam, vocabant et introrsus jactam murum. Post ea qui fiebat orbis urbis principium; qui quod erat post murum, postmoerium dictum eiusque auspicia urbana finiuntur.... Cippi pomeri stant et circum Ariciam et circum Romam.

Many founded towns in Latium by the Etruscan ritual; that is, with a team of cattle, a bull and a cow on the inside, they ran a furrow around with a plough. For reasons of religion they did this on an auspicious day, so that they might be fortified by a ditch and a wall. The place whence they had ploughed up the earth, they called a *fossa* "ditch," and the earth thrown inside it they called the *murus*, "wall." The *orbis*, "circle," which was made back of this, was the beginning of the *urbs*, "city"; because the circle was *post murum* "back of the wall," it was called a *postmoerium*; it sets the limits for the taking of the auspices for the city. Stone markers of the pomerium stand both around Aricia and around Rome.

> (Translation reprinted by permission of the publishers and the Trustees of the Loeb Classical Library from *Varro, On the Latin Language*, Loeb Classical Library, Vol. 1, translated by R. G. Kent, Cambridge, MA: Harvard University Press, 1938, p. 135. The Loeb

Classical Library © is a registered trademark of the President and Fellows of Harvard College.)

IV.3. Plutarch, *Life of Romulus* 11.

Ὁ δὲ Ῥωμύλος ἐν τῇ Ῥεμωνίᾳ θάψας τὸν Ῥέμον ὁμοῦ καὶ τοὺς τροφεῖς, ᾤκιζε τὴν πόλιν, ἐκ Τυρρηνίας μεταπεμψάμενος ἄνδρας ἱεροῖς τισι θεσμοῖς καὶ γράμμασιν ὑφηγουμένους ἕκαστα καὶ διδάσκοντας ὥσπερ ἐν τελετῇ. βόθρος γὰρ ὠρύγη περὶ τὸ νῦν Κομίτιον κυκλοτερής, ἀπαρχαί τε πάντων, ὅσοις νόμῳ μὲν ὡς καλοῖς ἐχρῶντο, φύσει δ' ὡς ἀναγκαίοις, ἀπετέθησαν ἐνταῦθα. καὶ τέλος ἐξ ἧς ἀφῖκτο γῆς ἕκαστος ὀλίγην κομίζων μοῖραν ἔβαλλον εἰς ταὐτὸ καὶ συνεμείγνυον. καλοῦσι δὲ τὸν βόθρον τοῦτον ᾧ καὶ τὸν ὄλυμπον ὀνόματι μοῦνδον. εἶθ' ὥσπερ κύκλον κέντρῳ περιέγραψαν τὴν πόλιν. ὁ δ' οἰκιστὴς ἐμβαλὼν ἀρότρῳ χαλκῆν ὕνιν, ὑποζεύξας δὲ βοῦν ἄρρενα καὶ θήλειαν, αὐτὸς μὲν ἐπάγει περιελαύνων αὔλακα βαθεῖαν τοῖς τέρμασι, τῶν δ' ἑπομένων ἔργον ἐστίν, ἃς ἀνίστησι βώλους τὸ ἄροτρον, καταστρέφειν εἴσω καὶ μηδεμίαν ἔξω περιορᾶν ἐκτρεπομένην. τῇ μὲν οὖν γραμμῇ τὸ τεῖχος ἀφορίζουσι, καὶ καλεῖται κατὰ συγκοπὴν πωμήριον, οἷον ὄπισθεν τείχους ἢ μετὰ τεῖχος· ὅπου δὲ πύλην ἐμβαλεῖν διανοοῦνται, τὴν ὕνιν ἐξελόντες καὶ τὸ ἄροτρον ὑπερθέντες διάλειμμα ποιοῦσιν. ὅθεν ἅπαν τὸ τεῖχος ἱερὸν πλὴν τῶν πυλῶν νομίζουσι· τὰς δὲ πύλας ἱερὰς νομίζοντας οὐκ ἦν ἄνευ δεισιδαιμονίας τὰ μὲν δέχεσθαι, τὰ δ' ἀποπέμπειν τῶν ἀναγκαίων καὶ μὴ καθαρῶν.

Romulus buried Remus, together with his foster-fathers, in the Remonia, and then set himself to building his city, after summoning from Tuscany [lit. "Tyrrhenia"] men who prescribed all the details in accordance with certain sacred ordinances and writings, and taught them to him as in a religious rite. A circular trench was dug around what is now the Comitium, and in this were deposited the first-fruits of all things the use of which was sanctioned by custom as good and by nature as necessary; and finally, every man brought a small portion of the soil of his native land, and these were cast in among the first fruits and mingled with them. They call this trench, as they do the heavens, by the name of *mundus*. Then, taking this as a centre, they marked out the city in a circle round it. And the founder, having shod a plough with a brazen ploughshare, and having yoked to it a bull and a cow, himself drove a deep furrow round the boundary lines, while those who followed after him had to turn the clods, which the plough threw up, inwards toward the city, and suffer no clod to lie turned outwards. With this line they marked out the course of the wall, and it is called, by contraction, "pomerium," that is "post murum," *behind* or *next the wall*. And where they purposed to put in a gate, there they took the share out of the ground, lifted the plough over, and left a vacant space. And this is the reason why they regard all the wall as sacred except the gates; but if they held the gates sacred, it would not be possible, without religious scruples, to bring into and send out of the city things which are necessary, and yet unclean.

(Translation reprinted by permission of the publishers and the Trustees of the Loeb Classical Library from *Plutarch's Lives, Alcibiades and Coriolanus, Lysander and Sulla,* Loeb Classical Library, Vol. 1, translated by B. Perrin, Cambridge, MA: Harvard University Press, 1968, pp. 119, 121. The Loeb Classical Library © is a registered trademark of the President and Fellows of Harvard College.)

IV.4. Columella, *De re rustica* 10.338–347.

Ipsa novas artis varia experientia rerum
et labor ostendit miseris ususque magister
tradidit agricolis ventos sedare furentis
et tempestatem Tuscis avertere sacris.
Hinc mala Rubigo viridis ne torreat herbas,
sanguine lactentis catuli placatur et extis.
Hinc caput Arcadici nudum cute fertur aselli
Tyrrhenus fixisse Tages in limite ruris,
utque Jouis magni prohiberet fulgura Tarchon,
saepe suas sedes praecinxit vitibus albis.
Hinc Amythaonius, docuit quem plurima Chiron,
nocturnas crucibus volucres suspendit et altis
culminibus vetuit feralia carmina flere.

Lest rustics suffer from these monstrous pests,
Varied experience of herself and toil
And use, their teacher novel arts have shown
To wretched husbandmen, how to appease
Fierce winds and to avert by Tuscan rites
The tempest. Hence, lest fell Rubigo parch
The fresh, green plants, her anger is appeased
With blood and entrails of a suckling whelp;
Hence Tages, Tuscan [lit. "Tyrrhenian"] seer, they say, set up
The skinless head of an Arcadian ass
At the field's edge; hence Tarchon, to avert
The bolts of mighty Jove, oft hedged his domain
With bryony; and Amythaon's son,
Whom Chiron taught much wisdom, hung aloft

Night-flying birds on crosses and forbade
Their sad funereal cries on housetops high.

> (Translation reprinted by permission of the publishers and the Trustees of the Loeb Classical Library from *Lucius Junius Columella On Agriculture and Trees*, Loeb Classical Library, Vol. 3, translated by E. S. Forster and E. H. Heffner, Cambridge, MA: Harvard University Press, 1955, p. 37. The Loeb Classical Library © is a registered trademark of the President and Fellows of Harvard College.)

IV.5. Macrobius, *Saturnalia* 5.19.13.

Sed Carmini curiossimi et docti verba ponam, qui in libro de Italia secundo sic ait prius itaque et Tuscos aeneo vomere uti, cum conderentur urbes, solitos, in Tageticis eorum sacris invenio et in Sabinis ex aere cultros, quibus sacerdotes tonderentur.

(Source of text: Thulin 3, 5.)

I shall set down the words of Carminius, a most curious and learned man, who in his second book *de Italia* [*Concerning Italy*] thus says, "Earlier the Tuscans, when they were going to found a city, were accustomed to use a bronze plow." I find in their own sacred Tagetic [books] and in Sabine [books] that there were plowshares of bronze with which the priests shaved.

IV.6. Macrobius, *Saturnalia* 3.7.2.

Est super hoc liber Tarquitii transcriptus ex Ostentario Tusco ibi repperitur purpureo aureove colore ovis ariesve si aspergetur, principi ordinis et generis summa cum felicitate largitatem auget, genus progeniem propagat in claritate laetioremque efficit.

(Source of text: Thulin 1, 11).

There is beyond this a book of Tarquitius transcribed from the *Ostentarium Tuscum* [*Tuscan Prognostics*] in which it is found that if a sheep or a ram is sprinkled with crimson or gold color it increases abundance with the greatest happiness for the initiator of the order and the genus. The genus propagates offspring in splendor and makes him more joyful.

IV.7. Cicero, *De divinatione* 2.38.80.

Omitte igitur lituum Romuli, quem in maximo incendio negas potuisse comburi; contemne cotem Atti Navii. Nihil debet esse in philosophia commenticiis fabellis loci; illud erat philosophi potius, totius augurii primum naturam ipsam videre, deinde inventionem, deinde constantiam. Quae est igitur natura, quae volucris huc et illuc passim vagantis efficiat ut significent aliquid et tum vetent agere, tum jubeant aut cantu aut volatu? cur autem aliis a laeva, aliis a dextra datum est avibus ut ratum auspicium facere possint? Quo modo autem haec aut quando aut a quibus inventa dicemus? Etrusci tamen habent exaratum puerum auctorem disciplinae suae; nos quem? Attumne Navium? At aliquot annis antiquior Romulus et Remus, ambo augures, ut accepimus. An Pisidarum aut Cilicum aut Phrygum ista inventa dicemus? Placet igitur humanitatis expertis habere divinitatis auctores?

Then dismiss Romulus' augural staff, which you say the hottest of fires was powerless to burn, and attach slight importance to the whetstone of Attus Navius. Myths should have no place in philosophy. It would have been more in keeping with your role as a philosopher to consider, first, the nature of divination generally, second, its origin, and third, its consistency. What, then, is the nature of an art which makes prophets out of birds that wander aimlessly about — now here, now there — and makes the action or inaction of men depend upon the song or flight of birds? And why was the power granted to some birds to give a favourable omen when on the left side and to others when on the right? Again, how, when, and by whom, shall we say that the system was invented? The Etruscans, it is true, find the author of their system in the boy who was ploughed up out of the ground; but whom have we? Attus Navius? But Romulus and Remus, both of whom, by tradition, were augurs, lived many years earlier. Are we to say that it was invented by the Pisidians, Cilicians, or Phrygians? It is your judgment, then, that those devoid of human learning are the authors of divine science!

> (Translation reprinted by permission of the publishers and the Trustees of the Loeb Classical Library from Cicero, *De senectute, De amicitia, De divinatione*, Loeb Classical Library, Vol. 20, translated by W. A. Falconer, Cambridge, MA: Harvard University Press, 1922, pp. 461, 463. The Loeb Classical Library © is a registered trademark of the President and Fellows of Harvard College.)

IV.8. Cicero, *De divinatione* 1.41.92.

Etruria autem de caelo tacta scientissime animadvertit eademque interpretatur, quid quibusque ostendatur monstris atque portentis. Quocirca bene apud maiores nostros senatus tum, cum florebat imperium, decrevit, ut de principum filiis sex* singulis Etruriae populis in disciplinam traderentur, ne ars tanta propter tenuitatem hominum a religionis auctoritate abduceretur ad mercedem atque quaestum. [*or x ex]

Etruria observes most skillfully lightning strikes from the sky, and they interpret the same, as to what is shown and with what signs and portents. Wherefore it was well devised among our forefathers in the Senate at that time when our power was growing that from the sons of the foremost men six [or ten] should be handed over to the individual peoples of Etruria for (learning) the discipline, in order that the art not be seduced away from the authority of religion toward reward and profit.

IV.9. Valerius Maximus 1.1.

Maiores statas sollemnesque caerimonias pontificum scientia, bene gerendarum rerum auctoritates augurum observatione, Apollinis praedictiones vatum libris, portentorum depulsi[one]s Etrusca disciplina explicari voluerunt.... Tantum autem studium antiquis non solum servandae sed etiam amplificandae religionis fuit, ut florentissima tum et opulentissima civitate decem principum filii senatus consulto singulis Etruriae populis percipiendae sacrorum disciplinae gratia traderentur.

Our ancestors willed that fixed and customary ceremonies be carried out by the priests, that the authority for conducting things well come from the observation of augurs, that the prophecies of Apollo proceed from the books of the seers, and that the turning away of bad omens come through the Etruscan discipline.... So great was the zeal of the ancients not only for the maintaining but also for the expanding of religion that at a time when Rome was most flourishing and wealthy, by decree of the senate, ten sons of nobles were handed over to the individual peoples of Etruria for the purpose of learning the discipline of sacred matters.

IV.10. Livy 7.17.2–6.

Falisci Tarquiniensesque alterum consulem prima pugna fuderunt. Inde terror maximus fuit quod sacerdotes eorum facibus ardentibus anguibusque praelatis incessu furiali militem Romanum insueta turbaverunt specie. Et tum quidem velut lymphati et attoniti munimentis suis trepido agmine inciderunt; deinde, ubi consul legatique ac tribuni puerorum ritu vana miracula paventes inridebant increpabantque, vertit animos repente pudor et in ea ipsa quae fugerant velut caeci ruebant. Discusso itaque vano apparatu hostium, cum in ipsos armatos se intulissent, averterunt totam aciem.

The Faliscans and Tarquinians routed the other consul in the first battle. The greatest terror came from the fact that their priests, carrying forward burning torches and serpents in the manner of attacking Furies, threw the Roman army into confusion at the unfamiliar sight. And then indeed like men out of their minds and dumbstruck they fell on their own works with a wavering battleline. Then, when the consul and legates and tribunes laughed at them and chided them because they trembled in the manner of children over the empty marvels, suddenly shame turned their spirits, and they rushed like blind men against the very things from which they had fled. And so while brushing aside the empty mechanisms of the enemy as they flung themselves on armed men, they turned the whole battle line.

V. ETRUSCAN TEMPLES, SHRINES, AND TOMBS

V.1. Livy 7.3.7.

Volsiniis quoque clavos indices numeri annorum fixos in templo Nortiae, Etruscae deae, comparere diligens talium monumentorum auctor Cincius adfirmat.

Cincius, a careful student of such memorials, asserts that at Volsinii, too, nails may be seen in the temple of Nortia, an Etruscan goddess, driven in to indicate the number of years.

> (Translation reprinted by permission of the publishers and the Trustees of the Loeb Classical Library from *Livy in Fourteen Volumes*, Loeb Classical Library, Vol. 3, translated by B. Foster, Cambridge, MA: Harvard University Press, 1919, p. 367. The Loeb Classical Library © is a registered trademark of the President and Fellows of Harvard College.)

V.2. Vitruvius 1.7.1–2.

Aedibus vero sacris, quorum deorum maxime in tutela civitas videtur esse, et Jovi et Junoni et Minervae, in excelsissimo loco, unde moenium maxima pars conspiciatur, areae distribuantur. Mercurio autem in foro aut etiam, ut Isidi et Serapi, in emporio; Apollini Patrique Libero secundum theatrum; Herculi, in quibus civitatibus non sunt gymnasia neque amphitheatra, ad circum; Marti extra urbem sed ad campum; itemque Veneri ad portum.

Id autem etiam Etruscis haruspicibus disciplinarum scripturis ita est dedicatum, extra murum Veneris, Volcani, Martis fana ideo conlocari, uti non insuescat in urbe adulescentibus seu matribus familiarum veneria libido, Volcanique vi e moenibus religionibus et sacrificiis evocata ab timore incendiorum aedificia videantur liberari. Martis vero divinitas cum sit extra moenia dedicata, non erit inter cives armigera dissensio, sed ab hostibus ea defensa belli periculo conservabit. Item Cereri extra urbem loco, quo nomine semper homines nisi per sacrificium necesse habeant adire; cum religione, caste sanctisque moribus is locus debet tueri. Ceterisque diis ad sacrificiorum rationes aptae templis areae sunt distribuendae.

But for sacred buildings of the gods under whose protection the city most seems to be, both for Jupiter and Juno and Minerva, the sites are to be distributed on the highest ground from which the most of the ramparts is to be seen. To Mercury, however, in the forum, or also, as to Isis and Serapis, in the business quarter; to Apollo and Father Bacchus against the theatre; to Hercules, in cities which have no gymnasia nor amphitheatres, at the circus; to Mars outside the walls but in the parade ground; and also to Venus near the harbour.

Now with Etruscan haruspices in the writings of their disciplines, the dedication is as follows: that the shrines of Venus, Volcanus, Mars are therefore to be situated outside the wall, so that venereal pleasure may not be customary to young men and matrons in the city, and, by summoning the power of Volcanus outside the ramparts with ritual and sacrifices, the buildings may seem to be freed from fear of fires. But since the divinity of Mars is dedicated outside the ramparts, there will not be armed quarrels among citizens, yet he will keep the ramparts defended from the danger of war. So also to Ceres in a place outside the city, under which name (i.e., Ceres extra urbem) men (unless by sacrifice) must always approach her; since that place must be kept religiously, purely and with strict manners. And to the other gods sites fit for temples with a view to the methods of sacrifice are to be arranged.

> (Translation reprinted by permission of the publishers and the Trustees of the Loeb Classical Library from *Vitruvius on Architecture*, Loeb Classical Library, translated by F. Granger, Cambridge, MA: Harvard University Press, 1931, pp. 67, 69. The Loeb Classical Library © is a registered trademark of the President and Fellows of Harvard College.)

V.3. Vitruvius 4.7.

Locus, in quo aedis constituetur, cum habuerit in longitudine sex partes, una dempta reliquum quod erit, latitudini detur. Longitudo autem dividatur bipertito, et quae pars erit interior, cellarum spatiis designetur, quae erit proxima fronti, columnarum dispositioni relinquatur. Item latitudo dividatur in partes x. Ex his ternae partes dextra ac sinistra cellis minoribus, sive ibi alae futurae sunt, dentur; reliquae quattuor mediae aedi attribuantur. Spatium, quod erit ante cellas in pronao, ita columnis designetur, ut angulares contra antas, parietum extremorum [e] regione, conlocentur; duae mediae e regione parietum, qui inter antas et mediam aedem fuerint, ita distribuantur; et inter antas et columnas priores per medium isdem regionibus alterae disponantur. Eaeque sint ima crassitudine altitudinis parte vii; altitudo tertia parte latitudinis templi; summaque columna quarta parte crassitudinis imae contrahatur. Spirae earum altae dimidia parte crassitudinis fiant. Habeant spirae earum plinthum ad circinum, altam suae crassitudinis dimidia parte, torum insuper cum apophysi crassum quantum plinthus. Capituli altitudo dimidia crassitudinis. Abaci latitudo quanta ima crassitudo columnae. Capitulique crassitudo dividatur in partes tres, e quibus una plintho, quae est abacus, detur, altera echino, tertia hypotrachelio cum apophysi. Supra columnas trabes compactiles inponantur ut altitudinis modulis is, qui a magnitudine operis postulabuntur. Eaeque trabes compactiles eam habeant crassitudinem, quanta summae columnae erithypotrachelium, et ita sint compactae subscudibus et securiclis, ut compactura duorum digitorum habeant laxationem. Cum enim inter se tangunt et non spiramentum et perflatum venti recipiunt, concalefaciuntur et celeriter putrescunt. Supra trabes et supra parietes trajecturae mutulorum parte iiii altitudinis columnae proiciantur; item in eorum frontibus antepagmenta figantur. Supraque is tympanum fastigii structura seu de materia conlocetur. Supraque eûm fastigium, columen, cantherii, templa ita sunt conlocanda, ut stillicidium tecti absoluti tertiario respondeat.

Let the site on which the temple is to be built be six parts in length; five parts are to be assigned to the breadth. Now the length is to be divided in two. The interior half is to be marked out by the dimensions of the sanctuary; the part on the front is to be left for the portico with its columns. Further, let the width be divided into 10 parts. Of these let three parts each on the right and left be given to the lesser sanctuaries, or alternately to the wings; the remaining four parts are to be given to the central shrine. Let the space which is before the sanctuaries in the forecourt be planned for the columns, in such a way that the corner columns are put opposite the pilasters, in line with the ends of the walls. The two middle columns are to be in line with the walls which are between the wings and the middle shrine. Between the pilasters and the columns in front, additional columns are to be put half way in line with them. At the bottom these are to have a diameter of 1/7 of the height. (The height is to be one third of the width of the temple.) The top of the column is to be diminished 1/4 of the diameter at the bottom. The bases are to be made half a diameter high. Let the bases have their plinths circular and half the height of the base, with a torus and *apophysis* as deep as the plinth. The height of the capital is to be half a diameter. The width of the abacus is as great as the diameter of the column at the base. The height of the capital is to be divided into three parts, of which one is to be given to the plinth or abacus, one to the echinus or ovolo, the third to the hypotrachelium with the apophysis. Above the columns, beams are to be placed bolted together, of such proportionate depth as shall be demanded by the magnitude of the work. And these coupled beams are to have a thickness equal to the hypotrachelium at the top of the column, and they are to be so coupled with dowels and mortices that the coupling allows an interval of two inches between the joists. For when they touch one another and do not admit a breathing space and passage of air, they are heated and quickly decay. Above the beams and walls the mutules are to project 1/4 of the height of the column. On the front of these, casings (antepagmenta) are to be fixed and above them the tympanum of the gable either of stone or wood. Above this the ridge-piece, rafters, and purlins, are to be so placed that the pitch of the roof is one in three.

> (Translation reprinted by permission of the publishers and the Trustees of the Loeb Classical Library from *Vitruvius on Architecture,* Loeb Classical Library, translated by F. Granger, Cambridge, MA: Harvard University Press, 1931, pp. 239, 241. The Loeb Classical Library © is a registered trademark of the President and Fellows of Harvard College.)

V.4. Aulus Gellius, *Noctes Atticae* 7.12.5-6.

Nam in libro de religionibus secundo: sacellum est, inquit, locus parvus deo sacratus cum ara. Deinde addit verba haec: Sacellum ex duobus verbis arbitror compositum sacri et cellae, quasi sacra cella. Hoc quidem scripsit Trebatius; sed quis ignorat sacellum et simplex verbum esse et non ex sacro et cella copulatum, sed ex sacro deminutum?

For he [Gaius Trebatius] says in the second book of his work *On Religions*: "A *sacellum,* or shrine, is a small place consecrated to a god and containing an altar." Then he adds these words: "*Sacellum,* I think, is made up of the two words *sacer* and *cella,* as if it were *sacra cella,* or a sacred chamber." This indeed is what Trebatius wrote, but who does not know both that *sacellum* is not a compound, and that it is not made up of *sacer* and *cella,* but is the diminutive of *sacrum*?

V.5. Pliny, *Historia Naturalis* 36.91-93.

Namque et Italicum dici convenit, quem fecit sibi Porsina, rex Etruriae, sepulchri causa, simul ut externorum regum vanitas quoque Italis superetur. sed cum excedat omnia fabulositas, utemur ipsius M. Varronis in expositione e[a] verbis: Sepultus sub urbe Clusio, in quo loco monimentum reliquit lapide quadrato quadratum, singula latera pedum tricenum, alta quinquagenum. In qua basi quadrata intus labyrinthum inextricabile, quo si quis introierit sine glomere lini, exitum invenire nequeat. supra id quadratum pyramides stant quinque, quattuor in angulis et in medio una, imae latae pedum quinum septuagenum, altae centenum quinquagenum, ita fastigatae, ut in summo orbis aeneus et petasus unus omnibus sit inpositus, ex quo pendeant exapta catenis tintinabula, quae vento agitata longe sonitus referant, ut Dodonae olim factum. Supra quem orbem quattuor pyramides insuper singulae stant altae pedum centenum. supra quas uno solo quinque pyramides. Quarum altitudinem Varronem puduit adicere; fabulae Etruscae tradunt eandem fuisse quam totius operis ad eas, vesana dementia, quaesisse gloriam inpendio nulli profuturo, praeterea fatigasse regni vires, ut tamen laus major artificis esset.

For it is appropriate to call "Italian" the labyrinth made by King Porsena of Etruria to serve as his tomb, with the result at the same time that even the vanity of foreign kings is surpassed by those of Italy. But since irresponsible storytelling here exceeds all bounds, I shall in describing the building make use of the very words of Marcus Varro himself: "He is buried close to the city of Clusium, in a place where he has left a square monument built of squared blocks of stone, each side being 300 feet long and 50 feet high. Inside this square pedestal there is a tangled labyrinth, which no one must enter without a ball of thread if he is to find his way out. On this square pedestal stand five pyramids, four at the corners and one at the centre, each of them being 75 feet broad at the base and 150 feet high. They taper in such a manner that on top of the whole group there rests a single bronze disk together with a conical cupola, from which hang bells fastened with chains: when these are set in motion by the wind, their sound carries to a great distance, as was formerly the case at Dodona. On this disk stand four more pyramids, each 100 feet high, and above these on a single platform, five more." The height of these last pyramids was a detail that Varro was ashamed to add to his account; but the Etruscan stories relate that it was equal to that of the whole work up to their level, insane folly as it was to have courted fame by spending for the benefit of none and to have exhausted furthermore the resources of a kingdom; and the result after all, was more honour for the designer than for the sponsor.

(Translation reprinted by permission of the publishers and the Trustees of the Loeb Classical Library from *Pliny, Natural History,* Loeb Classical Library, Vol. 10, translated by D. E. Eichholz, Cambridge, MA: Harvard University Press, 1962, pp. 73, 75. The Loeb Classical Library © is a registered trademark of the President and Fellows of Harvard College.)

VI. STATUES AND GODS

VI.1. Propertius 4.2.

Qui(d) mirare meas tot in uno corpore formas?
　accipe Vertumni signa paterna dei.
Tuscus ego Tuscis orior, nec paenitet inter
　proelia Volsinios deseruisse focos.
Haec mea turba iuvat, nec templo laetor eburno:
　Romanum satis est posse videre Forum.
Hac quondam Tiberinus iter faciebat, at aiunt
　remorum auditos per vada pulsa sonos:
at postquam ille suis tantum concessit alumnis,
　Vertumnus verso dicor ab amne deus.
Seu, quia vertentis fructum praecepimus anni,
　Vertumni rursus credis id esse sacrum.
Prima mihi variat liventibus uva racemis,
　et coma lactenti spicea fruge tumet;
hic dulces cerasos, hic autumnalia pruna
　cernis et aestivo mora rubere die;
insitor hic solvit pomosa vota corona,
　cum pirus invito stipite mala tulit.
Mendax fama vaces: alius mihi nominis index:
de se narranti tu modo crede deo.
Opportuna mea est cunctis natura figuris:
　in quamcumque voles verte, decorus ero.
Indue me Cois, fiam non dura puella:
　meque virum sumpta quis neget esse toga?
Da falcem et torto frontem mihi comprime faeno:
　iurabis nostra gramina secta manu.
Arma tuli quondam et, memini, laudabar in illis:
　corbis at imposito pondere messor eram.
Sobrius ad lites: at cum est imposta corona,
　clamabis capiti vina subisse meo.
Cinge caput mitra, speciem furabor Iacchi;
　furabor Phoebi, si modo plectra dabis.
Cassibus impositis venor: sed harundine sumpta
　fautor plumoso sum deus aucupio.
Est etiam aurigae species Vertumnus et eius,
　traicit alterno qui leve pondus equo.
Suppetat hoc, pisces calamo praedabor, et ibo
　mundus demissis institor in tunicis.
Pastor me ad baculum possum curvare vel idem
　sirpiculis medio pulvere ferre rosam.
Nam quid ego adiciam, de quo mihi maxima fama est,
　hortorum in manibus dona probata meis?
Caeruleus cucumis tumidoque cucurbita ventre
　me notat et iunco brassica vincta levi;
nec flos ullus hiat pratis, quin ille decenter
　impositus fronti langueat ante meae.
At mihi, quod formas unus vertebar in omnes,
　nomen ab aventu patria lingua dedit.
Et tu, Roma, meis tribuisti praemia Tuscis,
　(unde hodie Vicus nomina Tuscus habet),
tempore quo sociis venit Lycomedius armis
　atque Sabina feri contudit arma Tati
vidi ego labentes acies et tela caduca,
　atque hostes turpi terga dedisse fugae.
Sed facias, divum Sator, ut Romana per aevum
　transeat ante meos turba togata pedes.
Sex superant versus: te, qui ad vadimonia curris,
　non moror: haec spatiis ultima creta meis.
Stipes acernus eram, properanti falce dolatus,
　ante Numam grata pauper in urbe deus.
At tibi, Mamurri, formae caelator aenae,
　tellus artifices ne terat Osca manus,
qui me tam dociles potuisti fundere in usus.
　Unum opus est, operi non datur unus honos.[2]

Why do you wonder to see so many shapes belonging to one person? Listen: they are the inherited tokens of the god Vertumnus. I am a Tuscan, Tuscan born, and feel no remorse that I forsook the hearths of Volsinii in times of warfare. I like well this throng of mine, and I delight not in an ivory temple: it is enough that I can see the Roman Forum.

There was a time when Father Tiber took his road this way; indeed they say the noise of oars was heard upon the smitten reaches of water. But after he granted this much ground to his nurslings, I took my name from the *converting* of *amnis,* the river, and was called the god Vertumnus.

Or you may believe it is rather because we have a charge upon the first fruits of the *reverting annual* increase, that the god Vertumnus has his worship. For me the first grape among the yellow clusters begins to be spotted with purple, and the chevelure of the cornfield swells with a milky core of grain: at my feet you survey sweet cherries and autumn plums, and mulberries crimson at the midsummer time. Here the grafter pays his vows with a wreath of orchard stuff when his pear-tree has lent an unwilling stock to bear apples.

Attend, lying Hearsay! I have another key to expound my name; thou must believe none but the god's own tale about himself. My nature is easily trimmed to all shapes: turn me into which you please, I shall still be comely. Dress me in muslins of Cos, and I shall make none too prudish a girl: put me in a toga and who will gainsay that I am a man? Give me a scythe and bind my forehead tight with a wisp of hay; you shall swear that those hands have mown a grassfield. Time was, I carried arms, and I remember I was well spoken of in them; I saddled myself with the heavy panier, and in that style was a reaper. Sober enough at disputes, but when you put a garland on me you will vow that liquor has gone to my head. Give me a bonnet of my headgear, I will steal the semblance of Iacchus; and the semblance of Phoebus, if you will give me the quill. I shoulder the nets and go hunting: but if I take my cane, I am Faunus the god [or the Favoring God] of fowling for feathered game. Vertumnus is counterpart also of a charioteer and of one that shifts his agile poise from horse to horse. Let occasion offer and I will make a raid on the fishes with my rod; and I will go dapper as a peddler in loose-flowing tunic. I can play the shepherd stooping on his staff, and likewise carry roses in baskets through the dust of the lists. Nay, why should I add (what I am chiefly renowned for) that the gifts of gardens are well seen in my hands? The blue-green cucumber and the pot-bellied gourd is my emblem, and the kali-bundle tied up with a frail rush; and not a flower opens in the meadows but will droop forward becomingly if you put it on my forehead. Now because being one I could yet be *converted* into *omni-formity,* the tongue of my country named me from this circumstance. And thou, Rome, didst appoint a reward for my Tuscans (whence to this day the street of the Tuscans has its name) in the days when Lycomedius came with his confederate forces and shattered the Sabine forces of savage Tatius. I beheld the breaking ranks and the tumbling weapons, and how the enemy had turned tail in ignominious rout.

Now vouchsafe, O Father of the gods, that the gowned multitude of Rome may pass evermore before my feet.

I have six lines left over. I will not keep you long, Sir, who are hurrying to answer your bail; this is the last chalk mark and my race is run.

I was once a stump of maple, the scamped handiwork of some botcher's hook, before Numa was king; a needy god in my favourite city. It was thou, Mamurrius, graver of the bronze shape, who hadst the skill to found me so deftly to apply myself to all trades; and may the Oscan mould never bruise the craftsman's cunning of thy hands! The work is one, but more than one dignity is given to the work.

(From *Propertius,* tr. J. S. Phillimore, Oxford, Clarendon Press, 1906, pp. 144–146.)

VI.2. Ovid *Metamorphoses* 14.623–771.

(lines 623–660)
Rege sub hoc Pomona fuit, qua nulla Latinas
inter hamadryadas coluit sollertius hortos
nec fuit arborei studiosior altera fetus;
unde tenet nomen: non silvas illa nec amnes,
rus amat et ramos felicia poma ferentes;
nec jaculo gravis est, sed adunca dextera falce,
qua modo luxuriem premit et spatiantia passim
bracchia conpescit, fisso modo cortice virgam
inserit et sucos alieno praestat alumno;
nec sentire sitim patitur bibulaeque recurvas
radicis fibras labentibus inrigat undis.
Hic amor, hoc studium, Veneris quoque nulla cupido est;
vim tamen agrestum metuens pomaria claudit
intus et accessus prohibet refugitque viriles.
Quid non et Satyri, saltatibus apta juventus,
fecere et pinu praecincti cornua Panes
Silvanusque, suis semper juvenilior annis,
quique deus fures vel falce vel inguine terret,
ut poterentur ea? Sed enim superabat amando
hos quoque Vertumnus neque erat felicior illis.
O quotiens habitu duri messoris aristas

corbe tulit verique fuit messoris imago!
Tempora saepe gerens faeno religata recenti
desectum poterat gramen versasse videri;
saepe manu stimulos rigida portabat, ut illum
jurares fessos modo disjunxisse juvencos.
Falce data frondator erat vitisque putator;
induerat scalas: lecturum poma putares;
miles erat gladio, piscator harundine sumpta;
denique per multas aditum sibi saepe figuras
repperit, ut caperet spectatae gaudia formae.
Ille etiam picta redimitus tempora mitra,
innitens baculo, positis per tempora canis,
adsimulavit anum: cultosque intravit in hortos
pomaque mirata est tanto que potentior! inquit,
paucaque laudatae dedit oscula, qualia numquam
vera dedisset anus, glaebaque incurva resedit
suspiciens pandos autumni pondere ramos.
(lines 675–692)
Sed tu si sapies, si te bene jungere anumque
hanc audire voles, quae te plus omnibus illis,
plus, quam credis, amo: vulgares reice taedas
Vertumnumque tori socium tibi selige! Pro quo
me quoque pignus habe: neque enim sibi notior ille est,
quam mihi; nec passim toto vagus errat in orbe,
haec loca sola colit; nec, uti pars magna procorum,
quam modo vidit, amat: tu primus et ultimus illi
ardor eris, solique suos tibi devovet annos.
Adde, quod est juvenis, quod naturale decoris
munus habet formasque apte fingetur in omnes,
et quod erit iussus, iubeas licet omnia, fiet.
quid, quod amatis idem, quod, quae tibi poma coluntur,
primus habet laetaque tenet tua munera dextra!
Sed neque iam fetus desiderat arbore demptos
nec, quas hortus alit, cum sucis mitibus herbas
nec quicquam nisi te: miserere ardentis et ipsum,
qui petit, ore meo praesentem crede precari.
(lines 761–771)
Haec ubi nequiquam formae deus aptus anili
edidit, in juvenem rediit et anilia demit
instrumenta sibi talisque apparuit illi,
qualis ubi oppositas nitidissima solis imago
evicit nubes nullaque obstante reluxit,
vimque parat: sed vi non est opus, inque figura
capta dei nympha est et mutua vulnera sensit.

(lines 623–660)
Pomona flourished under this king [i.e., Proca], than whom there was no other Latian wood-nymph more skilled in garden-culture nor more zealous in the care of fruitful trees. Hence was her name. She cared nothing for woods and rivers, but only for the fields and branches laden with delicious fruits. She carried no javelin in her hand, but the curved pruning-hook with which now she repressed the too luxuriant growth and cut back the branches spreading out on every side, and now, making an incision in the bark, would engraft a twig and give juices to an adopted bough. Nor would she permit them to suffer thirst, but watered the twisted fibres of the thirsty roots with her trickling streams. This was her love; this was her chief desire; nor did she have any care for Venus; yet, fearing some clownish violence, she shut herself up within her orchard and so guarded herself against all approach of man. What did not the Satyrs, a young dancing band, do to win her, and the Pans, their horns encircled with wreaths of pine, and Silvanus, always more youthful than his years, and that god who warns off evil-doers with his sickle or his ugly shape? But, indeed, Vertumnus surpassed them all in love; yet he was no more fortunate than they. Oh, how often in the garb of a rough reaper did he bring her a basket of barley-ears! And he was the perfect image of a reaper, too. Often he would come with his temples wreathed with fresh hay, and could easily seem to have been turning the new-mown grass. Again he would appear carrying an ox-goad in his clumsy hand, so that you would swear that he had but now unyoked his weary cattle. He would be a leaf-gatherer and a vine-pruner with hook in hand; he would come along with a ladder on his shoulder and you would think him about to gather apples. He would be a soldier with a sword, or a fisherman with a rod. In fact, by means of his many disguises, he obtained frequent admission to her presence and had much joy in looking on her beauty. He also put on a wig of grey hair, bound his temples with a gaudy head-cloth, and, leaning on a staff, came in the disguise of an old woman, entered the well-kept garden and, after admiring the fruit, said: "But you are far more beautiful," and he kissed her several times as no real old woman ever would have done. The bent old creature sat down on the grass, gazing at the branches bending beneath the weight of autumn fruits.
(lines 675–692)
"If you will be wise, and consent to a good match and will listen to an old woman like me, who loves you more than all the rest, yes, more than you would believe, reject all common offers and choose Vertumnus as the consort of your couch. You may also have my guaranty for him; for he is not better known to himself than he is to me. He does not wander idly throughout the world, but he dwells in the neighbourhood here alone; nor, as most of your

suitors do, does he fall in love at first sight with every girl he meets. You will be his first love and his last, and to you alone he will devote his life. Consider also that he is young, blest with a native charm, can readily assume whatever form he will, and what you bid him, though without stint you bid, he will perform. Moreover your tastes are similar, and the fruit which you so cherish he is the first to have and with joyful hands he lays hold upon your gifts. But neither the fruit of your trees, nor the sweet, succulent herbs which your garden bears, nor anything at all does he desire save you alone. Pity his ardour, and believe that he himself who desires you is making his suit in person through words of mine."
(lines 761–771)
"Have thought of these things, I pray you, and put away, dear nymph, your stubborn scorn; yield to your lover. So may no late spring frost ever nip your budding fruit, and may no rude winds scatter them in their flower." When the god in the form of age had thus pleaded his cause in vain, he returned to his youthful form, put off the old woman's trappings, and stood revealed to the maiden as when the sun's most beaming face has conquered the opposing clouds and shines out with nothing to dim his radiance. He was all ready to force her will, but no force was necessary; and the nymph, smitten by the beauty of the god, felt an answering passion."

(Translation reprinted by permission of the publishers and the Trustees of the Loeb Classical Library from Ovid, *Metamorphoses 2*, Loeb Classical Library, Vol. 4, translated by F. J. Miller, Cambridge, MA: Harvard University Press, 2nd ed., 1984, pp. 345, 347, 349, 351, 353, 355. The Loeb Classical Library © is a registered trademark of the President and Fellows of Harvard College.)

VI.3. Varro, *De lingua Latina* 5.46.

In Subur[b]anae regionis parte princeps est C[a]elius mons a C[a]ele Vibenna, Tusco duce nobili, qui cum sua manu dicitur Romulo venisse auxilio contra Tati[n]um regem. Hinc post C[a]elis obitum, quod nimis munita loca tenerent neque sine suspicione essent, deducti dicuntur in planum. Ab eis dictus vicus Tuscus, et ideo ibi Vortumnum stare, quod is deus Etruriae princeps; de Caelianis qui a suspicione liberi essent, traductos in eum locum qui vocatur C[a]eliolum.

In the section of the Suburan region, the first shrine is located on the Caelian Hill, named from Caeles Vibenna, a Tuscan leader of distinction, who is said to have come with his followers to help Romulus against King Tatius. From this hill the followers of Caeles are said, after his death, to have been brought down into the level ground, because they were in possession of a location which was too strongly fortified and their loyalty was somewhat under suspicion. From them was named the Vicus Tuscus, "Tuscan Row," and therefore, they say, the statue of Vertumnus stands there, because he is the chief god of Etruria; but those of the Caelians who were free from suspicion were removed to that place which is called Caeliolum, "the little Caelian."

(Translation reprinted by permission of the publishers and the Trustees of the Loeb Classical Library from *Varro, On the Latin Language*, Loeb Classical Library, translated by R. G. Kent, Cambridge, MA: Harvard University Press, 1938, p. 43. The Loeb Classical Library © is a registered trademark of the President and Fellows of Harvard College.)

VI.4. Pliny, *Historia Naturalis* 34.16.34.

Signa quoque Tuscanica per terras dispersa qu[in] in Etruria factitata sint, non est dubium. Deorum tantum putarem ea fuisse, ni Metrodorus Scepsius, cui cognomen a Romani nominis odio inditum est, propter MM statuarum Volsinios expugnatos obiceret. Mirumque mihi videtur, cum statuarum origo tam vetus Italiae sit, lignea potius aut fictilia deorum simulacra in delubris dicata usque ad devictam Asiam, unde luxuria.

There is no doubt that the so-called Tuscanic images scattered all over the world were regularly made in Etruria. I should have supposed these to have been statues of deities only, were it not that Metrodorus of Scepsis, who received his surname from his hatred of the very name of Rome, reproached us with having taken by storm the city of Volsinii for the sake of the 2000 statues which it contained. And it seems to me surprising that although the initiation of the statuary in Italy dates so far back, the images of the gods dedicated in the shrines should have been more usually of wood or terracotta right down to the conquest of Asia, which introduced luxury here.

(Translation reprinted by permission of the publishers and the Trustees of the Loeb Classical Library from *Pliny, Natural History*, Loeb Classical Library, Vol. 19, translated by W. H. S. Jones, Cambridge, MA: Harvard University Press, 1962, p. 153. The Loeb Classical Library © is a registered trademark of the President and Fellows of Harvard College.)

VI.5. Livy 5.22.4.

Cum iam humanae opes egestae a Veiis essent, amoliri tum deum dona ipsosque deos, sed colentium magis quam rapientium modo, coepere. Namque delecti ex omni exercitu juvenes, pure lautis corporibus, candida veste, quibus deportanda Romam regina Iuno adsignata erat, venerabundi templum iniere, primo religiose admoventes manus, quod id signum more Etrusco nisi certae gentis sacerdos attractare non esset solitus. Dein cum quidam, seu spiritu divino tactus seu juuenali joco, visne Romam ire, Juno? dixisset, adnuisse ceteri deam conclamauerunt. Inde fabulae adjectum est vocem quoque dicentis velle auditam; motam certe sede sua parvi molimenti adminiculis, sequentis modo accepimus levem ac facilem tralatu fuisse, integramque in Aventinum aeternam sedem suam quo vota Romani dictatoris vocaverant perlatam, ubi templum ei postea idem qui voverat Camillus dedicavit.

When the wealth that belonged to men had now been carried away out of Veii, they began to remove the possessions of the gods and the gods themselves, but more in the manner of worshippers than pillagers. For out of all the army youths were chosen, and made to cleanse their bodies and to put on white garments, and to them the duty was assigned of conveying Queen Juno to Rome. Reverently entering her temple, they scrupled at first to approach her with their hands, because this image was one that according to Etruscan practice none but a priest of a certain family was wont to touch; when one of them, whether divinely inspired or out of youthful jocularity, asked "Wilt thou go, Juno, to Rome?"—whereat the others all cried out that the goddess had nodded assent. It was afterwards added to the story that she had also been heard to say that she was willing. At all events we are told that she was moved from her place with contrivances of little power, as though she accompanied them voluntarily, and was lightly and easily transferred and carried safe and sound to the Aventine, the eternal home to which the prayers of the Roman dictator had called her; and there Camillus afterwards dedicated to her the temple which he himself had vowed.

(Translation reprinted by permission of the publishers and the Trustees of the Loeb Classical Library from *Livy in Fourteen Volumes*, Loeb Classical Library, Vol. 3, translated by B. O. Foster, Cambridge, MA: Harvard University Press, 1924, pp. 77, 79. Loeb Classical Library © is a registered trademark of the President and Fellows of Harvard College.)

VII. RITUALS

VII.1. Livy 39.8–9.1.

Insequens annus Sp. Postumium Albinum et Q. Marcium Philippum consules ab exercitu bellorumque et provinciarum cura ad intestinae conjurationis vindictam avertit.... Consulibus ambobus quaestio de clandestinis conjurationibus decreta est. Graecus ignobilis in Etruriam primum venit nulla cum arte earum, quas multas ad animorum corporumque cultum nobis eruditissima omnium gens invexit, sacrificulus et vates; nec is qui aperta religione, propalam et quaestum et disciplinam profitendo, animos errore imbueret, sed occultorum et nocturnorum antistes sacrorum. Initia erant, quae primo paucis tradita sunt, deinde vulgari coepta sunt per viros mulieresque. Additae voluptates religioni vini et epularum, quo plurium animi illicerentur. Cum vinum animos [incendissent], et nox et mixti feminis mares, aetatis tenerae majoribus, discrimen omne pudoris exstinxissent, corruptelae primum omnis generis fieri coeptae, cum ad id quisque, quo natura pronioris libidinis esset, paratam voluptatem haberet. Nec unum genus noxae, stupra promiscua ingenuorum feminarumque erant, sed falsi testes, falsa signa testamentaque et indicia ex eadem officina exibant: venena indidem intestinaeque caedes, ita ut ne corpora quidem interdum ad sepulturam exstarent. Multa dolo, pleraque per vim audebantur. Occulebat vim quod prae ululatibus tympanorumque et cymbalorum strepitu nulla vox quiritantium inter stupra et caedes exaudiri poterat. Huius mali labes ex Etruria Romam veluti contagione morbi penetravit.

The following year [i.e., 186 BCE] diverted the consuls Spurius Postumius Albinus and Quintus Marcius Phillipus from the army and the administration of wars and provinces to the suppression of an internal conspiracy.... To both consuls the investigation of secret conspiracies was decreed. A nameless Greek came first to Etruria, possessed of none of those many arts which the Greek people, supreme as it is in learning, brought to us in numbers for the cultivation of mind and body, but a dabbler in sacrifices and a fortune-teller; nor was he one who, by frankly disclosing his creed and publicly proclaiming both his profession and his system, filled minds with error, but a priest of secret [Bacchic] rites performed by night. There were initiatory rites which at first were imparted to a few, then began to be generally known among men and women. To the religious element in them were added the delights of wine and feasts, that the minds of a larger number might be attracted. When wine had inflamed their minds, and night and the mingling of males with females, youth with age, had destroyed every sentiment of modesty, all varieties of corruption first began to be practised, since each one had at hand the pleasure of answering to that to which his nature was more inclined. There was not one form of vice alone, the promiscuous matings of free men and women, but perjured witnesses, forged seals and wills and evidence, all issued from this same workshop: likewise poisonings and secret murders, so that at times not even the bodies were found for burial. Much was ventured by craft, more by violence. This violence was concealed because amid the howlings and the crash of drums and cymbals no cry of the sufferers could be heard as the debauchery and murders proceeded.

The destructive power of this evil spread from Etruria to Rome like the contagion of a pestilence.

(Translation reprinted by permission of the publishers and the Trustees of the Loeb Classical Library from *Livy in Fourteen Volumes*, Loeb Classical Library, Vol. 12, translated by E. T. Sage, Cambridge, MA: Harvard University Press, 1936, pp. 241, 243. Loeb Classical Library © is a registered trademark of the President and Fellows of Harvard College.)

VII.2. Livy 7.15.9-11.

Eodem anno et a consulibus vario eventu bellatum; nam Hernici a C. Plautio devicti subactique sunt, Fabius collega eius incaute atque inconsulte adversus Tarquinienses pugnavit. Nec in acie tantum ibi cladis acceptum quam quod trecentos septem milites Romanos captos Tarquinienses immolarunt; qua foeditate supplicii aliquanto ignominia populi Romani insignitior fuit.

In the same year [i.e., 359-358 BCE] the consuls, too, waged war with varying success. Gaius Plautius defeated the Hernici and reduced them to subjection; his colleague Fabius showed neither prudence nor skill in his battle with the Tarquinienses. And yet the disaster experienced on the field was overshadowed by the fact that the Tarquinienses slew three hundred and seven captured Roman soldiers as a sacrifice — an act of savage cruelty that greatly emphasized the humiliation of the Roman People.

(Translation reprinted by permission of the publishers and the Trustees of the Loeb Classical Library from *Livy in Fourteen Volumes,* Loeb Classical Library, Vol. 3, translated by B. O. Foster, Cambridge, MA: Harvard University Press, 1924, p. 407. Loeb Classical Library © is a registered trademark of the President and Fellows of Harvard College.)

VII.3. Herodotos 1.167.

Τῶν δὲ διαφθαρεισέων νεῶν τοὺς ἄνδρας οἵ τε Καρχηδόνιοι καὶ οἱ Τυρσηνοὶ . . . ἔλαχόν τε αὐτῶν πολλῷ πλείστους καὶ τούτους ἐξαγαγόντες κατέλευσαν. Μετὰ δὲ Ἀγυλλαίοισι πάντα τὰ παριόντα τὸν χῶρον, ἐν τῷ οἱ Φωκαιέες καταλευσθέντες ἐκέατο, ἐγίνετο διάστροφα καὶ ἔμπηρα καὶ ἀπόπληκτα, ὁμοίως πρόβατα καὶ ὑποζύγια καὶ ἄνθρωποι. Οἱ δὲ Ἀγυλλαῖοι ἐς Δελφοὺς ἔπεμπον, βουλόμενοι ἀκέσασθαι τὴν ἁμαρτάδα. Ἡ δὲ Πυθίη σφέας ἐκέλευσε ποιέειν τὰ καὶ νῦν οἱ Ἀγυλλαῖοι ἔτι ἐπιτελέουσι· καὶ γὰρ ἐναγίζουσί σφι μεγάλως καὶ ἀγῶνα γυμνικὸν καὶ ἱππικὸν ἐπιστᾶσι. Καὶ οὗτοι μὲν Φωκαιέων τοιούτῳ μόρῳ διεχρήσαντο. Οἱ δὲ αὐτῶν ἐς τὸ Ῥήγιον καταφυγόντες ἐνθεῦτεν ὁρμώμενοι ἐκτήσαντο πόλιν γῆς τῆς Οἰνωτρίης ταύτην ἥτις νῦν Ὑέλη καλέεται. Ἔκτισαν δὲ ταύτην πρὸς ἀνδρὸς Ποσειδωνιήτεω μαθόντες ὡς τὸν Κύρνον σφι ἡ Πυθίη ἔχρησε κτίσαι ἥρων ἐόντα. ἀλλ' οὐ τὴν νῆσον. Φωκαίης μέν νυν πέρι τῆς ἐν Ἰωνίῃ οὕτως ἔσχε.

As for the crews of the destroyed ships [of Phocaeans], the Carchedonians and Tyrrhenians drew lots for them: and [by far the greater share of them falling to the Tyrrhenian city of Agylla] the Agyllaeans led them out and stoned them to death. But after this all from Agylla, whether sheep or beasts of burden or men, that passed the place where the stoned Phocaeans lay, became distorted and crippled and palsied. The Agyllaeans sent to Delphi, desiring to heal their offence; and the Pythian priestess bade them do what the people of Agylla to this day perform: for they pay great honors to the Phocaeans, with religious rites and games, and horse-races.

(Translation reprinted by permission of the publishers and the Trustees of the Loeb Classical Library from *Herodotus*, Loeb Classical Library, Vol. 1, translated by A. D. Godley, Cambridge, MA: Harvard University Press, 1920, p. 209. Loeb Classical Library © is a registered trademark of the President and Fellows of Harvard College.)

VIII. THUNDER AND LIGHTNING

VIII.1. Seneca, *Quaestiones Naturales* 2.32.2.

Hoc inter nos et Tuscos, quibus summa est fulgurum persequendorum scientia, interest: nos putamus, quia nubes collisae sunt, fulmina emitti; ipsi existimant nubes collidi ut fulmina emittantur; nam, cum omnia ad deum referant, in ea opinione sunt tamquam non, quia facta sunt, significent, sed quia significatura sunt, fiant.

This is the difference between us and the Etruscans, who have consummate skill in interpreting lightning: we think that because clouds collide, lightning is emitted. They believe that clouds collide in order that lightning may be emitted. Since they attribute everything to divine agency they are of the opinion that things do not reveal the future because they have occurred, but that they occur because they are meant to reveal the future.

(Translations of Selections VIII.1–6 reprinted by permission of the publishers and the Trustees of the Loeb Classical Library from *Seneca, Naturales quaestiones*, Loeb Classical Library, translated by T. H. Corcoran, Cambridge, MA: Harvard University Press, 1971, pp. 151, 163, 165, 167, 169, 173, 175, 177, 179. Loeb Classical Library © is a registered trademark of the President and Fellows of Harvard College.)

VIII.2. Seneca, *Quaestiones Naturales* 2.39.

Genera fulgurum tria esse ait Caecina, consiliarium, auctoritatis et quod status dicitur. Consiliarium ante rem fit sed post cogitationem, cum aliquid in animo versantibus aut suadetur fulminis ictu aut dissuadetur. Auctoritatis est ubi post rem factam venit, quam bono futuram malove significat. Status est ubi quietis nec agentibus quicquam nec cogitantibus quidem fulmen intervenit et aut minatur aut promittit aut monet. Hoc monitorium vocat, sed nescio quare non idem sit quod consiliarium, nam et qui monet consilium dat.

Caecina says there are three kinds of lightning, the advising, the confirming, and that which is called the conditional. The advising one happens before the event but after a thought has been conceived, when people who are planning something in their minds are either persuaded or dissuaded by a stroke of lightning. The confirming lightning comes after action has been done, indicating whether it will be good or bad. The conditional lightning comes to people who are quiet, doing nothing, not even thinking, and it either threatens, promises or warns.

(See credit under Section VIII.1 above.)

VIII.3. Seneca, *Quaestiones Naturales* 2.41.1–2.

Haec adhuc Etruscis philosophisque communia sunt. In illo dissentiunt quod fulmina a Jove dicunt mitti et tres illi manubias dant. Prima, ut aiunt, monet et placata est et ipsius Jouis consilio mittitur. Secundam mittit quidem Jupiter, sed ex consilii sententia, duodecim enim deos advocat; hoc fulmen boni aliquid aliquando facit, sed tunc quoque non aliter quam ut noceat; ne prodest quidem impune. Tertiam manubiam idem Jupiter mittit, sed adhibitis in consilium diis quos superiores et involutos vocant, quia vastat in quae incidit et utique mutat statum privatum et publicum quem invenit; ignis enim nihil esse quod fuit patitur.

The views up to this point are common to both Etruscans and philosophers. They disagree on this: namely, that the Etruscans say lightning is sent by Jupiter and they assign to him three types of equipment. The first type, so they say, gives a gentle warning and is sent by a decision of Jupiter himself. Jupiter also sends the second type but in accordance with the advice of his council, for he summons the twelve gods. This lightning occasionally brings about some good, but even then it causes some harm. It does not confer benefits without causing damage. Jupiter also sends the third type of lightning but he summons into council the gods whom the Etruscans call the Superior, or Veiled, Gods, because the lightning destroys whatever it strikes and, particularly, alters the state of private or public affairs that it finds existing. For the fire does not permit anything to remain as it was.

(See credit under Section VIII.1 above.)

VIII.4. Seneca, *Quaestiones naturales* 2.45.

Eundem quem nos Jovem intelligent, rectorem custodemque universi, animum ac spiritum mundi, operis huius dominum et artificem, cui nomen omne convenit. Vis illum fatum vocare, non errabis; hic est ex quo suspensa sunt omnia, causa causarum. Vis illum providentiam dicere, recte dices; est enim cuius consilio huic mundo providetur, ut inoffensus exeat et actus suos explicet. Vis illum naturam vocare, non peccabis; hic est ex quo nata sunt omnia, cuius spiritu vivimus. Vis illum vocare mundum, non falleris; ipse enim est hoc quod vides totum, partibus suis inditus, et se sustinens et sua. Idem Etruscis quoque visum est, et ideo fulmina mitti dixerunt a Iove quia sine illo nihil geritur.

They [ancient sages] recognize the same Jupiter, the controller and guardian of the universe, the mind and spirit of the world, the lord and artificer of this creation. Any name for him is suitable. You wish to call him Fate? You will not be wrong. It is he on whom all things depend, the cause of causes. You wish to call him Providence? You will still be right. It is by his planning that provision is made for this universe so that it may proceed without stumbling and fulfill its appropriate functions. You wish to call him Nature? You will not be mistaken. It is he from whom all things are naturally born, and we have life from his breath. You wish to call him the Universe? You will not be wrong. He himself is all that you see, infused throughout all his parts, sustaining both himself and his own. The Etruscans had the same concept, and so they said lightning was sent by Jupiter because nothing is done without him.

(See credit under Section VIII.1 above.)

VIII.5. Seneca, *Quaestiones naturales* 2.47.

Huic illorum divisioni non accedo. Aiunt aut perpetua esse fulmina, aut finita, aut prorogativa. Perpetua, quorum significatio in totam pertinet vitam nec unam rem denuntiat sed contextum rerum per omnem deinceps aetatem futurarum complectitur; haec sunt fulmina quae prima accepto patrimonio et in novo hominis aut [u]rbis statu fi[u]nt. Finita ad diem utique respondent. Prorogativa sunt quorum minae differri possunt, averti tollique non possunt.

I do not agree with the Etruscan classification: they say that lightning bolts are "perpetual," "limited," or "deferred." The prognostication of the perpetual ones pertains to the entire life; it does not give notice of a single event but embraces the chain of events which will happen throughout the whole subsequent lifetime. These are the lightning bolts which first occur when someone has received an inheritance or a new phase begins for a man or a city. Limited ones correspond exactly to a date. Deferred are those whose threats can be postponed but cannot be averted and cancelled.

(See credit under Section VIII.1 above.)

VIII.6. Seneca, *Quaestiones naturales* 2.49–50.1.

Nunc nomina fulgurum quae a Caecina ponuntur [per]stringam et quid de eis sentiam exponam. Ait esse postulatoria, quibus sacrificia intermissa aut non rite facta repetuntur; monitoria, quibus docetur quid cavendum sit; pestifera, quae mortem exiliumque portendunt; fallacia, quae per speciem alicuius boni nocent,–dant consulatum malo futurum gerentibus et hereditatem cuius compendium magno luendum sit incommodo–; dentanea, quae speciem periculi sine periculo afferunt; peremptalia, quibus tolluntur priorum fulminum minae; attestata, quae prioribus consentiunt; atterranea, quae in cluso fiunt; obruta, quibus iam prius percussa nec procurata feriuntur; regalia, cum [f]orum tangitur vel comitium vel principalia urbis liberae loca, quorum significatio regnum civitati minatur; inferna, cum e terra exiliuit ignis; hospitalia, quae sacrificiis ad nos Jovem arcessunt et, ut verbo eorum molliore utar, invitant,–sed non irasceretur invitatus; nunc venire eum magno invitantium periculo affirmant–; auxiliaria, quae invocata sed advocantium bono veniunt.

Quanto simplicior divisio est qua utebatur Attalus noster, vir egregius, qui Etruscorum disciplinam Graeca subtilitate miscuerat.

Now I will briefly give the names proposed for lightning flashes by Caecina and explain what I think about them. He says that there are the "demanding" ones, which demand that sacrifices be redone if interrupted or not performed properly; the "admonitory," which indicate what must be guarded against; the "deadly," which portend death and exile; the "deceptive," which do harm under the guise of some good; for example they give consulships which will be disastrous for the men in office, or bestow inheritance of which the profit must be compensated for by great trouble; the "threatening," which bear the appearance of danger without danger. The "cancelling" lightning flashes cancel the threats of prior lightning. The "confirming" agree with prior lightning flashes. The "earthy" occur in a closed place. The "overwhelming" strike things already previously struck but not expiated. The "royal" smite the forum or the assembly ground or the government quarters of a free city, and their meaning for a state is the threat of monarchy. The "infernal" cause fire to leap out of the ground. The "hospitable" summon, or to use their gentler term "invite," Jupiter to our company at sacrifices. But he would not be angry if "invited." As it is, they say he comes with great dangers to those "inviters." The "helping" lightning flashes are "called on," but they come for the good of the callers.

How much simpler is the division which our Attalus used, an outstanding man who mixed the skill of the Etruscans with Greek accuracy.

(See credit under Section VIII.1 above.)

VIII.7. Servius, *Ad Aen.* 1.42.

Cum Varro divinarum quinto quattuor diis fulmina adsignet, inter quos et Minervae, quaeritur, cur Minerva

Jovis fulmen miserit. Antiqui Jovis solius putaverunt esse fulmen, nec id unum esse, ut testantur Etrusci libri de fulguratura, in quibus duodecim genera fulminum scripta sunt, ita ut est Jovis Junonis Minervae, sic quoque aliorum . . . in libris Etruscorum lectum est jactus fulminum manubias dici et certa esse numina possidentia fulminum jactus, ut Jovem Vulcanum Minervam. Cavendum ergo est, ne aliis hoc numinibus demus.

Since Varro in his fifth book on divine matters assigns the lightning bolt to four gods, among whom is Minerva, it is asked why Minerva sent the lightning of Jupiter. The ancients thought the lightning belonged to Jupiter alone, but that was not one kind, as attested by the Etruscan books on lightning, in which twelve types of lightning are described, so that there is one of Jupiter, one of Juno, one of Minerva and thus also of others . . . in the books of the Etruscans it is read that bolts of lightning are called *manubiae*. And certain divinities possess the bolts of lightning, such as Jupiter, Vulcan, Minerva. We must beware lest we attribute this to other divinities.

VIII.8. Pliny, *Historia Naturalis* 2.138-140.

Tuscorum litterae novem deos emittere fulmina existimant, eaque esse undecim generum; Jovem enim trina iaculari. Romani duo tantum ex iis servavere, diurna attribuentes Jovi, nocturna Summano, rariora sane eadem de causa frigidioris caeli. Etruria erumpere terra quoque arbitratur, quae infera appellat, brumali tempore facta saeva maxime et exsecrabilia, cum sint omnia, quae terrena existimant, non illa generalia nec a sideribus venientia, sed ex proxima atque turbidiore natura. Argumentum evidens, quod omnia superiora e caelo decidentia obliquos habent ictus, haec autem, quae vocant terrena, rectos. E[t] qua[e] ex propiore materia cadunt, ideo creduntur e terra exire, quoniam ex repulsu nulla vestigia edunt, cum sit illa ratio non inferi ictus, sed adversi. A Saturni ea sidere proficisci subtilius ista consectati putant, sicut opulentissimum, totum concrematum est fulmine. Vocant et familiaria in totam vitam fatidica, quae prima fiunt familiam suam cuique indepto. Ceterum existimant non ultra decem annos portendere privata, praeterquam aut primo patrimonio facta aut natali die, publica non ultra tricesimum annum, praeterquam in deductione oppidi.

The Tuscan writers hold the view that there are nine gods who send thunderbolts, and that these are of eleven kinds, because Jupiter hurls three varieties. Only two of the deities have been retained by the Romans, who attribute thunderbolts in the daytime to Jupiter and those in the night to Summanus, the latter being naturally rare because the sky at night is colder. Tuscany [lit. "Etruria"] also believes that some burst out of the ground, which it calls "low bolts," and that these are rendered exceptionally direful and accursed by the season of winter, though all the bolts that they believe of earthly origin are not the ordinary ones and do not come from the stars but from the nearer and more disordered element: a clear proof of this being that all those coming from the upper heaven deliver slanting blows, whereas these which they call earthly strike straight. And those that fall from the nearer elements are supposed to come out of the earth because they leave no traces as a result of their rebound, although that is the principle not of a downward blow, but of a slanting one. Those who pursue these enquiries with more subtlety think that these come from the planet Saturn, just as the inflammatory ones come from Mars, as, for instance, when Bolsena [= Volsinii], the richest town in Tuscany, was entirely burnt up by a thunderbolt. Also the first ones that occur after a man sets up house for himself are called "family meteors," as foretelling his fortune for the whole of his life. However, people think that private meteors, except those that occur either at a man's first marriage or on his birthday, do not prophesy beyond ten years, nor public ones beyond the 30th year, except those occurring at the colonization of a town.

> (Translation reprinted by permission of the publishers and the Trustees of the Loeb Classical Library from *Pliny, Natural History*, Loeb Classical Library, Vol. 1, translated by H. Rackham, Cambridge, MA: Harvard University Press, 1938, pp. 275, 277. Loeb Classical Library © is a registered trademark of the President and Fellows of Harvard College.)

VIII.9. Zosimos 5.41.

Περὶ δὲ ταῦτα οὖσιν αὐτοῖς Πομπηιανὸς ὁ τῆς πόλεως ὕπαρχος ἐνέτυχέ τισιν ἐκ Τουσκίας εἰς τὴν Ῥώμην ἀφικομένοις, οἳ πόλιν ἔλεγόν τινα Ναρνίαν ὄνομα τῶν περιστάντων ἐλευθερῶσαι κινδύνων, καὶ τῇ πρὸς τὸ θεῖον εὐχῇ καὶ κατὰ τὰ πάτρια θεραπείᾳ βροντῶν ἐξαισίων καὶ πρηστήρων ἐπιγενομένων τοὺς ἐπικειμένους βαρβάρους ἀποδιῶξαι. Τούτοις διαλεχθεὶς ἔπεισιν ὅσα ἐκ τῶν ἱερατικῶν ὄφελος· ἐπεὶ δὲ τὴν κρατοῦσαν κατὰ νοῦν ἐλάμβανε δόξαν, ἀσφαλέστερον ἐθέλων πρᾶξαι τὸ σπουδαζόμενον ἀνατίθεται πάντα τῷ τῆς πόλεως ἐπισκόπῳ· ἦν δὲ Ἰννοκέντιος· ὁ δὲ τὴν τῆς πόλεως σωτηρίαν ἔμπροσθεν τῆς οἰκείας ποιησάμενος δόξης λάθρᾳ ἐφῆκεν ποιεῖν αὐτοῖς ἅπερ ἴσασιν. Ἐπεὶ δὲ οὐκ ἄλλως ἔφασαν τῇ πόλει τὰ γενόμενα συντελέσειν, εἰ μὴ δημοσίᾳ τὰ νομιζόμενα πραχθείη, τῆς γερουσίας εἰς τὸ Καπιτώλιον ἀναβαινούσης, αὐτόθι τε καὶ ἐν ταῖς τῆς πόλεως ἀγοραῖς ὅσα προσήκει πραττούσης, οὐκ ἐθάρρησεν οὐδεὶς τῆς κατὰ τὸ πάτριον μετασχεῖν ἁγιστείας, ἀλλὰ τοὺς μὲν ἀπὸ τῆς Τουσκίας παρῆκαν, ἐτράπησαν δὲ εἰς τὸ θεραπεῦσαι τὸν βάρβαρον καθ' ὅσον ἂν οἷοί τε γίνωνται.

While this was the situation, Pompeianus, the prefect of the city, met some people who came from Tuscia to Rome who said that they had freed a city, Narnia by name, from its surrounding dangers and had chased away the attacking barbarians by means of both a prayer to the divine and by cultivating the occurrence of extraordinary thunder and whirlwinds according to their ancestral rites. Having been told this, Pompeianus was convinced how great the help would be from the priestly offices. Then he adopted an opinion according to reason, wishing to do the necessary business with greater safety, that is, to entrust all matters to the bishop of the city. This man was Innocentius. Placing the salvation of the city over domestic common opinion, secretly he allowed them [the Tuscans] to perform the rites which they knew. Then they said things were not going to turn out differently in the city, unless the customary rites were performed in public, when the Senate met on the Capitolium and conducted its usual business either there or in the fora of the city. No one dared to participate in the holy rites contrary to their own custom, but they sent away those men from Tuscia, and turned to dealing with the barbarian as best they could.

(Translated by Svetla Slaveva-Griffin.)

IX. DEMONS AND SPIRITS

IX.1. Servius, *Ad Aen.* 3.168.

Id est unde originem ducimus, ut deos Penates quasi Troianos intellegas, et ad ritum referri, de quo dicit Labeo in libris qui appellantur de diis animalibus: in quibus ait, esse quaedam sacra quibus animae humanae vertantur in deos, qui appellantur animales, quod de animis fiant. Hi autem sunt dii Penates et viales.

That is whence we take the origin, so that you may understand the Penates gods as Trojan, and to the rite is to be referred that concerning which Labeo speaks, in the books which are named from the gods from whom there is an *animal* origin, in which he says that there are certain sacred acts by which human *animae* (souls) are turned into gods, who are called *animales,* because they come from *animae.* These, moreover, are the Penates gods and gods of the crossroads.

IX.2. Arnobius, *Adv. nat.* 2.62.

Quod Etruria libris in Acheronticis pollicentur, certorum animalium sanguine numinibus certis dato divinas animas fieri et ab legibus mortalitatis educi.

(Source of text: Thulin 1, 9)

And they promise this in the *Acherontic Books* in Etruria, that by the blood of certain animals divine souls become endowed with certain numinous spirits and they are led away from the laws of mortality.

IX.3. Arnobius, *Adv. nat.* 3.40.

Idem rursus [Nigidius] in libro sexto exponit et decimo, disciplinas Etruscas sequens, genera esse Penatium quattuor et esse Jovis ex his alios, alios Neptuni, inferorum tertios, mortalium hominum quartos.... Varro qui sunt introrsus atque in intimis penetralibus caeli deos esse censet quos loquimur (Penates) nec eorum numerum nec nomina sciri. Hos Consentes et Complices Etrusci aiunt et nominant, quod una oriantur et occidant una, sex mares et totidem feminas, nominibus ignotis et miserationis parcissimae; sed eos summi Jovis consiliarios ac principes existimari.

(Text: Thulin 1, 29–30.)

Likewise (Nigidius) explains in his sixth book and in his tenth, following the Etruscan teachings, that there are four types of Penates, and that the first of these is of Jupiter, the second of Neptune, the third of the inhabitants of the lower world, the fourth of mortal men.... Varro thinks that those of whom we speak (the Penates) are inside and within innermost chambers, and neither their number nor their names are known. The Etruscans say and call them Consentes and Complices, because they arise together and they fall together, six males and six females, with unknown names and of the most meager compassion. But they are thought to be counsellors and princes of highest Jupiter.

IX.4. Pliny, *Historia Naturalis* 2.154.

Exstat annalium memoria sacris quibusdam et precationibus vel cogi fulmina vel impetrari. Vetus fama Etruriae est, impetratum Volsinios urbem depopulatis agris subeunte monstro, quod vocavere Oltam, evocatum a Porsina suo rege.

Historical record also exists of thunderbolts being either caused by or vouchsafed in answer to certain rites and prayers. There is an old story of the latter in Etruria when the portent which they called Olta came to the city of Bolsena [= Volsinii] when its territory had been devastated; it was sent in answer to the prayer of its king Porsina.

(Translation reprinted by permission of the publishers and the Trustees of the Loeb Classical Library from *Pliny, Natural History,* Loeb Classical Library, Vol. 1, translated by H. Rackham, Cambridge, MA: Harvard University Press, 1938, pp. 277. Loeb Classical Library © is a registered trademark of the President and Fellows of Harvard College.)

NOTES

1. Minor editing changes in punctuation and orthography have been introduced in the interest of consistency. Consonantal *u* in Latin has been written as *v*, and consonantal *i* as *j*. Quotation marks are not used within the Latin and Greek texts.

2. The word order and particular details of the text given in *TLL* have been adjusted to conform to the sequence and translation of details as given below.

INDEX

Accademia Etrusca, 4
Achelous (Acheloos), 149, 156
Acheron, 1
Achillea, 139
Achilles, 41, 136
Aclus (June), 202
Acquarossa, 119
Acquarossa, "regia," 151
Acquasanta di Chianciano, 106
Admetos (Admetus), 19, 48, 80n24. *See also* Atmite
Adonis, 18, 50, 57, 94. *See also* Atunis
adyton, 150
aedes, 146, 147, 152
Aeginetan Apollo, 97
Aelius Donatus (fourth century CE), 7n12
Aeneas, 193
aesar. *See aiser*
Aeschylus, 62n46
aes rude, 97, 99, 139
Afuna family, 16
Afunei, Hasti, 58, 67, 68, 75
Agnone, 148
Agylla (Caere), 213
aiser (*aesar*), 13, 19, 198
Aita (Eita), 19, 46, 51, 56, 57, 71, 80n30. *See also* Hades
Aivas, 21
Ajax, 7n17
akroteria, 126, 142, 149, 155, 156, 158, 165n108
Alban Lake, 39, 195-196
Albinus, Spurius Postumius, 212
Alcstei, 19
Alkestis, 19, 80n24
Allah, 45
Alpan, 50, 55, 56, 57, 58
altar, altars, 6, 28, 98, 120, 132-143, 164n11, 76, 78
Althaia, 52, 63n58
Alu, 59
Amazons, 20, 51, 54, 62n54
Ambarvalia, 122
Amor, 46. *See also* Cupid; Eros, Erotes; Turnu
Ampharete, 91
Ampiles (May), 202
Amythaon, 203
Ana, 165n84

Anatolia, 46
Ancus Marcius, 147, 194
Andromache (Amazon), 20
Annio da Viterbo, 4, 7
anodos, 82n52
antefixes, 47, 49, 111n123, 147, 149, 150-151, 156
Apa, 139, 140
Apennine Mountains, 120
apex, 35-36, 43, 56
Aphrodite, 13, 46, 50, 55, 56, 57, 60, 61, 97, 109n67. *See also* Turan; Venus
Aplu. *See* Apulu
Apollo (Apollon), 46, 47, 48, 49, 57, 61, 77, 82n62, 109n58, 119, 139, 141, 151, 156, 205, 206. *See also* Apulu; Phoebus
Apollo Pythicus, 61
Apollo Soranus, 48
Apuleius Vicellius, 6n9
Apulu (Aplu), 18, 45-46, 49, 50-51, 57, 61, 82n62, 93, 156. *See also* Apollo
Ardea, 160
Ares, 46, 55, 56. *See also* Laran; Mars
Arezzo. *See* Arretium
Argive Heraion, 108n40, 109n59
Argos, 51
Aricia, 54, 57, 202
Aristophanes, 140
Aritimi, 45-46, 53, 57, 98. *See also* Artemis; Artumes
Arnobius (fl. ca. 300 BCE), xii, 3, 66, 217
Arno River, 116, 125
Arnza, 128n40
Arretium (Arezzo), 62n54, 103, 107, 124, 125, 141
Arretium (Arezzo), Fonte Veneziana, 98, 99, 111n108
Arretium (Arezzo), Monte Falterona, 99
Arretium (Arezzo), Paterno di Vallombrosa, 106
Arretium (Arezzo), Plowman, 117
Arretium (Arezzo), Porta Laurentina, 108n18
Arringatore ("Orator"), 92

Arruns, 48
Arruns Veltymnus, 30-31, 192
Artemis, 46, 54, 57. *See also* Aritimi; Artumes
Artile, 31
Artumes, 53, 54, 96, 106, 127, 155, 162. *See also* Aritimi; Artemis
arulae, 102, 103
aryballos, aryballoi, 81n47, 103
Ascanius, 61, 61n10
Asclepius, 20
Asilas, 3
Asklepieia, 105
Asklepios, 90, 104
askos, askoi, 103
Assyrian friezes, 84n102
Astarte, 13, 47, 61, 91, 101, 143, 144, 155, 109n52
Atalanta, 23, 53. *See also* Atlenta
Athena, 20, 46, 51, 59, 156, 160. *See also* Menrva; Minerva
Athenians, 202
Athens, 59
Athens, Acropolis, 95
Athens, Asklepieion, 103, 108n17, 110n106
Athrpa, 22, 23, 53, 57, 59. *See also* Atropos
ati, 20. *See also* Cel Ati
Atlenta, 22, 23. *See also* Atalanta
Atmite, 19. *See also* Admetos
atrium, 147, 161
Atropos, 23, 53. *See also* Athrpa
Attic black-figured *kylix*, 100
Attic black-figured *oenochoe*, 138
Attic black-figured vases, 135
Attic *kylix*, 139
Attic red-figured vases, 133
Atunis, 18, 19, 23, 50-51, 52, 53, 56, 57, 60, 106. *See also* Adonis
Aturmuca, 20
augur, augurs, xii, 2, 198, 204. *See also* priest, priests
auguraculum, 116, 118, 119
augural law, xii
augurium, 47
augury, 2, 3, 36, 41, 119
Augustus, 3, 43n42, 198. *See also* Caesar (Augustus)
Aurora, 46, 47, 60. *See also* Eos; Thesan

auspices, 118
Auster, 43n59
avl tarχunus, 29-30
Azoni, 200

baby, babies. *See* child, children
Bacchanalia, 212-213
Bacchant, 38
Bacchus, 13, 20, 38, 46, 206. *See also* Dionysos; Fufluns
Bakchos, 58, 59
balsamarium, balsamarii, 103
Bay of Naples, 47
Begoe. *See* Nymph Begoe
Bellerophon, 16
Bellona Victrix, 91
Bentz, Martin, 45
bird, birds, 3, 23n11, 32, 39, 41-42, 46-47, 54, 119, 194
Blera, 138
Blera, Grotta Dipinta, 79n19. *See also* Grotta Porcina
Bloch, Raymond, 7n28
blood, 76, 83n75, 133, 164n5, 217
Bologna, 101
Bologna, Via Fondazza, 143
Bologna, Villa Cassarini votive deposit, 108n33
Bolsena, 31, 58, 140
Bolsena, Poggio Casetta, 134, 147, 148, 151
Bolsena, Pozzarella, 128n51, 146
Bomarzo, Grotta Dipinta, 79n19
bothros, 91, 101, 135, 137, 141, 144
boulders and rocks, 74, 136
boundaries, 23, 30, 116-118, 120, 121, 122, 123, 125, 126
boundary stone, 6, 18, 23
Briquel, Dominique, 5
Brolio, 97, 99, 107
Brontoscopic Calendar, 2, 30, 39, 104, 173-190
bulla, bullae, 28, 108n20
Buonamici, Giulio, 5
burial ritual. *See* funerary ritual
Butades, 164n10
Byzantium (Constantinople), 173, 174

Cabreas (April), 202
Cacu, 31, 33, 47

219

Cadiz, 109n51
Caecina, Aulus (first century BCE), 2, 34, 141, 215
Caecus, Appius Claudius, 91
Caelestis Juno, 200
Caere (Cerveteri), 13, 17, 36, 38, 59, 60, 91, 92, 105, 111n129, 120, 121, 122, 124, 125, 146, 148, 156, 161. *See also* Agylla
Caere, Campana Tomb, 78, 140, 141, 151
Caere, Manganello, 102, 107, 110n91
Caere, Sant'Antonio, 160
Caere, Tomb of the Capitals (Capitelli), 154
Caere, Tomb of the Five Chairs (Cinque Sedie), 78, 109n57, 121, 140
Caere, Tomb of Giuseppe Moretti, 154
Caere, Tomb of the Greek Vases (Vasi Greci), 154
Caere, Tomb of the Marine Waves (Onde Marine), 79n19
Caere, Tomb of the Reliefs (Rilievi), 71-73
Caere, Tomb of the Shields and Chairs (Scudi e Sedie), 154
Caere, Tomb of the Ship (Nave) I, 83n71
Caere, Valle Zuccara, 165n84
Caesar, G. Julius, 2, 43n42
Caesar (Augustus), 198
Cafates, Larth, 39
Caicna, Vele, 82n71
calcei repandi, 51
calendar, calendars, 10, 23, 122, 173-190
Calu, 46, 51, 57, 80n30, 140
Calzni, Larth, 91
Camillus, M. Furius, 61
Campaccio, 123
Campania, 132
Capito (date unknown), 6n9, 193
Capo Monodendri, 142
Capua, 104, 146
Capua, Patturelli, 141-142
Capua Tile (Tabula Capuana; Tegola Capuana), 11, 12, 104, 146, 111n137, 119, 128n44
Carminius, 204
Carthage, 61
Carthaginians, 120
Castel d'Asso, 142, 152
Castiglione del Lago, 90
Castor, 19, 46, 60, 76
Castores, 60
Castur, 46, 76
Catha (Cath, Cautha, Cavatha, Kavtha), 11, 13, 19, 34, 46, 57, 59, 106, 139-140, 149, 151

Catharnai, Thanachvil, 101
Catiline, 174
Cato the Elder, xii
Cautha. *See* Catha
Cavatha, Cavtha. *See* Catha
Cel, 20, 46, 55, 57
Cel Ati, 48, 57, 90, 106
Celeritas, 200
celi, 10
Celius (September), 202
Celsclan, 20, 55, 57, 58
Cencnei, Thana, 91
Censorinus (third century CE), 3, 120, 200-201
cepen, 34
Cerca, 21. *See also* Circe; Kirke
Ceres, 46, 101, 103, 123, 146, 148, 200, 206. *See also* Demeter; Vei
Ceri, Tomb of the Statues (Statue), 78
Chalchas, 31, 33, 39, 42, 56, 57
Chalcidian Greeks, 47
Charchedonians, 213
Charon, 46, 58, 73, 74, 81n49
Charu(n), 43n43, 46, 57-58, 61, 67, 69, 74, 76, 79n11, 81n46, 83n97
Chianciano. *See* Fùcoli
Chianti, 122
child, children, 27, 28, 29, 92, 95, 96, 97, 101, 103, 104, 110n85, 128n40
Chimaera of Arretium (Arezzo), 15, 91
Chiron, 203
Chiusi. *See* Clusium
Christian beliefs, 174
Christianity, xi, xii, 45, 48
Christian votives, 91
Chthonic Hermes, 193
Cicero, Marcus Tullius (106-43 BCE), xi, xii, 2, 27, 34, 36, 39, 118, 119, 146, 174, 192, 199, 204
Cicero, Quintus Tullius, 2
Cilens, 11, 58, 107, 111n137, 164n21
Cincius, L., 165n59, 205
cippus (*cippi*), 36, 37, 100, 118, 123, 138, 142, 143
Cipus, 197-198
Circe, 21. *See also* Cerca; Kirke
Civil War (Roman), 174
Civita Castellana. *See* Falerii
Claudius (Tiberius Claudius Nero, 10 BCE-54 CE), xii, 34
Clemen, Carl, 5, 7n28
Clodius Pulcher, xii
Clusium (Chiusi), 30, 31, 43n42, 58, 59, 67, 70, 75, 77, 123, 124, 125, 207
Clusium (Chiusi), Tomb of Colle Casuccini, 82n66
Clusium (Chiusi), Tomb of Poggio al Moro, 82n66

collegium, xii, 34, 43n51
Colonna, Giovanni, 5, 45
Columella, Lucius Junius (first century CE), 203-204
Como, 58
Complices, 217
Concordia (Harmonia), 63n80
consaeptum sacellum, 146
Consentes, 217
Constantine, xii, 35
Constantinople, 4
Consus, 200
Corchiano, 152
Corinth, 108n40
Corinth, Asklepieion, 111n126
Corinth, Potters' Quarter, 109n46
Cortona, 4, 16, 18, 54, 56, 59, 92, 117, 123, 124, 142
Cortona, Melone del Sodo II, 141-142
Cortona lamp, 107
Cosa, 119, 121, 164
Cosa, Capitolium, 163
cosmos, 127, 198
cracna, 20
Crevole River, 125
Cristofani, Mauro, 5, 45
Culśanś, 16, 46, 56, 58, 59, 79n9, 93, 106, 117
Culśu, 13, 34, 58, 67, 68, 79n9
Cumae, 94, 141
cuniculi, 39
cupencus, 34
Cupid, 46. *See also* Amor; Eros; Turnu
Cures, 194
Cvinti (Cuinti), Velia, 16, 93, 108n23
Cypriote gods, 47, 58
Cyprus, 91, 95

Dardanians, 14
Daughter of Sol, 200
"Daybreak," 49
dea Syria Gravida, 95
"Death," 73
Decimviri (*Quindecimviri*) *sacris faciundis*, xii
Deecke, Wilhelm, 4
de Grummond, Nancy T., 45
Delos, 49
Delphi, 49, 58, 73, 94, 95, 108nn37,40, 141, 213
Delphic oracle, 57
delubrum, 146
Demeter, 46, 47, 81n52, 91, 97, 101, 140. *See also* Ceres; Vei
Demetreioi, 47
demons, 67, 68, 69, 73, 74, 76, 79nn10,15, 79-80n24, 81n46
Dempster, Thomas, 4

De Simone, Carlo, 45
Diana, 46, 54, 57, 127. *See also* Aritimi; Artemis; Artumes
Dii Consentes, 13, 40. *See also* Consentes
Dii Involuti, 41
Dii Manes, 200
Dii Novensiles, 200
Dii Publici, 200
Dio Cassius (late second-early third century CE), 198
Diocletian, xii
Diodorus Siculus (first century BCE), 116
Dionysios of Halikarnassos (second half of first century BCE), 41, 47, 117, 125
Dionysios (the Elder) of Syracuse, 98, 132, 151
Dionysos, 13, 20, 46, 49, 57, 58, 59, 77, 109n58. *See also* Bacchus; Fufluns; Pacha
Dioscuri, 46. *See also* Dioskouroi; Tinas Cliniar
Dioskorides, 139
Dioskouroi, 19, 46, 54, 56, 60. *See also* Dioscuri; Tinas Cliniar
Discordia, 200
Dis Pater, 48, 59, 139-140, 141
divination, 10, 14, 21, 23, 27, 33, 39-42, 174, 191-198
Dodona, 207
door, doors, 56, 58, 67, 75, 77, 79n9,11, 82n66, 136
Dumézil, Georges, 5
duodecim populi (Twelve Peoples), 27, 32, 35, 52, 192
Dyads, 19

earthquake, 27, 174
East Greek votives, 94
Ecile, 139
Egypt, 15
Egyptian gods, 48
Egyptians, 202
Eileithyia, 58, 91, 101
eisnev, 34
ekphora, 75, 82n59
Elcsntre, 52
Electra, 7n17
Eleusinian relief, 81n52
Elogia Tarquiniensia, 93, 96
Elpenor, 21
Elysian Fields, 82n62
entrails, 2, 3, 10, 27, 39, 46, 102
Eos, 46, 47, 60. *See also* Aurora; Thesan
Ephesus, 108n42
Epigonoi, 56
epileptic boy, 28, 96
Erichthonios, 59
Erinyes, 73, 81n47

Eros, Erotes, 46, 60, 61. *See also* Amor; Cupid; Turnu
eschara, 135
Espi (or Esti), 140
Esplace, 20
Ethausva, 20, 58, 59
Etrusca disciplina, xii, 1, 4, 6n9, 10, 27, 33, 34–35, 42, 67, 117, 127, 173, 202–205
Etruscheria, 4
Etruscus ritus. See ritus Etruscus
Eubouleus, 81–82n52
Euphronios, 18, 62n54
Euripides, 48
Eurynomos, 73, 81n45
Evander, 33
"Eye of the Sun," 140

Faesulae (Fiesole), 36, 124, 125, 163
Falerii, Celle, 151
Falerii, Scasato, 106, 107n14
Falerii (Civita Castellana), 103, 110n89, 120, 123, 141, 152
Faliscan gods, 61
Faliscan language, 62n31
Faliscans, 37, 139, 205
Faliscan territory, 119
fanum, 125, 146
Fanum Voltumna (Shrine of Voltumna), 2, 35, 94, 124, 125, 127
Farthan, 107n16, 140
Fasti, 11
Fata, 200
fate, 58
Father of Terra, 200
Father Tiber, 209
Faunus, 31, 209
favissa, 91, 100
Favor, 41, 200
Favores Opertanei, 41, 200
Favor Pastor, 200
Felsina (Bologna), 68
Felsinian stelai, 75, 77, 81n48, 82n66
Festus, Sextus Pompeius (second half of second century CE), 2, 7n13, 192, 202
Fiesole. *See* Faesulae
Figulus. *See* Nigidius Figulus, P.
fíisnú, 146
Fiora River, 123
Flaccus, M. Fulvius, 111n113
Flaccus, Verrius (first century BCE), 2, 3, 27
flamen, flamines, 35–36, 56
Floral Band Cups, 135, 137
Florence, 4
Florence, Poggio di Firenze, 123
Fons, 200
Fonteius (date unknown), 193
Fortuna, 94, 200

Fortuna Virilis, 111n113
fossa, 132
Fratta, 107
Fraus, 200
Fregellae, 104
Frontinus, Sextus Julius (ca. 30–104 CE), 117
Fùcoli (Chianciano), 134
Fufluns, 11, 13, 19, 20, 21, 34, 38, 46, 49, 50, 57, 58, 59, 77, 106, 139
fulguriator, 39
funerary ritual, 28, 66–67, 72–73, 75, 76, 78, 78n5, 95, 138
Funnel Group, 79n24
Furies, 73, 81n47
Furlani, G., 7n28

Gabii, 151
Gaia, 46
Galatomachia, 79n21
Galba, 2
galerus, 35–36, 56
gates, 120. *See also* door, doors
"Gates of Helios," 140
Gauls, 9, 195
Gaultier, Françoise, 5
Gellius, Aulus (ca. 130–180 CE), 207
Gelon, 91
Gemma Augustea, 43n42
Genius, 27, 46, 58, 192, 200
Genius of Juno Hospita, 200
Gerhard, Eduard, 5, 45
Ghiaccio Forte, 101
Giants, 55, 57, 58
Gigantomachy, 156
Giglioli, G. Q., 7n28
Glaukos, 91
Gorgon, 150
Gracchi, 14
Gracchus, Tiberius, xii
Grasceta dei Cavallari, 148, 151
Graviscae, 18
Graviscae (Gravisca), 18, 47, 50, 57, 61, 90, 92, 93, 94, 97, 102, 106, 110n106
Greco-Campanian temples, 155
Grenier, A., 7n28
groma, 116
Grotta Porcina (Blera), 78, 138, 139, 152
Grove of Diana, 125
Grove of Ferentina, 125

Hades, 46, 57, 80n30, 140, 150. *See also* Aita
Hamphiar, 21
Hannibal, 132
Harmonia, 55, 56, 57
haruspex (*haruspices*), xii, 2, 4, 33, 35, 39, 45, 46, 56, 57, 102, 105, 106, 111n108, 117, 119, 193, 206

haruspication, 32, 35
haruspicina, 10, 27
hatrencu, 34, 39
Hebrews, 21
Hector, 48
Helen, 54
Helios, 46, 47, 61, 139–140
Hephaistos, 46, 59. *See also* Sethlans; Vulcan
Hera, 15, 46, 51, 61, 97. *See also* Juno; Uni
Herakles, 15, 46, 58, 139, 156. *See also* Hercle; Hercules
Herbig, Gustav, 7n28
Herbig, R., 7n28
Hercle, 11, 15, 17, 18, 19, 23, 43n59, 46, 51, 53–54, 56, 58, 59, 61, 101, 106, 109n72, 156, 160. *See also* Hercules; Herakles
Hercules, 17, 34, 43n59, 46, 58, 155, 206. *See also* Herakles; Hercle
Hermes, 46, 51, 60, 109n58. *See also* Mercury; Turms
"Hermes of Hades," 51, 57
Hermes Psychopompos, 81n48
Hermius (August), 202
Hernici, 213
Herois, 49
Hesiod, 55
Heurgon, Jacques, 5, 7n28
Hieron, 94
Himera, 91
Hinthial Teraśiaś, 51, 53
hinθial, 20, 111n108
Hipukrates, Rutile, 109n63
Hirpi, 119
Hittites, 46–47
Homer, 47
Huinthnaia, 143
human sacrifice, 28, 95, 150
Hypnos, 81n45

Iberian vases, 101
Ides, 119
Ides of September, 120
Iguvine Tables, 173
impetrativa, 42
Indo-European, 5
Ionic order, 162
Iron Age Latium, 111n108
Isidore of Seville, 4
Isis, 7n17, 206
Islam, 45
Italic religion, 45, 46, 94, 101, 146, 148
Ithaka, 51
iynx, 50

Janitores Terrestris, 200
Janus, 46, 56, 58, 117, 200. *See also* Culśanś
Jewish religion, 45

John of Cappadocia, 174
John the Lydian. *See* Lydus, Johannes
Jovei, 16
Judgment of Paris, 52, 60
Julian, xii
July, 60
June, 173
Juno, 3, 16, 17, 34, 40, 45–46, 47, 61, 118, 127, 155, 200, 206, 212, 216. *See also* Hera; Uni
Juno Curites, 151
Juno Regina, 61
Juno Seispes, 51
Juno Sospita, 52, 61
Jupiter, 3, 17, 27, 29, 30, 36, 40, 41, 43n42, 45–46, 60, 117, 118, 121, 127, 155, 199, 200, 206, 215, 216, 217. *See also* Tinia; Zeus
Jupiter Capitolinus, 146
Jupiter Feretrius, 147
Jupiter of Opulentia, 200
Jupiter Secundanus, 200

Kadmos, 55
Kalchas, 57. *See also* Chalchas
Kalends, 119
kantharos, kantharoi, 38, 39, 139
Kapaneus, 156, 160
Kastor, 46, 60. *See also* Castor; Castur
katabasis, 81–82n52
katoptromanteia, 31
Kavatha. *See* Catha
Kharayeb, 109n50
Kirke, 20–21, 140. *See also* Circe
Kirrha, 108n37
Kleobis and Biton, 95
korai, 99
Kore, 97, 140. *See also* Persephone
Kos, 111n126
kouroi, 99
kourotrophos, kourotrophoi, 20, 59, 101, 103, 104
krater, kraters, 77, 83n89, 139
kratēriskos, 138
Kroisos, 109n67
Kuśakli, 47
Kyknos, 62n54
kylikeion, 69, 75, 83n89
kylix, kylikes, 100, 139
Kypselos, 94

Labeo, Cornelius (date unknown), 2, 42, 66, 69, 193
laena, 36
Lais, 110n107
Lake Nemi, 125
Lake Trasimene, 92, 128nn21,79
Lampredi, Giovanni Maria, 4, 7n23
Lapse, 139

Laran, 11, 46, 55, 56, 57, 58. *See also* Ares; Mars
Lares, 200
Laris Pule, the Greek, 13
Laris Pulenas. *See* Pulenas, L(a)ris
Larna family, 118
Lar Omnium Cunctalis, 200
Lars Caelestis, 200
Lars Militaris, 200
Larthia Zan Velchina. *See* Velchina, Larthia Zan
Lasa, 21, 23, 57, 60
Lasa Vecuvia (Lasa Vecu; Vecuvia), 30, 31-33. *See also* Nymph Begoe; Vegoia
Latin colonies, 164
Latin dedications, 107n14
Latin gods, 45, 58
Latin inscription, 101
Latin language, 174
Latin League, 54
Latin religion, 46
Latins, 9, 125, 140
Latin sanctuaries, 108n31
Latium, 58, 95, 103, 104, 125, 132, 146, 148, 151, 160, 202
lautni, 104
Lavinium, Tredeci altari, 91
Lavinium (Pratica di Mare), 59, 101, 140
lectisternium, 60, 77
Leinth, 55, 58
lekanomanteia, 31
lekythos, lekythoi, 135, 137
Leontinoi, 110n98
Leopold, H. M. R., 5, 7n28
Letham, 11, 58, 111n137
Leto, 156
Leukothea, 47
Levantine cults, 94, 95
Liber, 118, 200
Liber Linteus. *See* Zagreb Mummy
Libri Acheruntici (Acherontici), 1, 28, 66-67
Libri de fulguratura, 1
Libri fatales, 1
Libri haruspicini, 28
Libri rituales, 1
Libri Tagetici, 1, 28, 32
Libri Vegoici, 1, 30, 32
lightning, 2, 4, 27, 32, 37, 39, 40, 41, 43n59, 56, 60, 119, 156, 174, 204, 214-217
lituus, 36, 37, 38, 43n42
lituus/trumpet, 28, 29, 96, 147
liver, animal, 39, 46, 56, 105, 106. *See also* Piacenza liver
liver, human, 111n129
Livy (Titus Livius; 64 or 59 BCE–12 or 17 CE), 1, 2, 21, 35, 36, 37, 38, 39, 42, 47, 59, 98, 109n53, 117, 120, 122, 124, 125, 191, 193, 194-195, 196, 205, 212-213
Lokrian (Locrian) plaques, 110n106
Lokrians, 103
Lucan, 174
Lucera, Belvedere, 94
Lucumo, 194. *See also* Tarquinius Priscus
lucumo, lucumones, 27, 28
Lucus Feroniae, 94, 106
ludi saeculares, 140
Luna, 46
Luni, 164
L[?urs] Larunita, 151
Lycomedius, 209
Lydians, 109n67
Lydus, Johannes (Lydos; John the Lydian; 490-560 CE), 4, 27, 173, 174, 192-193
Lykainis, 91
Lymphae, 200
Lynsa Silvestris, 200

Macrobius, Ambrosius Theodosius (fifth century CE), 3, 204
Maenads, 58, 156
Maggiani, Adriano, 5
Magliano, 11, 13
magmentum, 132-133
Malta, 91
Mamurrius, 209
Manes, 200
Manth, 141
Mantiklos Apollo, 109n58
Manto, 56, 63n79
Mantua (Mantova), 3, 56, 141
Mantus, 141
manubia, 40
March (month), 11, 120
Mariś, 46, 55, 58
Mariśhalna, 58
Mariśhusrnana, 58
Mariśisminthians, 58
Mars, 40, 46, 56, 63n80, 110n85, 123, 206. *See also* Ares; Laran
Mars Quirinus, 200
Martianus Capella (first half of fifth century CE), 3, 4, 11, 34, 40, 41, 57, 118, 126, 199-200
maru, marunuχva, 34
Marzabotto, 47, 103, 107, 144, 146
Marzabotto, A (temple), 140, 155
Marzabotto, Acropolis, 141
Marzabotto, B (podium), 140-141, 142
Marzabotto, C (temple), 140, 160
Marzabotto, D (podium), 140, 142, 160
Marzabotto, E (temple), 160
Marzabotto, Santuario Fontile, 100
"master of animals," 53
Mater Matuta, 47, 53, 94, 111n113, 151, 156
Maxentius, xii
May (month), 122
Mean, 59
Medusa, 156
Melanippos, 160
Meleager, 22, 23, 52, 53
Meliacr, 22, 23
Melikertes, 91
Melqarth, 58
Memnon, 41
Menerva, 20, 31-32, 40, 41, 45-46, 51, 52, 53-54, 55, 58, 59, 60, 90, 98, 99, 101, 104, 106, 109nn72,74, 133, 151, 155, 164, 164n19. *See also* Athena; Minerva
Mephitis, 119
Mercury (Mercurius), 3, 4, 46, 56, 60, 200, 206. *See also* Hermes; Turms
Messana, 110n98
Messerschmidt, Franz, 5
Meteli, Aule, 92
Metrodorus of Scepsis, 211
Mettius, 43n42
mildew, 27, 30. *See also* Rubigo
Miletos, 142
Minerva, 3, 40, 45-46, 59, 118, 127, 155, 200, 206, 216. *See also* Athena; Menrva
Minerva Medica votives, 111n114
"mistress of animals," 53
Mistress of Horses, 49
Moirai, 53
Mons Albanus (Monte Cavo), 125
Montalcino, 91
Monte Amiata, 125
Monte (Monti) Falterona, 99-100, 103, 107, 119
Monte Giovi, 119, 127
Monteguragazza, 140, 146
Montescudaio, 78, 109n56
Monte Soracte, 141
Montetosto, 121, 144, 146
Monti della Tolfa, 148
Mother Earth, 48, 61
Mount Soracte, 48, 59, 119
Mugello, 122
Mulciber, 200
Müller, Karl Otfried, 4
mundus, 91, 98, 119, 140, 141
Murlo (Poggio Civitate), 36, 119, 125-126, 129n110, 119, 150, 151
Muśni family, 107
mutilation of objects, 95-96, 109n58

nail, nails, 23, 52, 53, 59, 120
Narce, 146
Narce, Le Ròte, 144, 146
Narnia, 217
Natis, gem of, 39-40
Naukratis, 109n67
Navius, Attus, 204
Near East, 15, 84n101
Near Eastern influence, 147
Nekyia, 51, 62n46, 69, 74, 80n26, 81n46
Nemi, 95, 103, 104, 108n31, 125
Neoplatonism, 174
Neptune (Neptunus), 11, 45-46, 59, 200, 217. *See also* Nethuns; Poseidon
Nereus, 91
Nethuns, 10, 11, 14, 45-46, 47, 59, 61, 107, 112n137. *See also* Neptune; Poseidon
netsvis, 39
Neverita, 200
Nigidius Figulus, P. (ca. 10-45 BCE), 2, 4, 30, 39, 42, 104, 173, 174-175, 193, 217
Nike, 59
nimbus, 61
Nocturnus, 58, 200
Nogara, Bartolomeo, 7n28
Nones, 119
Norchia, 142, 143, 152
Nortia, 52, 59, 120, 205
Numa Pompilius, 136, 111n118, 146, 194
numen, numina, 127
Nurtia, 59. *See also* Nortia
Nymph Begoe, 30-31, 32
Nymphs, 149, 165n84

oblativa, 42
October, 30, 120
Odysseus, 20-21, 51. *See also* Ulysses; Uthste
oikos shrine, 147, 150
oinochoe, oinochoai, 103, 107n16, 138
Olmo Bello, 109n56
olpe, 149
Olta, 218
Oltos cup from Tarquinii, 60, 111n134
Olympia, 51, 94, 108n37, 109n48
Olympian deities, 47-48
Ombra della Sera type, 103, 111n108
Ombrone River, 123, 125
opaion, 135
Opulentia, 200
opus quadratum, 137
orientation, 118, 164, 198-199
Orpheus, 31
Orphism, 80nn30,34, 104

Orvieto, 36, 43n43, 50, 55, 59, 121, 139. *See also* Volsinii
Orvieto, Belvedere temple, 140, 160, 161, 164
Orvieto, Campo della Fiera, 42–43
Orvieto, Cannicella sanctuary, 47, 49, 61, 99–100, 106, 107, 107n14, 147, 149–150
Orvieto, Crocefisso del Tufo, 122
Orvieto, Golini Tomb I, 70, II, 70
Orvieto, Tomb of the Hescanas, 70, 79n19
Oscan tablets, 148
Osiris, 7n17
Osteria dell'Osa, 95, 109n58
Ovid (P. Ovidius Naso; 43 BCE–17 CE), 3, 193, 197–198, 209–210

Pacha, 34, 46, 58, 59. *See also* Bacchus; Dionysos; Fufluns
Paktyes, 109n67
Pales, 200
Pallottino, Massimo, 5
Palma di Montechiaro, 111n108
Paris, 51–52, 61n10
Paris Painter, 51
patera, 39, 55, 93. *See also phiale, phialai*
Pater Pyrgensis, 140
Paulus Diaconus (eighth century CE), 3
Pava Tarchies, 29–30, 32, 35–36, 39, 47. *See also* Tages
Pegasus, 16
Peirithoua, 80nn24,28,32
Penates, 3, 13, 66, 217
Pentasila, 20
Penthesilea, 20
penus, 150
penus Vestae, 150
Perachora, 108n40
Persephone, 19, 46, 57, 82n52, 140, 150. *See also* Phersipnei; Proserpina
Persians, 202
Perusia (Perugia), 3, 18, 21, 51, 108, 124, 125
Perusia cippus, 23
Pettazzoni, R., 7n28
Pfiffig, Ambros J., 5, 7n28, 45
Phanyllis Group, 135, 137
Pharai, 164n11
Pharsalos, 174
Phersipnei (Phersipnai), 19, 46, 57, 69, 71, 80n30. *See also* Persephone; Proserpina
Phersu, 76, 83n76
phiale, phialai, 104, 107n16
Philadelphia (Lydia), 174
Philippus, Quintus Marcius, 212
Philologia (Philology), 3, 4, 200

Phoceans. *See* Phokaians
Phoebus (Apollo), 209
Phoenician gods, 58, 61
Phoenician influence, 147
Phoenician language, 13
Phoenicians, 47
Phoenician silver bowls, 95
Phokaians, 145, 155, 213
Phoroneus, 146
Phrygian dress, 61
Phrygians, 47
Piacenza liver, 4, 10, 11, 39, 47, 51, 57, 58, 59, 106, 111–112n132, 117, 118, 126, 127
Picus, 31
Pietrabbondante, 164
Pietra Zannoni, 78, 84n102
Pieve a Sòcana. *See* Sòcana
pigs, 3, 97
Pinarii, 34
Pindar (518–413 BCE), 140
Pisae (Pisa), 3, 123, 124, 125
Pithekoussai, 9
Plautius, Gaius, 213
Pliny the Elder (23/24–79 CE), 3, 40, 42, 47, 118, 164n10, 193, 207–208, 211, 217–218
plow, 27
Plowman from Arretium (Arezzo), 93
Plutarch (ca. 50–ca. 120 CE), 201–202, 203
Pluto, 46, 200
pocolom, 101
Poggio della Melonta, 134
Pollux, 19, 46, 60, 76. *See also* Polydeukes; Pultuce
Polybius (ca. 200–after 118 BCE), xi
Polydeukes, 46, 60
Polygnotos, 73
Polyxena, 136–137, 150
pomerium, 123
Pomona, 3, 209–211
pompa funebris, 67, 75
Pompeianus, 217
Pompey, 174
Pontecagnano, Via Verdi, 141
"Pontic" amphoras, 51, 53
Ponte di Nona, 111n110
Populonia, 21, 108n25, 123, 124, 125
Populonia, Tomba del Corridietro, 79n19
Po River, 141
Porsena (Porsina), 3, 207, 218
Poseidon, 9, 46, 47. *See also* Nethuns; Neptune
Postumius, 2
Potitii, 34
Po Valley, 73, 132
Praeneste, 62n31

Pratica di Mare. *See* Lavinium
precincts, 143–146. *See also* temenos
Priam, 61n10
priest, priests, 33–39
priestess, priestesses, 34, 38–39
Prisnius, 17
Proclus Diadochus, 193
prodigia, 96, 106
Prometheus, 20
Pronaia, 164n19
Propertius, Sextus (second half of first century BCE), 3, 91, 208–209
prophecy, 1, 6, 23, 27–33, 191–198. *See also* Cacu; Lasa Vecuvia; Pava Tarchies; Tages; Vegoia
Proserpina, 19, 46, 140, 151. *See also* Persephone
Proteus, 31
prothesis, 82n59
Prumathe, 20
Ptah, 109n51
Pulenas, L(a)ris, 13, 14, 22, 23, 34, 39, 79n24, 80n26, 136
Pultuce, 46, 76
Pumpus, Arnth Alitle, 106
Punic inscription, 101
Punicum, 98
Punta della Vipera (Santa Marinella), 11, 98, 102, 110n91, 133, 155
Pupluna, 21
Pyrgi, 6, 13, 23, 47, 55, 60, 61, 91, 92, 101, 102, 103, 105, 107n16, 110n91, 121, 132–141
Pyrgi, Alpha (shrine), 134–135, 136, 137, 148–149, 151
Pyrgi, Area C, 133, 143, 144, 146
Pyrgi, Beta (shrine), 133–134, 137, 148–149, 151
Pyrgi, Delta (altar), 137–138, 151
Pyrgi, Epsilon (altar), 137–138, 150
Pyrgi, Gamma (shrine), 137, 140, 148–149, 150, 151
Pyrgi, Iota (altar), 132–133, 135, 138, 144, 165n74
Pyrgi, Kappa (deposit), 135, 136, 139
Pyrgi, Lambda (altar), 138, 139, 140, 150
Pyrgi, North Area, 133, 148
Pyrgi, North Area, altar, 164n43
Pyrgi, Nu (altar), 133, 135
Pyrgi, Omicron (fossa), 132, 135
Pyrgi, Rho (deposit), 135, 136, 139
Pyrgi, South Area, 134, 136, 139, 148–149, 150
Pyrgi, temple A, 156, 159, 160
Pyrgi, temple A, 164
Pyrgi, temple B, 155

Pyrgi, terracotta antefixes, 47, 49
Pyrgi, Theta, 137, 149
Pyrgi, Zeta, 132, 133, 134, 135, 138
Pyrgi tablets, 128n44
Pythagoreanism, 4, 80n30
Pythia, 213

quadriga, 156
Quirinus, 197
Quirinus Mars, 200
Quirites, 198

Radke, Gerhard, 45
Rath, 30
Re, 48
Remonia, 203
Remus, 119, 193, 203, 204
Remzna, Arnth, 35–36
responsum, xii
Rhadamanthys, 80n34
Rhodes, 108n42
Richardson, Emeline, 45
ritus Etruscus, 3, 39, 127, 202
Riufri, Fasti, 93
Rix, Helmut, 45
Roman religion, xi, xii, 5
Rome, Ara Maxima of Hercules, 146
Rome, Ara Pacis Augustae, 36
Rome, Caelian Hill, 211
Rome, Campus Martius, 140
Rome, Capitoline Hill, 39, 120, 127, 197, 217
Rome, Comitium, 140
Rome, Forum Boarium, 146
Rome, Lapis Niger, 43n42
Rome, Ponte di Nona, 105
Rome, Quirinal Hill, 95
Rome, San Crisogono in Trastevere, 107n12
Rome, Sant'Omobono, 94, 103, 111n113, 155, 156
Rome, Tarentum, 140
Rome, temple of Castores (Castor and Pollux), 155, 156, 164
Rome, temple of Jupiter Feretrius, 147
Rome, temple of Jupiter Optimus Maximus, 59, 153, 154–155, 161
Rome, temple of Mater Matuta, 155
Rome, Tiber Island, 102, 104
Rome, Tomb of the Scipios, 13
Rome, Via Appia, Soleluna, 149
Rome, Via Praenestina votive deposit, 108n31
Rome, Vicus Tuscus, 211
Romulus, 36, 119, 147, 193, 203, 204, 211
Roncalli, Francesco, 5
Rose, H. J., 5
Rubigo, 128n69, 203

Index

Rusellae, 123, 124, 125, 146, 162, 165n58

Sabine, 34
sacellum, 146
sacerdos, 34, 35
saeculum, 31, 200
sakaraklúm, 146, 148
Salamis, 91
Samian vases, 164n10
Samnite sanctuary, 164
Samnium, 148. *See also* San Giovanni in Galdo
Samos, 51, 95, 108n42, 164n10
Samos, Heraion, 94, 103
Samothracian gods, 91
Sancus, 200
San Giovanni in Galdo (Samnium), 148
San Giovenale, 151, 152
San Giuliano, 152
Santa Marinella. *See* Punta della Vipera
Sardinian boat models, 78, 97
Sarissa, 47
Sarpedon, 48
Saties, Vel, 41, 42, 128n40
Satre, 59
Satricum, 47, 155, 156
Satricum, temple of Mater Matuta, 151
Saturn (Saturnus), 40, 59, 200
Satyr, Satyrs, 49–51, 58, 77, 139, 156, 210
Schnabelkanne, 41, 107n16
Secundanus Pales, 200
Seditio, 200
Selene, 46
Selvans, 59, 60, 106, 107n16, 117, 122, 127, 146. *See also* Silvanus
Selvans Tularias, 16, 17
Semele, 49
Semla, 19, 20, 49, 50
Semo Sancus, 95
Seneca, Lucius Annaeus (4 BCE?–65 CE), 2, 4, 213–214
Senenia, 102
seni crines, 39
Serapis, 206
Servius (fourth century CE), 3, 66, 69, 119, 120, 122, 141, 199, 202, 215–216, 217
Servius Danielis (seventh–eighth century CE), 7n12
Servius Tullius, 194, 195
Sethlans, 46, 59. *See also* Hephaistos; Vulcan
Seven against Thebes, 156, 160, 162
Seville, El Carambolo, 109n52
Shave Zion, 109n50
shrines, 146–152
Sibylline books, xii
Sibylline oracles, 47, 61

Sicily, 103, 116, 125
Siena, 36
Signia, 164
Sikyonian artist, 164n10
Silenus, 31
Silvanus, 59, 117, 127, 194, 210. *See also* Selvans
Silvanus-Terminus, 16
Sisyphos, 70, 79n24, 80n28
Sòcana (Pieve a Sòcana), 134, 135, 143
Sol, 46, 61, 140
Sol Indiges, 140
Sol Juvans, 140
Solis filia, 46
Sons of Jupiter, 200
Soranus, 59, 139
sors, sortes, 103, 135, 137, 139, 141
Sostratos of Aegina, 61, 93, 97, 106
Sotades, 81n46
South Italy, 103, 116
Southern Italic ritual, 94
Sovana, 100, 107, 125, 142
Spello, 35
Spina, 51, 81n46
Spina, Valle Trebba necropolis, 109n58
Spulare Aritimi, 93
Spuriaze, 144
Spurinas bowls, 101
Spurinna, 2
stele, stelai, 82n71, 84n102, 103, 140
stips, 91
Stoicism, 2, 4
Suda, The (tenth century CE), 4, 200
Suetonius Tranquillus, Gaius (b. ca. 69 CE–d. after 121 CE), 174, 198
Sulla, 2, 163
Summanus, 43n59, 216
Sun, 57
Supri, Fel, 90
Śuri, 47, 48, 57, 59, 139–140, 149, 151, 164n21
Surrina, 59
Suvlu, 91
suθina, 20
Sveitus, Vel, 35–36, 93
Syracuse, 94, 110n98, 138, 151
Syriskos Painter, 139

Tabula Capuana. *See* Capua tile
Tabula Cortonensis, 16, 18, 23
Tages, 1, 2, 4, 23, 27, 28–31, 32, 34, 109n61, 128n69, 173, 192, 193, 204. *See also* Pava Tarchies
Talamone, 55, 163
Tanaquil, 23, 42, 194, 195
Tarchon, 27, 28–31, 32, 34, 141, 193
Tarchon the Elder, 193
Tarchunus, Avl, 35–36

Tarquinians, 205, 213
Tarquinii (Tarquinia), xii, 18, 28, 54, 57, 60, 90, 92, 101, 105, 120, 123, 124, 125, 146, 148, 194
Tarquinii, Ara della Regina (temple), 47, 96, 107, 117, 151, 154, 155, 160–161, 162
Tarquinii, Ara della Regina, Beta (altar), 165n47
Tarquinii, Ara della Regina, winged horses, 108n20
Tarquinii, Bruschi Tomb, 38, 79n15
Tarquinii, Cardarelli Tomb, 82n66
Tarquinii, Fondo Scataglini, 165n90
Tarquinii, Giglioli Tomb, 80n35
Tarquinii, Labrouste Tomb, 82n66
Tarquinii, Pian di Civita, 27, 29, 90, 95, 102, 109n53, 110n96, 144, 147, 148, 151
Tarquinii, Querciola Tomb I, 75, 82n57
Tarquinii, Querciola Tomb II, 79n17, 82
Tarquinii, Tomb 1999, 83n88
Tarquinii, Tomb 4255, 82n66
Tarquinii, Tomb 5636, 67
Tarquinii, Tomb of the Aninas Family (Aninas), 67, 69
Tarquinii, Tomb of the Augurs (Auguri), 82n66, 83n76
Tarquinii, Tomb of the Baron (Barone), 54
Tarquinii, Tomb of the Biclinium (Biclinio), 83
Tarquinii, Tomb of the Black Sow (Scrofa Nera), 75
Tarquinii, Tomb of the Blue Demons (Demoni Azzurri), 73–75, 80n24, 81, 81nn45,46, 82
Tarquinii, Tomb of the Bronze Door (Porta di Bronzo), 82n66
Tarquinii, Tomb of the Bulls (Tori), 75, 76, 82n62
Tarquinii, Tomb of the Cardinal (del Cardinale), 68, 79n15
Tarquinii, Tomb of the Chariots (Bighe), 83n89
Tarquinii, Tomb of the Charons (Caronti), 67, 69, 70, 82n66, 152
Tarquinii, Tomb of the Citheroid (Citeroide), 82n66
Tarquinii, Tomb of the Convention (del Convento), 79n15
Tarquinii, Tomb of the Dead Man (Morto), 83n89
Tarquinii, Tomb of Dionysos and the Silenoi (Dioniso e Silenoi), 83n88
Tarquinii, Tomb of the Doors and Felines (Porte e Felini), 82n66

Tarquinii, Tomb of the Flagellation (Fustigazione), 82n66
Tarquinii, Tomb of Francesca Giustiniani, 82n57
Tarquinii, Tomb of the Funeral Couch (Letto Funebre), 54, 60, 76–77, 79n19
Tarquinii, Tomb of the Hunter (Cacciatore), 76
Tarquinii, Tomb of Hunting and Fishing (Caccia e Pesca), 76, 83n74, 103
Tarquinii, Tomb of the Hut (Capanna), 82n66
Tarquinii, Tomb of the Inscriptions (Iscrizioni), 82n66, 83n88
Tarquinii, Tomb of the Jade Lions (Leoni di Giada), 82n66
Tarquinii, Tomb of the Jugglers (Giocolieri), 43n43
Tarquinii, Tomb of the Lionesses (Leonesse), 67, 74, 79n19, 83, 83n89
Tarquinii, Tomb of the Marquis (Marchese), 82n66
Tarquinii, Tomb of the Mercareccia, 152
Tarquinii, Tomb of the Olympiads (Olimpiadi), 82n66, 83n76
Tarquinii, Tomb of Orcus (Orco), 80n26, 82n62; I, 72, 75; Orcus II, 69, 71, 72, 80n24
Tarquinii, Tomb of the Pygmies (Pigmei), 82n57
Tarquinii, Tomb of the Shields (Scudi), 70, 79n19
Tarquinii, Tomb of the Ship (Nave), 76
Tarquinii, Tomb of the Skull (Teschio), 82n66
Tarquinii, Tomb of the Tapestry (Tappezzeria), 152
Tarquinii, Tomb of the Triclinium (Triclinio), 38, 62n35, 79n19
Tarquinii, Tomb of the Typhon (Tifone), 37, 79n15
Tarquinii, Tomb of the Warrior (Guerriero), 82n57
Tarquinius Priscus, 42, 125, 146, 154, 194, 195
Tarquinius Superbus, 39, 155, 156
Tarquitius Priscus (first century BCE), 2, 30
Tatius, 194, 211
Tece, 92
Tec Sanś, 92, 106
Tecvm, 106
Tegola Capuana. *See* Capua Tile
Teiresias, 20, 31, 51, 56. *See also* Teriasa
Tel Dor, 95

Index

Telicles, Larth, 109n63
Tellurus, 200
temenos, 91, 118, 140
temples, 3, 101, 102, 119, 120, 123, 140, 141, 144, 151, 152-164, 205-207
templum, 82n62, 116, 118, 146, 147
Teriasa, 20
Terminus, 117-118
Terra, 200
Terra Mater, 46
Tessennano, 101
Testa Malavolta, 98
Thalna, 20
Thanatos, 73, 81n45
Thanr (Thanur), 11, 20, 58, 59
Theban myth, 56, 57
Thebes, 55, 56, 160
Thebes, Ptoion sanctuary, 108n40
Themistokles, 91
Theodosius, xii
Thesan, 13, 40, 41, 45-46, 47, 48, 49, 60, 61, 101, 156. *See also* Aurora; Eos
Theseus, 70, 80nn24,28
Thesmophoria, 97
Thethis (Thetis), 40, 41
Thiessen polygons, 123, 125
Thufltha, 91, 92, 106
Thulin, Carl O., 4, 7n28
thunder, 30-31, 32, 39-40, 119, 173-190
Thvariena, 144
thyrsos, 38
Tiber River, 116, 125
Tina Atalena Śea, 144
Tina Calusna, 140
Tinas Cliniar (Cliniiar), 19, 46, 54, 60, 77, 106
Tinia (Tina, Tin), 11, 14, 20, 27, 29, 30-31, 40, 41, 43n59, 45, 47, 51, 53-54, 56, 58, 60, 61, 101, 106, 107, 117, 127, 133, 156, 160
Tiples, Vel, 97, 101
Tivoli, 103
Tivr (Tiur), 11, 46, 100, 106
Todi, "Mars" of, 55, 92
Todi, ring bezel, 31, 33
Tolfa Mountains, 123-124
Tolonio, L., 101
Tolumnius, 98
tophet, 95
torch, 58, 61
Torelli, Mario, 5
Torre San Severo, sarcophagus from, 136, 137
Traneus (July), 60, 202
Trebatius Testa, Gaius (first century BCE), 146, 207

Troilos, 76
Trojans, 47, 61, 61n10, 76
Trojan War, 56
trutnvt frontac, 39
Tuchulcha, 68, 71, 80n24
Tul, 117
tular, 116-117, 122, 123
Tulumnes (Tulumnii), 93, 98. *See also* Tolonio
Tunisia, 14
Turan, 13, 18, 19, 22, 23, 45-46, 47, 50-51, 52, 53, 55, 56, 57, 58, 60, 61, 90, 97, 98, 106. *See also* Aphrodite; Venus
Turan Ati, 20
Turkey, 47
Turms, 46, 51, 54, 56, 57, 60
Turmś Aitaś, 51, 53, 57, 60
Turms of Calu, 53
Turms of Tin, 53
Turnu, 46, 50-51, 60, 61
Tuscania, 30, 47, 48, 56, 61, 122
Tuscania, Ara del Tufo, 152
Tuscania, Pian di Mola, 142
Tuscania, Tomb of the Curunas, 79n19
Tuscanic temple order, 151, 152, 154, 155
"Tuscanicus," 127n9
Tuscany, 116
Tuscia, 217
tutulus, 99
Twelve Peoples. *See duodecim populi* Tydeus, 156
Tyrrhenus, 7n17
Tyskiewicz Painter, 139

Ucernei, 30
Ulysses (Ulixes), 51, 80n26. *See also* Odysseus; Uthste
Umbria, 11, 31
Umbrian language, 92
Umbricius Melior, 2
Unata Zutas, M., 14
Uni, 11, 13, 18, 23, 45-46, 47, 51, 52, 53-54, 56, 57, 58, 59, 60, 61, 90, 97, 101, 106, 144, 155. *See also* Hera; Juno; Astarte
Unialastres, 101
Uni Chia, 144
Usil, 11, 46, 47, 49, 57, 59, 60, 61, 107
Uthste (Uthuze), 21, 51, 53. *See also* Odysseus; Ulysses
Ut-napishti, 84n101

Valerius Maximus (first half of first century BCE), 205
Valetudo, 200

Van Essen, C. C., 5, 7n28
Vanth, 58, 61, 67, 69, 78, 79n10, 80n30, 83n97
Vanth Group, 43n42
Varro, Marcus Terentius (116-27 BCE), 2, 3, 9, 34, 117, 127, 133, 136, 146, 154, 164n10, 174, 202, 207, 211, 216, 217
Vecuvia. *See* Lasa Vecuvia
Vegoia, xii, 1, 2, 16, 23, 30-31, 117, 121, 191-192. *See also* Lasa Vecuvia; Nymph Begoe
Vei, 18, 46, 47-48, 57, 61, 90, 97, 101, 103, 104, 106, 140, 143
Veii, 34, 35, 39, 47, 61, 92, 93, 103, 104, 105, 111n129, 120, 123, 124, 125, 160, 195-196, 212
Veii, Apollo from, 57
Veii, Campetti sanctuary, 101-102, 107
Veii, Piazza d'Armi, 148, 151
Veii, Portonaccio sanctuary, 48, 59, 98, 101, 103, 107, 107n14, 133, 151, 156, 157, 158, 165n47
Veii, Quattro Fontanili necropolis, 109n54
Veiovis, 200
Velchina, Larthia Zan, 20
Velcitanus (March), 202
Velianas, Thefarie, 101, 104, 155
Velkasnas, Laris, 103
Velletri, 149
Velparun, 21
Velthina family, 16
Veltune, 29, 31
Venetic cults, 94
Venus, 46, 56, 60, 63n80, 123, 206. *See also* Aphrodite; Turan
Venus Libitina, 142
Venuti, Filippo, 4
Vergil (Virgil; P. Vergilius Maro, 7-19 BCE), 3, 34, 36, 48, 60, 61, 75, 120, 141
Veris Fructus, 200
Vertumnus, 3, 29, 91, 127, 208-209, 210-211
Vesta, 146
Vestal Virgins, 39
Vetulonia, 31, 78, 124, 125
Vetulonia, Pietrera Tomb, 78
Vibenna, Caeles, 211. *See also* Vipenas brothers; Vipinas, Caile
Vicellius, Apuleius (date unknown), 193
Vignanello, 141, 146
Villanovan burials, 95
Vipenas brothers, 93

Vipiennas, Avile, 98, 103, 104
Vipinas, Avle, 31, 33
Vipinas, Caile, 31, 33
Virbius, 192
Virgil. *See* Vergil
Viterbo, 38, 59, 79n19, 141
Vitruvius Pollio (second half of first century BCE), 2, 3, 47, 123, 127n9, 155, 164, 205-207
Volaterrae (Volterra), 2, 23, 69, 56, 90, 103, 123, 124, 125, 164
Volaterrae, acropolis sanctuary, 164n34
Volaterrae, mirror with Hercle from, 14
Volcanus. *See* Vulcan
Volsinii (Orvieto), 20, 52, 59, 104, 111n113, 120, 123, 124, 125, 133, 205, 211, 216, 218. *See also* Orvieto
Volterra. *See* Volaterrae
Voltumna, 29, 91
Vulca of Veii, 59, 146
Vulcan (Vulcanus, Volcanus), 40, 46, 59, 123, 200, 206, 216
Vulci, 34, 56, 59, 75, 77, 79n24, 90, 92, 100, 105, 107, 111n129, 123, 124, 125, 140, 163
Vulci, Cuccumella, 152
Vulci, Cuccumelletta, 151
Vulci, Fontanile di Legnisina, 101, 143, 144, 146, 160
Vulci, François Tomb, 41-42, 70-73, 76
Vulci, great temple, 155, 156
Vulci, Isis Tomb, 78, 83n98
Vulci, Porta Nord, 101
Vulci, Tomb of the Inscriptions, 39
Vulcian incense burner, 109n48
Vulcian tripods, 95

Weinstock, Stefan, 5, 7n28

Xosfer (October), 202

Yahweh, 45

Zagreb mummy wrappings (*liber linteus*), 5, 10, 11, 13, 23, 34, 59, 60, 111n137, 119, 173
Zeus, 45-46, 51, 60, 61, 156, 160. *See also* Jupiter; Tinia
Zipna, 50
Zosimus (fifth century CE), 216-217
Zutas, M. Unata. *See* Unata Zutas, M.